BRITISH AIRCRAFT CARRIERS

BRITISH AIRCRAFT CARRIERS

Design, Development and Service Histories

DAVID HOBBS

Seaforth
PUBLISHING

FRONTISPIECE: *Ark Royal* after her 1970 refit. (AUTHOR'S COLLECTION)

First published in Great Britain in 2013 by
Seaforth Publishing
An imprint of Pen & Sword Books Ltd
47 Church Street, Barnsley
S Yorkshire S70 2AS

www.seaforthpublishing.com
Email info@seaforthpublishing.com

Reprinted 2014, 2017

British Library Cataloguing in Publication Data
A CIP data record for this book is available from the British Library

ISBN 978 1 84832 138 0

Typeset and designed by Neil Sayer
Printed and bound in China by 1010 Printing International Ltd

CONTENTS

ACKNOWLEDGEMENTS

This book has taken me some years to compile and, as always, I have relied on the support of my wife, Jandy, who encouraged and helped me with both research and collation and on my son Andrew who maintains his unfailing interest in my writings.

I would like to thank Jeremy Michel and Andrew Choong of the Historic Photographs & Ship Plans Department of the National Maritime Museum at the Brass Foundry in Woolwich who gave me access to the many ship's covers and drew my attention to the 'as-fitted' drawings reproduced in this book. Jennie Wraight, the Admiralty Librarian, has given me valuable assistance over the years as have Christopher Page, Steven Prince, Jock Gardner, Malcolm Llewellyn-Jones and Mike MacAloon and, of course, the late David Brown at the Naval Historical Branch. David Stevens, Director of Strategic and Historical Studies at the Sea Power Centre – Australia gave valuable help and information about the RAN and John Perryman helped with information and photographs. Joe Straczek helped with details of RN carrier movements in Australia and the Far East after 1945 and Terry Hetherington, Manager of the Fleet Air Arm Museum at RANAS Nowra, helped with the search for photographs. Mark Schweikert also helped me in my search for images. Michael Whitby, Chief of the Canadian Naval History Team at National Defence Headquarters in Ottawa gave information about the Canadian Fleet Air Arm. I would especially like to thank my friend Norman Friedman for the insight and understanding of world naval aviation that he has brought to our discussions at international conferences over the years; I value his opinions and encyclopaedic knowledge greatly.

A book like this requires considerable archival research and I would also like to thank Joe Kelly and other staff at the National Archives at Kew and the staff at the MOD Records Department who helped me when it was sited at Hayes. While I was Curator of the Fleet Air Arm Museum at Yeovilton I was able to carry out research in its extensive archive and I would like to thank staff there including Jan Keohane, Catherine Cooper, Jerry Shore, the late Len Lovell and the late Dennis White for their help and support.

I have gathered a large photographic archive of my own over many years and I have used it to illustrate a number of the carriers in this book but I found that there were significant gaps. Several people volunteered to help fill this deficiency and among them I would like to thank A D Baker III in the USA. I am also grateful to Steve Bush in the UK who was able to add images from the Ferrers-Walker collection to his own and make them available. My friends at the Crail Museum, Sue Bradman and Anne Mayes were also most helpful in providing images from the Museum archive. John Jordan and Ian Sturton helped with drawings at short notice and Conrad Waters also provided me with assistance. I have used a number of images which were made available by the US Navy and the Royal Australian Navy.

This publication contains Public Sector information licensed under the Open Government Licence v 1.0 in the UK.

Numerous other people have helped over the past few years by contributing data on equipment, tactics and technique that helped to shape the book; they are too numerous to name but I thank them all. Any errors that come to light are, however, my own responsibility. As always, I am grateful to Rob Gardiner and Seaforth Publishing for giving me the opportunity to publish this book which is the result of many years of research.

David Hobbs

INTRODUCTION

This book describes the development of aircraft carriers by the Royal Navy, from the first experiments in 1911 with aircraft that could operate from ships to the present day. It includes the early experimental vessels to show the line of development, and goes on to include all those ships which had the operation of aircraft as their primary purpose. It does not include battleships, cruisers, destroyers, frigates and fleet auxiliaries, many of which operated small numbers of aircraft as one among many purposes throughout the same period. The dividing line can become blurred, however, and details of fighter catapult ships are included, together with MAC-Ships, although the operation of aircraft from the latter was arguably secondary to their primary purpose as grain ships or tankers. I considered it important that they could be compared with British-built escort carriers.

With the exception of the *Invincible* and *Queen Elizabeth* classes and the commando helicopter carrier *Ocean*, all the ships covered were designed and built to Imperial measurements, and I have used these throughout to avoid the possibility of errors in translation. That said, I have used Imperial units for the three classes mentioned above so that they can more easily be compared with the earlier vessels, and to give a consistent form of measurement throughout. Where distances are referred to in miles, they are nautical miles, which are an exact distance of 6,080ft but usually taken as being 2,000 yards in any but the most precise navigational calculation. Gallons are given in Imperial measure, and American readers should note that one US gallon is the equivalent of 0.833 Imperial gallons.

The book is divided into chapters which contain details of British aircraft carriers by class, comparisons with foreign carriers at various stages of development, and descriptions of naval aircraft and their impact on ship design. After the Second World War the Australian, Canadian and, to an extent, Indian navies worked in close concert with the RN from which they had evolved and operated aircraft carriers of British design and construction that were either purchased outright or lent from the United Kingdom. They are, therefore, included in the chapters with their RN sister ships. Later ships have been purchased from other nations, operate less intimately with the RN and have therefore been allocated a chapter of their own. Each chapter covering an aircraft carrier class has a technical description of the design, drawings, photographs and an individual history of every ship in the class.

Unlike my previous books, in this one I have not used endnotes. In an encyclopædic work of this nature virtually every sentence would have required an endnote giving the source or some other amplification, and this would have proved impossible. The extensive bibliography gives sources and references for the data, facts and figures I have used, which were sourced both from published and unpublished documents. Amplification, where necessary, has been worked into the text, and I am responsible for any errors or omissions.

As I worked my way chronologically through the various aircraft carrier classes I found that some ships did not fit easily into this format because of long gestation periods or a massive mid-life reconstruction. I have therefore split them, and *Victorious*, *Eagle*, *Hermes* and *Ark Royal* have their initial design and early history described in their sister-ships' chapters but their reconstruction and later histories described in chapters of their own. To have done otherwise would have put the latter part of their service with steam catapults and transonic fighters in the same chapter as ships operating Swordfish and Seafires and would have been illogical. Effectively these ships had two distinct lives, and the list of contents and index will clarify any doubts the reader might have. As I made way through the decades describing the ships' activities in peace and war I became very aware of how the pace of operations has increased. The Korean War, Suez, Confrontation and the Falklands Conflict, NATO and other alliance exercises, together with the need to interact with other nations' forces on constant alert, meant that post-1945 RN carriers spent more time at sea than their wartime predecessors. In addition to the more usual images of operational ships, I have included several photographs of carriers being built, launched, laid up in reserve and scrapped, to give a wider feeling for the whole life of these intriguing vessels from beginning to end.

Once the RN resumed full control of its own air operations at sea, its professional aviators made great strides in designing new equipment and technique that literally led the world. The steam catapult, angled flight deck, mirror/projector landing aid, Stovl fighter technology and the 'ski-jump' continue to be used by other carrier navies. The ten year 'gap' in strike carrier capability inflicted on the RN in the 2010 by the UK Strategic Defence and Security Review could have spelt the end, but with the help of Great Britain's American and French allies it will, hopefully, be capable of resurrection when *Queen Elizabeth* and her sister ship *Prince of Wales* come into service. If it is not, the RN has a very limited future among the world's third-class fleets.

The British seem to have been very profligate with their aircraft carriers, and few of them have achieved the longevity that is common in the US Navy. Seventy-six CVs and CVEs are described in this book. Some achieved relatively long service lives, including the 1955 *Ark Royal*, which was paid off after twenty-three years, *Victorious*, which was withdrawn after twenty-six years, *Furious* after twenty-seven and the 1959 *Hermes* which was sold to India, also having achieved twenty-seven years' service. Taking all the ships into account, however, the average life of a British aircraft carrier to date is only 8.6 years. Even if the wartime CVEs are omitted because they were intended to be temporary 'hostilities only' expedients, the average age of the remaining thirty-two ships is still only 15.5 years. This makes the longevity of the recent *Invincible* Class seem quite remarkable, and when *Illustrious* pays off in 2014 she will be the longest-serving British aircraft carrier by far, with thirty-two years in service since 1982. All compare poorly with the USS *Enterprise*, which was decommissioned in 2012 after fifty-one years' service. These numbers illustrate the fact that the USN carrier force represents a well-understood long-term commitment, but that the vacillations in British defence policy have caused viable equipment to be discarded early by successive administrations that lack understanding and long-term vision, and have spent considerable sums of money on less effective weapons systems that lack similar reach, flexibility and capability.

The individual ship histories contain some details of visits to Commonwealth and foreign ports; I have included these because they are important diplomatic tools. For many people outside the UK, a visit by an RN warship and its ship's company may be the only time they have a first-hand encounter with anything British. A technologically advanced ship and its air group may well leave a lasting impression that should not be underestimated, and it is no coincidence that trade exhibitions accompanied carriers' visits to the Middle East and South America on several occasions. It is also worth pointing out that the UK shares with other maritime nations the responsibility for maintaining peace on the world's oceans and protecting the security of the global trade on which we all depend, but the deployment of an aircraft carrier gave the UK Government an influential say in the management of collaborative operations that a less capable warship would not. Hopefully this capability will resume from 2020; this time with a greater national comprehension of continuity and value.

This book is the result of years of research. It has been a joy to write, and I hope it describes adequately an important element of the RN that is better understood overseas than it has been, recently, in Great Britain. I hope it will help to redress that shortcoming.

David Hobbs MBE
Commander Royal Navy (Retired)
Crail, Scotland
2013

CHAPTER 1

ADMIRALTY INTEREST IN AVIATION 1908-1911

The Admiralty's interest in aviation followed an approach to new technology that had proved successful in the late-nineteenth and early-twentieth centuries. It was based on evaluation, the study of what other nations and potential enemies were doing, and the certainty that British industry would build new equipment faster and in greater quantity than the competition once a decision to proceed had been taken. New weapons had evolved over such short timescales that the same dynamic personalities were involved with the introduction of torpedoes, submarines, aircraft and the modifications that needed to be made to warships in order to deploy or support them. Although man's first powered flights in a heavier-than-air machine are generally accepted to have been achieved by the Wright Brothers in the USA on 17 December 1903, the first powered flight in Britain did not occur until 16 October 1908, when American Samuel Franklin Cowdery ('Colonel Cody') made a flight of 1,390ft at Farnborough, Hampshire, in British Army Aeroplane No. 1. There was little prospect of these early machines operating from a warship to achieve any practical naval purpose, or of operating in support of the fleet from an air station ashore, so it was hardly surprising that when the Wright Brothers offered their patents to the Admiralty in 1907, they had been politely refused. Balloons had been flying for over a hundred years, however, and the scientific establishment regarded motor-powered airships with their greater endurance and load-carrying

capability as having more potential for naval operations than the underpowered heavier-than-air aircraft that began to emerge after 1908. In Germany Count Zeppelin had achieved some success with his prototype rigid airships, although the majority had crashed or otherwise demonstrated unreliability that prevented the German Navy from ordering its own prototype. It was accepted that the design of practical aeroplanes depended on the development of engines of higher power and less weight. The Admiralty maintained close touch with progress in what was widely regarded as an eccentric gentleman's sport through studying the reports of naval officers who taught themselves to fly and, in some cases, designed their own aircraft, and by sending representatives to aviation meetings and conferences. The latter focused on what was then referred to as 'aerial navigation' and were held in France, the contemporary hub of aircraft and engine development.

In September 1909 Lieutenants Porte and Pirie RN, both serving in submarines and based at Fort Blockhouse, Gosport, designed and built a biplane glider. They hauled it on a specially designed trolley to the top of Portsdown Hill, overlooking Portsmouth, with the help of a number of sailors and attempted to take off in it. A wooden trackway was laid down on the grass slope and the trolley, with the aircraft on top, ran down it using gravity to accelerate until sufficient speed was reached to lift off. In common with current submarine

practice, the aircraft had two pilots or coxswains, one controlling up/down movement and the other left/right. Their combined weight proved too much; their co-ordination was unlikely to be perfect on this first flight and the machine crashed. Had it flown successfully, the next planned step was to fit a JAP engine and attempt prolonged, powered flight. The Admiralty was aware of the experiment and had sanctioned the use of sailors and material to support it, but refused to cover all the enthusiastic young officers' costs as the flight had proved to be a failure. Had it succeeded things might have moved forward in a different way.

The French Navy was the first to set up an investigative commission to establish the Service's aeronautical requirements, and Admiral Le Pord was charged with deciding whether airships or heavier-than-air aircraft were better suited to naval operations. In the summer of 1910 he recommended in favour of the latter, especially seaplanes, in a far-sighted report that recommended the conversion of a warship to support seaplane operations. His findings were

HM Rigid Airship Number 1 (R1) as designed. The lines drawn against the bottom of the cars show where the water level was to be when she floated while moored to the cruiser *Hermione* for replenishment and a crew change. She was painted silver on top to reflect sunlight and prevent it from causing excessive heat which would expand the gas in the seventeen internal gas bags, and yellow underneath so that she could be seen and identified by warships. (AUTHOR'S COLLECTION)

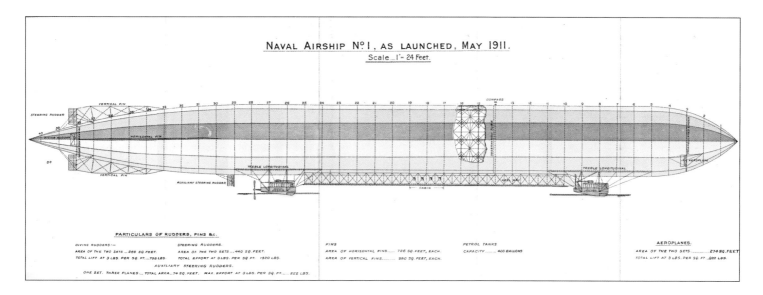

NAVAL AIRSHIP Nº 1, AS LAUNCHED, MAY 1911.
Scale _ 1'= 24 Feet.

PARTICULARS OF RUDDERS, FINS &c.

R1 is moved out to her mooring tower in Devonshire Basin, Barrow-in-Furness, in May 1911. Most of her weight is taken by the inflated gas bags, but her cars are resting on the surface. (AUTHOR'S COLLECTION)

reinforced in the autumn of 1910 when Henri Fabre became the first pilot take-off from and alight on the water, using a seaplane he had designed himself. The navy chose the destroyer depot ship *Foudre*, which already had extensive workshops, booms capable of raising and lowering seaplanes and useful clear deck space for aircraft to be prepared for flight. A canvas hangar was later replaced by a fixed metal structure and it was the first ship in any navy to be modified for the operation of aircraft.

In the USA, Captain Washington I Chambers of the US Navy (USN) secured funding to demonstrate the ability of aircraft to take-off from and to land on temporary wooden platforms rigged on cruisers, and the ability of such ships to hoist seaplanes in and out. On 14 November 1910 Eugene Ely, a demonstration pilot working for the Glenn Curtiss Aeroplane Company, successfully took off from a platform rigged over the forecastle of the USS *Birmingham*. Later, on 18 January 1911, he landed the same aeroplane on a larger platform built over the quarterdeck of the USS *Pennsylvania* and then took off again. On 17 February Glenn Curtiss himself became the second man to operate from the water when he made a very brief hop in his poorly balanced Tractor Hydro biplane to *Pennsylvania*, landed near the ship, was hoisted in by the boat crane and then hoisted out again for Curtiss to taxi back to the Curtiss shore-side camp. The demonstrations showed sufficient future promise for the USN to agree to the training of its first pilot by Curtiss. They also proved to be the catalyst that led the Royal Navy (RN) to set up its own formalised pilot training scheme at Eastchurch, Kent, later in 1911.

There were visionaries who wrote of the potential capability that fully-developed heavier-than-air aircraft could bring to naval warfare, among them Victor Loughheed (half brother of the two men who founded the Lockheed Corporation, using a revised spelling of the family name) in the USA and Clement Ader in France. In 1909 Loughheed described 'great, unarmoured, liner-like hulls designed with clear and level decks' for aircraft to launch from, provided with storage rooms for 'fuel, repair facilities and explosives' capable of destroying fleets of conventional ships operated by navies 'that refused to profit by the lessons of progress'. At about the same time Clement Ader wrote in a second edition of his book *L'Aviation Militaire* about a ship with a flight deck that must be 'as wide as possible, long, flat and unobstructed, not conforming to the lines of the hull for aircraft to take-off and land'. He went a step further than Loughheed, predicting that 'servicing the aircraft would have to be done below this deck with access by means of a lift long enough and wide enough to take an aircraft with its wings folded'. Workshops would run along either side of this maintenance area. Although both descriptions were regarded as futuristic in

1910, both authors might have been surprised if they could have seen how close their ideas actually were to fulfilment.

In 1911, although Captain Chambers's demonstrations had shown the technique to be possible, the RN was not yet convinced that take-off and landing from a ship by aircraft fitted with wheeled undercarriages represented the ideal solution. In the 1911/12 edition of *The Navy League Annual* it was stated in a chapter by Frank W B Hambling headed 'The Aeroplane in Naval Warfare' that 'a little common sense would indicate that the type necessary is one capable of acting with and from our Navy, of resting on and rising from the water. Its advantages for the work we require our scouts to perform are manifold. It could use a ship as a base, without requiring the erection of a special deck-landing platform; any number of aeroplanes could be accommodated in

Commander Schwann taxies his Avro biplane on Devonshire Basin, Barrow-in-Furness, during 1911.

one vessel; it could, while resting on the water recharge fuel tanks and effect minor repairs, save fuel, rest its pilot and engine. … in the event of a forced landing, it would always be at home. These are some of the advantages not possessed by the ordinary type.' Practical experience with seaplanes, as they became known, was to show them in a less favourable light, but the article illustrates contemporary naval thinking. Although his article did not say so specifically, Hambling clearly expected that ships intended to support aircraft operations would be moored in sheltered waters, lowering their aircraft into the water before take-off and recovering them after landing. Operation from the rough seas of the open ocean had yet to be demonstrated, and only a handful of landings in sheltered waters had been performed. The internal volume of a merchant ship would obviously be useful for the stowage of aircraft and spares, but the speed to operate with the battle fleet and the bulky machinery needed to achieve it were not, initially, considered important.

From February 1911 the officers standing by HM Airship R1 at Barrow-in-Furness studied the possibility of operating aircraft from ships. They took out a number of patents on devices ranging from catapults to quick-release hooks for use lowering seaplanes on to the water. Commander Schwann RN raised the money to purchase an Avro biplane which was fitted with a variety of floats, each of them an incremental improvement in design and constructed by sailors standing by R1 while it was under construction; they were made from the same type of duralumin used for the airship's frames. After a succession of taxiing trials

in Cavendish Dock, Schwann, who had not yet qualified as a pilot, became the first British aviator to take-off from water in November 1911. Unfortunately he crashed on landing, but a few weeks later Lieutenant A M Longmore RN, by then qualified as a pilot, landed Short S.38 naval biplane number 2 on floats on the River Medway. By 1912 naval aviation's practical steps forward were beginning to catch up with the theory.

The Clydeside shipbuilding firm of William Beardmore took theory a step further in 1912 when they proposed the construction of an 'aircraft parent ship' to the Admiralty. It was clearly intended to be a mobile base which would anchor in coastal waters rather than operate as a part of the battle fleet. It featured a long through-deck with workshops and hangarage on either side of it connected, over the deck, by a bridge from which both ship navigation and flying operations would have been controlled. The through-deck was level and ran for the full length of the hull, intended to allow convenient access for the aircraft between the hangars, workshops and working decks. In calm conditions, take-off into wind from the deck forward of the flying bridge might have been possible, but any attempt to land on the after deck, into the turbulence caused by the bridge structure and funnel gasses, would have been extremely hazardous. Booms would have been used to move aircraft from the deck into the water for flight and to recover them after landing. Wireless telegraphy (W/T) aerials fitted to tall masts would have allowed long-range communications commensurate with Admiral Fisher's concept of a 'Flying Squadron' of reconnaissance vessels and

The cruiser *Hermione* before her conversion into an airship support vessel. (A D BAKER III)

battlecruisers able to deploy to considerable distances from the UK to seek out an enemy force and destroy it. Rather broad in the beam, it would not have been a fast ship, and coal-fired boilers would have produced copious amounts of smoke and soot. With no experience of heavier-than-air aircraft operations, the Admiralty decided against placing order for such an experimental ship, but it provides an interesting starting point for the study of British aircraft carrier design.

The Royal Navy's first practical steps towards developing naval aviation began in 1908, when the Director of Naval Ordnance, Captain R H S Bacon RN, was sent to France to report on the first international aviation meeting at Reims,

Some idea of how *Hermione* would have appeared operating as an airship support vessel can be gained from this later photograph of a cruiser refuelling a non-rigid airship. (AUTHOR'S COLLECTION)

effectively an international 'showcase' for aircraft development. After his return he forwarded a paper to the First Sea Lord, Admiral Sir John Fisher, on 21 July 1908 in which he recommended the appointment of a Naval Air Assistant within the naval staff at the Admiralty; consultations with the War Office over the design and use of airships and the construction of a rigid airship for the Navy by Vickers, Sons and Maxim at Barrow-in-Furness. Within a remarkably short period of weeks the latter proposal was endorsed by the Committee of Imperial Defence and the RN entered the 'air age' when the sum of £35,000 was included in the 1909-10 Naval Estimates for the construction of a rigid airship. This was the same unit price as the submarines being built for the Admiralty by Vickers under an exclusive contract at the time. Bacon was one of the group of innovative officers who supported Admiral Fisher's reforms and who were known as the 'Fishpond'. After his appointment in charge of the embryo Submarine Branch, Bacon was the first captain of the revolutionary new battleship *Dreadnought* and then Director of Naval Ordnance, in charge of the Admiralty Directorate responsible for the development and introduction of new weapons. As the first Inspecting Captain of Submarines, Bacon had worked closely with Vickers and the firm clearly wanted to expand its portfolio into the new technology, and proposed another exclusive contract for the anticipated production of airships for the Royal Navy. As an inducement the firm built an airship construction shed in Cavendish Dock at Barrow-in-Furness at its own expense and agreed to cover the additional cost if construction of Rigid Airship number 1 exceeded the £35,000 allocated. In the twenty-first century their proposal would be known as a 'private finance initiative' with the catch in the eventual inflated price that the taxpayer would have to pay for the exclusive deal.

The R1 was the largest aircraft of its day and the first to have a structure made of duralumin. It successfully rode out a gale while tethered to a mast in Cavendish Dock during trials in May 1911, but it was too heavy to begin flying trials and had to be substantially lightened before they could be attempted. A number of structural alterations were made, but the airship was damaged while being pulled out of its shed in September 1911 and subsequently scrapped. It had a number of distinctly naval features, including an anchor and cable, a sea-boat that could be lowered into the water from a low hover and two wooden control/power cars which would allow the airship to float on the water if necessary. It also had a telephone exchange to connect the two control cars, the navigation position on top of the hull, the crew's quarters and the first wireless transmitter ever to be

fitted in an aircraft; a prototype device designed especially for this application by the Admiralty Signals Establishment. It was unusual in making no spark when transmitting in order to lessen the risk of explosion if hydrogen gas from one of the seventeen gas bags had leaked into the crew compartment within the rigid structure of the hull.

The R1's design has relevance, since the need to support its deployed operations with a fleet at sea led to the modification of first British warship intended to act as a base for aircraft. The *Astraea* class cruiser HMS *Hermione* was recommissioned in 1910 to act as a 'depot ship' for R1 and moored in Barrow-in-Furness, where it provided accommodation for two airship crews and a large handling party including 150 Royal Marines. The airship's entry in the January 1911 *Navy List* describes her as a twin-screw protected cruiser, second class, displacing 4,360 tons 'under the orders of the Inspecting Captain of Airships', Captain Murray F Sueter, with Commander Edwin H Edwards as his assistant. It also listed 'the following officers borne as additional': Commander Oliver Schwann, Lieutenants Neville F Usborne and Cecil P Talbot 'for service with Naval Airship Number 1' and Engineer Lieutenant Halliday G Paterson 'for temporary service with airships'. The

R1 had two crews which would have alternated to maximise its time airborne, with one of the two lieutenants in charge of each. They would have changed over while the airship was moored to *Hermione* for replenishment.

Physical alterations to the ship included a large boom to which R1 could be tethered by means of a special mooring point in its nose, the first device of its kind to be fitted to any airship. While thus tethered it would be able to swing head to wind whether 'flying' just above the sea surface or 'floating' with her cars on the sea surface. The device was designed to withstand a 'pull' of up to four tons and proved very satisfactory during R1's initial tethering trial in May 1911. A 'pull' of only 530lb was recorded during a breeze of 17 knots while tethered to a mast attached to a pontoon in the centre of Cavendish Dock and, although no accurate recordings were taken, it rode out a subsequent gale of 45 knots very successfully. *Hermione* was fitted with a hook, cable and winch to draw the airship's nose on to the boom attachment point. Another modification was the installation of an additional W/T set. The R1's

An artist's impression of the 'aircraft parent ship' designed by Beardmore in 1912. (STEPHEN MCLAUCHLIN)

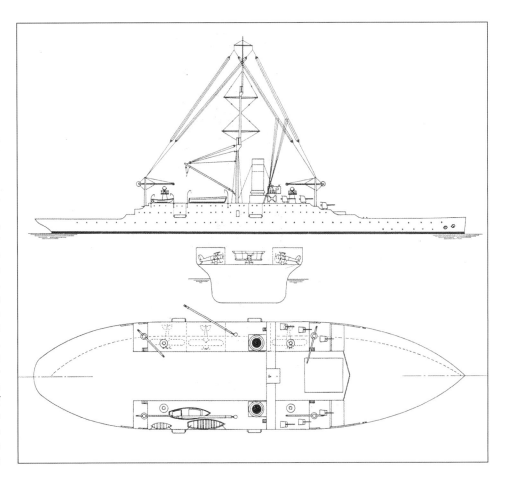

transmitter was relatively low-powered, with a range of only about 600 miles, and the airship would have sent its information to *Hermione*, which would rebroadcast it on its higher-powered sets to fleet flag officers and the Admiralty.

The most important modification, however, was the installation of a plant to produce the hydrogen gas with which R1's seventeen bags, containing a total of 700,000ft^3 of gas, were filled. Nothing on this scale had been attempted in the UK before, and for the first inflation in May 1911 Vickers had to procure 1,050 cylinders of gas from the Chemische Industrie of Amsterdam. Each was charged to 150 atmospheres and a number were connected at any one time through copper branch pipes, but the process took several days to complete. Later consignments were purchased from the Knowles Company of Wolverhampton but, to meet UK legislation, these could only be charged to 120 atmospheres, with the result that considerably more cylinders were required. The second inflation in August 1911 required 1,600 cylinders, 300 of which were recharged and reused. By then the leakage rate of the fragile bags had increased, and about 40 cylinders a day would be needed to top them up under what were expected to be 'normal' operating conditions. The R1 was specified to act as an aerial scout, maintaining a speed of up to 40 knots for 24hr at heights up to 1,500ft. A cabin with tables and chairs was provided under the keel to provide some comfort for the crew outside the engine and control cars, but the airship would have to return to *Hermione* every day to change crew, top up the gas bags and replenish with gasoline, water and ballast. The ship would have carried a number of hydrogen cylinders, although nowhere near enough for a major inflation, which could only be done at a specialised air station ashore. The delivery of cylinders from Wolverhampton to Barrow-in-Furness had filled eleven large railway freight wagons. To recharge the cylinders *Hermione* was fitted with a hydrogen manufacturing plant built on the upper deck. It was 13ft 6in long, 9ft 6in wide and 16ft tall. Unfortunately no photographs of the ship thus equipped seem to have survived. The plant had to be kept scrupulously clean and would have been run continually to charge

HMS *Hermione* technical details

Displacement:	4,360 tons deep load
Dimensions:	Length 339ft 6in
	Beam 49ft 6in
	Draught 19ft
Armament:	2 x 6in; 8 x 4.7in; 10 x 6pdr;
	1 x 3pdr
	4 x 18in above-water torpedo
	tubes.
Protection:	Full length deck 2in
	Engine hatch/ glacis plate 5in
Fuel:	1,000 tons coal.
Endurance:	not known
Complement:	318

cylinders. The R1's rate of leakage would have gradually increased as the gas bags deteriorated, steadily enlarging the depot-ship's production task, but since the airship was scrapped after the damage caused when it was extracted from her shed in September 1911, *Hermione* never operated in the role intended and the ship's potential success, or otherwise, cannot be evaluated.

Gasoline would have been carried in two-gallon cans obtained from the motor trade, stowed where they could be jettisoned over the side into the sea, if necessary, since they constituted a major fire hazard. A similar arrangement was subsequently adopted in battleships and cruisers that operated catapult-launched seaplanes. The R1 was designed to carry 182gal of gasoline in two gravity tanks and two main tanks distributed throughout the ship to provide an even distribution of weight. During replenishment it would have been transferred to the airship through hoses by hand-pump, a slow and laborious business that would have taken several hours. Water would have been drawn from *Hermione*'s domestic supply, also using hand-pumps. To compensate for the loss of gas in normal flight and through leakage and to change trim, airships carried ballast such as sand in bags; R1 carried up to a ton and this, too, would have to be replenished after every flight. Numerous other

engine, wireless and equipment spares would have to be carried to replace failed or worn out items, and the cruiser's workshops would have been utilised to carry out a variety of running repairs.

These details show that *Hermione* contained the essential features of an airship 'depot-ship' capable of acting as a mobile base in sheltered, coastal waters. It can therefore be considered the 'role model' for the first generation of British aircraft depot ships that followed.

Individual ship history

Hermione

Built by Devonport Dockyard, laid down on 17 December 1891 and launched on 7 November 1893, *Hermione* was completed on 14 January 1896 and commissioned for service with the 'Flying Squadron'. Later in 1896 she joined the CF until 1898, when she deployed to the China Station, remaining there until 1901. From 1901 to 1902 she was refitted in Malta and then joined the MF until 1904, when she returned to the UK and reduced to reserve with a nucleus crew. In 1907 she was recommissioned for service on the South African Station, based in Cape Town. After running aground off Zanzibar she was repaired in Cape Town and then returned to the UK in 1909 to join the 10 CS in the 3rd Fleet, which was maintained at a low state of readiness. *Hermione*'s period as the depot ship for airship trials began in 1910 and lasted until 1912, most of this time being spent at Barrow-in-Furness after modifications to suit her for the role had been carried out. Once these were removed she joined the 4th CS in the West Indies in 1913, but returned to the UK to become a depot ship for patrol vessels in Southampton on the outbreak of war in 1914. *Hermione* was badly damaged by fire in 1916 but continued in use as a depot ship. In 1921 she was sold for scrap but then resold to the Marine Society for use as a cadet training ship on the Thames in London, renamed TS *Warspite*. She was a familiar sight for many years in this role until she was finally broken up by T Ward & Co at Gravesend in 1940.

CHAPTER 2

EARLY SHIP TRIALS AND DEMONSTRATIONS

The most senior of the first four RN pilots trained at Eastchurch in 1911 was Commander C R Samson RN, a dynamic officer who sought to emulate and improve upon the demonstrations made by the USN earlier in the year. The Admiralty was keen to learn if the operation of aircraft from a ship at sea was a practical proposition and readily gave permission for a wooden take-off structure to be fitted over the forecastle of the *King Edward VII* class battleship *Africa*. Two downward-sloping troughs and a support structure were fabricated ashore and assembled on the ship in Sheerness Dockyard. Samson took off in Admiralty aeroplane number 2, alias Short S.38, fitted with a 50hp Gnome engine, on 10 January 1912 while the ship was moored to a buoy in the Dockyard. He used just over 100ft of the trackway and the flight was entirely successful, making Samson the second pilot, and the first naval officer, to take off from a ship. He subsequently landed at Eastchurch.

The next step was to take off from a ship under way, and for this the same wooden structure was reassembled on *Africa*'s sister-ship *Hibernia* with less of a downward slope. For the second take-off, on 2 May 1912, Samson used the same aircraft, which had by then been allocated the new Admiralty serial

number T2, using only 45ft of trackway while the ship steamed into wind at 10.5 knots off Portland Fleet Anchorage. He landed at Lodmore Marsh near Weymouth. A third launch using the same wooden structure, the second from a ship under way, was carried out on 9 July 1912; this time from the older battleship *London*. Samson flew T2 again, but by then it had been modified with a 70hp Gnome engine. Again the flight was successful, but this time Samson landed in the sea alongside and was hoisted inboard by derrick. Unfortunately the aircraft was damaged when it struck the ship as it swung while being hoisted and had to be returned to Eastchurch for repairs. Longer derricks would be needed to keep the aircraft further from the ship's side as it was hoisted and lowered.

These RN trial launches went further than the USN's earlier demonstrations and showed that the operation of aircraft from ships at sea was a practical proposition, but they also revealed some of the seaplane's shortcomings. The wooden structure covered the forward 12in-gun turret and would have hampered its movement; gun blast in action would have destroyed it. To recover the aircraft and its pilot the parent ship would have to stop and lower a hook from its derrick, in the process losing formation with other warships in its task force and,

while stopped for the recovery, becoming an easy target for enemy gunfire or a submarine's torpedo. While these limitations applied in action, the tendency of aircraft to swing and bump into the ship's side while being hoisted or lowered in any but the calmest conditions was an ever-present problem, and the damage suffered by T2 on the first occasion it was hoisted at sea gave a warning for the future.

Africa, *Hibernia* technical details

Displacement:	17,195 tons deep load
Dimensions:	length 453ft 9in overall
	Beam 78ft
	Draught 26ft 9in
Armament:	4 x 12in; 4 x 9.2in; 10 x 6in;
	14 x 12pdr; 14 x 3pdr; 2
	Maxim
Protection:	Belt 9in to 4in; bulkhead aft
	12in to 4in
	Conning tower 12in
	Decks; lower 2½ to 2in; middle
	2 to 1in; main 2 to 1½in
Machinery:	Two sets of 4-cylinder, vertical,
	triple-expansion reciprocating
	steam engines.
	12 Babcock + 6 cylindrical
	boilers.
	18,000hp at 210psi
	Giving 18.5 knots at 120rpm
Fuel:	2,200 tons coal
	380 tons FFO
Endurance:	7,000 miles at 10 knots
Complement:	777

Aircraft operating data

Wooden structure over forward 12in turret and forecastle supporting two trackways for aircraft wheels. Petrol stowed in 2gal cans. No aircraft support facilities.

Loading T2 on to *Hibernia*'s wooden runway in May 1912, using the derrick fitted on to the foremast for the purpose. Note the flotation bags fitted to the aircraft's undercarriage and the partly rigged canvas screen aft of the runway, intended to protect the open structure beneath the bridge aft of it from propeller blast. (AUTHOR'S COLLECTION)

Short S.38 T2 on *Hibernia*'s wooden runway. Sailors are completing the rigging of the canvas screen aft of the aircraft and working on the runway right forward near the bow. (Author's collection)

London technical details

Displacement:	15,640 tons deep load
Dimensions:	length 431ft 9in
	beam 75ft
	draught 26ft 6in
Armament:	4 x 12in; 12 x 6in; 16 x 12pdr;
	6 x 3pdr; 2 Maxims
	4 x submerged torpedo tubes
Protection:	Belt 9in to 3in; aft bulkhead
	12in to 9in;
	Decks; lower 2½ to 1in; middle
	2 to 1in; main 2 to 1½in
Machinery:	2 sets of Earle vertical triple-
	expansion steam reciprocating
	engines
	20 Belleville boilers with
	economisers
	15,000hp at 300psi giving 18
	knots
Fuel:	2,000 tons coal
Endurance:	8,000 miles at 10 knots
Complement:	733

Aircraft operating data

As in *Africa* and *Hibernia*

The early demonstrations convinced the British, French and American naval authorities that aviation had exciting potential that should be taken forward, and all three used aircraft in their 1913 manoeuvres. Commander Samson's flights from three different ships in 1912 convinced the Admiralty that the operation of seaplanes from platforms on warships or the sea alongside them was a practical proposition, but there were concerns that the need to operate aircraft would force the ships carrying them to act independently

rather than conforming to the movements of a squadron or fleet, thus hampering them in action and limiting the usefulness of their conventional weapons. The solution devised was to bring a ship out of reserve that could take part in the next

Hibernia fitted with the wooden runway, known as an 'aeroplane slipway', in May 1912. Two sailors are on the aircraft derrick, working on its rigging arrangements. (Author's collection)

Commander Samson's successful launch from *Hibernia* on 2 May 1912 off Portland, the first from a moving warship. The Isle of Portland is just visible beyond the bow. (AUTHOR'S COLLECTION)

annual fleet manoeuvres, operating in support of the battle fleet but with no other function than to operate aircraft. The vessel chosen was the *Highflyer* class cruiser *Hermes*, which was at reduced readiness with a nucleus crew as part of the 3rd Fleet at the Nore. She was modified into a 'state-of-the-art' aircraft support ship with a wooden platform over the forecastle, at the after end of which was a canvas hangar. A long boom was fitted to the fore-mast capable of lifting aircraft off the deck on to the sea and back. A second canvas hangar was rigged on the quarterdeck aft, using the boat boom on the mainmast to move aircraft, and a third aircraft could be carried on the boat deck amidships but with no protection from the elements.

The 1913 RN manoeuvres proved to be the most demanding and successful test of naval aviation before the outbreak of war in 1914, with a scenario that matched the Blue Fleet in the west against the Red Fleet in the east with 351 warships commissioned to match the exact ratio between the British and German main fleets. *Hermes* formed part of the Red or 'enemy' fleet based on Great Yarmouth, and when she sailed on 18 July 1913 she carried 80hp Borel monoplane RN number 48 on the forecastle and 160hp Short S.63 'Folder' RN number 81 aft. The latter had been designed with the help of Commander Samson and Lieutenant Longmore and was the first naval aeroplane to be built with folding wings, reducing its span for stowage from 56ft to 12ft. It also carried a wireless transmitter operated by an observer in addition to the pilot, but had insufficient power to carry a receiver as well. The Borel was damaged by waves which broke over the forecastle in rough seas and was replaced by a Caudron G.II, RN number 55. On 28 July Lieutenant Bowhill RN flew this aircraft off the short forward flight deck to land at RNAS Great Yarmouth, showing that the ability to launch from such a platform was becoming routine. Had the aircraft not been able to fly ashore, however, it would have had to ditch and would have been lost. The folder was a seaplane and managed to fly a number of reconnaissance sorties despite the choppy wave conditions experienced.

Hermes was given two functions during the exercises, both of which generated considerable interest in the fleet. First, she was to carry out reconnaissance sorties out to the Folder's radius of action, about 65 miles from the ship, which, coincidentally, was the working range of its W/T

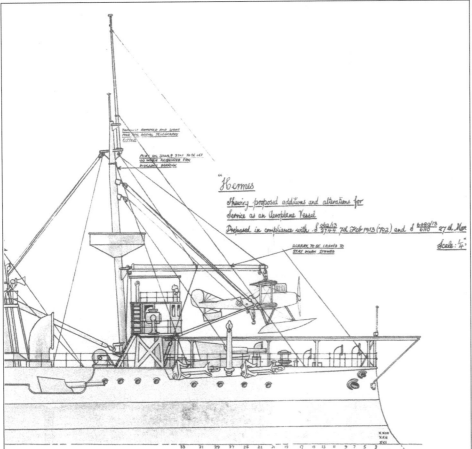

Detail of the forward flying deck fitted in *Hermes* for the 1913 fleet manoeuvres. (AUTHOR'S COLLECTION)

Hermes in 1913, with canvas hangars fore and aft and the prominent aircraft derrick on the foremast stowed fore and aft. (AUTHOR'S COLLECTION)

transmitter. These were intended both to seek out the enemy and to prove, in doing so, that it was possible for aircraft to operate from a warship with the fleet under average conditions in the North Sea. An idea of the capability expected from the *Hermione*/R1 Team can be gathered from *Hermes'* specific exercise instructions, which required the ship to simulate the operation of an airship. This involved steaming up to 340 miles from her base port and launching the Folder to complete the search. The Folder's weak W/T messages were to be picked up by *Hermes* and retransmitted to the battle fleet and Admiralty using the parent ship's more powerful sets. By the end of the fleet manoeuvres *Hermes* and its aircraft proved the concept of aircraft operating with the fleet and she was retained in commission to continue flying operations into the autumn. The months between July and October 1913 represented the longest period of sustained flying operations yet carried out by any navy, and showed the potential of aircraft in less-than-ideal weather conditions. Lessons included the imperative need for W/T transmitters in reconnaissance aircraft, since accurate information about the enemy was time sensitive and needed to be passed on immediately if it was to be of any value to the fleet commander. On a practical level, the *Hermes* trial showed the need for long booms to keep the aircraft clear of the ship's side as it was lowered on to the water or raised from it. The wings were particularly at risk during the lowering process since it was found

advisable to keep the aircraft with its nose forward so that the pilot could use rudder to turn away from the ship once his machine was on the water. Even a gentle bump could cause enough damage to the fragile wing structure to prevent the aircraft from flying. Another lesson, brought home by the practicality of handling on deck and the amount of minor damage caused by relatively rough water take-offs and landings, was the need for naval aircraft to be designed for their purpose, not simply adapted from machines intended for operation in the gentler environment ashore.

Hermes technical details

Displacement:	5,600 tons deep load
Dimensions:	length 372ft
	beam 54ft
	draught 22ft
Armament:	11 x 6in; 9 x 12pdr; 6 x 3pdr
	2 x submerged torpedo tubes
Protection:	Full length deck 3 to 2in
	Engine hatch/glacis 5in
Machinery:	2 sets vertical, triple-expansion
	steam reciprocating engines
	18 Babcock boilers
	10,000hp giving 20 knots
Fuel:	1,100 tons coal
Endurance:	not known
Complement:	450

Aircraft operating data

Wooden flight deck 70ft long over the forecastle; derricks to lift aircraft on to and off the water

alongside; 2,000gal of petrol carried in 2gal cans; oil carried in similar cans; a limited supply of aircraft tools and spares in portable boxes.

Individual ship histories

Africa

Built by Chatham Dockyard, laid down 27 January 1904, launched 20 May 1905 and completed in November 1906, she was commissioned for the AF at first but transferred to the CF in February 1907. In April 1909 she transferred to the 2nd Division of the HF, but in February 1911 she reduced to a nucleus crew at the Nore until April 1911, when she became flagship of the 3rd and 4th Divisions of the HF, both of which were maintained at a low state of readiness; in August the flag transferred to her sister-ship *King Edward VII* and she had resumed reserve status at the Nore with a nucleus crew when fitted with a temporary flight deck over the forecastle for the flying trial in January 1912. In May 1912 *Africa* recommissioned with a full crew for service in the 3rd BS, HF. In February 1913 she was lent to the 4th BS in the MF, returning to 3rd BS in July. War service was mainly with 3rd BS, at first with the GF but on detached service after 1915. In April 1917 she was attached to the 9th CS; in April 1919 she became an accommodation ship and was sold for scrap in June 1920.

Hermes sinking off the Ruylingen Bank in 1914. Note the aircraft in the remains of the canvas hangar aft. (AUTHOR'S COLLECTION)

Hibernia

Built by Devonport Dockyard, laid down on 6 January 1904; launched on 17 June 1905 and completed in January 1907. She commissioned for service with the AF on 2 January 1907 but transferred to the CF in February, flying the flag of the second-in-command. In January 1909 she became flagship of the CF, but in March she became flagship of the 2nd Division of the HF. In January 1912 she reduced to a nucleus crew at the Nore but recommissioned in April for service with the 3rd BS. In May *Hibernia* was fitted with a temporary flight deck forward, and on 2 May Commander Samson carried out the first ever take-off by an aircraft from a ship under way. She remained with 3rd BS after the outbreak of war in August 1914 but transferred to the task force off the Dardanelles as Admiral Freemantle's flagship in November 1915. In November 1919 she returned to the Nore Command for use as an accommodation ship before being sold to a German firm in 1921 to be broken up for scrap.

London

Built by Portsmouth Dockyard; laid down on 8 December 1898, launched on 21 September 1899 and commissioned in Portsmouth on 7 June 1902 for service as the flagship of King Edward VII's Coronation Review at Spithead. She then deployed to the MF but suffered from overheating bearings, leaky condensers and cracked engine cylinders during 1906. In April 1907 she was reduced to reserve as part of the HF based at the Nore. After a major refit in Chatham Dockyard *London* became the flagship of the second-in-command CF from 1908 to 1910, when she hoisted the flag of the second-in-command AF. In May 1912 she reduced to a nucleus crew as part of the 3rd BS and was fitted with a flight deck for seaplane experiments in July. After the removal of the flight deck she transferred to the 5th BS and served with it in the Channel after the outbreak of war in 1914. In March 1915 she was

ordered to the Dardanelles to make good losses. In 1917 she was converted into a minelayer; the ship's after barbette and all casemate guns were removed and a 6in gun placed on the quarterdeck between the mine rails. she was reduced to unmaintained reserve in 1919 and sold for scrap in 1920.

Hermes

Built by the Fairfield Shipbuilding and Engineering Company in Govan, laid down on 30 April 1897, launched on 7 April 1898 and completed on 5 October 1899. After commissioning she served as the flagship of the North America and West Indies Station until 1901, when she was taken in hand by Harland & Wolff in Belfast to be refitted with Babcock boilers. On completion she served in the CF from 1903 to 1904 before reducing to reserve in

Portsmouth in 1905. In 1906 *Hermes* became the flagship of the East Indies Station until 1907, when she became flagship of the South Atlantic Station, based in Cape Town. In 1913 she joined the 3rd Fleet at the Nore with a reduced complement and was refitted for duty as an 'aircraft depot ship' at Chatham. From July to the end of 1913 she carried out trials of aircraft operations both with the battle fleet and as an independent unit visiting a number of bases including the Humber, Cromarty and Scapa Flow. On completion of flying duties she reverted to reduced readiness at the Nore, but when war broke out in August 1914 she was brought forward for use as an aircraft ferry to carry Royal Naval Air Service (RNAS) aircraft to France. On 31 October 1914 she was torpedoed by U-27 off the Ruylingen Bank and subsequently sank with aircraft on board. Forty-four men were lost.

CHAPTER 3

SEAPLANE CARRIERS

Ark Royal (1914) renamed Pegasus in 1934

Technical background

The success of the trial with *Hermes* led the Admiralty to take urgent steps to provide the fleet with an aeroplane depot ship. In the 1914 estimates £81,000 was included for this purpose, and the design team included Constructor J H Narbeth, who was an aviation enthusiast; his assistant C J W Hopkins; Commodore Murray Sueter RN, the Director of the Admiralty Air department; and Commander L'Estrange Malone. They considered the Beardmore design but rejected it as containing too many unknown variables. A cruiser conversion was also rejected as being too expensive, besides withdrawing a significant warship from other duties. Narbeth listed what he considered to be the ideal properties an aircraft-carrying ship should possess. These included a large internal volume, aircraft stowage in hangars below the upper deck with easy access to the

flight deck and handling area; workshops; stowage for fuel, ammunition and spare parts, and many other features that are now accepted as normal in aircraft carriers. The ship would have no other function than the operation and maintenance of aircraft, so it was decided to adopt a mercantile rather than warship hull form. To save time the incomplete hull of a standard tramp steamer being built speculatively by the Blyth Shipbuilding Company was purchased in late 1913 and modified to a new design. (A 'tramp' steamer carried passengers and cargo to a variety of destinations on an opportunity basis, unlike a 'liner', which went to fixed destinations on standard routes.) The ship was framed and partly plated with the engine bearers in place amidships, but the design was recast to provide better aviation facilities, with the result that a number of changes were made on the slipway. The engines and boilers were moved right aft into what would have been the after hold, and the bridge structure moved as far aft as possible. The original sheer on the upper deck was removed to give a level 130ft-long flying-off deck at the bow. The forecastle with its facilities for working anchors and cables was placed under the flight deck with low headroom to minimise the space used for it.

The aircraft, spare parts and fuel carried would be considerably lighter than the original cargo in

Ark Royal at Kephalo in August 1915. (AUTHOR'S COLLECTION)

the holds, so the vessel was extensively ballasted, both to make it a steady platform in high seas and to reduce the freeboard to simplify the operation of lowering and raising seaplanes to and from the water. The forward hold and the space that would have contained the machinery amidships were transformed into a single hangar 150ft long, 45ft wide and 15ft high that was expected to be able to accommodate ten seaplanes. Two steam cranes were installed, one either side amidships, to hoist aircraft out of the hangar on to the deck for preparation, to lift them on to the water, and for the reverse processes. Each was capable of lifting 6,000lb, but Admiralty admitted that their selection was due to ready availability and electric alternatives would have been preferred. The hangar was surrounded by large cellular water tanks both to add the amount of ballast and to serve as protection against fire, since the petrol which fuelled the aircraft and especially the vapour it gave off had a low flashpoint and were known to be extremely dangerous, especially in confined spaces.

The bottom of the hangar rested on number 5 deck, the lowest continuous deck in the hull.

A view forward from *Ark Royal*'s bridge, showing the open hangar hatch with men visible in the workshop area. Two Short seaplanes are being maintained on the forward deck. (AUTHOR'S COLLECTION)

ship's company and the embarked air group was better than in other contemporary warships, partly because of the hull's mercantile origins but mainly due to the lack of guns, with their high demands for manpower to operate them and handle ammunition from the magazines. Air ordnance arrangements were well thought out, in advance of those considered in any other navy and coped well with rapid advances in the ability of naval aircraft to carry weapons. They included a bomb room, a torpedo warhead magazine, a separate torpedo body room and stowage for small-arms ammunition and grenades. There was an open area under the bridge, aft of the access hatch, in which an aircraft could be placed clear of other working areas to run up its engine or undergo maintenance.

The flight deck was the largest yet fitted in any warship when the vessel completed and, to help aircraft accelerate along it, it could be given a pronounced downward slope by flooding ballast tanks built into the bow. Unfortunately the low ship's speed of only 11 knots meant that unless there was a considerable natural wind, which would have made ranging and spreading extremely difficult, take-off from the deck was impractical. Instead, the area was used to prepare seaplanes, which were then craned on to the sea for take-off and the subsequent landing. The higher part of the water barrier around the hangar had the effect of reducing the ship's excessive metacentric height, with the result that rolling was less severe and aircraft swung less when being moved through the hatch and over the side. A unique feature was a mizzen mast aft, on which a sail could be hoisted to help keep the ship head to wind when operating seaplanes while it was at anchor.

Ark Royal's well equipped workshops gave her an important capability as a mobile naval air base and she was retained in service after 1918. In 1930 she was fitted with a catapult and used initially for trials and then for training seaplane crews destined for catapult flights in battleships and cruisers. Maintained at a low state of readiness, she was used for sea trials of equipment intended to improve the operation of seaplanes, including the unsuccessful Hein Mat towed astern, intended the lessen the effect of waves.

Above the hangar, airframe, engine and component workshops were built on to number 2 deck, just below the upper deck. Access to them was through a hatches in the upper and number 2 decks, which were 42ft long and 30ft wide. Aircraft, engines or bulky stores could be lowered in or hoisted out by either steam crane or a five-ton derrick attached to a kingpost on the port side, just forward of the bridge. Petrol was stowed in 2gal cans in a compartment forward of the workshops that was inside the water-tank barrier. Accommodation for the

Ark Royal seen from the air, with her steam cranes working. A canvas screen has been rigged across the hangar opening to provide shade, and the flying-off deck forward, which was never used for its intended purpose, is cluttered with boats and washing. (AUTHOR'S COLLECTION)

Ark Royal technical details

Displacement:	7,450 tons deep load
Dimensions:	length 366ft
	beam 50ft 6in
	draught 18ft 6in
Machinery:	1 shaft triple-expansion
	reciprocating steam engine
	3 x single-ended tank boilers
	3,000ihp delivering 11 knots
	maximum
Armament:	4 x single 12pdr; 2 single
	Maxim
Protection:	None
Fuel:	500 tons FFO
Endurance:	3,030 miles at 10 knots
Complement:	180

Aircraft operating data:

Flight deck:	130ft x 44ft
Hangar:	150ft x 45ft x 15ft
Catapult:	1 x 12,000lb at 55 knots fitted in 1930
Lifts:	None, aircraft lifted through 40ft x 30ft hatch by crane
Aircraft:	up to 10
Aircraft fuel:	4,000gal of petrol in 2gal cans 1,000gal of lubricating oil in cans
Air weapons:	torpedoes, light bombs, grenades and machine-gun ammunition

Engadine, Riviera

The pressing need for ships with greater speed than *Ark Royal* to operate aircraft with the fleet after the outbreak of war in August 1914 led to these two ships being requisitioned from the South Eastern and Chatham Railway Company on 11 August 1914. Both were well known for providing a regular, fast passenger service between Dover, Folkestone and the French Channel ports. They were fitted out in Chatham Dockyard with temporary arrangements including hangars sited forward and aft which had wooden decks surrounded by canvas screens and covered by canvas awnings. There was no flying deck, and seaplanes were winched on to and off the water by derricks worked by the vessels' capstans. They were smaller than *Ark Royal* but, at 22.5 knots, considerably faster and able to keep up with the battle fleet, although, since their boilers were coal fired, maximum speed depended on the quality of the coal, the number of stokers and their ability to keep the fires at peak thermal efficiency; it could only be maintained in short bursts. Their weakness was that they had to stop to launch and recover their aircraft and they could not, therefore, operate in formation with other warships. While stopped they were vulnerable to attack by U-boats or, during a fleet action, by enemy destroyers. They could each carry three seaplanes at first, and both their workshops and stowage for spare aircraft parts were less extensive than those in *Ark Royal*, limiting their use in extended operations.

Renamed *Pegasus*, the former *Ark Royal* is seen here in use as a fighter catapult ship during the Second World War. (AUTHOR'S COLLECTION)

In 1915 they were both reconstructed by Cunard in Liverpool. With more extensive aircraft-operating arrangements they were both subsequently able to carry four seaplanes. The most obvious change was the replacement of the canvas hangars by a more permanent weatherproof steel hangar structure aft. Aft of this were two cranes fitted in lieu of the derricks for operating aircraft, although a derrick was retained forward. The hangar was heated by fourteen steam radiators to keep the aircraft warm while they were stowed inside, and its interior bulkheads included stowage racks for bombs and air bottles. Rails were fitted on the deck for trolleys on which the bulky seaplanes were moved. The hangar was closed by roller shutters. The workshops were improved and extended to include armament, W/T and engine facilities. The last contained lathes, a milling machine, a vertical drilling machine, hand shearing machines, an emery wheel, a coppersmith brazing hearth, four benches with vices, an engine washing tank and trolleys for moving engines. There was even a portable forge and anvil, normally stowed in the hangar when not in use. A separate carpenters' workshop contained a circular saw, a spindle moulding machine, an emery wheel and five benches with vices. Stores and spare parts could be lowered and raised between the workshops and hangar through a trunking. There

Engadine in 1915, with a Short seaplane on its trolley on her after deck. She appears much as she did a year later, when she took part in the Battle of Jutland and launched the first aircraft to take part in a naval battle. (AUTHOR'S COLLECTION)

was also a darkroom for processing photographs and a W/T room with a Marconi set, both for communicating with aircraft that were airborne and for rebroadcasting their information with a stronger signal.

Both ships operated a carrier pigeon service with the necessary pigeon lofts and appliances for training the birds to return to the correct ship when released from aircraft. Given the unreliable nature of W/T, they were intended to bring back reconnaissance information and, in emergency, news of where and when their aircraft had ditched so that a search for the crew could be mounted.

Engadine, Riviera technical details

Displacement:	2,550 tons deep load
Dimensions:	length 316ft
	beam 41ft
	draught 13ft 8in
Machinery:	3 shaft Parsons steam turbines
	6 Babcock & Wilcox water-tube
	boilers
	13,800shp delivering up to
	22.5 knots for short periods
Armament:	4 x 12pdr, 2 x Maxim
Protection:	None
Fuel:	960 tons coal
Endurance:	1,250 miles at 15 knots
Complement:	197

Aircraft operating data

Flight Deck:	None
Hangar:	80ft x 36ft x 20ft after full
	conversion in 1915
Catapults:	None
Lifts:	None
Aircraft:	Four seaplanes
Aircraft fuel:	Variable amounts of petrol
	carried in 2gal cans
Air weapons:	18in torpedoes; 20lb and 100lb
	bombs; grenades; 0.303in
	ammunition; flares and
	pyrotechnics.

Empress

Another of the cross-Channel ferries taken up from the South Eastern and Chatham Railway by the Admiralty in 1914, *Empress* was closely similar to *Engadine* and *Riviera* but machinery of only 8,800shp gave her a maximum speed of only 18 knots. Her more extensive modifications were carried out slightly later than those to the first two ships and differed slightly in detail. For instance, the hangar was 2ft longer and 1ft wider. Overall her capability was the same, including the workshops and stowage arrangements.

Campania (1914)

After the outbreak of war in August 1914 the Admiralty took up such large numbers of merchant vessels that it proved difficult to identify large, fast ships suitable for conversion into seaplane carriers to work with the fleet. New construction was

expected to take too long and, in any case, the yards were full with orders for more cruisers, destroyers and other more conventional warship types. Efforts were made to expand the number of passenger ferries being modified for the role but, other than those mentioned above, most available vessels were converted for minesweeping, minelaying and other important tasks. In November 1914 the old Cunard liner *Campania* was identified and purchased for conversion to an auxiliary cruiser. Twenty years old, she had won the Blue Riband for the fastest Atlantic crossing in 1894, but was now worn out and had actually been sold to T W Ward & Co for scrapping. On the advice of the Director of the Air Department, however, she was converted into a seaplane carrier and her machinery overhauled to be able to maintain high speed with the fleet. The lack of watertight subdivision made her vulnerable to the effects of underwater damage but she proved to be an innovative and largely successful seaplane carrier.

The extensive modifications to convert *Campania* for her new role were carried out by Cammell Laird & Co of Birkenhead and included the construction of a large flying-off deck forward, from which it was hoped that seaplanes resting on wheeled trolleys could take off, thus obviating the need for the ship to stop and lower them into the water. In theory this made it possible for *Campania* to operate more closely with the battle fleet. A hangar capable of holding ten seaplanes was built under the flying-off deck. Workshops even more extensive than those in *Ark Royal* were fitted out and a considerable amount of space made available for the stowage of spares and stores. As with all the First World War aviation vessels it was assumed

Riviera in 1914, shortly after her initial conversion, with canvas hangars and derricks fitted in Chatham Dockyard. (AUTHOR'S COLLECTION)

Campania as she appeared in May 1916. (AUTHOR'S COLLECTION)

that many aircraft components would be made from scratch in workshops rather than delivered by manufacturers as spare parts.

A Sopwith Schneider seaplane was launched successfully from the deck in August 1915, albeit with little room to spare, and it was appreciated that the deck was too small to launch large

reconnaissance seaplanes successfully. Consequently the ship was returned to Cammell Laird for more extensive alterations to be carried out from November 1915. To make the deck as long as possible, the forward funnel was taken down and replaced by two smaller funnels, one on each side of the extended deck. A small navigating bridge

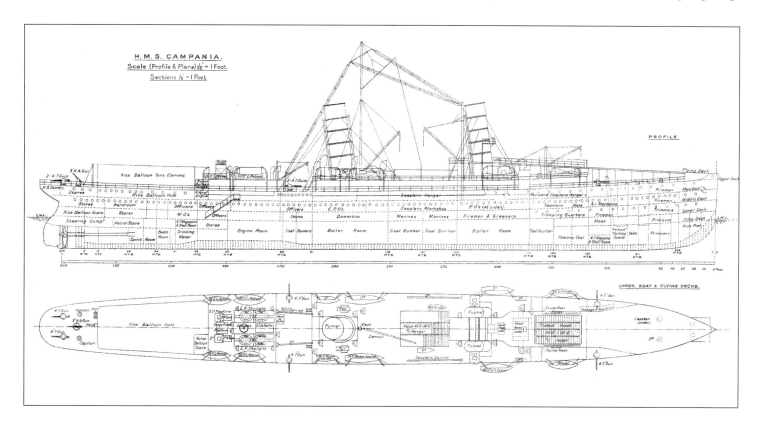

TOP *Campania* after her initial conversion into a seaplane carrier in 1915. Note the single forward funnel and the small flying-off deck, which had only a shallow downward slope. The small hangar is visible aft of the gun mounting, and the two aircraft derricks in their stowed position are conspicuous. (R A BURT COLLECTION)

LEFT *Campania* after the modification which extended the flying-off deck aft between the new, split fore-funnels. Note the slope of the deck, which was intended to help aircraft accelerate to flying speed in the short distance available. (AUTHOR'S COLLECTION)

BOTTOM LEFT A Short seaplane on its trolley is ranged ready for take-off from *Campania*. (AUTHOR'S COLLECTION)

was fitted between the funnels, high enough for aircraft to be passed underneath it on to the flying-off deck. The after part of the ship was cleared to make space for an inflated kite balloon to be stowed and winched up. A hydrogen-making plant to fill the balloon, and winches for hauling it down, were installed at the same time. The alterations were completed in April 1916 and *Campania* joined the GF in Scapa Flow with an air group of Sopwith Schneiders and Short Type 184s. She proved able to launch seaplanes given a reasonable amount of natural wind, but the ship's performance remained marginal and she still had to stop in the water to recover her aircraft once they had landed, making it difficult for her to stay close the battle fleet.

Campania earned a place in history as the evolutionary link between the early seaplane carriers and the first true aircraft carriers.

Campania technical details

Displacement:	20,611 tons at deep load
Dimensions:	length 622ft overall
	beam 65ft
	draught 29ft 3in

Anne in 1915. (Author's collection)

Machinery:	2 shaft reciprocating steam engines
	13 cylindrical boilers
	30,000shp giving up to 23 knots for short periods
Armament:	6 x single 4.7in LA; 1 x single 3in HA
Protection:	None
Fuel:	3,270 tons coal
Endurance:	2,600 miles at 21 knots
Complement:	600

Aircraft operating details

Flight deck:	245ft x 50ft (maximum)/30ft (minimum) wood planking
Hangars:	forward 210ft x 60ft x 20ft under flying-off deck
	Aft 100ft x 50ft narrowing to 40ft x 20ft canvas sides and cover
Lifts/hatches:	forward 45ft x 20ft
	Aft 45ft x 30ft through which aircraft were lifted by derricks
Aircraft:	Up to ten seaplanes; 1 kite balloon after 1915.
Aircraft fuel:	Variable amounts of petrol carried in 2gal cans
Air weapons:	18in torpedoes; 20lb and 100lb bombs; 0.303in gun ammunitions; flares and pyrotechnics

Anne

Originally the mercantile *Anne Rickmers* owned by the Rickmers Reismuhlen Reederai and Schiffbau, this vessel was captured by the RN in Port Said on the outbreak of war in August 1914 and given temporary modifications to allow her to operate as a seaplane carrier. She operated in the Eastern Mediterranean, where canvas hangars and awnings were sufficient to protect her aircraft against the elements. Workshops and stores facilities were extemporised since the vessel's service was expected to be temporary.

Anne technical details

Displacement:	4,083 tons deep load
Dimensions:	length 367ft 1in
	beam 47ft 7in
	draught 27ft 3in
Machinery:	single shaft triple-expansion reciprocating steam engine
	Coal-fired boilers
	11 knots maximum

Armament:	1 x 12pdr; 1 x 0.303in machine-gun
Protection:	none
Fuel:	coal
Endurance:	not known
Complement:	not known

Aircraft operating arrangements

Hangars:	canvas windbreaks
Aircraft:	Three seaplanes
Aircraft fuel:	petrol carried in 2gal cans
Air weapons:	grenades and 0.303in gun ammunition

Ben-my-Chree

Ben-my-Chree was requisitioned from the Isle of Man Steam Packet Company on 1 January 1915 and her modification into a seaplane carrier took advantage of the experience gained with the cross-Channel steamers that had been requisitioned a few months earlier. Her name translates into English as 'Woman of My Heart'. She was fitted with a small flying-off deck, 63ft long, over the forecastle but this proved too small to be able to launch even lightweight Sopwith Schneiders and was subsequently removed. Since she was considerably larger than *Engadine*, the conversion was more extensive and included a hangar that was slightly

larger and more sophisticated workshops capable of testing as well as manufacturing and repairing aircraft components.

The ship had the dubious distinction of being the only aircraft carrying vessel to be sunk in action during the First World War, after hits from Turkish shore batteries set her on fire. The situation was made worse by the explosion of petrol vapour from 'empty' 2gal aircraft fuel cans stowed in and around the hangar. Full petrol cans also contributed to her loss as they burned furiously and beat back all attempts to fight the fire. Subsequent analysis of the loss influenced all future British aircraft carrier designs, the majority having enclosed hangars that were isolated from the rest of the ship by airlocks and good ventilation to prevent petrol fumes building up. British hangars subsequently had metal decks, rather than wooden ones which could absorb fuel, and copious supplies of first-aid fire appliances. As with all ships fitted with coal-fired boilers, the maximum speed quoted could usually be maintained only for short periods, and performance varied with the type of coal in use. Welsh steam coal was considered the best.

Ben-my-Chree on fire aft and sinking off Castelorizo Island in 1917. (Author's collection)

Ben-my-Chree technical details

Displacement:	3,888 tons deep load
Dimensions:	length 375ft
	beam 46ft
	draught 16ft
Machinery:	3 shaft steam turbines
	4 cylindrical double-ended
	boilers
	14,500shp giving 22 knots for
	short periods
Armament:	4 x single 12pdr LA;
	1 single 12pdr HA;
	2 x single 3pdr
Protection:	none
Fuel:	552 tons coal

Endurance:	not known
Complement:	250

Aircraft operating data

Flight deck:	take-off deck forward 63ft long and 12ft wide
Hangar:	80ft x 42ft x 21ft
Lifts:	Derricks forward and aft for lifting seaplanes on and off the water
Aircraft:	Up to six seaplanes
Aircraft fuel:	Variable amounts of petrol stowed in 2gal cans
Air weapons:	18in torpedoes; small bombs; 0.303in gun ammunition; flares and pyrotechnics

Vindex, note the flying-off deck over the forecastle and derricks forward for lifting fighters out of the small hangar under the deck. (AUTHOR'S COLLECTION)

Vindex (1915)

Another of the Isle of man Steam Packet Company's vessels taken over by the Admiralty, *Vindex* was originally named *Viking*. She can be considered as the first of the 'second generation' of small aircraft carrying ships, and was intended from the outset to launch fighters from a deck forward to prevent German reconnaissance airships reporting the fleet's

Ben-my-Chree as she appeared after conversion to a seaplane carrier in 1915. (AUTHOR'S COLLECTION)

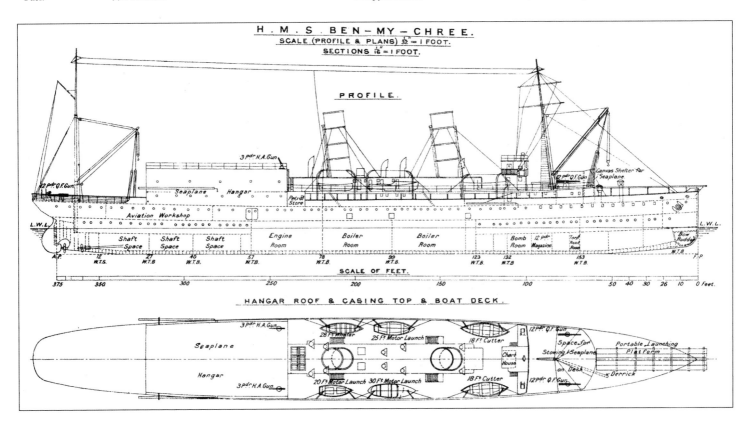

position. The arrangement for seaplanes aft followed the lines that were by then considered normal, supported by a general-purpose workshop. By early 1915, however, experience already showed that seaplane fighters were unable to intercept Germany's rigid airships over the North Sea. There were several reasons for this. The carrier had to stop to swing the fighter out on to the water, giving the enemy aircraft warning that a launch was imminent, and the floats limited the fighter's modest performance to the extent that the German airships could both out-climb and, usually, out-run them. If all else failed, the airship could dump ballast and climb rapidly above the fighter's ceiling. No German airship was successfully intercepted by a seaplane fighter in the entire war. The solution, already clear in 1915, was to embark wheeled high-performance fighters such as the Bristol Scout that could take off from a small deck and climb rapidly to intercept and engage. The only drawback before landing decks evolved was that, if the fighter could not fly to the nearest point of land, the pilot had to ditch close to a friendly warship. Apart from the obvious danger to the pilot, the aircraft was a write-off and had to be considered as a 'one-shot' system, rather like modern anti-aircraft missiles.

Vindex's conversion into a seaplane carrier included a box-type hangar aft. An operating deck was built aft of it and seaplanes were moved by two electric cranes fitted against the after hangar bulkhead. A second hangar was built forward under the small take-off deck. It was just large enough to carry two dismantled fighters which were carefully stowed to allow them to be quickly assembled (or dismantled). Two derricks, one either side of the ship, were fitted forward of the bridge to lift fighters out of the small forward hangar. At first these were to be Sopwith Babies, but the deck was too short for them and in October 1915 the ship's officers obtained Admiralty permission to evaluate a Bristol Scout C wheeled fighter, the fastest fighter in RN service at the time. On 3 November 1915 Flight Commander B F Fowler RNAS took off from *Vindex*, which was steaming at 12 knots into a 15 knot wind. It took 20ft to get the tail up and achieve flying attitude, but he was airborne in 46ft. The aircraft had no brakes and had to be restrained by a 'hold-back' device which was released only when the pilot was happy that he had full power and the bridge was happy that the ship was steady into wind.

Further experiments refined the technique by putting the tailskid on a trestle so that the aircraft was in the flying attitude from the outset, reducing the take-off run required and the minimum wind speed needed over the deck. It proved possible to launch two aircraft within ten minutes of each other, most of the time being taken to hoist the second aircraft out of the cramped hangar on to the deck and then assemble it.

Vindex technical details

Displacement:	2,950 tons deep load
Dimensions:	length 361ft
	beam 42ft
	draught 13ft 3in
Machinery:	3 shaft direct-drive turbines
	4 cylindrical, double-ended boilers
	11,000shp giving 22 knots for short periods
Armament:	2 x single 12pdr LA
Protection:	none
Fuel:	475 tons coal
Endurance:	995 miles at 10 knots
Complement:	218

Aircraft operating data

Flight deck:	64ft x 25ft
Hangar:	aft 80ft x 36ft x 20ft
	fwd not known
Aircraft:	up to seven, normally five seaplanes and two wheeled fighters
Aircraft fuel:	Variable amounts petrol in 2gal cans
Air weapons:	18in torpedoes; light bombs; 0.303in gun ammunition; flares and pyrotechnics

Raven II

Built as the merchant ship *Rabenfels* for the Deutsche Dampfschiffahrts Gesellschaft, this vessel was seized in Port Said at the same time as *Anne Rickmers* on the outbreak of war in 1914. She underwent a similar conversion and operated initially as a merchant auxiliary under the red ensign with a mixed Anglo-French air group.

Raven II technical details

Displacement:	4,706 tons deep load
Dimensions:	length 394ft 5in
	beam 51ft 6in
	draught 27ft 6in
Machinery:	single shaft quadruple-expansion reciprocating steam engine
	Coal-fired boilers
	10 knots
Armament:	1 x 12pdr LA
Protection:	none
Fuel:	coal
Endurance:	not known
Complement:	not known

Aircraft operating data

Flight deck:	none
Hangar:	temporary canvas screens to protect aircraft
Aircraft:	Up to six
Aircraft fuel:	petrol carried in 2gal cans
Air weapons:	grenades; 0.303in machine-gun ammunition; flares and pyrotechnics

Manxman

Manxman was built as a packet running to the Isle of Man and operated by the Midland Railway Company. She was slightly smaller but generally similar to *Vindex* and was converted into a seaplane carrier by Chatham Dockyard in 1916. The conversion took eight months and was more extensive than the work on any of her predecessors, allowing specialised workshops for aircraft maintenance to be fitted out. It reflected all the experience gained in two years of wartime operations. The steel hangar aft was large enough to accommodate four seaplanes, which were moved into and out of the hangar on trolleys running on rails to help with ranging and striking down in rough weather. They were handled by two electric jib cranes on the after corners of the hangar. *Manxman* was fitted with a Marconi W/T installation with an aircraft type set as a backup.

The first innovation in the design was a second hangar built in under a new bridge, aft of a small working space and accommodating four aeroplanes. Forward of the working space was a flying-off deck 86ft long, built up over the forecastle. This hangar could accommodate four fully-assembled fighters and was originally intended for Sopwith Baby seaplanes, but the ship's speed proved somewhat lower than the anticipated 21 knots and launching seaplanes proved to be impractical. Instead she embarked Sopwith Pups with wheels, which could be operated perfectly adequately. The aircraft were pushed forward out of the hangar on to a working space and then lifted on to the flight deck by derrick. The space between the flying-off deck and the hangar structure was covered by a portable hatch which was slid forward under the deck to allow aircraft to be hoisted off the working deck and ranged; once they were through it was replaced in position to form an after extension to the flight deck, allowing aircraft prepared for launch and in a flying position with a trestle under the tailskid the maximum deck run possible. The same derricks hoisted aircraft inboard from lighters in harbour to replace those that had ditched after an operational launch. *Manxman*'s early trials with Sopwith Pups in 1917 proved so successful that this aircraft type was adopted for use throughout

the GF. Given a suitable wind over the deck, a Pup could be airborne after a deck run of only 20ft.

The second innovation was a central cantilever gantry which extended aft from the hangar roof to a point beyond the stern, where a hook lowered from a trolley could be attached to a seaplane taxying at the same, slow, speed as the ship. The idea was that the ship would not have to stop to recover aircraft and, once the aircraft was attached to the hook, it was winched up clear of the water and the trolley moved it forward along the gantry to a point where it could be lowered on to a trolley on the working area and then wheeled into the hangar. The idea worked well in calm, sheltered water but was less successful in the open sea.

With a flight deck forward capable of launching fighters successfully but no means of landing them on, *Manxman* represented an intermediate step between the early seaplane carriers and *Argus*, the first truly practical aircraft carrier.

Manxman technical details

Displacement:	3,090 tons deep load
Dimensions:	length 343ft
	beam 43ft 1in
	draught 15ft 9in
Machinery:	3 shaft direct-drive steam
	turbines

Manxman, showing the cantilevered gantry aft which was intended to recover seaplanes while the ship remained in motion. (AUTHOR'S COLLECTION)

	3 boilers
	6,500shp giving a nominal 21
	knots
Armament:	2 x 12pdr LA; 1 x 6pdr HA
Protection:	none
Fuel:	430 tons coal
Endurance:	not known
Complement:	250

Pegasus with her two three-ton electric cranes aft of the hangar in their stowed position. (AUTHOR'S COLLECTION)

Aircraft operating data

Flight deck:	86ft x 28ft
Hangar:	forward 42ft x 36ft x 18ft
	aft 80ft x 36ft x 20ft
Aircraft:	8 (4 seaplanes aft; 4 wheeled
	fighters forward)
Aircraft fuel:	variable amounts of petrol
	stored in 2gal cans
Air weapons:	18in torpedoes; light bombs;
	0.303in machine-gun
	ammunition; flares and
	pyrotechnics

Pegasus

The next ship in sequence to be taken up for conversion was still under construction, and the Admiralty took the opportunity to carry out a more elaborate conversion and improve her machinery without unduly delaying the completion date. When taken over she had not been launched and, although the hull was fairly well advanced, there was an opportunity to make greater internal modifications than in earlier ships. The spaces originally intended for passengers, horses and cargo were completely rearranged to provide accommodation, and stores, magazines and workshops were created in the lower part of the vessel. The workshops were particularly well equipped and included shops for airframe and engine work and carpentry and specialist areas for the ship's hull, machinery and carpentry maintenance. She was also one of the first aircraft-carrying ships to have bulk stowage for aircraft fuel rather than stowing it in 2gal cans.

The structure and deckhouses above the awning deck were cut away to allow hangars to be constructed forward and aft which were similar to those in *Manxman*, the former being sited under a new bridge structure. By substituting Beardmore WB.IIIs, a folding-wing derivative of the Sopwith Pup intended specifically for embarked use, it proved possible to carry five fighters in the forward hangar, an improvement on the four fixed-wing Pups carried in *Manxman*. The central gantry aft was not repeated and two 3-ton electric cranes handled seaplanes and moved them on to and off the water. Derricks were provided forward to move wheeled fighters on to the flying deck. As in *Manxman*, a sliding hatch was fitted aft of the flying deck to allow movement of aircraft up from the hangar and to extend the deck once it was back in place. A Type 2 W/T installation was fitted.

Pegasus was fitted with Brown Curtis steam turbines direct-geared to two shafts. Her boilers had originally been fitted to burn coal but were modified to burn FFO and the former coal bunkers were modified to serve as oil tanks. These improvements gave her a realistic sea speed of 20 to 21 knots and allowed her to steam at high speed for up to three days.

Since her conversion was more elaborate than that of her predecessors, *Pegasus* proved successful in service and was retained after the First World War.

Pegasus technical details

Displacement:	3,315 tons deep load
Dimensions:	length 332ft 4in
	beam 43ft
	draught 18ft 9in
Machinery:	2 shaft Brown & Curtis direct-geared steam turbines
	6 oil-fired cylindrical boilers
	9,500shp giving over 20 knots
Armament:	2 single 3in HA; 2 single 12pdr HA
Protection:	none
Fuel:	360 tons FFO
Endurance:	1,500 miles at high speed
Complement:	258

Aircraft operating data

Flight deck:	82ft x 28ft
Hangar:	forward 40ft x 40ft x 20ft
	aft 80ft x 40ft x 20ft
Aircraft:	4 seaplanes aft; 5 fighters forward; total 9
Aircraft fuel:	1,300gal of petrol in bulk stowage
Air weapons:	18in torpedoes; light bombs; 0.303in machine-gun ammunition; flares and pyrotechnics.

Nairana

Nairana had been launched when she was taken over by the Admiralty for conversion to a seaplane carrier. Her machinery had not yet been installed but was at an advanced stage, so the boilers could not be modified to oil firing, limiting top speed to about 19 knots, but she was fitted out otherwise to the same standard as *Pegasus*, with extensive workshops and hangars fore and aft. She was slightly smaller, and thus able to carry only seven rather than nine aircraft. The arrangement of the flying-off deck forward was the same, with a sliding hatch to allow derricks to move aircraft out of the hangar on to the deck. Aft she had a gantry like the one in *Manxman* but considerably developed to allow it to be extended unsupported from the roof of the hangar for 50ft, and this variation proved more successful. The ship was fitted with a Type 2 W/T installation for communication with her aircraft and a secondary aircraft-type installation as backup.

Unlike previous ships that had been purchased

Nairana in a disruptive paint scheme in 1918, showing her enlarged and improved gantry aft. (AUTHOR'S COLLECTION)

outright by the Admiralty, *Nairana* was hired from her owners. The Admiralty had hoped that, together with *Manxman* and *Pegasus*, she would be able to form a 'Flying Squadron' capable of operating with the fleet without having to stop to launch and recover seaplanes, but their lack of top speed and the practical difficulties encountered with the gantry prevented realisation of this concept.

Nairana technical details

Displacement:	3,070 tons deep load
Dimensions:	length 352ft
	beam 45ft 6in
	draught 14ft 5in
Machinery:	2 shaft geared turbines
	6 water-tube coal-fired boilers
	7,000shp giving up to 19 knots
	for periods
Armament:	2 single 12pdr LA; 2 single
	12pdr HA
Protection:	none
Fuel:	448 tons coal
Endurance:	not known
Complement:	278

Aircraft operating data

Flight deck:	94ft x 23ft
Hangar:	forward 40ft x 36ft x 20ft
	aft 80ft x 36ft x 20ft
Aircraft:	4 seaplanes aft; 3 fighters
	forward; total 7
Aircraft fuel:	variable amounts of petrol
	carried in 2gal cans
Air weapons:	18in torpedoes; light bombs;
	0.303in machine-gun
	ammunition; flares and
	pyrotechnics

Albatross

The Royal Australian Navy (RAN) deployed three ships to the Grand Fleet from 1915 onwards and fully understood the need to have aircraft operating as an integral part of a modern fleet, but was unable to fund an aircraft carrier like *Argus* or *Hermes*. *Albatross* was designed by the Admiralty's Director of Naval Construction to meet the RAN requirement and was to be the first seaplane carrier to serve with the RAN and, after transfer, the last to serve with the RN. She was a logical progression from the First World War conversions but considerably larger. The high-sided forward two-thirds of the ship contained a hangar intended to contain nine seaplanes. The hangar roof was a working area with two cranes that could lift aircraft out of the hangar through a hatch like that in the original 1914 *Ark Royal*. The ship was designed to have an hydraulic catapult forward so that aircraft could be launched without the need for the ship to stop or turn into wind, but she still had to stop to lift them out of the water after landing. The catapult was not fitted on build, but was eventually installed in 1936. Her speed of 21 knots was adequate but slow by the latest standards, and she would not have been able to function effectively with a cruiser hunting or raiding force.

Given her later design in the light of considerable wartime experience she had extensive workshops, bulk stowage for petrol and relatively large bomb rooms.

Albatross technical details

Displacement:	6,350 tons deep load
Dimensions:	length 443ft 9in
	beam 68ft
	draught 16ft 6in
Machinery:	2 shaft Parsons geared turbines
	4 Yarrow small-tube boilers
	12,000shp delivering 21 knots
Armament:	4 single 4.7in HA; 4 quadruple
	2pdr 'pom-pom' (16)
Protection:	none
Fuel:	942 tons FFO
Endurance:	9,500 miles at 10 knots
Complement:	450

Aircraft operating data

Flight deck:	none
Hangar:	130ft x 60ft x 21ft
Catapult:	single EIII hydraulic capable of
	launching a 12,000lb aircraft at
	55 knots
Aircraft:	up to 9; 6 normally carried
Aircraft fuel:	8,300gal of avgas
Air weapons:	250lb SAP bombs; 100lb A/S
	bombs; Mark VII and Mark
	VIII depth charges; 0.303
	machine-gun ammunition;
	flares and pyrotechnics

Individual ship histories

Ark Royal/Pegasus

Laid down by the Blyth Shipbuilding and Engineering Company to a commercial design on 7 November 1913 and launched after extensive

An aerial view of HMAS *Albatross* before the installation of the catapult. (RAN)

redesign on 5 September 1914. Completed on 10 December 1914 and worked-up for service as a seaplane carrier. She sailed for the Dardanelles on 1 February 1915 and her aircraft flew their first combat mission on 15 February, dropping a 20lb bomb on a Turkish position. Her aircraft spotted for the battleship *Queen Elizabeth* in March, using wireless to transmit corrections for the first time in action. In June 1915 she was relieved by *Ben-my-Chree* and moved to Salonika. From March 1916 she acted as depot ship for No.2 Wing RNAS at Mudros, a task which continued until October 1918, when she ferried aircraft of the newly-formed RAF across the Black Sea for operations against the Bolsheviks in Russia.

After the Armistice she continued to give useful service, and in December 1918 she ferried 2 Squadron RAF to Somaliland and supported it during operations to put down a revolt by insurgents. In 1922 she ferried aircraft to Chanak during the crisis in the Dardanelles and supported them until the situation was resolved in 1923. After that she saw service as a fleet auxiliary, aircraft ferry and minesweeper depot ship until 1930, when she was fitted with a catapult for trials. Periods in reserve were varied with periods in commission to train seaplane crews in catapult launches and recoveries at sea by ship's crane and to carry out seaplane trials such those with the Hein Mat in 1933. On 21 December 1934 she was renamed *Pegasus* to free the name *Ark Royal* for the new aircraft carrier being built by Cammell Laird, and was reduced to reserve.

In September 1939 she was recommissioned for use as an aircraft ferry and used to transport naval

aircraft from the mainland to naval air stations in the Orkney Islands. After enemy aircraft began to operate from German-occupied France, the need for convoys to be defended against air attack became desperate, and *Pegasus* was allocated to WAC for use a fighter-catapult ship, with three Fairey Fulmars embarked, on convoys to and from Gibraltar despite initially having no radar or even VHF radio to communicate with the fighters. These were fitted later. As with other fighter-catapult ships the aircraft could be launched but not recovered, and had either to ditch near the convoy or, if possible, fly to the nearest friendly point of land. Her first convoy was OG 76 in December 1940, and subsequent launches were made on three occasions, in January, June and July 1941 while supporting convoys SL 60/HG 49; HG 63 and SL 78/OG 67. In the June launch the enemy aircraft was intercepted and driven off but not shot down; in the others the enemy evaded into cloud. After the last launch the pilot elected to fly back to Ireland rather than ditch near the convoy, but unfortunately flew into a hillside in bad weather and was killed.

Later in July 1941 she ceased operational flying and returned to catapult training duties in the Clyde. In February 1944, with the need to find manpower for the large number of ships nearing completion, she was reduced to reserve and used for a while as an accommodation vessel. In May 1946 she was de-stored and a month later she was placed on the list of ships for disposal. On 18 October 1946 she was sold for conversion into a merchant ship and renamed *Anita 1*. The

conversion was started but never finished, as more efficient merchant ships became available, and her hull was sold on to a succession of breakers before finally being scrapped at Grays in Essex during 1950.

Engadine

Built by William Denny and Brothers of Dumbarton for the South Eastern and Chatham Railway Company and completed in 1911, she was requisitioned by the Admiralty for naval service on 11 August 1914 and given temporary modifications in Chatham Dockyard to equip her as a seaplane carrier. She was commissioned on 1 September 1914 and allocated to the Harwich Force, taking part in a series of sweeps across the North Sea. On 25 December 1914 she launched aircraft against German Zeppelin sheds in the Cuxhaven Raid, in company with *Riviera* and *Empress*.

In February 1915 she was purchased outright by the Admiralty and taken in hand by the Cunard Steamship Company in Liverpool for improvements which included the fitting of a steel 'box' hangar aft with an operating platform and cranes positioned at the stern. After the modifications were completed in March 1915, she

Two merchant ships renamed as *Athene* and *Engadine* were purchased by the Admiralty from the Clan Line in 1939 and extensively modified for use as seaplane carriers. After their completion in 1941, however, they were used exclusively as aircraft transports and thus fall outside the scope of this work. This is *Engadine* in 1941. (AUTHOR'S COLLECTION)

rejoined the Harwich Force and was based at Granton. In October 1915 she joined the BCF based in the Firth of Forth and carried out a series of tests to evaluate the high-speed towing of kite balloons attached to warships which proved the viability of the concept. She was present at the battle of Jutland on 31 May 1916 and the aircraft she launched to locate the German fleet was the first ever to take part in a sea battle. Although the aircraft's successful reports were received by *Engadine*, their rebroadcast was, unfortunately, not taken in by the C-in-C in his flagship *Lion*. After the battle she took the damaged cruiser *Warrior* in tow and rescued her survivors when she foundered. In 1918 she was transferred to the MF and operated from Malta until the end of hostilities. In December the Admiralty sold her back to her former owners and she returned to use as a cross-Channel ferry. In 1923, with the regrouping of Britain's railways, her ownership transferred to the Southern Railway and in 1932 she was sold to a ship broker who sold her on to Hermanos Inc in the Philippines in 1933 and renamed her *Corregidor*. In December 1941, during the Japanese invasion, she was sunk by a mine in Manilla Bay, with heavy loss of life.

Riviera

Built by William Denny and Brothers of Dumbarton for the South Eastern and Chatham Railway and completed in 1911, she was requisitioned by the Admiralty with her sister ship *Engadine* on 11 August 1914 and given temporary alterations in Chatham Dockyard for use as a seaplane carrier. She joined the Harwich Force, together with *Engadine*, in October and took part in the Cuxhaven Raid on Christmas day 1914, together with her and *Empress*. She was fully converted into a seaplane carrier by the Cunard Steamship Company in Liverpool in February 1915, and on completion of the work she joined the Dover Patrol on 7 April 1915. Her seaplanes were used extensively to spot for the gunfire of monitors off the Belgian coast and other duties until 1918 when, with other early seaplane carriers, she transferred to the Mediterranean Fleet based in Malta. In 1919 she was sold back to her original owners and resumed duty as a cross-Channel ferry, transferring to the new Southern Railway in 1923. In 1932 she was sold to the Burns and Laird Lines and renamed *Laird's Isle*.

In September 1939 she was requisitioned again by the Admiralty, this time under her new name, and used at first as a torpedo training ship and then as an ocean boarding vessel. After modifications in 1944 she was used as an infantry landing ship. In 1945 she was demilitarised and returned to Burns and Laird, who continued to operate her until 1957, when she was sold for scrap.

Empress

Built as a cross-Channel ferry for the South Eastern and Chatham Railway by William Denny & Brothers of Dumbarton, she was completed in April 1907 and requisitioned by the Admiralty on 11 August 1914. Until space was available in Chatham Dockyard for her modification she was used as a dispatch vessel for the RNAS, carrying the men and equipment of the Eastchurch Squadron to France. After 30 August she was fitted out as a seaplane carrier, and when the work was completed in September she joined the Harwich Force and took part in North Sea sweeps. On 25 December 1914 she joined *Riviera* and *Engadine* in launching aircraft against Zeppelin bases in the Cuxhaven raid.

In May 1915 she was taken in hand by the Cunard Steamship Company of Liverpool and given more extensive modifications to operate seaplanes, the work being completed in July.

On 18 July 1915 she was based at Queenstown in Ireland for patrol work which lasted until January 1916, when she sailed to join the East Indies and Egypt Seaplane Squadron based at Port Said. In April 1916 she was detached for operations off the Bulgarian coast, for which she was based at various ports in the Aegean Sea. In November 1916 she used her seaplanes to support operations ashore in Sinai and the coast of Syria. From January 1918 she was based in Port Said again and used her seaplanes for antisubmarine patrols over the eastern Mediterranean. Later in the year she was based in Gibraltar to support patrols in the western Mediterranean.

Empress was handed back to her original owners in November 1919. She was transferred to the Southern Railway in 1923 and later in the same year sold to the French Société Anonyme de Gérance et d'Armement. She was eventually scrapped in France in 1933.

Campania

Built by the Fairfield Shipbuilding & Engineering Company in Glasgow and completed for the Cunard Steamship Company in 1894, she was purchased from T W Ward on 27 November 1914 and taken to Cammell Laird's yard in Birkenhead for conversion to a seaplane carrier. On completion of the work she was commissioned at Birkenhead on 17 April 1915 and subsequently joined the GF in Scapa Flow. On 11 June 1915 she carried out her first successful operational sortie with the GF. In August 1915 she successfully launched Sopwith Schneiders from her take-off platform, but it was demonstrably too short for larger aircraft to use. In consequence she was taken back into Cammell Laird's hands to have the deck lengthened and to have facilities for a kite balloon installed aft.

She emerged from this work and rejoined the

GF on 2 April 1916. Successful trials demonstrated her ability to launch aircraft under way, and she was regarded as an asset to the GF's reconnaissance capability but, due to a signalling error, she missed the battle of Jutland on 31 May 1916. She had actually sailed late when the error was realised and had the speed to catch up with the main fleet, but the C-in-C considered her too vulnerable on her own and ordered her to return to Scapa Flow. The potential usefulness of her aircraft remains one of the Battle of Jutland's imponderable questions.

She continued to operate with the GF throughout the remainder of the war, latterly based in the Firth of Forth, but mechanical defects caused escalating problems in 1918 and she was used increasingly in a training role after other large aircraft carriers joined the fleet. On 5 November she dragged her anchor during a gale in the Firth of Forth and collided with *Royal Oak* and *Glorious*. Her lack of underwater protection let her down and she sank about a mile south of Burntisland harbour. The ship's company were all taken off the stricken vessel without loss of life and she remains the largest vessel ever to sink in the Forth. Although she sank in 100ft of water, the tops of her masts and funnels still showed above the water and in 1921 they were cut down to give 6.5 fathoms clearance at low water. The hull remains intact on the seabed, although in 2013 it is said to be in a state of collapse. Given its history as one of the world's first practical aircraft carriers, the wreck has been declared a site of historic importance and is designated as a Protected Wreck under Section 1 of the protection Wrecks Act, 1973.

Anne

Built by Rickmers AG in Bremerhaven, *Anne Rickmers* was completed as a tramp cargo steamer in 1911. She was captured in Port Said in August 1914 and subsequently used as a temporary seaplane carrier. At first she retained her original name and flew the red ensign with a mixed RN and civilian ship's company, operating French Nieuport seaplanes manned by French pilots and British observers. She operated in the Eastern Mediterranean in early 1915 and reconnaissance missions flown by her aircraft contributed to the successful British naval and military actions that halted the Turkish thrust towards the Suez Canal. On 11 March 1915 she was torpedoed by the Turkish torpedo-boat *Demir Hisar* and deliberately beached at Mudros, after which her seaplanes were transferred to *Raven*. On 12 May 1915 she was refloated and towed to Alexandria for repairs and improvements to her aviation facilities. These were completed in July and she sailed for further operations off the Turkish coast, again with French seaplanes embarked.

On 5 August 1915 she was commissioned into

the RN and renamed *Anne* before joining the East Indies and Egypt Seaplane Squadron in January 1916. On 9 May 1916 she replaced her French aircraft with RNAS Short 184s and Sopwith Schneiders in Malta and returned to operations in the Eastern Mediterranean. By mid 1917 seaplane carriers that had been more extensively modified for the role in the UK arrived in the theatre, and on 8 August 1917 *Anne* was paid off.

On 29 January 1918 she was sold to F C Strick & Co for use as a collier. Sold on to a Greek shipping concern in 1922 and renamed *Ithaki*, in 1939 she was sold on to a Romanian company and renamed *Moldova*. In 1942 she was re-registered in Panama and in 1949 sold to the Panamanian firm of Wallen and Co. In 1954 she was renamed *Jagrahat* and in 1955 reverted to *Moldova*. After a long and varied career she was broken up for scrap in Hong Kong in 1958.

Ben-my-Chree

Built by Vickers at Barrow-in-Furness, launched on 23 April 1908 and completed on 8 August 1908 for the Isle of Man Steam Packet Company, she was requisitioned by the Admiralty on 1 January 1915 for conversion into a seaplane carrier. The work was carried out by Cammell Laird in Birkenhead and completed on 23 March 1915, when she commissioned in Birkenhead. In April 1915 she replaced *Empress* in the Harwich Force and operated in the North Sea with Sopwith Schneider seaplane fighters embarked. On 11 May 1915 attempts to launch a Schneider on a wooden trolley from the flying-off deck proved unsuccessful and the method was not used again.

On 12 June 1915 she replaced *Ark Royal* in the fleet off the Dardanelles with an air group that included the first Short Type 184 seaplanes to be used in operational service. On 12 and 17 August 1915 her aircraft carried out the first aerial-torpedo attacks in history; the targets were Turkish merchant ships. In January 1916 she became the flagship of the East Indies and Egypt Seaplane Squadron on its formation at Port Said. From then onwards she operated in the Eastern Mediterranean, Red and Aegean Seas. In March 1916 she was dry-docked in Suez for repairs.

On 9 January 1917, while anchored off Castelorizo Island, she was engaged and hit by Turkish shore batteries which started fires and explosions which became uncontrollable and she sank in shallow water. Her wreck was raised in 1921 and subsequently sold to a breaker's yard in Italy.

Vindex

Built by Sir W G Armstrong Whitworth & Co of Newcastle-upon-Tyne as *Viking* for the Isle of Man Steam packet Company, she was launched on 7 March 1905 and completed on 26 June 1905. On 26 March 1915 she was hired by the Admiralty, retaining the name *Viking,* and converted into a seaplane carrier by the Cunard Steamship Company of Liverpool. On 3 November 1915 she was the first vessel ever to launch a wheeled 'landplane' from a flight deck, and on 11 November 1915 she was purchased outright by the Admiralty, renamed *Vindex* and commissioned at Liverpool. She was allocated to the Harwich Force and used in the North Sea on anti-airship patrols off the Nore. On 2 August 1916 she launched a Bristol Scout against a Zeppelin, the first ever interception of an enemy aircraft by a carrier-based fighter. Unfortunately the Zeppelin, L17, managed to evade the fighter and escaped.

In 1918 she was allocated to the MF with a number of other early seaplane carriers. On 12 February 1920 the Admiralty sold her back to her original owner, who used her on the Isle of Man run again. In 1939 she was requisitioned by the Admiralty for the second time, this time as a troopship, retaining the name *Viking*. She was again restored to her original owner in 1945 and used on the Isle of Man run until 1954, when this grand old vessel was sold to British Shipbreakers for scrap.

Raven II

Rabenfels was built by Swan Hunter & Wigham Richardson at Wallsend-on-Tyne for the German shipping firm of Deutsche Dampfschiffahrts Gesellschaft and completed in December 1903. After being captured in Port Said she underwent a conversion into a temporary seaplane carrier that was similar in scope to *Anne*, and began operations in December 1914 with French seaplanes embarked. These had French pilots and British observers in an early example of a coalition force. In March 1915 she took over *Anne*'s aircraft and on 12 June 1915 she was commissioned formally into the Royal Navy and renamed *Raven II*.

In January 1916 she joined the East Indies and Egypt Seaplane Squadron and embarked a mixed group of Short 184 and 827 and Sopwith Schneider seaplanes. On 1 September 1916, while anchored in Port Said, she was damaged by a bomb dropped by a German aircraft. On 16 March 1917 she passed through the Suez Canal in company with the French cruiser *Pothuau* to form a hunting group searching for the German raider *Wolf* in the Indian Ocean. She returned to the Eastern Mediterranean on 10 June 1917 and paid off. In January 1918 she was bought by Graham & Co for mercantile service and renamed *Ravenrock*. In 1923 she was sold on to the British Dominion Steamship Company, which then sold her again to Karafuto KKK, who renamed her *Heiyei Maru 7*. She was sold for the last time to Innui KKK in 1935 and

was eventually sunk in the Pacific during the Second World War.

Manxman

Built by Vickers, Sons & Maxim at Barrow-in-Furness for the Midland Railway Company, she was completed in 1914 and ran on the Isle of Man packet service. She was purchased by the Admiralty on 17 April 1916 and taken in hand by Chatham Dockyard for conversion to a seaplane carrier. The work was completed in December 1916, and in early 1917 she carried out a series of trials with Sopwith Pup fighters and seaplanes, as a result of which the Pup was adopted as the GF's standard fighter and *Manxman* was allocated to the BCF rather than the Harwich Force, as had originally been the intention. In April 1917 she supported a minelaying operation in the North Sea, but her low speed meant that she could not operate with the battle cruisers, limiting her usefulness. In October 1917 she moved to the MF but acted more as a harbour depot ship for aircraft than as a fleet unit; she moved in turn from Syracuse to Taranto to Brindisi. In January 1918 she was ordered to embark aircraft and move to Mudros to prepare for a strike against the Turkish battle-cruiser *Goeben*, which was aground in the Dardanelles. The strike was, however, cancelled.

On 12 February 1920 she was sold to the Isle of Man Steam Packet Company, but she was requisitioned by the Admiralty for the second time in October 1941, modified for use as a radar training ship and recommissioned as HMS *Caduceus*. She was paid off again in 1945 and placed on the disposal list; this time she did not attract a buyer and she was broken up for scrap in 1949.

Pegasus

Laid down as *Stockholm* for the Great Eastern Railway Company by John Brown & Co of Clydebank, she was purchased incomplete by the Admiralty for completion as a seaplane carrier on 27 February 1917. She was launched on 9 June 1917 and completed on 14 August before commissioning on the Clyde as HMS *Pegasus* on 28 August 1917. She joined the GF and was based at Rosyth in the Firth of Forth, carrying out several sweeps of the North Sea with the BCF, but came to be used mainly for training RNAS pilots in shipborne operations as more-capable aircraft-carrying vessels joined the fleet. As the number of major warships with take-off platforms grew rapidly she was used to ferry replacement aircraft from the air yard at Donibristle out to ships in the Firth of Forth that had launched and lost their one-shot aircraft on operations.

In 1918 Sopwith 2F.1 'Ship' Camels replaced her Beardmore WB.IIIs and she continued to fill a variety of air functions for the GF. After the Armistice she was retained in service and in May 1919 she deployed to Archangel with Fairey IIICs embarked that were used to support British forces in action against the Bolsheviks. She returned to the UK in September 1919 and was used as an aircraft ferry until 1920, when she deployed to the Dardanelles during the 'Chanak Crisis' with 'L' Flight of 267 Squadron embarked. After the crisis she remained with the MF. In 1923 the forward flying-off deck was removed and in 1924 she reclassified as an aircraft tender. In early 1925 she ferried aircraft to Singapore, and on 5 July 1925 she paid off into reserve at Devonport. In 1929 she recommissioned for use as an aircraft ferry and was used to carry aircraft between naval bases in support of the growing number of aircraft carriers. She was paid off again after this service, being sold for scrap on 22 August 1931 and subsequently broken up at Morecambe.

Nairana

Built by William Denny & Brothers of Dumbarton for the Australian firm of Huddart & Parker as a mail packet and launched on 21 June 1915, she was taken up by the Admiralty in 1917 and converted for service as a seaplane carrier, completed on 25 August 1917 and commissioned for service with the BCF based at Rosyth. Like *Pegasus* she was used on some operational sweeps, but more often to train RNAS pilots in deck-launch techniques and to ferry replacement aircraft out to warships anchored in the Firth of Forth that were fitted with take-off platforms. In 1918 she was allocated to the MF with an air group of four Short 184 seaplanes and three Beardmore WB.III fighters embarked.

In 1919 she deployed with *Pegasus* to Archangel with four Fairey Campanias and three Sopwith 2F.1 'Ship' Camels embarked to support British operations against the Bolsheviks. After her return she was sold to Tasmanian Steamers Pty and refitted for mercantile service, reverting substantially to her original design. After an unusually long career she ran aground in Port Melbourne on 18 February 1951, and on survey was found to be beyond economic repair. She was subsequently broken up.

Albatross

Built in Cockatoo Island Dockyard, Sydney, she was laid down on 5 May 1926, launched on 23 February 1928 and completed in January 1929. Her first deployment was a patrol and survey of the dependent territories north of Australia with

six Supermarine Seagull III amphibious aircraft of 101 Flight, Royal Australian Air Force (RAAF), embarked. She paid off for a refit in December 1931 and recommissioned in 1932, primarily for use as a gunnery training ship but retaining four aircraft of 101 Flight on board. On 19 March 1932 she anchored in Sydney Harbour for the ceremonial opening of the Harbour Bridge, but on 26 April paid off into reserve at Garden Island Dockyard due to shortages of funding and manpower. Her aircraft were transferred to the new cruisers *Australia* and *Canberra* but her cranes were still used from time to time to support visiting seaplanes, using manpower from RAAF Richmond.

In 1936 she was fitted with the designed catapult for the first time and in August commissioned for trials with the new Supermarine Seagull V (Walrus) aircraft being procured for RAAF service. A proposed full reactivation was cancelled in September 1936 due to economic difficulties and she was placed in reserve again. In 1938 she was transferred to the RN in part payment for the light cruiser *Apollo,* which became HMAS *Hobart* and sailed for the UK manned by the ship's company intended for *Hobart*.

She arrived in Devonport on 9 September and commissioned into the RN, keeping the same name, on 29 September, after which she was used as a seaplane trials ship. On 15 December she reduced to reserve and the catapult was removed when she became an accommodation ship.

On 25 August 1939 she recommissioned at Devonport for operational service; embarked 710 NAS with six Walrus six days later and sailed for Sierra Leone on 14 September to use her aircraft for trade protection on the West African convoy routes. She was moored near Hastings while a naval air station was constructed ashore to take over her task. In June 1940 she led the Task Force which attempted to neutralise the French Fleet in Dakar, flying the flag of Vice-Admiral d'Oyley Lion, C-in-C South Atlantic. On 26 June one of her Walrus detected the breakout by the battleship *Richelieu*. She returned to Freetown on 3 July 1940 and her aircraft returned to antisubmarine duty. On 14 May 1941 her aircraft disembarked to the new RNAS Hastings and she proceeded to Simonstown for a refit, during which a replacement EIII catapult, removed from the cruiser *Orion*, was fitted. In September she returned to Hastings until 22 December 1941, when she sailed for Mobile, Alabama, USA, via Trinidad, to commence a refit which was completed on 2 April 1942. On 20 April she arrived off Hastings to embark 710 NAS and sailed to carry out antisubmarine patrols in the

Western Indian Ocean. In July she anchored off Mayotte in Madagascar for her aircraft to patrol the Mozambique Channel, and in September she moved to Majunga, from where her Walrus carried out patrols in support of military operations ashore and she was used as a command ship. In October she ferried 795 NAS, a fighter 'pool' unit, from Madagascar to RNAS Tanga in East Africa, and in November she started a refit in Durban.

In April 1943 she sailed for Bombay with 710 NAS embarked, and disembarked them to RAF Santa Cruz while she operated as a Combined Operations training ship. She re-embarked the squadron in July 1943 and sailed for Kilindini, where 710's aircraft and stores were landed, after which she sailed for the UK in August with 710's personnel. She arrived in Devonport on 6 October and landed the squadron personnel to disband formally on 14 October while the ship carried out sea trials with the new Supermarine Sea Otter amphibian. On 5 November 1943 she paid off into care and maintenance at Devonport.

In April 1944 she recommissioned for use as a landing craft repair ship, a task for which her extensive workshops suited her. On 2 June 1944 she moved to Southend, supporting the landing craft intended for 'Sword' Beach during the D-Day landings. On 6 June she was the flagship of Follow-Up Force L, used to repair landing craft and get them back into service quickly. While doing so she used her guns to engage shore batteries and shot down a German Junkers Ju 88. During Operation *Neptune* she saved 79 landing craft from total loss and repaired 132 others. On 24 June she was hit by a German shell which caused minor damage, and on 1 July she moved to support 'Gold' Beach.

On 11 August 1944 she was hit by a long-range German torpedo which killed fifty of her ship's company and caused extensive damage. She was towed to the UK and given temporary repairs to keep her afloat, and on 30 August she formally paid off into reserve. She recommissioned for use as a static minesweeper depot ship in Portsmouth in November 1944, but paid off finally in July 1945. In August she was towed to Falmouth and placed in unmaintained reserve. Subsequently she was towed to the Solent and placed on the disposal list. In August 1946 she was bought by a firm that intended to convert her into a luxury liner, but the deal was not proceeded with. On 21 November 1947 she was sold to the Greek Yannaulatos Group, which converted her into a passenger ship and renamed her *Hellenic Prince*. As an example of her new role, she carried 1,000 refugees from Europe to Australia in 1949. On 12 August 1954 she was sold to breakers in Hong Kong and subsequently scrapped.

CHAPTER 4

FURIOUS AND *VINDICTIVE*

Furious

Originally conceived as one of three large light battlecruisers by Admiral Fisher for his 'Baltic Project', *Furious* was designed to be a large, fast ship with single 18in guns in turrets forward and aft and a large, secondary battery of 5.5in guns. By 1917 the GF regarded the ship as too specialised and of little value against manoeuvring ship targets since the designed firing rate of the big guns was one round every four minutes. They were eventually fitted to monitors and a firing interval of 2min 38sec was found to be possible, but this was still too slow. In February 1917, therefore, the GF Aircraft Committee recommended that *Furious*, by then being fitted-out at Armstrong's Walker Naval Yard on the Tyne, would be of more use if completed as an aircraft carrier, since she would be able to embark a significant number of aircraft and had the speed to launch them from the deck while she remained in formation with the battle fleet. She was considered too valuable to stop to recover aircraft, however, and when they came down on the sea they would be recovered by more conventional and less valuable seaplane carriers, for return later.

The design was rapidly modified and she was completed on 4 July 1917.

Work on the forward turret was well advanced in March but the gun, which weighed 146 tons without the breech, had not been installed. The turret structure, roller path and part of the barbette armour were removed and replaced by a large hangar capable of containing 'about ten' aircraft, which was built over the forecastle deck. The roof of the hangar was extended to the bow to form a flight deck 228ft long and between 57ft and 36ft

Furious as completed, near the RNAS airfield at Smoogroo in Scapa Flow, Orkney. (AUTHOR'S COLLECTION)

wide, supported by a latticework structure of girders. The foremost section was plated in, but was believed to be vulnerable to damage if the ship were to be driven hard into a rough sea. Aft of the flight deck was a hatch through which aircraft were hoisted from the hangar by topping lifts attached to two derricks, one to port and one to

Furious' forward flight deck in 1917, showing the space in which Dunning had to land. Note the windbreaks, some of which are fully up, some only partly. The shapes to starboard of the after Pup are supports for the hatch covers removed from the hangar entrance. Note the starboard derrick just visible on the right-hand side of the picture, which marked the after limit of the landing area. (AUTHOR'S COLLECTION)

Dunning's first landing in Pup N6453, the first by an operational naval aircraft flown by a naval pilot on a ship under way at sea. Strops were not fitted to the aircraft at this stage, there is no Vickers gun forward of the cockpit, and there is a triangle of white paint on the aft starboard tip of the lower starboard aileron. The white line painted on the deck is an 'eye-line' to guide the pilot over the ideal landing spot. (AUTHOR'S COLLECTION)

starboard. Aircraft on deck near the hatch could, if necessary, be protected from wind blast by wooden palisades, attached vertically to the outboard hangar sides in metal brackets. Slid up and locked in position they formed a windbreak; slid down when not in use, their tops were flush with the deck and they were out of the way. They were an important feature, since the lightweight aircraft of the day could easily be blown over the side by a gust if not tied down or protected. Given the size of this deck and the ship's speed of over 30 knots, it was calculated that any reconnaissance or fighter aircraft could be flown off in almost any weather condition. Impressive as she appeared in 1917, she was still only an interim solution to the problem of operating aircraft with the fleet, however, as she could not land them on.

Furious technical details (as modified in 1918)

Displacement:	19,100 tons deep load
Dimensions:	length 735ft
	beam 88ft (extreme over
	bulges)
	draught 21ft 6in
Machinery:	4 shaft Brown Curtis geared
	turbines
	18 Yarrow boilers
	90,000shp giving 31 knots
	maximum speed
Armament:	10 x 5.5in; 5 x 3in HA; 12 x
	21in torpedo tubes
Protection:	2-3in side belt; 2-3in
	bulkheads; 1-2in magazine
	crowns; 3in magazine sides;
	bulges designed to defeat
	torpedo warheads up to 440lb.

Fuel:	3,400 tons FFO
Endurance:	3,500 miles at 20 knots
Complement:	658

Aircraft operating data

Flight decks:	forward 228ft x 50ft (tapering to 36ft)
	aft 284ft x 70ft
Hangars:	forward 120ft x 60ft x 15ft 6in
	aft 116ft x 33ft x 15ft 6in
Lifts:	forward 48ft x 18ft hydraulic; 6,000lb; 40ft/min
	Aft 48ft x 18ft electric (for comparison); 6,000lb; 40ft/min
Aircraft:	14
Aircraft fuel:	3,000gal in 2gal cans
Air weapons:	18in torpedoes; 20lb and 100lb bombs; 0.303in machine-gun ammunition; flares and pyrotechnics

The world's first carrier landing

Furious' first senior aviation officer was Squadron Commander E H Dunning DSC RNAS, a brave, skilled and resourceful pilot who had recently been involved with carrier flying experiments at the Deck Landing Trials Unit at the RN Experimental Air Station Isle of Grain, near Sheerness in Kent. With the full support of his commanding officer, Captain Wilmot Nicholson RN, he decided to investigate the possibility of landing on the large take-off deck. Both realised that if he succeeded and deck landing at sea proved to be a practical proposition, *Furious'* aircraft could be flown repeatedly rather than as 'single shots' that would be lost at the end of their

sorties. This would enormously increase the potential value of the air group and a demonstration would stimulate progress.

The air group fighters were Sopwith Pups, a delightful aircraft to fly and a type that inspired confidence in its pilots. Landing speed depended on weight ,which reduced as fuel and ammunition were used up, but 40 knots was a good average. Given sufficient ship's speed into a steady natural wind, the approach speed of a Pup relative to the deck could be very low. If *Furious* steamed at 20 knots into a 20-knot wind, a pilot could, in theory, side-slip over the deck from an approach alongside the ship and 'hover' over it, stationary relative to the deck. Initial tests were made while the ship lay at anchor close to the small naval air station at Smoogro, 7 miles south-west of Kirkwall on the north shore of Scapa Flow, where the Pups disembarked while she was in harbour. Whenever *Furious* lay head-to-wind Pup pilots would fly up the port side and, once forward of the bridge structure and derrick, carry out a flat or 'S' turn to starboard using rudder and then straighten up over the deck. Landing at, or near, stalling speed was dangerous, as a gust of wind or turbulence caused by the ship's hull could cause the pilot to lose control, but several pilots are believed to have bounced their wheels on the deck before climbing away.

Attempting to land a Sopwith Pup in front of the superstructure of a large warship was all the more remarkable when the aircraft's controls are fully explained. It had a very low wing loading, and any turbulence would cause the pilot to have to make constant adjustments to the primary flying controls. The 80hp Le Rhône 9C was a rotary engine, in which the cylinders rotated with the propeller about a fixed crankshaft. The rotating mass gave considerable torque and made left-hand turns easier to achieve than right; also the nose tended to rise when turning left and drop when turning right. The latter was never a good thing close to the surface of the sea, and the two effects made left-hand circuits the preferred option; they have remained so ever since. The engine operated over a very narrow range of revolutions, basically 'on' or 'off', and its manipulation needed to be as much part of the pilot's handling skill as the flying controls. The nearest equivalent to the control we now know as a throttle was a lever that adjusted the fuel/air mixture to achieve smooth running; with constant changes in height, speed, temperature and turning forces it needed constant adjustment. More

Pup N6454 being hoisted out of *Furious'* hangar by derrick, showing the narrow tolerances. Such a move would be extremely difficult in anything but the calm sea visible in this photograph. (AUTHOR'S COLLECTION)

instant control of engine power was achieved by means of a 'blip' switch on the control column, with which the pilot turned the engine ignition on and off. Speed was, therefore, achieved by a series of 'power/no-power' selections when necessary, giving the engine its characteristic 'blipping' sound.

On 2 August 1917 *Furious* sailed for gun-direction exercises near an island south of Scapa Flow. When these were complete Dunning was allowed to demonstrate the first deck landing by a naval pilot in an operational aircraft on an operational warship under way at sea. He flew a low, left-hand circuit off the ship's port side, controlling his height with the elevators and speed with ignition switch while constantly adjusting the mixture control. *Furious* steamed at 26 knots into a steady 21-knot wind, giving a 'wind over the deck' of 47 knots from directly ahead. This was slightly higher than ideal, and meant that he had to 'overtake' the deck as he drew alongside, turning in close ahead of the port derrick and encountering 'cliff-edge effect' as the wind was blown upwards against the ship's side. Once over the centre of the deck, Dunning would have centralised the controls and held the Pup, N6453, in a 'three-point' attitude about 10ft over the deck, 'blipping' the engine on and off to descend. He touched down at 1110 on the hangar roof at the widest part of the deck and was held firmly in place by officers briefed to prevent the Pup being blown over the side when it was lightened as he got out. The importance of the event was widely recognised, and a number of GF senior officers watched the dawn of a new era from the bridge.

Dunning attempted to repeat the demonstration on 7 August, but on his first landing the aircraft was blown backwards by a gust as it landed and struck the hatch coaming, causing some damage to the elevator. He elected to make another attempt in a second aircraft, N6452, at 1330, and flew three approaches before making his last at 1400. By then the wind was gusty and he moved over the deck too high and well forward of the ideal position. As his wheels touched the deck the handling party started to grab the aircraft, but he waved them away and 'blipped' the engine on to fly away, but it choked and lost power. Photographs show the port wing lifting, probably due to 'cliff-edge' effect at the narrower part of the deck. Without power and semi-stalled, the Pup rolled off the deck to starboard and ditched. There was no crash-boat, and it took *Furious* twenty minutes to return to the aircraft, which was kept afloat by the air bag in the rear fuselage. Dunning was found to have drowned after being knocked

unconscious when the aircraft hit the water. However, his initiative led to the recognition that landing aircraft on their carrier was indeed the best way forward, and that 'one-shot' operations represented a dead-end technology that was useful only as a short-term expedient. Dunning's initiative showed what could be achieved and undoubtedly hastened the pace of progress. Every carrier landing by every pilot in the last 95 years owes something to him.

Modification in 1918

Dunning's demonstration led Admiral Beatty, the Commander-in-Chief Grand Fleet, to recommend the removal of the after 18in gun and its replacement by a second flight deck intended for aircraft recoveries. *Furious'* pilots opposed the change because they believed that turbulence aft of the bridge structure and funnel would make the approach to the deck dangerous. Experience was to

Squadron Commander Edwin Harris Dunning DSC RNAS.

prove them right, but Admiralty approval was given in October 1917. There were also concerns that *Furious* was too valuable to lose, even for a short period, but the potential for landing-on aircraft was too attractive, and she returned to Armstrong's Walker Yard in the Tyne for the work to be carried out. The allocation of scarce shipyard capacity was a measure of the urgency given to the task. The design was based on that already prepared for the cruiser *Vindictive* and could thus be implemented quickly.

Furious emerged in March 1918 with an after flight deck nearly 300ft long, constructed over an after hangar. The forward hatch was replaced by an hydraulic-powered lift and the after structure was fitted with a similar sized electric lift, the two types being installed to enable a direct comparison to be made. The hydraulic lift was deemed superior. As in all subsequent British aircraft carriers, the lift platforms formed part of the flight deck when the lift was in the up position. The flight decks were connected by trackways 11ft wide fitted to port and starboard of the bridge structure, along which folded aircraft could be pushed by handling parties of sailors. At the after end of the after hangar there was a door through which seaplanes could be moved to be lowered on to the water by crane. In this way aircraft operations could continue when the ship was at anchor in sheltered water. The after flight deck was structured so that air could pass under as well as over in an attempt to reduce air turbulence aft of the ship, but the idea did not prove successful.

Dunning's loss had highlighted the vulnerability of aircraft on deck when the wind was at, or near, their flying speed. An attempt was made to hold them down using a system of fore-and-aft retaining wires which engaged with hooks on the aircraft undercarriage axles as they landed. These had been tested at Royal Naval Air Station (RNAS) Isle of Grain and, while they succeeded in holding the aircraft on deck, they made aircraft movement difficult, increased the necessary interval between landings and actually damaged some aircraft that landed with an element of sideslip. Landing trials were conspicuously unsuccessful, ten out of thirteen attempts ending in crashes. Turbulence aft of the bridge mixed with funnel exhaust made aircraft uncontrollable; the few landings that did succeed were made at low ship speed and consequently with little wind over the deck. As a consequence *Furious* finished the war as a 'take-off-only' carrier, although the extra hangar and deck parking space were obviously valuable in allowing her to carry more aircraft.

Major reconstruction

Clearly to the two-flight-deck arrangement with a central bridge and funnel had been a failure, but the Admiralty authorised DNC to design a reconstruction to a new flush-decked design for *Furious* on 5 July 1920. The estimated cost of the work was an incentive; at £1.3 million it was about one-third of the cost of a new ship. Despite the success of trials with an 'island' in *Argus*, it was believed at the time that a flush-decked arrangement offered more potential, as it would impose no limit on the wingspan of embarked aircraft. Funnel gases were a concern, however, as *Furious*'s more powerful machinery generated six times the amount of exhaust gas as *Argus* and J H Narbeth, the constructor in charge of the project,

Furious as she appeared in 1918, after the landing deck was built aft.
(AUTHOR'S COLLECTION)

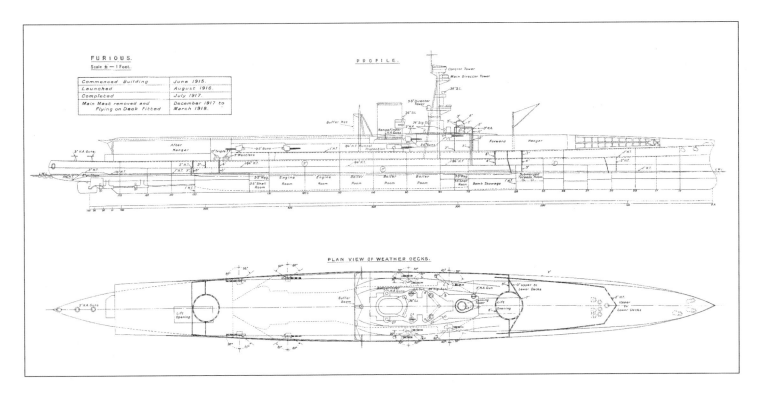

Furious in a disruptive pattern paint scheme in 1918, after modification with a landing-on deck aft. Note the prominent 'goal post' and rope barrier intended to prevent aircraft from crashing into the funnel. (AUTHOR'S COLLECTION)

was not certain that it could be trunked aft in a similar arrangement (see Chapter 5). An 'island' design was considered and tested in model form in a windtunnel, but eventually rejected in favour of a flush deck. Funnel gases were drawn into trunks which ran along either side of the hangar deck under the flight deck. To make up for this considerable loss of space Narbeth designed a second, lower hangar with the two combined

allowing the embarkation of a considerable number of aircraft on the existing lower hull. He estimated that the rebuilt *Furious* would carry as many aircraft as *Eagle* and *Hermes* combined.

The double hangar design led to concerns that the new ship would have a considerably higher freeboard than the original, and there were arguments about hangar height. Too low would impact on future aircraft designs and might, therefore, limit the ship's useful life; too high and the ship's stability might be impaired. The compromise solution was to make both hangars 15ft high and accept the consequences; her freeboard proved to be only 3ft greater than that of *Argus* with her single hangar deck. The new

flight deck ended well short of the bow, but below it two large doors opened from the upper hangar on to a short flying-off deck which allowed fighters to take off at short notice when the main flight deck had aircraft ranged on it. The idea had merit at the time with the lightweight fighters in service, but as heavier

Furious after the third reconstruction completed in 1925. The 'cruciform' lift forward was intended to allow aircraft to be struck down with their wings spread. It was also to prove useful for the early marks of Seafire, which did not have folding wings. Note the soot stains from the funnel exhausts aft. In this photograph she is still fitted with her fore-and-aft retaining wires. (AUTHOR'S COLLECTION)

Furious after her final reconstruction, with a small starboard-side island and in Second World War camouflage. Note the anti-aircraft guns and a director mounted on the former flying-off deck forward. (AUTHOR'S COLLECTION)

Fuel:	3,830 tons FFO
Endurance:	3,700 miles at 20 knots
Complement:	1,218

Aircraft operating data

Flight deck:	576ft x 91ft 6in
Arresting wires:	4 x 11,000lb at 60 knots
Hangars:	upper 456ft x 50ft x 15ft
	lower 436ft x 50ft x 15ft
Lifts:	forward 34ft long x 45ft wide
	aft 34ft long x 45ft wide both
	capable of lifting 12,000lb and
	serving both hangar decks
Aircraft:	over 30
Aircraft fuel:	20,800gal avgas in bulk
	stowage; two 600gal
	ready-use tanks
Air weapons:	36 18in torpedoes; 1,600lb AP
	bombs; 500lb SAP bombs;
	250lb SAP bombs; 250lb GP
	bombs; depth charges; aircraft
	mines; 0.303in gun
	ammunition; flares and
	pyrotechnics

aircraft replaced them from 1930 the idea ceased to be viable. Except for the mounting of close-range weapons the space was wasted, and the idea was repeated only in *Furious'* half-sisters *Glorious* and *Courageous*. A system of fore-and-aft retaining wires, like that first fitted in 1918, was fitted to hold aircraft on deck after landing, but it never proved practical or popular. It was removed in 1927, after which aircraft relied on their brakes when landing.

Approval for reconstruction was given by the Admiralty in October 1921, and *Furious* was stripped down to the upper deck at Rosyth and steamed to Devonport, where she was rebuilt. Both lifts served both hangars and she was fitted with a bulk aircraft fuel installation with two 600gal tanks on the upper deck for immediate use, which could be jettisoned in an emergency. Fuel from a lower bulk installation was pumped up daily to replenish them. There were three bomb rooms, one forward for larger weapons, two further aft for smaller stores and stowage for 36 torpedoes; three each for the twelve torpedo-bomber aircraft she was intended to carry.

With no island, she was controlled from two positions at the forward end of the flight deck. That to starboard was the compass platform from which the captain and his designated officers conned the ship. That to port was the flying control position from which air operations were directed. The two were connected by a passageway off which were doors to the charthouse, main signal office, air and intelligence offices. Like *Argus* she had a retractable charthouse in the centre of the flight deck forward.

In 1926 she was fitted with the first flight deck lighting equipment to facilitate night landing trials. These included the world's first landing on an aircraft carrier and night and proved entirely successful. She subsequently specialised in night operations and was involved in a number of trials that led to improved lighting and landing techniques that were used extensively in the early years of the Second World War.

The new flight deck was constructed of 1in plating riveted on top of a series of I-beams, with a leading edge of semi-circular planform about 200ft aft of the bow. In 1933 four arrester wires were installed. They were continually upgraded, and by 1944 were capable of handling aircraft of up to 11,000lb at 60 knots relative to the deck. The lower hangar was longer than the upper due to the smoke exhaust arrangements aft, and the smoke ducts running along the sides of the upper hangar reduced the amount of space available for workshops. Consequently part of the lower hangar had to be allocated as workshop space, reducing the number of aircraft that could be embarked from a potential forty to about thirty. She underwent a continual series of modifications and modernisations throughout her life, the last major one in 1938-39, during which the original 5.5in guns were removed and replaced by twin 4in dual-purpose guns and their directors. A small 'island' was added on the starboard side amidships. A low-profile structure intended for gunnery and flying control, it had a stump mast with a Type 72 aircraft homing beacon mounted on top of it. Ship's navigation continued to be carried out from the small bridge structure on the forward starboard side of the flight deck.

Furious technical details in 1939

Displacement:	27,165 tons deep load
Dimensions:	length 786ft 5in
	beam 90ft 1in
	draught 29ft 11in
Machinery:	4 shaft Brown Curtis geared
	turbines
	18 Yarrow boilers
	90,820shp giving 30 knots
Armament:	6 x twin 4in; 7 x 8-barrelled
	2pdr pom-pom
Protection:	2-3in side belt; 2-3in
	bulkheads; 1-2in magazine
	crowns; 3in magazine
	bulkheads; 1in plated flight
	deck; bulges designed to defeat
	torpedo warheads up to 440lb

Vindictive

Laid down as the cruiser *Cavendish* of the *Hawkins* class in 1916, she was renamed to perpetuate a name made famous by one of the ships that took part in the raid on Zeebrugge. The Admiralty decided to complete her as an aircraft carrier to increase the number of aircraft available to the GF. Her redesign included a small flying-off deck forward and a landing deck aft, and the drawings for the latter were used as the basis for the hasty design of *Furious'* larger landing deck. She was, in effect, a smaller *Furious* and retained four of her original battery of seven 7.5in guns, leading to some enthusiasm at first for the concept of hybrid gun and aviation cruiser. She proved to be a failure on both counts. By the time she was complete the initial attempts at landing on *Furious* had shown that the turbulence created by funnel gases and the central bridge and funnel structures would never allow safe recoveries, and only one landing was ever attempted on *Vindictive*. Surprisingly it proved successful, because the ship was under way at slow speed and the pilot elected to land at a slight angle across the deck, avoiding some of the turbulence. The 7.5in guns were hand loaded but fired a shell which was nearly twice the weight of the more common cruiser 6in gun, and was thus difficult

Vindictive at speed in 1918 in her original disruptive paint scheme. The forward flight deck is small but still has conspicuous windbreaks, seen in the raised position, and derricks. There is no hangar under the after flight deck. (AUTHOR'S COLLECTION)

and slow to reload in action. The ranges of the two weapons were about the same, so the larger gun, with its slower rate of fire, never proved popular in service.

Some consideration was given after the war to rebuilding *Vindictive* as an 'island' carrier, and a model was tested in the windtunnel at the National Physical Laboratory (NPL). She was clearly too small to be effective, however, and after the war the flight decks were removed and she was converted back into a cruiser. The hangar forward of the bridge was retained, however, with a working space for seaplanes on her roof and a crane to lift them out of the hangar and on to and off the water. In 1925 she was fitted with the prototype Carey Catapult for trials. It was capable of launching seaplanes up to 12,000lb at 55 knots and proved a success; she served on the China Station with a Flight of six Fairey IIIDs embarked, which were used to search for pirates. *Vindictive* eventually saw service as a cadet training ship and finally as a depot ship without any aircraft embarked.

Vindictive technical details

Displacement:	12,400 tons deep load
Dimensions:	length 605ft
	beam 65ft 2in
	draught 20ft 6in
Machinery:	4 shaft Parsons geared turbines
	12 Yarrow boilers
	60,000shp delivering 30 knots
Armament:	4 single 7.5in LA; 4 single 3in
	LA; 4 single 3in HA;
	6 x 21in torpedo tubes
Protection:	1.5-3in waterline belt; 1.5in
	upper deck; 1in magazine
	crowns

Fuel:	1,600 tons FFO; 800 tons coal
	as built
Endurance:	5,400 miles at 14 knots
Complement:	648

Aircraft operating data

Flight deck:	forward 78ft long x 49ft
	tapering to 44ft
	aft 193ft long x 57ft wide, both
	steel
Hangar:	78ft x 49ft tapering to 44ft
	under forward deck
Catapult:	1 x HIII hydraulic, 12,000lb at
	55 knots fitted in 1925
Lift:	Hatch giving access to the after
	part of the hangar. Aircraft
	lifted out by crane or derrick
Aircraft:	6 in 1926
Aircraft fuel:	Various amounts in 2gal cans
Air weapons:	light bombs; 0.303in gun
	ammunition; flares and
	pyrotechnics

Individual ship histories

Furious

HMS *Furious* was laid down as a light battlecruiser by Sir W G Armstrong-Whitworth & Co at its Walker Naval Yard at Newcastle-upon-Tyne on 8 June 1915 and launched on 15 August 1916. She was completed on 4 July 1917 and deployed to Scapa Flow to work up for service with the GF. Almost immediately her greatly improved flying arrangements led to flying experiments, and on 2 August 1917 her senior RNAS officer, Squadron Commander E H Dunning DSC RNAS, flying a Sopwith Pup, carried out the world's first-ever landing by an operational aircraft on a warship that was under way. Unfortunately he was killed on 7 August attempting to repeat the feat.

In November 1917 *Furious* returned to her builder's yard to have the after turret removed and a 'landing-on' deck installed aft. She recommissioned after the work on 15 March 1918 and rejoined the GF as flagship of Rear Admiral Phillimore, Admiral Commanding Aircraft. Flying trials in April proved that the after deck was too dangerous to use for landings, even in wartime, and she embarked an air group of Sopwith 2F.1 Camel fighters and Sopwith 1½ Strutter reconnaissance aircraft which could take off from the forward deck but not land back on board. On 19 July 1918 seven Camels from *Furious* attacked the German airship base at Tondern, destroying L54 and L60 in their sheds; the first successful strike operation by aircraft operating from a carrier in history.

After the Armistice she joined the AF and was used for a time in the Baltic, operating with British units that supported White Russian forces against the Bolsheviks. On 21 November 1919 she reduced to reserve at Rosyth, where she was eventually stripped down to upper-deck level before reconstruction as a flush-decked aircraft carrier. She steamed from Rosyth to Devonport in this condition in June 1922, after which she was built up to the new design. After the completion of work she recommissioned on 1 August 1925 and joined the AF in September with Nos 404 (Fairey Flycatcher), 420 (Blackburn Blackburn), 421 (Avro Bison), 443 (Fairey IIID), 461 and 462 (Blackburn Dart) Flights embarked. After working up she sailed on the Fleet's Spring Cruise to Gibraltar and Spanish waters, returning to the UK on 30 March 1926.

On 6 May 1926 she recovered a Blackburn Dart of 462 Flight flown by Flight Lieutenant Boyce RAF in the world's first night deck landing. Night trials continued in the English Channel and in the sea areas off Scotland. Number 405 (Flycatcher) Flight replaced 404 in 1926 and 447 (Fairey IIIF) Flight replaced 443 in 1929. In September 1930 she began a refit in Devonport, after which she joined the newly-formed HF in November 1931.

A starboard bow view of *Vindictive* in 1919 in 'peacetime' standard grey paint. Note how the mainmast is stepped to starboard, clear of the crash barrier. (AUTHOR'S COLLECTION)

In 1932 her air group comprised 401 and 407 (Flycatcher), 442 (Fairey IIIF), 465 and 466 (Blackburn Ripon) Flights, and she carried out a short cruise into the Mediterranean.

With the change from naval flights to squadrons in 1933, *Furious*'s air group consisted of 801 (Fairey Flycatcher/Hawker Nimrod/ Hawker Osprey), 811 (Blackburn Ripon) and 822 (Fairey IIIF) NAS. She subsequently exercised in UK, Mediterranean and West Indian waters before recommissioning with a new ship's company in 1935. Her new air group comprised 811 (Blackburn Baffin) and 822 (Fairey IIIF) NAS, the reduction in fighters reflecting the difficulty found in intercepting the new, fast bombers in the pre-radar era and the increasing reliance on guns. In 1936 Fairey Swordfish replaced Baffins in 811 NAS.

After her 1938-39 modifications she recommissioned with an air group comprising 801 (Blackburn Skua), 816 and 818 (Swordfish) NAS, and some of the latter attacked a U-boat east of Fair Isle on 22 September. She operated with *Repulse* after November, hunting enemy raiders in the Atlantic. On 10 December 1939 she sailed from Halifax, Nova Scotia, as part of the escort for the first Canadian troop convoy to the UK, and in April 1940, after a short maintenance period, she was the first British aircraft carrier to take part in the Norwegian Campaign, although, having sailed in haste without her fighter squadron, her

contribution was limited to Swordfish strikes. On 13 April 1940 her aircraft took part in the Second Battle of Narvik.

After operations off Norway she crossed the Atlantic at high speed, carrying £18 million worth of gold bullion from British reserves to be deposited in Canada. On the return voyage she ferried 40 Grumman Martlet and Brewster Buffalo fighters plus spares for the RN back to the UK. In September and October her aircraft struck at coastal targets in Norway before carrying out Operation *Stripe* in November, ferrying 34 RAF Hawker Hurricanes from Liverpool to Takoradi in West Africa, from where they were flown across the continent to the Middle East Air Force. After returning to Liverpool in December 1940 she ferried 40 Hurricanes to Takoradi during Operation *Monsoon* in January 1941. Operations *Pageant* and *Summer* in March saw a further 40 Hurricanes and 12 RN Fulmars delivered to Takoradi. In all of these operations the RAF aircraft were flown off 70 miles from the coast, but in the last only twenty-four RAF pilots had been embarked and some had to be flown back out to the ship in Fulmars to collect the remaining aircraft.

Furious was refitted in Belfast on completion of her first series of ferry missions, and was damaged by enemy bombing on 4 May 1941. On 12 May 1941 she embarked 807 (Fulmar) and 812 (Swordfish) NAS and sailed for Gibraltar, from

where she carried out a series of ferry missions with Force H to carry Hurricanes to Malta. These included Operation *Splice* in May and Operations *Rocket* and *Railway* in June, after which she returned to the HF in July 1941 to participate in strikes against Petsamo in company with *Victorious* and an escorting force. By then her air group included 800 (Fulmar), 812 (Swordfish), 817 (Fairey Albacore) and 880A (Sea Hurricane) NAS. Two Fulmars and an Albacore were shot down by the enemy and the harbour was found to be empty. In August her aircraft struck at shipping in Varanger Fjord before she returned to the Mediterranean in September for Operation *Status*, a further ferry trip taking Hurricanes to Malta.

Much of her war had involved fast steaming over large distances and *Furious*' machinery was beginning to show signs of strain. She was refitted in the USN's Philadelphia Navy Yard between October 1941 and April 1942, and then sailed for the Clyde, where new British equipment including search and fire control radars were installed. In July 1942 she embarked 801 and 807 (Supermarine Seafire) and 822 (Albacore) NAS, but later in the month she embarked 40 RAF Supermarine Spitfires in crates at Govan on the Clyde. Stowing and assembling these aircraft precluded flying, and she sailed for the Mediterranean in August, ferrying them to Malta as part of Operation *Bellows*. On 11 August 1942 she flew off 38 Spitfires in five ranges; one was found to be unserviceable and another had to land on *Indomitable* after a malfunction soon after launch. Later in the month more Spitfires were ferried to Malta in Operation *Baritone*. On 17 August thirty-two were launched; one went over the port side, killing the pilot, and two more had problems after getting airborne. Their pilots baled out and were successfully rescued. The remaining twenty-nine aircraft arrived safely in Malta. In October Operation *Train* saw more Spitfires ferried from Gibraltar to Malta, twenty-nine being launched on four ranges on the 29th. Two failed to start but the rest arrived safely.

In November *Furious* formed part of the centre naval task group of the Allied covering forces for Operation *Torch*, the invasion of North Africa, with 801 and 807 (Seafire) and 828 (Albacore) NAS embarked. On 8 November 1942 a force of eight Albacores and ten Seafires attacked La Senia Airfield very successfully, destroying forty-seven Vichy French aircraft in hangars and a further twenty-two parked in dispersals. There were a number of air combats in which more Vichy aircraft were destroyed. On 9 November Albacores bombed Vichy artillery and flew tactical reconnaissance sorties. By the next day the Allies were ashore in strength and *Furious* withdrew to Gibraltar.

She rejoined the HF in February 1943 after a maintenance period, and in July she carried out operations off the Norwegian coast as part of a strategic deception to confuse the enemy during the Allied landings on Sicily. On completion she was refitted in Liverpool and rejoined the HF for the last time in October 1943. Her air group by then comprised 801 (Seafire), 827 and 830 (Fairey Barracuda) NAS, and she carried out a series of strikes in Norwegian coastal waters. On 3 April 1944 she took part in Operation *Tungsten*, an air strike by the HF against *Tirpitz*, which was moored in Kaa Fjord. For this major attack *Furious* embarked 801 and 880 (Seafire), 830 and 831 (Barracuda) NAS; 830 formed part of 8 Torpedo Bomber Reconnaissance (TBR) Wing and 831 part of 52 TBR Wing. The other squadrons of these Wings flew from *Victorious*. Fighters from *Emperor, Pursuer* and *Searcher* supported the strike wings; aircraft from *Fencer* provided an antisubmarine

screen. A number of hits were obtained and *Tirpitz* suffered significant damage.

On 6 May 1944 *Furious* took part in Operation *Croquet*, a strike against shipping in Norwegian waters in company with *Searcher*. Barracudas hit two small merchant ships with bombs. Later in the month Operation *Brawn*, a repeat strike against *Tirpitz* in company with *Victorious*, had to be aborted because extensive low cloud obscured the target. On 1 June 1944 Operation *Lombard*, another strike against shipping off Norway with *Victorious*, saw two large merchant ships sunk by torpedoes launched by Barracudas. Operation *Blue*, another shipping strike, followed later in the month, and then on 17 July Operation *Mascot* was another attack against the *Tirpitz*. Smoke screens obscured the target and prevented accurate bombing. Another series of attacks on *Tirpitz* under the overall title Operation *Goodwood* were carried out in August, but the enemy detected the incoming aircraft in sufficient time to deploy smoke screens and frustrated attempts to bomb accurately.

Furious's last operational mission was Operation *Begonia*, an attack on enemy shipping off Norway on 12 September 1944. By then the old ship's machinery was deteriorating badly and trained manpower was needed urgently for the large number of aircraft carriers nearing completion in UK builders' yards. *Furious* paid off into reserve on 15 September 1944, the occasion being marked by signals from the C-in-C HF and the Admiralty that paid tribute to the ship's unique contribution to the development of naval aviation over more than a quarter of a century. After a short spell as an accommodation ship she was de-stored and towed to Loch Striven, near Rothesay, where she was used for bombing trials and the investigation of the effects of near misses on her hull and machinery. In 1948 she was sold to the British Iron and Steel Corporation to be broken up for scrap. She was beached at Troon for final destruction, which was not completed until 1954.

Vindictive

Laid down as *Cavendish*, the name-ship of a class of heavy cruisers by Harland & Wolff at its Belfast shipyard on 26 June 1916, she was renamed before launch on 17 January 1918 and completed as an aircraft carrier on 21 September 1918. She commissioned on 1 October 1918 and joined the GF's Flying Squadron, but by then *Furious* had already demonstrated the design's

failure and she saw no active service, being used instead for aircraft trials. The only landing on her after deck took place on 1 November 1918, when W W Wakefield landed a Sopwith Pup successfully.

In July 1919 she ferried aircraft to the Baltic, where they were landed to operate against the Bolsheviks from shore bases. They included Sopwith Camels, Short 184s, Sopwith 1½ Strutters and Grain Griffins. Later in the month *Vindictive* grounded off Reval (later Tallinn) and remained fast for eight days before being refloated. The aircraft ashore bombed Kronstadt and, as well as supporting them with maintenance facilities and weapons, *Vindictive* acted as depot ship for eight motor torpedo boats. She returned to the UK in December 1919 and paid off into reserve at Portsmouth. Of little value as either a carrier or a cruiser, she was brought out of reserve in 1920 for use as a troopship, and continued on these duties until March 1923, when she was taken in hand by Chatham Dockyard for the removal of the flight decks. Two extra 7.5in guns were added, for a total of six, but she retained the forward hangar for use by seaplanes and was the first British warship to be fitted with a catapult to launch them. The first aircraft to be launched was a Fairey IIID on 3 October 1925, and float-equipped Flycatchers were also launched.

On 1 January 1926 *Vindictive* sailed for the China Station with six Fairey IIIDs embarked. These were used for anti-piracy patrols as well as working with the fleet. She left the station to return to the UK on 14 March 1928 and arrived at Chatham Dockyard in May. During the subsequent refit all aircraft operating equipment was removed and the ship never operated aircraft again. She reduced to reserve in 1929, kept at readiness by a small working party.

In May 1937 *Vindictive* was partially demilitarised under the terms of the London Naval Treaty and modified for use as a cadet training ship. The former hangar was modified for use as a classroom. She recommissioned for service in the Dartmouth Training Squadron on 7 September 1937. In 1939 she was converted again, this time for use as a heavy repair ship, in which guise she operated throughout the Second World War. She saw service in Norway, the South Atlantic, Mediterranean and Home waters. On 8 September 1945 she paid off into unmaintained reserve, and on 24 January 1946 she was sold for scrap, later being broken up at Blyth.

CHAPTER 5

ARGUS

The world's first true aircraft carrier, designed to launch, recover and sustain embarked aircraft, *Argus* contained the essential elements subsequently found in every carrier in every navy. Her design also contained some features that appeared attractive in theory but which proved impracticable and have not been developed. It is noteworthy that her first deck landing took place on 24 September 1918, before the Armistice that ended the First World War and less than fifteen years after the Wright Brothers' first flight. The design evolved through several phases, and she was at first intended to be a seaplane carrier, effectively an improved *Campania*. To save time the incomplete hull of a fast liner ordered by the Italian Lloyd Sabaudo Line before the war was purchased by the Admiralty in August 1916 and modified on the slipway. As with the earlier aviation ships, J H Narbeth was the senior constructor responsible for the design.

The original passenger-ship hull was retained up to the shelter deck, but the commercial machinery was modified and destroyer-type boilers were substituted, with forced draught to provide sufficient steam for the 20,000shp the Admiralty required and to standardise equipment with that of other warships. Initially the design included two islands, one each to port and starboard, connected by a bridge from which the ship would be navigated. Aircraft would have been pushed between the islands from a preparation area aft to the take-off deck forward and seaplanes would have been lowered into the water and recovered by crane to and from the after part of the deck. Squadron Commander Dunning's landing on *Furious* in 1917, however, showed that a more advanced design was not only possible but urgently necessary, and the design was recast to include a flush flight deck with no island. Workshops forward and a hangar further aft were built up from

Argus as completed but after the end of hostilities. The flight deck is wider than that of the windtunnel model and there are fewer guns, but the cut-outs for them are still significant. The W/T masts and navigation bridge are all in the raised position. (AUTHOR'S COLLECTION)

the former shelter deck, the hangar roof forming the upper strength deck. The funnel uptakes were brought up on either side of the ship and then led to ducts which ran aft in the open space between the hangar roof and the flight deck. Annular casings surrounded the ducts, along which cooling air was driven by electric fans, and the funnel gases exhausted from under the after end of the flight deck. While aircraft did not usually fly through the funnel gases, turning finals and approaching the ship over them cannot have been pleasant. This was never a satisfactory arrangement as the casings took up a lot of space and, since lifts could not pass through them, none could be fitted in the after

An impression of *Argus'* original design, with two islands supporting a cross-over bridge structure, can be gathered from this windtunnel model. Note how narrow the take-off deck was made to give clear arcs of fire for the numerous forward gun mountings.

two-thirds of the hangar. The cooling arrangement never worked well and gave the hangar properties similar to a bread oven, so it is hardly surprising that this layout has never been repeated.

The flight deck was formed of light steel plating supported over the hangar roof and the funnel trunking; the gap between the top of the hangar and the bottom of the deck was 14ft 6in. The first deck landings were made on to a bare steel deck, with reliance on friction to bring the aircraft to rest, as they had no brakes. Fore-and-aft retaining wires were installed in October 1918, after the first landings were found to be a very easy operation, and

The canvas dummy island fitted to *Argus* for flying trials during 1918.
(AUTHOR'S COLLECTION)

used until 1923, when they were finally removed. An important aspect of the flying trials was the temporary installation of a wood-and-canvas island structure in Rosyth Dockyard on 4 October 1918 after the first two phases of flying trials had been completed successfully. Phase three involved landings and take-offs by two Sopwith 2F.1 Camels with the island in place to see what effect it had on flying operations. The structure resembled a large rectangular 'box' complete with a funnel shape but no mast; smoke generators at the after end showed that airflow closely matched the predictions made by windtunnel tests at the NPL. The first deck landing into the retaining wires with the island in place took place on 24 October 1918, and thirty-six more were completed successfully before trials ended. Contrary to the fears expressed by some 'doubters', the island caused very little turbulence over the deck and actually helped pilots to land by giving them a vertical reference against which they could judge their height and position relative to the ideal landing point. The island clearly offered the best solution for ship control, and positioning the

funnel and flying control, and the decision was taken at once to complete *Eagle* and *Hermes* with islands. The temporary structure was removed from *Argus* but no consideration appears to have been given to fitting her with an island, since she had a very narrow deck and an island was felt to unduly limit the wingspan of aircraft that could land on successfully. However, she had paved the way for the design of virtually every subsequent carrier.

Navigation when flying was in progress was carried out from positions on either side of the flight deck forward, as with the rebuilt *Furious*. Like her, there was a retractable charthouse in the centre of the flight deck forward. The hangar was 20ft high with overhead gantries so that aircraft trapped at the far end could be lifted and moved clear of other, obstructing aircraft and set down near the lift for movement to the flight deck. This bright idea solved a problem that has been present since 1918 when aircraft are being ranged, but proved too cumbersome to use in practice and it has never been repeated in a British carrier. Originally there were two lifts, but the after one was removed in 1936, leaving only the large one at the forward end of the hangar. A steel roller-shutter at the after end of the hangar allowed seaplanes to be manoeuvred on to the quarterdeck, when it was opened, and lifted on to and off the water by cranes under the after end of the deck. Another idea that has not been repeated was the provision of roller shutters which could cover the hole when the forward lift platform was at hangar level, to allow aircraft to take off when the lift platform was at hangar-deck level. Like her predecessors, *Argus* was completed without a bulk-fuel installation, and petrol was provided in 4,000 two-gallon cans which were stowed in a hold forward of the hangar. This had its own ventilation and was surrounded by void spaces filled with water.

Modernisation for use as a training carrier

In 1936 work was begun to modernise *Argus* for use as a training carrier and as a tender for de Havilland Queen Bee radio-controlled pilotless target aircraft. As rearmament gathered momentum it also gave the RN a useful 'spare' carrier capable of operating all contemporary naval aircraft, albeit in small numbers. The work included the installation of four transverse arrester wires capable of stopping an 11,000lb aircraft at up to 53 knots. A single hydraulic catapult was installed forward, capable of launching 12,000lb at an end speed of up to 66 knots. The single lift had a maximum loading of 13,440lb. No barrier was ever fitted, but in 1940 *Argus* was capable of operating all the carrier-capable aircraft in RN service. A bulk avgas installation with modern safety features was installed at the same time.

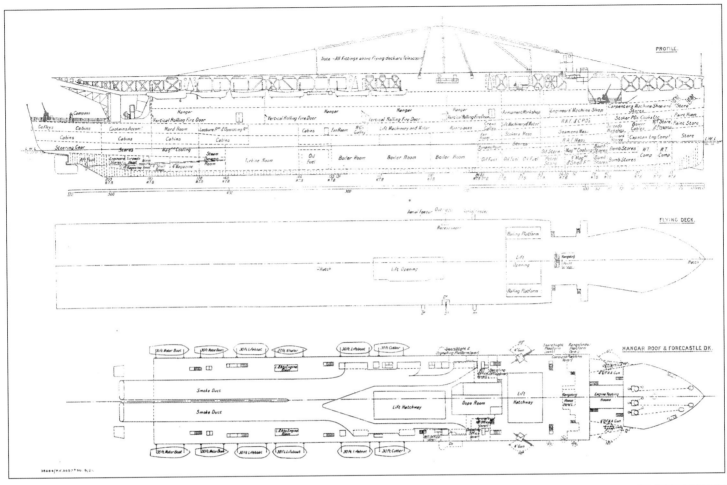

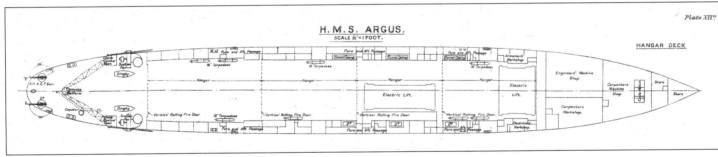

H.M.S. ARGUS.

SCALE ⅛" = 1 FOOT.

HANGAR DECK

Profile, flight deck and exhaust trunking drawings of *Argus* as completed. The lower drawing shows the hangar deck. (Author's collection)

Argus at the Spithead review held on 26 July 1924. The downward slope of the forward part of the flight deck is evident. (Author's collection)

Argus technical details in 1939

Displacement:	16,500 tons deep load
Dimensions:	length 560ft
	beam 79ft 6in
	draught 22ft 6in
Machinery:	4-shaft Parsons geared turbines
	12 cylindrical boilers with
	forced draught
	20,000shp delivering 20 knots
Armament:	6 single 4in; 4 single 3pdr; a
	number of single 20mm
	Oerlikons added during
	wartime
Protection:	2in crowns and sides on
	magazines; anti-torpedo bulges
	capable of defeating warheads
	up to 440lb
Fuel:	2,000 tons FFO
Endurance:	5,200 miles at 12 knots
Complement:	760

Aircraft operating data

Flight deck:	470ft x 85ft (extended to 548ft x 85ft in 1943)
Hangar:	350ft x 68ft x 20ft
Lift:	30ft long x 36ft wide; 13,440lb
Catapult:	1 hydraulic; 12,000lb at 66 knots
Arrester wires:	4 x 11,000lb at 53 knots
Aircraft:	Originally designed to take 20; up to 15 in 1941. Many more could be ferried partially dismantled
Aircraft fuel:	14,000gal avgas
Air weapons:	18in torpedoes; 500lb SAP bombs; 250lb GP bombs; 20lb bombs; depth-charges; 0.303in gun ammunition; flares and pyrotechnics

Individual ship history

Argus

Ordered from William Beardmore & Co of Dalmuir as a passenger ship for the Italian Lloyd Sabaudo Line, to be named *Conte Rosso*, and laid down in June 1914, the incomplete hull was purchased by the Admiralty in August 1916 and launched to a revised design as an aircraft carrier on 2 December 1917. She was commissioned as HMS *Argus* in Dalmuir on 14 September 1918 and handed over to the RN on her official completion date 16 September 1918.

Phase 1 of her flying trials began in the Firth of Forth on 24 September 1918, when Commander R Bell Davies VC RN made the first deck landing in a Sopwith 1½ Strutter. In early October she carried out successful trials with a dummy 'island' to validate the concept for the recast designs of *Hermes* and *Eagle*. On 10 October she embarked the world's first carrier-borne unit to be equipped with torpedo aircraft, the Sopwith T.1s of 185 Squadron. After working up to operational efficiency these were intended to attack the German High Sea Fleet in its bases, but the war ended days before the plan could be implemented. Operating the new type from a new type of carrier only weeks after its completion was a considerable achievement.

On 23 December 1918 the prototype system of retaining wires was replaced by the operational system, and on 21 March 1919 *Argus* began a series of flying trials intended to perfect the operation of aircraft from her flight deck. After the dispersal of the GF she was allocated to the AF in April 1919. On 23 June 1919 she ferried a number of Fairey IIID floatplanes to Archangel, where they were to be used in operations against the Bolsheviks by *Pegasus*. In January 1920 she embarked an air group comprising eight Sopwith 1½ Strutters, four Sopwith 2F.1 Camels, two de Havilland D.H.9As and two Fairey IIID floatplanes for the AF Spring Cruise to Gibraltar and the Western Mediterranean. When she returned in July she was taken in hand in Devonport Dockyard to have an improved system of retaining wires fitted. She rejoined the AF on completion of this work and carried out a further series of flying trials in UK and Mediterranean waters. Throughout 1921 she was used to train new pilots in deck-landing techniques. In November 1921 she underwent a refit and boiler-clean in Portsmouth.

During the Chanak Crisis *Argus* ferried twelve Bristol F.2B fighters to the Dardanelles in

Argus after modernisation into a target facilities and training carrier in 1938. The forward part of the flight deck has been rebuilt and strengthened to support the catapult. (Author's collection)

September 1922 and landed them on 11 October to operate with British and French Forces ashore. She rejoined the AF in June 1923 after a further refit in Portsmouth during which the retaining wires were finally removed, having been considered a failure. In November 1925 she paid off for a major refit in Chatham.

Argus recommissioned on 19 January 1927 for service on the China Station and deployed in February. She embarked 441 (Fairey IIID) Flight in Malta and finally arrived in Hong Kong in July. She left the Station on 26 March 1928 and reverted to the AF. In December 1929 she spent a period of defect rectification in Portsmouth and then sailed by a small steaming party to Devonport where she was reduced to reserve. In 1932 she was given a maintenance refit in Chatham Dockyard, after which she was towed to Rosyth and placed into extended reserve.

On 23 May 1936 approval was given for *Argus* to be modernised for use as a training carrier and Queen Bee pilotless aircraft tender. The work was carried out in Devonport Dockyard and she recommissioned on 30 July 1938 for trials with her new catapult and arrester wires. On completion of these she joined the HF and began her new training duties. In November 1939 she deployed to the Mediterranean to act as a deck-landing training carrier, based on Toulon with 767 (Swordfish) NAS embarked. The location offered better weather than UK waters with less risk of attack by German aircraft. By January 1940 770 (Swordfish) NAS was added to her training air group, but after the collapse of France in June she disembarked 767 NAS to Malta where it re-formed as an operational unit and *Argus* returned to the Clyde. On 27 June she sailed to ferry 701 (Walrus) NAS to Iceland, from where it was to fly antisubmarine patrols. On 2 August 1940 *Argus* sailed from the UK with twelve RAF Hurricane fighters embarked for Operation *Hurry*. She launched them from a point 300 miles west of Malta, where they flew off in two

ranges of six, each led by an RN Skua. The RAF ground crews were Ferried to Malta in the submarines *Proteus* and *Pandora*.

On 5 September she sailed for Operation *White*, a further reinforcement of RAF Hurricanes for Malta. In this case the launch position was further from the island and the Hurricanes had been fitted with modifications which reduced their range. These had not been explained to the pilots and, as a result, nine of the fourteen aircraft launched failed to arrive. On 17 November 1940 *Argus* delivered thirty RAF Hurricanes in crates to Takoradi to be assembled and flown across Africa to Egypt. In December 1940 *Argus* sailed loaded with RAF Hurricanes in company with *Furious* as part of convoy WS5A to deliver them to Takoradi. Three Swordfish of 821 NAS were embarked for antisubmarine defence. The convoy was attacked by the German cruiser *Hipper*, but she was driven off by the cruiser *Berwick*.

In January 1941 *Argus* returned to the Clyde for deck landing training duties, but in March she ferried another load of RAF fighters to Gibraltar, from where *Ark Royal* Ferried them to within range of Malta. This time Swordfish of 812 NAS were embarked for antisubmarine defence. In May 1941 she formed part of the escort for convoy WS8B to the Middle East before returning to resume deck landing training duties in the Clyde. On 3 August 1941 she embarked two Martlets of 802 NAS for air defence and twenty-four partly dismantled Hurricanes, sailing with them as part of Operation *Dervish*, the first convoy to Russia. Heavy cover was provided by the HF, and included the aircraft carrier *Victorious*. On 6 September the Martlets were flown off to *Victorious* and a day later the assembled Hurricanes were flown off to Vaenga; all arrived safely. *Argus* returned to Scapa Flow on 16 September.

In October 1941 *Argus* made further ferry trips to Gibraltar with RAF aircraft. Fulmars Of 807 NAS were embarked for self defence. On 14

November 1941 she joined Force H after the loss of *Ark Royal* and assumed the duties of an operational carrier. Aircraft of 807 (Fulmar) and 812 (Swordfish) NAS were embarked as required. In June 1942 she took part in Operation *Harpoon*, a resupply convoy to Malta with 807 (Fulmar) and 824 (Swordfish) NAS embarked. *Eagle* reinforced Force H for this operation. In September *Argus* returned to the Tyne for a refit, after which she resumed duties as a deck-landing training carrier in the Clyde.

In November 1942 she returned to operational duties to act as part of the Eastern Naval Task Force during Operation *Torch*, the Allied invasion of North Africa, with 880 (Seafire) NAS embarked. On 10 November she was hit aft by a 500lb bomb and near-missed by others, but her ability to operate aircraft was not impaired. After the landings she returned to the Clyde for repairs. In December 1942 she escorted convoy KMF5 to North Africa, and in January 1943 she escorted convoy KMF8. On 4 February 1943 she escorted the returning convoy MKF8 from North Africa to the Clyde.

On 9 February 1943 she underwent a period of defect rectification on the Clyde before commencing a final period of operation as a deck-landing training carrier in the Clyde areas in April. Her ageing machinery was proving difficult to maintain, and by 1944 the RN was suffering from an acute shortage of manpower. Escort carriers were available which could carry out the training task more effectively with less manpower, so *Argus* was paid off into reserve in August 1944. For a while she was used as an accommodation ship at Chatham, but when the immediate post-war demobilisation was complete she was de-stored and placed on the Disposal List without upkeep. In March 1947 she was sold to T W Ward and arrived at Inverkeithing to be broken up for scrap.

Argus operating Seafires in 1942. (AUTHOR'S COLLECTION)

CHAPTER 6

EAGLE

Two battleships ordered by the Chilean Government were under construction at Armstrong Whitworth's Walker Naval Yard on the Tyne in 1914. *Almirante Latorre*, the more advanced, was requisitioned by the Admiralty and served as HMS *Canada* during the First World War before being returned to Chile. The second, *Almirante Cochrane*, remained on the slipway until 1918, when she was purchased outright by the Admiralty for completion as an aircraft carrier. Her redesign benefited from the flying trials carried out in *Furious* and *Argus*, and she was the first aircraft carrier to be completed with a starboard-side island structure. She was renamed *Eagle* at her launch in 1918.

Technical background

The basic battleship hull was retained but antisubmarine bulges were added below the waterline. The original armoured belt was removed and replaced by another only 4.5in thick to protect the machinery and magazines against fire from cruisers and destroyers. The original 3in deck armour was retained and the original forecastle became the main strength deck, on top of which the 1,000-ton hangar, workshop complex and flight-deck structure were built. The flight deck itself was formed from 1in plates supported by

girders. Unlike *Argus*, the forward end of the flight deck was faired into the forecastle by plating to improve the airflow over the deck, and a cambered 'round-down' formed the after part of the flight deck to smooth the airflow immediately aft of the hull where aircraft would approach at low speed on finals. Models of *Eagle* were tested by the NPL in 1918 after the failure of *Furious*'s landing experiments.

Eagle's most distinctive new feature was the island on the starboard side of the flight deck amidships. This was 130ft long and 18ft wide and contained the compass platform, flying control, intelligence office and ready rooms for aircrew. It encroached into the deck, but by moving the painted deck centreline 6ft to port a clear area 72ft wide was left, sufficient to land-on any existing or planned naval aircraft. Contemporary thinking was that aircraft were too light to be kept permanently on deck, but the island arrangement did allow space clear to starboard of the runway in which fighters could be parked forward and aft of the island for short periods. The outstanding feature of *Eagle*'s design, however, was the ducting of the uptakes from the four boiler rooms horizontally across the ship below the hangar deck to the two funnels on top of the island. This elegant arrangement was far superior to the fore-and-aft trunking fitted in *Argus* and the reconstructed

Eagle in the China Station paint scheme during 1933. The large crane at the after end of the island was originally intended to lower seaplanes on to the water from the flight deck and recover them when she was at anchor. (AUTHOR'S COLLECTION)

Furious, and has been copied by the majority of the world's conventionally powered aircraft carriers ever since. Until the completion of the *Invincible* class from 1980, *Eagle* was the only British aircraft carrier to have two funnels.

The ship's early flying trials explored, among other things, the best way of ranging and launching aircraft. In the days before aircraft had wheel brakes the best way of preparing them for start-up and launch was found to be lining them and chocking them on the runway centreline. There had to be space enough for the forward aircraft to carry out a rolling take-off, and the last aircraft had to be chocked forward of the round-down; this left space enough for six aircraft arranged nose to tail on the centreline. The majority of contemporary aircraft had rotary engines which overheated if there was no significant airflow through them, and six proved to be a practical number to start up together and launch before overheating became a problem. For these reasons the standard units commissioned for operation from RN carriers before 1933 were

Eagle running partly complete in 1920 for flying trials; only one funnel is fitted and only some of her machinery was operable. (AUTHOR'S COLLECTION)

Taken in 1935, this photograph shows Eagle without arrester wires, although the retaining wires have been removed. The 'cruciform' shape of the forward lift allowed aircraft to be struck down with their wings still spread to save time, as the deck had to be clear with the lift up before the next aircraft could land on. (AUTHOR'S COLLECTION)

Flights of six aircraft numbered in the '400' series to differentiate them from shore-based RAF types.

Eagle was completed with fore-and-aft retaining wires between the lifts, but these were seldom used. In fact by 1925 aircraft were sufficiently heavy not to need retaining when they landed. The gear was removed in 1926 and aircraft landed on the bare deck for a number of years. Torpedo aircraft had never used the wires because their undercarriages had to be split to allow torpedoes to fit between the wheels, so there was no cross-axle on which to fit the hooks. They were among the first 'heavyweights' that needed no retaining. There were two lifts. The forward one was cruciform to allow aircraft to be struck down with their wings spread. It had a maximum length of 46ft and a maximum width of 47ft. The after lift could take only folded aircraft and was 33ft wide and 47ft long. Both lifts could handle aircraft up to 14,000lb and were electro-hydraulically powered. The shape of the forward lift reflected the original concept of landing aircraft on to a clear deck and striking it down before the next astern landed. Thus the interval between aircraft reflected the time taken to taxi the first on to the forward lift, strike it down, push it clear and bring the lift back up to flight-deck level. With pilots and deck crew who were not worked up this could take as much as five minutes, and while this was acceptable for the small launches in the 1920s, it was totally unacceptable for the larger launches which became common from 1933.

Unlike the earlier conversions, Eagle did not have a quarterdeck capable of operating seaplanes with access from an after opening in the hangar. Instead, she was fitted with a large crane aft of the island which could lift aircraft off the flight deck and lower them into the water and then back again after flight. The crane had a secondary use, lifting aircraft from the dockside on to the ship when they were not flown on board. It was put to an imaginative use on at least one occasion when it was used to pick a crashed aircraft up off the flight deck and swing it clear over the starboard side while other aircraft landed on. Once flying had ceased it was brought back over the deck and struck down into the hangar for repair.

Six arrester-wires were fitted in 1936, each capable of stopping an 11,000lb aircraft at 53 knots relative to the deck, but *Eagle* was never fitted with a barrier or catapults and was, thus, of limited use after 1939. Avgas was carried in a bulk stowage comprising tanks within water-filled compartments. On build there was sufficient tankage for 14,800gal, but this was increased to 17,750gal in 1942. In her last years *Eagle* was fitted with a number of improvements including Type 291 air-warning radar, radar-predicted barrage directors for an improved close-range armament and a Type 72 aircraft homing beacon on top of the gunnery control structure on the foremast. *Eagle's* original gun battery comprised 6in weapons intended to protect her against attack by destroyers armed with torpedoes.

Eagle technical details in 1942

Displacement:	27,500 tons deep load
Dimensions:	length 667ft 6in
	beam 115ft
	draught 26ft 8in
Machinery:	4 shaft Brown & Curtis HP turbines
	32 Yarrow boilers
	50,000shp delivering 24 knots
Armament:	9 x single 6in; 5 x single 4in HA; 2 x octuple 2pdr added in 1937; 12 x single 20mm Oerlikon added in 1942
Protection:	4.5in waterline belt; 4in bulkheads; 1.5in hangar deck; 1in flight deck
Fuel:	3,750 tons FFO as built
	2,810 tons in 1942
Endurance:	3,000 miles at 17 knots
Complement:	988

Aircraft operating data

Flight deck:	652ft x 96ft steel plate
Hangar:	400ft x 66ft x 20ft 6in
Arrester wires:	6 x 11,000lb at 53 knots fitted in 1936
Lifts:	forward 46ft long x 47ft wide
	Aft 46ft long x 33ft wide
	Both 14,000lb
Aircraft:	22 in 1942
Aircraft fuel:	8,300gal avgas in 1924
	17,750gal avgas in 1942
Air weapons:	18in torpedoes; 500lb SAP bombs; 250lb 'B' bombs, 100lb A/S bombs; depth charges; aircraft mines; 0.303in MG ammunition; flares and pyrotechnics

Eagle operational history

The hull that became HMS *Eagle* was laid down as the Chilean battleship *Almirante Cochrane* by Sir W G Armstrong Whitworth & Co at its Walker Naval Yard at Newcastle-upon-Tyne on 20 February 1913. Work on her was suspended after August 1914 but resumed after her purchase by the Admiralty in 1918 for completion as an aircraft carrier. She was launched as *Eagle* on 8 June 1918, but then work on her was suspended again while the design was recast in the light of trials with *Furious* and *Argus*. In November 1919 Board approval was given to complete her to a limited extent for flying trials to test, among other things, the validity of the starboard-side island arrangement. She raised steam for the first time on 3 March 1920 and sailed from the Tyne for Portsmouth on 23 April.

On 28 May 1920 *Eagle* began flying trials in the English Channel using a special '*Eagle* Flight' which was shore-based at RAF Gosport. To gain the widest experience, the Flight was equipped with the Sopwith 2F.1 Camel, Parnall Panther, Bristol Fighter, Sopwith T1 'Cuckoo' and de Havilland D.H.9A aircraft types. The first to land on was a 2F.1 Camel on 1 June 1920, and as the trial progressed the ship moved north to find bad weather in the Pentland Firth and evaluate its effect on flying operations. In all 143 landings

were made with only twelve minor incidents and no casualties, an outstanding achievement for the time. Although the trial was not yet complete, the Admiralty gave approval on 24 September for *Eagle* to be completed as a carrier and accepted the island and funnel arrangement as viable. The trial was finally completed on 27 October 1920. She paid off in Devonport in November and was moved to Portsmouth Dockyard on 21 February 1921 for completion to the new design.

After final completion, *Eagle* carried out sea trials in September 1923 and acceptance trials for the flying arrangements from 5 October 1923. These were completed on 20 February 1924 and she commissioned for service with the MF on 26 February. On 7 June 1924 she joined the MF and replaced the seaplane carrier *Ark Royal*. Her initial air group comprised 402 (Flycatcher); 422 (Blackburn); 460 (Dart) and 440 (Seagull III) Flights. Fairey IIIDs replaced the Seagulls in January 1925. On one day's flying off Malta on 1

This photograph was taken from the first Swordfish to get airborne from the range aft. It shows *Eagle's* slender but tall island and the crane turned out to starboard. In the event of a crash on deck it would be swung to port over the deck to pick up the wreck and would then be turned back to starboard with the aircraft beneath it, so that the recovery could continue quickly. The damaged aircraft could then be brought in for repair later or ditched if necessary. (AUTHOR'S COLLECTION)

Eagle in the floating dock at Singapore Dockyard for maintenance in November 1939. (Author's collection)

'Special Service Flight' equipped with new Hawker Nimrod and Osprey fighters together with Blackburn Ripon torpedo strike aircraft and sailed for Buenos Aires, where she supported an Exhibition of British Industry which was opened by the Prince of Wales on 14 March 1931. On her return to the UK she started a major refit in Devonport Dockyard, during which she was reboiled and fitted with improved close-range weapons and directors. The refit was actually completed 32 days early in November 1932, but recommissioning was delayed by a manpower shortage. Eventually she recommissioned on 9 January 1933 for service on the China Station.

Eagle sailed for the Far East in July with 803 (Osprey) and 824 (Fairey IIIF) NAS embarked, small Flights having given way to larger squadrons under the Rear Admiral Aircraft Carriers, Rear Admiral Henderson's reorganisation of naval air units. On the China Station her aircraft typically searched for pirate junks and attacked bands of 'robbers' on the coast when requested to do so by the Chinese authorities. In October 1934 she was relieved on station by *Hermes* and moved into the Mediterranean to replace *Furious*; 824 was renumbered as 825 NAS and 811 (Baffin) NAS from *Furious* embarked to replace 803. In June 1935 *Eagle* returned to Devonport and paid off into reserve to await refit. The refit was carried out in 1936 and included the fitting of transverse arrester wires and flight deck lighting to allow regular night flying to take place. The stowage for air weapons was increased and more close-range anti-aircraft weapons were fitted. She re-commissioned for service on the China Station in February 1937 and embarked 813 (Swordfish) NAS. On arrival in Hong Kong she relieved *Hermes* and embarked 824 (Fairey Seal) NAS from her. In 1938 824 re-equipped with Swordfish.

In 1939 *Eagle* was refitted in Singapore Dockyard and subsequently joined the cruisers *Cornwall* and *Dorsetshire* to form Force I and hunt for German commerce raiders in the Indian Ocean. In December she underwent a boiler clean in Durban, and on 1 February 1940 she sailed from Colombo with the battleship *Ramillies* as part of the escort for the first Australian troop convoy to the Middle East. A week later she left the convoy to rejoin Force I at Aden. On 14 March 1940 a 250lb bomb detonated as it was being moved in a bomb room, killing thirteen men and wounding three more. The flash penetrated the hangar and started fires which were extinguished by the spray system. She remained capable of operating aircraft but took passage to Singapore Dockyard where she was repaired.

May 1925 *Eagle*'s aircraft used 1,525gal of avgas. In 1926 she was refitted in Devonport Dockyard and the fore-and-aft retaining wires were permanently removed. In fact they were so unpopular that they had been left unrigged and had not been used in the ship's first operational commission. In 1927 she rejoined the MF with 448 (Bison) Flight embarked in place of 422 and carried out the world's first multiple carrier task group co-ordination exercises with the new *Courageous* in 1928. Later in 1928 she underwent a refit during which she was the first carrier to be fitted with a hangar spray fire-fighting system. She returned to the MF in 1930 and carried out successful night-flying trials before returning to the UK in January 1931. She then embarked a

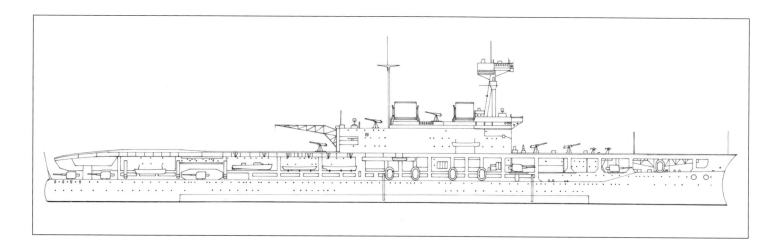

Eagle in profile. (Ian Sturton)

On 9 May 1940 *Eagle* sailed from Singapore to replace *Glorious* in the Mediterranean after she had been ordered back to the Home Fleet for operations off Norway. She passed through the Suez Canal on 26 May and began operations in support of convoy movements in the Eastern Mediterranean on 11 June, the day after Italy declared war on the British Empire. On 29 June her aircraft carried out an unsuccessful attack on an Italian submarine, and on 5 July disembarked Swordfish of 813 NAS carried out an attack on Tobruk while *Eagle* was in Alexandria. They sank four ships with torpedoes, including the passenger liner *Liguria*, and damaged two more. On 7 July three Gloster Sea Gladiator fighters were added to 813 NAS, flown by Commander Keighley-Peach, the Commander 'Air', and other volunteer pilots. *Eagle* provided cover for convoys carrying evacuees and stores from Malta to Alexandria. On 9 July during the Action off Calabria, 813 NAS spotted for the battle fleet's guns while 824 NAS carried out two unsuccessful torpedo attacks on the Italian Fleet as it withdrew. A day later 813 NAS Swordfish attacked Augusta Harbour, sinking a destroyer and damaging an oiler. On 11 July Italian aircraft attacked the fleet and 813 NAS Sea Gladiators shot down four Savoia Marchetti SM.79 bombers and damaged three others.

On 20 July 1940 813 and 824 NAS disembarked to bases in the Western Desert while *Eagle* was in Alexandria, and carried out a devastating series of attacks on Italian shipping in the enemy's forward supply ports. During attacks on Tobruk on 20 July and Bomba on 22 August, Swordfish sank two destroyers, one submarine and a depot ship for the expenditure of nine torpedoes and the loss of none of their aircraft. At sea again on 4 September, aircraft struck at Maritsa Airfield on the island of Rhodes

in company with aircraft from the new aircraft carrier *Illustrious*. Enemy aircraft and hangars were destroyed but four of 813 NAS's Swordfish were shot down by fighters. On 28 September *Eagle* was damaged by bombs which narrowly missed her and caused extensive damage, not all of which was appreciated at the time.

On 27 October *Eagle*'s aircraft attacked a seaplane station on the island of Stampalia as part of the operations that covered the first Commonwealth troop movements to Crete. On completion of this operation repairs had to be carried out to the aircraft fuel system, which had been found to be defective after the recent near misses. Consequently *Eagle* was not available for the attack on Taranto in early November, but five Swordfish and eight experienced crews were transferred to *Illustrious* to take part in the battle. The repair work was completed quickly, and by 16 November 1940 *Eagle* was at sea again covering convoy movements in the Eastern Mediterranean. On 26 November eight Swordfish dive-bombed an enemy freighter in Tripoli Harbour and subsequently 813 and 824 NAS disembarked to forward airstrips in the Western Desert to fly in

support of a variety of British operations. Among other tasks they flew escort sorties for coastal convoys and acted as pathfinders for RAF bombers which had proved unable to navigate over the featureless desert at night.

On 11 January 1941 *Eagle* sailed with her squadrons re-embarked to attack Axis forces in the Eastern Mediterranean as a diversion a day after *Illustrious* was badly damaged off Malta. Two Skuas were added to the fighter flight of 813 NAS. On 21 February four Swordfish and the Skuas were disembarked and replaced on board by 805 (Fulmar) NAS. Her squadrons spent another period disembarked after 25 March, this time operating from Port Sudan for strikes against Italian warships in the Red Sea. Success was achieved on 3 April when Swordfish sank two destroyers, damaged two more and forced a torpedo-boat to run aground. The air group re-embarked on 12 April, but *Eagle* passed through the Suez Canal to carry out a search for the German raider *Admiral Scheer* in the Indian Ocean. In

A Sea Hurricane of 801 NAS lands on *Eagle* during Operation *Harpoon*. (Author's collection)

Eagle in her final wartime paint scheme, photographed in 1942. (AUTHOR'S COLLECTION)

response to fears that *Bismarck* was about to break out and might succeed in moving into the South Atlantic, *Eagle* left Cape Town in company with *Nelson* to act as a 'long stop' on 13 May 1941; a planned boiler-clean was cancelled. On 6 June 1941 Swordfish found and sank the *Elbe*, one of *Bismarck*'s supply ships, and on 13 June a second supply ship, the *Lothringen*, surrendered intact to Swordfish. Following these successes *Eagle* remained in the South Atlantic, searching for German commerce raiders and their supply ships, but on 20 September an accidental hangar fire destroyed thirteen aircraft while the ship was operating near St Helena. The damaged it caused was so severe that *Eagle* had to return to the UK for repairs.

Eagle arrived in the Clyde on 26 October 1941 and disembarked her remaining aircraft. Four days later she entered Cammell Laird's shipyard at Birkenhead for repairs and a refit. The opportunity was also taken to make a number of alterations and additions to improve her operational capability. These included the installation of air- and surface-warning radars, fire-control radars, a Type 72 aircraft homing beacon and extra close-range weapons including 20mm Oerlikons. Aircraft fuel stowage was increased by taking up space formerly used for furnace fuel oil (FFO), and it is a measure of the scale of the protection given to avgas arrangements by the RN that the removal of stowage for 940 tons of FFO allowed an extra 9,450gal of avgas to be carried. At roughly 8lb per Imperial gallon that means that 38 tons of avgas were carried in the space that had formerly contained 940 tons of FFO, the balance being made up with the water-filled spaces that surrounded the avgas tanks. On completion of the refit she embarked 824 (Swordfish) and 813 (Sea Hurricane/Swordfish) NAS and worked up for operational service with Force H in the Western Mediterranean, replacing *Ark Royal*.

On 22 February 1942 *Eagle* landed her own aircraft at Gibraltar and embarked sixteen RAF Spitfires which had been ferried from the UK in SS *Clan Hawke*. To increase the range from Malta at which the aircraft could be launched, naval air mechanics fitted the Spitfires with drop tanks, but difficulty was encountered and one Spitfire had to be 'cannibalised' to provide spare parts. *Eagle* subsequently sailed for Operation *Spotter* to ferry the aircraft to Malta. Eight Spitfires were flown off in the first range on 6 March and met by two Bristol Blenheims which had flown from Gibraltar and flew on to Malta, providing navigational assistance for the Spitfires after 1020. The remaining seven Spitfires flew off in a second range at 1100 and were met by a single Blenheim. All landed safely in Malta. On 19 March a further seventeen Spitfires intended for Malta arrived in Gibraltar in SS *Queen Victoria* and were transferred to *Eagle*. A day later *Eagle* and *Argus* sailed in company for Operation *Picket 1* to ferry aircraft to Malta; nine Spitfires were flown off at 0824 but their Blenheim escort was late, and that for the second range did not arrive. The weather over Malta then deteriorated and *Eagle* returned to Gibraltar with eight Spitfires still on board.

On 27 March *Eagle* embarked six Albacores for passage to Malta and sailed with *Argus* for Operation *Picket 2*, which turned out to be a confused ferry operation. The Albacore launch was postponed on 28 March because of poor weather conditions over Malta, but seven Spitfires were successfully flown off on 29 March and picked up by two Blenheims and a Beaufort that were flying directly to the island from Gibraltar. An eighth Spitfire was found to be unserviceable and was not launched. On this day enemy shadowing aircraft closed the force but were driven off in a series of running fights with Fulmars from *Argus*. The danger from enemy aircraft caused the Albacore launch to be cancelled, and *Eagle* returned to Gibraltar on 30 March. In April she was docked in Gibraltar for repairs, but in May she was in action again, ferrying RAF Spitfires to Malta in company with the USS *Wasp*.

On 11 June 1942 *Eagle* sailed with *Argus* as part of the covering force for Operation *Harpoon*, a relief convoy to Malta. Some Swordfish were transferred to *Argus* and fighters from 801 (Sea Hurricane) and 807 (Fulmar) NAS were embarked in *Eagle* to balance the air groups. On 13 June *Eagle*'s fighters broke up a number of enemy air attacks on the convoy and shot down nine confirmed enemy aircraft. On 10 August 1942 *Eagle* sailed with *Indomitable* and *Victorious* in Operation *Pedestal*, the largest convoy to be fought through to Malta. *Furious* ferried Spitfires, making this the largest British carrier operation of the war to date. *Eagle*'s air group comprised the Sea Hurricane Flight of 813 NAS and 801 (Sea Hurricane) NAS.

Unfortunately, at 1311 on 11 August 1942 *Eagle* was hit by four torpedoes fired by U-73 in position 38 05N 03 02E, 584 miles west of Malta. By 1315 she had sunk, taking two officers and 158 men with her. There were 789 survivors, plus the four Sea Hurricanes of Red Section, which were airborne at the time and landed on other carriers.

CHAPTER 7

HERMES

Hermes in Plymouth Sound in November 1934. (AUTHOR'S COLLECTION)

*H*ermes was the first ship in the world to be designed, ordered and built from the keel up specifically to operate aircraft, and was named after the cruiser that had operated experimental seaplanes in the 1913 manoeuvres. She was originally intended to be a seaplane carrier with a low, sloping quarterdeck on to which aircraft could be hauled and placed on to trolleys before being pushed forward into the hangar. The order was placed in July 1917, but after her launch in 1919 work on her stopped for a while pending the outcome of flying trials in *Argus* and the partly-completed *Eagle*, and she was laid up for two years.

Technical background

Hermes' freeboard, at 32ft, was about half that of *Argus*, so the forward half of the hull, as far aft as the island, was plated in up to flight-deck level to improve her seaworthiness and flared to keep the deck as dry as possible. The results were successful and she was always regarded as a good, if lively, sea-boat. After the trials in *Eagle* the decision was taken to complete her with a starboard-side island, although it was shorter and narrower than the one fitted in the larger ship and had only one funnel. It was topped by a tripod mast with a huge

gunnery control position that always seemed much larger than really necessary to control her small battery of 5.5in guns. Apart from bulges, her only protection was a waterline thickness of 2in of high-tensile steel, not armour plate.

Like *Eagle*, her flight deck tapered to a point at the bow and was made of 1in high-tensile steel. *Hermes* had two lifts, both cruciform and identical to the forward lift in *Eagle*. The after lift was unusual in that it lowered into the open-sided quarterdeck, which was originally designed as a seaplane handling area with a very low freeboard. It was also accessible by means of a steel roller-shutter in the after bulkhead of the hangar. The after round-down was accentuated by a pronounced 'hump' in the flight deck just forward of it. This was intended to form the rear anchor point of the fore-and-aft retaining wire system, but it was kept when the wires were removed in 1926. The 'hump' served the secondary purpose of housing the lift structure inside the thickness of the flight deck, instead of projecting partly below it when in the raised position.

Four transverse arrester wires were installed in 1933 and proved to be capable of stopping Swordfish in 1938. She had a crane aft of the island but, unlike *Eagle*, it could lift only 7,850lb and was thus

Hermes in Plymouth Sound in November 1934. (AUTHOR'S COLLECTION)

incapable of lifting a fully-fuelled, float-equipped Swordfish. The hangar was divided into three bays by fire curtains; by 1939 each of these could accommodate only four Swordfish, limiting the ship's usefulness to trade protection in the distant oceans. To make matters worse her stability was marginal by RN standards, and although she was designed to take 2,600 tons of FFO, the full load made her trim by the bow and heel 4 degrees to port. These defects gave her an effective maximum bunkerage of 2,000 tons, which reduced her radius of action to about 4,000 miles at 18 knots. Her avgas bulk stowage was also marginal at 7,500gal, 500 of which were carried in a ready-use tank on the starboard side of the flight deck, intended for the gravity refuelling of aircraft on deck between sorties, and which could be jettisoned in an emergency.

The rapid development of naval aviation soon rendered *Hermes* obsolete and she was simply not big enough or fast enough for fleet operations. After the Washington Treaty, however, she was retained because she existed and because she had some value supporting cruisers on the imperial trade routes.

Hermes undergoing sea trials off Plymouth in 1923. The forward windbreak is raised and the tall mast next to it is a temporary, telescopic device with an anemometer on top, intended to give accurate readings of wind flow over the deck before flying trials. (AUTHOR'S COLLECTION)

Hermes technical details

Displacement:	13,700 tons deep load
Dimensions:	length 600ft
	beam 90ft
	draught 26ft 7in
Machinery:	2 shaft Parsons geared turbines
	6 Yarrow small-tube boilers
	40,000shp delivering 25 knots
Armament:	6 x single 5.5in LA; 3 x single
	4in HA; multiple machine-
	guns
Protection:	3in armoured waterline belt;
	1in tensile steel flight deck
Fuel:	2,000 tons FFO usable
Endurance:	2,930 miles at 18 knots
Complement:	700

Aircraft operating data

Flight deck:	570ft x 90ft
Hangar:	400ft long x 50ft wide x 16ft
	high
Arrester wires:	4 x 11,000lb at 53 knots fitted
	in 1933
Lifts:	forward 46ft long x 47ft wide
	cruciform
	Aft 46ft long x 47ft wide
	cruciform
Aircraft:	12 in 1939
Aircraft fuel:	7,500gal avgas in 1939
Air weapons:	18in torpedoes; 250lb GP
	bombs; 100lb bombs; depth
	charges; 0.303in gun
	ammunition; flares and
	pyrotechnics

Hermes Operational history

Laid down by Sir W G Armstrong, Whitworth & Co at Elswick-o-Tyne on 15 January 1918, *Hermes* was launched on 11 September 1919 by Mrs Cooper, the daughter of the First Lord of the Admiralty. In 1920 the ship was towed from Elswick to Devonport Dockyard, where she was to be completed. Work was essentially completed by August 1923, when she carried out steaming trials in Plymouth Sound. She commissioned for the first time on 18 February 1924 and carried out acceptance trials with 403 (Flycatcher) Flight and a single Parnall Panther embarked. In May 1924 she embarked officers from ships of the AF to witness flying operations off the Durnoch Firth so that they could learn about aircraft carriers and their capabilities. In June she carried out exercises with the AF off the west coast of Scotland and

anchored in Torbay for a visit from 11 July with other warships. On 26 July 1924 she was present at a Royal Review of the Fleet at Spithead by His Majesty King George V, on completion of which she sailed with *Argus* for combined flying exercises in the English Channel and then entered Portsmouth Dockyard for a short refit to set right the defects that had been identified since completion.

She sailed from Portsmouth for post-refit trials on 10 November 1924, and on their successful completion sailed to join the MF with 403 (Flycatcher), 440 and 442 (Fairey IIID) Flights

Hermes still has her fore-and-aft retaining wires fitted in this photograph, which shows how the 'cruciform' after lift lowered into the quarterdeck, a feature originally intended to help with seaplane operations in harbour. The after fighter is a Fairey Flycatcher. (AUTHOR'S COLLECTION)

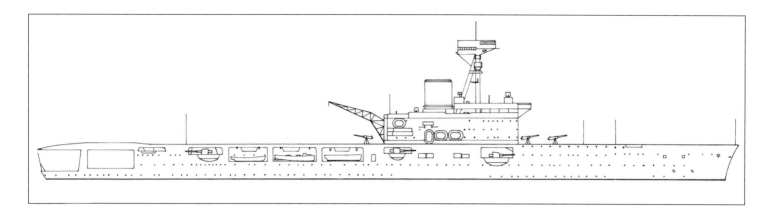

embarked. She arrived in Malta on 22 November and sailed on 5 January 1925 to demonstrate embarked flying operations to senior officers of the MF. In February she carried out joint exercises with the USS *Pittsburgh*, and in March combined flying exercises took place with aircraft from *Eagle*. On 27 March she entered Malta Dockyard for a short refit and then on 17 May she left Malta to return to the UK, pay off and recommission with a new ship's company for service on the China Station with the same air group.

Hermes recommissioned on 3 June 1925 and sailed for the Far East, passing through the Suez Canal on 18 July. She arrived in Hong Kong on 10 August after refuelling stops in Trincomalee and Singapore. She visited the Chinese 'treaty' port of Amoy in November and, having demonstrated her capabilities, began to return to the Mediterranean via Singapore and Colombo. She passed through

the Suez Canal again on 9 March 1926 and arrived in Malta on 15 March. On 5 August she was inspected by Sir Roger Keyes, the Commander-in-Chief Mediterranean, and in September passed through the Suez Canal again for a second period in the Far East, arriving in Hong Kong on 11 October. In April 1927 she supported operations by British forces at Woosung near Shanghai to protect British interests during fighting between rival Chinese factions. In July she moved with other ships from Hong Kong to Wei Hei Wei and remained in the area until relieved by *Argus* on 1 August. On 7 September 1927 she left Hong Kong to return to the UK, arriving at Portsmouth to pay off on 10 October before moving to Chatham Dockyard for a refit.

On 15 December 1927 she recommissioned in Chatham and then sailed for further service on the China Station on 21 January 1928. The same flights were embarked but Fairey IIIFs had replaced the earlier Fairey IIIDs. She passed through the Suez Canal on 5 February and visited

Bangkok on 9 March before relieving *Argus* on 20 March in Hong Kong. During the remainder of 1928 she visited the 'treaty' port of Chefoo, followed by Chingwangtao, North Borneo and Manilla. In 1929 she visited Nanking on the Yangtse River, Tsingtao and several ports in Japan. On 28 January 1930 *Hermes* deployed to Nanking, where she acted as guard-ship during talks between Sir Miles Lampson, the British Minister to China, and Chinese officials over the Japanese invasion of Manchuria. In March she visited Shanghai for a show of strength with other British warships. She sailed from Hong Kong for the UK on 7 August 1930 and arrived in Portsmouth to pay off on 23 September, moving to Chatham for a refit a few days later.

Anchored off Wei-Hei-Wei on the China Station, *Hermes* is seen operating Fairey IIIF seaplanes from her flight deck. The crane is about to lift the forward aircraft on to the water. Awnings have been spread over part of the flight deck to protect men working. The concept of operating seaplanes from a carrier at anchor was not finally discarded until 1940. (Author's collection)

Hermes recommissioned at Chatham for further service on the China Station on 3 October 1930 and sailed for the Far East on 12 November with 403 (Flycatcher) and 440 (Fairey IIIF) Flights embarked, together with six Ripons intended for *Eagle*. She passed through the Suez Canal on 1 December, and on 22 December entered the new Admiralty floating dock off the Singapore Dockyard which was still under construction at the time. She arrived in Hong Kong on 2 January 1931 and began an eventful year on the Station. In June she arrived at Wei Hei Wei to assist with rescue work when the submarine *Poseidon* sank. Six escapers reached the surface and were taken to *Hermes'* sick bay, but two of them unfortunately died there. In August Commissioner Hsu of Wei Hei Wei was flown in a Fairey IIIF and *Hermes* began a passage up the Yangtse River to Hangkow on 31 August.

On arrival in Hangkow on 4 September *Hermes* put landing parties ashore to quell mutinies in several British-owned merchant vessels and to assist with flood-relief work. Fairey IIIFs on floats were flown over a large area to assess the extent of flood damage in the region. The American Colonel Charles Lindbergh and his wife were in Hangkow, having flown from Japan in their Lockheed Sirius as part of a world tour. They too had helped with aerial survey work, and their aircraft was hoisted on board overnight. On being lowered into the swollen river the next day it capsized but was recovered on board. On 3 October *Hermes* slipped her mooring and proceeded to Shanghai, where the Lindberghs and their damaged aircraft were landed. On 3 November *Hermes* went to the aid of the Japanese merchant ship *Ryinjin Maru*, which had run aground, and rescued nine survivors. In March 1931 she began a refit in Hong Kong Dockyard; this was completed in April 1932. She operated from Wei Hei Wei during the summer months and visited Nagasaki and the Philippine Islands before returning to the UK in 1933, arriving in Chatham on 27 July 1933.

Hermes was open to the public during Chatham Navy Days in August and then sailed to Devonport, where she paid off for a long refit during which arrester wires were fitted. She recommissioned on 18 September 1934 and sailed to Portsmouth for trials with the new equipment

Hermes at speed after arrester wires had been fitted. (AUTHOR'S COLLECTION)

in November. On their successful completion she embarked 803 (Osprey) and 824 (Seal) NAS and sailed for the Far East. She anchored off the new naval base in Singapore on 31 December 1934 and relieved *Eagle* as the China Station carrier. In February 1935 her aircraft played a key role in rescuing the China Navigation Company steamer *Tungchow* from pirates, and on 8 November 1935 she joined the search for Air Commodore Sir Charles Kingsford-Smith MC AFC RAAF, who was missing off Burma with his copilot during an attempt to break the record time for a flight from London to Sydney. The search ended in early December without finding any sign of the pilots or their aircraft, the *Lady Southern Cross*. After a short refit in Hong Kong *Hermes* visited Kobe, Kagoshima, Nagasaki, Port Arthur and Tsingtao in 1936, and ports in the Dutch East Indies during 1937. After a few months based in Singapore she returned to the UK, arriving in Devonport on 3 May 1937. She took part in the Royal Review of

the Fleet at Spithead on 20 May 1937 and subsequently reduced to reserve at Devonport, where she was used as an accommodation ship. In July 1938 she was brought forward for use as an aviation training ship, based in Devonport with a reduced ship's company.

On 24 August 1939 *Hermes* was recommissioned for operational service and embarked 814 (Swordfish) NAS. She concentrated at Portland with other units of the HF on 1 September and subsequently carried out an antisubmarine sweep in the south-west approaches with the destroyers *Imogen* and *Isis*, returning to Devonport on 27 September. In October she joined a French squadron led by the battlecruiser *Strasbourg* based on Dakar which was used to hunt for German surface raiders in the South Atlantic shipping lanes. She was refitted briefly in Devonport in January 1940 and then returned to the Dakar-based group to resume searches. Her aircraft located the blockade-runner *Jobshaven* on 24 April and it was subsequently arrested.

After the collapse of France *Hermes* was ordered by the Admiralty to sail from Dakar on 29 June and initiate a blockade of French shipping off West Africa. She refuelled in Freetown on 2 July and then, on 18 July, one of her ship's boats was used to attack the new battleship *Richelieu* in Dakar. The intention was to disable the *Richelieu*'s rudder and propellers with depth charges but, because of the shallow water, they failed to explode. A more

successful attack was carried out by bomb-armed Swordfish a day later. On 10 August *Hermes* collided with the armed merchant cruiser *Corfu* in dense fog, suffering damage to her bow. Initial repairs were made in Freetown and more complete work was carried out in Simonstown Dockyard in South Africa. She was able to resume operations in the South Atlantic and Indian Oceans, searching for German commerce raiders. She still had 814 NAS embarked and it remained her only squadron throughout her war service.

In April 1941 *Hermes* supported the Anglo-Indian force that suppressed the German-supported uprising in Iraq. She subsequently searched for Vichy-French shipping in the Indian Ocean, refuelling when necessary in Colombo and Mombassa. In early October she had a brief self-maintenance period in Mombassa, during which her Swordfish disembarked to RNAS Port Reitz, and later in the month she joined *Repulse* to patrol Allied shipping routes.

On 18 November 1941 *Hermes* arrived in Simonstown Dockyard for a refit which was completed on 31 January 1942. The Admiralty's intention for her was that she would join the Australian Squadron to use her aircraft to support cruisers in operations against the Japanese. She was joined by HMAS *Vampire* and carried out an antisubmarine patrol with her south of Ceylon. The crisis that followed the rapid Japanese advances led to changes in her programme, however, and she was

Hermes in a camouflage paint scheme, shortly before her loss in 1942. Note the Type 72 aircraft homing beacon fitted at the highest point of the foremast over the spotting top structure. (AUTHOR'S COLLECTION)

retained near Ceylon while the new carrier *Indomitable* was misemployed ferrying RAF fighters to the Dutch East Indies. On 26 March she was ordered to leave Trincomalee with *Vampire* to join Allied forces assembling in Freemantle. Three days later she was recalled to form part of the EF in Trincomalee. However, when the Fleet Staff learnt of the imminent attack on Ceylon by Admiral Nagumo's Japanese fast carrier task force, *Hermes* was ordered to sail without aircraft embarked to clear the harbour with *Vampire*. Air cover for the ships was to be provided by the RAF from shore bases, but in the event it did not materialise and at 1100 on 9 April 1942 *Hermes* was attacked by aircraft from the Japanese carriers *Akagi*, *Hiryu*, *Shokaku* and *Zuikaku*. They scored over forty hits with 500lb bombs and at 1120 *Hermes* sank in position 07 35N 82 05E, off Batticaloa in Ceylon, now Sri Lanka, with the loss of 307 men. *Vampire* sank at 1130 with the loss of eight men. The corvette *Hollyhock* nearby was sunk at 1200 by aircraft from *Soryu* with the loss of fifty-three men, but the nearby hospital ship *Vita* was respected by the Japanese and rescued over 600 men from *Hermes* and *Vampire*. *Hermes* is the only British aircraft carrier ever to have been sunk by air attack.

CHAPTER 8

THE DEVELOPMENT OF CARRIERS
IN OTHER NAVIES

For four years after *Argus* was completed in September 1918 she was the world's only aircraft carrier. Other navies took a keen interest in aviation, however, and were given varying degrees of assistance by the Royal Navy in the design and construction of their first ships.

The United States Navy

When the United States entered the First World War on side of the Allies, a member of the Royal Corps of Naval Constructors, Stanley Goodall (later Sir Stanley Goodall KCB RCNC and Director of Naval Construction) was lent to the USN Bureau of Construction and Repair to brief on British warship projects. He took with him a number of plans, including those for *Eagle* and

Hermes, and briefed the Americans fully on RN policy for large aircraft carrying ships to work with the fleet. These were still evolving, but the USN was kept fully informed as changes were made, and officers were able to visit *Argus* shortly after her completion.

Langley

At first, Congress would not vote funds for a ship built from the outset as a carrier, but approved the conversion of a fleet auxiliary in 1919 and the collier *Jupiter*, AC-3, was selected. Work started in 1920 and the austere conversion was completed in March 1922 when, renamed the USS *Langley*, she became the world's second aircraft carrier. The basic collier hull and turboelectric machinery were retained, as was the

USS *Langley*, CV-1, off San Diego in 1928 with the destroyer USS *Somers* in the background. (USN VIA A D BAKER III)

original superstructure aft and the bridge right forward under the flight deck. The original single funnel was replaced by two hinged 'smoke stacks' on the port side aft, which lay horizontal during flight operations and were vertical when cruising. The former upper deck became the hangar deck and the rectangular flight deck was built above it, supported by a latticework structure which was completely open at the sides and allowed wind and wave to affect the hangar deck. Large gaps in the latticework were left in the sides amidships to allow seaplanes to be craned into the hangar from either side. Ship control remained in the original bridge under the flight deck, and flying control was exercised from netted sponsons on either side of the flight deck.

As a collier she had six holds. The foremost was modified to contain a large tank for avgas and the fourth was modified into a magazine for air weapons in the bottom half and a machinery space for the single lift in the upper half. The lift platform was in the centre of the flight deck and was locked at flight-deck level during flying operations. The remaining four holds, two forward and two aft of the lift, were used to stow dismantled aircraft which were raised on to the hangar deck by two three-ton travelling cranes installed under the flight deck. Each had a swivelling section which allowed aircraft to be lowered on to the lift for passage to the flight deck or removed from it to be struck down. This unusual arrangement led to Captain J M Reeves USN, her first captain, evolving ways to keep serviceable aircraft on deck and led directly to the evolution of barriers and catapult launching techniques. Two conventional cranes were installed, one on either side amidships at hangar deck level to lower seaplanes on to the water and recover them. The hangar sides were deliberately left open as it was felt that the benefit of ventilation to clear petrol fumes was more important than 'weather tightness'.

At 14 knots normal sea speed *Langley* was only just fast enough to operate the first generation of US carrierborne aircraft, but proved to be an ideal research 'tool' and could operate an increasing number of aircraft as Reeves's improvements in deck operation were incorporated. The USN's carrier operating technique rapidly caught up with and overtook that of the RN, which was hampered by the politically enforced 'dual control' arrangement with the RAF between 1918 and 1939.

Reeves was fully aware of the weapon system he had created for the USN, and after his promotion to Rear Admiral he confided to Admiral Moffett, the Head of the Bureau of Aeronautics, that he had concealed *Langley*'s true operational capability during a visit by Vice-Admiral Fuller of the RN during a visit in October 1928. 'Of course I did not tell Admiral Fuller that we operated not twenty-four but thirty-six aircraft and could operate forty-two and, possibly, forty-eight airplanes from the *Langley*,' he stated. Fuller may have been sharper than he was credited, however, and the RN followed American progress keenly, adopting arrester wires, barriers, landing control officers and hydraulic catapults to improve its own flying operations and increase the number of aircraft as soon as it was able.

In 1936 *Langley* was converted into a seaplane carrier with the forward third of the flight deck cut away to create a forward handling deck. By 1941 she was being used as an aircraft ferry, and on 27 February 1942, while ferrying US Army fighters to Java, she was located and sunk by land-based long-range bombers of the Imperial Japanese Navy.

Langley technical details

Displacement:	15,150 tons deep load
Dimensions:	length 542ft 2.5in
	beam 65ft 6 in
	draught 24ft
Machinery:	1 shaft turboelectric
	3 D.E. boilers working at 190psi
	7,150shp delivering 15 knots clean
Armament:	4 single 5in; numerous machine guns
Protection:	none
Fuel:	2,300 tons
Endurance:	12,260 miles at 10 knots
Complement:	468

Aircraft operating data

Flight deck:	534ft x 64ft
Hangar:	none as such, but space under flight deck for aircraft preparation
Catapults:	2 x 6,000lb at 40 knots
Arrester wires:	6 x 8,000lb at 60 knots; no barrier at first
Lift:	36ft long x 45ft 6in wide
Aircraft:	Average 33, with more stowed dismantled
Aircraft fuel:	134,000gal avgas
Air weapons:	torpedoes; bombs; 0.5in and 0.3in machine-gun ammunition; flares and pyrotechnics

Saratoga and *Lexington*

Two further aircraft carriers for the US Navy were converted from 33,500-ton battlecruiser hulls while they were still on the slipway, taking the full tonnage allowed under the terms of the Washington Naval Treaty. Named *Lexington* and *Saratoga*, they retained their battlecruiser form up to the original upper deck, but the conversion followed the British practice of continuing the hull up to the flight deck, which became the strength deck. The original upper deck became the hangar deck. They had two centreline lifts, eight arrester wires and a single catapult but, since the 888ft-long flight deck could allow free take-offs by aircraft from very large ranges aft, the catapult was removed in 1931. It was of a novel flywheel design and proved impractical in use because of the time taken to spin up the flywheel before each launch. The size of the flight deck was not exceeded until the *Midway* class of 1945, and in 1930 all ninety aircraft embarked could be launched from a single range. The ships' machinery comprised four shafts, each with a set of generating turbines and two electric motors per shaft developing 180,000shp. They were the most powerful warships built before 1939 and achieved 34 knots on trials. The uptakes from the twelve boilers were trunked to the starboard side into a single, enormous funnel that was the distinguishing recognition feature of these ships. Such was the electrical generating capacity of these ships that when the city of Tacoma's power station broke down in December 1929, *Lexington* supplied 4.25 million kilowatt hours of electricity over 31 days.

The USN was concerned that aircraft carriers operating as a strike force away from the battle fleet would be vulnerable to enemy cruisers, and both ships were built with eight 8in guns in four twin turrets, two forward and two abaft the starboard-side island. A further twelve 5in guns were fitted as singles in open mountings on sponsons around the deck edge. The original battlecruiser armour was replaced by a 6in belt on the waterline and thin horizontal decks over magazines and machinery. The 8in guns proved to be of little value and were removed in 1942 and replaced in *Saratoga* by four twin 5in mountings. The unarmoured steel flight deck was covered with Oregon Pine wooden planking laid athwartships, with athwartship slotted channels to which aircraft could be lashed, spaced at intervals. The wood was treated to be fire-retardant and offered a suitably non-skid surface, even when fuel or oil was spilt on it. A single safety barrier was added in 1931. The hangar was enclosed but not entered through air locks as in British carriers, and spaces near boat decks were open to the outside air to improve ventilation. The two centreline lifts were built at the fore and aft extremities of the hangar, the forward one being large enough to strike down aircraft with their wings spread. Although large, the hangar could not take all ninety of the aircraft in the initial air group, and these ships operated with a deck park, like *Langley*, from the outset. A second hangar with much less height and accessible only from the forward lift was used as a stowage for dismantled spare aircraft and components. The weakest aspect of an otherwise excellent design was the avgas stowage arrangement. To embark sufficient fuel for ninety aircraft over a prolonged period that was expected to include several deck-load strikes, avgas was stowed in integral bulk tanks, surrounded by void spaces which could be filled with inert carbon dioxide gas.

Saratoga took part in the war game that defined

The USS *Lexington*, CV-2, as built, showing her capability to launch an enormous deck-load strike. The first aircraft out of the range has just got airborne, and the two twin 8in turrets are visible forward of the island. The forward two twin 8in gun turrets can be seen before the island. (AUTHOR'S COLLECTION)

torpedoes and the mining effect of near-miss bombs distorted the hull and ruptured the avgas tanks and their surrounding bulkheads, allowing inflammable petrol vapour to spread throughout the ship. It detonated an hour after the initial damage, starting uncontrollable fires. These set off a second major explosion two hours later and she was abandoned when the fire reached her magazines. She still did not sink but salvage was impossible, and she had to be destroyed by torpedoes from the US destroyer *Phelps*.

Saratoga survived the war despite hits by Japanese torpedoes in January and August 1942 and severe damage when struck by a Kamikaze in February 1945. Rebuilt but reduced to reserve after VJ-Day, she was used as a target ship at the Bikini Atoll atomic bomb trial in 1946. Unmanned and with no pumps she flooded slowly and was allowed to sink several days after the first atomic explosion on 25 July 1946. It is interesting to speculate that, had she had an operational damage control organisation, she could have survived the blast.

Saratoga technical details

Displacement:	47,700 tons deep load
Dimensions:	length 888ft when completed
	beam 105ft 6in
	draught 32ft
Machinery:	4 shafts each with generating
	turbines and 2 electric motors
	16 White-Foster boilers
	working at 300psi
	184,000shp delivering 34 knots
Armament:	4 twin 8in; 12 single 5in
Protection:	6in waterline belt; 6in
	bulkheads; 3in main deck; 1 to
	3in lower deck; turrets up to
	3in; barbettes 6in
Fuel:	9,748 tons FFO
Endurance:	6,960 miles at 20 knots
Complement:	2,122

Aircraft operating data

Flight deck:	880ft x 90ft
Hangar:	393ft x 68ft x 20ft
Catapult:	single Norden flywheel type,
	soon removed, 6,000lb at 40
	knots
Arrester wires:	8 hydraulic, 8,000lb at 60
	knots; 1 barrier as built

the strike potential of a carrier task force; USN Fleet Problem IX in January 1929, which took place off Panama with Reeves, by now an Admiral commanding the Fleet's air component, flying his flag in her. The carrier detached from the main force to launch a strike against the 'enemy' Panama Canal by seventy aircraft from a range of 140 nautical miles. Using the new technique of dive-bombing to 'attack' the locks, they caught the defenders completely unawares, demonstrating the operational value of aircraft for 'independent' strike warfare rather than 'attendant' operations in support of battleships.

Lexington was hit by two Japanese torpedoes and two light bombs during the Battle of the Coral Sea on 8 May 1942. The whip effect of the

Lifts:	fwd 29ft 5in long x 59ft 5in wide
	aft 29ft 3in long x 34ft 11in wide
Aircraft:	90
Aircraft fuel:	110,140gal
Air weapons:	torpedoes; bombs; 0.5in and 0.3in machine-gun ammunition; flares and pyrotechnics

the boiler uptakes to three funnels at the starboard deck edge amidships, which were lowered to the horizontal during flying operations. Four 5.5in guns were mounted outboard of the hangar, together with several machine guns. The former upper deck became the hangar deck and the sides were continued up to the flight deck for two-thirds of the ship's length to make it semi-enclosed. The extra top weight was compensated for by a Sperry stabilisation system which worked well. The flight deck was supported by the hangar walls and pillars fore and aft. It was made of mild steel covered with

The USS *Saratoga*, CV-3, photographed from *Victorious*. (AUTHOR'S COLLECTION)

wooden planking laid fore and aft, and was originally stressed to take aircraft weights up to 8,800lb. This was later increased to 13,200lb, with lifts and the six arrester wires eventually fitted stressed to the same figure. Sections of the hangar sides amidships were left open to provide ventilation but, with the hangar deck only 15ft above the waterline, heavy seas could wash down

The Imperial Japanese Navy

Hosho

The Imperial Japanese Navy (IJN) received British help in the form of a Technical Mission of former RNAS officers led by the Master of Sempill. The Mission took RN carrier plans with them, and the IJN decided to convert an oiler that had been laid down in 1919 into its first carrier. Work on the ship was suspended while new drawings were prepared, but she was finally launched in November 1921 and towed to Yokosuka Navy Yard for fitting out. She was completed as the world's third aircraft carrier on 27 December 1922 and named *Hosho*, which translates as 'Swooping Dragon'. At about 10,000 tons she was smaller than *Argus* or *Langley*, but at 25 knots she was considerably faster owing to the removal of the designed reciprocating steam machinery and its replacement by two sets of destroyer-type geared turbines developing 30,000shp, for which steam was provided by twelve boilers in six boiler rooms.

Apart from the altered machinery, the original tanker hull was modified only by the trunking of

Hosho as built, with a small starboard-side island. (AUTHOR'S COLLECTION)

the hangar deck, and they were soon plated in.

She was originally completed with a small island comprising a bridge over a charthouse on the starboard side amidships but, with a deck only 59ft wide, pilots who carried out the initial flying trials warned that it was dangerous and it was immediately removed. The bridge arrangements were changed to wing platforms on either side of the forward end of the hangar 'box' and the charthouse was repositioned between the pillars supporting the forward overhang of the flight deck. Unlike the RN and USN, the IJN did not develop a system using 'batsmen' to control aircraft approach, but installed light projectors using red/amber/green lights at set angles to show pilots whether they were low, correct or high relative to the ideal glide slope.

After extensive use as a prototype operational carrier, *Hosho* was used mainly on training duties during the Second World War, although she did see action in the Midway operation. Unlike the majority of IJN carriers she survived the war and was used for a while on repatriation transport duties, extracting Japanese forces from island garrisons after VJ-Day. She was scrapped at Osaka in 1947.

Hosho technical details

Displacement:	9,630 tons deep load
Dimensions:	length 551ft 4in
	beam 59ft 1in
	draught 20ft 3in
Machinery:	2 shaft Parsons geared turbines
	12 Kampon boilers
	30,000shp delivering 25 knots
Armament:	4 single 5.51in; 2 single 3in
	plus 7.7mm machine guns
Protection:	None
Fuel:	550 tons FFO
Endurance:	Approximately 3,000 miles at
	14 knots
Complement:	550

Aircraft operating data

Flight deck:	519ft x 59ft
Hangar:	423ft 6in x 55ft maximum
	reducing to 40ft by funnel
	uptakes x 14ft
Arrester wires:	6 x 8,800lb at 60 knots when
	completed
Lifts:	fwd 44ft 11in long x 36ft 1in
	wide
	aft 42ft 4in long x 27ft 10in
	wide
Aircraft:	21
Aircraft fuel:	approximately 50,000gal in
	bulk stowage
Air weapons:	torpedoes; bombs; 20mm
	cannon and 7.7mm machine-
	gun ammunition; flares and
	pyrotechnics

Akagi

As in the RN and USN, the IJN elected to convert surplus battlecruiser hulls into aircraft carriers after the abandonment of capital ship construction agreed in the Washington Naval Treaty. Two incomplete hulls, *Akagi* and *Amagi*, were selected, but the latter was badly damaged by an earthquake while still on the slipway at Yokosuka in 1923 and her place was taken by the incomplete battleship *Kaga*.

Work on reconstructing *Akagi*, which translates as 'Red Castle', began in 1923 and she was completed on 25 March 1927. She had no island, a flight deck 632ft long and two hangars, one above the other, as in contemporary British carrier designs. Like the American battlecruiser conversions, a small hangar was built in under the main ones for the stowage of dismantled spare aircraft. Only 213ft long by 40ft wide, it could be accessed only by the after lift. The small flying-off decks were taken a stage further, however, with one

Akagi in the summer of 1941. Her small port-side island and the tapered stern make it difficult to work out which way she is heading. (AUTHOR'S COLLECTION)

for each hangar; the deck forward of the upper hangar was 60ft long and intended for fighters, and the deck forward of the lower hangar was 160ft long and intended for heavier aircraft. Neither proved successful, and both were removed in 1936 when she was refitted with a full-length flight deck and a third lift forward to give access to the extended hangar. A small port-side island was fitted at the same time, intended to facilitate left or right circuit patterns when carriers operated in close proximity. Like many Japanese warships of the period in which she was designed, her boilers were intended to operate with both domestically produced coal and FFO. After her 1936 reconstruction only FFO was used, despite the difficulty and expense of its procurement. Uptakes from the nineteen boilers were taken to one large funnel exhausting the smoke downwards on the starboard side amidships and a second, smaller funnel that exhausted upwards under the flight deck. Like the USN, the Japanese sought to protect these ships against cruisers, and 8in guns were fitted, six aft in casemates that proved difficult to use and four others in two twin turrets, one either side of the upper flying-off deck. The latter were removed during the 1936 refit when, in addition to lengthening the flight deck, the hangars were extended forward by 80ft.

Six electrically operated arrester wires were fitted initially, but were later replaced by nine hydraulically actuated units. No Japanese carrier was ever fitted with catapults. All IJN carrier-borne aircraft were capable of free take off and, unlike the British and American navies, seaplanes were operated from cruisers, freeing the carriers to operate nothing but fighters and strike aircraft. *Akagi*'s powerful machinery gave her a speed of just over 31 knots on trials. She was actually considerably heavier than the declared standard tonnage of 26,900, and when she recommissioned in 1938 her standard displacement was admitted to have risen to 36,500 tons despite the removal of the two heavy 8in gun turrets. Full-load displacement was 42,700 tons. There was no horizontal armour to protect the machinery or the poorly designed avgas stowage arrangements.

Akagi was lost on 4 June 1942 during the Battle of Midway, when she was hit by dive-bombers from the USS *Enterprise*. Fuelled and armed aircraft on deck and in the hangar exploded and started serious fires and, although she continued to steam and float at first, the spread of fires forced the machinery spaces to be abandoned. The consequent loss of power meant that the fires could not be brought under control and she had to be abandoned and scuttled.

Kaga

Kaga, named after a former Japanese province, differed in that she was laid down as a battleship. She was 62ft shorter than *Akagi* and her less-powerful machinery gave her a trial speed of only 27 knots. The hangars were carried further aft and were slightly wider, which meant that she was able to operate an air group of about the same size. Her funnel arrangements differed in that they were divided into port and starboard trunkings which were led aft down the outside of the upper hangar a distance of about 300ft to exhaust over the quarterdeck; an unsuccessful system very like that used in the rebuilt British *Furious*. To minimise the use of oil, which was expensive to import, her boilers were originally designed to burn both coal and FFO, but after her 1934 refit they were all modified to burn oil only.

Like *Akagi* she originally had two flying-off decks, but these were removed after 1934 when the flight deck was extended over the entire length of the hull and the hangars extended forward. The two 8in gun turrets were similarly removed, but in one sense her refit was more extensive than that of her contemporary; the hull was cut abaft the hangar and a new 34ft section inserted to preserve the length-to-beam ratio after anti-torpedo bulges were fitted outboard of the hull. New machinery of 127,400shp replaced the original 91,000shp units, giving a greater top speed of 28.5 knots. Deck strength, arrester wires and lifts were all designed to handle aircraft up to 13,200lb. She was the first Japanese carrier to be built with a permanent island on the starboard side amidships, like those in British and American carriers.

Kaga was also lost in the Battle of Midway on 4 June 1942, when she was hit by four 1,000lb bombs from the USS *Enterprise*'s dive-bombers. These burst through the unprotected flight and hangar decks as they exploded, causing extensive fires. Abandoned soon afterwards, she blew up and sank nine hours later when fire reached her avgas tanks. Eight hundred of her ship's company were lost.

Smoke emerges from *Kaga*'s distinctive starboard, downward-tilted funnel. (AUTHOR'S COLLECTION)

Akagi technical details

Displacement:	34,364 tons deep load
Dimensions:	length 857ft
	beam 95ft
	draught 26ft 6in
Machinery:	4 shaft Gijitsu Honbu geared turbines
	19 Kampon boilers
	131,000shp delivering 31 knots
Armament:	2 twin 8in turrets on upper flying off deck; 6 twin 4.7in on sponsons
Protection:	6in waterline belt; 3.1in deck over machinery
Fuel:	3,900 tons FFO; 2,100 tons coal
Endurance:	8,000 miles at 14 knots
Complement:	1,600

Aircraft operating data

Flight deck:	562ft x 95ft. Flying-off decks 160ft long at hangar deck levels
Hangars:	upper 354ft x 62ft (maximum) x 15ft
	lower 492ft x 59ft (maximum)x 15ft
Arrester wires:	6 electrically controlled, 13,200lb at 78 knots
Lifts:	fwd 38ft 6in long x 42ft 8in wide
	aft 42ft long x 29ft 6in wide
Aircraft:	60
Aircraft fuel:	100,000gal, approximately, in bulk stowage
Air weapons:	torpedoes; bombs; 20mm cannon and 7.7mm machine-gun ammunition; flares and pyrotechnics.

Kaga technical details

Displacement:	33,693 tons deep load
Dimensions:	length 782ft 6in
	beam 97ft
	draught 26ft
Machinery:	4 shaft Brown-Curtis geared turbines
	12 Kampon boilers
	91,000shp delivering 27.5 knots
Armament:	2 twin 8in turrets on upper flying off deck; 6 single 8in in casemates aft; 12 single 4.7in plus several machine guns
Protection:	6in waterline belt; 1.5in deck over magazines
Fuel:	3,600 tons FFO; 1,700 tons coal
Endurance:	8,000 miles at 14 knots
Complement:	1,340

Aircraft operating data

Flight deck:	560ft x 97ft
Hangars:	upper 415ft x 65ft x 15ft
	lower 470ft x 75ft x 15ft
Arrester wires:	6 x 13,200lb at 78 knots
Lifts:	fwd 37ft 8in long x 39ft 5in wide
	aft 35ft long x 52ft wide
Aircraft:	60
Aircraft fuel:	100,000gal avgas in unprotected bulk stowage
Air weapons:	torpedoes; bombs; 20mm cannon and 7.7mm machine-gun ammunition; flares and pyrotechnics

Béarn at speed, following the French battle-line. (AUTHOR'S COLLECTION)

The French Navy

Bearn was the only aircraft carrier to be built in France and completed before 1960. She was originally laid down in 1914 as a *Normandie*-class battleship but suspended incomplete throughout the First World War. Work on her resumed in 1919 and she was launched in April 1920. A short flight deck was erected over the quarterdeck, upon which landing trials were carried out in 1920/21. After the Washington Treaty had been signed in 1922 the French elected to complete her as an aircraft carrier. Work started on her conversion in August 1923 and was helped by the British Admiralty, which made drawings of *Eagle*'s aviation and island arrangements available. The ship's side aft was plated up to the flight deck, which was constructed of 1in armour and formed the upper strength deck of the hull. Horizontal armour 2.95in thick was fitted on the lower hangar deck, with 1in armour on the main deck over machinery and magazines. The machinery was unique, comprising two inner shafts driven by steam turbines and two outer shafts driven by steam reciprocating engines, in an attempt to combine the economy of the latter with the high-speed performance of the former. The arrangement was not a success and gave a maximum speed of only 21 knots, too slow for effective operation with the 29-knot battleships of the Force de Raid in 1939. Her gun armament was conventional for the time, comprising eight 6in guns in casemates and a number of smaller anti-aircraft weapons, but unconventionally she retained four underwater torpedo tubes from her original armament as a battleship.

Like British and Japanese carriers she had a double hangar arrangement, but the lower hangar was intended as a workshop area and stowage for reserve aircraft which were only partly assembled. The upper hangar was intended for operational aircraft, and although she was officially stated to be capable of carrying forty aircraft she could realistically operate only twenty-five. The flight deck ran the length of the hull, having pronounced taper and round-downs at either extremity. Fore and aft of the central hangar block it was supported by pillars over an open forecastle and quarterdeck, but the hangars were enclosed, following standard British practice. Another unique feature was the lift design, which connected the two hangars with the flight deck. The three lifts were electrically operated and had platforms which were normally kept at upper hangar level, leaving a lift well open under them at lower hangar level. In every other navy the lift platforms formed part of the flight deck when in the raised position, leaving a hole when it was lowered. In *Béarn* the apertures in the flight deck were closed by 'clamshell' doors which opened upwards to form fore and aft windbreaks when opened to allow the lift platforms to flight deck level. This cumbersome arrangement was no more successful than the unusual machinery installation.

French naval aviation was inadequately funded between the wars, and by 1939 her operational capability was further limited by obsolescent aircraft such as the Levasseur torpedo bomber and Dewoitine D.37 fighter. After a brief spell of operational duty she was used to ferry aircraft between the USA and France until the Franco/German armistice in June 1940, after which she lay inactive in Martinique for three years. When the island changed its allegiance from Vichy to the Free French Government she was refitted in the USA and used again as a ferry carrier for a number of years before becoming an accommodation ship. She was broken up for scrap in 1967.

Béarn's unique armoured lift doors in the open position.
(AUTHOR'S COLLECTION)

Béarn technical details

Displacement:	28,400 tons deep load
Dimensions:	length 599ft 1in
	beam 115ft 6in
	draught 30ft 6in
Machinery:	4 shaft; 2 steam turbine; 2 triple-expansion reciprocating steam
	12 boilers
	37,200shp delivering 21.5 knots
Armament:	8 single 6.1in; 6 single 75mm; 8 single 37mm
	4 x 550mm torpedo tubes
Protection:	3in waterline belt; 75mm lower hangar; 25mm main deck
Fuel:	2,037 tons FFO
Endurance:	6,000 miles at 10 knots
Complement:	875

Aircraft operating data

Flight deck:	599ft x 88ft
Hangars:	upper 406ft 10in x 64ft x 20ft
	lower 321ft 6in x 59ft x 20ft
Arrester wires:	6 x 8,800lb at 60 knots, electrically controlled
Lifts:	Three, largest 50ft long x 51ft 6in wide
Aircraft:	40 could be embarked, 25 operated
Aircraft fuel:	Not known
Air weapons:	torpedoes; bombs; 7.62 machine-gun ammunition; flares and pyrotechnics.

Early aircraft carrier completion dates

1.	HMS *Argus*	16 September 1918
2.	USS *Langley*	20 March 1922
3.	IJNS *Hosho*	27 December 1922
4.	HMS *Hermes*	18 February 1924
5.	HMS *Eagle*	26 February 1924
6.	HMS *Furious*	31 August 1925
7.	IJNS *Akagi*	25 March 1927
8.	FNS *Béarn*	May 1927
9.	USS *Saratoga*	16 November 1927
10.	USS *Lexington*	14 December 1927
11.	IJNS *Kaga*	31 March 1928
12.	HMS *Courageous*	5 May 1928
13.	HMS *Glorious*	10 March 1930

CHAPTER 9

COURAGEOUS CLASS

Technical background

Both ships saw service as light battlecruisers with the Grand Fleet, and some early thought was given to converting them into aviation ships like their half-sister *Furious*, but nothing was done until after the war. They were saved from the scrapyard by a decision taken by the Admiralty in 1920 to convert them into flush-deck aircraft carriers similar to *Furious*, and a team of constructors under J H Narbeth worked out the detailed redesign, which took advantage of the early experience with *Argus* and *Eagle*.

Even before *Furious* was completed it was clear that the trunked funnel arrangements and lack of an island were not successful, although the latter did allow aircraft with large wingspans to land-on without obstruction. Against that single positive, the trunking added about 200 tons in weight high in the ship, reduced the amount of workshop space available and reduced the number of aircraft that could be struck down into the upper hangar by

about ten. The temperature near the ducts was found to reach 63 degrees Celsius (or 146 degrees Fahrenheit), and made the after end of the ship hot, dirty and, at times, intolerable. The lack of an island made ship control difficult and made it difficult to find space for aerials, offices and aircrew briefing or ready rooms.

The idea of an island and funnel arrangement was first considered by Narbeth to make space for 8in gun turrets and their ammunition-hoist arrangements, to match similar weapons reported on American and Japanese carriers. Their advantages were deemed to be so great, however, that they were retained when the big guns were deleted from the design. Although the small island was important for ship and flying control, the trunked funnel gave the biggest advantage, and Narbeth referred to these ships at first as 'funnel carriers'.

The same double-hangar arrangement as *Furious* was adopted as a means of stowing the maximum number of aircraft in a relatively small hull. Deck parking was still not considered an option, as the relatively lightweight aircraft of the

Glorious in Plymouth Sound in 1935, after catapults and arrester wires had been fitted. Anti-aircraft guns have been mounted on the former flying-off deck. The long structure to port of the island was a bridge extension, intended to give the captain and navigating officer a view to port in pilotage waters. It was folded back flush with the island at sea during flying operations. (AUTHOR'S COLLECTION)

era could easily suffer wind damage even when lashed on deck. Without the trunking making inroads into the upper hangar, these two later ships were able to carry a useful air group of forty-eight aircraft as well as having more extensive workshop arrangements. The same cruciform lifts as those in *Eagle* and *Hermes* were fitted fore and aft. Like *Furious*, both ships had a flying-off deck over the forecastle connected to the upper hangar, from which fighters could be launched when the main deck was filled with parked aircraft. Windbreaks, which lay flush with the deck when not in use, were fitted at the forward end of both decks to protect aircraft ranged behind them as the ships accelerated into wind before starting a launch.

A Swordfish lands on *Glorious* while others join overhead in formation. The 'W' shaped bracket under the extended round-down is a distinctive recognition feature for this ship, but the letters GL painted on the after part of the flight deck confirm her identity. (AUTHOR'S COLLECTION)

catapulting the first aircraft out of a large range to increase the number of aircraft on deck beyond the amount of deck that would be needed for a free take-off was not appreciated until some years later. At the time the RN differentiated between catapults fitted in battleships, cruisers and specialised catapult ships and those fitted in aircraft carriers, the latter being referred to as accelerators. With the rapid disappearance of seaplane flights after 1943 the term catapult was applied universally and is used so throughout this work. The catapults fitted in *Courageous* and *Glorious* could launch an 8,000lb aircraft at an end speed of 56 knots or a 10,000lb aircraft at 53 knots. All naval aircraft of the 1930s were designed to operate either with wheels or floats, so that they could operate from either aircraft carriers or battleships and cruisers equipped with catapults. The aircraft floats were stressed to allow deck landings, although the metal-to-metal contact with the deck cannot have been good for either structure if carried out frequently.

The after ends of the two ships' flight decks were significantly different, and were a useful recognition feature by which they could be told apart. *Courageous'* flight deck ended abruptly with

With increasing aircraft weights leading to longer take-off runs the forward deck was no longer used after 1935, and the doors on to it from the upper hangar were welded shut.

Courageous was the first British carrier to be fitted with transverse arrester wires when she carried out flying trials of various different types in 1930. Both ships were fitted with production Mark III arrester wires from 1933, but neither was ever fitted with a barrier. At first there was some resistance to the new techniques in *Courageous* until Admiralty experts pointed out the marked improvement in landing intervals that followed the introduction of arrested landings and explained the progress that had been made by the US Navy. Both ships were also fitted with catapults, intended at first for launching aircraft fitted with floats. The potential for

Courageous as converted. (©JOHN JORDAN 2010)

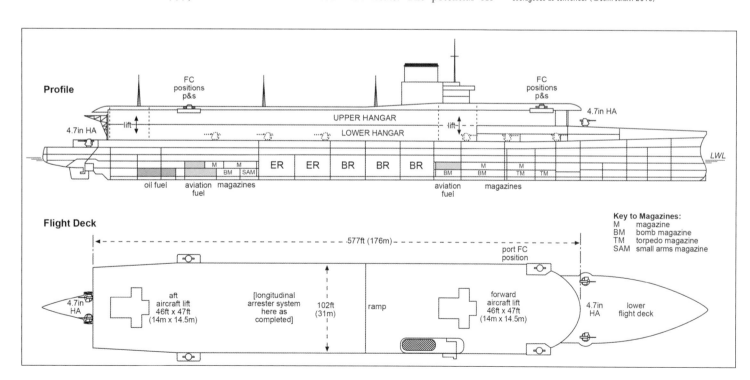

The sea water washing down *Glorious'* flying-off deck and crashing into the hangar door show the disadvantage of the design in rough weather. (AUTHOR'S COLLECTION)

Courageous Class technical details

Displacement:	27,560 tons deep load
Dimensions:	length 786ft 6in
	beam 110ft
	draught 28ft
Machinery:	4 shaft Parsons geared turbines
	18 Yarrow small-tube boilers
	90,670shp delivering 30 knots
Armament:	16 single 4.7in QF Mark VIII
	HA (12 in Glorious); 4 single
	3pdr; machine guns
Protection:	3in side belts; 3in forward and
	2in aft bulkheads; 1.75in over
	machinery and steering gear;
	ant-torpedo bulges designed to
	defeat 440lb warheads
Fuel:	3,685 tons FFO
Endurance:	2,920 miles at 24 knots
Complement:	1,260

Aircraft operating data

Flight deck:	530ft x 91ft 6in steel plate
Hangars:	upper 550ft x 50ft x 16ft
	lower 550ft x 50ft x 16ft
Catapults:	2 hydraulic, 10,000lb at 52
	knots
Arrester wires:	4 x 11,000lb at 53 knots
Lifts:	forward 46ft x 47ft
	cruciform
	aft 46ft x 47ft cruciform
Aircraft:	48
Aircraft fuel:	35,700gal avgas
Air weapons:	18in torpedoes; 500lb SAP
	bombs; 250lb SAP bombs;
	250lb GP bombs; 100lb
	bombs; 100lb A/S bombs; 20lb
	bombs; 0.303in machine-gun
	ammunition; flares and
	pyrotechnics

Individual ship histories

Courageous

a very short round-down at the after end of the hangar, and she had a seaplane handling deck built up above the quarterdeck. *Glorious* had a longer round-down that extended right aft, supported by a large W-shaped bracing at the after end of the quarterdeck. Her seaplane handling deck was lower, level with the lower hangar deck. Both ships had derricks for lowering seaplanes on to the water, these being folded flush with the after hangar bulkhead when stowed. There was more space in both ships for workshops than in *Furious* and they were relatively well equipped. Whatever their demerits, this class gave the RN the opportunity to evaluate the operation of relatively large numbers of aircraft in manoeuvres at sea, especially when two or more carriers operated together.

Both ships were originally completed with a main armament of four 15in guns in twin turrets, one forward and one aft. When the guns and mountings were removed they were kept in storage and eventually refurbished to equip the battleship *Vanguard* (those from *Courageous* being mounted forward and those from *Glorious* aft). Early in the carrier-conversion design process a number of options were considered for gun armament, including, as mentioned before, 8in weapons to match similar designs in other navies and provide a defence against cruisers. In the event they were fitted with twelve single 4.7in high-angle guns intended mainly for use against aircraft in barrage fire. They were controlled by four directors, two on each side just below the flight deck. Once the lower flight deck ceased to be used by aircraft, two eight-barrelled 'pom-poms' were mounted on it, and a third was mounted on the flight deck aft of the island in the late 1930s. Both ships had fittings for multiple machine guns for close-range defence against strafing aircraft.

The biggest design weakness of the class was that they had 'grown upwards' from light cruisers and not 'downwards' from a capital ship design. The protective arrangements could not be described as a cohesive system and had been designed and applied piecemeal. They were inadequate against the weapons deployed against them in 1939.

Courageous was laid down on 28 March 1915 in the Newcastle-upon-Tyne shipyard of Sir W G Armstrong Whitworth as a large, light battlecruiser and launched on 5 February 1916. She was completed on 4 November 1916 and subsequently served in the GF's 1st CS with her sister-ship, *Glorious*. After the end of the war she

was used as a turret drill ship attached to the Gunnery School in Portsmouth before being taken in hand for conversion into an aircraft carrier at Devonport Dockyard in June 1924. She recommissioned in Portsmouth on 21 February 1928 and subsequently joined the MF in June with 404 and 407 (Flycatcher); 445 and 446 (Fairey IIIF); 463 and 464 (Dart) Flights embarked.

She took part in the Fleet's manoeuvres and cruises and visited Skiathos, Argostoli, Zara, Venice, Taranto and Athens over the next year, and in August 1929 she embarked the 2nd Battalion, South Staffordshire Regiment, for passage to Jaffa, where they were used to restore peace after a period of inter-racial violence between the Arab and Jewish communities. Some of her aircraft were disembarked to Gaza, where they were used to support military operations ashore. On 12 October 1929 she passed through the Dardanelles with ships of the MF to visit Constantinople, and on 18 October her aircraft performed the first flying display ever held over the city.

In 1930 *Courageous* returned to the UK for a refit, during which she was fitted with prototype arrester wires. From 1931 she carried out flying trials of them, and new deck landing techniques were devised to take advantage of their use. Upon conclusion of the trials she was allocated to the HF. In 1935 she carried out flying training and tactical exercises in the Mediterranean which emphasised how important carrierborne aircraft had become in the evolving RN concept of operations. In February 1936 *Courageous* returned to the HF, and in June 1937, when the Fleet visited Copenhagen, HM the King of Denmark spent a day on board learning about carrier aviation. She paid off for a refit in 1938.

Courageous recommissioned for the last time on 31 July 1939 and joined the newly constituted Channel Force which was gathering at Portland. In September 1939 she formed part of the force that escorted the British Expeditionary Force (BEF) to France. On 16 September 1939 she sailed from Plymouth with 811 and 822 (Swordfish) NAS embarked for offensive antisubmarine operations in the Atlantic; four destroyers sailed with her as a screening force. A day later she was hit by one or possibly two torpedoes from U-29 in the South West Approaches and sank in position 50 18N 14 47W. The captain was lost with 517 other men out of a ship's company of 1,260. *Courageous'* sinking was an object lesson in how not to use an aircraft carrier, and the flawed tactic of 'trailing a coat' looking for submarines was not repeated.

Glorious

Glorious was laid down as a light battlecruiser by Harland & Wolff at its Belfast shipyard on 1 May 1915 and launched on 20 April 1916. She was fitted out remarkably quickly and was completed and commissioned into the RN on 14 October 1916. Unfortunately she struck a buoy when sailing from Belfast and had to be docked for repairs on 23 October. On 19 November she was struck by the Steamer *Corib* while still in the shipyard and further repairs were necessary before she finally left her builder's yard on 30 December. On 6 January 1917 she joined the 1st CS with the GF with *Courageous* and saw action against German forces off Heligoland in November. In February 1918 she commenced a refit in Devonport during which flying-off platforms were added to both gun

turrets and some stiffening was built into her light hull plating. After she rejoined the GF she was moored in the Firth of Forth off Burntisland on 5 November 1918 when the seaplane carrier *Campania* dragged her anchor during a gale and struck the battleship *Royal Oak*. Both ships then dragged on to *Glorious*, causing further damage, after which *Campania* sank. *Glorious* was at sea on 21 November to escort the surrendered German High Seas Fleet into internment in Scapa Flow, after which she paid off into reserve in 1919.

In January 1921 she was brought forward for use as a turret drill ship in Devonport, and in April became flagship of the Reserve Fleet in Devonport. In February 1924 she was towed to Rosyth to be stripped down before conversion into an aircraft carrier, and then towed to Devonport for the reconstruction work to the new design. She recommissioned as a carrier in Devonport on 7 January 1930, began sea trials in February and flying trials in March. Her air group was embarked in stages and eventually comprised 406 and 408 (Flycatcher); 461 and 462 (Ripon); 441 and 447 (Fairey IIIF) Flights. In July she arrived in Malta to join the MF, but three of her turbines were damaged on the voyage out from the UK and repairs in Malta Dockyard took five months, during which time her aircraft operated from Hal Far. Her final 'shake-down' cruise began on 8 December in the waters off Crete.

In January 1931 she took part in some of the first carrier-versus-carrier battle group exercises in the Adriatic, forming part of the 'Blue' fleet, with

Glorious turns into wind to launch RAF Hurricane fighters for disembarkation to Norway on 26 May 1940, seen from an escorting destroyer. (AUTHOR'S COLLECTION)

1935 as part of the concentration of the MF, reinforced by ships from the Home and other stations. On 5 October Italy invaded Abyssinia, and shortly afterwards sanctions were ordered against Italy by the League of Nations. Realistically, the RN was the only force that could implement them. *Glorious* remained with the Fleet in the Eastern Mediterranean, with a brief return to Malta for docking in December 1935, until sanctions ended in July 1936.

In July 1936 825 NAS re-equipped with Swordfish in Malta, the first unit to do so, and a month later *Glorious* carried out night deck-landing experiments with lighting designed on board. In March 1937 she took part in exercises with over a hundred ships of the HF and MF in the Atlantic. Emphasis was placed on night flying and torpedo attacks on 'enemy' ships when they were located. On 5 May 1937 she was reviewed with over 140 other warships during the Royal Review that marked the Coronation of His Majesty King George VI. Her aircraft took part in a Coronation Fly Past by the Fleet Air Arm on 21 May. In June she re-embarked her air group and took part in a major trade defence exercise, after which she deployed to the Mediterranean. From September onwards she was deployed into the Western Mediterranean to protect international shipping during the Spanish Civil War, but carried out a short maintenance period in Devonport at the end of 1937 between patrols. In March 1938 she took part in a major combined exercise off Gibraltar in which over eighty warships took part. A similar exercise was held a year later in February 1939, after which she concentrated at Alexandria with other ships of the MF, where Sea Gladiators replaced Ospreys in 802 NAS. A planned refit in Malta was cancelled in September 1939, and she passed through the Suez Canal on 9 October to carry out a maintenance period in Aden before hunting for German raiders in the Indian Ocean.

On Christmas Day 1939 she was in Trincomalee, and then sailed to cover a French troop convoy from Indo-China with *Kent* and *Suffren*. After a docking in Aden in January 1940 she returned to Alexandria, where she joined *Ark Royal*. In April, following the German invasion of Norway, she was ordered to join the HF with *Ark Royal*. On 18 April she arrived in the Clyde and disembarked 812 and 825 (Swordfish) NAS to Prestwick, leaving 802 (Sea Gladiator) and 823 (Swordfish) NAS on board. After sailing, eighteen Gladiators of 263 Squadron RAF were flown on board by naval pilots, and on 22 April 823 NAS disembarked and 803 (Skua) and 804 (Sea

Eagle in the opposing 'Red' fleet. In March combined exercises took place off Gibraltar with both the HF and MF taking part but, unfortunately, she collided with the French liner *Florida* in fog to the northeast of Gibraltar on 1 April. *Glorious* took the damaged liner's passengers on board and landed them at Malaga before proceeding to Gibraltar Dockyard for temporary repairs. When these were complete she sailed for Malta, arriving on 23 May for more permanent repairs which were not completed until September.

In January 1932 she took part in multiple carrier exercises under the direction of Admiral Henderson, the new Rear Admiral Aircraft Carriers who had previously commanded *Furious*. He was a convinced aviation enthusiast whose influence is still felt in the 21st Century. On 19 January aircraft from *Glorious* and *Courageous* 'struck' the Mediterranean Fleet anchored in a Southern Greek port with practice torpedoes and scored a number of hits on battleships and cruisers. In February the Flycatchers of 408 Flight were replaced by Nimrods and she then sailed to rejoin the Fleet in the eastern Mediterranean for its annual cruise. She sailed for the UK in November and began a refit in Devonport Dockyard.

In January 1933 she recommissioned for service in the Mediterranean again and took part in combined exercises with *Furious* and *Courageous* in March. Following the reorganisation of Flights into larger naval air squadrons, *Glorious'* air group changed to comprise 802 (Nimrod/Osprey), 812 (Ripon), and 823 and 825 (Fairey IIIF) NAS. After further exercises she spent the winter in Malta before carrying out exercises with the HF in the spring of 1934. On 11 March storm force waves smashed through the door from the forward flight deck into the upper hangar and destroyed six aircraft. She returned to the UK in April and commenced a refit in Devonport in May. During this the flight deck was extended aft, supported by the distinctive W-shaped bracket on the quarterdeck; four Mark III arrester wires were fitted aft and two hydraulic catapults were fitted forward.

Now a more capable and effective carrier, she recommissioned on 23 July 1935 and began trials with her new flight-deck equipment in August. After their successful conclusion she returned to Malta, where Blackburn Baffins replaced the Ripons in 812 NAS, having been stored at Hal Far after service in *Eagle*. When the Abyssinian Crisis developed she sailed for Alexandria on 3 August

Details of *Glorious'* island structure. The pilotage 'flying bridge' is secured in its stowage to port of the funnel. Note the compass binnacle at its after extremity, which would be well over to the port side of the ship when deployed. The square structure like a venetian blind at the after part of the funnel is the 'permission to land' signal with its shutters in the closed position. (AUTHOR'S COLLECTION)

May she returned to Scapa Flow to refuel for what was to be the last time.

After a fast turn-round she sailed immediately for Operation *Alphabet*, the evacuation of British forces from the area around Narvik, operating with *Ark Royal* again. *Glorious'* intended role was to recover RAF aircraft and take them back to the UK, and in order to have space for them she had only 802 and 823 NAS embarked. On 7 June she landed-on ten Gladiators of 264 Squadron RAF and seven Hurricanes of 46 Squadron RAF. This was the first time that high-performance monoplane fighters had landed on a British carrier and, since they could do so without arrester hooks, this recovery showed that it was a straightforward proposition. Tragically, *Glorious* was intercepted by the German battlecruisers *Scharnhorst* and *Gneisenau* southwest of Narvik, while on passage back to the UK on 8 June 1940. Between 1600 and 1730 she was hit by a number of 11in shells and sank in position 68 45N 04 30E. She had no aircraft airborne and her captain appeared to have given little thought to the potential danger posed by enemy surface forces. Her two escorting destroyers, *Ardent* and *Acasta*, were also sunk after gallant attempts to defend the carrier. *Glorious* is the only British aircraft carrier to have been sunk by enemy gunfire from surface warships.

Gladiator) NAS embarked. After a brief stop in Scapa Flow she sailed with *Ark Royal* for Operation *DX* to provide fighter cover for British forces landed in Namsos and Aandalsnes in Central Norway, and to fly-off the RAF Gladiators to an airfield marked out on the frozen lake Lesjaskou. On 27 April she transferred four aircraft of 803 NAS to *Ark Royal* and, having disembarked the RAF aircraft, she returned to Scapa Flow where she re-embarked 802 and 823 NAS and sailed with them, plus 804 NAS, which was already on board, for Norway. On 1 May she rejoined the force off the Norwegian coast to cover the evacuation from Aandalsnes. Late in the day she was ordered to transfer the balance of 803 NAS to *Ark Royal* and return to the UK.

She arrived off Greenock on 3 May, and eighteen Hurricanes of 46 Squadron RAF were craned on board from lighters. She also embarked 701 (Walrus) NAS and sailed on 14 May in company with *Furious*. On 18 May she arrived off Narvik and flew off 701 NAS to Harstadt. Bad weather prevented the Hurricanes from flying off, however. After continued bad weather she withdrew from Norwegian waters on 22 May and returned to Scapa Flow to refuel, retaining the Hurricanes on board. Two days later she sailed for Norway again, and on 26 May she managed to fly-off the Hurricanes to Skaanland, from where they subsequently flew on to Bardufoss. On 28 May three Sea Gladiators of 802 NAS shot down a shadowing Heinkel He 115 floatplane, and on 30

This is a poor-quality image, unfortunately, but it shows an RAF Hurricane taking off from *Glorious* for operations in Norway on 26 May 1940. (AUTHOR'S COLLECTION)

CHAPTER 10

ARK ROYAL

Technical background

Lack of funds had prevented the RN from ordering a new aircraft carrier until the mid-1930s, and even then a maximum limit of 22,000 tons was imposed for the sake of economy. The British Government had hoped to make this an international limitation by treaty, but the USA and Japan refused to accept it and the new ship was subsequently hampered by this unreasonably low figure. To save weight, extensive use was made of welding in the hull for the first time in a major British warship, saving about 500 tons.

The new design embodied the latest British thinking. However, she was only the second ship for the RN designed from the outset to be an aircraft carrier, and the first to be laid down for seventeen years. The lower flying-off decks in *Furious* and the *Courageous* class had been found to be a failure, often unusable due to sea and weather states and too small for the new generation of monoplanes. Furthermore, the completely flush decks of *Argus* and *Furious* were disliked by both pilots and ship's navigating officers, whereas both liked the island structures in the *Courageous* class, *Hermes* and *Eagle*, which gave the former a mark from which to judge their landing and the latter a more conventional bridge. The design aim of the

new ship was to put the largest possible flight deck on to the modest hull that was constrained by tonnage limitation and docking facilities. The ship that was to become *Ark Royal* was given a flight deck that ran the full length of the hull, with round-downs that overhung at both bow and stern. The after round-down was particularly pronounced, being designed to an aerodynamic shape to smooth the airflow on the final approach and completely overhanging the water aft of the stern. The round-downs meant that, although the flight deck was 800ft long between perpendiculars, only 720ft of it was level and therefore useable for ranging, launching and recovering aircraft. In order to carry as many aircraft as possible, the double hangar arrangement was retained.

Armour protection was not provided for the flight deck or hangars, but the lower hull was armoured to contemporary cruiser standards. The lower hangar deck was constructed of 3.5in armour plate which extended outboard to meet the top of the 4.5in waterline armoured belt. The end bulkheads were 3in, creating an armoured 'box' over machinery, magazines and steering gear. An improved form of bulge and an internal splinter-proof bulkhead were believed to be proof against a 750lb torpedo warhead or contact mine. The island

Ark Royal enters Grand Harbour, Malta, during her 'shake-down' Mediterranean cruise in early 1939. The S1 4.5in gun mounting is marked with the red, white and blue neutrality stripes which were painted on British warships during the Spanish Civil War, just coming to an end at the time. The poor state of the paintwork forward shows that she has been through rough weather. The area around the black boot-topping was often repainted by ships' companies as a short-term measure with inadequate preparation. The result, as seen here, was that it was easily washed off. (R A BURT COLLECTION)

housed the navigating bridge, flying control arrangements and the funnel. Since the gun armament was intended for anti-aircraft fire there was no requirement for a spotting top to control surface fire like those in *Eagle* and *Hermes,* and none was fitted.

Two BH 3 hydraulic catapults, each capable of launching 12,000lb at 56 knots, were fitted, one either side of the flight deck forward. Four arrester units were installed in the 'deep beams' between support girders under the flight deck aft, each of which had two arrester wires rove to it, capable of stopping an 11,000lb aircraft at a speed relative to the deck of 55 knots with an average pull-out of 140ft. Both the relative entry speed and pull-out varied between wires, decreasing for the wires nearest the barrier. For the first time in a British

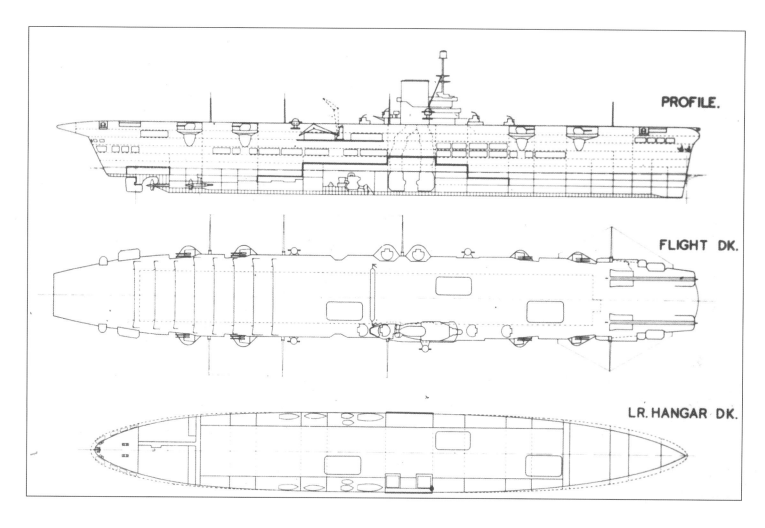

PROFILE.

FLIGHT DK.

LR. HANGAR DK.

aircraft carrier, a fifth unit was installed which controlled the safety barrier; this had the same entry limitations as the wires but a pull-out of only 40ft. The safety barrier was an American idea introduced by Captain Joseph Reeves USN, the first captain of the USS *Langley*. Noting that it

took time to range aircraft from the hangar, he wanted aircraft kept on deck, where they could be refuelled and rearmed quickly between sorties. He wanted a safe parking area, and achieved this by having a barrier of steel wire rope constructed across the flight deck amidships, supported on

Ark Royal as completed in 1938. (Author's collection)

Ark Royal anchored at Spithead in June 1939. The two port multiple 'pom-pom' mountings have not yet been fitted. (Author's collection)

The first aircraft airborne from *Ark Royal* out of a mixed range of aircraft during flying trials. (AUTHOR'S COLLECTION)

either side of the deck by collapsible metal stanchions. When raised it prevented aircraft that missed all the arrester wires from rolling forward into the new deck park. In use it was manned by an operator in the port catwalk. As soon as he saw that the next aircraft to land had caught a wire he would lower the barrier, allowing the aircraft to taxi forward safely into the parking area forward, known to aircraft handlers as 'Fly One'. As soon as the aircraft had passed over the barrier it was raised again to allow the next aircraft to land on.

With the introduction of the barrier in the USN, and the new techniques it allowed, aircraft in the landing circuit could back each other up more closely, reducing the landing interval between aircraft from about four minutes to less than one. The RN had wanted to introduce barriers as soon as the advantages became obvious, but the RAF had opposed the idea because of the possibility of aircraft being damaged. Once the Inskip Award allocated the control of carrierborne

aviation back to the navy, where it rightly belonged, the RN could insist on the equipment it needed for the most efficient operation of aircraft, and *Ark Royal* was designed to have a single barrier. By the time she was launched, similar devices had been in service with the USN for a decade. The new landing technique was further improved by the adoption of Deck Landing Control Officers (DLCO), known colloquially as 'batsmen', who took charge of the landing by signalling to pilots whether they were high, low, left or right and ordering them to cut the throttle when ideally placed for the hook to catch a wire. The landing was the DLCO's responsibility and, while there was some resistance from 'old hands' at first, the new system dramatically reduced the number of landing accidents, speeded up the whole process and was soon accepted as the best way forward.

The advantage of the double-hangar arrangement was that a large number of aircraft could be stowed in a ship with a relatively small displacement. In 1935, when *Ark Royal* was laid down, this seemed a good idea because aircraft were expected to operate around the clock,

launched in small numbers at any one time to search for an enemy fleet and to carry out small-scale torpedo attacks to slow an enemy force that sought to evade a surface action. By then the speed demonstrated by new monoplane bombers meant that the Admiralty was forced, reluctantly, to conclude that carrierborne fighters no longer represented the best way of defending the fleet against enemy air attack, since the time between visual sighting of enemy aircraft and bomb release would be too short to launch intercepting fighters with any chance of breaking up the attack. Fighters could, of course, be kept airborne on combat air patrol (CAP), but would be needed in impossibly large numbers flying all round the fleet to be effective. For this reason guns were deemed to offer the best defence, and the only fighters available when *Ark Royal* commissioned were the dual-purpose fighter/dive-bomber Blackburn Skuas intended to escort Swordfish strikes and attack ships in their own right with 500lb bombs. A solution to the fleet air defence problem emerged in the first days of the war, however, when radar proved capable of detecting enemy aircraft at long range and directing fighters accurately to

intercept them. Now a reasonable number of embarked fighters could be maintained on CAP during daylight hours with every chance of a successful interception. Unfortunately the discovery came after the heavily armoured carriers of the *Illustrious* class that followed *Ark Royal* had been designed, and it took some time to procure adequate high-performance fighters. *Ark Royal* herself was never fitted with radar, but evolved a successful technique of using the air warning radars of cruisers in company to direct her aircraft throughout 1940 and 1941. Had she survived, this shortcoming would have been addressed in a major refit during 1942.

Ark Royal's two hangars had a total deck area of 52,580ft^2, the largest yet achieved in a British carrier. Her original specification envisaged an air group of seventy-two aircraft, all to be stowed in the hangars, but the RAF objected that 'such a large number could not be operated safely'. Reluctantly, the Admiralty accepted that, while the larger number of aircraft could physically be struck down into the hangars, the ship would be completed with workshop capacity, spare part stowage, magazine space and 'hotel accommodation' based on support for an air group of only sixty aircraft, and in her short life this was never altered. She never used a deck park to add to the number of embarked aircraft.

Avgas capacity was 100,000gal, stowed in non-integral cylindrical tanks like those used in the *Courageous* class. Some changes were made as a further precaution against leakage and fire, and instead of the water-displacement system used since 1923 an air-pressure delivery system was used to avoid contamination of the fuel by salt water. As a further precaution CAFO 257/37 called for the compartments containing the avgas tanks to be

flooded when action was imminent. To avoid corrosion, the inside of the compartments and the outside of the tanks were to be coated with one coat of bitumastic solution and one coat of enamel, all existing paint to be removed and the metal surfaces thoroughly cleaned before their application.

For the first and only time the RN opted to have three lifts within the flight-deck perimeter. To maintain the flight deck's integrity as a strength deck the apertures were made as small as possible, with two offset to starboard and one to port of the centreline. This preserved the girder strength, but meant that only folded or partly dismantled aircraft could be struck down or ranged, unlike the cruciform lifts in previous British aircraft carriers. The lifts were grouped in the forward part of the hangars, making it difficult to extract aircraft from the after sections of both hangars, and only folded aircraft could be manoeuvred around the lift wells. The lifts themselves were unconventional in that each platform served only one deck. To get an aircraft from the lower hangar to the flight deck involved a handling party pushing it on to the lower platform, raising it to the upper hangar, pushing it clear, and lowering the platform to the lower hangar deck level. The upper platform could then be lowered to the upper hangar deck level, the aircraft pushed on, raised to the flight deck and pushed clear into the range. This cumbersome arrangement stemmed from the early concept that the lower hangar would be used for deep maintenance, and serviceable aircraft would be kept in the upper hangar. Wartime carrier operations required large numbers of operational aircraft to be ranged quickly from both hangars, and this cumbersome lift arrangement was never repeated.

Ark Royal alongside in Portsmouth early in the Second World War. The censor has made a halfhearted attempt to blank out the Type 72 aircraft homing beacon, but this photograph gives a good view of the structure that supported the two catapults. The recently fitted external degaussing coil also shows up well. (AUTHOR'S COLLECTION)

In the mid-1930s carriers were expected to operate 'in support' of the battle fleet but not 'the battle line'. The need for frequent turns into wind to launch and recover aircraft might take the carrier and its screening destroyers away from the main fleet, so high speed was considered essential for the carrier to resume station. The need to generate wind over the flight deck for flying operations was not considered important at the time, but became so as embarked aircraft weights increased dramatically after 1940. *Ark Royal* was specified to be capable of 31 knots, 3 knots faster than the projected *King George V* class battleships and considerably in excess of their predecessors. The power to develop this speed could not be achieved by a two-shaft installation, and a four-shaft installation would have led to an unacceptable increase in standard displacement and required considerable extra manpower. Therefore a three-shaft arrangement was adopted; this was unusual for the RN but had been used by the German Navy for a number of capital ships before 1918. The machinery developed 103,000shp, which developed 31.75 knots on trials with a clean hull. The original design called for four steam-driven turbogenerators and two diesel generators, but the latter were subsequently replaced during construction by two further steam generators to give added capacity for the full action load. Unfortunately this meant that electrical power

in the ship depended entirely on steam being available from the boilers.

In the years immediately before the introduction of practical air-warning radar in ships, *Ark Royal*'s primary defence against air attack was thought to be provided by guns. Eight twin 4.5in guns were disposed in pairs in four batteries near the 'corners' of the ship. They were mounted high on sponsons so that they could fire at low angles across the flight deck at targets on the opposite side of the ship. In practice this theoretical benefit was outweighed by the blast damage suffered by aircraft, flight deck and catwalk fittings, so it was seldom used in action. Each battery was controlled by a single director mounted on the deck edge near the guns. Each director could control the fire of its own battery;

the two batteries on its side of the ship or all batteries if required. They were never fitted with gun-direction radar, and relied on optical range-finding to control time-mechanical fused shells in barrage fire. Six eight-barrelled 2pdr 'pom-poms' were fitted, two forward of the island on the flight deck; one on the after end of the island; one on the flight deck aft of the island and two on a sponson at the port deck edge amidships. The latter were not fitted during initial flying trials in case they interfered with flying operations.

Ark Royal was never fitted with radar but she did have a Type 72 aircraft homing beacon. Had she not been lost she was programmed to carry out a major refit in the USA in early 1942 which would have seen considerable enhancements to her operational capability.

The overhang aft was the largest structure of its kind fitted to a British aircraft carrier, but aircraft could not be ranged on it or land on it because the of the slope of the round-down. It was a purely aerodynamic shape to smooth airflow over the after part of the deck. (AUTHOR'S COLLECTION)

Ark Royal's loss

She was hit at 1541 on 13 November 1941 by a single torpedo fired by U-81 thirty miles east of Gibraltar while the ship was steaming at 22 knots, returning from a sortie with Force H to ferry RAF fighters to Malta. Some of the blast vented up the bomb lift forward of the island, and the ship was felt to whip violently. Witnesses in the battleship *Malaya* 400 yards away saw the ship whip so severely that aircraft on deck were thrown into the air and bounced several times as they fell back into the deck (indicating that they had not been lashed to the deck after a recent recovery). The area of maximum damage appeared to be between the keel and the starboard side abreast the island structure, and subsequent analysis calculated that a hole approximately 130ft by 30ft had been blown in the bottom plating, indicating a failure of the internal anti-torpedo structure. The hole was larger than expected from a single hit, but it had taken some time for the ship to stop and her initial speed may have made the hole bigger.

After the explosion the starboard boiler room, air spaces, oil tanks and watertight compartments on the starboard side began to flood, together with the main switchboard room and the lower steering position. The port and centreline boilers continued to steam, but the centreline began to flood slowly from below. The engine rooms had lost

Ark Royal and *Argus* head towards Gibraltar after ferrying RAF aircraft to Malta in November 1941. They are seen from *Malaya*. (AUTHOR'S COLLECTION)

communications, which is why it took so long to stop the ship, and she immediately heeled 10 degrees to starboard, increasing to 18 degrees after 20min. The flooding of the main switchboard room and telephone exchange caused the failure of all lighting, electrical power and telephones, making the situation appear worse than it actually was, and the captain decided, half an hour after the explosion, to bring destroyers alongside to evacuate the ship, leaving the generators in the port and centre boiler rooms running. At about 1600 the destroyer *Legion* came alongside *Ark Royal*'s port quarter and took off over 1,000 men, casting off at 1648, by which time the captain had ordered damage control parties to save the ship. Unfortunately, however, a number of key men had already been taken off. Counter-flooding reduced the heel to 14 degrees. Electric power, feed water and pumps were supplied by *Laforey* for a time, but she slipped at 2224 when it appeared that *Ark Royal* had her own steam and power once more and that flooding was under control following the valiant efforts of a repair party of sailors from *Hermione* and *Legion* led by *Ark Royal*'s Gunner (T).

The ship was taken in tow at 2 knots by the tug *Thames*, with steam raised in the port boiler and lighting restored, but the starboard engine room continued to flood slowly, increasing the heel again

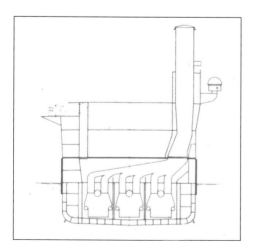

A section through *Ark Royal* shows how vulnerable the funnel uptake trunking was to a starboard list as the hull flooded and sank bodily in the water. (AUTHOR'S COLLECTION)

to 17 degrees and flooding the boiler uptakes at the point on the starboard side where they were taken vertically up to the funnel. With nowhere for the exhaust gas from the port boilers to go, fire broke out in the air casing and this led to the evacuation of the boiler room and a total loss of power again. The Senior Engineer and two of his men collapsed while attempting to keep the boilers working and had to be given artificial respiration. Viewed in hindsight, it is difficult to see why *Laforey* was not kept alongside to guarantee a power supply, given the importance of keeping the carrier afloat, but she was brought alongside again after power was lost for the second time. By then it was too late. The heel increased to 27 degrees at 0400 on 14 November, at which point the order was given to abandon ship, and everyone was taken off by 0430 except one man who had been in the main switchboard room during the initial impact. Twelve hours after the torpedo impact, all personnel had left the ship and the heel had increased to 35 degrees. She capsized and sank, after 'hanging' for a few minutes at 45 degrees, two hours later. The last 250 men to leave crossed over the tug *St Day* to *Laforey*.

The key vulnerability was the position of the boiler uptake trunking, but the steady spread of flooding into the centre and then port boiler rooms through the fan trunking was also a factor. The lack of diesel generators to provide electrical power was also a critical shortcoming. The early evacuation and the number of manhole covers and armoured doors left open by men leaving the ship led to an increased rate of flooding which lowered the hull in the water and immersed the funnel uptake trunking earlier than would otherwise have been the case. The subsequent Board of Enquiry noted that the size of the hole and the initial flooding it caused led to a list well beyond that envisaged in the ship's damage control books, which provided counter-flooding instructions for lists of only up to 8 degrees. Subsequent analysis showed that if the port engine and boiler rooms had been flooded after steam power had finally failed, *Ark Royal* could have been brought to an even keel, retaining enough buoyancy to reach harbour. The Board further noted that it considered it to be essential that the training and organisation of damage control personnel should, in future, be of the highest standard in order to deal satisfactorily with an emergency of this type.

Counter-flooding should be carried out quickly to correct a list in excess of 6 degrees. Changes in carrier design could not be carried out overnight, but the Board recommended that, as soon as possible, boiler uptakes and fan intakes should be carried higher where practical, and machinery should be run in units irrespective of the number of boilers alight. The positions of the main switchboard and telephone exchange should be reviewed to render them less liable to flooding, and control of the electrical ring main must be reviewed to avoid false operation in the event of flooding or wiring damage. Diesel generators must be fitted in all large ships. Lastly they stressed the need to have direct communication at all times between the bridge and engine rooms with alternative power supplies including sound-powered telephones.

The wreck was located on the sea bed at a depth of 3,497ft in 2002 by C & C Technologies Inc of Lafayette, Louisiana, funded by the BBC. They carried out a side-scan sonar survey and filmed the wreckage using a high-technology autonomous underwater vehicle which found that the forward 200ft of the hull and the island had become detached, and the former was lying about a quarter of a mile away from the main part of the hull. The discovery has allowed experts to speculate on what happened as the ship sank. As she went under, the hull planed to the north and broke up near the surface as it continued to roll during its initial dive to the bottom. The island and a large part of the flight deck tore away like the lid of a sardine can as she turned keel-up, and at about the same time a 200ft-long section of the bow broke away from the main hull and spiralled to the bottom, scattering debris as it did so. The break was exactly along the bulkhead that separated the hangars from the accommodation areas forward. The main hull continued to roll slowly as it plunged downwards, eventually righting itself before crashing into the sea floor, still heading in a northerly direction. The debris field lies between the main hull and the bow, and includes aircraft, gun mountings and lift platforms. This raises questions about the integrity of the welded hull, given the unexpected severity of the damage from a single torpedo hit and the catastrophic failure of the hull as it sank.

The silver *Ark Royal* bell

When *Ark Royal* was evacuated, the ship's office staff took with them the pay ledgers and the cash that constituted the ship's Canteen Fund. The Canteen Fund consisted of the profits from the ship's shop, which could be used as deemed fit by a committee of ratings. (After the Second World War, when the NAAFI took over the canteens, it evolved into what is now known as the Welfare

Stopped in the water and listing, this is *Ark Royal* at 1700 on 13 November 1941. (AUTHOR'S COLLECTION)

Fund). A meeting of the Canteen Committee was held in Gibraltar Dockyard on 16 November, close to *Ark Royal*'s old berth, at which decisions were taken on how the money was to be used. Grants were made to the ships which had taken off survivors, and £100 was allocated to the next of kin of the sailor who was lost. The balance, about £560, was allocated for the purchase of a silver bell, suitably inscribed with the ship's badge, the names of captains and battle honours, to be presented to future *Ark Royals* in perpetuity.

The bell was cast on 10 December 1943 by the famous firm of Gillett & Johnston at its Croydon foundry, in a ceremony attended by the First Lord of the Admiralty, Mr A V Alexander, and *Ark Royal* veterans. It was subsequently presented to the next *Ark Royal* on 26 March 1955, and to her successor on 12 October 1985, with inscriptions brought up to date. Because of its wartime origin the bell had not been hallmarked when new, but this oversight was corrected on 6 February 1985 at the Goldsmith's Hall in London in a small ceremony attended by Commander N Essenhigh RN, the new *Ark Royal*'s executive officer, and three ratings. Thus a bell cast in 1943 has the hallmarks for the London Assay Office, sterling silver (lion), London (leopard's head), and the year 1985 (L). When no *Ark Royal* is in commission, as is the case in 2012, the bell is kept on display to the public at the Fleet Air Arm element of the National Museum of the Royal Navy at RNAS Yeovilton.

At a postwar *Ark Royal* reunion, Captain R C Steele RN, the paymaster commander in November 1941, explained that the contents of the ship's main safe, including currency, postal orders and postage stamps with a value amounting to about £23,000, had been taken off in two large suitcases. As the cases were lowered on to *Legion*,

one of them fell into the sea but was recovered by a stoker at considerable personal risk. The large holding in cash was held on board as the ship was due to return to the UK in the near future to give Christmas leave, after which she was due to sail to the USA for a major refit.

Ark Royal technical details

Displacement:	27,720 tons deep load
Dimensions:	length 800ft
	beam 112ft
	draught 27ft 9in
Machinery:	3 shaft Parsons geared turbines
	6 Admiralty 3-drum boilers
	102,000shp delivering 31 knots
Armament:	8 twin 4.5in QF Mark 1 HA; 6 octuple 2 pdr 'pom-pom'; machine guns; saluting guns
Protection:	4.5in side belt; 3in bulkheads; 3.5in lower hangar deck
Fuel:	4,620 tons FFO
Endurance:	11,200 miles at 10 knots
Complement:	1,580

Aircraft operating data

Flight deck:	720ft usable x 95ft steel plate
Hangars:	upper 568ft x 60ft x 16ft
	lower 452ft x 60ft x 16ft
Catapults:	2 x BH3 hydraulic; 12,000lb at 56 knots end-speed relative to the deck
Arrester wires:	8 wires in total, numbered from aft to forward
	1 to 6 capable of stopping 11,000lb at 55 knots
	7 capable of stopping 11,000lb at 50 knots
	8 capable of stopping 11,000lb at 45 knots
	1 to 3 maximum pull-out 155ft
	4 to 6 maximum pull-out 137ft
	7 maximum pull-out 114ft
	8 maximum pull-out 90ft
	one barrier capable of stopping 11,000lb in 40ft
Lifts:	forward 45ft long x 25ft wide
	centre 45ft long x 22ft wide
	aft 45ft long x 22ft wide
	all 14,000lb with 2 platforms.
Aircraft:	designed to support 60, 54 embarked in 1941
Aircraft fuel:	bulk stowage for 100,000gal avgas
Air weapons:	18in torpedoes; 500lb SAP bombs; 250lb SAP bombs; 100lb GP bombs; depth charges; 0.303in gun ammunition; flares and pyrotechnics

Individual ship history

Ark Royal

Laid down by Cammell Laird & Co at its Birkenhead shipyard on 16 September 1935, the previous *Ark Royal* having been renamed *Pegasus* in December 1934 to make the name available, she was launched on 13 April 1937 and commissioned on the day of her formal completion, 16 November 1938. *Ark Royal* replaced *Courageous* as the flagship of the Rear Admiral Aircraft Carriers, RAAC. Her initial flying trials and work-up were carried out with Hawker Ospreys and Fairey Swordfish embarked, but by September 1939 her air group comprised 800 and 803 (Skua), 810 and 820 (Swordfish) NAS and she was serving with the HF.

She sailed for offensive air operations against U-boats in the Western Approaches and nearly met the same fate as *Courageous* on 14 September 1939, when U-39 fired two torpedoes at her, both of which missed. Escorting destroyers subsequently attacked and sank U-39, the first U-boat to be sunk in the Second World War. That afternoon two Skuas were lost in the detonation of their own bombs when they attacked U-30 at low level; the U-boat survived the attack and rescued both pilots. On 25 September *Ark Royal* sailed into the North Sea with the Home Fleet to cover the return of a

The destroyer *Legion* alongside *Ark Royal*'s port quarter. Smoke is issuing from one of the port boat bays, indicating that the normal exhaust trunking is already becoming blocked as flooding sinks the hull lower in the water and the starboard list is not corrected. (AUTHOR'S COLLECTION)

damaged British submarine, and Skuas of 803 NAS shot down a Dornier Do 18 flying boat that attempted to shadow the fleet; it was the first enemy aircraft to be shot down by a British fighter in the war. On 26 September she was attacked by German bombers. The pilot of one of them, Leutnant Adolf Francke, was awarded the Iron Cross and promoted for his claim to have sunk the ship, and for some time German radio continued to ask 'Where is the *Ark Royal?*', earning her international fame. During the next four months she formed part of Force K with *Renown* and searched the South Atlantic for enemy shipping.

In October her Swordfish sighted, but failed to identify, *Altmark*, which subsequently hid in Norwegian territorial waters until located by British destroyers. Positive success was achieved in November, however, when Swordfish identified and stopped *Uhenfels*, which was subsequently boarded and taken as a prize. Operating between Cape Verde and Pernambuco, *Ark Royal* was well placed to intercept German blockade-runners attempting to return to Europe. Her presence was threat enough to have a major influence upon the captain of *Graf Spee*'s decision to scuttle his ship off Montevideo on 17 December 1939. In March 1940 she was ordered to the Eastern Mediterranean without her Skua squadrons, which remained disembarked at RNAS Hatston in the Orkney Islands. She was recalled to the HF in April after the German invasion of Norway, but, before she could return, her Skuas of 800 and 803 NAS attacked the German cruiser *Konigsberg* at Bergen,

flying to the limit of their range on 10 April. Only a single Skua was lost, but the attack was remarkable in that it was the first in which aircraft destroyed a major surface vessel.

She sailed from Scapa Flow for the Norwegian littoral on 23 April 1940 with 800 and 801 (Skua/Roc) together with 810 and 820 (Swordfish) NAS embarked to carry out Operation *DX*, providing fighter cover for British troops landed at Namsos and Aandalsnes. On 25 April Skuas and Swordfish from *Ark Royal* and *Glorious* attacked Vaernes Airfield near Trondheim and caused heavy damage. Subsequently aircraft from *Ark Royal* attacked moored floatplanes, merchant shipping and a slipway at Trondheim. They then destroyed the last hangar at Vaernes on 28 April before returning to Scapa Flow to replenish and replace the aircraft lost in action.

On 4 May 1940 *Ark Royal* sailed again to cover the British forces sent to capture Narvik, which was too far away for the land-based aircraft of the RAF to reach. She operated aircraft on every day until 19 May, when she had to refuel at Tromso. On 21 May, when *Glorious* flew off her RAF fighters, *Ark Royal*'s Skuas provided cover for them until they were able to operate from Bardufoss. After refuelling in Scapa, *Ark Royal* returned to Northern Norway in early June, this time to cover the evacuation of British forces. She embarked the Walrus amphibians of 701 NAS on 7 June and was attacked by German bombers on 9 June, but one was shot down and the remainder driven off by Skuas. After the loss of *Glorious*, and once the British convoys were beyond enemy reach, *Ark Royal* closed Trondheim, where *Scharnhorst* was reported to be moored, to launch a dive-bombing attack by fifteen Skuas on 13 June 1940. The attack was to be co-ordinated with an attack on Vaernes Airfield by four RAF Beauforts and six

Blenheims, but all surprise was lost when they attacked too early and the RAF raid had the effect of alerting, rather than distracting, the enemy.

The port of Trondheim is 40 miles from the sea, at the inland extremity of Trondheim Fjord. Enemy fighters were waiting for the Skuas and there was intense flak as they pressed home their attacks. Only seven Skuas escaped, and among those killed or taken prisoner were the COs of 800 and 803 NAS, two experienced section leaders, while all the missing naval aircrew were veterans of the campaign and their loss was a disaster at this stage of the war. On 18 June, having made good her losses and added 818 (Swordfish) NAS to the air group, *Ark Royal* sailed from Scapa Flow to join the new Force H in Gibraltar together with *Hood*.

The first operation was the unhappy task of neutralising the French Fleet at Oran after diplomacy failed, and on 3 July *Ark Royal*'s Swordfish spotted for a dawn bombardment by capital ships. Subsequent strikes by Swordfish disabled the battleship *Dunkerque*, but *Strasbourg* managed to evade an air attack with torpedoes. On 2 August her Swordfish attacked Cagliari Airfield in Sardinia to provide a distraction for Operation *Hurry*, in which *Argus* ferried twelve RAF Hurricanes to Malta, and on 1 September they struck at Elmas, also in Sardinia, as a diversionary measure during the passage of *Illustrious* through the narrows to join the MF. On 23 September she was off West Africa with Force H for Operation *Menace*, an attempt to neutralise the French battleship *Richelieu* in Dakar. Envoys were flown ashore from *Ark Royal* in two Caudron Lucioles embarked for the purpose but, again, diplomacy failed and air strikes and bombardments by 15in guns were carried out. These, too, were unsuccessful, and after losing nine aircraft *Ark Royal* returned to the UK for a short refit.

An aerial view of *Ark Royal*'s final hours. (AUTHOR'S COLLECTION)

She rejoined Force H in Gibraltar during early November with an air group comprising 808 (Fulmar), 800 (Skua), 810, 818 and 820 (Swordfish) NAS. On 9 November 1940 her aircraft struck at Sicilian airfields to divert Italian attention away from the attack on Taranto by Swordfish from *Illustrious*, planned for two days later. On 17 November she covered *Argus* during Operation *White*, a second run ferrying RAF Hurricanes to Malta during which twelve were launched but, unfortunately, only four arrived. On 27 November three torpedo attacks were launched against an Italian force southwest of Sardinia. Little damage was achieved because the Swordfish squadrons were insufficiently

worked-up to carry out torpedo attacks efficiently, but at least the Italian warships withdrew at high speed. On 2 February 1941 Swordfish attacked the Tirso Dam in Northern Sicily with torpedoes; they damaged it but failed to cause a breach. On 8 February Swordfish spotted for a bombardment of Genoa by *Renown* and *Malaya* during a Force H attack while other Swordfish bombed La Spezia and Pisa.

Ark Royal was slightly damaged when a Swordfish armed with depth charges ditched ahead of the ship following an engine failure after take-off. The depth charges detonated as it sank and shook the hull, but there was no need for immediate repairs. On 3 April 1941 *Ark Royal* sailed for Operation *Winch* to ferry twelve RAF Hurricanes to Malta; all arrived safely, led by Fulmars which gave navigational assistance. On 27 April she ferried twenty-four RAF Hurricanes, twenty-three of which arrived safely in Operation *Dunlop*. On 21 May she joined *Furious* to ferry a combined total of forty-eight RAF Hurricanes to Malta in Operation *Splice*. They were led by 800X (Fulmar) NAS, but one Fulmar and two Hurricanes were lost in transit. On 24 May *Ark Royal* showed her versatility when she and Force H were ordered into the Atlantic as one of the long-stop forces positioned to cut off the German battleship *Bismarck*.

On 26 May 1941 a strike of Swordfish from *Ark Royal* scored a torpedo hit on *Bismarck*'s steering gear which made it possible for the Home Fleet battleships *King George V* and *Rodney* to intercept and sink her. An earlier strike had attacked a radar contact which proved to be the cruiser *Sheffield* in error, but their new, magnetic-fuzed torpedoes had fortunately failed to detonate. The error allowed the replacement torpedoes to be fitted with effective contact fuzes which proved to be more reliable. After her return to Gibraltar, 807 (Fulmar) NAS replaced the Skuas of 800 NAS, and in June 825 (Swordfish) NAS replaced 820.

On 6 June 1941 she steamed back into the Mediterranean with *Furious* for Operation *Rocket* to deliver forty-four RAF Hurricanes to Malta. They

were launched to join up with eight Blenheims flying directly from Gibraltar, but one Hurricane failed to arrive. The pace continued, and on 14 June she sailed with *Victorious* for Operation *Tracer*, this time to fly off forty-eight RAF Hurricanes, forty-five of which arrived after joining up with four Lockheed Hudsons from Gibraltar. *Ark Royal* was the only carrier in Operation *Railway I* on 27 June, when twenty-two RAF Hurricanes were flown off to join four Blenheims flying through from Gibraltar; twenty-one arrived. The month ended with Operation *Railway II* on 30 June, when *Furious* and *Ark Royal* combined again to fly-off forty-two RAF Hurricanes which were to join up with six Blenheims. Unfortunately one of *Furious'* Hurricanes crashed on take-off and seven more could not be launched as a consequence, so only thirty-four reached their destination. In July 816 (Swordfish) NAS replaced 818, and on 25 July *Ark Royal* carried out Operation *Substance*, ferrying seven replacement Swordfish for the naval air squadrons based ashore at Hal Far in Malta, all of which arrived safely.

In September 1941 the last of *Ark Royal*'s original squadrons, 810 NAS, was replaced on board by 812 NAS, and another series of ferry runs to Malta began with Operation *Status I* on 9 September, in which fourteen RAF Hurricanes joined two Blenheims that were flying direct from Gibraltar. All arrived safely. *Furious* joined *Ark Royal* for Operation *Status II* on 13 September, and between them they launched forty-six RAF Hurricanes for Malta which joined up with seven Blenheims; forty-five Hurricanes arrived in Malta. The only ferry run in October was Operation *Callboy* on the 18th, when *Ark Royal* sailed to ferry eleven Albacores towards Malta as replacements for the naval air squadrons based ashore. All of them arrived safely. The sortie that proved to be *Ark Royal*'s last was Operation *Perpetual*, for which she sailed on 12 November in company with *Argus*. The two carriers launched thirty-seven RAF Hurricanes, thirty-four of which joined seven Blenheims from Gibraltar to reach Malta safely.

On 13 November 1941 *Ark Royal* was hit by a single torpedo out of a salvo of four fired by U-81, 30 miles east of Gibraltar. She sank 14 hours later in position 36 06N 05 07E.

CHAPTER 11

ILLUSTRIOUS CLASS — FIRST GROUP

Illustrious shortly after completion in 1940. (AUTHOR'S COLLECTION)

Technical background

As rearmament gathered momentum in the mid-1930s, approval was given in the RN's 1936 building programme for two aircraft carriers as well as two battleships and seven cruisers. The aircraft carrier section within DNC was working close to capacity at the time on the detailed drawings for *Ark Royal*, and its initial proposal was to build virtual repeats with the benefit of an extra 1,000 tons to bring them up to the actual London Treaty limit of 23,000 tons, rather than the proposed limit of 22,000 tons against which *Ark Royal* had been designed. However, Admiral Sir Reginald Henderson, the Third Sea Lord and Controller, Admiralty Board member responsible for new construction, was determined not to build further *Ark Royals* because he regarded the design as being vulnerable to air attack by land-based bombers in the confined waters of the North Sea and Mediterranean. Henderson had commanded *Furious* and served as the first Rear Admiral Aircraft Carriers between 1931 and 1933, which gave him greater knowledge of carriers and their operation than his contemporaries, and he translated this into his demands for the new generation of ships that was intended to replace the earlier carriers. He forced the design work forward with unprecedented speed, instructing W A D Forbes, head of the aircraft carrier design department, who had just completed work on *Ark Royal*, to begin work after an informal briefing and before a detailed staff requirement had been prepared. Sir Arthur Johns, the Director of Naval Construction, was sick at the time and was in fact never to return the Branch. His deputy, Fred Bryant, ran DNC in his absence. The design of such vessels would conventionally have taken about two years, but Henderson's pressure led to a design being prepared in less than three months.

Henderson insisted that the new ships must have armoured hangars to protect their fragile aircraft against hits from 500lb bombs dropped from above 7,000ft, 1,000lb bombs dropped from below 4,500ft and cruiser shellfire from ranges outside 7,000 yards. They had to be capable of remaining in action after sustaining damage, rather than merely surviving to return to a dockyard for repairs. He briefed Forbes in a series of discussions in his office at the Admiralty, during which Forbes put forward alternative sketch proposals. Armouring the flight deck and hangar of a 23,000-ton, standard displacement ship was not a simple proposition, but Forbes achieved it. There could be no question of double hangars like *Ark Royal*'s, so a smaller air group would have to be accepted. The eventual design made the single hangar an 'armoured box' between the lifts, which were at the forward and aft extremities of the hangar, outside the 'box'. The flight deck itself comprised 3in armoured plates which were riveted and rabbeted in place to provide a smooth upper surface supported by athwartship beams which were 6ft deep and allowed the whole structure to form the upper strength deck of the hull. The hangar sides and ends were of 4.5in armoured plate. This adjoined 2.5in armour at hangar deck level which was taken outboard to meet the 4.5in waterline belt. There was no anti-torpedo bulge, but there was a 1.5in internal splinter bulkhead behind an area of 'sandwich' protection which was designed to be superior to that in *Ark Royal*.

As in previous British carriers, the hangar was fully enclosed by bulkheads which separated it from the rest of the ship. It could be entered only by lift from the flight deck or through air locks from the side passages outboard of the hangar. It was split into four sections by three steel fire curtains which could be lowered from a control position; care had to be taken to ensure that aircraft were not stowed under the curtains, preventing them from closing properly. A salt-water spray system was installed, taking water from the fire main.

As soon as Henderson was satisfied that the design was what he wanted he got board approval in a month, and in November 1936 the Admiralty invited tenders for the construction of two new aircraft carriers to be named *Illustrious* and *Victorious*. The lowest tender came from Vickers-

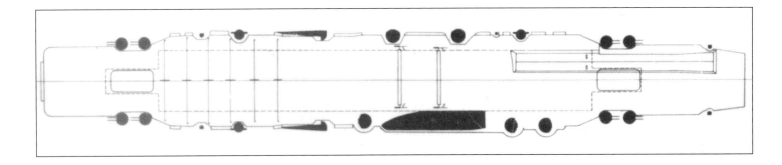

Illustrious' flight deck, showing the narrow areas fore and aft needed to incorporate the 4.5in medium-range-gun mountings. (AUTHOR'S COLLECTION)

Armstrongs, which was awarded the contracts on 13 April 1937 and built the ships in its yards at Barrow-in-Furness and Newcastle-upon-Tyne respectively. Cost per ship was estimated at £2,395,000. In all there was 5,000 tons of armour, of which 1,500 tons was in the flight-deck structure. Two further ships to the same design were ordered in 1937, to be named *Formidable* and *Indomitable*, but the latter was modified to a revised design on the slipway and will be dealt with separately in the next chapter. The first to complete was *Illustrious*, but delays with *Victorious* resulted in *Formidable* finishing second, followed by *Victorious*.

One of the biggest causes of delay stemmed from the run-down state of the British armour-plate industry, which had been virtually 'killed off' by lack of orders during the period of disarmament and the Depression. *Illustrious* was the least affected, *Victorious* the worst. The transverse bulkheads at the ends of the hangar and the armoured doors that closed off the lift wells were made slightly thinner than originally planned. The flight-deck armour was ordered from Vitkovice of Morava Ostrava in Czechoslovakia in 1938 and, fortunately, arrived before war broke out. It was this Czech armour that was penetrated by German bombs in January 1941.

The class was designed to operate thirty-six aircraft, each with a maximum overload weight of

14,000lb. A single BH-III hydraulic catapult was deemed sufficient, but the shuttle mechanism had to be mounted on top of the armour so as not to penetrate and therefore weaken it. It was placed on the port side forward, inside a shallow structure with sloping, faired-in sides, so that aircraft wheels could move over it when taking off or taxiing without it causing an obstruction. It could be fitted with a trolley for launching aircraft fitted with floats, or a shuttle to launch aircraft standing on their wheels in the 'tail-down' method, in which they were accelerated forward by a wire strop engaged with hooks on the underside of the aircraft. It was capable of launching a 12,500lb aircraft at an end-speed of 66 knots. The initial design included six arrester wires and two safety barriers of similar specification to those fitted in *Ark Royal*. Three further arrester wires were added aft while they were still building, and in *Victorious* and *Formidable* two arrester wires were installed forward to allow aft-facing landings over the bow.

Four wind breaks were fitted forward of the forward lift; each was 10ft high and designed to lie flush with the deck when not in use. They could be raised to shelter aircraft ranged on deck, but they were not very effective and tended to flex and distort as aircraft ran over them when they were down. *Illustrious* was the first British carrier to have a mobile crane on the flight deck when she was completed in 1940. Known as 'Jumbo', a generic name that persists into the twenty-first century, the original unit was a petrol-electric crane capable of lifting 5,000lb; its own weight was 6.75 tons. It was destroyed during the attack on 10 January 1941 and replaced by an American 'Jumbo' during the subsequent refit in Norfolk, Virginia. She also left the USA with two flight-deck tractors which

proved valuable in moving aircraft, and by 1945 she had four.

The two safety barriers were intended at first to give continuity should either fail or be damaged in use. By 1940, however, the landing interval had reduced and two barriers gave an added measure of safety. A third was added later to improve the margin of safety still further. In practice the aft-facing wires were seldom used, and they were unrigged in 1943. The hangar height was kept at 16ft, the minimum considered necessary to allow the contemporary Swordfish, Skuas and Rocs to be struck down on floats. All naval aircraft of the period were designed to be operable on floats so that they could operate from battleships or cruisers as well as aircraft carriers. From 1941 it was essential to increase the number of fighters embarked to take advantage of air warning radar and provide an effective air defence for the fleet. At first this was achieved with a deck park of aircraft which were pushed forward of the barrier by handling parties before aircraft could land-on, and pushed aft of the range for launches. The situation was eased slightly by outrigger stowages, U-shaped beams which projected outboard from the starboard deck edge and in which fighter tailwheels were guided to roll outwards until the main wheels were at the deck edge, clear of the landing area, and the aircraft could be chocked and lashed in place.

By 1945 these ships were operating an air group of fifty-four US-built Chance Vought Corsair fighters and Grumman Avenger torpedo-bombers. The latter's wings folded rearwards like earlier British-built types, but the Corsairs wings folded upwards, and at the vertical they just exceeded 16ft before lowering down with the tips

Illustrious' designed armour protection scheme. (AUTHOR'S COLLECTION)

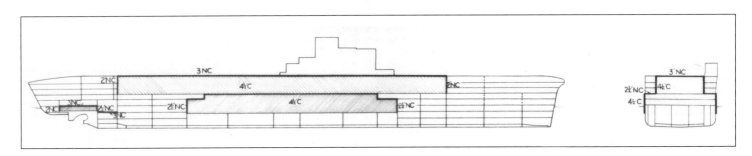

Illustrious after her limited reconstruction in 1946. The forward end of the flight deck has been completely reconstructed, and the island with its radar arrays and close-range armament looks very unlike its original appearance. (AUTHOR'S COLLECTION)

above the fuselage. It was felt that Corsairs would need to spread and fold their wings in the hangar for maintenance, so aircraft contracted for the RN had 6in cut off their wingtips, making them 'squared' rather than rounded. Despite fears that this might adversely affect performance, it was found that the modification actually improved the Corsair's rate of roll and deck-landing performance.

The bulk stowage for avgas was only 50,450gal, effectively half that in *Ark Royal* and reflecting the smaller air group originally envisaged. This was adequate in 1940 but totally inadequate by 1945, when nearly double the number of larger aircraft were embarked, with the result that frequent under-way replenishment was required.

Since they were designed before radar made fighter-interception techniques viable, these ships had a battery of eight twin 4.5in turrets rather than the open mountings in *Ark Royal*. They were disposed in groups of two on sponsons port forward and aft, and starboard forward and aft, designated 'A' and 'X' groups to starboard and 'B' and 'Y' to port. The turrets were countersunk into the sponsons but, since the staff requirement called for them to be able to fire across the flight deck on to the other beam, the turret tops stood 2ft 6in above deck level and interfered with aircraft movements. The turrets could not be positioned far outboard, and they formed a marked constriction in the width of the flight deck, especially aft, limiting the number of aircraft that could be ranged. The BD Mark II turrets were made by Vickers; the guns themselves were 4.5in Mark III made by the Royal Gun Factory and developed from an army anti-aircraft gun to provide commonality and use the same fixed ammunition. Six Mark VIII eight-

barrelled 2pdr 'pom-poms' were mounted in positions similar to those in *Ark Royal*; they were designated S1, S2, S3 and S4; P1 and P2. Large numbers of 20mm Oerlikons and eventually 40mm Bofors were added as the war progressed. Each group of 4.5in turrets had its own Mark IV director capable of directing its own group, more than one group or all four groups. The 'B' director had to be raised during construction to give it a better field of view, making it into a potential obstacle for aircraft that drifted left on take-off. In *Victorious* and *Formidable* this problem was solved by giving this director hydraulic lowering gear, but this was not available in time for *Illustrious*. It was eventually fitted in her 1946 refit.

Illustrious was the first aircraft carrier in the world to be completed with radar. In November 1939 it was decided to delay her completion by two months in order to fit a Type 79Z equipment. This had separate transmitting and receiving aerials; the latter was placed at the top of the foremast, but a new mainmast was stepped for the latter at the after end of the island. This was fixed in *Illustrious* but made telescopic in subsequent ships which had more time in the builder's yard before completion. Type 79 transmitted in two lobes and contact fade between them gave an indication of an aircraft's height. An aircraft flying towards the carrier at 10,000ft could be detected at about 60 miles; one at 20,000ft at about 100 miles. Radar revolutionised an aircraft carrier's ability to use its fighters to the best effect in intercepting enemy attacks, but *Illustrious*' officers had to overcome early misconceptions about the need for secrecy. When she arrived in the MF in 1940 the Fleet Standing Orders stated that radar

was turned on for only one minute in every hour and turned off immediately if an aircraft was detected in case the enemy learnt about it! No communication with fighters was to be made until the enemy was in sight. Fortunately common sense prevailed and *Illustrious* was able to use her radar and new Fulmar fighters to gain air superiority in the eastern Mediterranean.

Her Type 72DM aircraft homing beacon was moved down to a position on top of the foremast's tripod to make space for the Type 79 radar receiver at the masthead. She also had high- and medium-frequency direction finders and the best outfit of W/T and radio sets yet fitted in a British carrier. These included Types 56, 57, 52L and 52M, 52H, 405 and 49C.

Postwar modernisation

During her wartime refits *Illustrious* had a number of improvements made to her flight deck and was fitted with extra avgas tanks and extra structure to accommodate radar arrays, and given a considerable increase in the close-range armament. Her 1945 refit grew into a modernisation that consolidated wartime experience and made a number of improvements. She was given a new bow and stern at either end of a level flight deck, similar to those being built into the new light fleet carriers, giving the largest deck area that could be contrived on the hull. Consideration had been

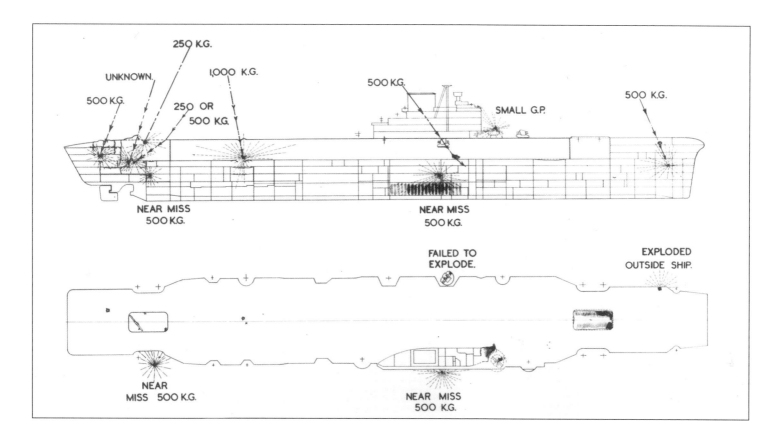

250 K.G.

UNKNOWN.

1,000 K.G.

500 K.G.

500 K.G.

500 K.G.

250 OR
500 K.G.

500 K.G.

SMALL G.P.

NEAR MISS
500 K.G.

NEAR MISS
500 K.G.

FAILED TO
EXPLODE.

EXPLODED
OUTSIDE SHIP.

NEAR
MISS 500 K.G.

NEAR MISS
500 K.G.

ABOVE Bomb damage suffered by *Illustrious* on 10 January 1941. (AUTHOR'S COLLECTION)

LEFT *Illustrious* carrying out flying trials in 1947. A Sea Fury F.10 is ranged aft, and a Seafire F.45 of 778 NAS is parked on an outrigger forward of the island. (AUTHOR'S COLLECTION)

given to removing the after 4.5in gun turrets and plating over the 'bottleneck' they created to give more space for ranging deck-load strikes, but in the event this was not done to save cost. Consideration was also given to fitting out the space under the flight deck as mess decks to ease the problem of cramped, inadequate accommodation, but cost considerations also prevented this. Between 1940 and 1945 her scheme of complement had risen from 1,280 to 2,000 because of the extra aircraft that could be embarked, radar and other new equipment and the significant increase in close-range guns.

Significant work included a rebuilt island with sponsons for single 40mm Bofors guns and a new outfit of radars on new fore and mainmasts. A 'YE' homing beacon on a mast attached to the funnel replaced the Type 72. Radars included Type 961, 281 and 293M. An American SM-1 radar replaced

'A' director, but this was replaced by a British Type 277 at the next refit. The gun directors had Type 285 range-finding gunnery radar. In her final refit in 1952 all remaining 2pdr 'pom-poms' and 20mm Oerlikons were removed, leaving her with an all-Bofors close-range armament. A five-bladed propeller was fitted to the centre shaft in 1946, which cured the major vibration problem, but over her remaining life some vibration was caused by the wing shafts at high speed.

The lifts were enlarged to 48ft long by 22ft 9in

wide with new platforms strengthened to take the new generation of naval aircraft under development. After the decision to complete her as a trials carrier, she was fitted with a boom aft, taken from *Pretoria Castle*, which was equipped with a television camera so that landings could be watched remotely and recorded.

Between 1940 and 1952 alterations and additions to *Illustrious* increased her deep load displacement from 28,210 tons to 31,630 tons, reducing the height of the flight deck above the

Illustrious under attack in Malta Dockyard in January 1941. (AUTHOR'S COLLECTION)

over the escort of four fast merchant ships headed for Alexandria from Force H. Shadowers had followed the fleet since 8 January, but the Fulmars had failed to intercept them. On 10 January, some hours after the rendezvous with the merchant ships, the MF was about 75 miles east of Malta when the enemy dive-bombers carried out a well planned set-piece attack on *Illustrious*. Five Fulmars were airborne at just after noon when a raid by two Italian SM.79 torpedo-bombers was detected; all five were drawn down to intercept and four Fulmars were launched, but this attack was a feint to achieve just that effect, as none of the Fulmars could then climb fast enough to disrupt an attack by Ju 87s from 12,000ft.

The attack was over in only 10 minutes, during which *Illustrious* was hit by six bombs of various sizes and a single Ju 87 that crashed into the ship out of control. The three bombs which hit forward inflicted little serious damage, but the three which hit aft put the flight deck out of action, although they failed to damage the machinery or affect the ship's watertight integrity. Two of the latter hit the unarmoured after lift, and their explosion in the confined space caused most of the damage and fire in the after part of the ship. The third was the only one to hit the armoured section of the flight deck. It defeated the armour forward of the after lift and exploded before hitting the hangar deck. A steering gear failure followed the bomb damage, and when it was rectified *Illustrious* began the 75-mile journey to Malta at 18 knots; she was still on fire aft and the machinery spaces were filled with smoke and fumes from the foam used to fight the fires. A second attack by Ju 87 dive-bombers added several near misses and a further hit in the after lift well, where it had the beneficial effect of blowing out the fires in some areas.

water from about 38ft to 36ft. This was less than ideal, and in rough conditions water could, occasionally, wash down the flight deck despite the flared bow design. The fact that the ship was still far below peacetime accommodation standards for an operational fleet carrier was a major factor in extending the 1945/46 refit, and every available space including, even including former boat bays, was turned into accommodation. In September 1945 it was decided to complete her as a trials and training carrier in order to run her with a ship's

company reduced to a practical number while retaining her for use as a fleet carrier in an emergency.

Damage to *Illustrious* on 10 January 1941

The German Luftwaffe contained a specialised anti-shipping unit known as *Fliegerkorps 10*, which had operated from Norway in 1940. The core capability was provided by the 54 Junkers Ju 87 dive-bombers of *Stukagruppes* 1 and 2. After the attack on Taranto it was deployed to Sicily with the specific aim of destroying *Illustrious*. Their opportunity came on 10 January 1941, during Operation *Excess*, as the MF closed Malta to take

Formidable shortly after completion. (AUTHOR'S COLLECTION)

Illustrious arrived at Parlatorio Wharf in Malta Dockyard at 2215 and firefighters from ashore joined the ship's company in extinguishing the fires at 0300 on 11 January. Casualties included a number of aircrew who were trapped in the vicinity of the wardroom aft when the fires broke out, and amounted to 126 dead and 91 wounded. The priority in Malta was to allow the steering gear to be repaired so that she could sail for Alexandria and, ultimately, repair in the USA. She was the focus of several air attacks while in Malta, but only one hit was scored; on 16 January a bomb hit the area of the after lift well again. A near miss on 19 January caused shock damage to the turbines.

Was the armoured hangar a good idea?
At the time of Admiral Henderson's insistent briefing the armoured carriers were unquestionably the right carriers for the RN, since radar was an untried theory, fighter interception was impractical and the ships would have to operate in the narrow seas against considerable air opposition. The lack of large air group at the time was, in part, realistic, since RAF opposition to carriers had prevented the navy from having a large air group to embark. Both situations were to change rapidly after 1940.

Although *Illustrious'* survival on 10 January 1941 is often ascribed to her armour, it is a fact that most bombs fell outside the armoured flight deck, and the one bomb that hit it defeated the armour and exploded in the closed hangar, causing considerable damage. A carrier with effective hangar deck armour and an open-sided hangar

topped by a light-structured flight deck might have survived as well or better and had the potential to operate considerably more aircraft when they were available and needed. The big positive of the design, however, was the protection arrangements for the bulk avgas storage. No British carrier was lost to fire during the war, but several US and Japanese carriers were.

The armoured deck did pay off in the Pacific in 1945, however, when all the *Illustrious* group carriers were hit at various times by kamikaze aircraft and managed to remain in action, although the damage was sometimes more severe than had been thought at the time. American carriers did not have armoured decks and suffered damage that had to be repaired in dockyard hands. The most negative aspect of the armoured hangar design, however, was the difficulty and expense of repairing damage such as that suffered by *Illustrious*, since the armoured 'box' formed a significant part of the structural strength of the hull. Postwar reconstructions were limited by the difficulty and cost of rebuilding the upper part of the hull to modify the hangar and flight deck. Despite plans for several ships being prepared, *Victorious* was the only ship of the class to be rebuilt for this reason, and she had to be stripped down to the hangar-deck level. In summary the design was a good compromise in 1936 but the development of radar and improved fighters made it less so by 1940. To their credit, despite everything thrown at them by three determined and resourceful enemies in a global war, none of the *Illustrious* group was sunk and all survived into the postwar era in one form or another.

Formidable at anchor after her US refit in 1941, flying a church pennant to show a religious service is taking place. A 'YE' homing beacon on a telescopic mast attached to the funnel has replaced the Type 72, but the forward round-down still limits the amount of deck space available for parking in Fly 1. (AUTHOR'S COLLECTION)

Illustrious Class technical details

Details are for *Illustrious* as built, with figures for 1946 in brackets

Displacement:	28,210 tons (31,630 tons)
Dimensions:	length 740ft (748ft 6in) beam 95ft 9in draught 28ft 10in (29ft 3in)
Machinery:	3-shaft Parsons geared turbines 6 Admiralty three-drum boilers 111,000shp delivering 30 knots
Armament:	8 x twin 4.5in; 6 octuple 2pdr 'pom-pom'; varying numbers of 40mm Bofors and 20mm Oerlikons added
Protection:	3in flight deck; 4.5in hangar bulkheads; 2.5in hangar deck; 4.5in waterline belt
Fuel:	4,850 tons (4,839 tons)
Endurance:	6,300 miles at 25 knots/11,000 miles at 12 knots
Complement:	1,229 (2,000 in BPF, 1,090 as trials carrier)

Aircraft operating data

Flight deck:	620ft x 95ft
	(740ft x 95ft)
Hangar:	456ft x 62ft x 16ft
Catapult:	1 x BH3; 14,000lb at 66 knots
	end speed
Arrester wires:	7 x 11,000lb at 55 knots
	3 barriers – after 2 10,000lb;
	forward 20,000lb
Lifts:	2, both 45ft long x 22ft wide,
	14,000lb; later enlarged and
	strengthened
Aircraft:	36
	(54)
Aircraft fuel:	50,660gal
	(50,540gal)
Air weapons:	42 x 18in torpedoes (30 x
	22.5in USN)
	72 depth charges (144)
	24 mines (none)
	250 x 500lb bombs (250)
	stowage for 500 smaller bombs,
	0.303in and 0.5in gun
	ammunition, flares and
	pyrotechnics

Individual ship histories

Illustrious

Laid down by Vickers-Armstrongs at Barrow-in-Furness on 27 April 1937, allocated Admiralty Job Number J3986 and Yard Number 732, *Illustrious* was launched by Lady Henderson on 5 April 1939. Tragically, ill-health had forced her husband to give up his position as Third Sea Lord in March and he died on 2 May. *Illustrious* was completed on 25 May 1940 and carried out a short period of trials before sailing to Bermuda to work-up her new air group, which comprised 806 (Fulmar), 815 and 819 (Swordfish) NAS. After a brief spell in Scapa Flow she sailed in August for the MF, flying the flag of Rear Admiral Lumley Lyster, Rear Admiral Aircraft Carriers Mediterranean. She was escorted through the Sicilian narrows by Force H, and on 2 September her fighters shot down three Italian aircraft and Swordfish struck enemy installations on Rhodes before she arrived in Alexandria and formally joined the Mediterranean Fleet on 5 September.

On 17 September nine Swordfish of 815 NAS attacked and sank an Italian destroyer and two merchant ships in Benghazi by dive-bombing them. Six aircraft of 819 NAS laid a minefield which subsequently sank another enemy destroyer and two merchant ships and damaged a third.

Later in the month her aircraft covered two convoys to Malta and struck at enemy installations on the island of Leros. In October, however, she was damaged by an accidental hangar fire.

On 11 November *Illustrious'* aircraft carried out Operation *Judgement*, the historic attack on the Italian Fleet in Taranto Harbour. The air group was augmented by Swordfish and crews from 813 and 824 NAS from the damaged *Eagle*. For the loss of two Swordfish and the expenditure of eleven torpedoes and a small number of bombs, the battleship *Conte di Cavour* was sunk and two other battleships, *Caio Duillio* and *Littorio*, beached and put out of action for many months. The aircraft of 806 NAS proved very successful in keeping enemy shadowers at bay. On 26 November Swordfish attacked Leros again, and on 12 December they struck at enemy positions near Bardia in support of an offensive operation begun by the Eighth Army. Five days later airfields on Rhodes and Stampalia were attacked successfully to limit enemy activity, and on 21 December Swordfish located and sank enemy merchant ships off Kerkeneh Island; a day later they attacked Tripoli.

On 7 January 1941 *Illustrious* sailed from Alexandria to cover a fast convoy to Malta; she was attacked on 10 January by dive-bombers of the German *Flieger Korps X*, which had just arrived in Sicily to reinforce the Italian Air Force. The unit had been trained to attack shipping, and 806 NAS fighters had been drawn down to intercept torpedo-carrying aircraft when dive-bombers attacked from high level, unopposed, to score several hits 75 miles east of Gibraltar. The armoured deck was penetrated and explosions in the hangar caused extensive fires, but *Illustrious* entered Malta Dockyard that evening still burning but under her own power. Despite German air raids, emergency repairs were made and she sailed for Alexandria on 23 January. When she arrived on 25 January further temporary repairs were carried out, and she finally sailed through the Suez Canal on 10 March, heading for Durban. On arrival she was docked to have underwater damage assessed.

Arrangements had been made for the ship to be repaired in Norfolk Navy Yard in Virginia, and she arrived there on 12 May 1941. The opportunity was taken to carry out a number of urgent alterations and additions, among which the curvature of the after round-down was significantly reduced, increasing the length of the usable flight deck by 50ft and making more space available to range larger numbers of aircraft. The steel fire curtains which had shattered into splinters in the explosions that followed enemy bomb hits were replaced by more flexible 'fear-nought' curtains. The repair and reconstruction work was completed on 28 November 1941, and she sailed for the UK on 2 December in company with *Formidable*.

Unfortunately, on 16 November she collided with *Formidable* in rough weather and suffered damage to the port side of the flight deck forward and the decks immediately beneath it, the ship's company recreation space on 2 deck and the cable working area on 3 deck. The damage was repaired by Cammell Laird in Birkenhead, after which *Illustrious* carried out deck-landing trials with a 'hooked Spitfire'; effectively the prototype Seafire.

In March 1942 *Illustrious* worked-up with a new air group comprising 881 and 882 (Martlet), 810 and 829 (Swordfish) NAS, sailing to join the Eastern Fleet on 23 March. Another accident occurred in Freetown, where she stopped for fuel, when a hangar fire destroyed eleven aircraft. Fortunately the fire curtains and spray system minimised and soon extinguished the fire and the damage was repaired by ship's staff. On 5 May 1942 she took part in Operation *Ironclad*, the British landings on Madagascar, in company with *Indomitable* and other ships. Swordfish torpedoed and sank the Vichy-French armed merchant-cruiser *Bougainville* during strikes on Diego Suarez on the first day of the operation, and the submarine *Le Heros* near the British assault transport anchorage a day later. On 7 May Diego Suarez was captured after *Illustrious'* fighters had shot down seven Vichy French aircraft for the loss of one Martlet. She subsequently supported the army in operations to occupy the southern part of Madagascar, before proceeding to Durban for a short refit, after which she returned to the UK.

Alterations and additions were carried out in Birkenhead after her return to the UK. These included a further 'levelling' of the round-downs to increase the usable flat area of the flight deck to increase the number of aircraft that could be ranged and launched for a single strike; the fitting of new and improved air search and fire-control radar, and an increase in the close-range armament. The work was completed on 7 June 1943. Her new air group reflected a general move towards larger numbers of embarked fighters rather than torpedo-bomber-reconnaissance aircraft, comprising 878 and 890 (Martlet), 894 (Seafire) and 810 (Barracuda) NAS. After working-up she joined the HF on 26 July for flying trials with new types of aircraft and carried out Operation *Governor* in company with *Unicorn*, a feint against Southern Norway intended to distract German attention from the Allied landings on Sicily. The operations showed how a carrier task force could operate with impunity 150 miles off an enemy-held coast.

On 5 August she escorted RMS *Queen Mary*, with Prime Minister Winston Churchill embarked for a working visit to the USA, until she was far enough out into the Atlantic to be clear of German air attack. She then deployed to Gibraltar, where she joined Force H. On 9 September 1943 Force H, which included *Illustrious* and *Formidable*, provided heavy cover for Operation *Avalanche*, the Allied landings at Salerno. On 29 October she returned to Birkenhead again for work to virtually eliminate the after round-down, giving a usable flight deck 740ft long (compared with only 620ft in the original design), allowing a deck park to increase the size of the air group to fifty-four aircraft. On 28 November, with work completed, she began to work-up in the Clyde with her largest air group to date, organised in a new way which reflected the larger number of aircraft the RN could now send to sea. It comprised 15 Naval Fighter Wing, which included 1830, 1833 and 1837 (Corsair) NAS and 21 TBR Wing which included 810 and 847 (Barracuda) NAS. When the work-up was completed she sailed to join the EF, arriving at its main base in Trincomalee on 31 January 1944.

In March she took part in a sweep searching for Japanese cruisers, and in April she carried out Operation *Cockpit*, a combined strike against shipping in Sabang, Sumatra, in company with the USS *Saratoga* and a number of eastern Fleet ships, during which fighters destroyed twenty-four enemy aircraft on the ground. She returned to Trincomalee on 21 April, when 832 and 851 (Avenger) NAS replaced 21 TBR Wing for Operation *Transom*. The force, which included *Illustrious* and *Saratoga*, sailed on 17 May and, after refuelling in Exmouth Bay in Australia, attacked oil refineries at Surabaya in Java. In June, 21 TBR Wing re-embarked and *Illustrious* sailed for Operation *Councillor*, a strike against Port Blair in the Andaman Islands on 21 June 1944. *Illustrious* had fifty-seven aircraft embarked, of which fifty-one were airborne together at one stage; the highest number ever achieved by this ship in a single operation. The CVE *Atheling* was in company as a 'spare deck' in case a crash blocked *Illustrious*' deck and prevented large numbers of aircraft from landing. In July 1944 the 1st ACS was expanded by the arrival of *Victorious* and *Indomitable*.

On 25 July the three carriers struck at Sabang in Operation *Crimson*. Number 15 Fighter Wing destroyed four enemy aircraft without loss and spotted for battleship gunfire against targets ashore. After the operation *Illustrious* sailed for a refit in Durban with only 810 NAS embarked for antisubmarine protection. The refit started on 14 August and ended on 10 October, after which she rejoined 1 ACS in the newly formed British Pacific Fleet (BPF). In November the Barracudas were permanently disembarked and replaced by 854 (Avenger) NAS with aircraft better suited to operations in the Far East; 1837 NAS was disbanded and its personnel distributed between the other two Corsair squadrons. On 20 December she sailed with *Indomitable* for Operation *Robson*, a strike against the oil refinery at Pangkalon

Brandon in Sumatra, but bad weather obscured the target and a secondary target at Belawan Deli was attacked instead.

On 16 January 1945 *Illustrious* sailed from Trincomalee with 1830 and 1833 (Corsair) and 854 (Avenger) NAS embarked to deploy into the Pacific in company with *Indomitable, Victorious, Indefatigable* and the remainder of the BPF. Operation *Meridian I* on 24 January was a set-piece attack by aircraft of the BPF on the oil refinery at Pladjoe near Palembang in Sumatra. Forty-three Avengers carrying 172 500lb bombs between them, twelve Fairey Fireflies and fifty escorting fighters achieved very successful results. On 29 January Operation *Meridian II* saw a similar number of aircraft attack Soengei Gerong refinery near Palembang. This raid proved equally successful and both refineries were considerably damaged, cutting the enemy's supply of aircraft fuel to a mere fraction of the pre-attack figure. These were among the largest attacks carried out by RN in the Second World War, and achieved strategic effect. Later on 29 January Japanese aircraft located and attacked the BPF. The cruiser *Euryalus* in the centre of the force engaged a fast-moving enemy aircraft at low level and, through bad gun discipline, hit *Illustrious* with two 5.25in shells. They killed twelve men, wounded twenty-one and damaged the island.

On 10 February the BPF arrived in its main base at Sydney and *Illustrious* was docked to investigate a severe vibration caused by the centre shaft. She was the first ship to enter the new Captain Cook dry dock in Garden Island Dockyard, which was operable but not formally opened until 24 March. In order to have her ready in time the drastic solution was to remove the centre propeller and lock the shaft, limiting her maximum speed to about 24 knots but reducing the vibration to an acceptable level. In March the BPF, now designated Task Force 57 in the USN system, moved to Manus to await orders. On 26 March TF 57 began strikes against Japanese airfields in the Sakashima Islands as part of Operation *Iceberg*, support for the American landings on Okinawa. The aim was to prevent enemy aircraft from Formosa from staging through the islands to attack the US fleet off Okinawa. A kamikaze aircraft crashed close alongside *Illustrious* on 6 April and exploded, causing damage to underwater plating and internal frames. Vibration worsened again. On 11 April aircraft from TF 57 attacked Japanese airfields on Formosa to neutralise kamikazes at source as far as possible. Since the start of the operation *Illustrious*' aircraft had flown 643 sorties on nine strike days for the loss of five aircraft in combat and seven in accidents. On 23 April TF 57 arrived in Leyte Gulf for a replenishment period. A survey found that *Illustrious*' damage was worse than had been

imagined, and most of her aircrew had continued to fly beyond what could be reasonably considered an extended tour of combat duty. She was therefore replaced by the newly-arrived *Formidable*, and passed spare parts and some aircraft over to other carriers.

Illustrious sailed from Leyte on 1 May and returned to Sydney where she disembarked her air group and underwent a period of urgent defect rectification before sailing for the UK on 24 May. On 27 June she arrived in Rosyth and commenced a refit that was scheduled to last four months but which was considerably extended after the end of hostilities. It effectively became the first modernisation applied to a ship of her class and was completed in June 1946, when she recommissioned with a reduced ship's company for use as a trials and training carrier to keep her active. During the manpower crisis in 1947 she was reduced to reserve with a skeleton ship's company, but she recommissioned in September 1948 to carry out trials with the first generation of turbojet and turboprop carrier aircraft. In November 1951 she ferried troops from the UK to Cyprus during a crisis in the Suez Canal Zone, and in September 1952 she embarked an operational air group comprising 824 (Firefly) NAS and the Dutch 860 (Hawker Sea Fury) NAS for Exercise *Mainbrace*, the largest NATO exercise held to that date. She was present in the line of aircraft carriers at the Coronation Review of the Fleet by HM Queen Elizabeth II in June 1953.

Illustrious' last training cruise for reserve aircrew took place in 1954, after which she was laid up in a state of preservation in the Gareloch in December. On 3 November 1956 she was sold to the British iron and Steel Corporation, and during 1957 she was broken up for scrap.

Victorious

The following paragraphs give the ship's history until 1950, when her modernisation began in Portsmouth Dockyard. Her subsequent operational history after modernisation is recounted in Chapter 28.

Victorious was ordered from Vickers-Armstrongs and laid down at its Walker Naval Yard in Newcastle-upon-Tyne on 4 May 1937, allocated Admiralty Job Number J4035 and Yard Number 11. She was launched by Lady Augusta Inskip, wife of Sir Thomas Inskip, the Minister for Defence Co-ordination, who was responsible for awarding complete control of embarked naval aviation back to the Admiralty and ending the period of dual control that had proved a failure. The ship's construction was delayed by the shortage of armour plate, but she commissioned in the shipyard on 29 March 1941 and was formally handed over on 16 April for sea trials and passage to Rosyth, where Admiralty-supplied items were

Formidable in the Captain Cook dry dock in Garden Island Dockyard, Sydney, in 1945. (Author's collection)

to be fitted. There was no time for a work-up, and on 14 May she was loaded with forty-eight crated Hurricanes for shipment to the RAF in Malta. On her nominal completion date, 15 May 1941, she sailed for Scapa Flow to join convoy WS8 for passage to the Middle East, but on 22 May she was allocated to the HF as part of a force hastily put together to contain the German battleship *Bismarck*, which had broken out into the Atlantic. Her scratch air group, originally intended to support the convoy escort, comprised 800Z (Fulmar) and 825 (Swordfish) NAS.

Although 800Z had only three aircraft, they carried out surface searches at night and in bad weather, during which one was lost, but its crew were recovered by a merchant ship. On 25 May 825 NAS carried out a torpedo attack on *Bismarck*

Victorious shortly before being launched by Lady Inskip. (Author's collection)

Victorious at speed in July 1942, with Fulmars and Albacores on deck. (R A Burt collection)

in terrible weather, scoring a hit despite their lack of current practice. After *Bismarck* was sunk, *Victorious* returned to the Clyde and refuelled before sailing with convoy WS8X, keeping her small air group for self defence. The Swordfish located the German *Gonzenheim* on 4 June, after which it was captured by the cruiser *Neptune*. The Hurricanes were assembled by ship's staff and flown off for Malta in Operation *Tracer* on 13 June. On 29 June *Victorious* rejoined the HF and embarked 809 (Fulmar), 827 and 828 (Albacore) NAS.

On 30 July, following a political decision to provide rapid support for Russia, aircraft from *Victorious* and *Furious* attacked German shipping in Petsamo and Kirkenes. Surprise was not achieved, but a 2,000-ton freighter was sunk, another damaged and five enemy aircraft shot down. Against this, the carriers lost eleven Albacores and two Fulmars; only one of the former returned undamaged. On 23 August 1941 *Victorious* sailed with the HF to cover Operation *Dervish*, the first Allied convoy to North Russia. For this, 817 and 832 (Albacore) NAS replaced 827 and 828, and the opportunity was taken to strike at targets in the Bodo area. In February 1941 *Victorious'* aircraft searched for *Lutzow* in the Norwegian Sea, but missed her in a heavy snowstorm. On 7 March she was at sea with the Home Fleet again, covering convoy PQ12 to North Russia, when a searching Albacore located *Tirpitz* at sea and shadowed it until a torpedo strike force arrived. *Tirpitz* steamed at high speed into a strong wind, which limited the aircraft to a relative overtaking speed of only about 30 knots. The leader lacked recent torpedo experience and the squadron pilots had no recent practice, so rather than spend time getting into ideal positions they attacked at once from a single direction. *Tirpitz* easily evaded the torpedoes and an opportunity that was never to be repeated was lost. Disappointment in the HF was countered by Hitler's decree that *Tirpitz* was never to sail again

if a British aircraft carrier was known to be at sea.

On 4 August *Victorious* sailed for the Mediterranean to form part of the fighting escort for a relief convoy to Malta. Her normal air group was augmented by 884 (Fulmar) and 885 (Sea Hurricane) NAS to keep the maximum number of fighters in the air. Operation *Pedestal* began on 10 August 1942, when *Victorious*, *Indomitable*, *Eagle* and *Furious*, together with many other warships, entered the Mediterranean. In the ensuing famous action they fought five merchant ships, including the damaged tanker *Ohio*, through to Malta and *Furious* flew off thirty-eight Spitfires to the island. Thirty enemy aircraft were shot down and numerous attacks beaten off, but *Eagle* and thirteen fleet fighters were lost. She sailed from Gibraltar to rejoin the HF on 16 August. On 8 November 1942 she left the Home Fleet again to join Force H to provide cover for Operation *Torch*, the Allied landings in North Africa. For this the air group was slightly modified, comprising 809 (Fulmar), 882 (Martlet), 884 (Seafire), 817 and 832 (Albacore) NAS. An unusual incident occurred when Lieutenant Nations of 882 NAS saw white flags raised over the Vichy French airfield at Blida and landed to take its surrender. His flight stayed overhead to cover him in the event of treachery. On the voyage back to the UK an Albacore on patrol detected and sank U-517 in mid-Atlantic.

Following a request from Admiral King, the US Chief of Naval Operations, the Admiralty agreed to lend *Victorious* to the American Pacific Fleet, so she anchored off Greenock on 23 November and landed all her squadrons including aircraft, personnel and stores. She embarked forty new Martlets and sufficient personnel to form new squadrons in the USA. Having completed her preparations she sailed for the USA on 20 December 1942, escorted by the destroyers *Racehorse* and *Redoubt*. *Victorious* arrived in Norfolk Navy Yard on 31 December and entered dry dock to have USN equipment, including SM-1 radar, fitted, and to be spray-painted with blue camouflage paint. She embarked a thirty-five-man USN liaison team under a commander and

including radio operators and coders to help with the USN signal procedures and ciphers that would be used. The team also included a Landing Signal Officer (LSO) to teach British pilots how to use American deck operating and landing procedures. The ship's company even wore USN working clothes, which proved so popular that, following *Victorious'* recommendation, they were adopted throughout the RN and, in developed form, are still worn in 2013. On 2 February she sailed with an air group that now comprised 882, 896 and 898 (Martlet) and 832 (Avenger) NAS. The Avengers were issued from USN stock and the aircrew trained on them locally, and all aircraft flew with US markings. On 14 February she passed through the Panama Canal into the Pacific and refuelled at Balboa, from where she was escorted westwards by the American destroyers *Bache*, *Converse* and *Pringle*. An outbreak of diphtheria was diagnosed on 21 February, and the limited amount of anti-toxin on board was quickly used up. Replacement stock was flown out to the ship by a USN Consolidated PB4Y Liberator and dropped into the sea in a canister that was recovered by sea boat. During this passage the decision was taken to adopt the USN name Wildcat in place of the RN name Martlet to avoid confusion; the whole RN followed suite on 1 January 1944. A total of 184 Wildcat sorties were flown, and sixty by Avengers. The latter revealed a problem, the Avenger's arrester-hook 'throat' proving too narrow for the RN arrester wires, which were thicker than those used in the USN. Worse, the arrester-wire tensioning was initially unsuitable for off-centre landings and, unless 1, 2 or 3 wires were caught, a barrier engagement was likely. Neither the ship's two fixed cranes nor 'Jumbo', the mobile crane, could lift an Avenger.

Admiral Nimitz, C-in-C Pacific Fleet, inspected *Victorious* when she arrived in Pearl Harbor on 4 March 1943, and a team of engineers came on board to modify the arrester gear. Simultaneously the Avengers were fitted with modified hooks. She subsequently sailed to Noumea, arriving on 17 May to join Carrier

Victorious in San Pedro Bay, Leyte Gulf, with the BPF in 1945, during the replenishment break in Operation *Iceberg*. (AUTHOR'S COLLECTION)

Division 1 (CARDIV 1), under Rear Admiral D W C Ramsey USN, flying his flag in *Saratoga*. The Division formed part of Task Force 14, which included the battleships *North Carolina*, *Massachusetts* and *Indiana*. A day later she sailed for a sweep searching for Japanese forces, during which antisubmarine and CAP sorties were flown. When she returned to Noumea on 24 May, six F4F-4 Wildcats were issued from USN stock to replace aircraft that had been lost in accidents, and victualling stores, including rum, arrived from Australia. In early June the battle group carried out exercises and *Saratoga* and *Victorious* practised cross-deck operations. Six Avengers and twelve Wildcats from the latter were exchanged for twelve Wildcats, eight Avengers and six Douglas

Dauntless of Carrier Air Group 3 (CVG-3). Flying went smoothly, with no incidents.

On 27 June the battle group, designated Task Force 36.3, sailed to cover landings on New Georgia in the Solomon Islands. With her better and more experienced fighter direction personnel and facilities, and with the difficulties of operating Avengers in mind, *Victorious* embarked sixty Wildcats while 832's Avengers embarked with CVG-3 in *Saratoga*. The force searched an area from 157 to 162 degrees east and 1 to 16 degrees south, flying out to 200 miles from the carriers, but no enemy ships were located. On 12 July *Victorious* replenished at sea from the USN oilers *Cimarron* and *Kaskaskia*, during which 3,270 tons of FFO, 30,283gal of avgas, 625gal of lubricating oil and 20gal of ice cream were taken on board. On 20 July *Victorious* ran out of potatoes and 800lb of dried potato powder was flown over from *Saratoga* in an Avenger dubbed the 'Spud Express', which

also brought a Chief Commissary steward to explain how to mix it to RN chefs. The result was four tons of mashed potato.

On 25 July 1943 *Victorious* returned to Noumea after twenty-eight days continuously at sea, a record for a British aircraft carrier. During the operation no Japanese warships had attempted to interfere with Allied operations, but *Victorious* had steamed 12,223 miles at an average of 18.1 knots. This compared most favourably with the monthly average for her first two years of operation, 4,905 miles. Her aircraft had flown 614 sorties, achieving the lowest accident rate yet achieved by the RN. Now that more USN carriers were becoming available the RN, perhaps unwisely in view of subsequent operations in the Pacific, asked for *Victorious* to return, and she left Noumea for Pearl Harbor in company with *Indiana*, *Converse*, *Boyd* and *Halford* on 31 July. In addition to her own ship's company she carried fifty-two USN aircrew

Victorious (nearest) and *Implacable* alongside in Sydney after the end of the war in the Pacific. The stern of a third fleet carrier is just visible in the Captain Cook dry dock. (AUTHOR'S COLLECTION)

from CVG-3 who had reached the end of their operational tours and two Japanese prisoners of war. The aircraft supplied from USN stocks were left behind as reserves for CVG-3. During the passage a further 165 accident-free CAP and antisubmarine sorties were flown. After short spells in Pearl Harbor and San Diego, *Victorious* passed through the Panama Canal on 26 August and arrived in Norfolk, Virginia, on 1 September to have her American equipment removed. She arrived back in the Clyde on 26 September and landed all her remaining aircraft and air stores to RNAS Arbroath. A day later she entered the Gladstone Dock in Liverpool for a refit.

Victorious rejoined the HF on 4 March 1944 and embarked a new air group which included 47 Fighter Wing, comprising 1834 and 1836 (Corsair) together with 827 and 829 (Barracuda) NAS. After working-up she took part in operation *Tungsten* on 3 April, the first strike against *Tirpitz* in Kaa Fjord, in company with *Furious, Pursuer, Emperor, Searcher* and *Fencer*. Forty Barracudas dive-bombed the battleship in a very short space of time, obtaining fourteen hits which caused extensive damage and 438 casualties; the supply ship *C A Larsen* was also damaged, but two Barracudas were shot down. A repeat attack, Operation *Planet*, two weeks later, had to be cancelled because of bad weather. On 26 April she took part in Operations *Ridge Able* and *Ridge Baker*, strikes against shipping in Bodo together with *Furious, Searcher, Emperor, Pursuer* and *Striker*. Twenty-seven Barracudas, each armed with three 500lb bombs, sank three ships totalling 15,000 tons and damaged another of 800 tons; attacks on shipping off Rorvik had to be aborted because of bad weather. On the same day six Corsairs carried out Operation *Veritas*, a low reconnaissance of Narvik to raise expectations of an Allied landing. In May two separate attempts to dive-bomb Tirpitz, Operations *Brawn* and *Tiger Claw*, had to be abandoned because of bad weather. On 1 June aircraft from *Victorious* and *Furious* attacked shipping in Aalesund area in Operation *Lombard*; sixteen Barracudas sank the 4,000-ton *Leonhart* and the 2,300-ton *Sperrbrecher 181*. They also damaged the 5,500-ton *Florida* and a second unnamed ship, both of which had to be beached. Her last action with the Home Fleet was Operation *Kruschen* on 8 June, an attack on shipping in the Norwegian leads which was curtailed by bad weather.

On 12 June 1944 *Victorious* sailed to join the EF, and on 25 July she joined *Illustrious* in Operation *Crimson*, a strike on Sabang Airfield and nearby radar installations followed by a shore

bombardment by *Queen Elizabeth, Renown* and *Richelieu*. Surprise was lost during a clumsy form-up, but Corsair pilots saw air combat for the first time and their spotting for bombardment was excellent. Operation *Banquet* on 19 August was a strike on Indaroeng cement works and Padang Airfield by aircraft from *Victorious* and *Indomitable*. Although the attack was well executed, intelligence had failed to discover that the enemy made little use of the port, and there were few targets. Operation *Light* on 18 September was a fighter sweep of airfields in the Medan and Belawan Deli areas of Sumatra by aircraft from *Victorious* and *Indomitable*. Mistakes were made, including the strafing of the British rescue submarine in its briefed position by fighters, but enemy reaction was negligible and lessons were learned that would be valuable when the new BPF was formed. On 17 October the same two carriers carried out Operation *Millet*, an attack on Japanese installations in the Nicobar Islands to distract attention from American landings at Leyte Gulf in the Philippine Islands. Operation *Millet II* two days later was an attack on opportunity targets in Nancowry, during which seven enemy aircraft were shot down and two small ships sunk. After this, Avengers replaced Barracudas and *Victorious* joined *Indomitable, Illustrious* and *Indefatigable* as part of the 1ˢᵗ ACS in the BPF. Her air group comprised 1834 and 1836 (Corsair) and 849 (Avenger) NAS.

On 4 January 1945 she joined *Indomitable* and

Indefatigable in striking at Pangkalan Brandan refinery in Sumatra, and on 16 January all four carriers in 1 ACS sailed from Trincomalee to attack refineries in the Palembang complex in Sumatra and then move on into the Pacific. On 24 January forty-three Avengers put their bombs accurately into Pladjoe refinery during Operation *Meridian I*. Oil in storage tanks was burnt and output halved over the next three months, and fighter 'Ramrods' destroyed thirty-four enemy aircraft on the ground. In Operation *Meridian II* on 29 January a similar force accurately bombed and damaged Songei Gerong, and full production was not resumed before the war ended. The BPF arrived in Sydney on 11 February 1945 and sailed to work-up near Manus Island on 27 February. While carrying out flying exercises on 14 March a fire broke out in the centre boiler room, but it was soon brought under control and repairs were carried out at sea by ship's staff. The BPF arrived at the USN forward operating base at Ulithi Atoll in the Caroline Islands on 20 March, where it joined the US Pacific Fleet and was designated Task Force 57. The Fleet sailed on 23 March for Operation *Iceberg*, the US landings on Okinawa, during which the BPF struck at airfields in the Sakashima Gunto to prevent Japanese aircraft staging from Formosa to Okinawa. On 5 May a kamikaze aircraft hit the port edge of the flight deck aft and cartwheeled into the sea, where it exploded, causing two casualties but minimal

Victorious in Malta on 11 November 1946. (Author's collection)

damage. On 12 April BPF aircraft struck at Japanese airfields in Formosa, and on 20 April TF 57 left the operating area for a period of replenishment in Leyte Gulf. *Victorious* had been at sea continuously for thirty-one days by the time she anchored.

On 1 May 1 ACS sailed for further operations off the Sakashima Gunto, *Formidable* having replaced *Illustrious*. On 9 May *Victorious* was hit by a kamikaze aircraft, which caused damage to the catapult and port forward gun mountings. Minutes later a second crashed into the deck park aft, destroying four Corsairs and causing fires, but good damage control kept her in action. A succession of barrier engagements destroyed the after barrier on 17 May. A jury barrier was rigged, but aircraft operations were limited until more permanent repairs could be made in Australia. On 19 May *Victorious* embarked 500lb bombs from the merchant auxiliary *Robert Maersk* at the rate of eighty-one per hour; a good achievement given the relative newness of under-way replenishment in the RN. The last strikes against the Sakashima Islands were carried out on 25 May, after which TF 57 sailed for Sydney to undergo a maintenance

period before the next phase of operations.

Redesignated TF 37 with the change of USN Pacific Fleet command, the BPF sailed for operations against the Japanese mainland on 25 June 1945. No specific name was given to this operation, which was thought at the time to be a precursor to Operation *Olympic*, the invasion of Japan planned for the autumn. The BPF joined the American Fast Carrier Task Force, TF 38, about 100 miles east of Honshu for combined strike operations. Sorties were flown against airfields, industry, shipping and targets of opportunity including railways. On 9 August the BPF flew the largest number of strike sorties and dropped the most ordnance by the RN on any single day in the Second World War. Even though the Japanese surrender was known to be imminent, the shortage of fuel in the fleet train forced most of the BPF to return to Australia for a pre-planned maintenance period, but the USN provided sufficient fuel to keep *Indefatigable*, *Duke of York*, *King George V* and their escorts in Japanese waters. *Victorious* was at sea on passage to Sydney on VJ Day; her war effectively ended when she disembarked her air group to RNAS Maryborough, the ground crews going ashore by boat in Moreton Bay.

A planned refit in Garden Island Dockyard, Sydney was cancelled, and *Victorious* returned to the UK with former prisoners of the Japanese and sailors due for early demobilisation embarked. She arrived in Portsmouth Dockyard on 27 October 1945, having steamed 268,000 miles since first

Victorious in rough weather, demonstrating the effectiveness of the British bow design in keeping water off the flight deck. (Author's collection)

Victorious sailing from Sydney in 1946, ferrying BPF staff to Hong Kong. Note the WRNS personnel fallen in on the forward part of the flight deck. (CRAIL MUSEUM COLLECTION).

commissioning and served throughout the world's oceans. She moved to Devonport for a refit, during which accommodation was built into her hangar and all air stores were landed. From December 1945 she was employed on 'trooping' runs between the UK and Australia, taking men east to replace 'hostilities-only' personnel and bringing back a variety of passengers including war brides, and 'Food for Britain' given by the people of Australia. This activity ended on 15 January 1947, when she reduced to reserve in Devonport with only a small care and maintenance party living on board. On 25 June she was steamed to Portsmouth and refitted with extra accommodation and classrooms for service in the HF training Squadron, relieving *Nelson* on 1 October 1947. In July 1948 she supported the sailing events in Portland Harbour during the 1948 Olympic Games. She was refitted in Rosyth in 1949 and visited a number of UK ports on training cruises. In July 1949 she took part in Exercise *Verity* with *Implacable* and *Anson*, a command and control training period with the new NATO alliance. Later in the year she took part in HF exercises with *Implacable* and *Vanguard*.

On 8 March 1950 she returned to Portsmouth,

where she transferred the training task to *Indefatigable*, all ammunition was landed and she was completely destored. She paid off into dockyard hands on 30 June 1950 for a modernisation. Details of *Victorious'* modernisation and her continued operational history are included in Chapter 28.

Formidable

Formidable was laid down by Harland & Wolff at its Belfast shipyard on 17 June 1936 and launched by Lady Kingsley Wood, wife of the Air Minister, on 17 August 1939. The ship was allocated Admiralty Job Number J3948 and Yard Number 1007. It launched itself and began to move thirty minutes early, but Lady Kingsley Wood had the presence of mind to hit the bow with the bottle of Empire wine as it gathered momentum. The wife of a shipyard worker was killed and several men injured, but the ship was undamaged. She was formally completed and commissioned in Belfast on 24 November 1940, and used in a hunt for German surface raiders off St Helena before sailing around the Cape to replace *Illustrious* in the MF,

striking at Italian targets in Somalia as she passed. On 28 March she took part in the Battle of Matapan with an air group comprising 803 and 806 (Fulmar), 826 (Albacore) and 829 (Swordfish/Albacore) NAS. Aircraft damaged *Vittorio Veneto* and *Pola*. In April she covered troop convoys during the evacuation of Commonwealth forces from Greece, and on 26 May her aircraft attacked Scarpanto during operations off Crete. Her fighters shot down six enemy aircraft, but others located *Formidable* and hit her with two 2,000lb bombs and she had to follow *Illustrious* to Norfolk, Virginia, for repairs. Her air group disembarked to North Africa and flew from a number of shore bases with distinction.

On completion of the work she collided with *Illustrious* on 16 December and had to undergo repairs in the UK before sailing to join the EF with 888 (Martlet) and 820 (Albacore) NAS embarked. She sailed around the Cape again and was in

Formidable as flagship of Vice-Admiral Sir Philip Vian, Flag Officer Aircraft Carriers British Pacific Fleet, arrives in Sydney Harbour on 24 August 1945 after operations off Japan. (AUTHOR'S COLLECTION)

Mombasa by the end of May. On 5 July she operated with Admiral Somerville's covering force 250 miles east of Diego Suarez during Operation *Ironclad*, to prevent Japanese intervention, and on 30 July sortied into the Bay of Bengal with *Illustrious* to distract Japanese attention from the landing by US Marines on Guadalcanal. The object was achieved when they were reported by a Japanese Kawanishi H6K 'Mavis' flying-boat and a second shadower was shot down by the CAP fighters. In September 1942 she returned to the UK for a refit in the Clyde. When this was complete she joined Force H with 885 (Seafire), 888 and 893 (Martlet) and 820 (Albacore) NAS embarked.

On 7 November 1942 she formed part of the covering force for Operation *Torch* with *Victorious*. *Furious*, *Biter*, *Dasher*, *Argus* and *Avenger* served with the task groups, providing air support for the landing forces. On 8 November three Albacores laid a smokescreen over the landings at 0400 and another carried out a front-gun attack on a searchlight on the Jette du Nord, extinguishing it. *Formidable*'s aircraft flew CAP and antisubmarine sorties, attacking a U-boat with depth charges on 14 November but with no observed result. On 17 November two Albacores attacked and sank U331

with torpedoes fitted with duplex fuses and set to run at a depth of 12ft and 40 knots. They hit the boat amidships and a Walrus of 700 NAS operating from Algiers subsequently picked up two survivors.

Once the other carriers left, *Formidable* was the only carrier in the Mediterranean for a while in early 1943. On 10 July she was joined in Force H by *Indomitable* and they gave cover for Operation *Husky*, the Allied landings in Sicily. From 9 September *Illustrious* joined *Formidable* in Force H to give cover for Operation *Avalanche*, the Allied landings at Salerno. The escort carriers of Force V provided air defence over the landing beaches and they, in turn, were covered by CAPs from the fleet carriers. *Formidable* flew seventy-four sorties on the first day, seventy-two on the second and eighty on the third. In October she returned to Belfast for a refit, after which she joined the HF with an air group comprising 1841 (Corsair), 827 and 830 (Barracuda) NAS. On 17 July she took part in Operation *Mascot*, an attack on *Tirpitz* in company with *Furious* and *Indefatigable*. In August her air group was enlarged to include 1841 and 1842 (Corsair), 826 and 828 (Barracuda) NAS, and she took part in Operation *Goodwood*, a series of strikes

against *Tirpitz* in company with *Furious*, *Indefatigable*, *Nabob* and *Trumpeter*. After a further refit she left the UK to join the BPF, eventually replacing *Illustrious* in Leyte Gulf on 1 May 1945 for participation in the second series of strikes against the Sakishima Islands as part of Operation *Iceberg*. By then her air group comprised 6 Naval Fighter Wing with 1841 and 1842 (Corsair) NAS and 848 (Avenger) NAS. On 4 May 1945 she was hit by a Mitsubishi A6M 'Zeke' kamikaze aircraft, which crashed into the deck park and put the deck out of action for five hours while temporary repairs were carried out. On 9 May a second kamikaze aircraft hit the flight deck, destroying six aircraft by blast and more in the subsequent fires. Again she was brought back into action, but on 17 May the guns of a Corsair in the hangar were accidentally fired into an Avenger, which exploded, starting a major hangar fire which destroyed or damaged seven Avengers and twenty-one Corsairs. Once again the ship was brought back into action, but she left TF 57 early for Garden Island Dockyard to undergo repairs and modifications to enable her to operate as a flagship.

On 1 July 1945 she replaced *Indomitable* as flagship of Rear Admiral Sir Phillip Vian, Flag Officer Aircraft Carriers BPF, and sailed with TF 37 for operations against the Japanese mainland with 1841 and 1842 (Corsair) NAS, 1844 (Grumman Hellcat) and 848 (Avenger) NAS embarked. On 9 August 1945 Lieutenant R H Grey DSC RCNVR, Senior Pilot of 1841 NAS,

was awarded the Victoria Cross for his conspicuous bravery in leading an attack on an enemy destroyer escort in Onagawa Wan. Like *Victorious*, she left the operational area before the Japanese surrender, disembarked her air group to naval air stations in the Sydney area and prepared for trooping duties. In 1946 she carried out two round trips between the UK and Australia before returning to Portsmouth in November to destore and pay off into reserve.

In March 1947 she was reduced to un-maintained reserve while a number of schemes to

modernise her were considered. However lack of funds delayed implementation and a survey found that the legacy of her extensive wartime damage and her poor material state meant that modernisation was not feasible. After a period moored in the Solent she was sold to breakers in 1953 and subsequently scrapped at Inverkeithing; the first ship of her class to be discarded.

Formidable after being hit by a kamikaze aircraft on 9 May 1945. The aircraft burning fiercely is a Corsair. (AUTHOR'S COLLECTION)

Chapter 12

INDOMITABLE

Technical background

Indomitable was originally intended as the fourth ship of the *Illustrious* class, and ordered as the second ship of the second group. In 1938, however, the Admiralty decided that the thirty-six aircraft her intended sister ships were designed to carry was too small an air group to be effective and that the ideal aircraft complement should be forty-eight. The design of this ship was therefore recast to allow the larger number of aircraft to be embarked. By reducing the thickness of the armour on the hangar sides to 1.5in it was found possible to raise the flight deck by 14ft without adversely affecting stability, and a new upper hangar was worked into this space. The original hangar now became the lower hangar; it was shortened to 168ft and could therefore only be served by the after lift, but retained its original height of 16ft. The area forward of it was converted into extra workshops and accommodation to support the larger air group. Unlike *Ark Royal*, the after lift had a single platform which stopped at flight-deck, upper- and lower-hangar-deck levels. The new upper hangar was only 14ft high, sufficient to give adequate overhead clearance for every aircraft type planned in 1938, since British naval aircraft all had aft-folding wings, but a severe limitation in the longer term. Aircraft on floats could not be struck down into the upper hangar, but it was felt that the lower hangar was available for the rare occasions when floats might be fitted. The flight deck was 14ft higher above the water level than that in *Illustrious*, making her less likely to ship 'green water' in rough seas and a better sea boat overall.

The other major change was the substitution of a larger forward lift for the original. At 33ft wide and 45ft long it allowed aircraft without folding wings to be positioned obliquely and struck down into the upper hangar. By 1942 *Indomitable* was able to carry up to twenty-two Sea Hurricanes, which were fitted on to special trolleys in the upper hangar and stowed obliquely. The remainder of the air group comprised Martlets, Fulmars and Albacores. Later in the war, as more powerful American aircraft became available under Lend/Lease arrangements, the low upper-hangar height became a distinct limitation. Corsairs could not be struck down into the upper hangar and, since she could carry less than her half-sisters in her constricted lower hangar, the decision was taken to operate Grumman F6F Hellcats, which had aft-folding wings and could be struck down into either. Thirty-three could be accommodated in the upper hangar, with Avengers split between both and more aircraft in the deck park, a total of fifty-six being embarked in 1945.

The larger-designed air group required enhanced spaces for workshops, air weapons and fuel, and extra accommodation for aircrew, maintenance personnel and aircraft handling parties. Their provision was the principle reason for shortening the lower hangar. Avgas stowage was increased by 25,000gal, weighing roughly 90 tons. The penalty for the RN's high standard of protection is illustrated by the fact that the tanks for this amount of fuel and their surrounding water reservoirs filled the space that was designed to contain 350 tons of FFO. Despite the major redesign *Indomitable* completed only five months later than *Victorious*, the last of the first group. Like her half-sisters she was completed with over-generous round-downs, especially aft, which were gradually removed in wartime refits. These extended the usable flight deck from 680ft to 745ft and increased the number of aircraft that could be ranged on it.

Indomitable's delayed completion allowed her to

Indomitable shortly after completion in 1941. (Author's collection)

be completed with an extensive array of air-warning and fire-control radars, and when she completed she was, without doubt, the best equipped and most capable British aircraft carrier.

Action damage

On 12 August 1942 at approximately 1845 *Indomitable* was hit by two armour-piercing bombs which defeated and penetrated the flight-deck armour, and by a near miss which caused a hole below the waterline on the port side. Fire broke out in 'A' turret and the captain ordered the forward magazines to be flooded and a 10 degree list to port to be corrected. The latter order was achieved by pumping out water from rapid flood positions to port, and flooding their equivalents to starboard. The hangar fire was contained by closing the armoured doors at either end, but only the forward fire curtains operated, the after one being damaged by blast. The spray system was activated and hoses were used successfully to fight fires in the torpedo body room and the aircraft fabric store. A number of compartments, including mess decks, were partly flooded and subsequently drained by mobile pumps. The flooded magazines were drained the next day. The ship's damage control organisation worked calmly and efficiently, and telephones remained operable. Information was received and orders passed and carried out with very little delay.

On 16 July 1943 at about 0025 *Indomitable* was hit on the lower strake of the port-side armour at 85 station by a torpedo dropped by a single Ju 88 while 90 miles northeast of Malta; it blew a hole 28ft long by 25ft high. Pieces of armour plate

destroyed P2 boiler, and the port boiler room was immediately and completely flooded. The ship immediately listed 12½ degrees to port, and damage control headquarters followed the ship's standing orders and immediately started counter-flooding. This proved to be vital, as the water was within a few inches of flooding the centre boiler room through the fan intake. The ship was upright by 0100 and a reserve of electrical power was available by 0130. There was considerable damage

Indomitable in 1943. (RAY BURT COLLECTION)

Indomitable's flight and hangar decks as built. (AUTHOR'S COLLECTION)

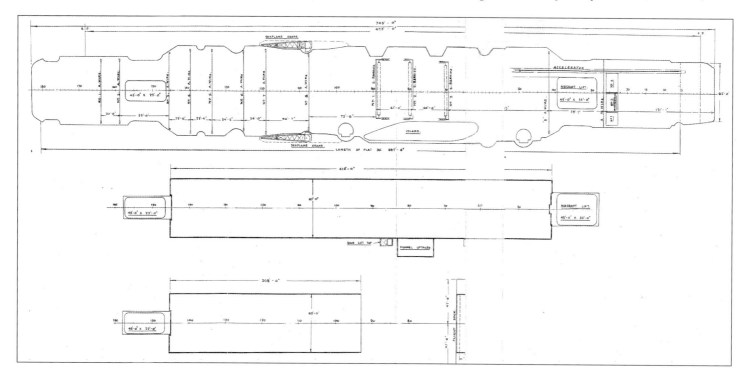

to the port side, but parties of shipwrights were able to shore up bulkheads and rig portable pumps. In summary, the damage control organisation knew their ship well and was able to act quickly and effectively to minimise the effects of the damage.

Accidental damage

On 3 February 1953, during combined HF/MF exercises in the Mediterranean, an explosion occurred below the after end of the island on the starboard side which killed eight men, wounded thirty-two more and caused extensive damage. The subsequent Board of Inquiry believed that a cigarette smoker had contravened orders and detonated vapour leaking from a defective avgas valve. Ten gallantry awards, including two George Medals, were made to men who had fought the fire and rescued survivors from the blast. The damaged compartment and the hole in the ship's side were never repaired, but filled with cement and the outside given a cosmetic coat of paint.

Post-war modernisation

Indomitable's modernisation in 1950 was similar to that carried out earlier with *Illustrious*. The forward part of the flight deck was widened, strengthened and streamlined to be rather like the those of the new light fleet carriers in appearance. It was also lengthened to give the longest possible flat space for ranging aircraft, and the catapult, arrester wires and barriers were upgraded to cope with aircraft up to 20,000lb. A comprehensive radar outfit was installed, including a Type 960 long-range air warning set; a Type 293Q search and target indication set at the top of the foremast, and two Type 277Q height-finding sets, one forward and one aft on the island. There was also a 'YE' aircraft-homing beacon on a mast attached to the funnel and a Type 963 carrier-controlled approach radar on the after part of the island. Some of the multiple 2pdr 'pom-poms' were retained, but the remainder of the close-range armament was standardised on twin and single 40mm Bofors guns.

As with *Indomitable*'s half-sisters, the Admiralty Board considered modernising her more extensively, but there were good reasons for their decision not to do so. The three ships of the first group and the two of the third were more attractive propositions, since design drawings for the reconstruction would apply to more than one hull, but those for *Indomitable* would be limited to the one hull. As work on *Victorious* grew to be more time consuming and expensive it was realised that the armoured hangar might offer solid protection, but as part of the hull structure it was extremely difficult to modify or repair. The repairs carried out in Norfolk, Virginia, during the war had also highlighted this difficulty. Any modernisation would have to result in a single hangar with a clear height of at least 17ft 6in, and that would mean scrapping the hull down to the lower-hangar-deck level and building a new ship upwards from there, probably after reboiling to provide a reasonable hull life expectancy. More limited modernisation was ruled out by the fact that the upper hangar was not high enough to take modern aircraft such as the Hawker Sea Hawk.

It is arguable that, had she been retained longer, 'cocooned' in the Gareloch, she might have made a viable amphibious assault ship or 'commando carrier' with space in the upper hangar for vehicles and overload marines' accommodation, but she would have been a relatively old and expensive ship to run by comparison with the former light fleet carriers that were chosen for the task from 1959. Westland Whirlwind helicopters were 15ft 4in high and could only be struck down into the lower hangar, which would have limited the number embarked to between nine and twelve, far short of the number required for an assault.

Indomitable technical details

Displacement:	29,730 tons deep load
Dimensions:	length 754ft
	beam 116ft 3in
	draught 29ft 5in
Machinery:	3-shaft Parsons geared turbines
	6 Admiralty three-drum boilers
	111,000shp delivering 30½
	knots
Armament:	8 twin 4.5in; 6 octuple 2pdr
	'pom-poms'; numerous 40mm
	Bofors and 20mm Oerlikon
	added after completion
Protection:	3in flight deck; 1.5in hangar
	sides; 4.5in waterline belt;
	1.5in hangar and magazine
	bulkheads; 2.5in magazine
	crowns
Fuel:	4,500 tons FFO
Endurance:	9,000 miles at 18 knots
Complement:	2,100 in 1945 as a flagship

A flight of Seafires over *Indomitable*. (AUTHOR'S COLLECTION)

Indomitable in Leyte Gulf with the BPF during Operation *Iceberg* in 1945. (AUTHOR'S COLLECTION)

Aircraft operating data

Flight deck:	680ft (extended to 745ft in 1943) x 95ft
Hangars:	upper 416ft x 62ft x 14ft
	lower 168ft x 62ft x 16ft
Catapult:	1 BH3 as built; capable of launching 14,000lb at 66 knots end-speed using the tail-down method.
Arrester wires:	7 aft all 11,000lb at 55 knots entry speed as built, pull-out 140ft
	2 forward both 11,000lb at 55 knots, pull-out 140ft
	3 barriers each 11,000lb at 55 knots, pull-out 40ft
Lifts:	forward 33ft wide x 45ft long, serving upper hangar only
	aft 22ft wide x 45ft long, serving upper and lower hangars
Aircraft:	56 in 1945
Aircraft fuel:	75,110gal avgas
Air weapons:	54 x 18in torpedoes as designed; 120 x 500lb bombs; 890 x 250lb bombs/depth charges; 0.303 and 0.5in gun ammunition; flares and pyrotechnics

Individual ship history

Indomitable

Indomitable was ordered from Vickers-Armstrongs and laid down at its Barrow-in-Furness shipyard on 10 November 1937, allocated Admiralty Job Number J3784 and Yard Number 735. Her construction was delayed by design changes but she was launched on 26 March 1940 and completed on 10 October 1941, commissioning in the shipyard on the same day. After sea trials she sailed for the relatively safe waters in the West Indies to work-up with 800 (Fulmar), 880 (Sea Hurricane), 827 and 831 (Albacore) NAS embarked. Later in the month she ran aground off Kingston in Jamaica and had to proceed to

Indomitable had a larger forward lift than her three earlier half-sisters; it can be seen clearly in the down position in this overhead view. The aerodynamic shaping of the island and funnel can also be seen. (AUTHOR'S COLLECTION)

Norfolk Navy Yard in Virginia, where a new lower bow section was fabricated and fitted in only ten days. Her work-up was originally intended to be complete on 22 November 1941, and she was due in Gibraltar on 29 November, after which she was intended to join the EF. This was the day after *Prince of Wales* and *Repulse* sailed for Singapore from Colombo, and the Admiralty War Diary for the period shows that although *Indomitable* was intended to join them, she would have to sail around the Cape as *Prince of Wales* had done, and could not have arrived before their loss on 10 December, even before her plans were delayed by the grounding and subsequent need for repair.

On 10 December she was in Cape Town, taking on board aircraft and spares that had been brought from the UK in the aircraft transport *Engadine*. On 14 January 1942 she arrived in Port Sudan, having disembarked 800 and 827 NAS at Aden and embarked fifty dismantled RAF Hurricanes of 261 Squadron, which were then assembled at sea by naval air mechanics. A day later she sailed, and on 21 January the Hurricanes were flown off in two ranges by RAF pilots to Batavia in Java. In late February a further batch of Hurricanes was ferried to Batavia from Port Sudan, after which *Indomitable* re-embarked her full air group and joined the EF, which already included *Formidable* and *Hermes* off Addu Atoll. In April the Fleet was concentrated as a potential counter to Japanese strikes against Ceylon but failed to bring it to action. This was probably a good thing, as it was outclassed and

Indomitable in February 1953, with Fireflies on deck. (AUTHOR'S COLLECTION)

outnumbered by the same Japanese fast carrier striking force that had attacked Pearl Harbor.

On 20 April *Indomitable* formed part of Force A with *Formidable* and searched island groups for enemy shipping without success. On 5 May she took part in Operation *Ironclad*, the occupation of Diego Suarez, in company with *Illustrious,* from which four Fulmars of 806 NAS were lent to the air group. Aircraft attacked enemy airfields and carried out offensive patrols over the harbour. The Vichy French sloop *D'Entrecasteaux* was sunk by aircraft from *Indomitable* and gunfire from the destroyer *Laforey* on 6 May. Sixty sorties were flown on each of the first two days of the operation, and after its successful outcome she spent a short period based on Kilindini. On 9 July *Indomitable* left Kilindini, escorted by the destroyer *Lightning*, and deployed to the Mediterranean via Mombasa, Durban, Cape Town and Freetown, where they stopped briefly to refuel.

On 8 August 1942 *Indomitable* took part in Operation *Bellows*, a work-up west of Gibraltar to give aircraft carriers from three different fleets the chance to work together before fighting a convoy through to Malta. They included *Indomitable* from the EF, *Victorious* and *Furious* from the HF, and *Eagle* and *Argus* from Force H. On completion *Argus* sailed for the UK and *Furious* went alongside in Gibraltar to pick up thirty-eight RAF Spitfires that were to be ferried to Malta. On 9 August the most heavily defended convoy to Malta passed through the narrows for Operation *Pedestal*; it included fourteen merchant ships and a fighting escort with *Indomitable*, *Victorious* and *Eagle*. *Furious* acted as a ferry carrier. *Indomitable*'s air group

comprised 800 and 880 (Sea Hurricane), 806 (Martlet), 827 and 831 (Albacore) NAS. In the heavy fighting that followed a number of air raids were broken up and thirty enemy aircraft shot down, five of them by Lieutenant R J Cork DSC RN of 880 NAS. On 11 August *Indomitable* was damaged by two bombs and holed by a near miss on the port side. Her damage control worked well and she entered Gibraltar Dockyard on 14 August for emergency repairs.

More extensive repairs were carried out in the Gladstone Dock in Liverpool from 25 August, and she was visited by King George VI and Queen Elizabeth on 18 November. Work was completed in February 1943 and she carried out a work-up in Scapa Flow and the Clyde areas in March. On 21 June she joined Force H in Gibraltar and in July she provided heavy cover for the Allied landings in Sicily, Operation *Husky*, in company with *Formidable*. By then her air group comprised 807, 880 and 899 (Seafire) and 817 (Albacore) NAS. On 16 July 1943 she was hit on the port side by a torpedo from a single Ju 88 which had approached her undetected 90 miles northeast of Malta. The port boiler room was extensively damaged, together with armour and hull plating, and she had to enter Malta Dockyard for emergency repairs, after which she went to Norfolk Navy Yard in Virginia for more extensive repair work. This was completed on 20 April 1944, after which she returned to the UK.

After her arrival she entered Rosyth Dockyard for modifications intended to suit her for operations in the Far East, and she sailed to join the EF on 12 June 1944 in company with *Victorious* and six destroyers. Her air group comprised 5 Naval Fighter Wing with 1839 and 1844 (Hellcat) NAS and 12 TBR Wing with 815 and 817

(Barracuda) NAS. By 24 July she was in Trincomalee, and on 29 August she took part in Operation *Banquet*, a strike against shipping in Emmahaven and Indaroeng with *Victorious*. In September she sailed with *Victorious* again for Operation *Light*, a series of Hellcat photographic reconnaissance missions and a strike against railway infrastructure at Sigli. In mid-October the same two carriers took part in Operation *Millet*, a strike against targets in the Nicobar Islands, after which *Indomitable* carried out a short maintenance period in Bombay before joining 1 ACS in the new BPF in Trincomalee as flagship of Rear Admiral Sir Philip Vian, Rear Admiral Aircraft Carriers BPF. The performance of the Barracuda in tropical temperatures was not good enough, and 815 and 817 NAS were disembarked and replaced by 857 (Avenger) NAS at this time. On 20 December 1944 her aircraft struck at Belawan Deli in company with others from *Illustrious* when bad weather obscured their primary target, the oil refinery at Pangkalan Brandon. On 4 January 1945 she joined *Victorious* and *Indefatigable* in Operation *Lentil*, a strike at Pangkalan Brandon in which accurate weapon delivery caused heavy damage to the refinery.

On 16 January 1945 the BPF left Ceylon for the last time and sailed for strikes against oil refineries in the Palembang complex and passage to Australia. Aircraft from *Indomitable*, *Illustrious*, *Victorious* and *Indefatigable* struck at Pladjoe in Operation *Meridian I* on 24 January, causing considerable damage. After refuelling they struck at Songei Gerong in *Meridian II* on 29 January, causing damage that the Japanese were unable to repair before the war ended and reducing their output of aviation fuel to 35 per cent of the 1944 figure. These were the largest set-piece air attacks

carried out by the RN in the Second World War. The BPF arrived in its new main base, Sydney, in February 1945, and sailed as Task Force 57 to operate with the US Pacific Fleet in March. On 23 March the British carriers joined in Operation *Iceberg*, protecting the left flank of the American amphibious landings on Okinawa against Japanese aircraft flown from Formosa. The British carried out two-day strike cycles before replenishing at sea; when not on task they were replaced by the USN carriers *Suwanee, Chenango, Santee* and *Steamer Bay*, although these smaller ships were not able to deliver the same weight of attack. On 20 April 1 ACS withdrew for a period of rest and replenishment in Leyte Gulf after 32 days at sea.

The BPF sailed from Leyte Gulf to return to operations off the Sakishima Gunto on the American left flank on 1 May 1945. On 4 May, while the battleships *King George V* and *Howe* were detached to bombard Miyako Island, a force of twenty Kamikaze aircraft attacked the BPF. Eight were shot down by CAP fighters, but the number of anti-aircraft guns for close-range defence was significantly reduced by the absence of the battleships and their escorts, with the result that two enemy aircraft broke through and

one of these crashed into *Indomitable*'s flight deck aft. It struck a glancing blow at high speed before going over the side, made no difference to her operational capability, and she continued to operate aircraft. On 25 May the BPF left the operational area and returned to Sydney, where preparations were made for the next operation off the coast of the Japanese mainland, and on 17 June ACS 1 transferred his flag to the repaired *Formidable* and *Indomitable* began a major refit in Garden Island Dockyard in Sydney.

When this work was completed in August she became the flagship of the 11th ACS, flying the flag of Rear Admiral C H J Harcourt. The remainder of the squadron comprised the new light fleet carriers *Vengeance, Colossus, Glory* and *Venerable*. The plan was for 1 ACS and 11 ACS to alternate in action as part of a vast Anglo/American Pacific Fleet for Operation *Olympic*, the invasion of Japan in the autumn, but the war ended earlier than anticipated and 11 ACS was used for a quite different purpose. On 27 August *Indomitable* sailed from Sydney in company with *Venerable* and the cruiser *Swiftsure* for the reoccupation of the British colony of Hong Kong. Four days later aircraft from the two carriers bombed and strafed Japanese

Indomitable in dry dock in Bombay during 1944. (Author's collection)

suicide boats that had sailed to attack British forces as they arrived, and they subsequently destroyed others hidden in a sheltered bay on Lamma Island near Aberdeen Harbour. On 1 September 1945 armed landing parties from *Indomitable* took over the Dockyard and the airfield at Kai Tak, which briefly became a naval air station. Admiral Harcourt became the acting Governor General and accepted the formal Japanese surrender, while parties of sailors from the growing fleet moored in the harbour got the trains, trams, power and port facilities running again. They even set up mounted patrols of the streets to keep order.

On 27 September *Indomitable* sailed for the British forward base at Manus in the Admiralty Islands, taking the opportunity to dump unwanted ammunition on the way. After Manus she returned to Sydney and landed all her aircraft and stores before embarking over 1,000 Service personnel as passengers for the voyage back to the UK. She arrived in Portsmouth on 20 November 1945 and recommissioned with a reduced ship's company for service on trooping duties between the UK and

Indomitable under tow to the breaker's yard at Inverkeithing. (FERRES WALKER COLLECTION VIA STEVE BUSH)

Australia. She carried out a number of return trips, the last commencing on 15 October 1946, when she left Portsmouth carrying replacement personnel, aircraft and even former German yachts to Malta, Singapore and Hong Kong. She returned to Portsmouth on 18 December 1946, paid off into reserve and was laid up in Fareham Creek in January 1947. In 1950 she was taken in hand in Portsmouth Dockyard for a limited modernisation to allow her to recommission with the HF as an operational carrier.

In 1951 she recommissioned and became the flagship of the HF, flying the flag of its C-in-C, Admiral Sir Philip Vian. Her new air group comprised 802 (Sea Fury), 820 (Firefly), 801 and 809 (de Havilland Sea Hornet) and 813 (Blackburn Firebrand) NAS. She was the first RN carrier to operate a helicopter permanently, having a single Westland Dragonfly embarked for air-sea rescue duties. In May 1952 *Indomitable* was relieved as fleet flagship by the battleship *Vanguard* and she became the flagship of the Heavy Squadron until relieved by *Eagle* in that role during 1953. On 3 February an explosion killed eight men and wounded others but, since the ship was nearing the end of its projected life, repairs were not carried out.

On 15 June 1953 she was present at HM Queen Elizabeth II's Coronation Review at Spithead, and a day later she sailed for her last spell of flying in a trial that links her to the modern era. On 16 June she embarked a de Havilland Sea Vampire fighter to fly a number of circuits to evaluate the prototype mirror landing aid, an optical landing system that evolved into the deck landing projector sight adopted by the RN, USN and every other carrier navy to this day. On 18 June 1953 the Sea Vampire carried out a free take-off to return to RNAS Culdrose, the last aircraft to use her deck. By 28 August 1953 *Indomitable* had been destored and she was decommissioned in Portsmouth Naval base. Her ship's company was reallocated to the new carriers *Ark Royal* and *Bulwark* as nucleus crews with carrier experience. On 5 October she left Portsmouth under tow for Rosyth, where she lay for a while in unmaintained reserve, and in October 1954 she was towed to the Gareloch and moored to a buoy. On 26 September 1955 she was sold to the British Iron and Steel Corporation and was subsequently broken up for scrap.

CHAPTER 13

IMPLACABLE GROUP

Implacable anchored in the Clyde on 21 August 1944. (AUTHOR'S COLLECTION)

Technical background

The Admiralty planned a significant expansion of its embarked air groups after Sir Thomas Inskip, the Minister for Defence Co-ordination, returned full control of embarked aviation to the Royal Navy in 1937. *Indomitable*'s modification had marked the first step away from the base-line *Illustrious* design, and the Board decided to go a step further for the two ships of the third group, which were to be ordered in 1938. The new requirement called for an air group of fifty-four, and an increase in speed to at least 32 knots and 35 knots if possible; optimistically it specified that there was to be no increase in the standard displacement from 23,000 tons. Before the first ship was laid down the Board also asked for an increase in the thickness of the armour on the hangar sides.

The two new ships, named *Implacable* and *Indefatigable*, underwent considerable redesign to meet the new requirement. They were 26ft longer than *Illustrious* but kept the same beam. The three-shaft arrangement could not deliver the power needed for the extra 2 knots, so a new four-shaft layout was 'shoehorned' into the same hull width as the first group. The increased quantity of exhaust gases required a larger funnel to clear them, and this was set in a larger island, a major

recognition feature that differentiated the third group from their earlier half-sisters. The armoured hangars used the same thicknesses of metal as *Indomitable* except for the bulkheads, which were 2in thick instead of 1.5in; compensation for the extra weight was achieved by lowering the height of the lower hangar to 14ft, the same as the upper. Thus freeboard at the flight deck was 50ft, 2ft less than *Indomitable* and 12ft higher than *Illustrious*.

Both ships were completed in 1944 after delays when manpower was taken from them to work on other projects which were given higher short-term priority. Their outfit reflected the progress made since the first ship was completed in 1940. Both had extensive air and surface warning, target indication and fire-control radars, and a considerably enhanced close-range armament that eventually included both 40mm Bofors and 20mm Oerlikon mountings. The 4.5in gun turrets were modified with flat tops and set slightly lower so that they did not obtrude above flight-deck level as they had done on the earlier ships, although their positioning still caused bottlenecks in deck width that adversely affected aircraft ranging.

Air arrangements were modified and the arrester wires, catapult and lifts were all strengthened to operate 20,000lb aircraft. The layout followed *Indomitable* in that the forward lift was larger but

served only the upper hangar. The smaller after lift served both the upper and lower hangars, and the lower hangar was extended 40ft further forward than that of *Indomitable*. The decision to accept the lower hangar height in both hangars followed acceptance that these ships would not be required to strike down aircraft on floats. They were the largest British aircraft carriers built to date and the first that were not required to operate floatplanes. While 14ft seemed a reasonable compromise in 1938, it soon limited the type of aircraft that could be embarked, and neither ship could embark Corsairs when they became available under Lend/Lease arrangements. With insufficient numbers of Hellcats available in 1945, both ships had to operate the fragile and short-ranged Seafire, which could be embarked in large numbers but was unsuited to operations in the Pacific. Some increase was made in the quantity of avgas that could be stowed, but these ships had enough for only five sorties for each aircraft embarked, hardly sufficient for sustained strike operations. Stowage for air weapons was also barely adequate by 1945.

Both ships were originally designed to go through the Panama Canal, but during their

Implacable being towed down the Clyde from her builder's yard in 1944. (AUTHOR'S COLLECTION)

construction it became obvious that it was important to achieve the maximum amount of space in the ranging area aft, and the deck was widened in the space forward of the after 4.5in turrets, allowing up to three more aircraft in the range. The structure to support it, however, precluded passage through Panama. Still more space was made available by making the top of the 4.5in turrets flat and flush with the flight deck, since it was realised that firing across the deck was impractical and likely to damage aircraft. The ability to wheel or taxi aircraft across the turret tops had the effect of widening the deck in the area that had been described as an undesirable 'gully' in the earlier ships of the group.

There were many design weaknesses which limited the usefulness of these large ships. The fourth machinery unit required considerably more stoker-mechanics than the earlier group designs,

and the number of radars and short-range weapons added during build added still further to the size of the ship's company that had to be accommodated. By 1945 these ships embarked forty-eight Seafires, twelve Fireflies and twenty-one Avengers, which needed roughly double the original estimate of manpower to fly, maintain and handle on deck and in the hangar. Workshops were inadequate and much of the space designed for use as the lower hangar had to be used to provide workshops and accommodation. By far the greatest weakness, however, was the hangar height of only 14ft, which proved to present too great a restriction on the type of aircraft that could be embarked. These weaknesses proved fatal after 1945, as larger and heavier aircraft came into service, and only *Implacable* saw operational service after 1945. The original design had failed to provide sufficient space to allow for aircraft growth in a period of dynamic advance. Consequently these two ships, which had taken five years to build and were the largest carriers yet completed for the RN, spent only three years and eighteen moths respectively in service.

Post-war modernisation plans

Implacable was meant to follow *Victorious* in the RN's planned aircraft carrier modernisation programme. Originally work on *Victorious* was expected to last from mid-1950 to 1955 and to cost an estimated £10,335,000. *Implacable* was to be taken in hand in November 1953, with completion projected for April 1957 at an estimated cost of £10,460,000. As the cost and complexity of work on *Victorious* spiralled upwards, however, the Board took the decision that it would be cheaper to build a new ship, and work on *Implacable* was cancelled.

The modernisation would have entailed stripping the hull down to the lower hangar deck level, reboilering while there was access and then building up a new hangar with at least 17ft 6in clear height, over which there was to be a new deck for accommodation and offices running the whole

Implacable's armour protection, showing how it differed from that of the basic *Illustrious* design. (AUTHOR'S COLLECTION)

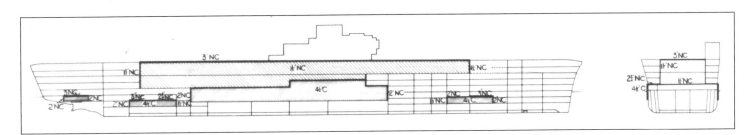

length of the ship under the flight deck, pierced by two large centreline lifts. Finally, there would have been a new armoured flight deck, a new island and a new armament of twin USN 3in/50 guns identical to those fitted in *Victorious*. Clearly lessons would have been read across from *Victorious*, but the timescale and cost would have been far beyond the estimates. She could not even have been considered for use, unmodified, as a commando carrier, since Westland Whirlwind helicopters had a height of 15ft 4in and could not be struck down into either hangar despite their usefulness as a vehicle 'garage'. The decision not to proceed and to seek approval to build a new ship instead was a sensible one.

Implacable Class technical details

Displacement:	32,110 tons deep load
Dimensions:	length 766ft 2in
	beam 131ft 3in
	draught 29ft 4in
Machinery:	4 shaft Parsons geared turbines
	8 Admiralty three-drum boilers
	148,000shp delivering 32 knots
Armament:	8 twin 4.5in turrets; 5 octuple
	2pdr 'pom-poms'; 3 quadruple
	2pdr 'pom-poms'; numerous
	40mm Bofors and 20mm
	Oerlikon
Protection:	3in flight deck; 4.5in waterline
	belt; 2in hangar sides and
	bulkheads; 4.5in magazine

	sides; 3in magazine crowns
Fuel:	4,690 tons FFO
Endurance:	12,000 miles at 10 knots
Complement:	2,300 in 1945

Aircraft operating data

Flight deck:	760ft x 90ft armoured steel
Hangars:	upper 456ft x 62ft x 14ft
	lower 208ft x 62ft x 14ft
Catapult:	1 BH3 – 20,000lb at 56 knots
	end speed
Arrester wires:	9 aft each 20,000lb at 60 knots
	entry speed
	3 forward each 20,000lb at 60
	knots entry speed
	3 barriers each 20,000lb with a
	40ft pull-out
Lifts:	forward 45ft long x 33ft wide,
	serving upper hangar only
	aft 45ft long x 22ft wide,
	serving both hangars
Aircraft:	81 in 1945
Aircraft fuel:	94,650gal avgas
Air weapons:	as designed
	54 x 18in torpedoes
	120 x 500lb SAP bombs
	890 x 250lb bombs
	1100 smaller bombs and depth
	charges
	0.303in gun ammunition; flares
	and pyrotechnics

Implacable arrives in Sydney in 1945 with 2,200 Australian Army personnel on board, having transported them from Borneo. (*Author's collection*)

Individual ship histories

Implacable

Implacable was ordered from the Fairfield Shipbuilding and Engineering Company on Clydeside in 1938 and laid down on 21 February 1939. She was allocated Admiralty Job Number J1672 and Yard Number 672. Work on her was suspended in 1940 when higher priority was given to the completion of destroyers and convoy escorts. After resumption of work she was launched on 10 December 1942 and eventually commissioned in Fairfield's shipyard on 22 May 1944. After that she carried out contractor's sea trials which revealed a considerable number of defects, these being rectified in Rosyth Dockyard between 16 June and 28 August, when she was formally accepted into service.

She embarked Number 2 TBR Wing comprising 828 and 841 (Barracuda) NAS in late August and began to work-up in the Clyde areas. On 22 September 1771 (Firefly) NAS joined the air group, but the Seafire Wing intended for her was still re-equipping and training replacement aircrew after service in *Furious*. On 7 October she joined the HF in Scapa Flow, and a week later

sailed to join ships searching for the *Tirpitz*, which had moved from Kaa Fjord to Tromso. A section of Fireflies located and photographed the German ship off Haakoy Island, but a request to launch a strike with Barracudas was firmly rejected by the Admiralty owing to the lack of any escort fighters. Subsequent sweeps by Fireflies damaged a 4,700-ton ship at Mosjoen and destroyed three enemy aircraft on the ground at Soreisen. On 26 October Number 24 Naval Fighter Wing, comprising 887 and 894 (Seafire) NAS, embarked and *Implacable* took part in Operation *Athletic*, strikes on Bodo, Rorvik and Lodings, during which forty Barracudas dropped 27 tons of bombs.

On 28 October 1944 her Barracudas carried out the last operational airborne torpedo attack by the RN. Six enemy merchant ships were sunk, including one of 2,693 tons, and seven other ships were damaged, for the loss of one Barracuda. Additionally, U-1060 was driven on to a reef and destroyed. On 30 October *Implacable* returned to Scapa Flow and disembarked 24 Wing. She sailed again on 8 November and embarked Number 38 Naval Fighter Wing, comprising 801 and 880 (Seafire) NAS together with the same Firefly and Barracuda units as before. The air group gave cover for aircraft from escort carriers that were laying mines off the Norwegian coast. On 27 November she took part in Operation *Provident*, in which Barracudas and Fireflies sank two enemy ships in a convoy off Alster Island and damaged four others. Fighters damaged the escorts with cannon fire. A day later high seas damaged *Implacable*'s bow and she returned to Scapa Flow for minor repairs by the fleet maintenance group. On 4 December she sailed to provide cover for another HF minelaying operation, and on 8 December she took part in Operation *Urbane*, during which Fireflies from 1771 NAS and Wildcats from *Trumpeter* sank a German minesweeper. On 15 December 1944 she entered Rosyth Dockyard for a refit to prepare her for service with the BPF.

The refit was completed on 10 March 1945 and she embarked an air group comprising an expanded 38 Naval Fighter Wing with forty-eight Seafires; 1771 (Firefly) NAS with twelve aircraft and 828 (Avenger) NAS with twenty-one aircraft, the largest air group embarked in a British carrier up to that time. She sailed on 16 March to join the BPF, working-up off Ceylon in April and arriving in Sydney in May. In June 1945 she joined the other carriers of 1 ACS at the forward operating base at Manus Island as they returned from Operation *Iceberg*, and on 16 June she sailed for Operation *Inmate*, strikes against the Japanese base on Truk Island, with *Ruler* acting as a spare deck.

In early July *Implacable* worked-up off Manus in company with *Victorious* and *Formidable*, and on 6 July she sailed with task Force 37 of the BPF for operations off the Japanese mainland. The British task force joined the US Fast carrier Task Force, TF 38, off Honshu on 16 July, the combined fleets 'stretching as far as the eye could see' in the words of one RN pilot.

On 17 July 1945 aircraft from 1 ACS struck at targets in the Tokyo Plain, and over the next 25 days bad weather, replenishment cycles and the need to stay clear of atomic bomb attacks limited operational flying to only eight days, but *Implacable*'s aircraft flew over 1,000 sorties and hit airfields, shipyards, shipping, factories and railway installations. On 10 August she flew seventy offensive sorties against targets in Honshu. After replenishment on 11 August she withdrew for passage to Sydney in company with *Victorious* and *Formidable*. She arrived in Sydney on 24 August and then spent two months repatriating Allied former prisoners of the Japanese to Australia and Canada. On 18 October she sailed from Vancouver to repatriate Dutch personnel to Balikpapan in Borneo, after which she ferried Australian Army personnel home from New Guinea.

In December 1945 she carried out a defect rectification period in Sydney to prepare for operational flying once more, after which she embarked 801 (Seafire), 828 (Avenger) and 1790 (Firefly) NAS for a tour of Australian and New Zealand waters. On 23 January 1946 she arrived at Melbourne for a very successful visit in company with *Indefatigable*, *Glory*, *Armada* and *Tuscan*. On 25 January a thousand sailors from the combined ship's companies marched through Melbourne, watched by

over a quarter of a million Australians. The fleet sailed on 31 January, and *Implacable* was refitted in Garden Island Dockyard in Sydney. On completion she sailed for the UK on 5 May 1946, arriving at Portsmouth after disembarking the air group on 3 June. She subsequently joined the HF with a reduced ship's company as a deck landing training carrier.

In February 1947 she took part in exercises in the Western Mediterranean with *Ocean*, but had no air group of her own embarked. In April 1947 she was refitted for further operational service and recommissioned in October. Her new air group included new aircraft types which were not ready, so she replaced *Illustrious* temporarily as a trials carrier. She underwent a further short refit in Rosyth in October 1948 to equip her to be the flagship of the HF, emerging in December. In April 1949 she embarked her new air group, now designated the 1st Carrier Air Group and comprising 801 (Sea Hornet) and 813 (Firebrand) NAS. On 29 April she hoisted the flag of Admiral Sir Philip Vian. Her air group remained small because of a shortage of aircrew, but it was augmented for the Autumn Cruise with 702 (Sea Vampire) NAS, the jet fighter evaluation unit, which operated very successfully from the deck. In 1950 the air group was temporarily augmented by 815 (Barracuda) NAS, which was normally employed on antisubmarine trials at RNAS Eglinton in Northern Ireland.

Implacable paid off into reserve on 13 September 1950 after disembarking her air group. She was maintained by a small ship's company and work was slowly taken forward to equip her with extra accommodation and classrooms in the former hangars to equip her as a training ship. She

Indefatigable steams up the Channel on the last leg of her journey home from the BPF in 1946. The Seafire on deck appears to have hit the forward barrier and is being removed by 'Jumbo', the mobile crane. (AUTHOR'S COLLECTION)

recommissioned in January 1952 as flagship of the HF Training Squadron, a task which involved some sea time and kept her in running condition. She was present at the Coronation Review for HM Queen Elizabeth II at Spithead on 15 June 1953, and on 10 October she sailed with a battalion of the Argyle and Sutherland Highlanders from Plymouth to Trinidad as part of a reinforcement operation to deal with a crisis ashore in British Guiana. On 19 August 1954 the battleship *Vanguard* took over as flagship of the Training Squadron and *Implacable* was destored before being decommissioned on 1 September 1954. The plan to modernise her having been cancelled, she was placed on the Disposal List and sold to breakers on 27 October 1955. Subsequently towed to Inverkeithing, she was broken up for scrap from November 1955 onwards.

Indefatigable

Ordered from John Brown and Company of Clydebank in 1938 and laid down on 3 November 1939, *Indefatigable* was allocated Admiralty Job Number J1565, Yard Number 565 and was

Amidships detail of *Implacable* as she enters Vancouver with repatriated former prisoners of the Japanese in 1945. Temporary sports pitches have been marked out on the flight deck to help keep her passengers entertained. (AUTHOR'S COLLECTION)

Implacable coming alongside in Melbourne for a port visit in January 1946. (Author's collection)

launched on 8 December 1942. She was formally completed and commissioned at Clydebank On 3 May 1944, after which she carried out sea trials before joining the HF at Scapa Flow in July and embarking an air group comprising 24 Naval Fighter Wing with 894, 880 and 887 (Seafire) NAS; 1770 (Firefly) NAS and 9 TBR Wing with 820 and 825 (Barracuda) NAS. Her first operational sortie was Operation *Mascot*, a strike against *Tirpitz* in Kaa Fjord which was frustrated by a smokescreen up to 800ft which obscured the target.

On 2 August she sailed for Operation *Turbine*, a sweep through the Norwegian Leads during which fighters strafed and destroyed German radar and communications installations ashore. A week later she provided cover during Operation *Offspring* with a reduced air group comprising 894 and 897 (Seafire) and 852 (Avenger) NAS while aircraft from *Nabob* and *Trumpeter* laid mines off the Norwegian coast. Fighters attacked Gossen Airfield and destroyed six Messerschmitt Bf 110

fighters on the ground and a radar station. On 22 August she took part in Operation *Goodwood*, a series of strikes against *Tirpitz* in Kaa Fjord which damaged the battleship but failed to inflict fatal damage. Operation *Divan*, intended strikes on targets north of the Lofoten Islands in September, had to be cancelled because of bad weather.

In November 1944 *Indefatigable* was allocated to the new BPF, and she sailed from Portsmouth on 19 November with an air group made up with 24 Naval Fighter Wing comprising 887 and 894 (Seafire) NAS, 1770 (Firefly) and 820 (Avenger) NAS. She arrived in Colombo on 10 December, joined 1 ACS and worked-up before taking part in Operation *Lentil*, a strike against the oil refinery at Pangkalan Brandan in Sumatra in company with *Victorious*. On 16 January 1945 she sailed with the BPF for Operation *Meridian*, strikes against the oil refineries at Pladjoe and Songei Gerong near Palembang in Sumatra. In both strikes 24 Wing was limited to providing CAP over the fleet, but the Avengers and Fireflies joined in the striking forces. In *Meridian II* on 29 January Seafires destroyed five out of seven Kawasaki Ki-48 'Lily' bombers that attacked the fleet; a Corsair from *Victorious* and a

Hellcat from *Indomitable* splashed the other two. *Indefatigable* arrived in Sydney on 10 February together with the bulk of the BPF to prepare for operations against the Japanese in the Pacific.

On 15 March 1945 she concentrated with the BPF, now designated Task Force 57 in the USN system, and prepared for Operation *Iceberg*, supporting the Fifth Fleet's left flank during the amphibious landings in Okinawa. Strikes against airfields in the Sakishima Islands were sustained to prevent Japanese aircraft staging through them to attack American shipping off the invasion beaches. Operations started after a refuelling stop at Ulithi Atoll at the end of March. On 25 March *Indefatigable* received two replacement Seafires and a Firefly from the replenishment carrier *Striker* while the fleet refuelled at sea. Back in action on 26 March, deck movement caused some strike sorties to be cancelled and caused a number of deck landing accidents involving Seafires, and a day later two Seafires collided while forming up after take-off; both pilots were lost.

On 1 April 1945 *Indefatigable* was the first of the BPF carriers to be hit by a kamikaze aircraft. It hit at the base of the island, killing twenty-one men and wounding a further twenty-seven, but the flight deck was operable after only thirty minutes and the ship was 'reasonably operational' that evening. On 5 April she received three Seafires, an Avenger and a Firefly from *Striker*, but when she resumed strikes Seafires continued to be damaged in deck landing accidents at a rate beyond that at which they could be replaced, and the number available continued to decline. On 9 April one Seafire, one Avenger and one Firefly were flown on from *Striker*, but a day later a Seafire crashed into the after-barrier stanchion, destroying both itself and the stanchion. A temporary replacement was rigged by sunset to keep her in action. By this stage *Indefatigable* was short of seventeen Seafires and a Firefly, and a further eleven Seafires, two Fireflies and two Avengers were damaged beyond the ability of ship's staff to repair. On 16 April a Seafire bounced over two barriers and crashed into the forward deck park, Fly 1, killing a maintenance rating and writing off both itself and an Avenger. It is hardly surprising that 1 ACS complained that the Seafire was totally unsuited to Pacific operations, and there was concern that a second Seafire-equipped carrier was due to join the fleet. On 7 June *Indefatigable* returned to Sydney with the BPF for an operational turn-round. Machinery defects had to be rectified, and her departure was delayed until after the other three carriers had sailed for operations off the Japanese mainland.

Indefatigable finally sailed from Sydney on 12 July 1945, and made a high-speed passage to the operational area. Improvements had been made to the Seafires, including the procurement of larger drop-tanks which gave them the radius of action to escort Avenger strikes and even carry out interdiction operations of their own with bombs. A concentrated period of pilot training had also reduced the number of deck landing incidents by the time she returned to action. By August she was in action with the BPF, which formed TF 37 of the Anglo/American Third fleet, and on 9 August her aircraft flew sweeps over airfields on the Japanese mainland which resulted in the destruction of over fifty enemy aircraft for the loss of seven RN aircraft and five pilots. The last day of planned operations before the BPF was due to withdraw to Australia to prepare for Operation *Olympic*, the Allied invasion of Japan in the autumn, was 10 August. However, with the unforeseen collapse of Japan and the imminent surrender, a token BPF force including *Indefatigable,* two battleships, cruisers and destroyers remained with the Third Fleet to be 'in at the finish'. The force came under the direct orders of Admiral McCain USN and formed part of TF 38. On 13 August strikes were carried

out in the Tokyo area, after which the carriers refuelled at sea.

On 15 August 1945, in the absence of news about the timing of the ceasefire, dawn strikes were launched and *Indefatigable*'s Avengers were attacked by twelve Mitsubishi 'Zero' fighters. In the last air combat of the war 24 Wing Seafires shot down eight Zeros for the loss of one of their own. An Avenger gunner destroyed a ninth Japanese aircraft during an attack on a chemical factory. Operations were halted at 0700, but several kamikaze aircraft subsequently attacked the fleet, one of them narrowly missing *Indefatigable*. She joined the American carriers *Essex*, *Wasp* and *Randolph* in Task Group 38.3 and flew CAP sorties over the fleet and tactical reconnaissance sorties looking for Allied prisoners of war in their camps and dropping supplies to them. On completion of this task she anchored near the flagships in Tokyo Bay. After the Japanese surrender, signed on the USS *Missouri* on 2 September 1945, *Indefatigable* spent several moths ferrying Commonwealth former prisoners and internees to Australia.

At the end of 1945 she resumed duty as an operational carrier within the BPF, and in January 1946 she visited Melbourne with *Implacable*, *Glory*, *Armada* and *Tuscan*. After returning to the UK she

was destored and reduced to reserve in Portsmouth during December. Shortages of manpower prevented her being brought forward for operational service, and her low hangar height limited the number of aircraft she could embark. In 1949 she was brought out of reserve and had messdecks and classrooms built into the former hangars to fit her for use as a training ship; she recommissioned for service in the HF Training Squadron in 1950. In February 1952 she was secured in Dover Harbour to act as a saluting ship when foreign royal families arrived for the state funeral of His Late Majesty King George VI. On 15 June 1953 she was present at the Coronation Review of the Fleet at Spithead by Her Majesty Queen Elizabeth II.

In August 1954 the light fleet carriers *Ocean* and *Theseus* assumed duty as training ships within the HF, since their requirement for manpower was less and they were cheaper to operate than the big fleet carriers. In September 1954 *Indefatigable* was destored and reduced to reserve at Rosyth, and in June 1955 she was towed to the Gareloch and placed on the Disposal List. She was subsequently sold to the British iron and Steel Corporation and towed out of the Gareloch on 4 November 1956 to be broken up for scrap at Dalmuir.

Indefatigable visiting Wellington, New Zealand, in 1946, with Seafires, Fireflies and Avengers on deck. (AUTHOR'S COLLECTION)

CHAPTER 14

BRITISH-BUILT ESCORT CARRIERS AND MAC-SHIPS

B etween 1918 and 1940 the Admiralty concentrated on the development of aircraft carriers capable of supporting the battle fleet in action, and opposition from the RAF had made it difficult to equip and man even the modest force that was created. Some attention was given to trade protection, but Coastal Command of the RAF had responsibility for operations to detect and attack hostile shipping in European waters and active sonar, known originally as Asdic, was believed to have given escorts the edge against submarines. In the 1914-18 war most U-boat operations had been confined to coastal waters, and even after Nazi Germany was perceived as a threat in the mid-1930s it was by no means obvious that, in the event of war, a new generation of U-boats could break through the Coastal Command 'barrier' to operate in the open ocean. Surface raiders were seen as a greater threat, and these would be contained by the battle fleet and detached forces created for the purpose, which could include aircraft carriers.

Technical background

The Admiralty showed some interest in trade protection carriers in 1936, but came to the conclusion that there were insufficient funds to build, equip and operate such ships in the

peacetime fleet. Despite this, DNC was tasked to produce sketch designs for conversions that could be taken forward in an emergency; these included the Union Castle liner *Winchester Castle* of 20,109 tons, completed in 1930, and the Shaw, Savill Line *Waipawa* of 12,500 tons, completed in 1934. The pressure of rearmament work prevented any detailed drawings being prepared, but the genesis of the concept of converting suitable merchant ships into utilitarian carriers for tasks unconnected with main fleets survived. 'Auxiliary aircraft carriers', as they were termed, appeared on the agenda of conferences held in 1937 and 1938 to discuss the protection of seaborne trade in the war that appeared increasingly likely, but they were rejected on both occasions on the basis that merchant shipping was required for 'other more important services'. Even the outbreak of war in 1939 failed to change this view, since 'auxiliary carrier' conversions were expected to take a year or more to convert using scarce shipbuilding resources, and the Ministry of War Transport refused to allocate merchant ships for the purpose.

Initially the war followed the anticipated pattern. Cruisers were formed into hunting groups, some of them with carriers, to search the oceans for German raiders, but the 1939 'Fighting Instructions' failed to see the need for control of the third dimension over convoys and stated that 'small escort forces and evasion can be relied upon

to provide sufficient security during the ocean passage'. Coastal Command and local flotillas were to augment the close escort in the littoral danger areas approaching ports. However, the fall of Norway and France in the summer of 1940 changed the picture dramatically. Germany's U-boats could range far out into the Atlantic from bases such as Lorient, unlike their First World War predecessors, and attack convoys where their ocean escorts were minimal and Coastal Command could not reach. Aircraft such as the Focke-Wulf Fw 200s of KG40 could locate convoys without opposition, especially those heading for Gibraltar and in the eastern Atlantic, and attack them with bombs. Desperate measures were taken to counter this air threat, including fighter catapult ships manned by the RN, with a handful of fighters that could be launched by catapult but not recovered, and catapult-armed merchants ships or CAM-Ships. The latter were cargo-carrying merchant ships fitted with a single RAF-manned Hurricane fighter on a catapult fitted over the bow. If launched out of range of land, the fighter had to be ditched near the convoy, with the certain loss of the aircraft and the possible loss of the pilot. This led to an understandable reluctance to launch in any but the most ideal circumstances.

In the autumn of 1940 Captain Mathew Slattery RN, the Director of Air Material at the Admiralty, proposed fitting the simplest possible flight deck and arrester wires on to suitable merchant hulls so that they could launch fighters in defence of convoys and, critically, recover them after combat. The Ministry of War Transport still refused to allow merchant ships to be taken up from trade for the purpose but, after Prime Minister Winston Churchill's 'Atlantic Directive', agreed that ships already under Admiralty control could be used. Steps to convert the first operational escort carrier followed. The Admiralty subsequently drew up a table of features to be taken into account in ships considered for conversion, including size, speed and propulsion. Three broad classes were designated A, B and C, the first having the best features and the last being the most austere.

Because the RN had too few fleet carriers, the Admiralty saw the new escort carriers as general-purpose vessels capable of a wide range of tasks. Some were fitted as 'assault' carriers capable of operating fighters in support of amphibious operations. Others were fitted for antisubmarine operations, and both received British radars and sophisticated operations rooms capable of bringing together information from a wide range of sensors and 'fusing' it to build up a tactical picture for the command.

Following Captain Slattery's proposal, a captured German merchant ship renamed *Empire Audacity* and originally intended for use as an ocean boarding vessel was allocated for conversion into an auxiliary aircraft carrier, and work was completed in six months. The bridge, funnel and masts were removed and a flight deck built over the accommodation structure amidships. Unlike previous British aircraft carriers, the flight deck was a lightweight superstructure and incorporated expansion joints. The space between the hull and the flight deck was partly plated-in aft, but there was no hangar and therefore no need for a lift, and no workshops. The exhaust from the single diesel engine was led out through new trunking to starboard below flight-deck level, and platforms were fitted to port and starboard about 100ft aft of the bow for ship control and visual signalling. They were about 4ft below flight-deck level and joined by a cross-connecting passageway under the flight deck. These positions offered only a limited arc of visibility to the officer conning the ship. Little could be seen to port from the starboard

position, for instance, and the captain was known to be unhappy about operating inside the convoy at night as a consequence. This may have contributed to his decision to remain outside the convoy and, ultimately, to the ship's loss. The installation of an island from which the ship could be adequately controlled in close proximity to other vessels was considered to be an essential development for subsequent types of escort carrier. A single mast was stepped by the starboard conning position. Windbreaks were fitted to the side of the deck aft which could be pulled up to provide some protection for the aircraft against the elements, but all maintenance, refuelling and rearming had to be carried out on deck. A single 4in gun and several close-range weapons were fitted. Aircraft maintenance personnel used portable outfits of tools and spare parts.

In view of the limited engineering facilities on board, a special, simplified arrester gear system was installed capable of stopping a 9,000lb aircraft at an entry speed of 55 knots relative to the deck. The work to produce the gear was justified by the expectation that a number of mercantile conversions would follow. There was some discussion about the number and type of aircraft she would embark, and a mixture of fighters and Swordfish was considered, but an all-fighter air group was eventually chosen, to offset the lack of air-defence capability in escort groups. The American-built Grumman Martlet was chosen as the most robust carrier fighter available at the time, and the only one available to the RN that

had been designed for operation at sea. Since her machinery was of a type with which the RN was not familiar, most of *Audacity*'s technical sailors came from the Merchant Navy, serving with the RN under T.142X articles. Pilots were accommodated in the former passenger cabins, and very little of the ship below the flight deck was altered.

There was just enough space on the flight deck to range six Martlets in a 'herring-bone' pattern aft, leaving just enough space for the furthest forward to carry out a free take-off. There were two arrester wires, a third 'safety' wire and a single barrier. An aircraft that engaged the safety wire was likely to engage the barrier, but at a reduced speed which would cause less damage. Aircraft were usually launched in sections of two, and for recoveries the aircraft on deck were pushed by hand forward of the barrier, and then aft into the range again when it was complete. The aircraft were not flown at night, and, since the ship operated fully darkened, maintenance to prepare for dawn launches had to be carried out by dim torchlight. Aircraft ammunition and avgas were stowed in the former holds, the latter meeting the usual RN safety standards, which reduced the amount that could be carried.

To offer effective air defence of a convoy with her limited number of fighters, it was essential that *Audacity* was fitted with radar, and during her conversion she received the second prototype Type 79B 'single-masted' air warning set. This carried both transmitter and receiver on the same mast and was fitted at the very top of the single pole-mast just aft of the starboard conning position. Her fighter direction officer was an RNVR former Cambridge don who had just taken part in the first course at the new fighter direction school at RNAS Yeovilton. He was promoted and awarded the MBE for his services.

Initially she retained the name *Empire Audacity* and was referred to as an 'auxiliary aircraft carrier', but it was soon learnt that senior officers failed to recognise the ship as an operational aircraft carrier, especially since the name prefix 'Empire' was usually applied to merchant ships in government service and the term 'auxiliary' was usually applied to fleet support ships such as tankers and stores vessels. The misunderstanding was resolved by changing her name to *Audacity* and referring to her as an escort aircraft carrier. Stability was affected by the ship's lightened structure, and she was fitted with 3,000 tons of ballast during the conversion.

Audacity technical details

Displacement:	11,000 tons deep load
Dimensions:	length 467ft 3in
	beam 56ft 3in
	draught 21ft 7in
Machinery:	1 shaft Vulkan diesel
	5,200bhp delivering 14½ knots
Armament:	1 x 4in HA; 1 x 6pdr; 4 x
	single 2pdr 'pom-pom'; 4 x
	single 20mm Oerlikon
Fuel:	649 tons diesel
Endurance:	12,000 miles at 14 knots
Complement:	210

Aircraft operating data

Flight deck:	453ft x 60ft steel plate
Arrester wires:	2 x 9,000lb at 55 knots; 1 x
	9,000lb at 55 knots 'safety
	wire';1 barrier 9,000lb at 55
	knots with 40ft pull-out
Aircraft:	Up to 8
Aircraft fuel:	10,000gal avgas
Air weapons:	0.5in gun ammunition; flares
	and pyrotechnics

Audacity operational history

The cargo liner *Hannover* was completed by the German shipbuilder Vulkan in Bremen on 10 May 1939 and put into commercial service with the Nordeutscher-Lloyd Line for trade with the West Indies. She was captured by the cruiser *Dunedin* and the Canadian destroyer *Assiniboine* while trying to evade the British blockade in March 1940, and converted initially for use as an ocean boarding vessel, renamed *Empire Audacity*. In January 1941 she was taken in hand by the Blyth Drydock and Shipbuilding Company in Northumberland for conversion into an escort carrier. The work was completed in June and she was commissioned as *Empire Audacity* on 20 June 1941, sailing for trials in the Clyde soon afterwards. On 10 July a Martlet of 802 NAS was the first aircraft to land on her deck, and on 31 July she was renamed *Audacity*.

After a work-up she sailed as part of the escort for convoy OG74 to Gibraltar on 13 September, during which her aircraft shot down one Fw 200 and sighted a U-boat. She returned to the UK with convoy HG74, which was unopposed. On 29 October she sailed from the Clyde as part of the escort for convoy OG 76 to Gibraltar. In the next ten days her Martlets shot down two Fw 200s and chased off a third. On 14 December 1941 she sailed with the escort for HG76, the return convoy to the UK, in what was to prove her last action. Although 802 NAS had only four serviceable fighters left, in six flying days they shot down two Fw 200s, damaged three more and chased off a further three. They also sighted or assisted surface escorts in the destruction of eight U-boats in one

of the most decisive convoy actions of the war.

Unfortunately, on the night of 21 December 1941 *Audacity* was left outside the convoy screen without her own escort. She was hit by a torpedo from U-751, which flooded the engine room, stopped her and caused her to settle by the stern. A surfaced U-boat was seen on the port side and she engaged it with P1 and P2 'pom-poms' before being hit by two more torpedoes which caused her to sink at 2210, bows first, 10 miles to starboard of HG76 in position 43 45N 19 54W. Her short but brilliant career had shown the escort carrier to be a vital component of convoy defence, and immediate steps were made to increase the number being made available by the USN. The Ministry of War Transport withdrew its opposition to suitable merchant ships being converted, and the next was *Activity*.

Audacity's success led to urgent studies to provide more escort carriers, including orders for ships to be built in the USA, which will be described in a later chapter. The conversion of *Winchester Castle* was reconsidered, but by 1941 she was too valuable as a troopship. New construction was considered to be too time-consuming, and there was insufficient capacity for it in the UK, but one suitable hull under construction was identified. This was the diesel-powered, fast refrigerated transport *Telemachus*, building in Dundee for the Ocean Steam Ship Line. She was requisitioned in January 1942 and converted over the next ten months as an 'improved *Audacity*'. As in other escort carriers, the ship's company technical staff was largely made up by merchant navy sailors serving under T.142X articles.

The principal improvements were a small hangar aft capable of holding six folded Swordfish and served by a single lift; a small island on the starboard side forward of amidships from which ship and flying control were exercised, aft of which there was a pole mast for her Type 79B air and Type 272 surface warning radars and 'YE' aircraft homing beacon. A second control position at flight-deck level was sited to port, level with the island, for signalling, and limited ship control when appropriate; a cross-passage under the flight deck linked the two. Basic workshops were fitted forward of the hangar. The designed aircraft complement was three Swordfish and seven Martlets, to be operated by a single, composite naval air squadron. The avgas stowage was doubled while still meeting RN standards of safety, and the hangar was fully enclosed in the normal British practice, only accessible via the lift or air-locks.

While she represented a considerable advance on *Audacity*, she was considerably less capable than contemporary American escort carriers, and this limited her usefulness. The single lift meant that it was sometimes necessary to range a number of aircraft to get at a serviceable machine if it was 'blocked in' at the forward end of the hangar. The limited avgas supply could pose problems on prolonged convoy operations, but on the other hand her riveted hull was thought to be more robust in rough, northern seas than the welded hulls of her American contemporaries. She had to keep some aircraft in a deck park as not all could be struck down into the hangar, and windbreaks could be raised around the after part of the flight deck to protect the range. The ship's sides were plated in up to flight-deck level in order to improve her sea-keeping qualities in rough weather.

Activity technical details

Displacement:	14,250 tons deep load
Dimensions:	length 512ft
	beam 66ft 6in
	draught 25ft 1in
Machinery:	2-shaft Burmeister & Wain diesels 12,000bhp delivering 18 knots
Armament:	1 x twin 4in; 6 x twin 20mm Oerlikon; 8 single 20mm Oerlikon
Fuel:	2,000 tons diesel
Endurance:	4,500 miles at 18 knots
Complement:	700

Aircraft operating data

Flight deck:	498ft x 66ft steel plate
Hangar:	87ft x 59ft x 21ft
Arrester wires:	2 x 15,500lb at 60 knots; 2 x 15,500lb at 55 knots; 1 x 15,500lb at 55 knots 'safety wire'; 1 barrier 15,500lb at 55knots with 40ft pull-out
Lift:	42ft long x 20ft wide
Aircraft:	Up to 15
Aircraft fuel:	20,000gal avgas
Air weapons:	18in torpedoes; 500lb SAP bombs; 250lb GP bombs; 3in rocket projectiles; depth charges; 0.303in gun ammunition; flares and pyrotechnics

Pretoria Castle was already in Admiralty hands as an armed merchant cruiser when it was decided to convert her into an aircraft carrier in 1942. The work took about a year and was broadly based on the prewar *Winchester Castle* design. She was by far the largest and most sophisticated escort carrier, and was stripped down to the former upper deck, which was strengthened before the hangar and

flight deck were built up on top of it. The hangar was capable of taking about fifteen aircraft and had a clear height of 17ft 6in; the steel flight deck was built as superstructure and incorporated expansion joints. It was not a strength deck. The hangar was fully enclosed in the usual British way, and the ship's side outboard of it was continued up to flight-deck level apart from the areas around the cable deck forward and the 4in gun mountings aft. She had an island and pole mast with a sophisticated array of radar and homing aids, but 2,500 tons of ballast had to be added low in the hull to compensate for the added topweight.

She was fitted with an experimental catapult powered by slow-burning cordite. This was a common source of power in the catapults fitted to battleships and cruisers, but the installation in *Pretoria Castle* was unique in a British aircraft carrier. The lift was the prototype for the type used later in the *Colossus* class light fleet carriers. For most of her short life she was used as a trials carrier in the Clyde areas, and the work included proving that new aircraft could fly to and from the deck, as well as compatibility tests with lifts, lashings, tractors and all the other elements of shipboard life. She was refitted in late 1945 for further service in the role, but when the war in the Pacific ended earlier than expected, larger fleet carriers became available and she was sold out of service.

As a trials carrier she was fitted with gantries for cameras to film deck landings and with sensitive devices to measure the wind over the deck accurately. When her final refit was terminated, many of these were removed and fitted to *Illustrious*, which was to take over the role.

Pretoria Castle technical details

Displacement:	23,450 tons deep load
Dimensions:	length 592ft
	beam 76ft 4in
	draught 29ft 10in
Machinery:	2-shaft Burmeister & Wain diesels 16,000 bhp delivering 18 knots
Armament:	2 x twin 4in; 10 x twin 20mm Oerlikon; 2 x quadruple 'pom-pom'
Protection:	1in plating over bomb-room, magazines and steering gear
Fuel:	2,430 tons diesel
Endurance:	16,000 miles at 16 knots
Complement:	580

Aircraft operating data

Flight deck:	550ft x 76ft steel plate
Hangar:	354ft x 46ft x 17ft
Catapult:	1 x CII slow-burning cordite, 14,000lb at 66 knots end speed
Arrester wires:	6 x 15,000lb at 60 knots; 2 barriers each 15,000lb at 60 knots with 40ft pull-out
Lift:	45ft long x 39ft wide
Aircraft:	21
Aircraft fuel:	74,000gal avgas
Air weapons:	18in torpedoes; 500lb SAP bombs; 250lb bombs; 3in rocket projectiles; depth charges; 0.303in, 0.5in and 20mm cannon ammunition; flares and pyrotechnics

Nairana, Vindex and *Campania* were requisitioned in 1942 and built as escort carriers; they can be considered as sister-ships although *Campania* was slightly larger and faster than the other two. The first two were at an early stage of construction on the slipway; the third had not even been laid down. The hull sides were continued up to the flight deck, which became a strength deck as in the larger fleet carriers but, unusually for British carriers, the hangar took up the entire width of the hull inboard of the side plating, with access hatches leading to the decks below. Fore and aft passageways were on the deck below the hangar.

All three were designed to operate aircraft up to 15,500lb and had a reasonably long but narrow flight deck. The hangar was considerably larger than that of *Activity* but suffered from having only one lift sited at its after end, making it difficult to range aircraft from the forward end of the hangar. The narrow deck limited the size of the deck park, and the single barrier was sited by the small island only about 150ft from the bow, limiting the number of aircraft that could occupy Fly 1 after a single recovery. Although more aircraft could be embarked, these factors limited the size of the air group to a practical total of about twenty. As in *Activity* there was a small island well forward on the starboard side and a small control position at flight-deck level opposite to port, used for signalling.

The conversion and completion of these ships took over a year, and the opportunity was taken to give them an exceptionally complete outfit of radar, identification friend or foe (IFF) and homing beacons. The weight of the equipment led to them being fitted with lattice masts rather than the pole masts of the earlier conversions. On completion *Nairana* had Type 271, 277, 281B and 293 radars; Type 242 and 243 IFF interrogators and Type 251M, 252 and 253 IFF transponders; a 'YE' homing beacon and Type 87 VHF radio dipoles on her single mast. 'Hockey-stick' masts at the deck edge, which were lowered during flying operations, carried the long wires of the Type 89 HF W/T installation. At the after end of the flight deck she was fitted with

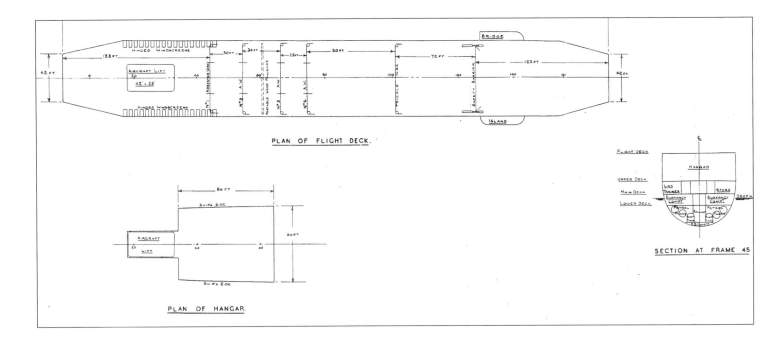

the dipole transmitter and receiver aerials for the Type 257 Blind Approach Beacon System (BABS), intended to guide pilots back to a position at night or in bad weather from where they could see the flight-deck lighting and land visually. When she was completed *Campania* had the most advanced operations room yet fitted in a British escort carrier, capable of controlling fighters for convoy air defence and directing strikes against submarines that were plotted from various sensor inputs.

All three ships had 1in plating around their magazines but no other protection. They had a twin 4in mounting right aft and numerous close-range 2pdr and 20mm Oerlikon mountings. The sponsons angled out on each quarter contained depth charge throwers. The diagonal shape on the starboard side amidships was the donkey-boiler funnel casing, and the larger rectangular shape aft of it was the diesel exhaust casing from the motor room.

All three had riveted hulls, which the Admiralty considered to be better suited to operations north of the Arctic Circle than the welded hulls of

Activity's flight deck and hangar. The section shows the typical arrangement of avgas tanks in a British design. (AUTHOR'S COLLECTION)

American escort carriers. This explains why these ships were used extensively on the Russian convoys, and probably why they were fitted with such a sophisticated outfit of electronics, including BABS.

Activity with Swordfish and Martlets on deck. (AUTHOR'S COLLECTION)

Nairana lent to the Royal Netherlands Navy in 1946

The RN had no further use for *Nairana* at the end of the war but she was well-equipped and immediately available when the Royal Netherlands Navy (RNethN) asked for the loan of an aircraft carrier to gain experience before purchasing a light fleet carrier as part of its postwar fleet. Dutch pilots had flown with the RN during the Second World War, and two MAC-Ships had been operated by Dutch crews. Renamed *Karel Doorman*, she provided a straightforward transition and was allocated the pennant number QH 1.

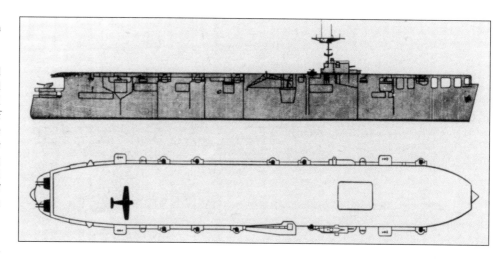

Nairana, *Vindex* (*Campania* in brackets) technical details

Displacement:	17,210 (15,970) tons deep load
Dimensions:	length 524ft (540)ft
	beam 68ft (70)ft
	draught 23ft 7in (25ft 9in)
Machinery:	2-shaft Doxford (Burmeister & Wain) diesels
	10,700 (13,250) bhp delivering 17 (18) knots
Armament:	1 x twin 4in; 4 x quadruple 2pdr 'pom-pom'; 8 x twin 20mm Oerlikon
Fuel:	1,655 (2,230) tons diesel
Endurance:	13,000 (17,000) miles at 16 (17) knots
Complement:	554 (639)

Aircraft operating data

Flight deck:	502ft (515ft) x 66ft (70ft) steel plate
Hangar:	231ft (198ft) x 61ft (63ft) x 17ft 6in
Arrester wires:	8 (4) x 15,500lb at 60 knots; 2 (1) barriers 15,500lb at 60 knots with 40ft pull-out
Lift:	45ft long x 34ft wide
Aircraft:	Up to 20
Aircraft fuel:	52,000gal avgas
Air weapons:	Mark XXIV mines (homing torpedoes); 18in torpedoes; 3in rocket projectiles; depth charges; 20mm cannon and 0.303 gun ammunition; flares and pyrotechnics

Individual ship histories

Activity

Laid down by Caledon Shipbuilding and Engineering Company in its Dundee shipyard as yard number 388 for the Ocean Steamship Line,

Pretoria Castle; the aircraft shown on deck for scale is a Grumman Martlet/Wildcat. (AUTHOR'S COLLECTION)

and to have been named *Telemachus* as a refrigerated merchant ship, she was requisitioned by the Admiralty in January 1942 and converted into an escort aircraft carrier on the slipway. She was allocated Admiralty Job Number J11801. She was launched on 30 May 1942 and commissioned as *Activity* in Dundee on 30 May 1942. On 9 October she sailed to Rosyth Dockyard, where Admiralty-supplied items were installed and stores taken on board before her formal completion on 14 October. On 18 October she sailed for the Clyde and worked-up based at Lamlash. Post-work-up defects were rectified in the Clyde from 20 December, and from 1 January 1943 she was allocated to WAC as a deck landing training carrier based in the Clyde.

On 4 October 1943 she arrived in Liverpool,

Pretoria Castle in August 1943. The port twin 4in gun mounting right aft is just visible, trained to port. (AUTHOR'S COLLECTION)

Nairana in January 1944 with an American-built CVE on her starboard side. (AUTHOR'S COLLECTION)

where she was subsequently refitted for operational service, rejoining WAC on 12 January 1944 and working-up in the Clyde for the remainder of January with 819 (Swordfish/Wildcat) NAS embarked. In February 1944 she provided air cover for a series of slow convoys bound for West Africa and the Mediterranean. In early March she was in Gibraltar, from where she escorted a fast convoy to the Clyde before joining the escort for convoy JW58 to North Russia in Scapa Flow on 27 March. The convoy sailed a day later with forty-eight merchant ships, all of which arrived safely. On 7 April she sailed with the return convoy RA58. Her aircraft flew a total of sixty-seven hours protecting the two convoys. On 19 April she sailed with the escort for JW59, the next convoy to North Russia, which delivered forty-four out of forty-five merchant ships safely, and during which thirty-six hours were flown. In May she underwent a refit in a Clyde shipyard, then returned to providing air defence for convoys to and from Gibraltar and West Africa between late May and 27 August 1944, when she returned to the Clyde and was redesignated a ferry carrier.

Activity subsequently sailed for the Far East with a load of replacement naval aircraft which were unloaded at Trincomalee on 23 October, after which she returned to the UK and carried out a maintenance period in the Clyde and a docking in Portsmouth. On 17 January she sailed for Belfast, where she was loaded with aircraft for the EIF. She sailed from the UK at the end of January and arrived in Colombo on 20 February. A day later she was lent to the BPF and sailed for Australia with a load of replacement aircraft. She returned to the EIF at the end of March and was then used to ferry RN aircraft between Cochin and Colombo.

On 1 September 1945 she sailed from Colombo to Singapore, arriving on 6 September. She was present in Singapore Roads with a number of other

RN warships when Admiral Mountbatten, Supreme Allied Commander South East Asia, took the surrender of Japanese forces in the area on 12 September. Ten days later she sailed for the UK and arrived in the Clyde on 20 October. There was no further use for her as a warship, and she was immediately destored and reduced to unmaintained reserve. The Admiralty sold her to the Glen Line on 25 April 1946 for conversion back into a merchant ship. Renamed *Breconshire*, she served until 1967, when she was broken up at Mihara in Japan.

Pretoria Castle

Pretoria Castle was originally completed as a passenger liner for the Union Castle Line by Harland & Wolff at its Belfast shipyard on 12 October 1939, and was immediately requisitioned for use as an armed merchant cruiser. After guns were fitted she was commissioned as *Pretoria Castle* on 28 November and sailed for service on the South Atlantic Station as a long-range convoy escort based on Freetown in Sierra Leone. After the decision was taken to convert her into an aircraft carrier she arrived in the Tyne on 30 June 1942 and the work was carried out by Swan Hunter and Wigham Richardson at its Wallsend Shipyard. On 16 July she was purchased outright by the Admiralty.

She recommissioned on the Tyne on 29 July 1943, and the conversion was formally completed on 9 August. On 12 August she arrived in Rosyth, where she was stored and prepared for service as a trials carrier, after which she was allocated to WAC. Most of her trial work was carried out in the Clyde areas, and she normally anchored overnight off Rothesay so that trial teams could embark by boat early in the morning.

Pretoria Castle carried out one operational

Vindex with Swordfish ranged aft. (AUTHOR'S COLLECTION)

mission, when she embarked 825 (Swordfish/Sea Hurricane) NAS and sailed with the escort for convoy DS46 to Iceland on 27 October 1943. She came back with the return convoy SD46 on 30 October, after which she disembarked 825 NAS and resumed her normal duties. On 29 November she collided with *Ravager* in the Clyde and had to undergo repairs, but by January 1944 she was able to resume trials.

Between 20 January and 25 April she conducted trials with a 'hooked [North American] Harvard', Seafire, Hellcat, Avenger, Wildcat and Corsair, which included deck qualification, expansion of the types' flight envelope and other important parameters. In April she began a docking in Admiralty Floating Dock IV which was completed in early June, after which she carried out radar intercept trials with Seafires, but on 14

July she collided with the mercantile *Edith* in the Clyde and had to be repaired again. The Clyde in wartime was a crowded space.

Trial work resumed after a run through the degaussing range in October. It included deck-landing trials for new or modified Seafires, Avengers, Hellcats and even Swordfish, which operated at ever-higher weights with improved radar and other sensors. Late in the month she was involved in aerodynamic trials with a modified Wildcat and deck-landing trials with the new Supermarine Sea Otter amphibian. In November she carried out deck-landing trials with new marks of Firefly and Barracuda, and from December she underwent machinery refits and repairs, first in Belfast and then in the Clyde before carrying out trials of new catapult launching techniques in April 1945. On 11 August she hoisted a 'hooked [Gloster] Meteor' on board to evaluate the type for sea service, but it was not flown from the deck at that stage. After that she was used to evaluate new flight-deck lighting to support night flying, and in September she started a refit in Portsmouth Dockyard.

The war ended while she was in refit and, with no further use for her, the Admiralty sold her back to the Union Castle Line on 26 January 1946. She was destored in Portsmouth during February and paid off on 21 March 1946 at Belfast, where she was converted back into a passenger liner. She was subsequently renamed *Warwick Castle* and operated until 1962, when she was sold to Spanish breakers and scrapped.

Nairana

Laid down by John Brown at its Clydebank shipyard on 6 November 1941 as Yard Number 577, *Nairana* was requisitioned by the Admiralty in 1942, allocated Admiralty Job Number J1577 and launched on 20 May 1943. She was commissioned as *Nairana* in the shipbuilder's yard on 26 November 1943, and formally completed and handed over on 12 December. Her work-up in the Clyde areas began after sea trials on 17 December, and on 25 January 1944 she embarked 835 (Swordfish/Sea Hurricane) composite NAS and joined WAC. On 29 January 1944 she sailed in company with the 2nd Escort Group to provide air cover for a number of convoys in the Eastern Atlantic throughout February. In early March she was in Gibraltar, and sailed with *Activity* on 9 March to cover a fast convoy from the Mediterranean to the Clyde. Her fighters shot down two Luftwaffe Junkers Ju 290B aircraft.

On 24 March she sailed to cover more convoys on the route between Gibraltar and the Clyde before carrying out an anti-U-boat sweep off Londonderry in May. On 16 May 1944 she joined the 15th Escort Group to provide cover for more convoys on the UK to Gibraltar route and the return. This pattern continued until she underwent a docking in the Clyde in July, and then again from 24 August to 14 September, when she returned to a Clyde yard for defect rectification. Wildcats replaced the Sea Hurricanes in 835 NAS while the squadron was disembarked during this period.

On 15 October she was lent to the HF for operations in support of Russian convoys; 835 NAS was expanded with extra Swordfish to bring it up to twenty aircraft, the split being fourteen Swordfish and six Wildcats. *Nairana* sailed on 21 October for operation *Trial* with *Vindex*, *Tracker* and two support groups to give cover to convoy JW61 to North Russia. On 31 October the force sailed with the return convoy, RA61. Her aircraft flew 104 hours in support of the convoys, nearly all of them at night. After a period of defect rectification in the Clyde she returned to Scapa Flow and sailed for Operation *Acumen* on 30 November in company with *Campania* and support groups. Fighters from the two carriers shot down a Luftwaffe Blohm und Voss Bv 138 and two Ju 88s, but lost a Wildcat and its pilot in combat. They sailed from the Kola Inlet with the return convoy on 10 December, and *Nairana*'s total of flying hours for the two convoys was 162, again nearly all at night. On 20 December she entered a Clyde yard for a short defect rectification period.

She sailed on 1 January 1945 for Operation *Sampler*, a planned strike against enemy shipping near Vaagso which had to be aborted because of bad weather. This was followed on 28 January by Operation *Winded*, in which she joined *Premier* to provide cover for a night strike on shipping near Vaagso by Swordfish from *Campania*. Two days later they covered a further Swordfish strike, against shipping in Stadtlandet. On 3 February she sailed with *Campania* as part of the covering force for Operation *Hotbed*, convoy JW64 to North Russia. The enemy used massed attacks by twenty-five torpedo-carrying aircraft against the convoy, but lost twenty-one of them. Four 'kills' and five 'probables' were credited to fighters from the carriers, and the remainder to anti-aircraft fire and the very bad weather. The return convoy sailed from the Kola Inlet on 17 February and *Nairana* flew a total of 148 hours in the operation, forty-six of them at night.

On 26 March she sailed with *Puncher* for Operation *Prefix*, a strike against enemy shipping in Aalesund by Wildcats with a single Firefly acting as navigation leader, which went ahead despite rain, sleet and poor visibility. A W/T station at Vikero was strafed and set on fire. Three days later she returned to Scapa Flow and then left the HF for a major refit in Belfast, which began on 31 March 1945. Unfortunately she hit a jetty when being manoeuvred out of dry dock on 7 August, and had to be docked again for repairs which took until October, by which time the war was over. She was allocated to duty as a deck landing training carrier in the Irish Sea, with no dedicated air group.

In January 1946 she carried out a period of defect rectification in the Clyde, and on 23 March 1946 she was handed over to the RNethN on loan as the first Dutch aircraft carrier. She was returned to the RN at Devonport on 28 May 1948 and immediately sold to her originally planned owner, the Port Line, for mercantile conversion and renamed *Port Victor*. She was broken up for scrap in 1971.

Vindex

Originally ordered from Swan Hunter and Wigham Richardson at its Wallsend shipyard with the Yard Number 1667 by the Ministry of War Transport for operation by the Port Line, *Vindex* was purchased by the Admiralty on 29 June 1942, two days before her keel was laid down, and allocated Admiralty Job Number J4698. She was launched on 4 May 1943 and commissioned at Wallsend on 15 November 1943. Formal completion was on 3 December, after which she sailed to Rosyth for the installation of new Admiralty-supplied items. On 11 December she was allocated to WAC and moved to the Clyde areas to work-up with 825 (Swordfish/Sea Hurricane) composite NAS embarked. Post-work-up defect rectification work was carried out in a Clyde yard from 21 January 1944, the opportunity being taken to repair minor damage caused by a collision.

Vindex arrived in Londonderry on 2 March and subsequently carried out an antisubmarine sweep with the 2nd Support Group. On 15 March her Swordfish shared in the sinking of U-653 with surface escorts, but on 24 March a Swordfish crashed on deck, detonating its depth charges and causing a major fire and damage, after which she had to enter a Clyde yard at short notice for repairs from 28 March. These were completed by 26 April, and she sailed for an antisubmarine sweep with the 6th Escort Group. Swordfish shared the destruction of U-765 with surface escorts on 6 May 1944. In June she carried out a further series of sweeps in the Western Approaches to the UK, and on 11 August she was lent to the HF and arrived in Scapa Flow.

On 16 August 1944 she sailed for Operation *Victual* as part of the escort for Convoy JW59 to North Russia, in company with *Striker*. On 22 August one of her Swordfish sank U-354, and two days later Swordfish shared with surface escorts in the destruction of U-344. The convoy arrived in the Kola Inlet on 25 August, and three days later the escort sailed with Convoy RA59A for the return to the UK. Swordfish and surface escorts shared in the destruction of U-394 on 2 September, and no merchant ships were lost in either the outward or homeward convoys. The two carriers flew sorties totalling 529 hours. After a short maintenance period *Vindex* collided with the liner *Queen Mary* in the Clyde and had to undergo repairs until 15 October, when she returned to Scapa Flow. On 21 October she sailed for Operation *Trial* with the escort for Convoy JW61 to North Russia, which also included *Tracker*, *Nairana* and two support groups. The convoy arrived in the Kola Inlet on 28 October and the escort sailed with the return convoy, RA63, on 31 October. Both convoys encountered bad weather, and *Vindex's* aircraft flew only seventy-six hours, forty-two of them at night. She carried out an assisted maintenance period in the Clyde from 10 November and returned to Scapa Flow on 27 December 1944.

On 31 December 1944 she sailed for Operation *Greystoke* as part of the escort for Convoy JW63 to North Russia, arriving in the Kola Inlet on 8 January 1945. On 11 January she sailed with the escort for the return convoy, RA63, to the UK. Very bad weather was encountered throughout, but there was no contact with the enemy. *Vindex* aircraft flew 110 hours, seventy of them at night, and the convoy suffered no losses. She returned to Scapa Flow on 21 January and moved straight to the Clyde to have storm damage repaired. *Vindex* sailed from Scapa Flow for Operation *Roundel*, escorting Convoy JW66 to North Russia, on 17 April 1945, and returned with RA66 to the UK. For this operation she embarked 813 (Swordfish/Wildcat) composite NAS, and they flew for 150 hours and neither convoy suffered any

loss. On 17 May 1945 she arrived in the Clyde for modifications to suit her for use a replenishment carrier with the BPF.

On 1 July 1945 *Vindex* sailed to join 30 ACS in the Far East with 1790 (Firefly nightfighter) NAS embarked for passage. She arrived off Brisbane on 11 August to join the 30th ACS and unloaded aircraft and stores, on completion of which she sailed for Sydney. Once there, she embarked a draft of 300 men and humanitarian stores for the relief of Hong Kong and sailed for Brisbane on 20 August to take on more stores. She finally set off for Hong Kong on 23 August, stopping to refuel at Leyte Gulf and Manus on passage and arriving on 8 September. While going alongside her designated berth in Kowloon she struck an unmarked wreck and damaged her port propeller, although not seriously. On 14 September she embarked 300 Australian former prisoners of war and civilians who had been held in Stanley Internment Camp and repatriated them to Australia, arriving in Sydney on 3 October. She spent the remainder of 1945 ferrying passengers, stores and deck cargoes of aircraft between Australia, Hong Kong and Iwakuni in Japan. On 30 November she collided with a junk in Hong Kong Harbour but suffered only minor damage.

On 9 February 1946 *Vindex* began a refit in Garden Island Dockyard in Sydney, after which she was used to transport the shore headquarters of the BPF to Hong Kong. When that task was completed she carried Lend/Lease aircraft out to sea, where they were dumped over the side to avoid having to pay the US Government for them under the terms of the agreement, which stated that they must be paid for, returned to the USA or destroyed. On 23 September 1947 she returned to Rosyth, where she was stripped of naval equipment and laid up. In October she was purchased by the

Port Line and renamed *Port Vindex*. She was towed to Wallsend for conversion back to her original design as a fast cargo ship, and was operated by the Port Line until 1971, when she was broken up for scrap in Taiwan.

Campania

The largest and most capable of the three 'half-sisters', *Campania* was laid down by Harland & Wolff at its Belfast shipyard as Yard Number 1091 before being purchased by the Admiralty on 29 July 1942 and allocated Admiralty Job Number J3317. Her extensive conversion took another year before she was launched on 17 June 1943, and she was commissioned in Belfast on 9 February 1944. Formal completion was achieved on 7 March, after which she sailed for a work-up in the Clyde areas, but in April she had to return to Belfast for engine defects to be repaired. On 3 June 1944 she was allocated to WAC and embarked 813 (Swordfish/nightfighter Fulmar/Wildcat) composite NAS and sailed to cover convoys to Gibraltar, West Africa and the Mediterranean during July and August.

On 14 September 1944 she was attached to the HF and deployed to Scapa Flow, sailing again two days later for Operation *Rigmarole* as part of the escort for Convoy JW60 to North Russia. On 28 September she sailed from the Kola Inlet for the return voyage with RA60, and her aircraft sank U-921 on 30 September. She returned to Scapa Flow on 21 October but sailed for Operation *Hardy* two days later with a HF force including *Trumpeter*, from which aircraft were to lay mines near Lepsorev and Haarhamsfjord. By 27 October she was back in Scapa Flow, and on 1 November she sailed for Operation *Golden* as part of the escort for convoy JW61A to North Russia. Within this convoy two liners carried home 11,000 Russian former prisoners of war who had been liberated by Allied forces in the west. Fighters shot down a Bv 138. The return convoy, RA61A, sailed from the Kola Inlet on 10 November with the two liners carrying Russian sailors who were to take over RN warships, including the battleship *Royal Sovereign*, that were to be lent to the Soviet Navy. Again, fighters shot down a single Bv 138.

On 30 November she sailed for Operation *Acumen* as part of the escort for convoy JW62 to North Russia, returning from the Kola Inlet on 10 December. During the whole operation her aircraft flew 180 hours, seventy of which were at night. *Campania's* aircraft sank U-365 on 13 December, and after her return she carried a maintenance period in the Clyde from 20 December. She returned to Scapa Flow in January 1945 and took

Campania photographed in 1944. (STEVE BUSH COLLECTION).

The 'grain' MAC-Ship *Empire MacKendrick* in December 1944. (AUTHOR'S COLLECTION)

part in Operation *Winded* from 28 January. This was an attack by her Swordfish on shipping near Vaagso during a full-moon period, covered by aircraft from *Premier* and *Nairana*. Four Wildcats of 842 NAS were added to the air group for this mission, and for the strike six Swordfish were armed with eight 25lb rockets with solid heads and four others carried flares to illuminate targets. Three fishing boats totalling 398 tons were located and sunk in Rovdafjord.

On 2 February she sailed for Operation *Hotbed* as part of the escort for convoy JW64 to North Russia, and on 17 February she sailed from the Kola Inlet with the return convoy, RA64. Seventy-five hours were flown in support of these convoys, seventeen of them at night. After a short defect repair period on the Clyde she returned to Scapa Flow on 12 March and sailed for Operation *Scottish* with the escort for convoy JW65 for North Russia. The return trip from the Kola Inlet started on 23 March, and during the two runs her aircraft flew eighty-seven hours, of which nineteen were at night. This was her last Russian convoy, and on 7 April she went into a Clyde yard for a refit. When she emerged from the dry dock on 5 June she hit the dock gate and had to be taken to London for the damage to be repaired. When this work was complete she was allocated to the Nore Command for trooping duties.

On 9 September she sailed for Trinidad on the first of a series of runs back and forth across the

Atlantic to the island that continued until she arrived in Devonport Dockyard on 10 December 1945. She was then destored, and at the end of the month moved to Rosyth, where she was laid up in Category B reserve. In 1947 some thought was given to bringing her out of reserve as an RFA-manned ferry carrier, but the idea was not carried through. In 1950 she was converted into a civilian-manned exhibition ship, and in 1951 she toured the UK in support of the Festival of Britain. The exhibition equipment was then removed, and in early 1952 she was fitted out as a headquarters ship for the Flotilla supporting the British atomic bomb tests carried out at Monte Bello Island on the northwest coast of Australia. She anchored off the lagoon east of the island on 8 August 1952 and remained there for Operation *Hurricane*, the detonation of the first British atomic device in the frigate *Plym*. Her operations room had been modified to act as a control centre for the operations; she provided accommodation for the scientists and officials who attended the test and operated a small ship's flight in support of the technical teams. These included Dragonfly helicopters that flew from the deck and Sea Otter amphibians that were lowered into the sea to fly. She was modified with a large crane on the flight deck aft with several deckhouses, and was thus no longer able to operate conventional fixed-wing aircraft. Derricks were provided along the deck sides for a large number of small boats and landing craft to support the trials parties. A close-range armament of twin and single Bofors was fitted. She returned from Australia in 1953 and was laid up

in reserve again, this time at Chatham. Unlike her half-sisters she was not converted for mercantile use, eventually being sold to breakers and towed to Blyth on 11 November 1955 to be broken up for scrap.

MAC-Ships

Technical background

By February 1942 the value of escort carriers was fully appreciated, but the Admiralty feared that, with the future demands on their services anticipated for amphibious operations in 1943, the existing rate of construction would not produce enough ships for the surrogate carrier tasks required by the RN in addition to the need for transatlantic trade protection. A proposal was therefore put forward that grain-carrying merchant ships should be modified with flight decks to act as rudimentary aircraft carriers and, after considerable discussion, approval to proceed was given in June1942. To be known as Merchant Aircraft Carriers, or MAC-Ships, they would retain most of their cargo-carrying capacity, be manned by Merchant Navy crews flying the red ensign and have a small RN detachment to handle, maintain and control a detachment of four Swordfish aircraft each. There was to be a small flight deck 410ft long by 62ft wide with four arrester wires, each capable of recovering 15,000lb at an entry speed of 55 knots, and a single barrier. Grain-carrying MAC-Ships had a small hangar aft of the original superstructure under the flight deck. It was 142ft long by 38ft wide and 24ft high, and was accessed by a single lift towards the after end of the flight deck. A small island containing a bridge, wheelhouse and flyco was positioned on the starboard side just forward of amidships.

In October it was decided to go ahead with another twelve MAC-Ship conversions, six of which were to be grain ships and six tankers, despite misgivings about their cargoes. While serving as MAC-Ships, tankers were restricted to carrying crude oil. The tankers had a slightly larger flight deck, which was 460ft long and the same width, but had no hangar because of the after superstructure on the original hull. They carried a detachment of only three Swordfish which were protected from the elements, as far as possible, by windbreaks which could be slid up from the deck sides aft around the parking area. They had the same wires and a single barrier. Aircraft on deck had to be pushed forward of the barrier by hand for a recovery and aft of the serviceable aircraft before a launch. Later on more conversions were

The 'tanker' MAC-Ship *Amastra* with two of her Swordfish ranged aft and windbreaks down. (AUTHOR'S COLLECTION)

Nova Scotia in the west. Besides carrying out antisubmarine searches, Swordfish also provided a valuable service to convoy commodores by locating and helping to 'round up' merchant ships that had strayed from the convoy. No fighters were ever embarked in a MAC-Ship, although the idea was considered. As these ships came to the end of their service as temporary carriers, one of them achieved an historic event in the history of aircraft operations in the RN. On 28 June 1945 *Empire Mackay* launched a Swordfish for what was to be the last operational flight by a Royal Navy biplane.

Grain MAC-Ships

Empire MacAlpine	April 1943
Empire MacAndrew	July 1943
Empire MacRae	September 1943
Empire MacCallum	December 1943
Empire MacKendrick	December 1943
Empire MacDermott	March 1944

authorised and the USN showed interest in the concept at first, but as the number of escort carriers under construction increased rapidly it was decided to concentrate on them and no US MAC-Ships were built. In the event the Admiralty cancelled many of the later conversions and only nineteen were built, two of which were Dutch manned.

The first MAC-Ship, *Empire MacAlpine*, was built by the Burntisland Shipbuilding Company and converted by William Denny & Brothers at Dumbarton. She joined Convoy ONS 9 on 29 May 1943. The last MAC-Ship to be built entered service in June 1944. Although MAC-Ships filled an important niche they will be described only in brief detail in this work, but their effectiveness can be judged by the fact that only one of the 217 convoys in which one or more MAC-Ships were included was successfully attacked by U-boats. The embarked Flights were provided by 836 NAS, which absorbed 840 NAS in 1943 to become the largest squadron in the RN. The Dutch Navy formed its own unit, designated 860 NAS, to operate from the Dutch MAC-Ships. The squadrons were shore-based at RNAS Belfast initially, but moved to RNAS Maydown, also in Northern Ireland, which specialised in MAC-Ship support. By January 1944 836 NAS had ninety-two Swordfish on charge. No U-boats were sunk by MAC-Ship Swordfish, but their constant presence, often in the most appalling weather, forced the enemy to dive and made their attempts to intercept convoys more difficult. They filled the gap left by the later-than-planned appearance of

escort carriers in sufficient numbers, and boosted the morale of every convoy in which they sailed. Merchant Navy officers and men came to regard them as 'their own', and responded with enthusiasm to the responsibility of operating aircraft from their ships, and, despite being flown by RN aircrew, many Swordfish had 'MERCHANT NAVY' painted on their fuselage sides. An Air Staff Officer was embarked to advise ships' masters on purely flying matters, but the master alone was responsible for tactical matters within the convoy, and the decision on whether to take advice was his own.

In March and April 1944 tanker MAC-Ships were used to ferry aircraft from New York to the UK, carrying 212 in eleven non-operational voyages. In July 1944 four MAC-Ships reverted to normal trading, leaving fifteen in operation. Up to four MAC-Ships sometimes accompanied convoys, but two were more usual in east-bound sailings and at least one in west-bound convoys until the end of 1944. In 1945 it became unusual to have more than one MAC-Ship in any convoy. Some tanker MAC-Ships were used to provide fuel for escorts, using the astern hose method. Early fears that MAC-Ships might prove 'too lively' in a heavy sea proved unfounded, and in some instances it was found that they could continue to operate aircraft in rough weather when an escort carrier could not. Aircraft had to have thirty-hour inspections at the end of every convoy, and these were carried out at Maydown in the east and at the Royal Canadian Air Force (RCAF) air station at Dartmouth in

Technical Details

(Exact details vary; those below are for *Empire MacAlpine*)

Displacement:	12,000 tons deep load
Dimensions:	length 459ft
	beam 62ft
	draught 24ft 6in
Machinery:	1 shaft Doxford diesel
	3,500bhp delivering 12.5 knots
Armament:	one 4in; two single 40mm
	Bofors; four single 20mm
	Oerlikon
Protection:	none
Fuel:	3,000 tons diesel
Endurance:	?
Complement:	107
Cargo capacity:	80 per cent of amount carried as
	standard merchant ship

Aircraft operating data

Flight deck:	410ft x 62ft
Hangar:	142ft x 38ft x 24ft
Arrester wires:	4 x 15,000lb at 55 knots; 1
	barrier
Lift:	42ft long x 20ft wide; 10,000lb
Aircraft:	4 Swordfish
Aircraft fuel:	5,000gal avgas
Air weapons:	Homing torpedoes, depth
	charges, 100lb A/S bombs; 3in
	RP; 0.303in MG ammunition;
	flares and pyrotechnics

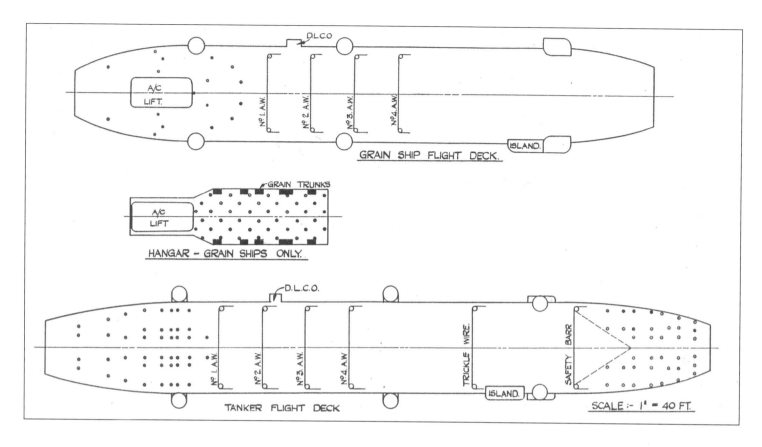

Grain and tanker MAC-Ship flight decks. (Author's collection)

Tanker MAC-Ships

Rapana	July 1943
Amastra	September 1943
Ancylus	October 1943
Acavus	October 1943
Empire MacKay	October 1943
Empire MacColl	November 1943
Empire MacMahon	December 1943
Empire MacCabe	December 1943
Alexia	December 1943
Miralda	January 1944
Adula	February 1944
Gadila (Dutch)	March 1944
Macoma (Dutch)	May 1944

Technical Details

(Exact details vary; those below are for *Rapana*)

Displacement:	16,000 tons deep load
Dimensions:	length 482ft 9in
	beam 62ft
	draught 27ft 6in
Machinery:	1 shaft Sulzer diesel
	4,000 bhp delivering 12.5 knots
Armament:	one 4in; 2 single 40mm Bofors; 6 single 20mm Oerlikon
Protection:	none
Fuel:	3,100 tons diesel
Endurance:	?
Complement:	118
Cargo capacity:	90 per cent of the amount carried as a standard merchant ship

Aircraft operating data

Flight deck:	462ft x 62ft
Arrester wires:	4 x 15,000lb at 55 knots; 1 barrier
Aircraft:	3 Swordfish
Aircraft fuel:	5,000gal avgas
Air weapons:	Homing torpedoes; depth charges; 100lb A/S bombs; 3in RP; 0.303in MG ammunition; flares and pyrotechnics

Collective achievements (based on Admiralty Trade Division records)

In 1943 MAC-Ships spent 378 days at sea and flew 282 operational sorties, an average of twenty-one flying hours for each ship on a convoy passage. These amounted to 567 flying hours in 349 days in convoy. Nineteen aircraft were lost or damaged beyond repair.

In 1944 MAC-Ships spent 2,938 days at sea and flew 2,603 operational sorties, an average of twenty-six flying hours for each ship on a convoy passage. These amounted to 5,626 flying hours in 1,748 days in convoy. Seventy-four aircraft were lost or damaged beyond repair.

In 1945 MAC-Ships spent 1,131 days at sea and flew 1,292 operational sorties, an average of thirty-five flying hours for each ship on a convoy passage. These amounted to 2,823 flying hours in 960 days in convoy. Twenty-one aircraft were lost or damaged beyond repair.

Brief individual ship histories

Empire MacAlpine

Built by the Burntisland Shipbuilding Company from August 1942, she was launched on 23 December 1943 and converted by William Denny & Brothers of Dumbarton for completion in 21 April 1943. Her austere facilities allowed a much faster build time than the more comprehensively equipped escort carriers. In May 1943 the commanding officer of 836 NAS landed-on,

Empire MacAlpine on sea trials shortly after completion. (AUTHOR'S COLLECTION)

achieving the first landing on a merchant ship by an RN aircraft, and on 29 May 1943 she sailed with the Swordfish of 836B Flight embarked as part of ONS 9. On 22 September, while she was with ONS 18, a Swordfish sighted a surfaced U-boat and attacked it but failed to sink it. In February 1944 836D Flight replaced 836B until December 1944, when it disembarked to RNAS Maydown.

In April 1945 she embarked her last Flight, 836Y, and on 12 April one of its Swordfish sighted and attacked a schnorkelling U-boat and possibly damaged it, as three hours later U-1024 surfaced and surrendered to the surface escorts. After the war she was laid up for a while until 1947, when she was converted back into a conventional grain ship, sold by the Ministry of War Transport and renamed *Derrynane*. She was renamed *Huntsbrook* in 1951, then *Suna Breeze* in 1960, and subsequently resold as *Djatinegeleh* and then *San Ernesto*. Her last name was *Pacific Endeavour* before being sold to the Wise Investment Company and scrapped in Hong Kong in April 1970.

Empire MacAndrew

Built by William Denny & Brothers in Dumbarton, she was launched on 3 May 1943 and completed as a MAC-Ship in July. After a short work-up she embarked 836M Flight in August and began convoy duty in the North Atlantic. In November 836H Flight replaced 836M, and in June 1944 836R Flight replaced 836H. By then the number of aircrew in the Flight had been reduced to provide extra crews for naval air squadrons involved in Operation *Neptune*, the naval element of the D-Day landings in Normandy.

On 26 September 1944, while with ON 255, a

Swordfish on a dusk patrol saw a U-boat dive but was unable to carry out a successful attack on it. In November 1944 836B Flight replaced 836R, and in March 1945 836Z Flight replaced 836B. On 26 April 1945, while with ON 298, a Swordfish sighted a U-boat periscope and carried out a depth-charge attack but failed to sink it. In May 1945 836Z was disembarked to RNAS Maydown for the last time and she was laid up for a while before being converted back into a grain carrier in 1947. In that year she was sold by the Ministry of War Transport and renamed *Derryheen*. In 1951 she was sold on and renamed *Cape Grafton*, and in 1964 she was sold again and renamed *Patricia*. In 1970 she was sold to Chinese shipbreakers and scrapped.

Empire MacRae

Built by Lithgow in Port Glasgow, she was launched on 21 June 1943 and completed in September. After a short work-up she embarked 836C Flight in October and began to operate on the North Atlantic convoy routes. In May 1944 836L Flight replaced 836C, and in November 1944 836U replaced 836L. The last flight to be embarked was 836D in March 1945, disembarking to RNAS Maydown for the last time in June 1945 to be disbanded.

After conversion back to normal mercantile standard she was sold in 1947 and renamed *Alpha Zambesi*. In 1954 she was sold again and renamed *Tobon*, and again in 1967 when she was renamed *Despina P*. Her eventual fate has not been found.

Empire MacCallum

Built by Lithgow in Port Glasgow, she was launched on 12 October 1943 and completed for the Ministry of War Transport as a MAC-Ship in December. After working-up she embarked 836K Flight and began convoy operations in the North

Atlantic. In February 1944 836R Flight replaced 836K, and 836T Flight replaced 836K in June 1944. On 8 July 1944 three Swordfish from *Empire MacCallum* and *Empire MacColl* attacked and probably damaged an unidentified U-boat. In September 1944 836Y Flight replaced 836T, and it was in turn replaced by 836K Flight in February 1945.

In May 1945 836K disembarked to RNAS Maydown for the last time and the ship was converted back to mercantile standard. She was sold in 1947 and renamed *Doris Clunies*. In 1951 she was sold on and renamed *Sunrover*. In 1959 she was sold twice, being renamed *Eudoxia* first and then *Phorkyss* before being sold to Japanese shipbreakers in 1960.

Empire MacKendrick

Built by the Burntisland Shipbuilding Company, she was launched on 29 September 1943 and completed as a MAC-Ship in December. After her work-up she embarked 836M Flight in January 1944 and began to operate on the North Atlantic convoy routes. On 29 May 1944, while with ON 237, three Swordfish from *Ancylus* and *Empire MacKendrick* sighted a U-boat on the surface and attacked it with 3in rocket projectiles. The U-boat was not sunk, and all three aircraft were slightly damaged by its anti-aircraft fire as it chose to stay on the surface rather than dive.

In September 1944 836Z Flight replaced 836M, and in January 1945 it was, in turn, replaced by 836L. The last embarked flight was 836V, which joined in March 1945 and disembarked for the last time in June 1945 to disband. She was converted back into a standard grain ship and sold in 1951, when she was renamed *Granpond*. In 1954 she was sold again and renamed *Condor*. In 1959 she was resold twice, first being renamed *Saltersgate* and then *Vassil Levsky*. In 1967 she was one of the merchant ships trapped

A detailed view of *Empire MacAlpine's* island and forward flight deck. The angled white lines show the direction of the wind over the deck from a steam jet positioned at their forward end. (AUTHOR'S COLLECTION)

in the Bitter Lakes on passage through the Suez Canal during the Arab/Israeli 'Six-Day War', but her eventual fate is not known.

Empire MacDermott

Built by William Denny & Brothers in Dumbarton, she was launched on 24 January 1944 and completed in March. After working-up she embarked 836K Flight in April and began work on the North Atlantic convoy routes. On 26 September 1944 Swordfish on a dusk patrol from *Empire MacDermott* and *Empire MacAndrew* saw a U-boat dive but were unable to attack it. In November 1944 836N Flight replaced 836K, and in April 1945 836B Flight replaced 836N. It disembarked for the last time in May 1945 and the ship was converted back into a standard grain ship in 1946. In 1948 she was sold and renamed *La*

Cumbre. In 1959 she was sold again and renamed *Parnon*. In 1969 she was sold on and renamed *Starlight*. Her eventual fate is unknown.

Rapana

Built by Wilton-Fijenoord, Schiedam and launched in April 1935, she was converted into a MAC-Ship by Smith's Dock Company of North Shields and completed in July 1943. The first tanker MAC-Ship to be completed, she worked-up for convoy service in the North Atlantic in July 1943. In August she embarked 836L Flight and in October, while with SC 143, one of her Swordfish carried out an attack on a U-boat that was thought to have been damaged, but this was not confirmed. In February 1944 836L disembarked and in April 1944 836X Flight was embarked. It disembarked to RNAS Maydown in

October 1944, and for the rest of the war *Rapana* sailed without aircraft embarked. In 1945 she was converted back into a normal mercantile tanker, and in 1950 she was sold and renamed *Rotula*. She was broken up in Hong Kong in January 1958.

Amastra

Built by Lithgow in Port Glasgow, she was launched on 18 December 1934 and converted into a MAC-Ship in 1943 by Smith's Dock Company, completed in September. After working-up she embarked 836E Flight in October and worked on the North Atlantic convoy routes.

A view of *Empire MacAlpine's* hangar from forward to aft, showing the lift platform stopped just below flight-deck level to provide light. The main hangar lighting was quite dim. (AUTHOR'S COLLECTION)

In July 1944 836C Flight replaced 836E, and disembarked for the last time in September. She ran for the remainder of the war without Swordfish embarked, but her deck was used to ferry aircraft from the USA to the UK. In 1946 she was converted back into mercantile configuration, and 1951 she was sold and renamed *Idas*. In 1955 she was sold to Italian shipbreakers and arrived in La Spezia on 27 June for scrapping.

Ancylus

Built by Swan Hunter at Wallsend-on-Tyne and launched on 9 October 1934, she was converted into a MAC-Ship by Palmers at Hebburn-on-Tyne and completed in October 1943. After working-up she embarked 836G Flight in November and worked on the North Atlantic convoy routes. In May 1944 836G disembarked to RNAS Maydown and she operated without aircraft until August, when 836D Flight embarked. It was disembarked in October, and for the remainder of the war her deck was used to ferry aircraft from the USA to the UK. In 1945 she was converted

back into a mercantile oil tanker, and in 1952 she was sold and renamed *Imbricaria*. In December 1954 she was sold to Italian shipbreakers and scrapped in La Spezia.

Acavus

Built by Workman Clark in Belfast and launched on 24 November 1934, she was converted into a MAC-Ship by Silley Cox & Co of Falmouth and completed in October 1943. After completion and work-up she embarked 836F Flight for runs with ON and HX convoys in the North Atlantic. In January 1944 the Dutch-manned 860F Flight embarked until March 1944 to gain experience before embarking in the Dutch *Macoma*, then 836V Flight replaced it until disembarking in July. Subsequently her deck was used to ferry aircraft from the USA to the UK. After a postwar period laid up she was converted back to mercantile tanker configuration and sold in 1952, when she was renamed *Iacra*. In 1963 she was sold to Italian shipbreakers and scrapped in La Spezia.

Empire MacKay

Built in Harland & Wolff's yard at Govan and launched on 17 June 1943, she was converted by her builder and completed as a MAC-Ship in October.

After working-up she embarked 836D Flight and began to work on the North Atlantic convoy routes. In July 1944 836W Flight replaced 836D, and in December 1944 836R Flight replaced 836W. The Flight remained with the ship then until June 1945, when it disembarked to RNAS Maydown to disband. After the war she was retained by BP, which owned her and converted her back to mercantile oil tanker standard; she was renamed *British Swordfish* as a tribute to those who had flown from her during the war. In 1959 she was sold to Dutch shipbreakers and broken up in Rotterdam from May.

Empire MacColl

Built by Cammell Laird in Birkenhead, she was launched on 24 July 1943 and converted while still under construction. She was completed in November 1943 and, after working-up, embarked 836A Flight for runs on the North Atlantic convoy routes. On 8 July 1944 three Swordfish from *Empire MacColl* and *Empire MacCallum* attacked a U-boat that was threatening ONM 243. The U-boat dived and was believed to be damaged, but this was not confirmed. Later in July 836J Flight replaced 836A. In August 836E Flight replaced 836J, and in November 836V Flight replaced 836J. In January 1945 836V disembarked to RNAS Maydown and the ship ran without a Flight

Acavus ferrying Republic P-47 Thunderbolt fighters to the UK with her flight of Swordfish parked right aft, protected by boxes of stores and the windbreaks. (AUTHOR'S COLLECTION)

until March, when 836Q was embarked. This was to be the last Flight, and it disembarked to RNAS Maydown in May 1945 to disband.

After the war she was retained by BP, converted back to mercantile standard and renamed *British Pilot* in 1946, a tribute to her wartime aircrew. In 1962 she was sold to Metal Industries and broken up for scrap at Faslane.

Empire MacMahon

Built by Swan Hunter at Wallsend-on-Tyne, she was launched on 2 July 1943 and modified into a MAC-Ship before being completed in December. She worked-up for service on the North Atlantic convoy routes and embarked 836J Flight later in the month. In April 1944 836B Flight replaced 836J, and in October 1944 836G Flight replaced 836B. In March 1945 836W Flight replaced

836G and remained with the ship until it disembarked to disband in June 1945. In 1946 she was converted back to the original mercantile design, sold and renamed *Navinia*. In 1960 she was scrapped in Hong Kong.

Empire MacCabe

Built by Swan Hunter at Wallsend-on-Tyne and launched on 18 May 1943, she was converted by her builder and completed as a MAC-Ship in December 1943. After working-up she embarked 836N Flight in January 1944 and operated on the North Atlantic convoy routes. In September 1944 836A Flight replaced 836N, and on 18 January 1945, while with ONS 40, a Swordfish sighted a U-boat on the surface but was unable to attack it. In May 1945 836H Flight replaced 836A and remained with the ship until June,

when it disembarked for the last time. After the war she was retained by BP, converted back into standard tanker configuration and renamed *British Escort*. In 1959 she was sold and renamed *Easthill Escort*, and in 1962 she was scrapped in Hong Kong.

Alexia

Built by Vulkan, Vegesack and launched on 20 December 1934, she was converted into a MAC-Ship by T W Greenwell & Co of Sunderland and completed in December 1943. After working-up she embarked 836F Flight and started operations on the North Atlantic convoy routes. In May 1944 836J Flight replaced 836F, and in July 1944 836Q Flight replaced 836J. In December 1944 836Q disembarked and the ship ran without a Flight, ferrying aircraft from the USA to the UK until 836L was embarked for a final convoy in May 1945. After the war she was converted back into a normal tanker and sold in 1951, when she was renamed *Ianthina*. In 1954 she was sold to Hughes Bolkow and arrived at Blyth to be scrapped.

Miralda

Built by the Netherlands Dock & Shipbuilding Company and launched in July 1936, she was converted by Palmers of Hebburn-on-Tyne and completed as a MAC-Ship in January 1944. After working-up she embarked 836Q Flight in February 1944 and began work on the North Atlantic convoy routes. On 21 June 1944, while with ON 240, two Swordfish sighted a U-boat but were unable to attack it. Both were damaged landing on but were repaired on board. In August 1944 836H Flight replaced 836Q, and on 27 December 1944, while with ON 274, a Swordfish attacked a U-boat with 100lb antisubmarine bombs with no confirmed result. On 26 January 1945 a Swordfish sighted a U-boat schnorkel but could not get into a position to attack it.

In February 1945 836P Flight replaced 836H and remained with the ship until May 1945, when it disembarked to RNAS Maydown to disband. After the war she was converted back into mercantile oil tanker configuration. She was sold in 1950 and renamed *Marisa*, and was eventually scrapped in Hong Kong in 1960.

Adula

Built by Blythwood of Scotstoun and launched on 28 January 1937, she was converted by Silley, Cox

The Dutch-manned MAC-Ship *Macoma*. (AUTHOR'S COLLECTION)

& Company in Falmouth and completed as a MAC-Ship in February 1944. After working-up she embarked 836P Flight and operated on the North Atlantic convoy routes. In July 1944 836G Flight replaced 836P, and in September it was in turn replaced by 836P Flight again. Her last Flight was 836M Flight, which replaced 836P in December 1944 and stayed with the ship until it disembarked for the last time to RNAS Maydown in May 1945. After the war she was converted back into normal tanker configuration and operated commercially until she was sold to T W Ward and scrapped at Briton Ferry in 1953.

Gadilla (Dutch)

Built by Howaldstswerke of Kiel and launched on 1 December 1934, she was operated by the Anglo Saxon Petroleum Company, which had an international fleet, and she flew the Dutch mercantile ensign. After conversion she remained Dutch-manned for operation on the North Atlantic convoy routes, and embarked 860S Flight of the Dutch-manned 860 NAS between February 1944 and May 1945, when the Flight disbanded. After the war she was converted back into a standard tanker and remained with her owners until 1958, when she was scrapped in Hong Kong.

Macoma (Dutch)

Built by the Netherlands Dock and Shipbuilding Company in Amsterdam for the Anglo Saxon petroleum Company's international fleet, she was launched on 31 December 1935. After her conversion to a MAC-Ship she remained Dutch-manned and flew the Dutch mercantile flag while operating on the North Atlantic convoy routes. She embarked 860O Flight in June 1944 and operated with it until October, when it was redesignated 860F Flight. As F Flight it remained with the ship until it disembarked to RNAS Maydown in May 1945 to disband. Like 836 NAS, 860 was shore-based at RNAS Maydown in Northern Ireland and had support facilities at RCAF Dartmouth in Nova Scotia. After the war she was restored to her original design and operated commercially until 1959, when she was broken up in Hong Kong.

CHAPTER 15

ARCHER CLASS

Ideas in the USA paralleled those in Britain, and at about the same time that Captain Slattery proposed an austere carrier for convoy escort work, Rear Admiral Halsey, the Commander of the Battle Force Aircraft Carrier Component, proposed a new type of small auxiliary carrier for use in pilot training and for the transport of aircraft to deployed fleets in the event of the USA being drawn into the war. There was considerable debate over the level of sophistication to be built into the new ships, and the USN initially wanted a warship hull with much of the capability of a fleet carrier. President Roosevelt, a former Secretary of the Navy, intervened and insisted on a simpler conversion of mercantile hulls.

Technical background

By January 1941 the C-3 merchant ship design was selected; it was being built in large numbers in the USA for use by the British and American Merchant Navies. The conversion of a number of hulls would have little adverse effect on the overall programme. Initially the USN designation for these ships reflected their early concept and they were referred to as aircraft tenders, general purpose, or AVG. Two incomplete diesel-powered C-3 hulls, *Mormacmail* and *Mormacland*, were selected for conversion in January 1941, and the first of these commissioned as the USS *Long Island* on 2 June, a few days before *Audacity*. On 1 April the Admiralty asked the USN to act as its agent for the procurement of six escort carriers in the USA, as British shipyards lacked the capacity to build or convert ships in the numbers required. At first they requested a design based on the *Winchester Castle* drawings, but the USN shared its plans and

pointed out that its own C-3 conversion carried more aircraft and could be built far more quickly and in greater numbers for service in both navies. To make the concept still more attractive, the new Lend/Lease Act meant that the UK would not have to pay for the ships on delivery. In May 1941 three further C-3 hulls were requisitioned for conversion into escort carriers, known initially as British AVGs or BAVGs and numbered 1, 2 and 3. Three more were subsequently added to what was to be known as the *Archer* Class in the RN, with *Archer*, the first, commissioned in November 1941. One of the six, BAVG-4, named *Charger*, was retained by the USN for training and did not serve with the RN, and *Tracker*, the last, was completed to a modified design, effectively becoming the prototype for the subsequent *Attacker* class.

The conversion was basic and the first two ships retained the original mercantile bridge structure amidships, with the wings extended outboard of the flight deck to give the navigating officers an adequate view. After arrival in the UK, port and starboard conning positions were constructed, similar to those in *Activity*. The third ship, *Biter*, and subsequent CVEs were all fitted with a small box-shaped island to starboard during their conversion or build. A small pole mast was stepped aft of the island and the ships were fitted with British Type 79B air-warning and Type 272 surface-warning radar sets. The flight deck was shorter but wider than those in the early British conversions, and was built up as superstructure over the original bridge structure. It comprised steel plate over which planks of Oregon Pine were laid athwartships, which gave a rough surface to prevent aircraft skidding and which could be easily replaced after action damage. Unlike the British practice of welding individual ring bolts for aircraft lashings

A port side view of *Archer* in late 1941, shortly after her completion. The open, unused, space forward of the hangar stands out clearly from this angle. (R A BURT COLLECTION)

to the deck, these ships followed the American method of laying metal strips across the deck at regular intervals, in which there were slots to which the deck-end of lashings could be attached. The hangar was built in aft of the structure and served by a single lift, but aircraft movements were complicated by the fact that its deck followed the original curvature of the ship's upper deck, which meant that they had to be pushed up a slope on to the lift platform for ranging and 'downhill' when being pushed off the lift on being struck down into the hangar. The ship's side forward between the original hull and the flight deck was left open to save on structural work and allow sufficient view from the original bridge.

Aircraft operating arrangements were considerably better than those in *Activity*. The lift was larger; there was a single hydraulic catapult forward capable of launching a 7,000lb aircraft at an end speed of 60 knots using the USN tail-down method with a strop. They could not launch early British-built naval aircraft without hooks for the strops and which needed a trolley on to which they had to be loaded. There were nine arrester wires, each capable of stopping a 10,000lb aircraft at 60 knots relative to the deck, and three barriers capable of stopping aircraft of the same weight with a pull-out of 30ft. After arrival in the UK most ships had the length of the flight deck extended to 442ft from the original 438ft, and a small round-down fitted at the after end of the flight deck. The inclusion of large lifts and a catapult in the US designed CVEs had obvious operational utility, but they also

reflected the difference between the original RN and USN concepts of operation. The lift enabled a wide variety of aircraft types to be struck down during ferry missions, and the catapult allowed aircraft to be launched from a tightly packed deck park which left insufficient deck run available for free take-offs. The limited number of aircraft embarked by the RN at first needed neither. The 3,205 tons of diesel fuel these ships carried not only gave them an endurance in excess of 14,000 miles at economical speed, but also gave them the important capability to refuel escort destroyers on long-range or extended missions, reducing the need for RFA tankers.

The weakest feature of these ships was their machinery. *Archer* had two Sulzer diesels connected to a single shaft, but these proved so unreliable that she was withdrawn from active service in August 1943. Subsequent ships had Doxford diesels that proved to be slightly more reliable, and *Tracker* introduced a steam turbine which gave an extra 2 knots and proved to be more reliable once teething problems had been overcome. As in the British conversions the technical personnel were Merchant Navy men serving under T.142X articles. Some of the early technical problems may have been exacerbated by lack of British familiarity with American standard equipment. After their conversion the ships were found to have inadequate stability and 1,000lb of ballast was fitted in low down. This was subsequently increased to 1,500lb as more equipment was added high up.

As these ships entered service they were redesignated as escort aircraft carriers, or CVE, by the USN, and the RN adopted the same description. Such was the urgency to get the ships into action that the first ships were operated

without modifications to improve their very basic standards of safety. The loss of two ships led to modifications in the other ships which were subsequently applied to all RN escort carriers.

Loss of *Avenger*

On 15 November 1942 *Avenger* blew up and sank after being hit by a single torpedo which detonated weapons in the bomb room. The subsequent Board of Enquiry found that splinters from the torpedo warhead had detonated bombs and depth charges stowed against the plating of the ship's side. There were only twelve survivors and the ship broke up and sank in under five minutes. To provide protection against a reccurrence the Admiralty designed the installation of a longitudinal bulkhead in all subsequent CVEs which would keep charges 10 to 15ft away from the ship's side. The USN instituted a similar alteration.

Loss of *Dasher*

Dasher sank on 27 March 1943 while at anchor off Little Cumbrae Island in the Clyde, following an accidental petrol vapour explosion and fire, probably caused by someone smoking near a leaking avgas pump. She sank in only three minutes, but 149 members of her ship's company were rescued. The Admiralty blamed the accident on the poor design of the avgas stowage and handling arrangements, especially with regard to the pipework, valves that led to the flight deck, and the tanks themselves, which were hull spaces like those used for diesel fuel with its higher flash point. The USN obviously took a keen interest in the accident and felt that RN regulations, especially those concerned with smoking in the

Archer in 1943, fitted with British Type 79B air-warning and Type 272 surface-warning radars. The small bridge with its wind baffles was fitted in the UK. Swordfish of 819 and Martlets of 892 NAS are parked in Fly 1 after a recovery. Smoke is being discharged from the small funnel on the starboard side aft. (AUTHOR'S COLLECTION)

vicinity of avgas valves, were inadequate. There was truth in both views, since the basic avgas stowage arrangements did leave much to be desired, but the RN was used to the safer stowage arrangements in British-built ships and had not emphasised the need for extreme care in ships that did not measure up to those standards. In consequence all CVEs in RN service were modified to RN avgas stowage standards, with the fuel stored in tanks inside compartments filled with water. This reduced the amount of avgas that could be carried from 75,000gal or more to 36,000gal.

Improvements in *Tracker*

In addition to her steam turbine machinery, *Tracker* introduced a number of detailed improvements. These included nine watertight bulkheads up to the main deck, and a further two up to the lower deck. A larger island with a compass platform from which the ship was controlled gave a good all-round view for ship and flying control, and a lattice mast supported an enhanced radar fit and a 'YE' aircraft homing beacon. The original superstructure was deleted and the hangar extended much further forward. Two lifts, sited at the extremities of the hangar, made it much easier to range and strike down the larger number of aircraft, although the original curvature of the hull was retained, giving the hangar a pronounced 'dip' amidships.

Avenger on 26 October 1942, with Sea Hurricanes and Swordfish ranged aft. The camouflaged flight deck must have made flying visual circuits difficult in some light conditions. (AUTHOR'S COLLECTION)

Archer Class technical details

(*Tracker* in brackets)

Displacement:	12,860 tons deep load
Dimensions:	length 492ft
	beam 102ft 3in
	draught 24ft 3in
Machinery:	1 shaft through clutches (Allis-Chalmers geared turbine)
	4 Busche-Sulzer diesels (2 Foster-Wheeler boilers)
	8,500shp delivering 17 knots (8,500shp delivering 18½ knots)
Armament:	3 (2) single 4in; (4 twin 40mm Bofors); 6 (8) twin 20mm Oerlikon; 7 (10) single 20mm Oerlikon.
Fuel:	1,430 tons diesel (3,196 tons FFO)
Endurance:	14,550 miles at 10 knots (27,300 miles at 11 knots)
Complement:	555 (646)

Aircraft operating data

Flight deck:	438ft (442ft) x 70ft (80ft) wood covered steel plate
Hangar:	260ft x 62ft x 18ft 9in
Catapult:	1 x H2; 7,000lb at 60 knots end speed
Arrester wires:	9 x 10,000lb (19,800lb) at 60 (55) knots entry speed
	3 barriers capable of stopping 10,000lb (19,800lb) aircraft
Lift:	aft 38ft long x 34ft wide capable of raising 12,000lb (fwd 42ft long x 34ft wide, 14,000lb)
	(aft 34ft long x 42ft wide, 14,000lb)
Aircraft:	up to 15 (20); up to 90 could be ferried
Aircraft fuel:	36,000gal (44,600gal) avgas
Air weapons:	18in torpedoes; homing torpedoes; 22.4in torpedoes; 500lb SAP bombs; 250lb bombs; 3in rocket projectiles; depth charges; 0.5in and 0.303in gun ammunition; flares and pyrotechnics

Individual ship histories

Archer

The hull that was to become *Archer* was laid down by the Sun Shipbuilding & Dry Dock Corporation in Chester, USA, on 7 June 1939 and launched as the MV *Mormacland* on 14 December 1939. She was completed on 24 April 1940 and subsequently purchased by the USN on behalf of the Admiralty for conversion into an escort aircraft carrier just before the implementation of the US Lend/Lease legislation. The work was undertaken by the Newport News Shipbuilding & Dry Dock Company, Newport News, USA, and completed on 17 November 1941. She was commissioned on the same day and sailed for sea trials on 23 December, which revealed a number of defects which had to be rectified in Philadelphia Navy Yard.

On 10 January 1942 she arrived in Norfolk, Virginia, to embark aircraft for passage to the UK, but two days later she collided with the USS *Brazos* and had to be towed to Charleston, South Carolina, for repairs. Once these were completed she joined WAC and embarked 834 (Swordfish) NAS and twelve Martlet airframes for transit, and sailed on 19 March 1942 in company with *Devonshire* for operations off Sierra Leone. She suffered a machinery breakdown, however, and had to be towed into Freetown on 4 April. After local repairs she sailed on 13 May for Cape Town, where she embarked gold bullion which she then carried to New York with a refuelling stop in Bermuda. The gold was used to pay for armaments bought by Britain in the USA before the Lend/Lease Act.

While she was in New York, repairs were made to her machinery and USN-inspired alterations were fitted which improved her ability to ferry aircraft. The work was completed and she sailed on 2 November 1942 with convoy UGS 2, carrying US personnel and aircraft to Morocco.

Having disembarked the Americans, she sailed for Casablanca and then Gibraltar, arriving on 18 November. On 27 November she joined a fast convoy from the Mediterranean to the UK, after which she underwent a refit in Liverpool, starting on 4 December, during which her flight deck was lengthened. She recommissioned for service with WAC on 17 February 1943 and worked-up in the Clyde areas and at Scapa Flow. On 20 March she was inspected by His Majesty King George VI during his visit to the Home Fleet. A further period of defect rectification was carried out in Belfast between 21 March and 2 May 1943, after which she embarked 819 (Swordfish) and 892 (Martlet) NAS and sailed to join the 4th Escort Group off Hvalfjord in Iceland. She acted in support of North Atlantic convoys with the group, and on 23 May Swordfish 'B' of 819 NAS sank U-752 using rocket projectiles. This was the first U-boat to be sunk by 3in rocket projectiles with solid 25lb warheads, and only the second to be sunk by an aircraft from an escort carrier.

In June she exercised in the Irish Sea, and in July she was allocated to the C-in-C Plymouth for anti-U-boat patrols in the Bay of Biscay. When these proved unsuccessful she was taken in hand in Devonport Dockyard for another period of defect rectification. These could not cure her problems, and on 3 August she moved to a Clyde yard for major engine repairs. By November it had to be admitted that these were of such severity that she could not be repaired, and she was paid off into care and maintenance, subsequently being moored in the Gareloch for use as a stores hulk. In March

Biter's flight deck was painted grey rather than camouflaged. She is at recovery stations in this photograph, with her W/T masts lowered, but the barriers abreast the small island have not been raised. (AUTHOR'S COLLECTION)

1944 she was moved to Loch Alsh for use as an accommodation ship until August, when she was taken to Belfast. The main gearing was removed and replaced and she was fitted out for service as an aircraft ferry.

The work was completed on 15 March 1945, but she was not recommissioned for RN service. Instead she was transferred to the Ministry of War Transport and renamed MV *Empire Lagan* for use as an aircraft transport. On 8 January 1946 she was returned to the USN at Norfolk, Virginia, and subsequently sold for mercantile service. From late 1946 she was operated by Swedish, Greek and Taiwanese shipowners and renamed *Anna Saelen*, *Tasmania* and then *Union Reliance*. She was finally broken up for scrap at New Orleans in March 1962, having shown greater reliability in her mercantile career than she had demonstrated in the RN.

Avenger

Laid down as the merchant ship MV *Rio Hudson* by the Sun Shipbuilding & Dry Dock Corporation in Chester, USA, on 28 November 1939, the hull was purchased incomplete by the USN for conversion into the second escort carrier for loan to the RN. She was launched on 17 November 1940 and moved to the Bethlehem Steel Corporation's yard at Staten Island, New York, for conversion and completion. Completed on 1 March 1942, she was commissioned into the RN as *Avenger* a day later. On 18 April she broke down during sea trials and had to be towed back into the Staten Island yard for repairs, finally sailing for the Clyde as part of a

troopship convoy on 30 April. Work, including the lengthening of the flight deck, was carried out on her in a Clyde shipyard between May and July 1942, after which she joined the HF.

During August she embarked 825 (Swordfish), 802 and 883 (Sea Hurricane) NAS and worked-up in the Clyde areas. On 2 September she sailed for Operation *EV* as part of the escort for convoy PQ18 to North Russia. Twenty-seven ships arrived, six having been sunk by U-boats and a further ten by enemy torpedo bombers. *Avenger* contributed to the defence by shooting down five enemy Ju 88 and Heinkel torpedo-bombers but lost five Sea Hurricanes, one of their pilots and a single Swordfish. On 8 September Swordfish shared the destruction of two U-boats with surface escorts which had already sunk two boats in a series of running battles. On 12 September *Avenger* reversed to cover convoy QP14 to Sedisfjord; twelve merchant ships arrived of the fifteen that had sailed. *Avenger* returned to Scapa Flow on 24 September and disembarked her squadrons to prepare for operations in support of amphibious landings.

On 22 October 1942 *Avenger* sailed for Operation *Torch*, the Allied invasion of North Africa, with 802 and 883 (Sea Hurricane) and 833B (Swordfish) NAS embarked as part of a slow convoy to Gibraltar, where 833B disembarked. She then formed part of the Eastern Naval Task Force. Her operations were limited by mechanical defects, however, and on 10 November she transferred four serviceable Sea Hurricanes to *Argus* and went to Algiers, where repairs were made to her diesel engines. Once the work was completed she sailed

for the UK with a slow convoy, but on 15 November she was hit by a single torpedo from U-155 at 0415 to the west of Gibraltar in position 36 15N 07 45W. The torpedo hit and detonated in the bomb room, causing a massive explosion, after which the ship broke up and sank in minutes, leaving only twelve survivors.

Biter

The third US-built CVE for the RN was laid down by the Sun Shipbuilding & Dry Dock Corporation at Chester in the USA on 28 December 1939. She was a diesel-powered C-3 merchant hull originally named *Rio Parana*, and was launched on 18 December 1940 before being purchased by the USN for conversion into an escort carrier for Britain. The conversion work was undertaken by the Atlantic Basin Iron Works in Brooklyn, and the ship commissioned as *Biter* in the company's yard on 6 April 1942. Work on the ship was formally completed on 1 May 1942, after which she carried out sea trials and sailed in convoy to the UK, where she was allocated to the HF in June. After work to modify her to RN standards she embarked 800 (Sea Hurricane) NAS and worked-up for operations in the Western Mediterranean.

On 22 October 1942 *Biter* embarked 833 (Swordfish) NAS for antisubmarine defence and sailed from the UK with a fast convoy for Gibraltar, where she disembarked the Swordfish. On 8 November she formed part of the Centre Naval Task Force off Oran, in company with *Furious* and *Dasher* for Operation *Torch*, the landings in North Africa, and flew a number of sorties in support of the Allied armies as they moved ashore. Five Vichy French Dewoitine D.520 fighters were shot down by 800 NAS aircraft while they were escorting a strike against La Senia by Albacores of 822 NAS. Other aircraft flew a number of tactical reconnaissance sorties in direct support of the army ashore.

On completion of *Torch* she returned to the UK and was allocated to WAC on 21 April 1943, when she commenced antisubmarine operations with 811 (Swordfish/Wildcat) composite NAS embarked. She operated at first with the 5th Escort Group in support of North Atlantic convoys. On 25 April U-203 was sunk by a combination of depth-charge attacks by Swordfish of 811 NAS, the destroyer *Pathfinder* and *Biter* herself; the first occasion on which a CVE had directly attacked a U-boat with its own weapons. Support operations for several convoys continued into May, and on 11 May her aircraft shared in the destruction of U-89. After a refit she joined the 7th Escort Group in October and sailed for further convoy support operations in the North Atlantic, refuelling in Argentia before helping to fight several convoys through a heavy U-boat concentration to reach the UK without loss. On 16 November a Swordfish suffered an engine failure on take-off and ditched just ahead of the ship. Its homing torpedo did not detonate but broke free and struck *Biter*'s rudder, damaging it, and she needed repairs which lasted a month after her return to the UK.

In February 1944 *Biter* joined *Tracker* to operate west of Finisterre with the 7th and 9th Escort Groups in support of several slow North Atlantic convoys approaching the UK. On 16 February Wildcats (Martlets were renamed Wildcats on 1 January 1944 to conform with USN nomenclature) of 811 NAS shot down a Ju 290 that had attempted to attack a convoy, and later in the day

Biter's fighter direction officers controlled an interception by Bristol Beaufighters of RAF Coastal Command that led to the destruction of a second Ju 290. Support for slow convoys to Gibraltar and the Mediterranean continued through March, April, May and June, and on 14 April the sloop *Pelican* sank U-448, which had attempted to torpedo *Biter*. After this spell of operational activity she returned to the UK, and in August 1944 she arrived in Greenock, where work started to prepare her for duty as a ferry carrier since, by then, a number of larger and better-equipped CVEs were available for operational duties and there was insufficient manpower to run them all. On 21 August 1944 she was transferred to merchant naval charge for use as a ferry carrier, but three days later she was damaged by a major fire while still alongside in the yard. No shipyard capacity was available to repair her, and she was laid up in the Gareloch off Faslane.

On 9 April 1945 *Biter* was returned to USN charge 'as lying' in the Gareloch. She was subsequently refitted at American expense and lent to the French Navy, renamed *Dixmunde*. She was used initially to ferry aircraft from the USA to France and then, from 1946, was used operationally off French Indo-China, where her Douglas Dauntless dive-bombers were used to support the French army ashore against Viet-Minh insurgents. In 1947 she returned to ferrying duties when *Arromanches* became operational, continuing to perform a useful role. In 1956 she became an accommodation ship at St Mandrier; there was some interest in converting her into an assault helicopter carrier and the USN was asked for assistance, but the idea was not taken forward. In 1966 she was returned to USN ownership and subsequently broken up locally for scrap.

Dasher

Laid down by the Sun Shipbuilding and Dry Dock Corporation at Chester, USA, on 14 March 1940 as a diesel-powered C-3 merchant ship, the hull

was launched on 12 April 1941 as MV *Rio de Janeiro* and acquired by the USN in November for conversion into a CVE for the RN. She was moved to Tietjens & Lang Dry Dock Company for the conversion, which was completed on 1 July 1942. She was completed and handed over to the USN on the same day at Hoboken Navy Yard, and transferred and commissioned into the RN as *Dasher* at the same place a day later. During engine trials while she was still alongside a fire broke out in the engine room and the subsequent repair work took a month. When it was completed she embarked 837 (Swordfish) NAS and sailed for the UK with convoy HX205 from Halifax, Nova Scotia, on 30 August. After arriving she underwent some modification work in a Clyde yard to equip her to operate fighters and worked-up for operational service.

On 27 October 1942 she sailed from the UK with 804 and 891 (Sea Hurricane) NAS embarked to take part in Operation *Torch*, the Allied landings in North Africa. On 8 November she formed part of the Eastern Naval Task Force and her Sea Hurricanes joined the escort for the Albacores of 822 NAS that attacked La Senia Airfield. Others flew tactical reconnaissance and CAP sorties which continued on 9 November. On the two days her aircraft flew a combined total of thirty sorties, after which she returned to the UK as part of a fast convoy from Gibraltar. On arrival she was taken in hand in Liverpool for defect rectification and the installation and fitting-out of an air-defence operations room. When the work was completed, in January 1943, she was allocated to the HF, arriving at Scapa Flow on 1 February, after which she worked-up with 891 (Sea Hurricane), 816 and 837 (Swordfish) NAS embarked. She sailed on 15 February as part of the escort for convoy JW53 to North Russia, but two days later ran into a severe storm off Iceland which caused structural damage, and she had to return to Dundee for repairs. Without her the convoy was subsequently attacked

Dasher launching a Sea Hurricane. (AUTHOR'S COLLECTION)

Seafires and Swordfish of 816 NAS ranged aft on *Tracker*. The HF/DF mast on the starboard side right forward is conspicuous. (AUTHOR'S COLLECTION)

by up to thirty enemy aircraft but suffered no losses, and all of its twenty-two merchant ships arrived safely.

After her repairs, *Dasher* moved to the Clyde to work-up again on 24 March, but on 27 March she suffered a massive internal explosion caused by the detonation of avgas vapour while at anchor off Little Cumbrae Island, 55 40N 04 57W. She sank in three minutes, leaving only 149 survivors.

Tracker

The last of the ships requisitioned by the USN for loan to the RN to form the *Attacker* Class, the hull was laid down by the Seattle-Tacoma Shipbuilding Corporation in Seattle as the SS *Mormacmail* on 3 November 1941. Conversion started while she was still on the slipway, and she was launched on 7 March 1942. She was commissioned as *Tracker* at Seattle on the same day as her formal completion, 31 January 1943. After sea trials and defect rectification she sailed for New York, passing through the Panama Canal on 23 March to arrive on 4 April. Once there she was loaded with US aircraft and sailed with a fast convoy for Casablanca on 3 May 1943, arriving a week later. From there she moved to Gibraltar, where she joined a fast convoy for Belfast, arriving on 4 June, after which she was taken in hand for modification to RN standards.

The work was completed in August and she embarked 816 (Swordfish/Seafire) composite NAS to work-up for duty with WAC. Plans were changed in September, however, and she was employed as a training carrier in the Clyde with aircraft of 768 training NAS embarked while *Argus* was in refit. On 23 September she re-embarked 816 NAS and sailed with the 4th Escort Group in support of North Atlantic convoys. She returned to the Clyde for a few days in October and then sailed with Captain Walker's 2nd Escort Group, which gave support to a number of convoys in the North East Atlantic. On 28 October 816 NAS Swordfish flew antisubmarine patrols while *Tracker* refuelled the escorts close to convoy HX262. On 1 November storm force winds caused her to roll heavily, causing damage to several aircraft in the hangar. The group moved south to an area of calmer weather and, after investigating HF/DF bearings of U-boat transmissions, escorts sank U-226 and U-842. *Tracker* was narrowly missed by a torpedo on 8 November, but arrived safely at Argentia in Newfoundland on 12 November to carry out initial repairs to machinery defects. On 23 November she sailed for Norfolk,

Virginia, where further repair work was carried out before she sailed on 5 December to cross the Atlantic eastbound, giving support to a succession of convoys. On 28 December she disembarked 816 NAS to RNAS Donibristle, and on 5 January 1944 she embarked 846 (Avenger/Wildcat) composite NAS and worked-up with the new unit.

After a short maintenance period in a Clyde yard she sailed on 13 February in company with *Biter* to act in support of North Atlantic convoys until 12 March, when she returned to the Clyde for further machinery repairs. On 25 March she was lent to the HF and sailed for Scapa Flow, where she joined the escort for Operation *FY*, convoy JW58 to North Russia, which comprised forty-eight merchant ships. During a series of successful actions *Tracker*'s Avengers shared in the destruction of U-288 with 819 NAS Swordfish, the destruction of U-355 with the destroyer *Beagle*, and contributed to damaging U-362, U-673 and U-990. Wildcats shot down three Fw 200s, two Ju 88s and a Bv 138. On 7 April she sailed with the escort for the return convoy RA58. During its passage she was damaged by one of her aircraft, which crashed on deck, and she had to undergo repairs in Belfast from mid-April. At the end of April she took part in a sweep which gave cover to North Atlantic convoys in company with the 1st and 2nd Escort Groups, returning to Scapa Flow on 7 May.

Later in May she carried out a maintenance period in the Clyde and then joined other escorts for Operation *Neptune*, the maritime element of the D-Day landings in Normandy. Her role was to cover units that blocked the entrances to the English Channel while the invasion shipping made

its initial passage. On 10 June she collided with *Teme* and suffered damage that needed shipyard assistance to repair. Consequently 846 NAS was disembarked to Limavady and she moved to Liverpool for work to begin on 19 June. When this was complete the ship embarked 853 (Avenger/Wildcat) composite NAS and began a fresh work-up in the Clyde areas. She returned to Scapa Flow on 15 October 1944 and sailed a week later for Operation *Trial* as part of the escort for convoy JW61A for North Russia. After a spell refuelling in the Kola Inlet she sailed with the return convoy, RA61. Neither convoy suffered any loss, but this was to be *Tracker*'s last operational mission. When she returned she disembarked her aircraft and their stores and support equipment before sailing from the Clyde for New York on 10 November 1944. For the remainder of the war she was lent to the USN for use as a ferry carrier, retaining her RN ship's company.

On 1 January 1945 she sailed from New York for San Diego, California. From there she ferried aircraft to forward areas for the US Pacific Fleet, continuing to do so for the next six months. On 19 July she left San Pedro Bay in the Philippine Islands for the long journey back to the UK, eventually arriving in the Clyde on 9 August 1945 to be destored and placed in reserve. On 10 November a skeleton crew steamed her first to Portsmouth and then to Norfolk Navy Yard in Virginia. She arrived on 29 November and was immediately handed back to USN custody. She was subsequently sold by the USN for conversion back into a merchant ship and renamed *Corrientes*. She was broken up for scrap at Antwerp in September 1964.

CHAPTER 16

ATTACKER CLASS

Tracker, the last of the initial group of CVEs built in the US for the RN, was effectively the prototype for forty-four more ships built under the 1942 and 1943 war programmes. All were based on the C-3 merchant hull and reflected 'production-line' manufacturing techniques, especially in new shipyards on the American west coast. Even this vast capacity was not capable of delivering the number of hulls required and, although the USN requested twenty-four ships in its 1942 programme, only twenty hulls could be spared. Half of these were allocated to the RN under Lend/Lease arrangements.

Known as the *Bogue* Class in the USN and the *Attacker* Class in the RN, these ships followed the *Archer* Class in being allocated names ending in 'er'.

Technical background

The small island was standardised on this class. It was 14ft long, 6ft wide and positioned so that only 4ft projected into the flight deck. A lattice mast carried Type 279 air warning radar and a 'YE' homing beacon, and Type 272 surface search radar was mounted on the island structure. Space was allocated in the tiny 'box' for captain and navigating officer's sea cabins, a chart room, compass platform/bridge and a flying control position known in the RN as 'Flyco'. Overall, the ships of this class were acquired earlier in build than the previous ships of the *Archer* Class, making it possible to fit them out to standards that approximated more closely to those of more

conventional warships, including the provision of extra bulkheads to give better watertight subdivision. The operations rooms fitted in some of these ships were exceptionally well fitted-out for the time and served as 'patterns' for later RN construction. The amount of space available in the former holds made it relatively easy to fit arrester gear, catapult and lift machinery and to gain access to it for maintenance. These were practical warships, capable of a wide variety of uses that made up for the shortage of fleet carriers in the RN.

Like *Tracker*, the ten ships of this class had nine arrester wires, each capable of stopping a 19,800lb aircraft with an entry speed of 55 knots relative to the deck, and three barriers capable of stopping aircraft of the same weight. The barriers were somewhat harsher than those designed in the UK, and were intended to stop an aircraft in only 20ft. The hangar was the same size as that in the preceding ships but had a lift at each end. Both lifts were 42ft by 34ft; the forward lift had the longer dimension fore and aft, and the after one had it athwartships. This was intended to offer flexibility, but practical difficulties were encountered in making use of the longer dimension aft, especially in rough seas, forcing handlers to manoeuvre aircraft on to the lift at an angle. A Martlet/Wildcat fitted comfortably on to the after lift, but a Swordfish was 2ft 4in longer and had to be angled. Aircraft are basically positioned fore and aft on the flight deck and in the hangar, so any requirement to manoeuvre them athwartships unnecessarily greatly complicates the processes of ranging and striking down. As in all

Ravager before sailing for the UK, with an Avenger of 846 NAS parked in Fly 1. (AUTHOR'S COLLECTION)

C-3 conversions, the hangar deck followed the curvature of the original upper deck, with the result that aircraft had to be manoeuvred up or down a significant slope when being pushed on to or off the lifts.

The steam turbine machinery proved to be more reliable than the diesels fitted in the earlier ships. Funnel gases were exhausted through curved trunks aft of amidships at flight-deck level. Surprisingly, in view of the early difficulties experienced by the RN in carrier development, they caused very little trouble. As with other merchant ship conversions, the machinery was largely manned by men with a mercantile background serving under T.142X articles. The C-3 hull proved to be remarkably adaptable and the former holds were used as machinery spaces for the lift motors, arrester wire and catapult equipment, and as bomb rooms. Since there were few scuttles in the hull, these more developed conversions came with extensive air conditioning and fan trunking which actually made them better ships in which to serve in hot climates than the cramped and airless fleet carriers. All ships were fitted out to USN standards with bunks instead of hammocks, ice-cream machines and soda 'fountains'. Early ships were laid down as mercantile hulls before being requisitioned and given USN names. Those lent to the RN were

A Swordfish on *Attacker*'s deck during January 1943, off the US east coast, before she sailed for the UK. (AUTHOR'S COLLECTION)

A Swordfish of 834 NAS lands on *Battler* in 1944. Although US-built CVEs had wider decks than their British-built equivalents, there was still little margin for error. (AUTHOR'S COLLECTION)

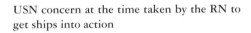

renamed on commissioning in America. Later units were actually laid down as warships.

By 1943 there was a steady flow of equipment from the USA to the UK with Hellcat, Corsair and Avenger NAS eventually being formed and commissioned at the rate of one per month. Whenever possible their passage to the UK was linked with the delivery voyage of a CVE.

USN concern at the time taken by the RN to get ships into action

In late August 1943 the Allied Anti-Submarine Survey Board complained that there was a delay of from twenty-four to thirty weeks between the completion of CVEs allocated to the RN and their deployment on their first operational mission. They regarded this as unacceptable, and Admiral King, Commander-in-Chief of the USN, agreed, although he stopped short of agreeing with the Board that the number of ships allocated to the RN should be reduced.

The Admiralty made its reply through the British Admiralty Delegation in Washington in a document dated 7 September 1943 and classified 'Most Secret'. It pointed out that the RN differed from the USN in having fewer fleet carriers in service and building and had, therefore, to make greater use of CVEs in fleet operations. As well as modifying the avgas system and installing British radar, other British equipment had to be fitted, and this could only, realistically, be done after arrival in the UK. The document noted that some delays had been caused by defects found in American shipyards over which the Admiralty had no control, and that construction on the west coast introduced delays because of the long passage times needed to reach the UK. In some cases it took between six and twelve weeks from completion before ships were ready to sail from Norfolk, Virginia, in convoy to the UK. Some ships had been further delayed by use ferrying American aircraft and personnel from Norfolk to Casablanca before they could even arrive in the UK for modification work to begin. This had been

The 'White Lady' singing for *Battler* in Durban in 1944. The photograph gives a good view of the structure that supported the starboard sponsons. (AUTHOR'S COLLECTION)

Attacker Class technical details

Displacement:	14,400 tons deep load
Dimensions:	length 491ft 7in
	beam 105ft 1in
	draught 21ft
Machinery:	1 shaft General Electric geared turbine
	2 Foster-Wheeler D Type boilers
	8,500shp delivering 18 knots
Armament:	2 single 4in; 4 twin 40mm Bofors; 8 twin 20mm Oerlikon; various single 20mm Oerlikon (there were differences between individual ships)
Fuel:	3,123 tons FFO
Endurance:	27,300 miles at 11 knots
Complement:	646

Aircraft operating data

Flight deck:	442ft x 88ft wood (Oregon pine) over steel plate
Hangar:	262ft x 62ft x 18ft
Catapult:	1 x H2 hydraulic; 7,000lb at 61 knots (tail-down method only)
Arrester wires:	9 x 19,800lb at 55 knots entry speed
	3 barriers with 20ft pull-out
Lifts:	forward 42ft long x 34ft wide aft 34ft long x 42ft wide. Both 14,000lb
Aircraft:	Up 20 normally for operations. Up to 90 could be ferried
Aircraft fuel:	44,800gal avgas
Air weapons:	Homing torpedoes; torpedoes; 500lb bombs; 250lb bombs; depth charges; 3in rocket projectiles; 20mm cannon ammunition; 0.303in gun ammunition; flares and pyrotechnics. Actual load depended on the ship's role at the time

the case in the most extreme cases of delay cited in the original Board complaint.

A further factor was the congestion which limited the amount and timing of work that could be undertaken in UK shipbuilding and repair yards. This was not understood in the USA until it was explained at the 'Quadrant' conference in September 1943. To speed up the process the Admiralty undertook to carry out post-build defect rectification and modification work in shipyards in Vancouver, Canada, which could handle three

ships concurrently. As so often happens when staffs thousands of miles apart study a problem, the clarified picture that emerged from the subsequent discussion showed that there were good reasons for the time taken to bring CVEs into action, not all of which were under Admiralty control. The CVEs modified for use as assault and fighter carriers had benefited the Allied cause in areas where the RN was unable to deploy fleet carriers. It also emerged that the USN could not have manned any extra CVEs 'taken back' from the RN.

Individual ship histories

Attacker

Laid down by the Western Pipe and Steel Corporation at San Francisco as the mercantile *Steel*

Artisan on 17 April 1941, the hull was acquired by the USN before launch as AVG 7 and converted into an escort carrier by the builder. She was launched as the USS *Barnes* on 27 September 1941 and subsequently transferred to the RN and commissioned as HMS *Attacker* on 30 September 1942. After completion she carried out sea trials off San Francisco in November and passed through the Panama Canal on 22 December 1942, but did not finally arrive in the UK until 1 April 1943, after which she was modified to RN standards in Liverpool.

In June 1943 she began to work-up to operational efficiency as a fighter CVE, with 879 and 886 (Seafire) NAS embarked, and on 3 August she sailed for the Mediterranean. After a further work-up she sailed from Malta on 8 September for Operation *Avalanche* as part of Force V in company with *Battler*, *Hunter*, *Stalker* and *Unicorn*, all with Seafires embarked. Their task was to provide fighter cover over the Allied landings at Salerno in Italy. On 9 September her aircraft flew fifty-two sorties; the next day forty-six and on the third day twenty-four. Aircraft damage, caused by a combination of the ship's low top speed and a lack of natural wind that led to a number of deck landing accidents, reduced the number of Seafires available, but on 12 September her aircraft still managed to fly ten sorties, in one of which an enemy aircraft was engaged and damaged.

Attacker returned to the UK after *Avalanche*, and on 10 October she was taken in hand in Rosyth Dockyard for modification into an assault carrier. The work was completed in March 1944, when she worked-up for her new role with 879 (Seafire) NAS embarked. She sailed for the Mediterranean again on 14 May 1944, and after further spell working-up joined Task Group 88.1 for Operation *Dragoon*, the invasion of Southern France from 15 August 1944. The Group comprised *Attacker*, *Khedive*, *Emperor*, *Pursuer* and *Searcher*. The second CVE group involved was TG 88.2 with *Hunter*, *Stalker* and the US CVEs *Tulagi* and *Kasaan Bay*. On 16 August *Attacker*'s Seafires dive-bombed coastal defences and attacked enemy motor transport inland with cannon fire. They also spotted for a bombardment by the cruiser *Aurora* and flew tactical reconnaissance missions in support of the army. Similar sortie profiles continued until 23 August, when she withdrew from the area of operations after flying a total of 183 missions.

On 2 September 1944 she arrived in Alexandria for a period of rest and replenishment before sailing on 14 September for Operation *Outing*, a series of strike operations to neutralise German garrisons in the Aegean Sea. She formed part of Force A with *Pursuer*, *Emperor*, *Searcher* and *Khedive*, and her Seafires flew extensive armed-reconnaissance sorties in which they destroyed a

quantity of motor vehicles but found few shipping targets. On 19 September her Seafires dive-bombed shipping in Rhodes Harbour, and a day later she returned to Alexandria for replenishment. A further series of Aegean strikes coded Operation *Outing II* began on 30 September, and on 3 October eight Seafires strafed Levitha wireless station. A day later aircraft spotted for a bombardment by the cruiser *Royalist*, after which *Attacker* returned to Alexandria again, having flown 102 aircraft sorties without loss.

By 13 October *Attacker* had completed her replenishment period, and sailed for further Aegean operations coded Operation *Manna* in company with *Stalker* and *Emperor*. Over the next few days her aircraft strafed motor transport and railway rolling stock on the island of Kos, and an extensive period of dive-bombing brought the system to a standstill by 24 October. After leaving briefly to refuel in Alexandria, she returned to cover amphibious landings on Mitylene on 26 October and Piskopi on 29 October. That marked the end of CVE operations in the Aegean, and she returned to the UK, arriving in Devonport on 10 November.

On 7 December she arrived in the Italian Dockyard at Taranto, now working for the Allies, and began a refit which lasted until March 1945. On 1 April she sailed, still with 879 (Seafire) NAS embarked, to join the 21st ACS in the EIF. She arrived in Trincomalee in early August, and on 17 August took part in Operation *Jurist*, the reoccupation of Penang in Malaya. On 4 September she formed part of the fleet that was present at the British reoccupation of Singapore, and remained there until 14 September, when she sailed to return to the UK.

Attacker arrived in the Clyde on 11 November 1945 and was immediately destored and reduced to reserve. On 9 December a steaming party took her back to the USA and she was formally returned to the USN at Norfolk, Virginia, on 5 January 1946. She was sold immediately for conversion

Chaser with Swordfish and Wildcats of 816 NAS ranged aft on 29 February 1944. The HF/DF mast to starboard in Fly 1 is prominent. (AUTHOR'S COLLECTION)

back into a merchant ship and renamed *Castel Forte* and later *Fairsky*. She had a lengthy mercantile career, but on 23 June 1977 she hit a submerged wreck and had to be beached. She was subsequently refloated, towed to Hong Kong and sold to interests that intended to convert her into a floating hotel named *Philippine Tourist*. In November 1979, however, she was gutted by fire in Mariveles and then towed to Hong Kong, where she was broken up for scrap in May 1980 after a long and varied career.

Battler

Laid down by Ingalls Shipbuilding Corporation in Pacagoula as the merchant ship *Mormactern*, the hull was acquired by the USN before launch and converted into an escort carrier designated AVG 6. She was launched as the USS *Altamaha* on 4 April 1942 and subsequently handed over to the RN, commissioning as HMS *Battler* at Pascagoula on 31 October 1942. Her sea trials were interrupted by a collision with a jetty on 9 November, after which repairs in New Orleans took a week before she was declared to be complete on 15 November 1942, but still had to undergo a period of defect rectification in Norfolk Navy Yard that lasted until 21 December, when she embarked 890, 892 and 894 (Martlet) NAS and sailed for passage to the UK in convoy HX220. On 12 January 1943 she entered Liverpool Docks for modifications and fitting out as a fighter carrier, emerging on 4 April, when she was allocated to WAC and worked-up off Greenock. On 4 June she sailed with a slow convoy to the Mediterranean as a ferry carrier, returning in a slow convoy from Gibraltar to the Clyde.

After a further period working-up with 807

and 808 (Seafire) NAS embarked, she sailed for the Mediterranean on 1 September for Operation *Avalanche* to provide fighter cover for the amphibious beach-head as part of Force V with *Hunter, Stalker, Attacker* and *Unicorn*, all of which operated Seafires. Between them they flew 713 sorties during forty-two daylight hours, over half the Allied effort in this critical period. On 20 September she arrived in Gibraltar and landed her Seafire squadrons, replacing them with 834 (Swordfish/Seafire/Martlet) composite NAS to act as a trade protection carrier in the EF, based on Bombay. Between November 1943 and January 1944 she supported a number of convoys between Aden and Bombay. Later in January she carried out an antisubmarine sweep off East Africa and Madagascar before joining *Newcastle, Suffolk, Roebuck* and *Quadrant* to hunt for the U-boat supply vessel *Brake*. On 12 March a Swordfish sighted *Brake* with two U-boats alongside her. Rocket-armed Swordfish were launched to shadow the enemy, and *Roebuck* was ordered to intercept and destroy them. *Brake* was subsequently sunk and one of the U-boats damaged by rocket projectiles.

On 21 March 1944 *Battler* arrived in Durban for a refit, emerging in June with only the Swordfish of 834 NAS embarked owing to the low threat of enemy air attack. She gave support to

convoys between Cape Town and Kilindini in late June and moved to Colombo in July, after which she carried out antisubmarine patrols between Ceylon and Addu Atoll. In November she was redesignated a ferry carrier and sailed for the UK via the South Pacific, Panama Canal and Norfolk, Virginia. On her return in March 1945 she was redesignated again, this time as a deck-landing training carrier in the Clyde areas. In May she carried out trials in the Belfast areas, and in June she was allocated to Rosyth Command to resume duty as a deck-landing training carrier off the Scottish east coast. On 6 January 1946 her flying task ended and she returned to the Clyde to be destored. A fortnight later a reduced ship's company steamed her back to Norfolk, Virginia, where she was returned to USN custody on 12 February. Unlike many of her sister ships that were reconverted for mercantile use, she was sold in June 1946 and immediately broken up for scrap.

Chaser

Laid down by Ingalls Shipbuilding Corporation in Pascagoula as the merchant ship *Mormacgulf* on 28 June 1941, she was acquired by the USN and converted to a CVE on the slipway. She was launched as the USS *Breton*, CVE 10, on 15

January 1942 but not completed by the USN until 9 April 1943, when she was transferred to the RN and commissioned as HMS *Chaser* at Pascagoula. No further work was needed before she arrived in Norfolk Navy Yard on 23 April. By then a number of naval air squadrons were being equipped and commissioned in the USA, and it was convenient to embark them in new CVEs for passage to the UK, although neither was in a worked-up state. On 23 June 1943 845 (Avenger) NAS embarked in *Chaser* and both sailed for the UK with convoy HX245. She arrived in the Clyde on 6 July, but a day later suffered an explosion in the boiler room and had to proceed to Rosyth Dockyard for repairs.

The repairs were completed at the end of October 1943 and she embarked 835 (Swordfish/Sea Hurricane) composite NAS to work-up in the Clyde areas, after which she was allocated to WAC. After a period of defect rectification in November and December she was lent to the HF in early 1944, embarked 816 (Swordfish/Wildcat) NAS and moved to Scapa Flow. On 21 February 1944 she sailed for Operation *FX* and formed part of the escort for

Chaser operating as a ferry carrier with the BPF in July 1945. She has a deck-load of Corsairs, Seafires and Avengers. (AUTHOR'S COLLECTION)

convoy JW57 to North Russia. The convoy comprised forty-two merchant ships, all of which made their destination through rough seas, snow storms and low temperatures. The Swordfish managed to maintain antisubmarine patrols despite the appalling conditions. In March she escorted the return convoy RA57 back to Scotland, and on 4 March Swordfish 'B' shared in the sinking of U-472 with surface escorts, having hit it with 3in rocket projectiles. A day later Swordfish 'F' sank U-366 with rockets, and on 6 March Swordfish 'X' sank U-973, also with rockets. Despite its success, this was *Chaser*'s last operation as an antisubmarine carrier.

On 13 March she dragged her anchor and grounded, causing damage to the hull which had to be repaired in Rosyth after she was towed clear. On completion of the repair work she was taken to Belfast and modified for use as a ferry carrier. When she emerged from this work she was allocated to the BPF and sailed on 4 February 1945 in convoy for Gibraltar. She then made refuelling stops in Suez, Aden, Cochin and Colombo before arriving in Sydney in May 1945. She was redesignated a replenishment carrier capable of carrying a broad range of serviceable aircraft and sailed, as soon as she was loaded, for Leyte Gulf and then the replenishment areas off the Sakishima Gunto, to provide replacement aircraft for 1 ACS. On 18 May she transferred three Seafires, two Hellcats, a Firefly, two Avengers and a Corsair to

the fleet carriers. She recovered four flyable 'duds', three Avengers and a Firefly, for repair by the Fleet Aircraft Maintenance Group (FAMG).

On 22 May she transferred a further ten aircraft to the fleet carriers, although two aircraft and their pilots were lost in accidents which were put down to their lack of recent flying practice. Another four were transferred the next day, after which she returned to Manus to pick up more aircraft from the forward aircraft pool. By July she was supporting 1 ACS in the logistic areas off Japan, where she provided replacement aircraft on 31 July and 6 August. There was a shortage of tankers, and *Chaser* was used on several occasions to refuel destroyers, using a buoyant hose trailed astern. She returned to Manus in August and then to Sydney, where she underwent a period of defect rectification. In October she took maintenance personnel and two Walrus aircraft from RNAS Ponam back to Australia as part of the BPF's initial run-down, and then spent some months as a transport, moving men and equipment. In March 1946 she was in Surabaya before returning to the UK to destore and pay off. She was returned to the USN at Norfolk, Virginia, on 12 May 1946, and sold quickly for conversion to a merchant ship. She was subsequently renamed *Aagtekerk* and later *E Yung*, and had a long mercantile life. Unfortunately she foundered in December 1972 and was subsequently salvaged and broken up for scrap in Taiwan in 1973.

Fencer during Operation *Tungsten* in April 1944, with *Furious* in the background. (AUTHOR'S COLLECTION)

Fencer

Laid down by the Western Pipe & Steel Corporation of San Francisco on 5 September 1941 as a merchant ship, but requisitioned by the USN shortly after work started and never given a mercantile name, this ship was launched on 4 April 1942 as the USS *Croatan*. She was commissioned into the USN at San Francisco on 20 February 1943, the date of her formal completion, and subsequently transferred to the RN on 27 February. On 1 March 1943 she was commissioned as HMS *Fencer* in San Francisco. By May she had arrived in New York, and she subsequently sailed for the UK as part of a North Atlantic convoy from Halifax. Work to modify her to RN standards was carried out in Liverpool between late May and the end of July, when she was allocated to WAC and embarked 842 (Swordfish/Seafire) composite NAS for a work-up period in the Clyde areas.

Her first deployment was Operation *Alacrity*, for which she sailed on 3 October 1943 to provide air cover for the Allied occupation of the Azores as a maritime air base. She returned to the Clyde on 5 November and Martlets replaced Seafires in 842 NAS. *Fencer* subsequently sailed to provide air cover for a series of slow convoys to and from

Fencer off Sheerness Dockyard in September 1946. She has two Sea Otters on deck and aircraft derricks rigged. The vessel alongside is a tank landing craft. (AUTHOR'S COLLECTION)

Hunter

Originally allocated the mercantile name *Mormacpen*, this ship was laid down by the Ingalls Shipbuilding Corporation in Pascagoula on 15 May 1941, but requisitioned soon afterwards for conversion into an escort carrier. She was launched as the USS *Block Island*, AVG-8, on 22 May 1942, but transferred to the RN on her nominal completion date on 9 January 1943. At first the RN intended to name her *Trailer*, but this rather undistinguished name was changed and she emerged as *Hunter* on the day of her completion. She carried out post-build trials in the West Indies before joining a convoy in Norfolk, Virginia, to ferry American aircraft to Casablanca in March. She eventually arrived in the UK and was taken in hand at Dundee for modification to RN standards on 12 April 1943. Emerging as a fighter carrier, she worked-up in the Clyde areas and subsequently Malta with 899 and 834 (Seafire) NAS embarked.

On 9 September 1943 she sailed from Malta as part of Force V in company with *Attacker*, *Battler*, *Stalker* and *Unicorn* for Operation *Avalanche*, to provide fighter cover over the Allied landings at Salerno. As in the other CVEs, Seafires proved to be fragile in the low wind conditions and a number were damaged in landing accidents, but *Hunter* was still able to land five to the forward airstrip at Paestum once it was in Allied hands on 12 September, whereupon the carriers withdrew. On 30 September *Hunter* returned to Dundee for repairs, but suffered a mishap when hangar deck plating fractured while she was being taken out of dry dock on 3 December. This needed further repair work in a Clyde shipyard, which lasted until the end of February. On 1 March she embarked 807 (Seafire) NAS and began to work-up, based in Scapa Flow.

On 14 May she sailed for the Mediterranean, where she continued to work-up before giving fighter cover for Operation *Dragoon*, the Allied invasion of Southern France on 15 August 1944. She formed part of Task Group 88.2 with *Stalker* and the USN CVEs *Tulagi* and *Kasaan Bay*. Her part in the operation lasted until 22 August, when she withdrew to Magdalena for a break after her Seafires had flown 219 sorties. She returned to the operation on 24 August and withdrew for the last time on 27 August after a further eighty-eight sorties. During *Dragoon* 807 NAS had flown thirty-six dive-bombing and fifty-six armed reconnaissance sorties; ninety-six combat air patrols and forty-eight target patrols; sixteen photographic reconnaissance sorties and fifty-five

Gibraltar and the Mediterranean between 19 November and 24 December 1943, when she returned to a Clyde shipyard for a period of defect rectification. On 8 February 1944 she sailed with *Striker* and the 16th Escort Group to provide cover for convoys in the North Atlantic, achieving success on 10 February when one of her Swordfish sank U-666. At the end of February she gave cover for convoys to and from Gibraltar.

On 17 March 1944 *Fencer* was lent to the HF and arrived at Scapa Flow. She subsequently took part in Operation *Tungsten*, a strike by Barracudas from the fleet carriers *Victorious* and *Furious* against the battleship *Tirpitz* in Kaafjord, Northern Norway. *Fencer* provided antisubmarine cover for the force, and *Emperor*, *Pursuer* and *Searcher* provided fighter cover. The strike damaged *Tirpitz* but failed to sink her, so a planned repeat, Operation *Planet*, with the same forces, sailed later in April, but bad weather caused the strike to be aborted.

On 28 April 1944 *Fencer* sailed for Operation *FZ* as part of the escort for convoy RA59 from North Russia, in company with *Activity*. The rough sea caused a considerable amount of deck motion, and snow on the flight deck delayed aircraft movements but never prevented launches. Despite the conditions 842 NAS Swordfish did particularly well and sank U-277 on 1 May and U-674 and U-959 on 2 May. On the same day fighters shot down a Bv 138C shadowing aircraft. *Fencer* suffered some storm damage during the operation, and this was repaired in a Clyde yard between 5 May and late June 1944. On 20 June she sailed in company with *Striker*, the cruiser *Sheffield* and six destroyers for Operation *Wanderers*, a hunt for U-boats in North Norwegian waters which was intended to simulate both a convoy to North Russia and a potential Allied landing in Norway to tie down enemy forces, but no U-boats were located. For this sortie 881 (Wildcat) NAS was added to 842 NAS.

On 13 July 1944 *Fencer* returned to WAC and sailed with 842 NAS embarked to give support for slow convoys to and from Gibraltar. In August she participated in Operation *CX*, an antisubmarine

sweep off the west coast of Scotland, and in September she returned to the HF and was involved in operations off the Norwegian coast that had to be cancelled because of bad weather. On 14 October she took part, with *Trumpeter*, in Operation *Lycidas* with the Avengers of 852 NAS and the Wildcat Flight of 842 NAS embarked. Avengers from both carriers laid mines off Haarhamsfjord, Lepsorev and Ramsoysund over two days; those on the first were laid out of position due to an inaccurate landfall, but the second lay was more successful. This was *Fencer's* last operational mission, and on her return she disembarked all her aircraft and their stores at the end of October and was allocated to the BPF for use as a ferry carrier.

Fencer arrived at Trincomalee on 22 November 1944 and was used at first to ferry replacement aircraft from RN Air Yards in India and Ceylon to RN Air Stations in Australia, where they were prepared for issue to operational NAS. On 31 March 1945 she sailed from Sydney to Leyte Gulf with serviceable aircraft for transfer to 1 ACS via the maintenance ships of the FAMG. The ferry task continued until 13 June 1945, when she sailed for Simonstown Dockyard in South Africa for a refit, after which she was allocated to 30 ACS in the EIF. On 31 August she was in Colombo, but the ferry tasking ended with the unexpectedly early end of the war and she sailed for the UK on 4 September, arriving in the Clyde three weeks later.

She arrived in London Docks on 30 September for conversion to trooping duties, and was subsequently allocated to Rosyth Command. On 13 December she sailed for Colombo, returning to Plymouth on 20 February 1946. The RN had no further use for her and after a period of defect rectification in Sheerness Dockyard she was returned to the USN at Norfolk, Virginia, on 21 November 1946. She was subsequently sold for conversion into a merchant ship and renamed *Sydney* until 1967, when she was sold on and, in quick succession, renamed *Roma*, *Galaxy Queen*, *Lady Dina* and *Caribia*. She was finally sold for scrap in September 1975 and broken up at La Spezia.

A tactical signalman sending a semaphore message from *Royalist* to *Hunter* while the cruiser takes on fuel from a buoyant hose towed astern of the CVE. The escort carriers' large fuel stowage made them additionally useful for replenishing other warships at sea. (AUTHOR'S COLLECTION)

strike escort missions for the loss of three aircraft to anti-aircraft fire, one ditching and eleven deck-landing accidents.

On 2 September *Hunter* arrived in Alexandria to prepare for Operation *Outing*, for which she sailed on 9 September 1944 in company with *Searcher*, *Pursuer* and *Khedive* to strike at German shipping and other targets in the Aegean Sea. She returned to Alexandria on 15 September, leaving again for Operation *Outing II* in the Aegean Sea on 30 September. In both sorties her aircraft flew CAPs over the fleet and targets that were being attacked by aircraft from other carriers. On 3 October her Seafires dive-bombed a W/T station at Levitha, and on 5 October they flew close-support missions for a landing by British troops on Levitha and spotted for a shore bombardment by the cruiser *Aurora*. Further dive-bombing sorties sank a small enemy merchant ship on 7 October and a 600-ton barge on 9 October. On 11 October

she returned to Alexandria, having flown a total of 135 sorties in both *Outings*.

In November she returned to the UK in company with *Attacker*, but was allocated to 21 ACS in the EIF and promptly sailed for Malta, where she commenced a refit on 6 December. This was completed in February, and she sailed for Trincomalee on 21 February 1945, still with 807 (Seafire) NAS embarked, arriving on 8 March. On 30 April 1945 she took part in Operation *Dracula*, a strike on the Burmese Coast between Tenasserim and Rangoon, in company with *Emperor*, *Khedive* and *Stalker*. On 10 May she participated in Operation *Dukedom*, a search for the Japanese cruiser *Haguro* and a sweep across the Andaman Sea in company with *Khedive*, *Emperor* and *Shah*. *Hunter*'s last operational sortie was Operation *Zipper*, the reoccupation of Singapore in company with *Khedive*, *Emperor*, *Ameer*, *Empress*, *Stalker* and a large number of other warships, although the war had ended by the time she entered Singapore on 10 September 1945.

There was no further use for her in the EIF, so *Hunter* sailed for the UK on 9 October, arriving in the Clyde on 31 October, where she was destored and her ship's company reduced to a minimal

steaming party who took the ship to Portsmouth for the removal of British equipment, arriving on 28 November. She sailed for the USA on 2 December and was returned to the USN at Norfolk, Virginia, on 29 December 1945. The USN sold her for conversion to a merchant ship and she was renamed *Almdijk*, serving as such until November 1965, when she was broken up for scrap at Valencia.

Pursuer

Laid down as a merchant ship by the Ingalls Shipbuilding Corporation at Pacagoula and originally to have been named *Mormacland*, the hull was requisitioned by the US Navy for conversion into an escort carrier at an early stage of construction. She was launched as the USS *St George*, CVE17, on 18 July 1942 and completed on 14 June 1943. On the same day she was formally transferred to the RN under Lend/Lease arrangements, renamed and commissioned as HMS *Pursuer* at Pascagoula. A fortnight later she arrived in Norfolk, Virginia, for the installation of equipment and modifications before sailing for the UK as part of convoy HX250 on 30 July 1943. She arrived in Liverpool on 11 August and was taken in hand for modifications to RN standard and to be fitted as an assault carrier. The work was completed on 16 November, when she sailed to work-up in the Clyde areas after being allocated to WAC. After a period of defect rectification in Belfast she embarked 881 and 896 (Wildcat) NAS on 19 December and carried out a further work-up.

In February 1944 she provided cover for slow convoys to and from Gibraltar and the Mediterranean before returning to the Clyde in March. She was then lent to the HF with the same air group and deployed to Scapa Flow, where she joined the carrier task force that was to strike at the German battleship *Tirpitz*. She sailed on 30 March for operation *Tungsten* in company with *Victorious*, *Furious*, *Emperor*, *Searcher* and *Fencer* to provide fighter cover for the strike on 3 April 1944 against *Tirpitz*, which was moored in Kaafjord. Later in April she took part in Operations *Ridge Able* and *Ridge Baker* with *Victorious*, *Furious*,

Her improved bridge structure is evident in this photograph of *Pursuer*, taken in July 1945 after her refit in Durban. (AUTHOR'S COLLECTION)

Searcher, *Emperor* and *Striker*. These were strikes against shipping in and around Bodo in which three vessels were sunk, but similar attacks off Rorvik had to be called off because of stormy seas which damaged *Pursuer* and several other ships. Repairs lasting a month were carried out in Liverpool, after which she sailed on 1 June for Operation *Neptune*, the naval element of the D-Day landings, during which *Pursuer* formed part of the forces that secured the English Channel against enemy intervention. She subsequently operated in the Irish Sea for a short spell, after which 896 NAS disembarked.

Pursuer was subsequently allocated to the MF, and sailed for Malta with 881 (Wildcat) NAS embarked on 25 July 1944. From 12 August onwards she took part in Operation *Dragoon*, the Allied invasion of Southern France, forming part of Task Group 88.1 with *Attacker*, *Khedive*, *Emperor* and *Searcher*. Her aircraft flew spotting, armed reconnaissance, dive-bombing and target-CAP missions, and when she withdrew from the operating area on 23 August they had flown a total of 180 sorties. Out of an air group of twenty-four Wildcats, two were shot down by anti-aircraft fire,

one forced-landed after damage by enemy fire, two ditched after running out of fuel and two suffered barrier engagements. Seventeen aircraft were damaged by enemy fire, one of them badly.

On 2 September 1944 *Pursuer* arrived in Alexandria, and a week later she sailed for Operation *Outing*, strike operations against enemy forces in the Aegean Sea in company with *Searcher*, *Khedive* and *Hunter*. For the first three days of the operation her aircraft flew CAP sorties, and on 16 September they sank four enemy caiques and damaged a further six with bombs. They also strafed transport ashore and spotted for shore bombardment. Armed reconnaissance sorties were flown over the islands of Milos and Thia, and on 19 September shipping was strafed in Rhodes Harbour. When she left the operating area on 20 September, *Pursuer*'s Wildcats had flown 136 sorties. She subsequently sailed for the UK and rejoined the HF at Scapa Flow on 28 October, retaining 881 NAS with its Wildcats as her embarked squadron.

On 13 November 1944 she sailed for Operation *Counterblast*, an attack on shipping off the Norwegian coast during which cruisers sank the

Wildcats form up over *Pursuer* during strike operations in the Norwegian littoral during 1944. (AUTHOR'S COLLECTION)

major part of an enemy convoy near Egersund. A day later she participated in Operation *Steak*, during which a German armed trawler was sunk and a wireless station at Titran was destroyed. On 20 November she sailed with *Premier* for Operation *Handfast*, in which a minefield was laid off Salhusstrommen. A week later she sailed with *Implacable* and *Premier* for Operation *Provident*, which was intended to attack shipping between Mosjoen and Rorvik, but bad weather forced the two escort carriers to turn back. Aircraft from *Implacable* sank two ships and damaged a third.

After a period of defect rectification in a Clyde yard during early September, *Premier* sailed for the USA in convoy UC48B without aircraft embarked on 12 December 1944. She was refitted in Norfolk Navy Yard throughout January 1945 and embarked 1831 (Corsair) NAS for passage to the UK on 4 February, arriving in Belfast on 15

February. In March she was allocated to 21 ACS in the EIF, and sailed with 898 (Hellcat) NAS embarked as part of a fast convoy to Gibraltar. From there she sailed for Cape Town and then to Durban, where she was refitted in May and June. On 7 July she sailed for Colombo, and eventually arrived at the fleet base in Trincomalee on 1 August. In September she took part in the reoccupation of Port Swettenham, returning to Trincomalee on 6 October.

For a while she was used after the end of hostilities on local trooping voyages, but on 20 November she sailed for the UK, arriving in the Clyde on 12 December 1945. While there she came under the administrative control of Rosyth Command while she was destored and her ship's company reduced to a small steaming party. On 12 January 1946 she sailed for a brief stop in Portsmouth, after which she sailed for Norfolk, Virginia, where she was returned to the USN on 12 February 1946. Unlike many of her sister ships, she was not sold for mercantile conversion, and in May 1946 she was sold to shipbreakers to be scrapped.

Ravager

Laid down by the Seattle-Tacoma Shipbuilding Corporation on the Williamette River on 30 April 1942, she was acquired by the USN a day later, and can thus be said to have been built as a CVE from the outset. She was never allocated a name by the USN, but launched with the hull number ACV 24 on 16 July 1942. The RN originally considered the name *Charger* for her, but she was eventually transferred to the RN and commissioned as *Ravager* on 25 April 1943, with formal completion a day later. On 25 May she sailed for the US east coast, having completed sea trials. On 2 July she embarked 846 (Avenger) NAS at Norfolk, Virginia, for passage to the UK, sailing with convoy HX248 on 15 July. On 27 July she disembarked the squadron to RNAS Macrihanish before moving to Greenock, where she underwent modification to basic RN standards.

She was allocated to Western Approaches Command, but used initially as a deck-landing training carrier in the Clyde areas. This involved numerous short embarkations by training

Ravager in the Williamette River near Portland, Oregon, shortly after completion. (AUTHOR'S COLLECTION)

squadrons and their *ab initio* pilots. On 29 November 1943 she collided with *Pretoria Castle* and had to undergo repairs in a Clyde shipyard until 8 December, when she resumed deck-landing training. In April 1944 she underwent modification for duty as a ferry carrier in a Clyde yard, but resumed duty as a training carrier when the work was completed in May.

On 20 October she sailed, loaded with aircraft, as part of a fast convoy to Gibraltar. From there she went to Norfolk, Virginia, and loaded with aircraft

A Hellcat, Fulmars, Avengers and Barracudas in *Ravager's* hangar while she operated as a deck-landing training carrier in 1945. The overhead hoist system was used for the removal and replacement of heavy components. (AUTHOR'S COLLECTION)

for the UK, eventually returning to Belfast at the end of November. After a short refit in London she returned to the deck-landing training role, based now in Rosyth. For some weeks in January 1945 she was employed on Asdic (sonar) trials, but on 28 January she collided with the merchant ship *Ben Lomond* and had to undergo repairs in Rosyth. Training was resumed on their completion and continued until the end of April, when she began a refit in a Clyde yard.

When the refit was complete she resumed deck-landing training from 8 November, but ceased flying operations on 28 December 1945, after which she was destored and had her ship's company reduced in size. She was returned to the USN at Norfolk Navy Yard on 27 February 1946 and subsequently sold for conversion to a merchant ship. Renamed *Robin Trent* at first and then *Trent*, she was eventually broken up for scrap in Taiwan in July 1973.

Searcher

Laid down by the Seattle-Tacoma Shipbuilding Corporation on 20 February 1942, she was acquired by the USN and allocated hull number ACV22 but not named when she was launched on 20 June 1942. She was subsequently transferred to the RN under Lend/Lease arrangements and commissioned as *Searcher* on 7 April 1943, a day before her formal completion. In May she moved to Seattle, where some modifications to RN standards were carried out. Further modifications were carried out in Norfolk Navy Yard when she arrived there in June, and she sailed with convoy HX246 for Liverpool on 30 June. More work was

done in Liverpool to bring her to RN standards as a fighter carrier.

On 6 October 1943 she embarked 882 and 898 (Wildcat) NAS and worked-up in the Clyde areas before sailing on 22 October to provide cover for North Atlantic convoys, a task which continued until she docked for repairs in New York in January 1944. When she returned to the UK in February she worked-up with the same squadrons embarked for strike operations with the HF, arriving at Scapa Flow on 18 March. On 3 April she took part in Operation *Tungsten*, the Barracuda strike against *Tirpitz* in Kaafjord with *Victorious*, *Furious*, *Emperor*, *Pursuer* and *Fencer*. Later in April she took part in Operations *Ridge Able* and *Ridge Baker*, strikes against shipping in the regions of Bodo and Rorvik with *Victorious*, *Furious*, *Emperor*, *Pursuer* and *Striker*. Bad weather caused the strikes off Rorvik to be cancelled, but three enemy ships were sunk off Bodo. On 6 May, with *Furious*, she took part in Operation *Croquet*, a strike against enemy shipping between Bud and the island of Smolen. Despite bad weather, five large enemy ships were hit by torpedoes and bombs and two Bv 138s were shot down. Two days later she joined *Emperor* and *Striker* in Operation *Hoops*, during which oil tanks at Kjehn and a fish-oil factory at Fossevaag were destroyed and one Fw 190, two Messerschmitt Bf 109s and two flying boats were shot down.

In mid-May *Searcher* reverted to WAC and, after a brief defect rectification period in Rosyth, sailed to cover slow convoys to Gibraltar and the Mediterranean in June. In July she returned to the Clyde and 882 and 898 NAS were amalgamated

to form a single, enlarged 882 NAS. On 15 July 1944 she sailed for operations in the Western Mediterranean, arriving in Malta on 25 July, where she joined *Attacker*, *Khedive*, *Emperor*, *Pursuer*, *Hunter*, *Stalker* and the USN CVEs *Tulagi* and *Kasaan Bay* to form Task Group 88 and work-up as a cohesive force. On 15 August they took part in Operation *Dragoon*, the Allied invasion of Southern France. The RN CVEs flew a total of 1,673 sorties in the operation, of which 552 were CAPs over the fleet and the remainder offensive strikes against German troops, railways, aircraft and coast defences. Twenty-one RN and fourteen USN aircraft were lost to enemy action, and a combined total of sixty in deck-landing accidents.

When *Searcher* left the operational area on 23 August her Wildcats had flown 167 operational sorties for the loss of three aircraft missing, one ditched with engine failure and one barrier engagement. On 2 September she arrived in Alexandria to prepare for operations in the Aegean Sea, and from 9 September she took part in Operation *Outing*, strikes on German shipping and island garrisons in company with *Hunter*, *Khedive* and *Pursuer*. The Wildcats of 882 NAS flew CAP sorties over the fleet and escorted a Catalina flying boat which searched for mines in the Kithera Channel. On 17 September *Searcher*'s aircraft bombed a radar station at Cape Sparta and flew armed reconnaissance sorties over Crete. She left the Aegean on 21 September and returned to Alexandria, and from there she returned to the UK via Gibraltar, arriving at Belfast on 12 October to disembark 882 NAS while she underwent a refit in a Clyde yard from mid-October. When the refit was complete she re-embarked 882 NAS at the end of January 1945 and rejoined the HF to work-up for further strike operations.

Searcher arrived in Scapa Flow on 4 March 1945 and added 746A (Firefly nightfighter development) NAS to the air group. On 20 March she sailed with *Premier* and *Queen* for Operation *Cupola*, in which mines were laid in Oranesund by aircraft, and fighters strafed coastal batteries and a patrol vessel. A week later she took part in Operation *Prefix* with *Queen*, during which her Wildcats shot down three Bf 109s and damaged two more, but Avengers from *Queen* found no targets for their bombs. On 6 April Operation *Newmarket* was intended as a strike on U-boat depot ships in Kilbotn in company with *Puncher*, *Queen* and *Trumpeter*, but prolonged bad weather caused it to be aborted. Another attempt, codenamed Operation *Judgement*, on 4 May 1945 with *Trumpeter* and *Queen*, succeeded in sinking

Searcher turns out of wind after landing-on a number of 882 NAS Wildcats. Handling teams have started to move aircraft aft out of Fly 1 into the range aft. (AUTHOR'S COLLECTION)

A number of RN escort carriers with other ships moored in Trincomalee during 1945. (AUTHOR'S COLLECTION)

Black Watch and U-711 and damaging *Senja*. This was the last combat operation by the HF in the Second World War, but *Searcher*, *Trumpeter* and *Queen* remained at sea to take part in Operation *Cleaver*, the liberation of Copenhagen by British naval forces on 6 May 1945. Royal Navy fighters intercepted a number of Ju 88 bombers in flight to Norway, but allowed them to fly on unmolested. *Searcher* returned to Scapa Flow on 10 May to disembark her aircraft, and began a refit in a Clyde yard five days later.

When the refit was completed she was allocated to 21 ACS in the EIF and, after re-embarking 882 NAS, sailed for Trincomalee on 1 July. By the time she arrived, however, the war had ended, and after a brief spell in Ceylon she sailed to return to the UK on 19 September. On 9 October she arrived in the Clyde, disembarked 882 NAS to disband and ceased active operations. She was destored and her ship's company was reduced in size to the minimum necessary to take her across the Atlantic. On 14 November she sailed for the USA, and 29 November 1945 she was returned to the USN at Norfolk, Virginia. The USN subsequently sold her for conversion to a merchant ship and she was renamed *Captain Theo* and later *Oriental Banker* from 1964. She was broken up for scrap in Taiwan in April 1976.

Stalker

Laid down by the Western Pipe & Steel Corporation in San Francisco on 6 October 1941, the hull was acquired by the USN shortly afterwards for conversion to a CVE. She was launched on 5 March 1942 as the USS *Hamlin*, ACV15, but subsequently transferred to the RN under Lend/Lease arrangements and commissioned as HMS *Stalker* in San Francisco on 21 December 1942. Formal completion was achieved on 30 December and after sea trials she sailed for New York on 30 January 1943. From there her progress towards operational capability was slow. She was loaded with US aircraft and sailed for Casablanca as part of convoy UGF6 on 5 March. After unloading the aircraft she refuelled in Gibraltar on 20 March and subsequently sailed with a fast convoy to the Clyde, arriving on 5 April. On 17 April she was taken in hand by Chatham Dockyard for modification to RN standards. When the work was completed at the end of June she returned to the Clyde areas to embark 833 (Swordfish/Seafire) composite NAS.

She was allocated to WAC and worked-up for duty as an escort carrier, but in early August she was allocated to Force V in the Western Mediterranean

and sailed for Gibraltar, arriving on 9 August. Once there she disembarked the Swordfish Flight of 833 NAS, embarked 880 (Seafire) NAS and prepared for operations as a fighter carrier. On 1 September she sailed for Malta to work-up with Force V, and on 9 September she took part Operation *Avalanche*, joining *Attacker*, *Battler*, *Hunter* and *Unicorn* to provide CAP over the Allied landings. *Illustrious* and *Formidable* provided distant cover. Once ground forces had captured an airfield at Paestum, *Stalker* disembarked two Seafires to it on 12 September and Force V withdrew. On 13 September she was in Bizerta, and on 20 September she re-embarked 833 NAS Swordfish in Gibraltar before returning in convoy to the Clyde, where both squadrons were disembarked. On 11 October she began a refit in Liverpool which lasted until mid-December, when she embarked 809 and 897 (Seafire) NAS and worked-up off Belfast. More modifications to equip her as an assault carrier were undertaken in a Thames yard in March and April 1944, and she then embarked 809 (Seafire) NAS and sailed for Gibraltar on 14 May with a slow convoy. In early June she was in Algiers, and in early August she worked-up off Malta with *Hunter* and the USN CVEs *Tulagi* and *Kasaan Bay* as part of Task Group 88.2.

From 15 August 1944 *Stalker* took part in Operation *Dragoon*, the Allied invasion of Southern France. By the time she left the operational area on 27 August her aircraft had flown 337 sorties, including CAPs, spotting, and both tactical and armed reconnaissance missions. On 2 September she arrived in Alexandria to prepare for operations in the Aegean, starting with Operation *Cablegram* on 25 September. In the following days her aircraft destroyed enemy aircraft, motor transport and coastal shipping around Rhodes and Leros. By the time she

returned to Alexandria at the end of the month her aircraft had flown 107 sorties. On 6 October she returned to strike at coastal shipping and then, after replenishment in Alexandria, she returned for Operation *Manna*, a concerted attack on railway infrastructure and coastal shipping in the Northern Aegean. By the time she left the operational area at the end of October, *Stalker*'s aircraft had flown a total of 277 strike sorties, during which five Seafires were lost to anti-aircraft fire. After a brief spell in Alexandria she returned to Devonport Dockyard for two weeks before returning to Gibraltar Dockyard, with 809 NAS still embarked, for a refit which began on 3 December.

When the refit was completed on 21 February 1945 she was allocated to 21 ACS in the EIF and sailed for Trincomalee. On 30 April she participated in Operation *Dracula*, a series of strikes against Japanese positions on the Rangoon and Tenasserim coasts of Burma in company with *Emperor*, *Khedive*, and *Hunter*. During this, 809 NAS flew CAPs over the fleet and both fighter-bomber and strafing missions, totalling 124 sorties. On 18 June she took part in Operation *Balsam*, a photographic reconnaissance of Southern Malaya and strikes against airfields in Sumatra in company with *Ameer* and *Khedive*. A Walrus amphibian of 1700 NAS was embarked for air-sea-rescue duties during this operation. In July she carried out operational training for the reoccupation of Singapore and Malaya, but Operation *Zipper* actually took place after the end of hostilities on 15 August. Stalker entered Singapore on 10 September in company with *Khedive*, *Emperor* and *Hunter*. She was in Singapore for only three days, leaving for Trincomalee on 13 September and then sailing for the UK on 2 October.

The RN had no further use for *Stalker*, and she was destored when she arrived in the Clyde on 22 October, after nearly a year away. Her ship's company was reduced in size to a steaming party which sailed her to the USA on 2 December. She was returned to USN custody on 29 December 1945 and sold by the USN for conversion to a merchant ship, being renamed *Riouw* at first and then *Lobito* in 1968. She was eventually broken up for scrap in Taiwan in September 1975.

Striker

Laid down on 15 December 1941 by the Western Pipe & Steel Corporation in San Francisco, she was subsequently acquired by the USN and launched on 7 May 1942 as the USS *Prince William*, CVE19 (not to be confused with the subsequent USN ship of that name given hull number CVE31). On 29 April 1943 she was completed, transferred to the RN under Lend/Lease arrangements and commissioned in San Francisco as HMS *Striker*. A month later she sailed for Norfolk, Virginia, after her sea trials and spent time in Norfolk before sailing for the UK as part of convoy HX246. She arrived first in Liverpool on 13 July, and on 18 July was taken in hand by Chatham Dockyard for modification to RN standards as a trade protection carrier. On completion of dockyard work she

embarked 824 (Swordfish/Sea Hurricane) composite NAS on 18 October and worked-up in the Irish Sea for allocation to WAC.

After a short period of defect rectification in a Clyde yard she sailed on 16 December 1943 to support slow convoys between the UK and Gibraltar, returning on 17 January 1944 for a period of defect rectification on the Clyde. On 8 February she sailed with the 16th Escort Group to provide support for two North Atlantic convoys before returning to support slow Gibraltar-bound convoys in March. Short periods of defect rectification work were carried out in the Clyde between convoys, and on 18 April she was transferred to the HF for operations in the Norwegian littoral. On 21 April she took part in Operations *Ridge Able* and *Ridge Baker* with *Victorious*, *Furious*, *Searcher, Emperor* and *Pursuer*, during which she provided antisubmarine cover for the force. On 7 May she sailed for Operation *Hoops* with *Searcher* and *Emperor*, to provide antisubmarine cover for the other carriers as their aircraft struck at coastal targets including a fish-oil factory at Fossevaag. On 11 May she embarked 898 (Wildcat) NAS in addition to 824 to increase the number of fighters available for CAPs.

In May she supported a Gibraltar-bound convoy before returning to the HF for Operations *Potluck A* and *B* on 12 June, attacks on shipping

Chaser at Circular Quay, near the famous harbour bridge in Sydney, showing her USN-allocated BPF pennant number R306. (RAN)

near Rorvik in company with *Emperor*. On 20 June she took part in Operation *Wanderers* with *Fencer* and a force of cruisers and destroyers intended to simulate both a Russian convoy and an impending invasion of Norway, to keep U-boats concentrated in the north away from the D-Day landings. At the end of June she had another defect rectification period in the Clyde and then sailed for an antisubmarine sweep off Cape Wrath in company with *Vindex* and the 3rd Escort Group. This was the last protracted hunt by escort carriers in the European war, and saw carrier aircraft landing in visibility of less than 200 yards, while RAF Coastal Command aircraft engaged in the operation were ordered to return to their bases because of the fog. On 1 August she sailed for Operation *Kinetic*, in which she provided antisubmarine protection for a force of cruisers destroyers that searched unsuccessfully for enemy convoys off the coast of Western France.

On 16 August 1944 *Striker* sailed with *Vindex* for Operation *Victual*, as part of the escort for convoy JW59 to North Russia, returning after a few days in the Kola Inlet with the return convoy, RA59A. On 16 September she sailed for Operation *Rigmarole* with

Fencer in Grand Harbour, Malta, during a trooping run. (RAN)

Campania as part of the escort for convoy JW60 to North Russia, returning with RA60, during which 824 NAS Swordfish flew extensive night antisubmarine patrols. This was to be her last operational sortie with the HF, and in October she was allocated to 30 ACS in the BPF as a replenishment carrier after a short refit on the Clyde. She arrived in Sydney on 7 January 1945, and after preparation, sailed for Ulithi Atoll via the BPF forward base at Manus and then to the logistic support areas off Sakashima Gunto, where 1 ACS was taking part in Operation *Iceberg*. She had eighteen replacement aircraft on board and flew four off to Task Force 57 on 25 March. On 28 she flew off thirteen replacement aircraft to the fleet carriers and recovered three unserviceable 'duds' for repair by the FAMG. She transferred a replacement Avenger crew to *Illustrious* and then departed for Leyte Gulf.

In Leyte Gulf she received more serviceable aircraft that had been brought from RN air stations in Australia in ferry carriers, and she sailed for the logistic support areas on 5 April 1945 with fourteen replacement aircraft. On 8 April she transferred twelve replacement aircraft of various types to the fleet carriers and an Avenger crew to 854 NAS in *Illustrious* before recovering four flyable 'duds' for repair. On 6 May she flew off fifteen replacement aircraft to the fleet carriers and embarked thirty-four casualties from *Formidable* for transfer to hospital ships. She flew off a further fourteen replacement aircraft and recovered a flyable 'dud' on 14 May, and six replacements a day later, again recovering a single 'dud' for repair. At the end of May she returned to Manus for a period of logistic consolidation with the forward aircraft pool.

On 9 July *Striker* sailed from Manus with *Arbiter* for the replenishment areas off Japan. By then she was flagship of 30 ACS, which formed part of Task Force 112, the logistic support element of the BPF. She transferred replacement aircraft to the fleet carriers on 20 July and again on 27 July before returning to Manus for more. On 4 August she sailed from Manus with a further load of replacement aircraft, but on 6 August it became clear that the war would end before she could deliver them, and she was ordered to return. By the end of the month she was in Sydney, being prepared for trooping duties.

On 18 September 1945 she sailed from Sydney with men and equipment for the recently liberated colony of Hong Kong. In October she returned to Sydney for a maintenance period and then sailed for Singapore, where she spent a month before sailing to return to the UK. She eventually arrived in the Clyde on 16 December to be destored and have a large portion of her ship's company demobilised. She sailed for her last voyage on 20 January and was handed back to the USN on 12 February 1946. The USN sold her for scrap and she was broken up in June 1946.

CHAPTER 17

RULER CLASS

Ameer with Hellcats on deck. (AUTHOR'S COLLECTION)

Effectively repeats of *Tracker*, the last ship of the *Attacker* class, the twenty-three units of the *Ruler* class were all built from the outset as warships but still based on the C-3 design. The USN construction programme for 1943 included twenty-four units of the *Prince William* class based on the C-3 hull and the fifty specially designed ships of the *Casablanca* class to be built by Kaiser in only twelve months. Significant numbers of both classes were intended for the RN, and in November 1942 the Admiralty formalised a bid for five C-3 types and fourteen of the *Casablanca* class. This was approved, but a further request for another twelve of the latter was refused. By May 1943, however, it was evident that the Kaiser-built ships would not appear as quickly as anticipated, and in June the Admiralty agreed to accept an equal number of C-3s in exchange for the Kaisers. Subsequently the USN transferred four more C-3s to provide the RN with a standardised class and retained only the name-ship, *Prince William*, for itself. The entire *Casablanca* class was retained for USN service, but some were actually allocated names in early 1943 by the RN which were subsequently reallocated to C-3 hulls after the change. These included CVE-55, *Casablanca* herself, which was to have been HMS *Ameer*; CVE-59 was to have been HMS *Atheling* but became the USS *Mission Bay*, and CVE-62 was to have been HMS *Begum* but became USS *Natoma Bay*.

These changes occurred before US concerns arose in August 1943 about the time taken by the RN to bring CVEs into action, but the USN subsequently decided that no further CVEs would be allocated to

the British other than those already earmarked, because it was evident that the RN lacked sufficient personnel to man them effectively. Engine-room and supply departments in these ships were largely manned by Merchant Navy personnel under T.142X articles, and even then there were insufficient flight-deck and air-maintenance personnel to use all the ships operationally. Of the fifteen CVEs delivered after August 1943, nine were used as aircraft ferries or for training tasks. By 1944 the Admiralty was making plans to run down the number of CVEs in operation in order to find men to man the new light fleet carriers.

Technical background

Although superficially identical to the *Attacker* class, the *Ruler* class incorporated a number of detail changes. The *Attackers* were fitted with British radars and guns on arrival in the UK, but the *Rulers* were accepted complete with USN SG and SK radars. The former was a 10cm surface-search set, and the latter a 1.5m air-search set; both had powered continuous aerial rotation and plan position indicators well before most British sets were so fitted, and were the envy of many British officers. They also retained their American fire-control radars and weapons. The ships were transferred with complete USN stores outfits including steel helmets.

Although the American equipment worked well in service, the weapons required different ammunition, and even screw threads and electrical

systems were different, requiring maintenance personnel to undergo specialised training, some of it in the USA, and even to have tool kits containing spanners and other tools that could not be used on British equipment. The *Ruler* Class had improved H-4C hydraulic catapults capable of launching heavier aircraft than the *Attackers*, but could only use the 'tail-down' method with a strop. This effectively limited them to launching American-built aircraft, as British aircraft mostly used the trolley method, but as the deck was large enough for Seafires and Swordfish to carry out free take-offs, the limitation was not a major one in practice. Both types could be fitted with rocket-assisted take-off gear (RATOG), in extremely light wind conditions.

The major disadvantage with the *Ruler* class was the hangar deck, which followed the sloping contour of the original C-3 upper deck like that in the previous class. This made it difficult to move aircraft in rough weather, with the result that winches and wires sometimes had to be used to haul aircraft 'up the slope' on to the lift platforms when the ship was pitching. The after-lift posed another problem. Although it was the same size as the forward lift, its longer dimension was athwartships. This meant that aircraft which were stowed fore-and-aft in the hangar and on deck had to be manoeuvred through 90 degrees to fit them on to the lift. For example, the length of a Grumman Avenger was 40ft, but the fore-and-aft dimension of the after lift was only 34ft. Its athwartship dimension was only 42ft, so positioning an aircraft on to it was a difficult and time-consuming task. Fitting lifts at the forward and after extremities of the hangar was a good design feature, but while fitting the after one at right angles to the forward one might have been seen as a flexible idea on the drawing board, it did not work in practice. Since the ships were mass-produced using production-line techniques there was no prospect of changing the design without losing an unacceptable amount of valuable time.

Conversion of the avgas stowage arrangements and modifications to the magazine protection arrangements were similar to those carried out in the *Attacker* Class.

Ruler Class technical details

Displacement:	15,390 tons deep load
Dimensions:	length 492ft
	beam 108ft 6in
	draught 25ft 5in
Machinery:	1 shaft Allis-Chalmers geared turbine
	2 Foster-Wheeler boilers 8,500shp delivering 18 knots
Armament:	2 single 5in USN Mark 9; 8 twin 40mm Bofors; 14 twin 20mm Oerlikon; 7 single 20mm Oerlikon (individual ships varied in number of 20mm fitted)
Fuel:	3,290 tons FFO
Endurance:	27,500nm at 11 knots; 18,750nm at 18 knots
Complement:	646

Aircraft operating data

Flight deck:	450ft x 80ft wood covered steel plate
Hangar:	260ft x 62ft x 18ft
Catapult:	1 x H4C hydraulic; 16,000lb at 74 knots end speed
Arrester wires:	9 x 19,800lb at 55 knots entry speed
	3 barriers capable of stopping 19,800lb aircraft
Lifts:	forward 42ft long x 34ft wide, 14,000lb
	aft 34ft long x 42ft wide, 14,000lb
Aircraft:	up to 30; up to 90 could be ferried
Aircraft fuel:	36,000gal avgas
Air weapons:	18in, 22.4in and homing torpedoes; 500lb SAP bombs; 250lb bombs; 3in rocket projectiles; depth charges; 0.5in and 0.303in gun ammunition; flares and pyrotechnics. (Individual outfits varied significantly with the role on which the ship was employed)

The *Ruler* class was the largest class of aircraft carriers to serve with the RN. The ships' operational histories that follow are listed in the

Slinger turns into wind to launch two Seafires of 768 NAS in November 1944. (AUTHOR'S COLLECTION)

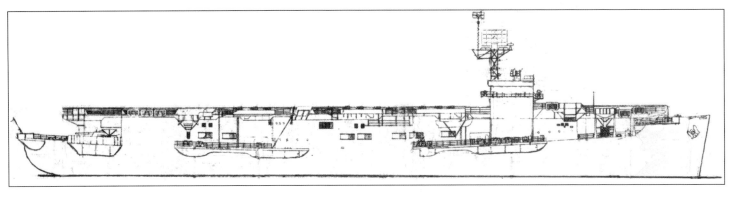

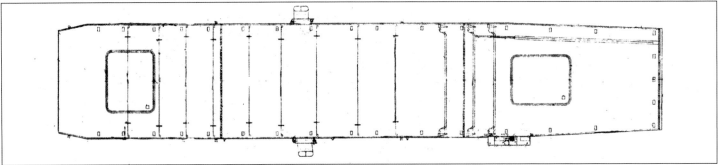

Top *Ruler* Class profile. (Author's collection)

Above *Ruler* Class flight deck. (Author's collection)

order in which they were laid down; their original USN hull numbers are therefore sequential. The original name ship of the class, *Prince William*, retained in service with the USN, was CVE-31. All twenty-three ships were built by the Seattle-Tacoma Shipbuilding Corporation in the same shipyard in Seattle and, as work on them progressed, improving production-line techniques reduced their building time from fourteen-and-a-half months for the first ship to eight-and-a-half for the last. This was a remarkable achievement in itself, but the company managed to reduce build times for subsequent CVEs to three-and-a-half months, and the tempo of construction can be seen from the short intervals between the dates on which new hulls were laid down.

To reduce the time taken to get these ships into service, a number were taken from their builders directly to Burrard's Shipyard in Vancouver, where three CVEs at a time were modified to RN standards. The work entailed 150 separate modifications, including lengthening the flight deck, fitting an improved flying control position (Flyco) and fitting a redesigned fighter direction room, as well as making improvements to the hangar and modifying the avgas stowage and pumping arrangements. Only 2 per cent of Burrard's workforce had ever worked on a ship before the war, and each new man or woman was

taught to carry out a single task in the interest of speeding completion. The cost of the work was funded by the Canadian Government as part of its contribution to the British war effort. The ships were moved to Vancouver by a steaming party made up with men from other ships in Burrard's yard, as no T.142X men were available at first. For a while *Thane* was used as an accommodation ship for a pool of sailors in Vancouver that could be used for a variety of essential tasks. Stores for every CVE arrived in boxes which were immediately stowed away, as there was no supply staff or time to check them. Since the ships were fitted with USN-pattern guns, ammunition was taken on board from Bremerton Navy Yard. At the end of the work there was a single day of builder's sea trials, after which the ship's senior officer signed for his ship on behalf of the Admiralty and set off for the UK.

Individual ship histories

Slinger

Originally given the hull number CVE-32, this ship was laid down on 25 May 1942 and launched as the USS *Chatham* on 15 December. On 11 August 1943 she was completed, transferred to the RN and commissioned as HMS *Slinger*. She passed through the Panama Canal on 29 September and arrived in Norfolk Navy Yard on 6 October, where she was allocated to WAC for use a ferry carrier. She

embarked 1830 (Corsair) NAS for passage to the UK on 9 October and sailed for the UK, in convoy, on 15 October 1943. After disembarking the squadron to RNAY Belfast she was taken in hand at Chatham Dockyard in November for modifications to RN standards, but on leaving the yard on 5 February 1944 she was mined in the River Medway and extensively damaged. At first there was no dockyard capacity to repair her, and she returned to Chatham to be cannibalised for spare parts for other carriers. Her forward lift went to *Stalker* and had to be replaced by another in due course.

She was eventually taken to a shipyard on the Thames, where repairs were carried out that lasted until mid-October 1944, when she sailed for the Clyde. After a brief work-up she was used as a deck-landing training carrier in November, with fighters of 768 NAS embarked. In December she was allocated for duty with the BPF as a replenishment carrier, and she sailed for the Far east in early January 1945 with 1845 (Corsair) NAS embarked. After refuelling stops in Gibraltar, Port Said and Colombo she arrived in Sydney on 22 February 1945. A typical load for a BPF replenishment carrier at this time was ten Corsairs, seven Hellcats, three Seafires, one Avenger and one Firefly, and she sailed on 11 March 1945 to join Task Force 112, the Fleet Train, joining *Speaker*, *Ruler*, *Striker* and *Chaser*. After brief stops in Manus and Leyte Gulf to refuel she rendezvoused with the BPF at sea with twenty-five replacement aircraft embarked. On 5 April she transferred twenty-two of them to the operational carriers in Task Force 57 and recovered two 'flyable duds' for repair by the FAMG.

In July 1945 she was in Sydney, and in August she was used to repatriate former prisoners of the Japanese from Hong Kong to Australia. In October 1945 she carried out a defect rectification period in Sydney, then sailed on 10 November to carry Service personnel back to the UK. She arrived in Devonport on 24 December 1945, and her operational career effectively ended on 16 January 1946, when she arrived in the Clyde to be destored. She sailed for the USA on 25 January with a small steaming party, and was officially returned to the USN in Norfolk Navy Yard on 27 February 1946. The USN subsequently sold her for conversion into a merchant ship, and she became the mercantile *Robin Mowbray*. On 29 January 1970 she arrived in Taiwan to be broken up for scrap.

Atheling

Laid down on 9 June 1942 and launched as the USS *Glacier* on 7 September, CVE-33 was commissioned into the US Navy on 3 July 1943 in Puget Sound Navy Yard. On 31 July she was decommissioned and handed over to the RN before moving to Vancouver, where she was modified to RN standards. Initially she was to have been named *Setter*, but she eventually commissioned as HMS *Atheling* at Burrard's shipyard in Vancouver on 28 October 1943. She arrived at New York on 22 December 1943, and sailed in convoy for the

UK with 1836 (Corsair) NAS embarked for passage on 1 January 1944.

On 10 January work began to modify her with an operations room for use as a fighter carrier, and this was completed in mid-February, when she was allocated to the EF. She sailed from the UK on 3 March 1944 with 822 and 823 (Barracuda) NAS plus 1837 and 1838 (Corsair) NAS embarked for passage. She formed part of convoy KMF 29A to Port Said and passed through the Suez Canal on 23 March. On 28 March she sailed with convoy AJ 2 from Aden to Colombo, and later convoy JC 34A from Colombo to Madras, where the squadrons disembarked. On 13 May she embarked 899 (Seafire) and 890 (Wildcat) NAS and worked-up as a fighter carrier before taking part in Operation *Councillor*, a diversionary sweep into the Indian Ocean with *Illustrious* in June, intended to divert Japanese attention from American operations in the Marianas. On 21 July 1944 she embarked 818 (Swordfish) NAS for duty as a trade protection carrier. On 25 August she left Trincomalee with 818 NAS embarked to ferry 1838 (Corsair) NAS to RNAS Wingfield in South Africa before carrying out antisubmarine operations between Mauritius and Cape Town. She then disembarked 818 NAS to RNAS Cochin and prepared for duty as a ferry carrier on loan to the USN.

After a brief defect rectification period in Sydney she ferried American aircraft across the Pacific before reverting to RN operational control

Unlike the earlier classes of CVE in the RN, the *Rulers* were fitted with USN SK air-search and SG surface-search radars. Their aerials stand out in this photograph, together with the 'YE' homing beacon aerial on the tallest mast. (AUTHOR'S COLLECTION)

at Norfolk Navy Yard in August 1945, but she saw no more use as a carrier. Her first task was to ferry Service personnel from Trinidad to the UK, after which she carried out a variety of trooping duties to and from the Far East, during which she visited Australia, New Zealand, Trincomalee and Aden. Trooping duties ended in November 1946, when she returned to the Clyde to be destored. She was returned to the USN by a reduced ship's company on 13 December 1946 and subsequently sold for mercantile conversion. In 1950 she was renamed *Roma*, and operated until November 1967, when she was sold for scrap in Italy.

Emperor

Laid down on 23 June 1942, CVE-34 was launched as the USS *Pybus* on 7 October 1942 and moved to Puget Sound Navy Yard for completion. She was completed on 31 May 1943 and entered service with the USN, but following the decision to transfer more C-3 hulls to the RN instead of *Casablanca* class ships, she was transferred to the RN in New York on 6 August 1943 and commissioned as HMS *Emperor*. At one stage the

Hellcats of 800 NAS ranged on *Emperor*. (AUTHOR'S COLLECTION)

name *Stinger* was considered for her but not adopted. She subsequently sailed for the UK in convoy and arrived in the Clyde on 3 September to be allocated to WAC. Modifications to RN standards and the installation of an operations room to fit her for use as a fighter carrier were carried out in Belfast between September 1943 and February 1944, after which she embarked 800 and 804 (Hellcat) NAS and worked-up in the Clyde areas.

After convoy support operations in the North Atlantic she transferred to the HF to take part in Operation *Tungsten* on 3 April 1944, the first strike on *Tirpitz* by aircraft of the HF, in company with *Victorious*, *Furious*, *Pursuer*, *Searcher* and *Fencer*. Extensive damage was caused to the primary target, and the supply ship *C A Larsen* was also damaged. A repeat attack by the same force, codenamed Operation *Planet*, had to be cancelled on 24 April because of bad weather, but two days later *Emperor* took part in Operations *Ridge Able* and *Ridge Baker* in company with *Victorious*, *Furious*, *Searcher*, *Pursuer* and *Striker*. These were planned as strikes against enemy shipping in Bodo and Rorvik. Bad weather caused *Able* to be cancelled, but three ships were sunk off Bodo in *Baker*, and a fourth damaged. On 8 May 1944 she joined *Searcher* and *Striker* in Operation *Hoops*, a strike against shipping between Gossen and Kristiansand North, oil tanks at Kjehn and a fish-oil factory at Fossevag. Her aircraft shot down five enemy fighters for the loss of two Hellcats, and an enemy patrol vessel, V-5704, was set on fire. Intensive operations in the Norwegian littoral continued, and on 14 May *Emperor* joined *Striker*

in Operation *Potluck A*, a strike on shipping in Rorvik. Three enemy merchant ships, including the 3,000-ton *Tyrifjord*, were hit by bombs and damaged, and five Heinkel He 115 floatplanes were strafed and destroyed. A day later the fish-oil factory at Fossevag was struck again in Operation *Potluck B* and two enemy armed trawlers were strafed and sunk. On 23 May 1944 she rejoined WAC and supported slow convoys from Liverpool to the Mediterranean and West Africa.

On 6 June 1944 she operated in company with *Pursuer* and *Tracker* to give fighter cover over the western approaches to the English Channel during Operation *Neptune*, the naval element of the D-Day landings in Normandy. Later in June 804 NAS was absorbed into 800 NAS to form a single, large fighter squadron, and *Emperor* deployed to the Mediterranean on 15 July 1944. A single Walrus was embarked for ASR duties. On 12 August she joined *Attacker*, *Khedive*, *Pursuer* and *Searcher* to form Task Group 88.1 and provide fighter cover for Operation *Dragoon*, the Allied landings in the south of France. *Hunter* and *Stalker* joined the USN CVEs *Tulagi* and *Kasaan Bay* in Task Group 88.2. Between 15 and 23 August *Emperor*'s fighters flew 252 operational sorties for the loss of eleven Hellcats. Tasking included CAPs, TARCAPs and dive-bombing as well as interdiction missions. With their greater radius of action, *Emperor*'s Hellcats were able to fly long-range interdiction sorties up the Rhône Valley and over much of southern France, strafing motor transport, railways, road intersections and horse-drawn transport. On 24 August she anchored in Maddalena with ten serviceable aircraft embarked plus four that were repairable.

On 2 September 1944 she arrived in Alexandria with other CVEs to prepare for operations in the

Aegean Sea, beginning with Operation *Outing* on 14 September, a series of attacks on shipping, motor transport and German garrisons in the Aegean islands. After a brief return to Alexandria to refuel and rearm in late September, she sailed for Operation *Outing II* on 30 September and destroyed landing craft, caiques and small craft for the loss of a single Hellcat to anti-aircraft fire. Another had to divert to an airfield in Turkey when its undercarriage failed to lower. On 12 October Hellcats dive-bombed and destroyed Plimiri radar station on Rhodes before a brief return to Alexandria for fuel, after which *Emperor* joined *Stalker* and *Attacker* with supporting cruisers and destroyers for Operation *Manna*, a series of strikes against motor transport, coastal shipping and road bridges during which Hellcats dive-bombed and destroyed a radar station on Milos, but a damaged Hellcat had to make a forced landing on Mount Olympus. The final phase was Operation *Contempt*, in which fighter cover was provided for the occupation of Milos by British troops. Throughout the Aegean operations *Emperor*'s Hellcats flew 455 operational sorties, more than double the total flown by any other CVE. On 20 November 1944 she returned to the UK for a refit in Newport, after which she was allocated to the 21st ACS in the EIF.

She sailed with 800 NAS embarked on 1 March 1945, arrived in Colombo on 25 March and began operations in the Indian Ocean with Operation *Sunfish* on 4 April, a photographic reconnaissance of Port Swettenham and strike on Emmahaven in company with *Khedive*. For this operation detachments from 808 (Hellcat) and 845 (Avenger) NAS were also embarked. For Operation *Dracula* on 21 April, 800 NAS was the only squadron embarked. This was a strike against the

Rangoon and Tenasserim coast regions in company with *Khedive*, *Hunter* and *Stalker*. Operation *Collie* on 2 July 1945 was a strike on the Nicobar islands in company with *Ameer*, and the provision of fighter cover for minesweeping forces off Phuket Island by both carriers.

On 4 September 1945 *Emperor* sailed for Operation *Zipper*, the reoccupation of Singapore, and she anchored in Keppel Harbour a day later in company with *Khedive*, *Ameer*, *Empress*, *Hunter* and *Stalker*. This marked the end of her active service, however, and she sailed for the UK on 30 October and arrived in the Clyde on 4 December 1945 for destoring, after which she moved to Plymouth on 8 January 1946. The RN had no further use for her, and a steaming party sailed her to the USA on 23 January. She was returned to the USN at Norfolk Navy Yard on 12 February 1946. She was not sold for mercantile conversion but was subsequently sold for scrap.

Ameer

Laid down on 18 July 1942, CVE-35 was launched as the USS *Baffins* on 18 October 1942 and nominally completed on 28 June 1943, when she was commissioned into the USN. On 19 July she was deactivated and transferred to the RN, commissioning a day later as HMS *Ameer*. Some

months of defect rectification and modification to British standards followed at Burrard's yard in Vancouver before she moved to New York to join a UK-bound convoy, sailing on 2 January 1944. After her arrival in the Clyde she was converted into an assault carrier, and when the work was complete she sailed to join the EF on 6 May 1944, arriving in Trincomalee on 27 June 1944, almost exactly a year after her original acceptance by the USN.

At first she was employed as a ferry carrier, but on 26 July she embarked 845 (Avenger) NAS for operations as a trade protection carrier in the Indian Ocean until the end of December, when she disembarked the Avengers and prepared to carry out her intended role as an assault carrier. On 18 January 1945 she embarked a re-formed 804 (Hellcat) NAS and sailed to provide fighter cover for the battleship *Queen Elizabeth* and the cruiser *Phoebe*, which bombarded Japanese positions ashore as part of Operation *Matador*, the British landings on Ramree Island. On 26 January she gave fighter cover for Royal Marines landing on Cheduba island in Operation *Sankey*, and on 26 February her Hellcats escorted photographic reconnaissance Hellcats of 888 NAS in *Empress* which carried out a reconnaissance of the Kra Isthmus, Penang and Northern Sumatra as a prelude to the recovery of Singapore and Malaya from Japanese occupation.

On 1 March 1945 804 NAS shot down three Japanese aircraft for no loss while engaged on escort duties.

On 18 June 1945 a detachment of 888 NAS joined 804 NAS and *Ameer* began Operation *Balsam*, a photographic reconnaissance of Southern Malaya and strikes against airfields in Northern Sumatra. On 5 July she disembarked her normal squadron and embarked 896 (Hellcat) NAS for strikes against the Nicobar Islands and cover for minesweeping operations near Phuket Island as part of Operation *Collie*. On 24 July 804 NAS was re-embarked, together with an ASR Walrus for Operation *Livery*, strikes on Northern Malaya and cover for further minesweeping operations. In three days Hellcats from *Ameer* and *Emperor* flew over 150 sorties and destroyed more than thirty Japanese aircraft on the ground, together with road and rail transport.

On 26 July 1945 *Ameer* became the only British aircraft carrier to be attacked by a Japanese kamikaze aircraft in the Bay of Bengal. A single Mitsubishi Ki-51 'Sonia' dived at the ship but was hit by anti-aircraft fire which first deflected it and then shot it down into the water 500 yards clear

Begum in the Eastern Fleet during 1944, with the Avengers and Wildcats of 832 NAS on deck. (AUTHOR'S COLLECTION)

of the ship. After the Japanese surrender *Ameer* embarked 808 (Hellcat) NAS and a single ASR Walrus of 1700 NAS for her last operational activity, Operation *Zipper*, the reoccupation of Singapore. She sailed for the UK on 30 October and arrived in the Clyde to be destored on 18 November 1945. A reduced ship's company sailed her to Norfolk Navy Yard on 22 December, and she was formally returned to the USN there on 17 January 1946. In September the USN sold her for mercantile conversion and she became the SS *Robin Kirk* in 1948. In 1969 she was broken up for scrap in Taiwan.

Begum

Laid down on 3 August 1942 as CVE-36, she was launched on 11 November 1942 as the USS *Bolinas* and completed on 22 July 1943. She was commissioned into the USN on the same day. On 2 August 1943 she was deactivated by the USN and transferred to the RN as part of the adjustment of CVE allocations, being commissioned as HMS *Begum* on that day. The name had originally been allocated to a unit of the *Casablanca* Class, and was transferred with the revised allocation. She is, to date, the only RN warship ever to have been commissioned with the name. Later in August she moved to Burrard's yard for modifications to RN standards. She eventually passed through the Panama Canal on 4 January 1944 and eventually sailed in convoy from New York for the UK with 1837 and 1838 (Corsair) NAS embarked for passage. On 1 February 1944 she entered a Clyde shipyard for minor modifications which were completed by the end of the month.

On 3 March 1944 she was allocated to the EF and sailed with 1839 (Corsair), 1844 (Hellcat), 815 and 817 (Barracuda) NAS embarked for passage, arriving in Colombo on 26 April. On 11 June 1944 she embarked 832 (Avenger/Wildcat) composite NAS and carried out antisubmarine sweeps in the Indian Ocean until mid-January 1945, when she returned to the UK for a refit and

modification for use as a ferry carrier in a Clyde shipyard. After being allocated to the BPF she embarked 721 (Vultee Vengeance) and 1701 (Sea Otter) NAS in early April for passage, and sailed for Australia on 17 April 1945, arriving in Sydney on 5 June 1945. She was immediately loaded with replacement aircraft for the operational task force, and ferried them to the forward base at RNAS Ponam in the Admiralty Islands, arriving on 15 June. Her period as a ferry carrier was short-lived, however, and in July she was allocated to the EIF as a deck-landing training carrier for operation in the Ceylon areas, allowing pilots in transit to the BPF to maintain flying currency. The end of the war brought this task to an end in October, and she sailed for the UK on 23 October 1945.

Begum arrived on the Clyde to be destored on 10 November 1945, and sailed for the USA a month later. She was formally returned to the USN at Norfolk Navy Yard on 5 January 1946 and subsequently sold for mercantile conversion in April 1947. She became the SS *Raki* and then, in 1966, the *I Yung*. She was broken up for scrap in Taiwan during March 1974.

Trumpeter

Laid down as CVE-37 on 25 August 1942, she was launched as the USS *Bastian* on 15 December and moved to Commercial Ironworks for completion. On 4 August 1943 she was completed, transferred to the RN under Lend/Lease arrangements and commissioned as HMS *Trumpeter* in Portland, Oregon. She subsequently sailed for Norfolk Navy Yard and passed through the Panama Canal on 29 September 1943, arriving on 6 October. After embarking 848 (Avenger), 1831 and 1833 (Corsair) NAS for passage to the UK she sailed in convoy via New York on 23 October and arrived in Belfast on 1 November 1943. She was allocated to WAC as a ferry carrier, and made two Atlantic crossings to ferry aircraft from new York to the Clyde.

In February 1944 she began a refit in Dundee which was completed in May, when she moved to

Rosyth Dockyard for modifications to RN standards to be incorporated. On 4 June she was allocated to the HF and embarked 846 (Avenger/Wildcat) composite NAS to work-up in the Clyde areas. On 10 August 1944 she took part in Operation *Offspring*, a fighter sweep against Gossen Airfield and minelaying by aircraft in Haarhamsfjord and Lepsorev in company with *Indefatigable* and *Nabob*. On 22 October 1944 she took part in Operation *Goodwood*, a strike against the *Tirpitz* in Kaafjord, in company with *Indefatigable*, *Formidable*, *Furious* and *Nabob* which was synchronised with cover for the passage of convoy JW 59 to North Russia and fighter 'Ramrods' against airfields in Hammerfest and Banak. Unfortunately low cloud obscured the target and caused the attack to be aborted. On 12 September she took part in Operation *Begonia*, minelaying and attacks on shipping off Vorkso, with 846 and 852 (Avenger) NAS embarked. Seventeen mines were laid, and Seafires from *Furious* sank a minesweeper and two coasters. In October *Trumpeter* joined an antisubmarine sweep in support of convoy RA 60.

Further minelaying sorties included Operation *Lycidas* off Haarhamsfjord on 14 October in company with *Fencer*, and Operation *Hardy* off Lepsorev on 24 October 1944 in company with *Campania*. Bad weather limited concurrent strikes against shipping, but fighters strafed Gossen Airfield. On 7 December Operation *Urbane* involved minelaying off Sulhusstrommen with 856 (Avenger) and 881 (Wildcat) NAS embarked. A day later *Trumpeter* joined *Implacable* for an armed coastal reconnaissance during which several merchant ships were set on fire and an 'R' boat sunk in Bommelnfjord. Operation *Lacerate* on 14 December 1944 involved minelaying in Ramsoysund with the same air group embarked, in company with *Premier*. Twelve mines were laid, but five Ju 88s attacked the force; they caused no damage and one was shot down by anti-aircraft fire. The weather deteriorated, and an Avenger ranged on *Trumpeter*'s flight deck was blown over the stern. Operation *Fretsaw* on 21 December was planned as a strike against shipping off Stadlandet with 846 (Avenger/Wildcat) composite NAS embarked, but no targets were found and the operation proved unsuccessful.

The year 1945 started with Operation *Spellbinder* in company with *Premier*; antisubmarine patrols to cover surface forces that attacked an enemy convoy off Egersund. Operation *Gratis* a day later involved minelaying in the Haugesund area, after which fighters strafed and destroyed Utsira radar as the force withdrew.

On 5 February 1945 *Trumpeter* arrived at a Clyde shipyard for a refit which lasted until late March. On 6 April she sailed for Operation *Newmarket*, a strike against U-boat depot ships in Kilbotn in company with *Puncher*, *Queen* and *Searcher*. Despite cruising off the target area for several days, bad weather prevented flying and the attack was postponed. Another attempt, Operation *Judgement*, was made with the same squadron embarked in company with *Searcher* and *Queen* on 4 May 1945. This time the weather was perfect and the German depot ship *Black Watch* of 5,000 tons was sunk, together with the *Senja* and U-711, which had been alongside her. This proved to be the last offensive operation by the HF before the end of the war in Europe four days later. Before the task group could return to Scapa Flow it was ordered to implement Operation *Cleaver* to provide air and antisubmarine protection for British naval forces entering Copenhagen, in case they were attacked by German forces that refused to surrender. On VE Day, 8 May 1945, *Trumpeter* returned to Scapa Flow, and on 15 May she commenced a refit in a Clyde shipyard.

When it was completed, in July, she was allocated to the EIF as a deck-landing training carrier without an allocated air group, but she did not arrive in Ceylon until after the Japanese surrender. In September she was allocated for trooping duties within the EIF area, and carried men and equipment between Port Swettenham,

Singapore, Trincomalee, Bombay and Cochin. The task ended in January 1946 and she sailed from Colombo for the UK on 5 January, arriving in the Clyde to destore on 10 February. Her active life as a warship ended on 6 April 1946, when a small RN steaming party formally returned her to the USN under the terms of the Lend/Lease agreement. She was subsequently sold for conversion to a merchant ship and became the SS *Alblasserdjik*. In 1966 she was sold on and renamed *Irene Valmas* before ending her days in a scrapyard at Castellon in May 1971.

Empress

Ordered as CVE-38 and laid down on 9 September 1942, she was launched as the USS *Carnegie* on 30 December 1942 but transferred to the RN on 8 June 1943. She was completed on 9 September and moved to Burrard's yard in Vancouver, where she was commissioned as HMS *Empress* on 12 September and subsequently modified to RN standards. The work was completed in early 1944, and she sailed for New York on 17 February, passing through the Panama Canal on 9 March. Once in New York she embarked 850 (Avenger) NAS for passage and sailed in convoy for the UK on 26 March. After her arrival in the Clyde on 8 April 1944 she spent a considerable period in Clyde shipyards and Rosyth Dockyard undergoing defect rectification before being allocated to the EIF.

Empress in 1944 with her aircraft derricks rigged aft. Interestingly, although she is at anchor, there appears to be no jack on the jack-staff, which is almost exactly in line with the FH4 HF/DF aerial sited on the starboard side of Fly 1. (R A BURT COLLECTION)

She sailed in convoy from the UK on 6 January 1945 and arrived in Trincomalee on 4 February, where she joined the 21st ACS and prepared for operational service. Her first active mission was Operation *Stacey* in company with *Ameer*, with detachments of 888 (Hellcat PR), 845 (Avenger) and 804 (Hellcat) NAS embarked. This involved photographic reconnaissance of the Kra Isthmus and Sumatra. Next she took part in Operation *Bishop*, strikes against Japanese installations in the Nicobar and Andaman Islands in company with *Shah*, with 804 (Hellcat) NAS and an ASR Walrus of 1700 NAS embarked. The same aircraft were embarked for Operation *Livery* in company with *Ameer*, during which strikes were carried out against targets in northern Malaya and cover was provided for minesweepers off Phuket Island. On 8 September 1945 she participated in Operation *Zipper*, the reoccupation of Singapore, with 896 (Hellcat) NAS and an ASR Walrus of 1700 NAS embarked.

This was her last active deployment and she returned to Colombo in October, but in November she visited Wellington in New Zealand before returning to the UK via Ceylon. She arrived in the Clyde on 19 December 1945 and subsequently sailed for the USA on 6 January. Formally returned to the USN on 4 February 1946, no further use was found for her and she was sold for scrap on 21 June.

Khedive

Laid down on 22 September 1942, CVE-39 was launched as the USS *Cordova* on 30 January 1943 and moved to Williamette Valley ironworks for completion. Before she was completed she was transferred to the RN under Lend/Lease arrangements, commissioned as HMS *Khedive* on 23 August 1943 and moved to Burrard's yard in Vancouver by a small steaming party for modification to RN standards. She sailed for Norfolk Navy Yard on 24 September 1943. Once there she embarked 849 (Avenger) and 1834 (Corsair) NAS for passage, and sailed in convoy for Liverpool, arriving on 16 November 1943. She was allocated to WAC but immediately taken in hand by Rosyth Dockyard for modifications to assault carrier standard. These lasted until March 1944 but, unfortunately, she collided with *Stuart Queen* shortly after their completion and had to undergo repairs in a Clyde yard until May.

On 15 May 1944 she embarked 899 (Seafire) NAS and began a work-up to operational efficiency, based in Scapa Flow. On 15 July she

Khedive in 1945. Apart from her pennant number, 62, she can be identified from the air by the letter 'K' painted on her forward lift. (AUTHOR'S COLLECTION)

sailed for Malta, and from 15 August she took part in Operation *Dragoon*, the Allied landings in the south of France, in which she formed part of TG 88.1 with *Attacker*, *Emperor*, *Pursuer* and *Searcher*. When she withdrew from the area on 23 August her aircraft had flown 201 combat sorties, during which they had dive-bombed coastal gun batteries and strafed troop movements and transport, dropping ninety-four 500lb and forty-four 250lb bombs. On 2 September 1944 she arrived in Alexandria to prepare for operations in the Aegean Sea, and sailed for Operation *Outing* on 9 September in company with *Searcher*, *Pursuer* and *Hunter*. This involved CAPs over minesweepers operating in the Kithera Channel and strafing targets of opportunity on Rhodes and Crete. On completion of this operation she returned to the UK and underwent a period of defect rectification in London Docks from 23 October.

The work was completed on 11 January 1945 and she embarked 808 (Hellcat) NAS for service in the EIF. She passed through the Suez Canal on 24 January and arrived in Cochin on 3 February to join 21 ACS. At first she was used as a ferry carrier between India and Ceylon, but on 11 April she embarked 808 NAS for Operation *Sunfish*, a photographic reconnaissance of the Port Swettenham area in company with *Emperor*. On 30 April she sailed for Operation *Dracula*, a series of strikes in the Rangoon and Tenasserim coastal areas in company with *Emperor* and *Stalker*. A single ASR Walrus of 1700 NAS was embarked.

In May 1945 she took part in the search for the Japanese cruiser *Haguro*, and from 18 June she took part in Operation *Balsam*, a photographic reconnaissance of southern Malaya and strikes on targets in Sumatra in company with *Ameer* and *Stalker*.

On 10 August 1945 she sailed from Trincomalee for the reoccupation of Penang, and on 8 September she sailed for Operation *Zipper*, the reoccupation of Singapore. On 10 September she entered Keppel Harbour in company with *Emperor*, *Hunter*, *Stalker* and a number of other warships. She was there for only three days, however, sailing for Trincomalee on 13 September. After visiting Durban she sailed for the UK with 808 NAS embarked on 13 November 1945. The squadron disembarked to disband on 5 December and *Khedive* entered the Clyde to be destored on 8 December. On 4 January 1946 she sailed for Halifax, Nova Scotia, and from there to Norfolk Navy Yard, where she was handed back to the USN on 26 January. She lay idle for a year, but was sold for mercantile conversion on 23 January 1947 and subsequently renamed *Rempang*. In 1968 she was renamed *Daphne* and in January 1976 she arrived at Gandria to be broken up for scrap.

Speaker

Laid down as CVE-40 on 9 October 1942, she was launched as the USS *Delgada* on 20 February 1943 and moved to the Williamette Iron & Steel

Speaker with both her radar and pennant number painted out by a particularly zealous wartime censor. (AUTHOR'S COLLECTION)

Corporation for completion. She was transferred to the RN, completed and commissioned as HMS *Speaker* on 20 November 1943. A steaming party took her to Burrard's yard in Vancouver on 8 December, and work there was completed in late February. She passed through the Panama Canal on 7 March 1944 en route to Norfolk Navy Yard, joining *Empress* and the USS *Tulagi* for the final part of the passage. While at sea an Avenger from *Emperor* made her first deck landing, and defects were discovered in the main gearing. These were subsequently rectified in Norfolk, after which she sailed to New York, where she was loaded with eighty-two aircraft and stores at Staten Island by US Transportation Service personnel, and fifty-four women and children embarked as passengers. She then sailed in convoy for the UK and arrived at the Gladstone Dock in Liverpool on 8 April to disembark aircraft, stores and passengers. She subsequently made another trip ferrying aircraft across the Atlantic before being taken in hand by Caledon at Dundee for work to convert her to an assault carrier. This entailed fitting one of the first Type 277 radars, a new, improved bridge, a 100-line operational telephone system, a new aircrew briefing room and 'Army Plot' room together with extra W/T and R/T sets. She was fitted with 140 extra bunks, heads and bathrooms for the expanded operations team, and twin power-operated 20mm Oerlikons replaced the hand-held single mounts with which she had been built. While she was in Dundee the Speaker of the House of Commons

presented the ship with a silver cigarette box, since she was the only warship in the modern era to be allocated the name.

On 12 September she carried out a docking in Rosyth Dockyard, after which she was allocated for duty as a training carrier for DLCOs in the Firth of Forth areas. She operated Swordfish and Barracudas of 768 NAS, and between 16 October and 28 November 1944 she carried out 1,460 deck landings, of which 160 were in a single day and forty-three of those in 38min. In December she carried out a brief defect repair period in a Glasgow shipyard and then embarked 1840 (Hellcat) NAS to work-up for operational service. On 11 January 1945 she sailed for service with 30 ACS in the BPF, arriving in Sydney on 23 February 1945. She was used as a CAP carrier to provide fighter cover over the task force during RAS operations, giving the aircrew from the fleet carriers a rest. After a boiler-clean in Sydney she sailed for Operation *Iceberg* on 9 March 1945. While she was at sea four Hellcats were maintained at readiness on non-RAS days, and these initially had to be scrambled frequently to intercept unidentified aircraft that proved to be American transport or patrol aircraft whose pilots had not switched on their IFF. Once the US programme and appropriate call-signs were received it proved possible to identify these aircraft by radio without having to intercept them. On RAS days *Speaker* maintained eight aircraft on CAP from dawn to dusk in two-hour sorties.

On 23 April she anchored in Leyte Gulf with the Fleet Train, which included the maintenance carrier *Unicorn*, and changed roles from CAP carrier to replenishment carrier. Consequently 1840 NAS's most experienced pilots and seventy

maintenance ratings were transferred to *Indomitable* and the aircraft, together with the less experienced pilots and the balance of the maintenance personnel, went to *Ruler*, which became a CAP carrier. In May she took part in the second phase of *Iceberg*, transferring serviceable aircraft to the fleet carriers and recovering flyable 'duds' for repair by the FAMG. She also transferred casualties from the big carriers to hospital ships. On 14 May she returned to Leyte for a short spell to transfer stores to *Ruler*. Her part in *Iceberg* ended on 29 May; by then 30 ACS had carried 190 aircraft to the combat area off Okinawa and transferred 140 of them to the BPF.

Speaker was in Sydney on 5 June to load aircraft, stores and personnel for RNAS Ponam, and landed them there on 9 July before embarking a replenishment load and proceeding to the new operational area off Japan. Most of the BPF's Task Force 37 had to leave the operational area on 10 August 1945, but *Speaker* remained to support *Indefatigable*, which remained with the US Pacific Fleet as TG 38.5 to be present at the Japanese surrender. On 20 August she transferred ten Seafires and a Firefly to *Indefatigable*, which continued to fly patrols off the Japanese coast in case renegade kamikazes refused to surrender. On completion of this she was ordered to fly-off her remaining aircraft to *Ruler* and make as much accommodation as possible available. On 28 August 1945 she was ordered into Tokyo Bay, and was the first Allied carrier to arrive there a day later. *Ruler* followed on 31 August and took off all her remaining air maintenance personnel, after which *Speaker* embarked 477 Commonwealth former prisoners of the Japanese. She sailed with

most of them on deck on 3 September, taking a circuitous route around Tokyo Bay so that they could be cheered by every Commonwealth warship in what proved to be a remarkable send-off. They were put ashore in Manila on 9 September, after which *Speaker* carried out two further repatriation runs; the first carrying 899 Americans from Japan to Okinawa and the second 645 Americans to the same destination.

On 28 September she refuelled from the Fleet Train in Hong Kong and then ferried Australian former prisoners from Manila to Sydney, where she underwent a short period of defect rectification. While she was alongside in Sydney a diesel pipe burst and poured fuel into a dynamo room, which caught fire. Repairs, delayed by strikes, lasted until December. On 28 December she ferried 721 (Seafire/Vengeance) NAS, a Fleet Requirements Unit from RNAS Archerfield in Australia, to the RN Air Facility at Kai Tak in Hong Kong. She also carried 4,076 stores items and 38,400 bottles of beer to the recently liberated colony. Her operational career was now over, and she was used to carry 459 passengers from Hong Kong to Sydney in mid January, and another group when she sailed for the UK on 30 January 1946.

She eventually arrived in the Clyde to be destored in June 1946, and sailed for the USA on 6 July. The terms of the Lend/Lease agreement stated that the ships must be returned in operational condition, and she had to spend a few days in Bermuda Dockyard having boiler defects repaired before being formally returned to the USN in Norfolk Navy Yard on 17 July 1946. She was subsequently sold for mercantile conversion and renamed *Lancero*. In 1965 she was renamed *Presidente Osmena*, and in 1971 she was renamed *Lucky Three* for her last voyage to the breaker's yard in Taiwan.

Nabob

Laid down as CVE-41 on 20 October 1942 and launched as the USS *Edisto* on 9 March 1943, she was completed, transferred to the RN and commissioned as HMS *Nabob* on 7 September 1943. She then moved to Vancouver for modification to RN standards. The Royal Canadian Navy (RCN) wanted to gain carrier experience before taking over one of the new light fleet carriers, but the terms of the Lend/Lease agreement stipulated that the CVEs could only be commissioned into the RN. A compromise was reached whereby *Nabob* was commissioned into the RN but most of her seaman department were provided by the RCN. The RCN did not have sufficient experienced sailors to man the air department, so this was provided by the RN. Many of the aircrew in her squadrons came from New Zealand, and some adjustment had to be made to pay scales to avoid friction but, overall, the Commonwealth ship's company proved to be a success. She called at Esquimalt in January 1944 to take on her Canadian sailors before sailing to New York, where she embarked 852 (Avenger) NAS for passage in convoy to the UK.

She arrived in Liverpool in April and subsequently had defects repaired in a Clyde yard before moving back to Liverpool for further rectification work on 18 April. On 29 June she re-embarked 852 NAS and worked-up for operational service with the HF. On 10 August she sailed from Scapa Flow for Operation *Offspring* in company with *Indefatigable* and *Trumpeter*. This was the largest HF minelaying operation of the war, forty-seven being successfully laid off Haarhamsfjord and Lepsorev by the Avengers of 852 and 846 NAS. Fighters sank the minesweeper R-89 and destroyed a W/T station on Vigra Island as well as six Bf 110 fighters on the

Nabob makes her way slowly back to Scapa Flow after suffering torpedo damage. She is still down by the stern, but aircraft have been parked right forward in Fly 1 to provide weight which helped to keep the bow down. She even managed to launch aircraft in this condition. (AUTHOR'S COLLECTION)

ground at Gossen Airfield. One Avenger, one Firefly and three Seafires were lost.

On 22 August 1944, in company with *Formidable*, *Furious*, *Indefatigable* and *Trumpeter*, she took part in Operation *Goodwood*, one of a series of strikes against the battleship *Tirpitz* in Kaafjord. Bad weather spoiled the main attack, but two ships were damaged in Altafjord and enemy aircraft were strafed at Banak. During the operation *Nabob* was hit aft by an acoustic torpedo fired by U-354, which blew a hole 50ft by 40ft below the waterline and bent the propeller shaft. Bulkheads were shored and, greatly to the credit of her ship's company, she was able to return to Scapa Flow under her own steam on 27 August 1944. She even managed to fly-off two Avengers for an antisubmarine patrol despite being well down by the stern. At Scapa Flow emergency work was done to keep her afloat, but there was insufficient industrial capacity in the UK or the USA to repair her.

On 30 September 1944 she was de-commissioned and left, unrepaired, on a mud bank on the south shore of the Firth of Forth, being allocated to Rosyth Command in nominal reserve. On 16 March 1945 she was returned to the USN in 'as lying' condition in the Firth of Forth, but in March 1947 she was sold to a Dutch shipyard which towed her to Rotterdam, where she was rebuilt as a merchant ship. Work was completed in 1952 and she retained the name *Nabob* for a number of years. In 1968 she was renamed *Glory* and eventually, in December 1977, she was broken up for scrap in Taiwan.

Premier

Laid down on 31 October 1942, CVE-42 was launched as the USS *Estero* on 22 March 1943 and completed on 3 November 1943, when she was transferred to the RN and commissioned as HMS *Premier* on the same day. On 11 November she moved to Burrard's Yard in Vancouver for modification to RN standards and storing, before sailing for the long delivery voyage to the UK on 9 January 1944. She passed through the Panama Canal on 17 February and arrived in Norfolk Navy Yard on 25 February, eventually sailing in convoy for the UK on 6 March. On arrival she was allocated to WAC and used as a ferry carrier until the end of May, carrying aircraft between Norfolk, Virginia, and Liverpool. On 31 May she began a period of defect rectification in Liverpool which lasted until 5 September, when WAC designated her an operational carrier. On 13 September 1944 she embarked 856 (Avenger) NAS and worked-up in the Clyde areas.

On 10 November 1944 she was transferred to the HF and moved to Scapa Flow. Her first operational sortie, Operation *Handfast* in company

Premier unloading aircraft in the King George V Dock in Glasgow. (AUTHOR'S COLLECTION)

with *Pursuer*, entailed Avengers laying mines in Salhusstrommen near Haugesund. Operation *Provident* followed on 26 November; this was an attack on shipping between Mosjoen and Rorvik by aircraft from *Implacable*, *Premier* and *Pursuer*. Storm-force winds and high seas forced the two CVEs to turn back, but Barracudas from *Implacable* attacked an enemy convoy, sinking two ships and damaging others. Operation *Urbane* on 6 December involved further minelaying off Salhusstrommen in company with *Trumpeter*. Stormy weather was a factor in Operation *Lacerate*, minelaying off Ramsoysund on 12 December in company with *Trumpeter*, and *Premier* had to undergo repairs in a Clyde yard which were completed by 6 January 1945, when she returned to Scapa Flow.

For Operation *Spellbinder* on 11 January 1945, 881 (Wildcat) NAS was added to the air group, tasked with providing air cover for surface forces that attacked an enemy convoy off Egersund. *Premier* remained at sea to carry out Operation *Gratis*, which involved minelaying off Haugesund in company with *Trumpeter*. On 28 January she took part in Operation *Winded*, a night attack on shipping near Vaagso in company with *Campania* and *Nairana*, during which three fishing vessels were sunk. In mid-February she took part in Operations *Selenium 1* and *2* in company with

Puncher, during which aircraft gave cover for surface forces which attacked shipping near Hustadviken and laid mines off Skatestrommen. From 21 February 1945 she took part in Operations *Shred* and *Groundsheet* with *Puncher*. The former was a sweep of the Salhusstrommen Channel; the latter minelaying by Barracudas from *Puncher*. Fighters of 881 NAS strafed a W/T station on Feisten Island and destroyed a Dornier Do 24 flying boat at its moorings. Operation *Cupola* on 18 March involved minelaying in company with *Searcher* and *Queen* while 881 NAS fighters strafed a coastal gun battery and a patrol vessel.

After a brief defect rectification period in a Clyde yard, *Premier* returned to Scapa Flow to prepare for Operation *Roundel*, providing cover for convoy JW66 to North Russia from 17 April 1945. She arrived in the Kola Inlet on 25 April and sailed with convoy RA66 to the UK on 29 April, returning to Scapa Flow on 5 May 1945, where she disembarked her aircraft. On 21 May 1945 she was allocated to Rosyth Command, without squadrons embarked, for a short refit in a Clyde yard, after which she was to be used as a deck-landing training carrier in the Clyde areas. Training began on 24 July and continued until 27 September, when she returned to a Clyde yard for a further refit. She saw no further active service,

however, and commenced destoring in the Clyde in November. A steaming party returned her to the USN at Norfolk Navy Yard on 20 April 1946, where she lay idle until 1947, when she was sold for conversion into a merchant ship. She was subsequently renamed *Rhodesia Star*, and then *Hong Kong Knight* in 1967. She arrived in Taiwan to be scrapped on 10 February 1974.

Shah

Laid down on 13 November 1942, CVE-43 was launched as the USS *Jamaica* on 21 April 1943 and completed on 27 September 1943. She was transferred to the RN and commissioned on the same day as HMS *Shah* before being moved to Burrard's yard in Vancouver for modification to RN standards on 18 October. When the work was completed she was allocated to the EIF and sailed for San Francisco, where she embarked 851 (Avenger) NAS on 7 January 1944. The squadron had formed-up at NAS Norfolk, and flew across America in stages to join the ship. She sailed for Melbourne on 15 January and eventually arrived in Colombo on 19 March 1945. Initially she was used to ferry aircraft between RN air stations and air yards in India and Ceylon, but on 13 May she re-embarked 851 NAS, which had been expanded with a flight of Wildcats to form a composite squadron for trade protection.

On 17 June she sailed for an antisubmarine patrol off Trincomalee, and subsequently carried out a series of trade-protection and convoy-support

Shah with Avengers of 851 NAS on deck. (AUTHOR'S COLLECTION)

operations throughout the Indian Ocean until 23 February 1945, when she arrived in Durban for a refit. By 15 April 1945 she was in Trincomalee, where she prepared for a resumption of operational activity. On 27 April 1945 she embarked 852 (Avenger), 809 (Seafire) and a detachment of 804 (Hellcat) NAS and sailed for Operation *Bishop*, a strike on the Nicobar and Andaman Islands in company with *Empress*. On 10 May 1945 she sailed from Trincomalee in company with *Emperor* to intercept the Japanese heavy cruiser *Haguro*. Unfortunately *Shah*'s catapult became unserviceable and she had to transfer her Avengers, lightly loaded, to *Emperor*, which, as an assault carrier, did not have the facilities to brief or arm a torpedo strike. *Haguro* was sunk in a classic torpedo attack by the 8th Destroyer Flotilla.

After a spell in Trincomalee she resumed antisubmarine operations in August, which ceased when the war ended. On 12 September she sailed for the UK with the aircrew of 845 and 851 NAS on board, their aircraft having been left behind to be destroyed under the terms of the Lend/Lease agreement. *Shah* arrived in the UK for the first time on 7 October 1945; she was remarkable among British aircraft carriers in that she only ever spent a month in the UK, and that was to be destored in the Clyde at the end of her operational service. A reduced ship's company sailed her for the USA on 16 November, and she was formally returned to the USN at Norfolk Navy Yard on 6 December 1945. After she had spent a period lying idle the USN sold her for conversion to a merchant ship in June 1947, and she became the SS *Salta*. She was eventually broken up for scrap in Buenos Aires in 1966.

Patroller

Laid down on 27 November 1942, CVE-44 was launched as the USS *Keweenam* on 6 May 1943 but transferred to the RN and commissioned as HMS *Patroller* on 22 October 1943. She was nominally completed two days later, and sailed for San Francisco on 22 November. Allocated to the EF as a ferry carrier, she sailed directly to the Indian Ocean via Melbourne. On 22 January 1944 she was in Cochin and, for a few weeks, ferried RN aircraft between India and Ceylon, but in February she returned to the US West Coast via Wellington, New Zealand. She arrived in San Francisco on 7 March and for a short spell was allocated to the US Army as a ferry carrier. On 23 April she arrived in Esquimalt, and on 2 May 1944 she reverted to RN control and moved to Burrard's yard in Vancouver, where she was modified to RN standards. On completion of this work she began her delivery voyage to the UK, arriving in Liverpool on 7 September 1944.

Again used as a ferry carrier, she ferried aircraft between Norfolk Navy Yard and the UK until 21 December 1944, when she operated in the Clyde areas to provide deck-landing practice for 1843 (Corsair) NAS. On 28 January 1945 she was lent to the USN for use as a ferry carrier and sailed for San Diego, arriving on 25 February. She eventually reverted to RN control at Norfolk Navy Yard on 1 May 1945, and embarked 1852 (Corsair) NAS for passage to the UK, arriving in the Clyde on 21 May. On 26 May she began a refit in Liverpool, on completion of which she was allocated to Rosyth Command, but with the end of the war in the Pacific there was no further operational use for her,

Patroller in 1945. (AUTHOR'S COLLECTION)

and she moved to the Clyde, where she landed her air stores and entered a shipyard for modification to trooping duties.

This work was completed in November, and she sailed for Devonport where a new, smaller ship's company took her over to carry out trooping runs to and from Colombo until February 1946, when she sailed for Fremantle and subsequently back to the UK. In May 1946 she left the UK for a trooping run to Sydney and return. In August she left the UK for a trooping run to Hong Kong and return, and in November she carried out her

last run to Bermuda and back. With no stores to land, she sailed for America in December and was formally handed back to the USN at Norfolk Navy Yard on 13 December 1946. She was subsequently sold for conversion to a merchant ship and became the SS *Almkerk*. In 1968 she was renamed *Pacific Alliance*, and in February 1974 she was broken up for scrap in Taiwan.

Rajah

Laid down on 17 December 1942, CVE-45 was originally to have been named *Prince* by the USN, but this was changed to *McClure* before she was launched on 18 may 1943. She was subsequently

moved to the Williamette Iron & Steel Corporation for completion, transferred to the RN in Tacoma on 17 January 1944, and commissioned as HMS *Rajah* on the day of her completion, 17 January 1944. At the end of the month she moved to Burrard's yard in Vancouver for modification to RN standards, but while she was there damage was discovered in the turbine gearing and had to be repaired before she could sail. Work was finally completed at the end of May, and she started her

Rajah secured to a buoy shortly after her completion. Her paint has lost its initial pristine finish and she is high in the water, indicating that she has not yet been fully fuelled and stored. (AUTHOR'S COLLECTION)

Trouncer shortly after completion. (Author's collection)

delivery voyage to the UK on 26 May 1944. She embarked 1842 (Corsair) and 857 (Avenger) NAS for passage to the UK in New York, and sailed in convoy for Liverpool on 30 June 1944, arriving on 12 July.

After a defect rectification period in a Clyde shipyard she was allocated to WAC as a deck-landing training carrier, and began operations in the Clyde areas on 30 July 1944 using a variety of aircraft types from 767, 768 and 769 NAS. The task did not last long, and on 10 September she embarked 849 and 857 (Avenger) NAS together with 888 PR (Hellcat) NAS to ferry them to the BPF. In Ceylon on 19 October she embarked the personnel of 822 NAS, but no aircraft, for the passage back to the UK. After a period of defect rectification on the Clyde from 10 November she emerged on 20 December 1944 to be allocated to the USN as a ferry carrier. Her new duties began after arrival in San Diego on 15 January 1945, and for six months she ferried USN aircraft between San Diego and Pearl Harbor. On 7 July she reverted to RN control and sailed first for New York and then the Clyde, arriving on 5 August. Once there she unloaded her air stores and was modified for trooping duties, carrying out several runs between Plymouth, India and Ceylon. Once this tasking ended she was returned to the USN at Norfolk Navy Yard on 13 December 1946. She was subsequently sold for conversion to a merchant ship and became the SS *Drenthe*. In 1966 she was renamed *Lambros*, and in 1969 *Ulisse*. She was eventually broken up for scrap from 23 June 1975 in Savona.

Ranee

Laid down on 5 January 1943, CVE-46 was launched as the USS *Niantic* on 2 June 1943 and transferred to the RN, completed and commissioned as HMS *Ranee* on 8 November 1943. Later in the month she moved to Burrard's yard in Vancouver for modification to RN

standards, after which she was lent to the USN as a ferry carrier and sailed for San Francisco on 4 February. Her duties took her all over the Pacific, including Australia and New Zealand, until she returned to Vancouver in May for a refit. When this was complete she resumed ferrying operations until 18 October, when she reverted to RN control in New York, where she embarked 1846 (Corsair) NAS for passage in convoy to the UK. She returned to Norfolk Navy Yard in November and ferried 1848 (Corsair) NAS to the UK, after which she was refitted in Rosyth Dockyard before being loaned to the USN again for ferry duties in the Pacific from the end of January 1945. She returned to the Clyde to be destored at the end of May, and was refitted again in Rosyth Dockyard from 4 June, during which she was modified for use as a troopship. Further modification work was carried out on the Tyne from 12 September, after which she made a number of runs to Australia and India before being returned to the USN on 8 November 1946. She was subsequently sold for conversion into a merchant ship and renamed *Friesland*. In 1967 she was renamed *Pacific Breeze*; she was finally broken up for scrap in Taiwan from 11 May 1974.

Trouncer

Laid down on 1 February 1943, CVE-47 was launched as the USS *Perdido* on 16 July 1943 and moved to Commercial Ironworks for completion. She was transferred to the RN, completed and commissioned as HMS *Trouncer* on 31 January 1944. On 29 February she moved to Burrard's yard in Vancouver for modifications to RN standards, and on 15 May sailed for Norfolk Navy Yard via the Panama Canal. Once there she was lent to the USN as a ferry carrier, and sailed for Casablanca with a load of US aircraft on 18 June 1944. From there she sailed for New York, reverted to RN control and embarked 1843 (Corsair) NAS for passage to the UK. She eventually arrived in Liverpool on 22 August, but there was no shipyard

capacity to bring her up to operational capability, so she was allocated for duty as a ferry carrier, transporting aircraft between the USA and UK. This task lasted until 2 November 1944, when she was used temporarily as a deck-landing training carrier in the Clyde areas

Further ferrying duties followed until 5 March 1945, when she arrived in Belfast for a refit. On 14 September she was allocated to the EIF and embarked 1702 (Firefly) NAS for passage to Malta. After disembarking the squadron she continued to Colombo, but returned to the UK soon afterwards via Durban and Cape Town. She arrived back in the Clyde on 14 December 1945 and destored on completion of her active service. On 26 January 1946 she sailed for the USA, stopping at Trinidad and Bermuda Dockyard for short spells in February. She was finally returned to the USN on 3 March 1946 in Norfolk Navy Yard. Subsequently sold for mercantile conversion, she became SS *Greystoke Castle*. She was renamed *Gallic* in 1954 and *Benrinnes* in 1959. She ended her days being broken up for scrap in Taiwan from 3 November 1973.

Thane

Laid down on 23 February 1943, CVE-48 was launched as the USS *Sunset* on 15 July 1943. She was subsequently completed, transferred to the RN and commissioned as HMS *Thane* on 19 November 1943. She was then moved to Burrard's yard in Vancouver, where she was used as an accommodation ship until sufficient specialised sailors were accumulated to man and store her. Work to modify her to RN standards started on 15 April 1944 and was completed in early June, when she sailed for Norfolk Navy Yard. After a period having defects rectified, she was allocated to WAC as a ferry carrier and sailed for Cape Town, loaded

Thane shortly after completion. (AUTHOR'S COLLECTION)

with aircraft, on 14 August 1944. She subsequently ferried aircraft between Norfolk, the UK, Gibraltar and ports in the Mediterranean.

On 28 December 1944 she embarked 1851 (Corsair) NAS for passage to the UK and disembarked it to RNAY Belfast on 14 January 1945. A day later she was torpedoed by U-482 in the approaches to the Firth of Clyde. She survived afloat with extensive damage aft, and was towed to Faslane in a damaged state and destored into reserve as there was no dockyard capacity available to carry out the extensive repairs needed to restore her to operational capability. On 21 July 1945 she was allocated to the Reserve Fleet laid up in Faslane, with a small care and maintenance party left on board. On 5 December 1945 she was returned to USN custody 'as lying', and was subsequently sold to Metal Industries to be broken up for scrap at Faslane.

Queen

Laid down on 12 March 1943, CVE-49 was launched as the USS *St Andrews* on 2 August and completed on 7 December 1943. Transferred to the RN and commissioned as HMS *Queen* on the same day, she was moved to Vancouver on 17 December for modification to RN standards. Unfortunately she ran aground on 26 February 1944 while carrying out contractor's sea trials, and had to return to Vancouver to be docked for repairs to be carried out before finally sailing for Norfolk Navy Yard on 22 March, passing through the Panama Canal on 15 April 1944. While in Norfolk she embarked 855 (Avenger) NAS for passage to the UK, and sailed for the UK in convoy via New York, eventually arriving in the Clyde on 23 May 1944. She was initially allocated to WAC as a ferry carrier, and returned to New York, from where she embarked a load of American aircraft for passage to Casablanca. She arrived in Casablanca on 27 June and then made her way back to the Clyde in a series of convoys via West Africa, arriving on 10 August 1944 and then undergoing a period of defect rectification in a Clyde yard. This was completed at the end of August and was followed by a refit in Dundee, completed on 23 December 1944. On 27 December she entered Rosyth Dockyard to have RN operational equipment fitted, and finally arrived in the Clyde to work-up for operational service with the HF on 23 January 1945.

Queen arrived in Scapa Flow on 2 March 1945 with 853 (Avenger/Wildcat) composite NAS, and

Queen, clearly showing her aircraft signal panels on the port side of the flight deck amidships. (AUTHOR'S COLLECTION)

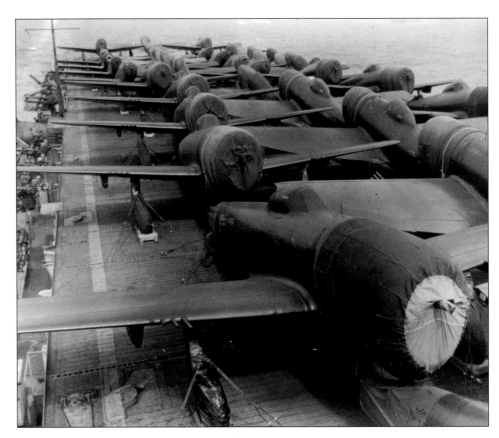

Queen ferrying USAAF P-47 Thunderbolt and P-51 Mustang fighters from New York to Casablanca in June 1944. (AUTHOR'S COLLECTION)

sailed on 20 March 1945 for her first operational mission, Operation *Cupola*, a minelaying sortie off Oranesund in company with *Searcher* and *Premier* which was partly hampered by bad weather and a heavy swell which limited flying operations. On 26 March she sailed for Operation *Prefix*, an attack on shipping in Trondheim Leads in company with *Searcher*. No enemy shipping was sunk, but fighters shot down three Luftwaffe Bf 109s. On 3 April 1945 she sailed in company with *Puncher*, *Searcher* and *Trumpeter* for Operation *Newmarket*, an attack on U-boat depot ships in Kilbotn which had to be postponed because of bad weather. She sailed in company with *Trumpeter* and *Searcher* for a further attempt codenamed Operation *Judgement* on 30 April, and on 4 May Avengers from the three carriers sank U-711, the depot ship *Black Watch* and the merchant ship *Senja*. Fighters shot down three enemy aircraft.

Queen, *Trumpeter* and *Searcher* joined other warships in Operation *Cleaver* to provide escort cover for the British naval forces that were to liberate Copenhagen before returning to Scapa Flow on 10 May 1945. On 14 May 1945 she sailed as part of the covering force for Operation *Timeless*, convoy JW67 to North Russia. The convoy was sailed as planned, despite the end of the European war six days earlier, in case some U-boat captains on long patrols had not received the order to surrender or had elected to carry on fighting. The convoy arrived in the Kola Inlet on 20 May, and *Queen* sailed with the return convoy, RA67, on 23 May, arriving in Scapa Flow on 30 May 1945. On 7 July 1945 she was allocated to Rosyth Command, as WAC was being disbanded, and entered a Clyde yard for a refit. On 18 September she moved to Barrow-in-Furness for the refit work to be completed, finally sailing for Portsmouth on 18 November 1945.

By then, *Queen*'s short operational career was over and she was used for trooping duties, sailing on 24 November 1945 on a voyage that took her to Colombo, Fremantle, Sydney and then back to Devonport Dockyard in the UK on 15 February 1946. After further runs as a troopship she was damaged by a storm in the North Atlantic September 1946, during her return voyage to the USA. Notwithstanding the damage, she was formally returned to the USN at Norfolk Navy Yard on 31 October 1946. She was sold by the USN for conversion into a merchant ship in July 1947 and was subsequently renamed *Roebiah*. In 1967 she was renamed *President Marcos*, and in 1972 she was renamed *Lucky One* for her last voyage to the breaker's yard. She was broken up for scrap in Taiwan from July 1972.

Ruler

Laid down on 25 March 1943 as CVE-50 and launched as the USS *St Joseph* on 21 August 1943, she was completed, transferred to the RN and commissioned as HMS *Ruler* on 22 December 1943. On 31 December she moved to Vancouver for modification to RN standards, this being completed on 20 March 1944, when she sailed for Norfolk Navy Yard. She arrived on 8 April and was loaded with aircraft for the UK, arriving with them in Liverpool on 6 May. Allocated to WAC as a ferry carrier, she sailed for New York on 9 May, sailing at the end of May with a further load of aircraft.

From 24 June 1945 she was refitted in Liverpool before carrying a further aircraft ferrying run across the North Atlantic. On 18 November 1944 she carried out a defect rectification period in a Clyde yard before commencing an operational work-up with 885 (Hellcat) NAS embarked. On 28 January 1945 she was allocated to the BPF as a fighter carrier to provide CAP fighters over under-way replenishment operations, and sailed for the Far East via Gibraltar, Alexandria and Colombo. In addition to 885 NAS she embarked 1772 (Firefly) NAS for passage to Australia. She arrived in Sydney on 16 March 1945, and in April sailed for the BPF anchorage in San Pedro Bay, Leyte Gulf. On 3 May she sailed from Leyte Gulf to cover

fleet replenishment operations off Okinawa. By then 885 NAS had been expanded into a composite Avenger/Hellcat NAS capable of providing fighter and antisubmarine cover for the BPF while the fleet carriers were replenished and their aircrew relaxed. Cover for replenishment operations with Task Force 57 was given on 6, 10, 14 and 18 May before she returned to Leyte Gulf. From there she returned to Sydney for replenishment before sailing again on 12 June to support the BPF, by then redesignated Task Force 37, in operations off the Japanese mainland. On 31 August 1945 she entered Tokyo Bay and took off air maintenance ratings from *Speaker* to make space available in her for the repatriation of former prisoners of war.

She was present in Tokyo Bay for the Japanese surrender on 2 September 1945, but her operational career then came rapidly to an end. She sailed for Sydney on 19 September, and from there she sailed to return to the UK on 22 October 1945. On 3 December she arrived in the Clyde, where she ceased to be operational and was destored. On 4 January 1946 she sailed for the USA with a reduced ship's company, and on 29 January 1946 she was formally returned to the USN at Norfolk Navy Yard. She saw no further service, and after only a few moths idle at Norfolk she was sold to be broken up for scrap on 31 May 1946.

Ruler in Sydney Harbour during 1945. (RAN)

Arbiter

Laid down on 26 April 1943 as CVE-51, she was launched as the USS *St Simon* on 9 September 1943 and subsequently completed by Commercial ironworks before being commissioned into the USN for a short while. On 30 December 1943 she was decommissioned before being completed, transferred to the RN and commissioned as HMS *Arbiter* a day later, on 31 December 1943. On 9 January 1944 she moved to Vancouver for modification to RN standards, and on 25 April she passed through the Panama Canal. On 2 June 1944 she was allocated to WAC as a ferry carrier and was used to ferry newly commissioned naval air squadrons between the USA, where they had formed, and the UK. These included 853 (Avenger), 1820 (Curtiss Helldiver) and 1843 (Corsair) NAS. On 12 September 1944 she began a refit in Belfast, and on 30 January 1945 she was allocated to the BPF as a replenishment carrier.

On 1 March 1945 she sailed from the Clyde for the Pacific with 1843 (Corsair) NAS embarked for passage. In May 1945 she sailed from Sydney with her first replenishment load of aircraft, and after refuelling at Manus she moved north to support Task Force 57. A typical replenishment load at this time was nine Seafires, seven Avengers, six Corsairs, one Hellcat and one Firefly. In July she supported the redesignated Task Force 37 off Japan with replacement aircraft before returning to Australia in August. A plan had been considered in July to convert her into a fleet oiler due to the shortage of tankers available to the BPF but, with the unexpectedly rapid end to hostilities, it was not carried forward. Instead she was used for several weeks as a deck-landing training carrier by 899 (Seafire) NAS, which trained former Royal Australian Air Force (RAAF) pilots as sub-

lieutenants RANVR (A) to fly Seafires. When that task was completed she sailed to Hong Kong, arriving on 11 October to embark former prisoners of the Japanese for repatriation to Australia. She returned to Hong Kong on 3 December to embark 300 further former prisoners for repatriation to the UK, arriving in the Clyde on 10 January 1946. Reallocated administratively to Rosyth Command,

Arbiter in 1945. (AUTHOR'S COLLECTION)

she was destored in Portsmouth from 6 February and sailed for the USA with a reduced ship's company on 12 February. She was formally returned to the USN at Norfolk Navy Yard on 3 March 1946 and almost immediately sold for conversion into a merchant ship. Later that year she was renamed *Coracero*. In 1965 she was renamed *President Macapagal* and, finally, for her voyage to the breaker's yard, *Lucky Two*. She was broken up for scrap in Taiwan from may 1972.

Smiter

Laid down on 10 May 1943 as CVE-52, and launched as the USS *Vermillion* on 27 September 1943, she was completed, transferred to the RN and commissioned as HMS *Smiter* on 20 January 1944. She moved to Vancouver on 15 February, where modification work was completed on 31 March 1944, when she sailed for Norfolk Navy Yard via San Francisco and the Panama Canal. A period of defect rectification was carried out in Norfolk, after which she sailed for New York with 856 (Avenger) NAS embarked for passage to the UK. In New York 1841 (Corsair) NAS was added, and she sailed in convoy for Liverpool, where she was allocated to WAC as a ferry carrier on arrival. After another transatlantic ferry run she arrived in a Clyde yard for defect rectification on 21 July, and then Newport for repairs to her electrical system on 14 September 1944.

For a few weeks in December 1944 she was used as a deck-landing training carrier in the Clyde, but in January 1945 she was taken into Rosyth Dockyard for a refit. When this was completed, in May, she moved to a Clyde yard for modification into a general-purpose carrier. In July she was allocated for operational duty with the EIF and sailed for Ceylon without an air group. On 1 September she was in Trincomalee, and a day later sailed for Singapore. On 11 September she sailed for Hong Kong, returning to Singapore on 26 September. She was subsequently used to repatriate former prisoners of the Japanese from Singapore to Ceylon. On 21 November 1945 she was in Trincomalee, and on 16 December she embarked 888 (Hellcat) NAS for passage to RNAS Sembawang, Singapore, disembarking it on 27 December. A day later she sailed for the UK, arriving in the Clyde on 11 February 1946. She ceased to be operational and was destored before sailing for the USA with a reduced ship's company. On 6 April 1946 she was formally returned to the USN and subsequently sold for conversion into a merchant ship. Later in 1946 she was renamed *Artillero*. In 1965 she was renamed *Presidente Garcia*, and on 24 November 1967 she arrived in Hamburg to be broken up for scrap.

A Wildcat lands on *Puncher*. Both barriers are down, and marshallers are guiding the aircraft forward into Fly 1. (AUTHOR'S COLLECTION)

Reaper ferrying USN aircraft in April 1945. (AUTHOR'S COLLECTION)

Reaper ferrying USN aircraft in April 1945. (AUTHOR'S COLLECTION)

Puncher

Laid down on 21 May 1943, CVE-53 was launched as the USS *Willapa* on 8 November 1943 and completed, transferred to the RN and commissioned as HMS *Puncher* on 5 February 1944. As with *Nabob*, the executive branch of her ship's company was provided by the RCN to provide experience of carrier operations, but the RN provided the air department. She moved to Vancouver for modification work on 15 March, sailing for New York when it was completed on 9 June 1944. After arriving in New York she had to undergo defect rectification work in Norfolk Navy Yard, after which she was allocated to WAC as a ferry carrier. At the end of July she returned to New York and loaded American aircraft for passage in convoy to Casablanca. She arrived in Casablanca on 8 August and returned to Norfolk Navy Yard on 27 August 1944. Once there she loaded 1845 (Corsair) NAS for passage to the UK and sailed for the Clyde in convoy, arriving on 15 September. After another North Atlantic aircraft ferry run she arrived in a Clyde shipyard on 21 October 1944 for defect rectification.

On 12 November 1944 she embarked 821 (Barracuda) NAS for torpedo-bomber trials in the Clyde areas, but on 27 November she suffered a main gearing failure and had to be repaired in a Clyde yard with a gearbox removed from *Nabob*. After repairs she was allocated to the Home Fleet and deployed to Scapa Flow with 881 (Wildcat) and 821 (Barracuda) NAS embarked. Her first operational sortie was Operation *Selenium I*, in which she provided fighter cover for an attack on shipping in Hustadviken Lead near Haugesund in company with *Premier*. It was followed immediately by *Selenium II*, in which Barracudas laid mines off Skatestrommen near Skaten Lighthouse, escorted by Wildcats. After the mines were laid the fighters strafed targets of opportunity ashore. On 22 February she sailed with *Premier* for Operations *Shred* and *Groundsheet*, an armed sweep of the Salhusstrommen Channel which had to be aborted because of bad weather, followed by minelaying in the Karmoy Channel near Stavanger, during which two Barracudas were shot down by enemy gunfire.

After her return to Scapa Flow on 23 February she dragged her anchor and ran aground, suffering significant damage that took a month to repair, but she was able to take part in Operation *Prefix* on 28 March 1945. This was an attack on shipping in Aalesund in company with *Nairana*. No ships were sunk, but buildings and a W/T station ashore were destroyed. She sailed for Operation *Newmarket*

on 6 April 1945 in company with *Queen*, *Searcher* and *Trumpeter* for an attack on U-boats and their depot ships in Kilbotn, which had to be postponed because of bad weather. This proved to be her last operational sortie, and on 21 April she was taken in hand in a Clyde shipyard for defect rectification.

She emerged on 13 May 1945 to be allocated administratively to Rosyth Command and embarked 1790 (Firefly) and 1791 (Firefly nightfighter) NAS for training. This proved to be her last air group, and on 25 June 1945 she was allocated for trooping duties and sailed for Halifax, Nova Scotia. She spent the remainder of 1945 on runs between the UK and Halifax, New York and Norfolk Navy Yard, returning to the latter for the last time to be formally returned to the USN on 16 January 1946. She was subsequently sold for conversion into a merchant ship and renamed *Bardic*. In 1959 she was renamed *Ben Nevis*, and in June 1973 she was sold to be broken up for scrap in Taiwan.

Reaper

The last USN-built CVE to be commissioned into the RN was laid down as CVE-54 on 5 June 1943 and launched as the USS *Winjah* on 22 November. She was transferred to the RN and commissioned as HMS *Reaper* on 18 February 1944 and completed three days later. On 31 March she moved to Vancouver for modification to RN standards by Burrard's. The work was completed on 24 May 1944, when she sailed for San Francisco. From there she sailed for Norfolk Navy Yard, arriving on 9 July 1944. She was subsequently allocated to WAC as a ferry carrier, and spent the remainder of 1944 carrying aircraft

between the Clyde, Gibraltar and the east coast of the USA.

On 22 November 1944 she embarked 1849 and 1850 (Corsair) NAS in New York for passage to the UK, and disembarked them to RNAY Belfast in early December. On 9 December she collided with *Tegelburg* in the Clyde and had to undergo repairs until 5 January 1945, when she was allocated to USN control for duty as a ferry carrier in the Pacific. She arrived in San Diego Navy Yard on 29 January 1945, after which she was employed to carry aircraft off the west coast of the USA until late May, when she returned to the Clyde and reverted to RN operational control. On 31 May 1945 she entered Rosyth Dockyard for a refit, after which she was allocated to the BPF as a ferry carrier. She sailed for the Pacific via the Panama Canal with a full load of aircraft on 23 July and arrived in Sydney on 13 September 1945. While she was on passage the war had ended and her tasking changed.

On 3 October 1945 she sailed for RNAS Ponam, where she loaded equipment and a Sea Otter amphibian before sailing for Hong Kong. By 4 November 1945 she was back in Sydney, and she made one trip to Auckland, New Zealand, before returning to the UK via Singapore. She arrived back in the Clyde on 27 March 1946 and was allocated to Rosyth Command administratively while she was destored and removed from operational service. A reduced ship's company subsequently steamed her to Norfolk Navy Yard, where she was formally returned to the USN on 20 May 1946. She was subsequently sold for conversion into a merchant ship and renamed *South Africa Star* later in 1946. She arrived at Nikara in Japan to be broken up for scrap on 25 May 1967.

CHAPTER 18

PROJECT HABBAKUK

The Director of Programmes at Combined Operations Headquarters in 1942 was a man named Geoffrey Pyke, who had no technical training but a flair for unusual inventions. His most bizarre idea was a gigantic 'iceberg aircraft carrier', which fired the imagination of Prime Minister Winston Churchill and the Head of Combined Operations, Admiral Lord Louis Mountbatten. Churchill seized on the proposal, writing that: 'The advantages of a floating island or islands, if used only as refuelling depots for aircraft, are so dazzling that they do not, at the moment, need to be discussed. There would be no difficulty in finding a place to put such a stepping stone in any of the plans of war now under consideration.' The project was given the name 'Habbakuk', a miss-spelling of the Old Testament prophet Habbakkuk.

In September 1942 an investigative committee was set up to look into the detailed practicality of designing and constructing such a vessel. The original idea had been that a huge ice block could be frozen inside a giant wooden mould created at a suitable northern latitude, but the committee found that ice alone was not sufficiently strong as a building material for the hull contemplated. Pyke proposed a solution which involved incorporating a binding substance such as wood pulp or sawdust into water to form a material that could be frozen into the shape of the hull. Imaginatively named 'Pykrete', the material had a compressive resistance similar to concrete, about $3,000lb/in^2$. It was made under laboratory conditions in the UK, but it was considered that the vast quantities needed for Habbakuk could be made only in arctic Northern Canada. Canadian scientists found a further major problem when they calculated that it could take up to seven years to freeze an object of the size contemplated under natural conditions, and that suitable refrigerating machinery would therefore have to be specially designed, built and transported to the building site. This defeated the original object of using natural resources, and it was noted that lake ice rarely exceeded two feet in thickness, even after a hard winter. Moving further into the Arctic would improve freezing conditions but make it more difficult to build the site and accommodate construction staff.

The investigative team included Pyke and naval constructors, who were sent from the UK in early 1943 to work with representatives from the Canadian National Research Council and the British Admiralty Technical Mission, both based in Ottawa. Their directive required them to study a number of different hull applications, including a 3,000ft-long base for refuelling long-range aircraft; an aircraft carrier 2,000ft long; an advanced fighter base 1,250ft to 1,500ft long and, last, a cargo-ship, oil tanker or combination of the two. All of them were required to be unsinkable. Faced with a growing realisation of the complexity of design and construction, the group dismissed all but one of these, finding the long-range base to be beyond the existing knowledge of materials and

The 2,113,000-ton Pykrete aircraft carrier as proposed in 1943. (AUTHOR'S COLLECTION)

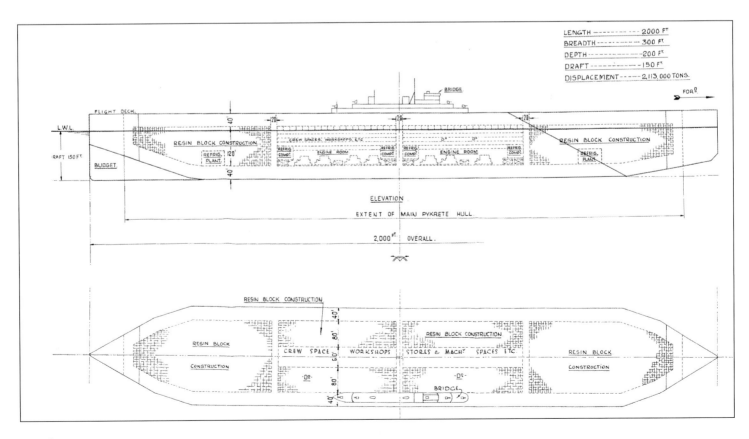

facilities, and the fighter base to be too small to incorporate the necessary wall thickness and machinery. The cargo and tanker versions had cargo capacities that were tiny in comparison with the size and cost of the projected vessels, only about 5 per cent of their displacement, making them uneconomical to operate in commercial terms. Their inability to enter any port would severely restrict methods of loading and unloading their cargoes.

Attention therefore focussed on the aircraft-carrier version, and a design evolved for a Pykrete ship estimated at 2,000ft long and 300ft wide with a draught of 150ft and a freeboard of 50ft, to be built during the winter of 1943/44. It would have displaced approximately 2,000,000 tons and would have been propelled by steam-powered turboelectric machinery driving propellers in twenty-six electric motor pods mounted along the sides of the hull, giving a maximum speed estimated at 6 knots. Huge refrigeration plants and extensive piping would have been used to maintain the Pykrete structure at its ideal temperature, and the hot machinery would have needed large quantities of insulation to protect the hull structure from melting. Timber construction would have been used to create the 'ship shapes' at the bow and stern, keeping the weight and bulk

of the Pykrete hull amidships. Wooden sheathing would have been required to maintain the hull shape, and the amount of timber needed to make sawdust or pulp for Pykrete and to cover the outer hull would have been considerable.

The sides, bottom and top of the Pykrete central area of the hull would have been 40ft thick and insulated inside and out. The rectangular 'box' in the centre would have contained machinery and crew accommodation space, flanked by port and starboard upper and lower hangars. Each of the twenty-six propulsion pods would have contained a single electric propulsion motor directly driving a shaft and screw without an intermediate gearbox. Fuel would have been stored in tanks under the central 'box', and a box girder structure on top of it was intended to provide fore and aft strength for the hull. The funnels, uptakes and conventional, if somewhat large, island structure would have been fabricated from mild steel. Design sketches show a single, large T-shaped lift aft giving access to all four hangars, and a large number of dual-purpose and close-range guns fitted on sponsons around the flight deck. The exact number was probably never finalised.

Studies indicated that three million cubic yards of Pykrete would be needed to build the hull at a cost estimated at up to £13 million, not taking into account the cost of machinery, insulation and

ABOVE AND OVERLEAF An impression of the *Habbakuk* aircraft carrier drawn by G. H. Davies and published in the *Illustrated London News* on 2 March 1946. (ILLUSTRATED LONDON NEWS)

refrigeration ducts. Three ways of building up the central Pykrete hull were evaluated. The first was by freezing by layers within giant wooden moulds; the second involved pumping pre-cooled Pykrete into a suitable mould; and the last entailed building the hull with pre-cast frozen blocks. The first two would have required specialised machinery which had not been designed, and the third seemed extremely doubtful as block bonding was imperfectly understood and could not be guaranteed. The project had moved a long way from the iceberg aircraft carrier using natural materials that had seemed so attractive in London, and further study showed greater problems at every stage. Even without explosive tests against a representative structure, estimates showed that Habbakuk was very far from being unsinkable. A hole 24ft square in the hull, such as might be caused by the impact of a torpedo, would lead to the Pykrete around it melting at the rate of 6in, or 4.5 tons, per hour in a sea water temperature of 65 degrees. Dislocation or rupture of the refrigeration ducts would allow water to spread quickly through them, and the situation would deteriorate, leading quickly to a dangerous condition. The study group could not envisage any practical method of carrying out repairs, especially to the bottom, since the hull would rapidly become unstable and could not be dry-docked. Model testing also revealed that, if all or part of the hull grounded, the structure would suffer irreparable damage and quickly break up.

A model Habbakuk was tested at the NPL at Teddington in the UK, and an experimental Pykrete ship 60ft long was built and tested on Lake Jasper in Canada. The latter suffered from water ingress into the refrigeration ducts, which were found to complicate manufacture in the first place, besides making the finished vessel more vulnerable. Despite, or perhaps because of, these small-scale experiments, the study group had no real confidence that such a vessel could be built. Canadian engineers evaluated five construction sites and found Corner Brook in Newfoundland to have the fewest drawbacks, but it was closed by ice from December to April, had no local labour and was considered largely inaccessible. They stated that the ideal site must have ample supplies of power, pulpwood and labour; a long winter freezing period with no intermediate thaws; and very deep water close inshore but a shelving beach with easy access to the sea. The construction workers would need good, warm accommodation, and the site would need good road and rail transport links with a large power station nearby. Needless to say, such a site did not exist in Northern Canada in 1943.

The study group grew increasingly alarmed at the scale of construction effort that would need to be created at a remote Arctic site to build one of these monsters, and calculated that the cost would be considerably more than double that of a conventional fleet carrier for a hull that might have only a relatively short life. As the practical difficulties were realised the group decided that such a vessel was beyond any practical consideration of construction or operation and, on hearing that that manpower was being earmarked in 1944 planning for the first Habbakuk, the study group recommended that no personnel should be allocated for the project. In late 1943 they concluded that: 'In view of the proposed vessel's serious limitations, we regret we cannot see advantages that would be commensurate with the diversions of war effort needed for the construction', and recommended its termination.

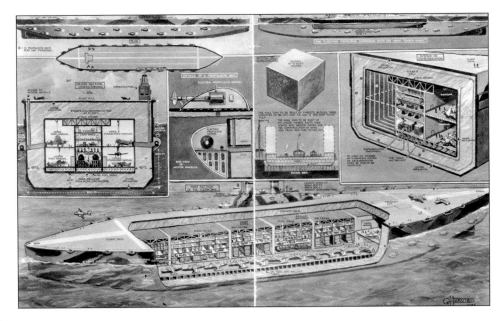

Mercifully, this recommendation was accepted.

The Pykrete carrier was never developed beyond the detailed drawing stage, but the NPL model showed that it could ride waves up to a thousand feet long and fifty feet high without significant deck motion, and the hangars were large enough to take aircraft as large as the de Havilland Mosquito, without folding wings. In the Atlantic there was usually sufficient natural wind to allow free take-off by heavily loaded aircraft from a deck that size, but turning the massive hull into wind at only 6 knots might not always have been possible. Calculations showed that, after a year, marine growth on the hull would reduce the maximum speed to 4.75 knots, making the vessel unmanoeuvrable. Machinery would have been difficult to maintain because, with its enormous draught, Habbakuk could not have entered any dockyard or dry dock for refit. Nor, with its enormous mass, could it realistically have been anchored in deep water. The inability to enter any dry dock meant that even the need to clean marine growth off the vast wooden hull underwater would have required an expensive and difficult solution. Habbakuk was a wartime 'mad idea' that was taken further than it deserved because it attracted the interest of men in high places who should have known better. It did, at least, raise RN awareness of the value of size in more conventional aircraft carriers, however, so the study was not completely without value.

Habbakuk estimated technical details

Displacement:	2,113,000 tons
Dimensions:	length 2,000ft
	beam 300ft
	draught 150ft
Machinery:	26 podded shaft steam
	turboelectric
	16 boilers
	6 knots estimated
Armament:	Twin 4in; twin and single
	40mm Bofors and 20mm
	Oerlikon
Protection:	none in conventional terms
Fuel:	Not estimated
Endurance:	Not estimated
Complement:	Not finalised

Aircraft operating data

Flight deck:	1,800ft x 250ft usable
Hangars:	Four, each 1,000ft x 80ft x 20ft
Arrester wires:	unknown
Lifts:	one T-shaped aft 100ft x 100ft
	maximum
Aircraft:	unknown
Aircraft fuel:	avgas in unknown quantity
Air weapons:	unknown

CHAPTER 19

AUDACIOUS CLASS

The Admiralty's 1940 Supplementary Building Programme included a third unit of the *Implacable* Class, which was to be ordered in the spring of 1941. The inclusion of the ship in the programme underlined the Admiralty's recognition of the importance of naval aviation, but the subsequent complicated series of changes to the specification reflected a period of dynamic change in aircraft carriers and their aircraft. At first the ship was conceived as a repeat *Implacable*, but before any order was placed the Design Department was asked to make modifications to allow fifty-four aircraft to be stowed in the hangars, and to widen the flight deck, especially aft, to increase the number of aircraft that could be ranged for a single launch. Improvements in avgas stowage and flight-deck armour, without making fundamental changes to the basic design or detracting from stability, were also requested. Detailed design work began in March 1941, by which time it was obvious that the ship was no longer a repeat *Implacable* and no order was placed.

Technical background

In August 1941 three design options were put forward for consideration; a slightly modified *Implacable* with 4in flight deck armour; a bigger carrier with a 4in deck and long double hangars, and a compromise between the two with 3in deck armour and big double hangars. The bigger carrier with a 4in deck was selected, and detailed design work began in October 1941. It represented a significant departure from the earlier armoured deck carriers and, while treated as a new class, contained a number of compromises as a legacy from its design origins. The lower hangar had to be reduced in length from 208ft to 150ft in order to provide accommodation space for the extra men needed to operate the larger air group. The flight deck was 10ft wider than the earlier ships and the forward lift was enlarged to 45ft by 33ft to take the new generation of aircraft under development, but the hangar height remained at the inadequate 14ft of *Implacable* and her sister. Approval was given to proceed with the new design at a standard displacement of 27,000 tons on 28 November 1941, with the name *Irresistible* tentatively allocated to the single ship. It was cancelled only two days later, however, and a new Staff Requirement was issued for a much larger carrier with fewer compromises.

Design work on what was now referred to as the *Audacious* class continued into 1942 and had to be amended to take into account the recommendations of the Joint Technical

Eagle recovering Attackers of 800 and 803 NAS. Eight have already landed-on, and another is about to catch a wire. Just visible to port of the island are the two nylon barriers which had to be rigged for Attacker recoveries, since, without an engine in front of the pilot to absorb the impact, they could not use the normal steel wire barriers. (AUTHOR'S COLLECTION)

Committee on future naval aircraft. The maximum all-up weight allowed for naval aircraft was to rise from 11,000lb to 30,000lb, with a commensurate increase in size. Catapult end-speed was to be 75 knots at the higher weight, requiring machinery of increased size and complexity, and low hangar heights were recognised as a crippling limitation. By 1942 the RN relied on the USN as a primary source of aircraft supply, and the USN standard hangar height of 17ft 6in was adopted. This also provided an adequate margin for future aircraft designs through the projected life of the ship. However, the new hangar height required an increase in the depth of the hull of 6ft which, in turn, required a 4ft increase in beam to maintain stability and increased the standard displacement to 32,500 tons. A number of other improvements were made, including dividing the machinery into two widely separated units of boiler rooms, engine rooms and gear rooms. The forward unit comprised A and B boiler rooms, with A and B engine rooms and A and B gear rooms driving the

outer shafts, the space between them being used for feed tanks, auxiliary machinery and stores. The after unit comprised X and Y boiler rooms with X and Y engine rooms and gear rooms driving the inner shafts. Designed shaft horsepower was 152,000, intended to deliver 32 knots with a clean hull. Both completed ships were heavier than the original design, however, and on trials *Eagle* achieved 30.5 knots on 156,630shp during initial sea trials. The beam was increased to allow the latest standard of protection against underwater charges of up to 2,000lb. The eventual design represented a big improvement over *Implacable* and overcame most of the undesirable compromises in the earlier design studies. At the time they were laid down, the first two ships were the largest aircraft carriers under construction in the world.

Improvements to the design were incorporated during build, which reflected wartime experience. Both lifts were lengthened to 54ft in 1943 to take bigger aircraft, and the forward lift was moved aft by 50ft to make room for an aircraft repair shop forward of the lift. This answered criticism that there was no space outside the normal flow of hangar movement where aircraft could be spread for repair and have welding appliances or power tools used on them. The space created could take one aircraft at a time and had enlarged ventilators that allowed engines to be started and tested for

short periods. Bomb lifts were enlarged to enable them to move 2,000lb bombs, and bomb rooms were made less cluttered so that various types of weapon could be stowed as operational requirements dictated. Assuming that about eighty aircraft could be carried, some of which would be in a deck park, there was space for approximately nine weapon loads per aircraft. Improved fire control for the 4.5in guns was fitted, based on the USN Mark 37 director modified with British Type 275 radar. Both hangars were offset slightly to port as a result of the lesson learnt from the loss of the *Ark Royal* in 1941, allowing watertight integrity of the boiler uptake trunking to the funnel to be carried to a higher level than in previous carriers. The lifts were aligned with the centre of the hangars and were, thus, also to port of the ship's centreline. The redesign gave the opportunity to allow welding rather than riveting techniques to be employed, and both the ships that were completed had hulls that were 90 per cent welded.

After the loss of *Ark Royal* in November 1941 the name was allocated to the 1940 Supplementary ship in place of *Irresistible*. Three ships, *Ark Royal*, *Audacious* and *Eagle*, were ordered under the 1942 programme. The order for *Eagle* originally went to Swan Hunter, but when the beam was increased it made the hull too big for the company's available slipway and the contract was transferred to

Eagle shortly after her completion as the largest aircraft carrier in the RN. She was finished to substantially the original *Audacious* design, but has the most extensive radar outfit yet installed, including two Type 982, two Type 983 and a single Type 960 for long-range air search as well as fire-control and navigation sets. The aircraft on deck is a Dragonfly helicopter. (AUTHOR'S COLLECTION)

Vickers-Armstrongs' Walker Naval Yard on the Tyne in November 1942. A fourth ship was ordered under the 1943 programme. Initially unnamed, the order for this ship was subsequently changed to become the fourth unit of the later *Malta* Class and she was allocated the name *Africa*. No work on her was ever started under either order, and she was eventually cancelled in October 1945. Work on the other three ships slowed in 1945 so that modifications to reflect war experience could be incorporated and the latest standard of equipment fitted. *Eagle* was the least advanced, with £1,950,000 spent on her and the hull about 26 per cent complete, although most of her machinery was built ready for installation.

The flight deck design for the *Audacious* Class in 1945. Note the four barriers, sixteen arrester wires and the numerous close-range anti-aircraft weapons in addition to the 4.5in batteries. Widening the hull has made more space available to range aircraft between the after 4.5in turrets. (AUTHOR'S COLLECTION)

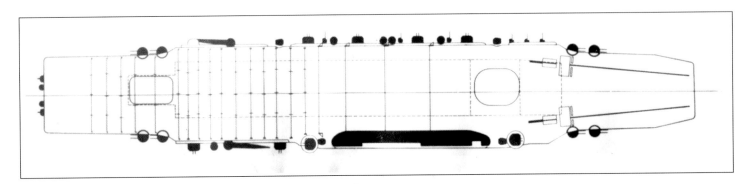

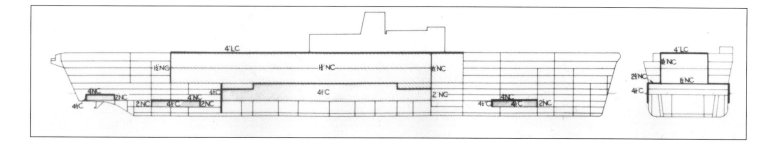

The armour protection designed for the *Audacious* Class. (AUTHOR'S COLLECTION)

After arguments that it was at least worth completing her to a point where she could be launched and then preserved for potential completion at some later date, the Admiralty Board decided at its meeting on 21 December 1945 that only two ships would be completed, and *Eagle* cancelled. Work on her stopped in January 1946 and she was subsequently scrapped on the slipway. The more advanced *Audacious* was renamed *Eagle* to perpetuate the name, and launched as such just over two months later.

Air arrangements underwent substantial modification even after the ships were laid down. They were originally to be fitted with eight arrester wires and three safety barriers. In July 1946 the requirement was amended and called for sixteen arrester wires, each capable of stopping a 30,000lb aircraft at 75 knots entry speed, and four safety barriers with the same limits. Later, two further barriers were proposed to act as 'immediate spares' for use if any of the others were damaged. The original intention to fit the British two-track trolley-type hydraulic catapults was changed in 1943 to the USN style two-point, tail-down method using a strop which fell away from the aircraft after launch. The island was larger than any in previous carriers and contained a split-level operations room, the upper part forming the surface plot on a mezzanine deck from which officers could look down into the aircraft direction room, which had a large 'tote' on a bulkhead showing the tactical air picture. The original specification called for 7,000 tons of FFO and 103,000gal of avgas, the latter contained in three groups of cylindrical tanks positioned inside flooded compartments. It was appreciated that this was hardly enough to sustain an embarked air group that might be as large as 100 aircraft under wartime conditions, but fortunately, by the time the first ship entered service, turbojet and turboprop aircraft made up a large part of the air group. They used a turbine fuel, avcat, which had a relatively high flashpoint and so could be stowed unprotected. The design was modified to retain the avgas stowage for the remaining piston-engined types and to stow avcat

in tanks originally designed for FFO, reducing stowage of the latter to 5,500 tons. *Eagle* was the only ship completed to the original design; work on *Ark Royal* proceeded more slowly and the design was considerably modified in the early 1950s to incorporate steam catapults, the angled deck, a side lift and new visual landing aids. Her modified technical history and complete operational history will be found in chapter 30.

The radar outfit was the most advanced yet installed in a British aircraft carrier, and *Eagle* was completed with Type 960 long-range air warning radar, a development of the wartime Type 281B with improved display facilities, including the Skiatron horizontal display system. Two Type 982 aerials were fitted for fighter direction, one at the forward end of the island and one aft. Both had a range of about 60 nautical miles. A pair of Type 983 height finding radars with a stabilised vertical parabolic array were fitted close to the Type 982 aerials on the island. A Type 293Q radar was carried on the foremast for gun direction and tactical plot compilation, and a Type 974 was used for navigation. A 'YE' aircraft homing beacon was fitted at the highest point of the foremast, and a Type 961 carrier-controlled approach radar was fitted at the after end of the island. A full outfit of IFF interrogators and responders was fitted on the island and, shortly after completion, *Eagle* was fitted with a receiver for the AN/APS-20 airborne early warning (AEW) radar fitted in the Douglas Skyraider aircraft which was to be supplied to the RN by the USN under the Mutual Defence Assistance Programme (MDAP). The sixteen 4.5in guns were arranged in groups of four in two turrets at each 'corner' of the flight deck. As in *Implacable*, the turret roofs were level with the flight deck and flat, so that aircraft wheels could pass over them and they did not create an obstruction like the 'domed' turrets in *Illustrious* and her sisters. The fire of each group was controlled by a Mark 37 director with twin Type 275 radar dishes. The six-barrelled Bofors mountings were controlled by close-range blind-fire directors (CRBFD), fitted with the single dish of a Type 262 radar. The considerable close-range armament was completely made up with 40mm Bofors in single, twin and six-barrelled mountings.

Audacious Class technical details

(Details are for *Eagle* as completed, rather than the earlier versions of the design)

Displacement:	49,950 tons deep load
Dimensions:	length 803ft 9in
	beam: 112ft 9in
	draught: 35ft 7in
Machinery:	4 shaft Parsons geared turbines
	8 Admiralty 3-drum boilers
	152,000shp delivering 30.5 knots
Armament:	8 twin 4.5in; 8 six-barrelled 40mm Bofors; 2 twin 40mm Bofors; 9 single 40mm Bofors; 4 single 3pdr saluting guns.
Protection:	4.5in waterline belt; 4in tapering to 1.5in flight deck; 1.5in hangar sides; 2.5in tapering to 1.5in hangar deck
Fuel:	5,500 tons FFO
Endurance:	7,000nm at 14 knots
Complement:	2,750

Aircraft operating data

Flight deck:	800ft x 100ft
Hangars:	upper 364ft x 67ft x 17ft 6in plus 45ft extension forward of the forward lift
	lower 172ft x 54ft x 17ft 6in
Catapults:	Two BH5 hydraulic; 30,000lb at 75 knots end speed
Arrester wires:	Sixteen 30,000lb at 75 knots entry speed; three barriers
Lifts:	forward 54ft long x 44ft wide aft 54ft long x 33ft wide. Both capable of lifting 40,000lb aircraft on a 35sec cycle; only the forward lift served both hangars
Aircraft:	Up to 100, depending on type
Aircraft fuel:	103,000gal avgas 279,000gal avcat
Air weapons:	18in torpedoes; 1,000lb MC bombs; 500lb bombs; 3in RP; 2in RP; Mark 11 depth charges; 20mm cannon ammunition; flares and pyrotechnics

Individual ship histories

Ark Royal

The name *Irresistible* had been allocated to the ship intended as a third unit of the *Implacable Class* in the 1940 Supplementary Estimates, but it was eventually ordered as a unit of the *Audacious* Class on 19 March 1942. It was allocated Admiralty Job Number J 3699 and named *Ark Royal* from the outset to perpetuate the famous name of the earlier *Ark Royal*, lost in November 1941. The order was given to Cammell Laird & Company in Birkenhead, which gave her the Yard Number

1119 and laid her down on 3 May 1943. She was the largest warship ever built by the firm. Despite being the first of the class to be ordered, she was the second to be laid down and work on her proceeded slowly, stopping altogether in 1945 while the design was recast to incorporate the latest developments. When she finally emerged in 1955 she differed significantly from the original design, and even from her sister ship, *Eagle*. Her divergent technical background and complete operational history will be found in chapter 30.

Eagle (laid down as Audacious)

Allocated the Admiralty Job Number J 3375, she was ordered on 19 May 1942, given the Yard Number 1220 and laid down by Harland & Wolff

Eagle turns into wind to start a launch, with an Attacker on the starboard catapult. Other aircraft in the range include more Attackers, Fireflies, Sea Hornets and Skyraiders. (AUTHOR'S COLLECTION)

at its Belfast yard on 24 October 1942 as *Audacious*, but renamed *Eagle* just before her launch on 19 March 1946 by Her Royal Highness Princess Elizabeth. She was the first of the class to be laid down and, as the most advanced of the three ships of her class, work continued on her at a slow pace after 1945 and she was finished, largely, to the original design, albeit with a revised and modernised radar outfit. She was completed on 1 October 1951 as the largest aircraft carrier ever built for the RN, and carried out extensive sea trials. On 1 March 1952 she was accepted from the builders and commissioned into the RN, after which she worked-up to operational efficiency in the Portsmouth areas. During May she carried out deck-landing trials with new aircraft types including the Fairey Gannet, de Havilland Sea Venom and Hawker Sea Hawk before taking part in Exercise *Castanets*, designed to test NATO command arrangements in the NATO area in June. In August 1952 she replaced *Indomitable* as flagship of the Heavy Squadron (HF), and on 2 September she sailed from Devonport for the HF autumn cruise with 800, 803 and 890 (Supermarine Attacker), 827 (Firebrand) 812 and 814 (Firefly) NAS embarked. Later in the month she took part in Exercise *Mainbrace*, the largest peacetime naval exercise to be held up to that time. Post-exercise discussions were held on board on 27 September, during a visit to Oslo.

On 20 January 1953 she sailed for the HF spring cruise; by then 890 NAS had disbanded but 809 (Sea Hornet nightfighter) NAS was added to the air group, together with 849A (Skyraider

Eagle at anchor, with Sea Hornets, Attackers, Skyraiders and Avengers on deck. (AUTHOR'S COLLECTION)

AEW) NAS. Combined exercises with the MF took place in the Gibraltar areas before she returned to Devonport on 26 March for a docking. After a short summer cruise in May she anchored in the Solent on 9 June 1953 for the Coronation Review of Her Majesty Queen Elizabeth II. For the autumn cruise in September she embarked 800 and 803 (Attacker), 825 and 814 (Firefly), 809 (Sea Hornet nightfighter) and 849C (Skyraider AEW) NAS and took part in Exercise *Mariner* with over 300 NATO warships. The air group was modified again for the spring cruise in 1954, and comprised 800 and 803 (Attacker), 806 (Sea Hawk), 815 (Avenger ASW), 849A and 849B (Skyraider AEW) and 809 (Sea Hornet nightfighter) NAS. In March 1954 she transferred to the MF and in early April she took part in a search for wreckage and bodies from the BOAC Comet airliner which crashed into the sea 60 miles north of the Straits of Messina. Five bodies were located and recovered. In May 1954 she left the MF and returned to Devonport for a refit; FO Heavy Squadron transferred his flag to *Glory*.

The refit was completed in February 1955, and she carried out trials in home waters. On 21 May she embarked 826 (Gannet), 802 and 804 (Sea Hawk), 813 and 827 (Westland Wyvern) and 849A

(Skyraider AEW) NAS and sailed to work-up in the Mediterranean, culminating on 23 August 1955, when her aircraft flew 201 sorties in a single day, a record that is still unsurpassed in the RN in 2013. On 8 September she rejoined the HF as flagship of the Heavy Squadron and took part in Exercise *Sea Enterprise* with ships from Canada, the USA and Norway as well as the UK. The RN contribution to the exercise was five aircraft carriers, twenty-six other surface ships and six submarines. Exercise *Phoenix I* in October was a test of the HF defences against high-flying jet bombers, after which she returned to Devonport for a defect rectification period in November. This was completed in April 1956, and she joined the MF with 812 (Gannet), 849A (Skyraider AEW), 897 and 899 (Sea Hawk) and 830 (Wyvern) NAS embarked. Delayed by technical problems, 892 and 893 (Sea Venom) NAS joined her in July. In May she embarked FOAC and carried out a firepower demonstration off Izmir. A month later she tested the air defences of Malta in Exercise *Maltex*, and in October she prepared for operations in the Eastern Mediterranean.

On 1 November 1956 she joined *Albion* and *Bulwark* for Operation *Musketeer*, and her aircraft struck at targets in Egypt to neutralise potential

LEFT *Eagle's* upper hangar, looking from aft to forward, in October 1955. The aircraft are Sea Hawk fighters. (AUTHOR'S COLLECTION)

TOP RIGHT *Eagle* after her flight deck was modified with an interim 4-degree angle. The new centreline passes over the port forward 4.5in gun turrets, which have been plated over. Later 'hay-rake' Type 982 radar aerials have replaced the earlier variety. The aircraft on deck include Sea Venoms, Sea Hawks and Gannets. (AUTHOR'S COLLECTION)

BOTTOM RIGHT *Eagle* launching her aircraft. Those on the catapults are Sea Hawks; further aft the first of three Skyraiders is beginning to taxi forward, while three antisubmarine Gannets are running, awaiting their turn to move up the deck. (AUTHOR'S COLLECTION)

opposition to the Anglo/French landings. Between 1 and 6 November her aircraft flew 621 sorties despite her starboard catapult becoming unserviceable on the day before the operation started. During the same period *Albion* flew 415 sorties, *Bulwark* 580 and the French carriers 166. The operation was a political failure, but from a strike carrier perspective it was very successful and emphasised the RN capability to neutralise a significant land-based air force and naval forces in the littoral area when required to do so in advance of an amphibious assault. In January 1957 she returned to Devonport for modifications and repairs, after which she carried out trials in June. For the HF autumn cruise in September she embarked 849A (Skyraider AEW), 813 (Wyvern), 803 and 806 (Sea Hawk), 814 (Gannet) and 894 (Sea Venom) NAS to participate in Exercises *Strike Back*, *Pipe Down* and *Phoenix II* before returning to Devonport to give leave in December. She sailed with same air group plus 701A (Westland Whirlwind) SAR Flight at the end of January 1958 to join the MF, and took part in Exercise *Dawn Breeze IV* in March. In July she provided fighter escorts for RAF transport aircraft from Cyprus that flew British troops in Jordan as part of Anglo/US moves to protect Lebanon and Jordan against Iraqi aggression. After that she moved west to take part in Exercise *Petrel 1*, a combined

amphibious exercise with the Libyan Army in early September, and then returned to Devonport in December for leave. In January 1959 she returned to the MF with 802, 806 and 898 (Sea Hawk), 814 (Gannet), 849A (Skyraider AEW) and 894 (Sea Venom) NAS embarked and took part in Exercise *Dawn Breeze V* in March. She visited Brest on her way back to the UK in April, and on 11 May 1959 she paid off in Devonport for a major modernisation.

The modernisation completely altered the ship, and technical details, together with the rest of her operational history will be found in Chapter 28.

The original *Eagle*

The third unit of the *Audacious* Class was originally allocated Admiralty Job Number J 4670 and was named *Eagle* from the outset. The contract was awarded to Swan Hunter at its Wallsend-on-Tyne yard on 4 August 1942 and the ship was given the yard number 1703, but design changes called for a wider hull which would be too big for the available slipway. Consequently the order was allocated the new Job Number J 4715 and transferred to Vickers-Armstrongs' Walker Naval Yard further up the Tyne. They allocated it Yard Number 73 and she was laid down on 23 December 1943. She was the

least far advanced of the three *Audacious* Class ships when the war ended, and at a Board Meeting on 21 December 1945 the Admiralty decided to terminate her construction as an economy measure despite arguments that she should be finished up to the point where she could be launched and then preserved as an asset for potential future use. At the time the hull was close to being structurally complete, and most of the machinery and fittings were fabricated ready for installation. Work to terminate construction activity was completed in January 1946, after which she was scrapped on the slipway.

The initially unnamed fourth ship

The Admiralty intended to add a fourth ship to the *Audacious* Class as part of the 1942 programme. It was allocated Job Number J 1722 and the order was placed with the Fairfield Shipbuilding and Engineering Company, but it was not laid down and its existence is ephemeral. On 12 July 1943 the order was changed to become a unit of the larger *Gibraltar* Class. After this the name *Africa* was allocated, associated with the Fairfield Yard Number 722. Subsequent details will be found in chapter 22.

CHAPTER 20

COLOSSUS CLASS

By the end of the Norwegian Campaign in 1940, experience had taught the RN that only high-performance fighter aircraft embarked in ships of the fleet could provide an effective counter to attacks by enemy aircraft. To improve the situation, consideration was at first given to adding fighters to *King George V* Class battleships, which already had hangars and catapults to operate Walrus amphibians for reconnaissance. Fighters needed a deck in order to land back on their ship, however, and the conversion of the new battleships into hybrid carriers was unacceptable in terms of cost, time and the loss of gun armament. Studies

were then made into cruiser and fast merchant ship conversions, but these were also time-consuming and expensive for the limited capability they offered. Like a later generation of studies into small 'Harrier carriers', they suffered from the drawback that providing the necessary workshops, stores and maintenance personnel in each of a number of small ships was not the most effective or economical way of deploying aircraft.

By 1941 Admiralty attention focused on what were referred to as 'aircraft destroyers'; these were not destroyers designed to operate aircraft, but aircraft-carrying ships designed to destroy enemy

Ocean sailing from Malta in 1952, with Sea Furies and Fireflies ranged aft. (AUTHOR'S COLLECTION)

aircraft, the name owing its origin to the earlier concept of torpedo-boat destroyers. The term caused confusion and was gradually replaced by the simpler description of 'fighter carrier', and it was accepted that an austere carrier designed for the purpose would be more effective, cheaper and quicker to produce than hybrids or conversions. Urgency was added to the requirement for fighter carriers by the loss of *Prince of Wales* and *Repulse* to

Colossus in the eastern Mediterranean in 1945, with Barracudas and Corsairs on deck. (AUTHOR'S COLLECTION)

Japanese naval aircraft off the coast of Malaya on 10 December 1941, when land-based fighters failed to provide them with adequate defence.

Technical background

The Controller passed a draft statement of requirement to DNC on 7 January 1942, only days after its agreement by the Admiralty Board. In it the vessel was referred to as a fighter support ship. The DNC's carrier section under naval architect A Mitchell produced a sketch design on 14 January 1942 which featured a flight deck 600ft long, a single hangar 14ft 6in high and two centreline lifts, each 45ft long by 34ft wide. Fifteen fighters, each up to 15,000lb, could be carried in the hangar. There were two twin 4in mountings right aft, numerous close-range weapons, and speed was 25 knots. The Board found the sketch to be broadly acceptable but asked for the 4in mountings and their control to be removed to reduce complexity and to allow the flight deck to be lengthened to allow free take-off by the planned new generation of high-performance fighters. The DNC was overloaded with other work at the time, and design work on the project was passed to Vickers, which set up a team under their chief naval architect, J S Redshaw, who produced one of the most outstanding warship designs of all time.

The first Vickers sketch, produced on 23 January 1942, incorporated a number of changes

The *Colossus* Class flight and hangar deck design to which the first ships were completed in 1945. (AUTHOR'S COLLECTION)

including an increase in hangar height to the new standard of 17ft 6in and an increase in avgas stowage to 80,000gal, nearly double that of *Illustrious*. Further modifications included the extension of the flight deck right aft and the deletion of the 4in guns as required by the Admiralty. There was some debate about the time it would take to build these ships; the Admiralty wanted twenty-one months, Vickers countered that twenty-seven was more practical, and twenty-four was finally accepted as a compromise. After a detailed design process that had lasted less than three months, the first three ships were ordered in March 1942, followed shortly by a fourth, and

nine more were ordered in August. A review in September showed that there was capacity to build two more ships at Harland & Wolff's yard in Belfast and one at Devonport Dockyard; orders were placed with these, bringing the total to sixteen. However, two of these were modified into maintenance carriers while still building, and the last six were completed to an improved design and known subsequently as the *Magnificent* Class. They were referred to collectively as the '1942 Light Fleet Carriers'.

To save time the two-shaft machinery was to be half of the four-shaft installation designed for *Fiji* Class cruisers, and the first two ships, *Colossus* and

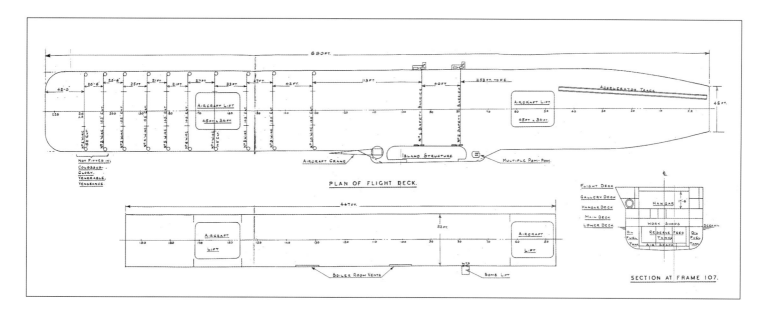

Edgar, were built with boilers, turbines and shafts that had been ordered for the cancelled cruiser *Bellerophon*. The machinery was divided into two units, which were widely separated to offer the best chance of survival after a torpedo hit. Each unit comprised two boilers and a turbine, and they were separated by a water-filled space in which were fitted cylinders for avgas stowage. There was no armour or torpedo impact protection, but there were a number of transverse bulkheads, and the design team believed that the these ships would stay afloat with four principal compartments flooded. Wing compartments with steel thick enough to prevent splinter damage were arranged outboard of machinery spaces, magazines, bomb rooms and avgas stowage; these were filled with empty drums to maintain buoyancy and stability after underwater damage. They would also crush and absorb some of the explosive force of a torpedo hit. Hardened steel mantlets were built in over the stowage for up to thirty-two torpedo warheads.

The design team had experience of both warship and merchant ship construction, and used this to good effect. The *Colossus* Class had structures which were built in a manner previously used for merchant shipping but slightly lighter than that stipulated in Lloyd's rules. The design allowed shipbuilders who had not previously specialised in warship construction to participate in the programme, and gave rise to an erroneous belief after the war that they were intended for conversion into merchant ships. They were not, but the design led to excellent ships that had very short build times. *Venerable*, built by Cammell Laird, was the shortest at twenty-five months, others averaged twenty-seven months. This compared very favourably with other warships such as the first batch of *Battle* Class destroyers; *Barfleur*, for instance, took twenty-three months to build. Cost averaged £2.5 million, under a quarter of the cost of a fleet carrier, showing the advantages of accepting a low top speed, simple close-range gun armament, and structure built to mercantile standards. Running costs were projected to be much lower than those of fleet carriers.

During the design phase carrier commanding officers had been asked to state the priorities they gave to various parameters, including speed and gun armament; the final design reflected their views. While the Admiralty did not consider the original 'aircraft destroyers' to be an expendable type, they considered that a hull designed for only two years' war service would be adequate. Later statements of requirement spoke of the ships being designed for three years' service or the remaining duration of the war, whichever was less. The ships that emerged had some remarkably long lives, one of them lasting into the twenty-first century.

The original radar outfit was comprehensive and included both Type 79 and Type 281 long-range air-warning sets to give gap-free all-round coverage. Types 293 and 277 were fitted for fighter direction, except in *Ocean*, which was initially fitted as a nightfighter carrier and had the superior USN SM-1 radar fitted. All ships had a 'YE' aircraft homing beacon; some of them had it at the top of the foremast, and some on a small mast fitted to the outboard side of the funnel. The SM-1 had a range of about 70 miles against an aircraft at 10,000ft, could be used as a height-finder and was accurate to within 500ft at 30 miles. Type 277 was less accurate, and its range was only about 40 miles. Initially the close-range armament was all aimed visually and had no specialised fire-control equipment.

The flight deck was 690ft long, with a width of 75ft abeam the island and a minimum width of 45ft at the bow, without the narrow encroachments caused by the 4.5in gun mountings in the fleet carriers. It was capable of having a larger launch range aft than the first four units of the *Illustrious* group, and was stressed for aircraft up to 15,000lb. The two centreline lifts were both 45ft long by 34ft wide and capable of moving 15,000lb aircraft in a 36sec working cycle. The hangar was 342ft long, 52ft wide and 17ft 6in high, capable of taking any aircraft in service or projected at the time. Asbestos fire curtains divided it into four bays, and there were comprehensive flooding arrangements. As in the fleet carriers the hangar was fully enclosed, entered through air locks (apart from the lifts) and treated like a magazine because of the inherent risk from avgas vapour and oils.

A single BH3 hydraulic catapult was fitted on the port forward part of the flight deck, capable of launching 16,000lb aircraft at an end speed of 66 knots. Eight arrester wires reeved to four Mark 8 operating units were fitted during build, and a further operating unit with two wires was added in most ships after trials to make a total of ten wires, each capable of stopping a 15,000lb aircraft at an entry speed of 60 knots. Two barriers were fitted, each capable of stopping aircraft of the same weight at 40 knots. During the Korean War some operational naval air squadrons achieved remarkable landing intervals; *Ocean*'s Sea Furies achieved intervals of 18.6sec in 1952, and the Fireflies were only slightly slower at 20.2sec between aircraft landing. The potential capability of these ships was realised as they were built, and the anticipated air group doubled in size when it was decided to maintain a permanent deck park of aircraft. This increased the size of the ship's company from the original 1,054 to 1,336 by the time the first ship was completed. Workshop arrangements and stowage for spares were good by contemporary standards, but accommodation was cramped and inadequate. The bomb rooms were originally designed to cater for thirty-two 18in torpedoes, thirty-six 2,000lb bombs, 300 500lb bombs, 200 Mark 11 depth charges and 1.5 million rounds of 20mm gun ammunition. During the ships' lives the space was used for a variety of different combinations of aircraft armament.

The increased size of the air group gave these ships capabilities that were not far short of those of fleet carriers, and in some cases exceeded them. The name fighter carrier was clearly no longer relevant, and the Admiralty adopted the new title light fleet carrier, which described them perfectly. By the time the first ships joined the BPF the standard air group comprised 21 Corsair fighters and 18 Barracuda TBR aircraft.

The 1942 light fleet carriers were the largest class of major warships ever ordered for the RN, ten of them being ordered on a single day, 7 August 1942. Postwar they achieved the largest total of overseas sales ever achieved by major British warships, and by the late 1950s every navy that operated aircraft carriers, with the sole exception of the USA, did so with one or more 1942 light fleet carriers purchased from the UK. This was a remarkable achievement and, given the success of the design, it is surprising that the RN itself did not make more use of them. For the decade until 1955 they certainly formed the 'backbone' of the operational carrier fleet, and there were plans to modernise some of them, but with the drastic reductions that followed the 1957 Defence Review only *Warrior* was modernised and she was soon sold. Originally these ships were designed to operate any naval aircraft in service; the larger fleet carriers were to operate the same aircraft in larger numbers. The effect of the economies forced on the RN after 1957 encouraged the use of a smaller number of larger carriers to reduce the cost of manpower and ownership, if not that of replacement construction. The decision to procure large aircraft capable of nuclear strike and multiple roles also favoured larger ships, but it is interesting to see how well other navies did operating Sea Hawks, Sea Venoms, Douglas A-4 Skyhawks and Grumman S-2 Trackers from these outstanding ships.

The design was adaptable, and in addition to the two ships converted into aircraft maintenance ships, a third was converted into a fleet maintenance ship. One of the two aircraft maintenance ships was to have been further converted into a submarine depot ship in 1956, but the work was cancelled after the 1957 Defence Review. Their use as assault helicopter carriers, trials, training and transport ships also stands out. There was a plan to convert *Glory* into a commando carrier, but the availability of a 1943 light fleet carrier by 1959 led to it being cancelled.

Glory with Corsairs and Fireflies on deck off Melbourne in January 1946.
(AUTHOR'S COLLECTION)

COLOSSUS Class technical details

Displacement:	18,040 tons deep load
Dimensions:	length 695ft
	beam 112ft 6in
	draught 23ft 6in
Machinery:	2 shaft Parsons geared turbines
	4 Admiralty 3-drum boilers
	40,000shp delivering 25 knots
Armament:	All close-range, typically 4
	quadruple 2pdr pom-pom; 16
	single 40mm Bofors; 4
	single 3pdr saluting guns
Protection:	Armoured mantlets over
	torpedo warheads
Fuel:	3,196 tons FFO
Endurance:	8,300 miles at 20 knots
Complement:	1,300

Aircraft operating data

Flight deck:	690ft x 75ft mild steel plate
Hangar:	275ft plus 57ft extension aft of
	after lift x 52ft x 17ft 6in
Catapult:	1 BH 3 capable of launching
	16,000lb at 66 knots end speed
Arrester wires:	10 x 15,000lb at 60 knots entry
	speed; 2 barriers 15,000lb at 40
	knots entry speed
Lifts:	2 centreline, both 45ft long x
	34ft wide, both 15,000lb
Aircraft:	42; double that number could
	be ferried
Aircraft fuel:	98,600gal avgas
Air weapons:	18in torpedoes; 1,000lb bombs;
	500lb bombs; 250lb bombs; 'B'
	bombs; 3in RP with 60lb and
	25lb warheads; Mark 11 depth
	charges; 20mm cannon
	ammunition; flares and
	pyrotechnics

Individual ship histories

Colossus

Allocated Admiralty Job Number J 4576, *Colossus* was ordered from Vickers-Armstrongs' Walker Naval Yard on the Tyne on 14 March 1942, given Yard Number 55 and laid down on 1 June 1942. She was launched on 30 September 1943 and was the first ship of the class to be completed;

would join 1 ACS for Operation *Olympic*, the projected amphibious landings on the Japanese mainland, in the autumn of 1945.

On 26 July she was operational with the BPF with 1846 (Corsair) and 827 (Barracuda) NAS embarked. After the Japanese surrender she joined the cruisers *Bermuda* and *Argonaut* and two destroyers to form TG 111.3, and sailed for Formosa, arriving on 6 September 1945. While other British warships went in Kiirun Harbour, she remained at sea to operate her aircraft as cover against enemy forces that refused to surrender. Later she gave air cover for British forces that landed in Shanghai, before anchoring at the mouth of the Yangtze River on 18 September. Next she was ordered to make as much space as possible available for accommodation and ordered to proceed to Inchon in Korea, where she picked up 354 British and Australian former prisoners of war and carried them to Manila, arriving on 4 October. On 12 October 1945 she was in Hong Kong, and in November she transferred from the BPF to the EIF, adopting a peacetime routine but retaining her operational capability.

She returned to Portsmouth on 23 July 1946 and was decommissioned, although her full outfit of stores was left on board following an agreement that she would be lent to the French Navy for an initial period of five years. She was commissioned as the French Ship *Arromanches* in Portsmouth on 6 August 1946, and subsequently worked-up with an embarked air group of Seafires with RN assistance. In 1949 she deployed to South East Asia to operate in support of French forces in Indo China with an air group of Seafires and Dauntless dive-bombers. The French Navy purchased her outright in 1950, and she subsequently operated an air group of Hellcats and Helldivers provided by the USN under MDAP funding.

In November 1956 she had an air group of Corsairs and took part in Operation *Musketeer*, the Anglo/French landings in Egypt. A year later she was modernised with a 4 degree angled deck and mirror landing aid. In 1968 she was refitted for use as an antisubmarine carrier with an air group of Breguet Alizé turboprops and helicopters before finally paying off at Toulon in 1973 after nearly thirty years service in the two navies. Her original ship's bell was returned to the RN during a ceremony held on board *Hermes* during a visit to Toulon on 31 October 1974. She was eventually broken up for scrap in Toulon in 1978.

Edgar

The second light fleet carrier was also ordered from Vickers-Armstrongs' Walker Naval Yard on 14

commissioned at Walker Yard on 1 December 1944, completed on 16 December and handed over to the RN for sea trials on the same day. After working-up to operational efficiency she was allocated to 11 ACS and sailed for further operational training off Malta with other ships of the squadron. The deployment to the Pacific was continued without urgency since, at the time, the war was expected to continue into 1946 and the build-up of the BPF was being paced to match the ability of the Fleet Train to support protracted operations at sea. It was expected that 11 ACS

March 1942. She was allocated Job Number J 4578 and was originally to have been named *Edgar*. Allocated the Yard Number 56, she was laid down on 1 June 1942, the same day as *Colossus*, and launched as *Edgar* on 26 March 1944. She was renamed *Perseus*, however, in June 1944, when it was decided to convert her into an aircraft maintenance carrier for service in the Pacific. Her details will be found with the other maintenance carriers in chapter 24.

Glory

The third ship in the initial order for light fleet carriers was *Glory*, Admiralty Job Number J 3318, ordered from Harland & Wolff's Belfast yard on 14 March 1942 and given Yard Number 1191. She was laid down on 27 August 1942 and launched on 27 November 1943, completion being signed on 2 April 1945, the day she commissioned in Belfast. After an initial work-up in the Clyde areas she sailed for the Mediterranean with 1831 (Corsair) and 837 (Barracuda) NAS embarked to continue working-up for service in 11 ACS with the BPF. By the middle of July she was in Trincomalee, and she arrived in Sydney in August, just too late for active operations against the Japanese.

In early September 1945, in response to a request from the Australian Government, *Glory* sailed for Rabaul to take the surrender of Japanese forces in New Britain, escorted by the sloops *Hart* and *Amethyst*. The ceremony of surrender took place on her flight deck at 0147 GMT while *Glory* lay stopped in St George's Channel, 28 miles southeast of Rabaul. General B A H Sturdee of the Australian Army took the surrender of all Japanese

forces in the area. On 12 September she returned to Sydney, disembarked her aircraft to RNAS Schofields and had hundreds of bunks installed in the hangar to enable her to ferry former prisoners of the Japanese to safety. Five QARNNS sisters and sixteen VAD nurses were added to the ship's company; they were among the first women to serve at sea with the RN. In October she ferried 1,350 British and Canadian former prisoners from Manila to Esquimalt, British Columbia; sadly one died and was buried at sea near Eniwetok. After a visit to Vancouver *Glory* sailed to Hong Kong, from where she carried displaced persons to Manila and then took Dutch Army personnel to Balikpapan in Borneo, arriving in November 1945. Next she picked up Australian Army and RAAF personnel from Tarakan in Borneo and carried them home to Sydney, arriving in December. The bunks were then removed and she reverted to duty as an operational carrier with the BPF.

In January 1946 she worked-up in Jervis Bay with 1831 (Corsair) and 837 (Firefly) NAS embarked, and on 23 January she entered Melbourne for a memorable visit with *Indefatigable*, *Implacable*, *Armada* and *Tuscan*. A march through the streets by the combined ship's companies, watched by 250,000 people, took place on 25 January, and 50,000 people toured the ship when she was open to visitors two days later. In March she visited New Zealand and then ferried 14 (Corsair) Squadron of the RNZAF to Japan for duty with the British Commonwealth Occupation Force. After visiting Kure in Japan she returned to Australian waters in April and operated with the BPF until 18 August 1947, when she sailed from Brisbane for the UK, flying her 'paying-off' pennant. She arrived in Devonport after more than

two years away on 14 October 1947, paid off into reserve immediately and was used as an accommodation ship for RAN personnel as they arrived to stand by the new HMAS *Sydney*, the former *Terrible*.

In January 1948 *Glory* commenced a major refit in which her flight deck was strengthened to operate heavier aircraft, her catapult and arrester wires were also modified to take heavier aircraft, her bridge and operations room were improved to the latest standard, Bofors guns replaced Oerlikons, and her accommodation was improved, although it was always to be cramped. She recommissioned on 24 October 1949 for service with the MF and embarked 14 CAG comprising 804 (Sea Fury) and 812 (Firefly) NAS before working-up. She arrived in Malta on 11 November 1949 and was visited by HRH Princess Elizabeth on 14 December. The next months were spent in peacetime routine, visiting a number of Mediterranean ports and carrying out exercises with USN and French warships. Late in the year she was selected to replace *Theseus* in Korean War operations; she disembarked her air squadrons to RNAS Hal Far in Malta and returned to Devonport to pay off on 16 December. She recommissioned on 29 December 1950 with a ship's company brought up to war strength for operations in the Far East. She arrived in Malta to re-embark her aircraft on 2 February 1951 and worked-up until March, when she sailed for Korea, stopping to refuel at Aden and Hong Kong before

Ocean enters Devonport Dockyard while serving as a training ship in 1955. She was used to give sea training both to officers and ratings. (AUTHOR'S COLLECTION)

Glory in her first paint scheme, photographed on 27 June 1945. (AUTHOR'S COLLECTION)

arriving at Sasebo, where she took on board aircraft, stores and ammunition from *Theseus* and *Unicorn* and embarked a USN Sikorsky S-51 Dragonfly helicopter for SAR duties.

Glory sailed for her first war patrol on 26 April 1951. It was off the west coast of Korea and targets included railway lines, bridges, enemy logistics and junks. Sea Furies flew CAPs over the task force and Fireflies few antisubmarine patrols. On 14 May 1951 Stoker McPherson fell overboard and was rescued by the SAR helicopter, the first such rescue in the RN. During her first period of war duty off Korea, *Glory* carried out nine operational periods at sea during which her aircraft set a record for a light fleet carrier of eighty-four sorties in a single day. Between April and 27 September 1951 *Glory*'s air group flew for 2,875 hours in 107 days at sea with only nine accidents. Targets destroyed included 679 junks, 794 ox carts and 236 railway wagons for the expenditure of ninety-four 1,000lb bombs, 1,450 500lb bombs, over 9,000 3in rocket projectiles and 538,000 rounds of cannon ammunition. She was relieved in the Korean war zone by HMAS *Sydney* and left for a refit in Garden Island Dockyard, Sydney.

She returned to Sasebo to relieve *Sydney* on 2 February 1952, and began a further series of war operations during which her air group set a new record for light fleet carrier operations of 105 sorties in a single day. In April close air support was provided for the Commonwealth Division as it made its stand on the Imjin River and rail bridges were destroyed north of Chinnampo. *Glory*'s second tour of operations off Korea ended on 1 May 1952, when she completed her fifth patrol and sailed for Hong Kong, where she handed over pilots, aircraft and stores to *Ocean*, which was to relieve her. The cumulative total of her flying operations in the Korean Theatre was 4,835 flying hours for the loss of twenty-seven aircraft and nine aircrew. On 11 May she left the FEF for the Mediterranean, arriving in Malta on 26 May, where she disembarked 14 CAG for the last time and entered Malta Dockyard for a docking and assisted maintenance period.

On completion of the work she rejoined the MF with 898, 807 (Sea Fury) and 810 (Firefly) NAS embarked. She visited Istanbul with HMCS *Magnificent* in July, but had to sail unexpectedly and stand-by off Cyprus during the crisis when King Farouk of Egypt abdicated. Normal MF routine followed until October, when she returned to Malta to embark 801 (Sea Fury) and 821 (Firefly) NAS, ammunition and war stores for a return to Korean operations. *Glory* left Malta to rejoin the FEF on 9 October 1952, and in November took part in Exercise *Taipan*, a test of Hong Kong's air defences, in company with *Ocean*.

Glory's third Korean War deployment began on 10 November 1952 and continued into 1953. On 5 April 1953 her aircraft equalled the record of 123 sorties in a single day set by *Ocean*; it was deliberately not exceeded to end potentially dangerous rivalry between air groups. To achieve the total every squadron pilot flew four sorties during the day; Commander (Air), the Flight Deck Officer and the Landing Signals Officer flew two each. Targets destroyed included seven bridges, twenty-eight houses and five ox carts, plus four bridges and three gun positions damaged. The ammunition expended included 104 bombs and 384 rocket projectiles. She sailed for the eleventh and last patrol of her third period of operations on 5 May 1953, with instructions that, since the war appeared to be drawing to a close, no unnecessary risks were to be taken attacking heavily defended targets. The last day of operational flying was 14 May 1952, and *Glory* returned to Sasebo, where she handed over to *Ocean* for the last few weeks of the war. In two years *Glory* had made a considerable contribution to the British war effort in Korea. Since leaving the UK in January 1951 she had steamed 157,000 miles and flown 13,700 sorties, 9,500 of which were operational over Korea. Her aircraft had destroyed 70 bridges, 392 vehicles and 449 railway trucks for the loss of twenty aircrew. Ammunition expended included 278 1,000lb bombs, 7,080 500lb bombs, 24,238 3in rocket projectiles and 1,441,000 rounds of 20mm cannon ammunition.

Glory returned to Portsmouth on 8 July 1953 and commenced a refit, after which she returned to the MF with the same air group, arriving in Gibraltar on 9 November 1953. After a short spell during which she carried out several visits, she returned to the UK on 1 March 1954 and was modified for use a ferry carrier to transport aircraft, personnel and equipment to and from the Far East. She was loaded with aircraft from RNAS Abbotsinch at Glasgow in September and delivered them to Singapore in October, returning to the UK in December. In January 1955 *Glory* played a principal role in Operation *Snowdrop*, acting as a base in Loch Eriboll for naval helicopters that carried out relief work in snow-bound Scotland. On completion she steamed to Rosyth, where she reduced to care and maintenance with a small ship's company. In June 1956 she was reduced to reserve at Rosyth, and in 1957 she was placed on the Disposal List. On 23

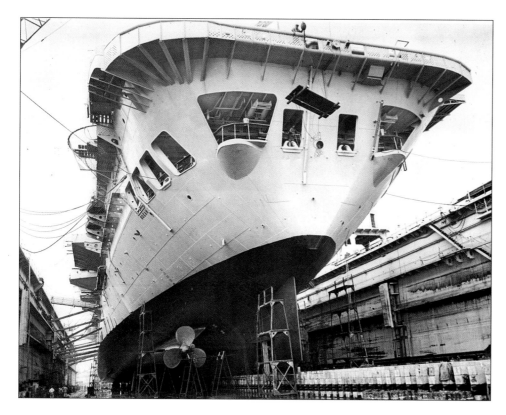

August 1961 she was sold to T W Ward Ltd and towed the short distance to Inverkeithing, where she was broken up for scrap. The work was complete by 1962.

Mars

Mars was allocated Admiralty Job Number J 3898 and was ordered from Vickers-Armstrongs' yard at Barrow-in-Furness on 7 August 1942, where she was given the Yard Number 884. The name *Ethalion* had been considered for her at an early stage but was not allocated. She was laid down on 2 December 1942 and launched as *Mars* on 20 May 1944, but subsequently it was decided to convert her into an aircraft maintenance carrier and she was renamed *Pioneer* in July 1944. Her details will be found with the other maintenance carriers in chapter 24.

Ocean

Admiralty Job Number J 1498 was given the name *Ocean* from the outset and ordered from Alexander Stephen & Sons at Linthouse, Govan, on 7 August 1942, a yard that was more usually associated with cruiser and destroyer construction. The firm gave the new ship their Yard Number 598. She was laid down on 8 November 1942 and launched on Saturday 8 July 1944 by Lady Olive Willis, wife of the Second Sea Lord, Admiral Sir Algernon Willis. The ship was completed and commissioned in the shipyard on 8 August 1945,

exactly a week before VJ-Day and the end of the Second World War. While she was fitting-out she had been selected for modification into a nightfighter carrier, as experience in the BPF had shown such a ship to be vitally necessary. Despite the end of the war the Admiralty decided to go ahead with the modification to gain experience with night carrier operations, and *Ocean* arrived at Cammell Laird's yard in Birkenhead for the work to be carried out. Major changes included the substitution of a USN supplied SM-1 radar instead of the inferior British Type 277 for fighter control, Type 961 carrier-controlled approach radar and improved direction-finding equipment. The flight deck lighting was also improved, and a box-like structure was added to the forward part of the island to house the SM-1 office; a useful recognition feature of the ship in her early years. When the work was completed she was allocated to Rosyth Command for flying trials on 16 November 1945.

The first trials included carrier compatibility trials of the Sea Hornet and a number of landings and take-offs to clear the type for operational use. During this period a Swordfish from the Torpedo Development Unit was embarked and launched to mark the end of the type's long and distinguished Service career with a final carrier take-off. By far the most significant event, however, was the world's first carrier landing by a jet aircraft on 3 December 1945. Sea Vampire LZ551/G was flown by Lieutenant Commander E M Brown DSC RN,

who safely carried out a total of fifteen landings and take-offs over a two-day period in less than ideal sea and weather conditions. On 7 December 1945 she embarked 892 (Hellcat nightfighter) and 1792 (Firefly nightfighter) NAS and sailed for the Mediterranean for an extended trial intended to evaluate night carrier operations. It was also intended to evaluate the difference in capability between the single-seat Hellcat and the two-seat Firefly nightfighters. The importance placed on the trial can be judged from the fact that the Admiralty had to pay in dollars to retain the Hellcats and SM-1 radar after the end of Lend/Lease arrangements. The Hellcats were the equivalent of the USN F6F-5N, equipped with AN/APS-6 radar in a wing-mounted pod. The Fireflies were fitted with a pod under the fuselage which contained a USN AN/APS-4 radar set. While the APS-6 had a slightly better performance, the APS-4 had a useful surface search capability and the pod and control 'boxes' could easily be fitted into any Firefly to equip it as a nightfighter. The two-man crew, in which the observer could concentrate on the radar interception and the pilot on flying the aircraft, was also thought to be a better and safer option, especially in bad weather. The trial ended in April 1946 with the conclusion that intensive night carrier operations were entirely practical and that the British-built Firefly was the better nightfighter in the short term because it was available in large numbers and was also used for a number of other roles. During her four-month deployment *Ocean*'s squadrons carried out 1,100 day and 250 night deck landings. Both squadrons were disbanded after disembarking when the ship returned to the UK on 16 April.

In May 1946 she embarked 20 CAG, comprising 805 (Seafire) and 816 (Firefly) NAS, and sailed to join the MF. In August Fireflies temporarily replaced the Seafires in 805 when the latter were grounded owing to a technical defect, and in October medical and technical assistance was given to the destroyers *Saumarez* and *Volage* when they were damaged by Albanian mines in the Corfu Channel. In April 1947 Seafires replaced the Fireflies in 805 NAS, and *Ocean* took part in the MF summer cruise, which included a visit to Istanbul. In May 1948 she formed part of the RN task force that covered the final withdrawal of British forces from Palestine. Her squadrons provided the only air cover once RAF bases ashore were evacuated. In June 1948 her squadrons disembarked to re-form as part of the RAN and *Ocean* embarked 804 (Seafire) and 812 (Firefly) NAS to replace them. In June 1949 the air group

was disembarked and she was used to carry troops to the Mediterranean and Far East. She made a total of four runs, the last two carrying reinforcements and equipment for the Commonwealth forces in Korea. In January 1951 she commenced a refit and on 27 June 1951 she recommissioned for service in the MF.

In January 1952 she sailed from Malta for the Far East to replace *Glory* in the Korean war zone, with 802 (Sea Fury) and 825 (Firefly) NAS embarked together with two Dragonfly helicopters. Her first war patrol began on 10 May 1952, and only a week later she set a new operating record for a light fleet carrier of 123 sorties in a single day and dropping 90 tons of bombs, showing the influence of her outstanding captain, Captain C L G Evans DSO DSC RN. On 11 July she took part in Operation *Pressure Pump*, a combined RN, USN, US Marine Corps (USMC), United States Air Force (USAF) and RAAF strike on Pyongyang, the North Korean capital, co-ordinated by the US 5th Air Force. *Ocean*'s aircraft

Whirlwinds of 845 NAS from HMS *Theseus* carrying out the first helicopter-borne assault in history during the Suez intervention in 1956. (AUTHOR'S COLLECTION).

contributed thirty-nine out of a total of 1,254 Allied offensive sorties, their targets including a railway marshalling yard thought to contain crated Mikoyan and Gurevich MiG-15 fighters, which was successfully destroyed. On 9 August 1952 Lieutenant Carmichael of 802 NAS and his section shot down a MiG-15, the first jet to be destroyed by British armed forces. Her first period of operations off Korea ended on 30 October 1952 with a church service on the flight deck and a wreath dropped into the sea in memory of the nine aircrew who had died in action. In one of her last patrols *Ocean*'s squadrons had achieved 749 combat sorties in nine days. Priority targets were trucks and road transport, but on 28 October her aircraft attacked sluice gates at Yonan. In recognition of their outstanding contribution to Korean operations, 802 and 825 NAS were awarded the Boyd Trophy for 1952.

In November 1952 *Ocean* joined *Glory* for Exercise *Taipan*, which practised the air defence of Hong Kong; on its completion *Glory* relieved *Ocean* in the war zone. She returned to the war zone to relieve *Glory* for the last time on 17 May 1953, and began a war patrol two days later. On 31 May she returned to Sasebo, and on 1 June 1953 she launched fourteen Sea Furies in harbour using RATOG, to take part in a fly-past to celebrate the Coronation of HM Queen Elizabeth II. This was the first time RATOG had been used for a large harbour launch, and was necessary because fog and low cloud had prevented the aircraft from disembarking to Iwakuni while the ship was on passage to Sasebo. To celebrate Coronation day itself on 2 June 1953, all Commonwealth ships in harbour dressed overall and a parade was held in *Ocean*'s hangar. Further war patrols followed while armistice talks brought the conflict to a conclusion. On 16 July three Fireflies were disembarked to K-6

Airfield at Pyongtaek to act as nightfighters against slow-flying North Korean nuisance raiders. They proved very successful. After the signing of the armistice in Panmunjon in July, *Ocean* carried out a further four patrols off Korea to ensure that the terms of the armistice were upheld. On 31 October she sailed for Hong Kong flying her paying-off pennant, and in November she was relieved as the FEF carrier by HMAS *Sydney*.

Ocean returned to Devonport Dockyard in December 1953 after two-and-a-half years away, to be refitted and modified for use a training ship, recommissioning on 19 August 1954 to relieve *Indefatigable* in the HF Training Squadron. She was used occasionally for other tasks, and in 1955 she was used twice to ferry troops and equipment to Cyprus. During the build-up of forces in the Eastern Mediterranean before the Suez intervention in 1956 she joined *Theseus* and the cruiser *Cumberland* to carry the 16th Parachute Brigade to Cyprus in August. In September 1956 she was hastily modified for use as a helicopter carrier, using the accommodation in the training spaces to carry Royal Marines Commandos. In October she embarked 845 (Whirlwind) NAS and elements of 45 RM Commando to carry out assault exercises in the English Channel, and later off Malta together with *Theseus*, which had been similarly modified. Later 845 NAS transferred to *Theseus* and *Ocean* embarked the Joint Helicopter Development Unit, equipped with Whirlwinds and Bristol Sycamores. On 6 November 1956 *Ocean* and *Theseus* took part in Operation *Musketeer*, the Anglo/French landings in Suez. In the first operational 'vertical envelopment' in history, 45 RM Commando was landed by helicopters from the two carriers, 415 marines and 23 tons of stores being flown ashore to Port Said in one-and-a-half hours and casualties returned to the ships for treatment. *Ocean* returned to Devonport Dockyard after what was to be her last operational deployment on 12 December 1956, for modification back into the training role.

To give her trainees sea experience and to 'show the flag', *Ocean* carried out a number of visits during 1957. These included Weymouth, Milford Haven, Rothesay, Glasgow, Rosyth and Anwerp in the first part of the year. After a maintenance period in Devonport in May she visited Rosyth, Invergordon, Reykjavik, Hamburg, Penzance, Helsinki and Oslo. Her last visits, in October and November, were to Gibraltar, Bilbao, Rosyth, Liverpool and Portsmouth. She returned to Devonport for the last time on 5 December 1957 and paid off. She was subsequently destored and moved to buoys in the River Tamar, with no plans for her further use. Placed on the Disposal List in March 1958 and stripped of all useful fittings and equipment, she was sold to the British Iron & Steel Corporation and towed out of Devonport for Faslane to be scrapped on 6 May 1962. Her demolition was effectively complete by the end of August.

Theseus

Ordered on 7 August 1942 from the Fairfield Shipbuilding & Engineering Company of Govan, *Theseus* was allocated Admiralty Job Number J 1709 and Yard Number 709 by her builder. She was laid down on 6 January 1943 and launched on 6 July 1944. She was not completed before the end of the war, and work on her slowed after VJ-Day, but she was eventually completed, handed over to the RN and commissioned at the shipyard on 9 February 1946. Initially she was allocated to

Rosyth Command without an air group and used as a deck-landing training carrier, replacing escort carriers. This task ended a year later when she embarked 804 (Seafire) and 812 (Firefly) NAS and sailed to join the BPF on 1 February 1947. She returned on 20 December 1947 and entered Rosyth Dockyard for a refit.

In 1948 she emerged to join the HF and embarked 807 (Sea Fury) and 810 (Firefly) NAS. On 19 June 1950 a Sea Vampire from 703 NAS at RNAS Ford carried out the first night deck landing by a jet on a British aircraft carrier. Two months later she was ordered to sail for the Far East to relieve *Triumph* in the Korean war zone, and she left Portsmouth on 18 August with 17 CAG, comprising 807 (Sea Fury) and 813 (Firefly) NAS, embarked together with a Sea Otter amphibian for SAR duties. Her first war patrol began on 8 October and she subsequently flew a number of sorties off the west coast, supporting the left flank of the advancing UN forces. On 27 October her catapult became unserviceable and sorties had to be flown without bombs, rockets or drop tanks, relying on free take-off. She returned to Sasebo and then sailed for Hong Kong on 8 November. While on passage the catapult wires were re-reeved, a remarkable achievement by the engineering department in a ship under way. Catapult deadweight launches and then real launches with aircraft were carried out off Hong Kong, after which *Theseus* returned to Korea in December to join other UN forces in trying to stem the communist

Theseus loaded with military vehicles and equipment in 1956. (Author's collection)

winter offensive after the Chinese intervention. During her third war patrol in the bitter winter of 1950 *Theseus* flew 338 sorties in seven days with 95 per cent aircraft serviceability, attacking bridges, rolling-stock and enemy troops in the field and earning a signal of congratulation from the First Sea Lord. During the critical month of December she spent twenty-three days at sea and had flown 630 sorties, expending 38,000 rounds of 20mm ammunition and 1,412 3in rocket projectiles.

In January 1951 she flew what was then a record number of sorties from a light fleet carrier, sixty in a single day, in attacks against railways, trucks and junks. On 18 January the Admiralty announced that 17 CAG had been awarded the Boyd Trophy for its operations off Korea. At the end of January a USN S-51 helicopter was embarked to replace the Sea Otter for SAR duties, and on 2 February a run of 1,463 accident-free deck landings ended when a Sea Fury landed heavily and broke its undercarriage. A new record of sixty-six sorties was achieved a day later. She sailed for her tenth and last war patrol on 8 April 1951; this was off the east coast of Korea in company with the USS *Bataan*, and was intended to deter potential Chinese attacks on Formosa, but reconnaissance of the west coast was maintained by aircraft flying across the peninsula. On 17 April she moved back to the west

Theseus enters Sasebo for the last time on 20 April 1951, after her final Korean War patrol. (AUTHOR'S COLLECTION)

coast, and on 20 April she entered Sasebo for the last time, with her ship's company spelling *Theseus* on the flight deck. *Glory* relieved her on 23 April and two days later she sailed for the UK. On 29 May 1951 she arrived in Portsmouth, where the First Sea Lord, Admiral of the Fleet Lord Fraser of North Cape, presented the Boyd Trophy.

After a short refit she recommissioned for service in the MF in January 1952 and then alternated between the HF and MF until October 1953, when she returned to Portsmouth for conversion into a training ship. On 19 August 1954 she relieved *Implacable* as flagship of the HF Training Squadron and began a series of training courses and port visits. In August 1956 she carried part of 16 Parachute Brigade from the UK to Cyprus during the build-up for the Suez operation. She was then prepared for duty as an operational helicopter carrier, using the training accommodation to carry Royal Marines Commandos, and worked-up with *Ocean* in the English Channel and Malta areas. On 6 November 1956 she took part in Operation *Musketeer*, the Anglo/French landings in Suez, with 845 (Whirlwind) NAS embarked, in company with *Eagle, Albion, Bulwark* and *Ocean*. Together with the Joint Helicopter Development Unit (JHDU) in *Ocean* her helicopters landed over 400 RM commandos and 23 tons of stores at Port Said in the first-ever 'vertical envelopment' and flew casualties back to the ship for medical treatment. This was to be her last operation, however, and on 21 December 1956 she returned to Portsmouth, where she was paid off and destored before being reduced to extended reserve, moored in Fareham

Creek. In March 1958 the Admiralty gave approval for her to be scrapped, and on 29 November 1961 she was sold to the British Iron & Steel Corporation, towed out of Portsmouth and subsequently broken up at Inverkeithing.

Triumph

Admiralty Job Number J 4677 was given the name *Triumph* from the outset and ordered from Hawthorn Leslie of Hebburn-on-Tyne on 7 August 1942, being given Yard Number 662. Again this was a yard that had not, previously, built carriers, and its slipway was only five feet longer than the overall length of the ship. She was laid down on 27 January 1943 and launched on 2 October 1944 by Lady Mountbatten, but was too late for war service and was finally completed on 9 May 1946, being commissioned the same day. She was used initially as a trials and training carrier without a dedicated air group, although she did have a ship's flight. In July 1946 she visited Kronstadt, flying the flag of the C-in-C Home Fleet, and in 1947 she embarked 13 CAG, comprising 800 (Seafire) and 827 (Firefly) NAS. In May she escorted the battleship *Vanguard*, which had HM King George VI and the Royal Family on board, back into UK waters after their Royal Tour of South Africa. In June 1947 she joined the MF, visiting Istanbul in July and taking King Paul I of Greece to sea to witness flying operations in August. She returned to the UK late in 1948 for a refit, and recommissioned in Sheerness Dockyard on 21 April 1949 for service in the FEF, leaving in July after a period working-up with 13 CAG embarked together with a Sea Otter SAR amphibian.

While on passage to Singapore her aircraft carried out strikes against communist terrorists in the Malayan jungle. On 8 June 1950 she visited

Ominato in Japan, and six days later began operational training exercises in Japanese waters with ships of the FEF and the USN. Their timing and location soon proved to be of critical importance after the communist North Korea attacked South Korea in an unprovoked and unexpected act of aggression on 25 June. On 29 June the Admiralty ordered the FEF to concentrate and join forces under US command to support UN operations in defence of South Korea. *Triumph* flew constant antisubmarine patrols and kept Seafires at readiness on deck before joining the USS *Valley Forge* in TF 77 on 2 July. Aircraft from both carriers flew familiarisation sorties around the combined TF to allow gunners to recognise unfamiliar shapes, and a day later both carriers launched strikes against North Korean targets. Seafires were notoriously difficult to maintain, but 800 produced all twelve of its aircraft serviceable on this day and, together with nine Fireflies, they attacked Haeju Airfield, causing damage to hangars and installations. On 6 July 1950 *Triumph* entered into Sasebo for replenishment. Black and white stripes were painted on the aircraft because it was feared that, with their in-line engines, they might be mistaken for communist Yakovlev Yak-9s by US forces, and these markings remained in use on RN and RAN aircraft throughout the Korean conflict.

On 15 July 1950 *Triumph* rejoined *Valley Forge* for a series of strikes from the east coast. Because of their more limited range, Fireflies flew antisubmarine patrols and Seafires flew CAPs over the task force. On 19 July the Sea Otter rescued a USN Corsair pilot from the sea; the last recorded occasion when the type carried out an operational rescue. A leaking stern gland required repairs in Sasebo for two days, but by 24 July *Triumph* was back with TF 77. On 26 July more USN carriers

Triumph in June 1950. The aircraft in the range are Seafires and Fireflies. (AUTHOR'S COLLECTION)

arrived and *Triumph* left TF 77 to join the Commonwealth TF off the west coast. On 28 July a Seafire was shot down in error by a USAF Boeing B-29 bomber which had closed the fleet without showing the correct IFF signal. The Seafire was investigating it when the B-29 opened fire and hit it in the fuel tank. The pilot, Warrant Officer White RN, baled out, having suffered burns, and was rescued by the USS *Eversole* and returned to *Triumph*. On 29 August 1950 a Firefly missed all the arrester wires and hit the barrier; the propeller blades broke up in the impact and a large piece of one of them bounced off the bottom of the Flyco structure, smashed through the operations room scuttle and fatally injured Lieutenant Commander I M MacLachlan RN, the CO of 800 NAS. He was buried at sea that evening off South Korea with full naval honours. Lieutenant Handley, the Senior Pilot, took over command.

On 5 September *Triumph* moved back to the east coast to replace the USN carriers while they replenished, and later in the month she moved back to the west to support the landing of the 1st US Marine Division at Inchon. By then her few remaining aircraft were difficult to maintain and support, there being no spare Seafires or early-model Fireflies left in the FEF. Consequently FO2 FEF decided that she had reached the end of her operational usefulness on 20 September and ordered her withdrawal, to be replaced by *Theseus* in a few days' time. She returned to Portsmouth in November and was refitted for use as a ferry carrier. For the next year she carried troops backward and forward between the UK and the Middle East until February 1952, when she was used to assess the new angled deck, initially known in the RN as the 'skew deck'. A 3 degree angled deck was painted on the flight deck and a variety of jet- and piston-engined aircraft flew approaches to it which proved the validity of the concept. The arrester wires had not been 'angled', so they were removed and all landings were 'touch-and-go'. The trials were so successful that the USN immediately fitted the USS *Antietam* with a full 8 degree angled deck with arrester wires modified to match it. Combined RN/USN proof-of-concept trials were carried out on her in 1953.

In 1953 *Triumph* was refitted with extra accommodation and classrooms built into the former hangar and recommissioned in September to relieve *Devonshire* for duty as a cadet training ship. Aircraft operating facilities on the flight deck were retained, and she embarked a flight of Boulton Paul Sea Balliols to give air experience to young officers. In October 1953 she visited Leningrad in return for a visit to the UK by Soviet

cruisers. Frigates took over the role of cadet training in 1956 and the Admiralty announced that *Triumph* was to be converted into a fleet repair ship. Work on this project started in December 1957, using resources that became available as *Victorious* finished her long modernisation. Work had to be suspended in 1960 due to a shortage of dockyard manpower, but recommenced in 1961 and she eventually began post-conversion sea trials in October 1964.

On 7 January 1965 she recommissioned in Portsmouth as a fleet repair ship and subsequently sailed to join the FEF, based in Singapore, where

she maintained destroyers and frigates. Structures externally similar to those in *Perseus* and *Pioneer* had been built on the flight deck, but helicopters could operate from a spot right forward, and a hangar was fitted-out for use by Westland Wasp and Wessex helicopter flights from ships undergoing maintenance. She spent several periods at sea during exercises, and took part in the Beira patrol and flood relief operations in the bay of Bengal before returning to the UK in February 1972 when the FEF was stood down. In March 1972 she began an extended refit in Chatham Dockyard before being placed in long-term, maintained reserve

Triumph after conversion into a fleet repair ship, refuelling at sea from RFA *Blue Rover*, with *Minerva* on the other side of the tanker. The box-like structure to port of the island is a hangar for helicopters disembarked from ships alongside for maintenance; the circle painted on the deck near the bow is their designated landing spot. A Wasp helicopter is parked aft of the spot, with the crane 'Jumbo' secured astern of it. (AUTHOR'S COLLECTION)

there. Despite being in excellent condition she was placed on the Disposal List after the 1981 Defence Review and towed from Chatham to be broken up for scrap in Spain on 9 December 1981. Her disposal was an ill-considered political move to reduce the size of the fleet, and within weeks she was sorely missed when the Falklands Conflict, not anticipated by politicians, broke out. Desperate measures had to be taken to provide a fleet repair ship in the South Atlantic, and the RN bought the *Stena Inspector* for £25 million and then had to fit her out for use at further expense.

Venerable

Admiralty Job Number J 3697, *Venerable* was ordered from Cammell Laird & Company of Birkenhead on 7 August 1942 and given Yard Number 1126. She was laid down on 3 December 1942 and the firm achieved one of the fastest build times for the class, launching her on 30 December 1943 and completing her on 17 January 1945. She was first commissioned in the shipyard and subsequently embarked 1851 (Corsair) and 814 (Barracuda) NAS to work-up to operational efficiency. By March she was the flagship of 11

ACS and sailed with *Vengeance* and *Colossus* to join the BPF. The Admiralty expected the war to last into 1946, so progress to the Pacific was measured and intended to reach a peak in time for the invasion of the Japanese mainland in the autumn of 1945. For this reason 11 ACS spent two months of intensive work-up in Malta before resuming their passage to the Pacific on 22 May 1945. *Venerable* arrived in Sydney on 22 July 1945 and Rear Admiral Harcourt, ACS 11, transferred his flag to *Indomitable*. The expanded squadron now comprised *Indomitable*, *Venerable*, *Vengeance*, *Glory* and *Colossus*, and was intended to join 1 ACS in operations against the Japanese mainland.

New plans followed the sudden and unexpected end of the war on 15 August, and *Venerable* sailed with *Indomitable* and other ships to liberate Hong Kong from Japanese occupation. On 31 August 1945 the two carriers launched aircraft to destroy Japanese forces which refused to surrender. Suicide boats that had sortied to attack were dive-bombed, strafed and sunk. Other craft concealed to the north of Hong Kong Island were destroyed, and a continuous CAP was maintained in daylight. On 2 September the remaining Japanese forces surrendered, and *Venerable* landed members of her ship's company to help with restoration work ashore. She sailed for Trincomalee on 20 October with Indian former prisoners of war, and spent the remainder of 1945 repatriating former prisoners and internees, soldiers and military equipment between Bombay, Singapore, Batavia and Fremantle.

On 1 January 1946 she arrived at Garden Island Dockyard in Sydney for a refit, and subsequently

resumed operations in the BPF with the same air group embarked. She was refitted in Singapore Dockyard from October 1946 and finally sailed for the UK in February 1947, arriving in Devonport Dockyard on 30 March 1947 after two years away. With the RN being reduced in size, *Venerable* was considered surplus to requirements and was destored, paid off into reserve and placed on the Disposal List. On 1 April 1948 the unwanted carrier was sold to the Dutch Government, and on 28 May she was commissioned into the RNethN as *Karel Doorman*, replacing the escort carrier *Nairana*, which had been on loan. She embarked a Dutch air group equipped with Sea Furies and Fireflies.

From 1954 she underwent an extensive modernisation at Wilton-Fijenoord Shipyard in Holland, during which she was fitted with a new steam catapult, an angled deck, a mirror landing sight and an extremely tall and distinctive combined mast and funnel which supported an air-search radar. She recommissioned in 1958 and subsequently operated an air group of Sea Hawks and Grumman S-2 Trackers. Sikorsky S-58 antisubmarine helicopters were added later. In 1968 she was damaged by a major fire in the machinery spaces and subsequently sold to Argentina 'as lying', to be refitted in Wilton-Fijenoord Shipyard for further service. Replacement boilers and turbines were taken from the incomplete *Leviathan* in Portsmouth Dockyard to replace those damaged in the fire.

She was renamed *25 de Mayo* and commissioned into the Argentine Navy on 1 September 1969 to

Venerable on 1 May 1945. (AUTHOR'S COLLECTION)

operate an air group of A-4 Skyhawks and S-2 Trackers. In 1981 the Argentine Navy procured Dassault Super Etendard strike fighters and a small batch of Exocet air-to-surface missiles, and *25 de Mayo* underwent modifications to be able to operate them. During the South Atlantic War in 1982 *25 de Mayo* sortied against the RN Task Force, but the loss of the cruiser *General Belgrano* to a torpedo attack by the submarine *Conqueror* led to her being withdrawn into a safe harbour. Her aircraft subsequently operated from shore bases. By 1988 her machinery was in a poor state and she began a long, slow refit from which she was never to emerge. In 1990 Fincantieri was given an initial contract to provide technical assistance on replacing the Parsons geared turbines with gas turbines, installing a new steam plant for the catapult and making improvements to the flight deck and lifts as well as providing a new command system. In 1994 the old machinery was stripped out, but further work finally came to a halt as funding ran out. Finally, in 2000, she was towed to Alang in India to be broken up for scrap.

Vengeance

Ordered from Swan Hunter & Wigham Richardson at its Wallsend-on-Tyne yard on 7 August 1942, *Vengeance* was allocated Admiralty Job Number J 4675 and builder's Yard Number 1699. Laid down on 16 November 1942 and launched on 23 February 1944, she was completed and commissioned in the shipyard on 15 January 1945 and subsequently embarked 1850 (Corsair)

and 812 (Barracuda) NAS to work-up before service with 11 ACS in the BPF. She sailed for the Mediterranean on 12 March in company with *Colossus* and *Venerable* and, with them, spent two months working-up in the Malta areas before finally sailing to join the BPF on 18 April 1945. She passed through the Suez Canal on 28 May and arrived in Sydney on 23 July 1945. On VJ Day, 15 August, she sailed for Manus but was diverted to join other BPF ships in liberating Hong Kong. Once moored in the harbour she remained there for the remainder of 1945, using her sailors to help repair the Dockyard and restore the colony to normality.

On 16 January she returned to Sydney for a refit in Garden Island Dockyard, on completion of which she was allocated to the EIF and used, from March, to ferry aircraft from Singapore to Kure in Japan for use by the Commonwealth Occupation Force. She finally left Colombo on 20 July 1946 to return to the UK, arriving in Devonport Dockyard on 13 August to pay off for a refit. *Vengeance* was to be retained in service, and improvements were made to her accommodation as well as to the bridge and aircraft operating arrangements. She recommissioned on 14 December 1946 and was allocated to Rosyth Command for use as a training carrier without a dedicated air group, although she did have a ship's flight. In June 1947 she visited Oslo, flying the flag of the First Sea Lord and with her ship's flight Barracuda painted blue as an 'admiral's barge', and subsequently visited other Norwegian ports as a private ship after he flew back to the UK. In July 1947 she joined in the HF visit to Liverpool that expressed the RN's gratitude for the work done by the city's population during the war. After a brief docking she sailed for the Far

East in September to rejoin the BPF briefly, returning to the UK in February 1948.

After a refit in Rosyth she joined the HF with 15 CAG embarked, comprising 802 (Sea Fury) and 814 (Firefly) NAS. After a work-up she took part in HF cruises to the West Indies and South Africa. In December 1948 she was modified for Arctic operations and subsequently took part in Operation *Rusty*, a six-week deployment into the Arctic to evaluate the effect of extremely cold weather on men, ships and aircraft. Flying operations involved a number of aircraft types including Sea Vampires and Dragonfly helicopters. Overall it proved very successful, but it was found that the wartime-grade mild steel from which the light fleet carriers were constructed became brittle at low temperatures, and a serious crack developed across *Vengeance*'s flight deck. This had to be repaired during the post-trial refit at Rosyth Dockyard from 8 March 1949. On completion of the refit she rejoined the HF until January 1951, when she relieved *Illustrious* temporarily as the trials and training carrier. In August 1951 she arrived in Portsmouth Dockyard to have temporary accommodation built into the hangar so that she could be used for trooping duties to and from the Far East in support of the British contribution to the Korean War. She sailed for Singapore with a load of replacement aircraft and personnel in January 1952, arriving in February and returning to Portsmouth in March. In June she took aircraft to Malta and then sailed for Singapore again. On 28 August she returned to Portsmouth for a docking and essential defect repair period, and to have the accommodation removed from the hangar to prepare her for operational service with the RAN.

On 13 November 1952 she was commissioned

in Devonport Dockyard as HMAS *Vengeance*, on loan because of the delayed completion of HMAS *Melbourne*. After a short work-up in UK waters she sailed for Australia on 22 January 1953. She arrived in Sydney on 11 March to form 5 ACS with *Sydney* and to embark an air group comprising 808,

Vengeance in the Arctic during Operation Rusty *in February 1949.* (AUTHOR'S COLLECTION)

850 (Sea Fury) and 817 (Firefly) NAS. In September 850 NAS transferred to *Sydney* and in 1954 she was employed as a training ship, although still fully capable of operating aircraft. She joined other ships of the RAN to escort HM Queen Elizabeth II during her tour of Australian waters in SS *Gothic* during 1954. During this period Her Majesty presented Captain Burrell with a signed photograph, and he had the idea of using sailors to reproduce the signature in large on the

Vengeance on 3 May 1945, in her initial paint scheme and with Barracudas on deck. (AUTHOR'S COLLECTION)

flight deck. This was successfully achieved and a photograph was taken and sent to HM the Queen in *Gothic*, to which she replied that it was 'a most original forgery'. In June 1955 *Vengeance* sailed from Sydney for the UK with a ship's company that would take over the new *Melbourne*.

Vengeance loaded with equipment and stores while trooping in 1952.
(AUTHOR'S COLLECTION)

Vengeance was returned to the RN on 13 August 1955 and immediately destored and reduced to extended reserve. The RN had no further use for her and she was placed on the Disposals List. On 13 December 1956 she was sold to the Brazilian Government and renamed *Minas Gerais*. In 1957 she was taken in hand by the Rosenburg Yard of Verolme United Shipyards at Rotterdam, Holland, and modernised to a standard similar to her sister ship *Karel Doorman*, formerly *Venerable*. She had the largest angled deck that could engineered, including a section on the ship's starboard quarter, to achieve a landing area angled at 8.5 degrees to port. She also had a steam catapult, mirror landing aid and both flight deck and lifts strengthened to operate aircraft up to 20,000lb. The refit was completed in December 1960 and she commissioned into the Brazilian Navy on 13 January 1961.

She was employed as an antisubmarine carrier with an air group made up with S-2 Trackers and ASH-3A Sea King helicopters. She was regularly refitted with an upgraded command system, and between 1991 and 1993 she was modernised with new CCA radars and improved communications including data links and electronics. The boilers were retubed, the turbines refurbished and Mistral surface-to-air missiles replaced Bofors guns. In the late 1990s, however, the Brazilian Navy acquired a number of A-4 Skyhawks which were refurbished to give a strike and limited air-defence capability. Although these could operate from *Minas Gerais*,

the Brazilian Navy sought a larger ship and acquired the *Foch* from France in 2001. She was renamed *Sao Paulo*, and after she entered service *Minas Gerais* was deactivated on 16 October 2001. Over fifty years old, she was the last wartime carrier in service and a remarkable testament to what the light fleet carrier design could achieve. In 2004 she was towed to Alang in India to be broken up for scrap.

Warrior

The name *Brave* was considered for this ship at an early stage, but changed to *Warrior* before work started. Given Admiralty Job Number J 3393, she was ordered on 7 August 1942 from Harland & Wolff in Belfast, allocated Yard Number 1224, laid down on 12 December 1942 and launched on 20 May 1944. The RCN had discussed with the Admiralty the possibility of operating a carrier after the war, and had partly manned two CVEs to gain experience. To help take the concept forward the Admiralty agreed in May 1945 to transfer *Warrior* to the RCN on loan when she was completed. The last of the *Colossus* Class to finish construction, she was completed, handed over to the RCN and commissioned as HMCS *Warrior* at Belfast on 24 January 1946. After working-up with RN assistance she embarked 19 CAG, comprising 803 (Seafire) and 825 (Firefly) NAS, and joined the Canadian Atlantic Fleet on 23 March 1946. Her time with the RCN was relatively short, and in March 1948 she returned to Belfast, where her ship's company took over the new HMCS *Magnificent* and *Warrior* reverted to RN control at Portsmouth on 23 March 1948.

She was recommissioned and fitted with an experimental flexible 'rubber' flight deck for landing trials by aircraft without undercarriages. The idea was that, by removing the undercarriage and its hydraulic actuating mechanisms, carrierborne aircraft could be made lighter, thus improving their performance or allowing more fuel to be carried. The weakness of the concept was, of course, the inability of the aircraft to move once it had landed until it had been lifted on to a trolley by a crane. Recovery times could have hardly been better than one aircraft every five minutes in good weather, and would have been considerably worse in bad weather. While the system worked, albeit slowly, with 'clean' Sea Vampires, it was never tried and could not have worked with propeller-driven aircraft, helicopters or jets fitted with pylons for bombs, rockets or drop tanks. The trials took place between November 1948 and March 1949, with Lieutenant Commander E M Brown DSC RN and five other pilots carrying out landings in specially modified Sea Vampire fighters. The aircraft had undercarriages for landing ashore, but these were kept retracted for the trial landings on the 'rubber' deck. Brown was awarded the Boyd Trophy for this work, which proved to have no useful value operationally but led indirectly to the concept of the angled deck. Once the trials were complete the flexible deck was removed and *Warrior* was reduced to reserve in Portsmouth.

Reactivated in June 1950 and modified to ferry men and aircraft to reinforce the Far East Station after the outbreak of the Korean War, she sailed in August for the first run. In June 1951 she ferried 16 Parachute Brigade from the UK to Cyprus during a crisis in the Middle East, and in 1952 she

Warrior in March 1946. (AUTHOR'S COLLECTION)

was taken in hand in Devonport Dockyard for modernisation. When she recommissioned on 8 September 1953 she was the only ship of her class to be fitted with a lattice mast in RN service, intended to take an improved Type 293Q radar and a 'YE' homing beacon. Improved Type 277Q radars were fitted fore and aft on the island, and a Type 281Q radar and IFF aerials were mounted on a mainmast abaft the funnel. The bridge was enlarged and enclosed, a modification carried out on all the active ships of the class. Twin Mark 5 Bofors replaced the pom-pom mountings, and single Bofors replaced Oerlikons. After sea trials she embarked 811 (Sea Fury) and 825 (Firefly) NAS and worked-up for operational service with the FEF. On 12 May 1954 she relieved *Sydney* off Korea in operations to monitor the ceasefire on behalf of the UN. On 25 August she was ordered to evacuate refugees from the North to South Vietnam following a request to the British Government by the Vietnamese Prime Minister. She sailed from Hong Kong on 31 August after bunk beds and extra heads had been hastily fitted into the hangar by Hong Kong Dockyard. The evacuation began on 4 September, and by 13 September 1954 3,000 refugees had been evacuated, three babies being born at sea with the help of the ship's medical staff. From 23 September the extra bunks and heads were removed and *Warrior* began her return passage to the UK. In October 1954 she was awarded a Special Unit Citation by the President of Vietnam.

After her arrival back in the UK she began a major modernisation in Devonport Dockyard on 14 December 1954. She was fitted with an angled flight deck and was the only ship of her class to be so modified in RN service. Some of the port-side sponsons were removed and a flight-deck extension fitted on the port side amidships. The flight deck was strengthened to take aircraft up to 20,000lb,

the arrester gear was upgraded to take aircraft at this weight with an entry speed of 60 knots, and the BH3 hydraulic catapult was uprated to launch 20,000lb aircraft at an end speed of 60 knots. She was also fitted with a mirror landing aid and Type 961 CCA radar. Although small, she could operate a broad range of aircraft and it was intended that she should relieve *Bulwark* as the trials and training carrier. After a short spell on this task, however, she was selected to be the flagship of the RN task force supporting the British nuclear tests at Christmas Island in the Pacific, Operation *Grapple*. She sailed in February 1957 with a ship's flight of Avengers and Whirlwind helicopters embarked. When the thermonuclear bombs were detonated the Whirlwinds were used to collect air samples from the area surrounding the test site and the Avengers were used to fly them ashore for onward transport to the UK for analysis.

The homeward passage through the Straits of Magellan included several port visits, including one to Buenos Aires. She eventually returned to

Devonport in February and was paid off and decommissioned, with no further service planned in the RN after the large reductions in the number of active ships announced in the 1957 Defence Review. The significance of the port visit became apparent when it was announced in July 1958 that she had been bought by Argentina. She was recommissioned as ARA *Independencia* on 24 July 1958, and sailed for Argentina after a work-up in UK waters on 10 December. She operated an air group that included F4U Corsairs and AT-6 Harvards for just over a decade before being withdrawn from service in 1971, when she was replaced by her more heavily modified sister ship *25 de Mayo*, formerly *Venerable*. She was broken up locally after 1971.

Warrior sailing from Devonport after her initial modernisation, which included the installation of a lattice mast. (AUTHOR'S COLLECTION)

CHAPTER 21

MAJESTIC CLASS

Technical background

The last six of the light fleet carriers ordered in 1942 were modified early in their construction to allow the operation of heavier aircraft. The flight deck was strengthened to take aircraft up to 20,000lb, and larger lifts 54ft long and 34ft wide were installed. Internal subdivision was modified to improve survivability, and improvements were made to the standard of accommodation, including partial air conditioning and the provision of cafeteria-style dining halls for junior rates and more spacious sleeping areas in mess decks. The close-range armament was standardised as power-operated 40mm Bofors in twin Mark 5 and single Mark 7 mountings. The radar outfit was also improved, and was to consist of Type 281BQ, Type 293Q and two separate Type 277Q installations, one forward and one aft on the island. The 'YE' beacon remained the standard aircraft homing aid. Avgas stowage was increased to over 100,000gal in some ships, and electrical generation capacity was doubled. Nothing could be done to bring the flight deck up to the strength required for projected postwar aircraft, but the lifts and hangar deck were strengthened to take static aircraft up to 24,000lb. However, 20,000lb remained the heaviest weight at which aircraft could be landed-on.

None of the ships was completed before VJ-Day, and with a number of *Colossus* Class ships already in service and eight of the larger 1943 light fleet carriers on order, the six *Majestics* were surplus to the requirements of the peacetime fleet. The three most advanced, *Majestic, Magnificent* and *Terrible*, were being fitted out and were offered for sale or long-term loan to the RAN and RCN. The remaining three were less advanced, and *Hercules* was not launched until September 1945. An Admiralty Board meeting that same month decided that construction of these three should be suspended and that they should be laid up pending a decision on their future. None of them served with the RN, although consideration was given to completing at least one hull as a helicopter carrier in either the antisubmarine or commando assault roles, or even as a missile-carrying cruiser.

Sales to Commonwealth Navies

Although the RN never operated any of these ships, three were modernised to a British design in order to operate jet fighters, sophisticated antisubmarine aircraft and helicopters, and they demonstrated what could be achieved in a small, relatively inexpensive hull. Two other ships were completed to the original design for Commonwealth navies and one was never completed. The fully modernised ships had angled

A Fairey Gannet antisubmarine aircraft lands on HMAS *Melbourne*. Two more Gannets and a Wessex helicopter are parked forward. (RAN)

decks up to 7.5 degrees, steam catapults, mirror landing aids and both sophisticated radars and adequate operations rooms to make use of them, maintain an air plot and control the fighters. Aircraft operated included Sea Venoms, A-4 Skyhawks, McDonnell F2H Banshees, S-2 Trackers, Sea Hawks and Alizés, although it must be admitted that some of these stretched the design capability to its limit. There had been interest in fitting a longer steam catapult, known tentatively as the 'Scheme B' modernisation, but this would have entailed removing the forward lift and would have been an extensive and expensive modification for which DNC did not have the capacity, as the Department was fully extended with work for the RN. The limited British steam catapult production facilities may well have struggled to produce longer catapults in time to meet the ships' completion programmes. There is evidence that the Indian Navy had hoped to procure the French Dassault Etendard IV strike fighter rather than the Sea Hawk, and complained at British 'unwillingness' to modify the design of *Hercules/Vikrant*. The Indian purchase was a 'cut-price' deal, however, and should be seen in that light. To operate A-4 Skyhawks, HMAS *Melbourne* was forced to operate routinely with boiler

199

pressures 15psi above the designed levels in order to provide catapult steam. She was the world's third aircraft carrier to be completed with steam catapult, angled deck and mirror landing aid installed during build rather than modified subsequently, following shortly after *Ark Royal* and *Forrestal*. Despite reaching their design limit with new generations of aircraft, some of these ships had remarkably long and effective lives. Their machinery and equipment was closely similar to that of other contemporary British designs and was easy and economical for the RAN and RCN both to assimilate and operate without the need for specialised training and support.

Majestic Class technical details

There were differences between the ships from completion onwards; the details below are for *Terrible* as she was completed in 1948.

Displacement:	19,550 tons deep load
Dimensions:	length 695ft
	beam 112ft 6in
	draught 25ft
Machinery:	2 shaft Parsons single-reduction geared turbines
	4 Admiralty 3-drum boilers
	40,000shp delivering 25 knots
Armament:	6 twin 40mm Bofors; 18 single 40mm Bofors; 4 x 3pdr saluting guns
Protection:	Armoured mantlets over torpedo warheads.
Fuel:	3,175 tons FFO
Endurance:	8,300 miles at 20 knots
Complement:	1,300

Aircraft operating data

Flight deck:	690ft x 75ft steel plate
Hangar:	275ft long plus 57ft extension aft of after lift x 52ft x 17ft 6in
Catapult:	1 x BH-3, 20,000lb at 56 knots
Arrester wires:	10 x 20,000lb at 87 knots; 2 barriers.
Lifts:	forward 54ft long x 34ft wide aft 54ft long x 34ft wide, both 20,000lb
Aircraft:	Up to 42 operationally; 70 could be ferried
Aircraft fuel:	98,600gal avgas
Air weapons:	18in torpedoes; 1,000lb bombs; 500lb bombs; 3in rocket projectiles; Mark 11 depth charges; 20mm cannon ammunition; flares and pyrotechnics.

HMAS *Melbourne* after modification to operate Skyhawks and Trackers, photographed in UK waters during 1977, when she formed part of HM Queen Elizabeth II's Silver Jubilee Fleet Review at Spithead. (RAN)

Individual ship histories

Majestic — completed as HMAS *Melbourne*

Ordered on 7 August 1942, on the same day as seven *Colossus* Class ships and two other *Majestics*, *Majestic* was given Admiralty Job Number J 3876. The order was placed with Vickers-Armstrongs at its Barrow-in-Furness shipyard, which allocated her the Yard Number 885, and she was laid down on 15 April 1943. She was launched on 28 February 1945 by Lady Anderson, the wife of Sir John Anderson, the British Chancellor of the Exchequer. The ship's construction was halted from 1946, however, and she remained at Barrow incomplete until 1949, when she was purchased by the Australian Government. Work resumed in 1949 to an improved design, but slowed again in 1952 when the design was recast to incorporate the new steam catapult, angled deck and mirror landing aid.

On 28 October 1955 she was officially renamed HMAS *Melbourne* and commissioned at Barrow-in-Furness by Lady White, wife of Sir Thomas White, the Australian High Commissioner in the UK. Her ship's company had previously steamed *Vengeance* back to the UK after a period on loan to the RAN. After a brief docking in the Gladstone Dock in Liverpool she carried out acceptance trials in the Clyde before working-up in the Channel areas off Portsmouth. The first aircraft to land-on was an RN Sea Hawk on 9 January 1956, and she was visited by HRH the Duke of Edinburgh in February. In March she went alongside the King

George V Dock in Glasgow to embark her first air group by crane, the aircraft being delivered by road from RNAS Abbotsinch. This comprised 808 (Sea Venom), 816 and 817 (Gannet) NAS and the two Sycamore helicopters of the ship's flight. On 12 March she sailed for Australia, passing through the Suez Canal on 30 March.

She disembarked her aircraft to RANAS Nowra on 7 May and entered Sydney Harbour on 9 May in company with *Sydney*. On 14 May she became flagship of the Australian Fleet and subsequently worked-up to prepare for operational service. After a spell in Australian waters she took part in Exercise *Albatross* on passage to Singapore in September 1956, and subsequently gave a flying display for the President of the Philippines in October and carried out tropical trials with the Mark 30 homing torpedo at Manus in November. In March 1957 she demonstrated her capabilities to senior officers off Sydney, then took part in Exercise *Tradewind* in April, visited Singapore and demonstrated her capabilities to senior Thai officers in April during Exercise *Astra*. A series of exercises and demonstrations in the South China Sea, together with port visits, followed. Typical of these was Exercise *Oceanlink* in May 1958 and *Red580scar* with the USN in June 1958. In July she began a refit at Garden Island Dockyard in Sydney, but was operational again by the end of the year. In January 1959 she was involved in filming *On the Beach*, and in April she took part in Exercise *Fotex 59*, one of the largest Commonwealth naval exercises in the area. A series of exercises and port visits to New Zealand, Japan, Singapore, Indonesia, Hong Kong and Australia itself followed, and from

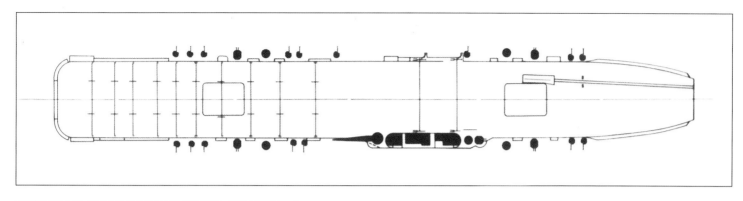

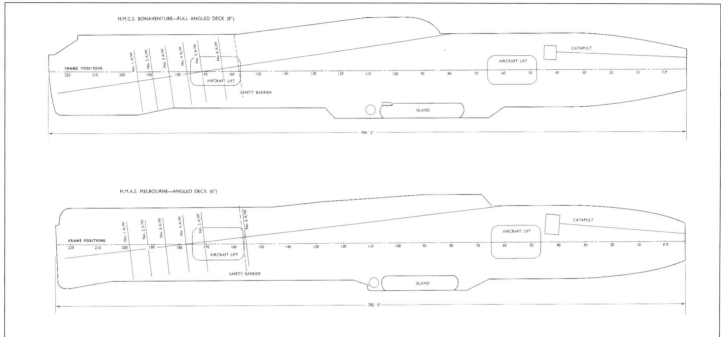

Top The original flight deck design for the *Majestic* Class. (Author's collection)

Above The flight decks of HMCS *Bonaventure* and HMAS *Melbourne* compared after their completion with angled decks and steam catapults. (Author's collection)

June 1959 her air group comprised 805 (Sea Venom) and 816 (Gannet) NAS.

In 1961 she took part in another major Commonwealth exercise, *Jet 61*, after which she visited Bombay, Trincomalee and Karachi. Later in the year she took part in Exercises *Pony Express* and *Tucker Box* as well as a series of port visits. Exercise *Sea Devil* in April 1962 was the largest of its kind in the SEATO region, and included *Ark Royal* and the USS *Bennington* as well as other warships from Australia, New Zealand, Pakistan, the UK and the

USA. She then entered a major refit in September 1962. After working-up with the same air group she disembarked 805 NAS in Singapore in April 1963 and embarked 814 NAS from RNAS Sembawang for Exercise *Python*, an antisubmarine work-up in the Pulau Tioman area during which the RAN evaluated the Wessex helicopter. SEATO Exercise *Sea Serpent* followed, after which 805 replaced 814 NAS. In August 817 (Wessex) NAS joined the air group, the

other squadrons being slightly reduced in size to compensate, and *Melbourne* began to work-up in the antisubmarine role.

On 10 February 1964 the destroyer *Voyager* cut across *Melbourne*'s bow during night manoeuvres off Jervis Bay and, after the ensuing collision, *Voyager* sank with the loss of 82 lives. Repairs to the carrier were carried out in Sydney and lasted until May 1964, after which she resumed her

The incomplete *Majestic* at Barrow-in-Furness on 14 October 1947. (RAN)

The incomplete *Hercules* laid up in the Gareloch in September 1954.
(AUTHOR'S COLLECTION)

programme of exercises and port visits throughout the Far East, beginning with Exercise *Fotex 64* with ships of the RN FEF. A year later, in March 1965, she took part in *Fotex 65*, an even bigger exercise with *Victorious* and *Eagle*, together with over twenty Commonwealth destroyers and frigates. In May she took part in Exercise *Seahorse* with other SEATO warships, in which it was intended to practice running a convoy from Manilla to Bangkok against air and submarine opposition. After a visit to Subic Bay she joined *Sydney*, which was carrying Australian troops to Vietnam, in the Sulu Sea and escorted her to Saigon in May 1965. Further runs escorting *Sydney* were carried out in September 1965 and April 1966, after which she reverted to the more usual routines of exercises and visits. In October 1967 she visited Vancouver and then called at various US ports to load the A-4 Skyhawks and S-2 Trackers that had been purchased by the RAN, together with stocks of stores, missiles and torpedoes, returning via Pearl Harbor and Fiji. Aircraft and stores were unloaded in November, and in December 1967 *Melbourne* began a special refit to enable her to operate the new aircraft types, while her squadrons converted to them at RANAS Nowra.

Sea Acceptance trials began in February 1969, after which she worked-up with 805 (Skyhawk), 816 (Tracker) and 817 (Wessex) NAS. In May she took part in Exercise *Sea Spirit*, during which the USS *Frank E Evans* cut across her bow in the South China Sea. The destroyer was cut in half, and the forward half subsequently sank with the loss of 74 American sailors; the exercise was curtailed and *Melbourne* proceeded to Singapore for emergency repairs. She was docked in the King George VI Dock in Singapore Dockyard on 9 June, and left for Australia at the end of the month. More extensive repairs to the bow were carried out in the Sutherland Dock, Cockatoo Island Dockyard, from 16 July 1969. Operational deployment resumed with a ceremonial fleet entry into Sydney in

November, followed by a planned routine of regional exercises and port visits. During October 1971 she took part in Exercise *Rimpac 71*, the first in a series of major naval exercises involving navies from around the Pacific rim, followed by further visits to 'show the flag' and small-scale exercises. In August 1972 *Rimpac 72* took place, after which she was refitted in Sydney before returning to her normal routine.

In February 1972 *Melbourne* visited the west cost of the USA without her air group and collected a number of Boeing-Vertol CH-47 helicopters that had been procured for the Australian Defence Force, returning to Brisbane and then Sydney in April. Late in December 1974 she sailed at short notice for Operation *Navy Help Darwin*, after Cyclone Tracy devastated the city. *Melbourne* and the fleet oiler *Supply* led the largest relief operation in Australia up to that date, with shore parties and helicopters working around the clock. *Rimpac 75* followed in March 1975, and then the usual routine of maintenance periods, exercises and port visits. Sea Kings replaced the Wessex helicopters in 817 NAS during 1976, giving an enormous increase in fleet antisubmarine capability. In August 1976 she took part in a ceremonial fleet entry into Sydney, and in October she visited Melbourne to celebrate the 21st anniversary of her first commissioning. *Rimpac 77* took place in February 1977, after which she sailed to San Diego in March to collect replacement S-2G aircraft for 816 NAS. At the end of April she sailed for the UK with 805 (Skyhawk), 816 (Tracker) and 817 (Sea King) NAS embarked. She took part in the Silver Jubilee Review for HM Queen Elizabeth II in the Solent on 28 June 1977, and subsequently in Exercise *Highwood* in July. This was a major NATO air defence training period, with a number of warships taking part. On return to Sydney she was refitted before taking part in *Rimpac 78* in March.

By 1978 *Melbourne* was beginning to show her

age, and she underwent a major overhaul in Garden Island Dockyard between June 1978 and August 1979. After working-up she returned to her normal routine and took part in *Rimpac 80* during February 1980. Exercise *Elephant Walk* in September forged closer links with the Indian Navy, but on 21 October a Skyhawk was lost over the bow after a premature catapult shot, the second to be lost in matter of days. Sub-Lieutenant Baddams RAN, the pilot, ejected safely, but all fixed-wing flying was suspended. Tracker launches were resumed on 25 October, and *Melbourne* celebrated her 25th birthday at sea carrying out Exercise *Che Sara 80* off Socotra. After catapult dead-load trials in early 1981 she worked-up off Jervis Bay, but there was a catapult 'hang-fire' while launching a Tracker, the second in twenty launches, and *Melbourne* returned to Garden Island for further repair work in early April. Exercises with the Royal New Zealand Navy (RNZN) and USN followed, and in June 1981 *Melbourne* and *Torrens* rescued over 100 survivors from two unseaworthy refugee boats off Malaysia. Later in June Exercise *Starfish* provided an annual training period for ships and aircraft from the Five-Power Defence Agreement to work together. On 23 July 1981 she disembarked 816, 817 NAS and the ship's Wessex SAR Flight to RANAS Nowra, and returned to Sydney a day later to prepare for a planned major refit in 1982. It had already been decided that further operations with A-4 Skyhawks were unsafe and the relevant spares were landed, effectively ending the era of embarked fighter operations in the RAN.

In September 1981 she embarked aircraft from 816, 817 NAS and the Wessex SAR Flight to act as escort for HM Royal Yacht *Britannia*, after which she took part in Exercises *Sea Eagle* and *Kangaroo 81*. On 10 November 1981 she disembarked 816 NAS to RANAS Nowra; although it was not appreciated at the time, this was to be her last fixed-wing launch. The helicopters were also disembarked and she prepared for a refit, but on 25 February 1982 the Minister for Defence announced that the refit would not now take place, and that *Melbourne* would be reduced to 'contingency reserve' after a safety check in dry dock. The Australian White Ensign was hauled down for the last time at a ceremony on the flight deck on 30 June 1982, and destoring was finally completed on 31 August. She was docked for a period to allow equipment and fittings common to other ships to be removed and then laid up in Sydney Harbour. In April 1985 she was sold the ship breakers at Dallan, near Shanghai, and towed out of Sydney. The tug broke down at one stage

A starboard-bow view of INS *Vikrant* in UK waters shortly after completion. (AUTHOR'S COLLECTION)

and, after drifting, *Melbourne* ran aground near Moreton Bay before completing her last voyage.

Hercules — completed as INS *Vikrant*

Ordered from Vickers-Armstrongs' Walker Naval Yard on the Tyne on 7 August 1942 and given the name *Hercules*, she was allocated Admiralty Job Number J 4673 and the Yard Number 61. She was laid down on 14 October 1943 and launched on 22 September 1945; the only 1942 light fleet carrier to be launched after the end of hostilities. Construction work was suspended in May 1946 after the hull had been made safe and preserved, and in May 1947 she was laid up in the Gareloch off the Clyde. She lay there for nearly ten years before being sold to the Indian Government in January 1957, after which she was towed to Belfast, where she was reconstructed to a modernised design by Harland & Wolff. This incorporated the new angled deck, steam catapult and mirror landing aid, together with modern radar and improved air direction and operations rooms.

She was finally completed to the new design on 4 March 1961, renamed and commissioned as INS *Vikrant* on the same day. The first deck landing was carried out by an Indian Navy Sea Hawk off Portsmouth on 18 May 1961, and in July she embarked 300 (Sea Hawk) NAS and sailed from the UK to work-up off Malta. *Vikrant* arrived at her home port of Bombay, later renamed Mumbai, on 3 November 1961, and subsequently embarked 310 (Alizé) NAS and an SAR Flight with Sud-Aviation Alouette III helicopters. In December 1961 she took part in Operation *Vijay*, and formed

part of the covering force off the coast when Indian forces seized the Portuguese colonies of Goa, Daman and Diu. With the growth of other navies in the region *Vikrant*'s roles were seen as anti-ship strike as well as antisubmarine warfare. Subsequently she took part in a routine of training exercises and port visits in the Indian Ocean area, but she played no part in the 1965 war between India and Pakistan, being in refit at the time. Extra Sea Hawks, including some bought from the German Navy, were procured to maintain the type in service. In 1969 the Indian Navy (IN) attempted to procure A-4 Skyhawks but the USN was unwilling to supply them. *Vikrant*'s strike capability was increased by the progressive allocation of more Sea Hawks to the air group, but the number of Alizés was reduced to four for task force protection.

In December 1971 she took part in operations in the Bay of Bengal during the fighting which led to East Pakistan becoming the independent state of Bangladesh. At least one of her boilers was inoperable, limiting her speed to 16 knots and reducing the amount of steam available for the catapult, but she moved close to the coast with four frigates acting as escorts. Her first strike, against Cox's Bazaar Airfield on 4 December 1971, was followed by a raid on Chittagong and a succession of other locations. Additionally, the armed merchant ship *Ondarda* and several Pakistani small craft were sunk. Operations continued around the clock, with Sea Hawks striking at airfield targets by day and Alizés operating by night. From 8 December *Vikrant*'s aircraft targeted retreating Pakistani troops. Calm conditions on 10 and 11 December meant that the Sea Hawks could not be launched, and Alizés had to be used for all strikes, scoring a minor success when they located and damaged the patrol boat *Jessore*, which was attempting to rescue senior officers from Chittagong. Sea Hawk flights resumed on 12 December with twenty-eight sorties

flown against shipping and shore targets. *Vikrant* eventually retired to Paradip to refuel. By the time the conflict ended in January 1972 the success of *Vikrant*'s operations and the benefits of IN control of long-range maritime patrol aircraft gave a considerable boost to IN plans for the future.

In July 1972 the British Aerospace V/Stol demonstration aircraft G-VTOL landed on board as part of an overseas sales tour and stimulated interest which led to India procuring Sea Harriers to replace the Sea Hawks. Her antisubmarine capability was improved by the procurement of Sea Kings to equip 330 NAS. In 1979 she was reboilered, and in February 1984 she embarked the new 300 NAS, equipped with Sea Harriers, for the first time. In 1986 *Vikrant* was extensively modernised with new radar and command systems after INS *Viraat*, formerly HMS *Hermes*, joined the fleet. A year later the steam catapult, which had become difficult to maintain, was removed and a 12 degree ski-jump was fitted at the bow to allow her to operate a mixed air group of Sea Harriers and Sea Kings until 1994, when she suffered a serious fire. In 1995 she was reduced to reserve status, fifty years after her launch. For most of her life she had been capable only of a limited strike capability, but, as IN commentators observed, it was better to have a limited capability when facing opponents who had less. She was finally decommissioned from the IN on 31 January 1997 and marked for preservation as a museum ship in Mumbai, but lack of funding has so far prevented this from happening. In 2013 she still exists, however, and is the oldest British-built aircraft carrier in existence. She has been opened to the public for short periods by the IN.

Leviathan

The hull that was to be named *Leviathan* was originally ordered from Vickers-Armstrongs' Walker Naval Yard on the Tyne on 7 August 1942,

The incomplete *Leviathan* laid up in Portsmouth in 1962. (Author's collection)

the last of ten aircraft carriers to be ordered for the RN on that day. She was allocated Job Number J 4696 and the Yard Number 62. However, when Swan Hunter found that Job Number J 4715, *Eagle*, had become too wide for its slipway after the latest design modifications, the order was moved to Vickers-Armstrongs' Walker Yard and given the new Yard Number 73 on 2 December 1942. To compensate, the order for *Leviathan* was switched to Swan Hunter on the same day and allocated the new Yard Number 1703. After this complicated start she was not laid down until 18 October 1943, and was finally launched on 7 June 1945, after the end of the war in Europe and only three months before the end of the war in the Pacific. Work continued slowly and finally ended in May 1946, when she was structurally 80 per cent complete.

In July 1946 she was towed to Portsmouth for preservation but kept alongside for use as an accommodation ship for dockyard personnel. From 1950 onwards she was used as a lay-apart store and for many other functions connected with the modernisation of the fleet carrier *Victorious* in Portsmouth Dockyard. The modernisation eventually lasted for eight years as the design was continually modified and the latest developments were incorporated. During this time no preservative work was carried out on *Leviathan* herself, and her material state declined beyond the point where it would have been economical to complete her, although plans were considered for converting her into a helicopter carrier and even a missile-armed cruiser.

When she was no longer required for the dockyard task she was towed out and moored in Fareham Creek in an unmaintained state. Unlike her sisters, no foreign interest led to her purchase, but in July 1966 she was brought back alongside to have her boilers, turbines and other useful spare parts removed to replace the fire-damaged

equipment in *Karel Doorman*, formally *Venerable*, in preparation for her sale to Argentina as *25 de Mayo*. She had little further value since she could not now be completed, and was eventually sold for scrap, arriving at Faslane on 27 May 1968.

Magnificent

Magnificent was one of the last three 1942 light fleet carriers, authorised when it was found that there was sufficient shipbuilding capacity in the UK to increase the number of aircraft carriers under construction. She was ordered from Harland & Wolff in Belfast on 16 October 1942, which gave her Yard Number 1228. Her Admiralty Job Number was J 3329. Having already laid down *Glory* and *Warrior*, the shipbuilder was able to move relatively quickly, and *Magnificent* was laid down on 29 July 1943. She was launched on 16 November 1944 by Lady Hyacinth Needham, daughter of the Earl of Kilmorey, the hereditary Vice-Admiral of Ireland. Work on the ship slowed after the end of the war, but when an agreement was reached between the Admiralty and the Canadian Government on her long-term loan to the RCN, work was accelerated to complete her to the original design. A large contingent of men from *Warrior*, which had returned to the RN after a short-term loan, transferred to her in Belfast during March 1948, and *Magnificent* was completed and commissioned into the RCN as HMCS *Magnificent* on 17 April 1948. After flying trials off the Isle of Wight she embarked naval and air stores in Portsmouth during May and then embarked the new Canadian 19 CAG from RNAY Sydenham in Belfast. This comprised 803 (Seafire) and 825 (Firefly) NAS, and she also embarked the RN's 806 (Sea Vampire/Sea Hornet/Sea Fury) NAS for passage to North America, where it was to give a season of air displays.

Magnificent sailed for Canada on 25 May 1948 and arrived in Halifax on 1 June. Her subsequent work-up period included 171 deck landings, but two aircraft were lost in crashes. After a series of

exercises she ferried Mark 4 Fireflies back to the UK in February 1949 and returned with new Mark 5s before taking part in exercises in the West Indies during March. During these her aircraft located HMS *Jamaica* at 210 miles and 'attacked' her at 162 miles. In June she grounded off Port Mouton in Nova Scotia, but was refloated with the aid of destroyers; she had to be docked stern-first in St John for repairs. In November she joined the search for the crew of a missing American B-29 bomber, and then visited the US Naval Bases at Guantanamo Bay in Cuba and Roosevelt Roads in Puerto Rico. In January 1950 she embarked the new Canadian 18 CAG, a specialised anti-submarine unit comprising 825 and 826 (Firefly) NAS and, after working-up, sailed for exercises with RN and USN ships in the Caribbean. In August 1950 she re-embarked 19 CAG and sailed for exercises in the eastern Atlantic to strengthen ties with NATO navies. After a visit to the Joint Anti-Submarine School (JASS) at Londonderry she searched for HMAS *Sydney*, which was working-up in the Moray Firth, and launched strikes against her before visiting Oslo, Gothenburg and Rotterdam. While secured between two buoys at the last-named location she was struck on the port side by the barge *Shell 25*, which crushed the captain's barge and a motorboat. In November she visited Gibraltar and took part in Exercise *Maple Flag* with units of the HF including *Vengeance* and *Vanguard*, after which she returned to Canada, being located and 'attacked' by the recently acquired Avengers of 826 NAS.

After a docking at St John *Magnificent* embarked 18 CAG, which now comprised 883 (Sea Fury) and 825 (Avenger) NAS, and resumed the routine of exercises off Bermuda and the West Indies from February 1951. In May the RCN air squadrons were reorganised to free several squadron numbers for use in the RN; 18 CAG became 30 CAG, and within it 883 NAS was renumbered to become 871 NAS and 826 NAS became 881 NAS; 19 CAG became 31 (Support) CAG, and within it 803 NAS was renumbered

870 NAS and 825 NAS became 880 NAS. In August she sailed for exercises in the Mediterranean which included intensive flying off Malta and participation in Exercise *Symphonie Deux* with the MF, which included *Ocean*. After returning to Canada she embarked the Royal Canadian Air Force's (RCAF) 410 Squadron with forty-eight North American Sabre jet fighters and ferried them to Glasgow, from where they deployed to Canadian air bases in the NATO area. On the return voyage she ferried new Sea Fury fighters for the RCN and then commenced a refit in Halifax Dockyard in December 1951.

After post-refit trials in April 1952 she took part in Exercise *Castanets* in June, during which she operated with the Heavy Squadron of the HF under Rear Admiral Caspar John, who flew his flag in *Indomitable*. On completion she visited Malta and Greece, joining the MF Regatta at Navarino. On 25 July she visited Istanbul with *Glory*, but the visit was cut short when the RN ships sailed at short notice following the abdication of King Farouk of Egypt and his replacement by a military government under General Naguib. After a work-up off Malta she returned to the Atlantic in September 1952 to take part in Exercise *Mainbrace*, the largest NATO maritime training period to date, involving over 160 warships. She formed part of the carrier support group with *Theseus*, USS *Mindoro*, HMNZS *Bellona* and eight USN destroyers. In

HMCS *Magnificent* in Port Said, Egypt, in January 1957, with RCAF Otters on deck. She has the hull number '21' painted on deck, rather than deck recognition letter carried by other Commonwealth carriers at the time. (AUTHOR'S COLLECTION)

October Exercise *Emigrant* practised convoy support between Londonderry and New York.

In May 1953 *Magnificent* sailed for the UK with the cruisers *Quebec*, *Ontario* and three destroyers, and on 15 June 1953 they were present at the Coronation Fleet Review by HM Queen Elizabeth II at Spithead. Eight Sea Furies and eight Avengers disembarked to RNAS Lee-on-Solent and took part in the Coronation fly-past over the fleet. By July she was back in Canada, and after a visit to New York she took part in Exercise *Mariner* from 16 September 1953. This was even larger than the previous year's exercise, and involved 300 warships, 1,000 aircraft and over 500,000 men from nine NATO countries. The alliance was represented by 'Blue Force', which was opposed by 'Orange Force' submarines, surface raiders and land-based aircraft. *Magnificent* flew sorties around the clock as part of a Commonwealth force that included *Eagle* and the battleship *Vanguard*. In the autumn she provided deck-landing training for 31 CAG, and in March 1954 she was refitted in Portsmouth Dockyard while many of her sailors carried out shore training courses with the RN.

After returning to Canada in June she took part in Exercise *New Broom II* in the North Atlantic, and then passed through the Panama Canal in September to visit Esquimalt on the Canadian west coast and the USN base at San Diego. By December 1954 she was back in Halifax for a refit, and in 1955 she took part in routine training periods with the Atlantic Fleet, highlighted by a visit to New York in August for a combined USN/RCN Navy Week. In September 1955 the CAG system was discontinued by the RCN and USN-style designation letters were adopted for squadrons. *Magnificent* took part in Exercises *New*

Broom IV and *Sea Enterprise* with VF-871 (Sea Fury) and VS-881 (Avenger) NAS embarked; both tested convoy protection tactics. The remainder of 1955 was spent visiting European ports, and she returned to Halifax for a maintenance period in December. In February 1956 *Magnificent* took part in Exercise *Spring Tide* with VS-881 (Avenger), HS-50 (Sikorsky HO4S-3) and HU-21 (HO4S) NAS embarked, marking the first major use of antisubmarine helicopters by the RCN. A further work-up with the same air group was carried out with the USN in the weapons ranges off Roosevelt Roads in Puerto Rico in March, and Exercise *New Broom V* in May had as its principle objective the demonstration of antisubmarine helicopters' ability to work within a task force.

Routine training followed, after which she took part in antisubmarine exercises with VS-881 and HS-50 NAS embarked which included Exercise *New Broom VI* in September. On 10 October 1956 an Avenger made what was to be the ship's last fixed-wing landing, and at the end of the month she sailed with the frigate *Buckingham*, which had been fitted with an experimental flight deck aft, to carry out deep-water helicopter operating trials. On completion of these she sailed for Belfast without aircraft embarked to deliver stores for the new *Bonaventure*. On 7 November she called at Glasgow to load fifty RCAF Sabre jet fighters that were to be ferried back to Canada, but in the evening she was ordered to return to Halifax with despatch to be fitted-out as a troopship and headquarters vessel for the Canadian contingent that was to be sent to Egypt as part of UN peacekeeping operations after the Suez Crisis. *Magnificent* arrived back in Halifax after a stormy Atlantic crossing, her ship's company was reduced

HMCS *Bonaventure* leaving her builder's yard in 1957. The angled deck and mirror landing aid on a sponson to port stand out well in this photograph. Unusually, *Bonaventure* retained a batsman's position at the base of the VHF/DF mast on the port side right aft. The little compartment on the port quarter was for the preparation and launching of meteorological balloons. (AUTHOR'S COLLECTION)

to 600 and accommodation for 500 troops and their kit was constructed in the hangar. Once this work, known as Operation *Rapid Step*, was complete, she waited at eight hours' notice to sail while the UN pondered what best to do with its peacekeeping force. In December Operation *Rapid Step II* followed, with further modifications to modify the ship for use as a troop transport. She finally sailed for Egypt on 29 December 1956 with 406 Army personnel, 100 tons of supplies, 233 vehicles, four RCAF de Havilland Canada Otter aircraft and a single ship's flight HO4S helicopter.

Magnificent arrived in Port Said on 9 January 1957 and stores were landed by UN working parties. The Otters were flown off on 19 January, and on 20 January the ship sailed for a visit to Naples. In February she arrived in Glasgow to load fifty-nine RCAF Sabres which were to be ferried back to Canada. The ship's flight helicopter and several members of the ship's company were left behind to join *Bonaventure* in Belfast. In March she returned to Halifax, where she was destored and RCN items of equipment were removed, and on 10 April 1957 she left Canada for the last time to be returned to the RN at Devonport. The official handover took place on 14 June 1957, and her commanding officer and ship's company moved to Belfast, where they commissioned HMCS *Bonaventure*. Although the ship was in a sound physical state the RN had no immediate use for *Magnificent*, and she was laid up between two buoys in the River Tamar and left in unmaintained reserve. In 1961 she was placed on the Disposal List, and on 12 July 1965 she arrived at Faslane on the Gareloch to be broken up for scrap.

Powerful — completed as HMCS *Bonaventure*

The second 1942 light fleet carrier to be ordered on 16 October 1942, when space for extra construction was identified at Harland & Wolff's Belfast Yard, was Admiralty Job Number J 3395, allocated the name *Powerful*. The builder identified her as Yard Number 1229, and she was laid down on 27 November 1943 and launched on 27 February 1945. Work on her slowed when the war ended, and in May 1946 the Admiralty ordered work on her to be suspended; she was laid up incomplete in Belfast. In 1952 she was purchased by the Canadian

Government and taken into Harland & Wolff's Yard to be completed to a modernised design with a fully-angled flight deck, steam catapult and mirror landing aid. Unlike her sister ships in the RN, RAN, IN and other navies, however, she was completed with USN radars, including an SPS-8A height finder and an SPS-12 air search set. The armament differed too, and she was fitted with four USN-pattern twin 3in 50-calibre mountings, like those fitted by the RN to the reconstructed *Victorious*, instead of 40mm Bofors.

She was eventually completed on 17 January 1957, renamed and commissioned as HMCS *Bonaventure* in Belfast on the same day by Mrs Ralph Campney, wife of the Canadian Minister of National Defence.

In March 1957 she took on stores in Devonport, and flying trials began in the English Channel on 2 April. For these she embarked the

HO4S helicopter transferred from *Magnificent* together with F-2H Banshee fighters and S-2 Trackers flown across the Atlantic for the purpose. She sailed for Canada on 19 June and arrived in Halifax on 26 June for a period of trials and training. Her operational work-up began in September with VF-870 (Banshee) and VS-881 (Tracker) NAS embarked, plus the ship's flight helicopter. In early 1958 she carried out an operational training period in the Caribbean which included cross-deck operations with aircraft from *Bulwark*. Exercise *New Broom VII* followed, and the ship settled into a routine of training, exercises and port visits to encourage NATO solidarity. In 1959 Exercises *New Broom IX* and *Sharp Squall IV* were followed by visits to the UK and a refit in St John.

Bonaventure rejoined the operational fleet in November 1960 with VF-870 (Banshee), VS-880 (Tracker) and HS-50 (HO4S) NAS embarked.

HMCS *Bonaventure* prepares to launch a large range of Trackers. (AUTHOR'S COLLECTION)

Exercise *Toput Droit* in February 1961 was followed by exercises with the US Atlantic Fleet in July and exercise *Trapline* in October, an antisubmarine trial in Canadian arctic waters. In April 1962 Tracker 550 made the ship's 10,000th arrested deck landing. Operations by the F-2H Banshee had always been near the limit on such a small carrier, and in September 1962 the RCN decided to end fighter operations, despite having considered the A-4 Skyhawk as a potential replacement. Consequently VF-870 NAS was disbanded and *Bonaventure* operated an antisubmarine air group comprising VS-880 and HS-50 NAS. On 17 September, while on passage to Rotterdam, *Bonaventure* joined in the search for survivors from a Flying Tiger Line Lockheed Super Constellation that had ditched off Land's End in Cornwall. In October she took part in Exercise *Sharp Squall VI* with RN, Danish and Norwegian warships, and in November she joined ships of the US Atlantic Fleet for operations during the Cuban Missile Crisis.

In January 1963 *Bonaventure* began a refit in St John, New Brunswick, during which she was modified to operate the new Sea King helicopter which was to give a major improvement to her antisubmarine capability. She rejoined the operational fleet in May but suffered a boiler uptake explosion while flashing-up in Halifax. Repairs took six weeks and were followed by another *Sharp Squall* exercise in September 1963

which tested the antisubmarine defences of the Greenland-Iceland-UK gaps. In October she carried out cross-deck operations with *Karel Doorman*, and in January 1964 she took part in Exercise *Gooey Duck*, a training period off Bermuda. February saw her in the Mediterranean for exercise *Magic Lantern*, but she was withdrawn at short notice and ordered back to Halifax with despatch to embark Canadian troops for UN peacekeeping operations. She sailed for Operation *Snow Goose* on 18 March 1964 with ninety-five soldiers, fifty-four vehicles and 400 tons of stores embarked for Cyprus. Trackers were retained on

board and could, with difficulty, still have operated if required. *Bonaventure* anchored off Famagusta on 30 March, disembarked the troops and military equipment and returned to Canada.

On 22 April 1964 she carried out trials with USN A-4 Skyhawks off Norfolk, Virginia. The A-4 had been considered as a Banshee replacement and the trials were completely successful, but the idea was not taken further for financial reasons and

HMCS *Bonaventure* in Malta, with Trackers and Whirlwind helicopters on deck. (AUTHOR'S COLLECTION)

Terrible on the slipway in Devonport Dockyard. (D K Brown via the author)

first time in any navy the helicopter was salvaged at sea by being craned on to the carrier's flight deck. In March she visited New Orleans as part of the US 'Canada Week', and in June she took part in Exercise *Racer Run*, an amphibious training period with the USN. The major NATO Exercise *Silver Tower* followed in August, with *Eagle* and a number of other warships. She trained with the USN in the AFWR in January 1969 and spent some months in Canadian waters. In September she carried out a *Shop Window* demonstration for a Canadian Parliamentary Sub-Committee tasked to decide on the future of carrier aviation in the CAF. On its completion she took part in Exercise *Peace Keeper* off the west coast of Ireland, during which she flew a record number of sorties despite atrocious weather. Despite this the committee decided against her retention. After a visit to Portsmouth she sailed for Canada on 22 October 1969. The last night deck landing by a Canadian fixed-wing aircraft took place on 28 October and, after a visit to Boston, the last catapult launch took place on 12 December 1969.

In January 1970 she carried troops of the Loyal 22nd Regiment to Jamaica for exercises ashore, but the Parliamentary Committee seem to have been blind to her potential as an amphibious transport as well as her role as a valuable antisubmarine asset. Exercise *Maple Spring* in February 1970 was her last; she was used as a tanker to support frigates but had six Sea Kings of HS-50 embarked. In April she collected Canadian military forces from

Bonaventure was to remain without a fast-jet capability. The results were, however, made available to the RAN and helped with the decision to procure A-4s to operate from *Melbourne*. Sea acceptance trials with the new Sea King helicopters of HS-50 NAS were carried out in December 1964, and in January 1965 she operated in the AFWR with VS-880 (Tracker), HS-50 (Sea King) embarked together with an HO4 plane-guard helicopter from HU-21 and a COD Tracker from VU-32. Exercises *Springboard* and *Maple Springboard* followed in February and March before she visited the UK from May. Antisubmarine training with the Joint Anti-Submarine School (JASS) at Londonderry took place in June, followed by a self-maintenance period in Halifax and then operations

in the South West Approaches to the UK in company with *Ark Royal* and *Karel Doorman*. In January 1966 she sailed with six frigates and other ships of the Atlantic Fleet for the largest period of training yet carried out by the RCN in Caribbean and South American waters. She visited Rio de Janeiro in February and returned to Halifax in March to prepare for what was planned to be a major 'half-life' refit in Lauzon, Quebec.

The refit ended in September 1967 and she rejoined the operational fleet in November. On 31 January 1968 the RCN ceased to exist and both *Bonaventure* and Canadian naval aviation were absorbed into the new integrated Canadian Armed Forces (CAF). Exercise *Maple Spring* took place in February 1968 and Sea King 305 ditched; for the

HMAS *Sydney* leaving UK waters loaded with cocooned aircraft for the RAN. (Author's collection)

HMAS *Sydney* after conversion to a fast troop transport, loaded with troops and equipment for Vietnam. Note the two cranes added to the flight deck forward. (RAN)

Narvik after exercise *Arctic Express* and visited Portsmouth for the last time. She was decommissioned in Halifax on 3 July 1970 and put up for disposal, but despite her recent refit and obvious capability there was no foreign interest. In March 1971 she was sold to the Tung-Chen Iron & Steel Company of Taiwan to be broken up for scrap.

Terrible - completed as HMAS *Sydney*

The last 1942 light fleet carrier was ordered on 7 December 1942, when sufficient capacity to build her was identified at Devonport Dockyard. She was allocated Admiralty Job Number D 1182 but had no Yard Number as they were not allocated by Dockyards. The name *Terrible* was allocated from the outset. She was laid down on 19 April 1943 in a ceremony attended by Viscountess Astor, and her turbine machinery was provided by Parsons. She was launched on 30 September 1944 by Mrs Duncan Sandys, daughter of Winston Churchill. In August 1945, however, work on her stopped and she was laid-up incomplete in Devonport Dockyard. She was the only aircraft carrier ever built in a Royal Dockyard.

On 3 June 1947 *Terrible* and *Majestic* were bought by the Australian Government for a combined total price of £2,750,000, less than the build cost of a single ship. Work on *Terrible* resumed immediately to complete her with the design modifications agreed by the Admiralty and DNC in 1946 in the light of war experience. Work on *Majestic* proceeded more slowly and incorporated planned improvements. Key members of her ship's company began to join in

December 1948 and were accommodated in *Glory*, which was, herself, just emerging from a long refit in which postwar modifications and improvements had been carried out. In February 1949 *Terrible* was renamed HMAS *Sydney* and commissioned in Devonport Dockyard by Mrs J A Beasley, the wife of the Australian High Commissioner in London. A sum of £427,000 could be set against her purchase price, having been raised for a new ship to perpetuate the name by public subscription in Australia after the loss of the previous *Sydney* in 1941. She commenced flying trials on 8 February with RN Seafires, Sea Furies and Avengers in the English Channel. Five days later she sailed to Belfast Lough in Northern Ireland and embarked 20 CAG off Bangor. This comprised 805 (Sea Fury) and 816 (Firefly) NAS. In March 1949 she worked-up off Scotland, and on 12 April she sailed from Devonport for Australia. In addition to her own ship's company she carried 438 former RN personnel who had volunteered to transfer to the RAN, fifty-two aircraft and 400 tons of stores. Her only refuelling stop in the passage was at Aden.

On 12 May she arrived in Fremantle and then visited Melbourne and Jervis Bay, landing aircraft for RANAS Nowra at the latter. On 28 May 1949 she arrived at Garden Island Dockyard in Sydney, and on 3 June her ship's company marched through the city to attend a civic reception at the town hall. She embarked 805 (Sea Fury) and 816 (Firefly) NAS of 20 CAG in July and worked-up in the Jervis Bay areas before hoisting the flag of the Flag Officer Commanding HM Australian Fleet on 25 August. The following months were spent in fleet exercises and port visits to demonstrate the RAN's growing operational capability until June 1950, when she returned to

HMAS *Sydney* after conversion to a fast troop transport, loaded with troops and equipment for Vietnam. Note the two cranes added to the flight deck forward. (RAN)

the UK to embark 21 CAG, which comprised 808 (Sea Fury) and 817 (Firefly) NAS. A work-up with her new squadrons began off Torbay in August and she carried out operational training in Scottish waters during which she was located and 'attacked' by aircraft from HMCS *Magnificent*, which was also working-up in UK waters. In October 1950 she carried out an antisubmarine exercise with the JASS, after which she loaded twenty-three Fireflies, thirty-two Sea Furies and a quantity of air stores from RNAS Abbotsinch in Glasgow. She finally sailed for Australia again on 26 October, securing alongside Garden Island on 8 December.

In January 1951 she re-embarked 20 CAG and worked-up off the east coast. A Firefly hit her mast on 25 January and she had to return to Sydney for repairs, but she was ready for fleet exercises in February. *Sydney*'s first night launch was carried out on 13 March 1951, after which she embarked 21 CAG for operational training. On 19 May she returned to Sydney to prepare for an operational tour in the Korean War Zone, replacing *Glory*, which was to be refitted at Garden Island. On 9 July she embarked 805, 808 (Sea Fury) and 817 (Firefly) NAS and prepared for operational service, securing alongside *Glory* in Kure, Japan, on 27 September to transfer aircraft, personnel and stores. These included the USN Sikorsky S-51 helicopter used for SAR duties, together with its air and ground crew. *Sydney* sailed for her first war patrol on 3 October 1951, sending aircraft into action off the east coast of Korea two days later; the first time

HMAS *Melbourne* with an 'Alpha-Range' of Skyhawks, Trackers and Wessex helicopters ranged smartly on deck. (RAN)

that an Australian aircraft carrier had sent its aircraft into action. On 14 October she had to avoid Hurricane Ruth and, although she avoided the epicentre, storm-force winds and high seas destroyed six aircraft in the deck park. Her seventh and last war patrol began on 16 January 1952 and, when it was concluded, FO2 FEF, who commanded the Commonwealth naval task force, described her work as 'quite excellent'. She had flown 2,366 sorties on forty-three operational flying days, an average of 55.2 per day at a cost of three pilots and fifteen aircraft lost. Ammunition expended included 73,440 rounds of 20mm ammunition, 1,197 3in rocket projectiles and 144 500lb bombs. On only her fifth day of operations she had equalled the record for the number of sorties flown in a single day by a light fleet carrier; eighty-nine, previously set by *Glory*. Judged by the standards of its peers with their wartime carrier operating experience, the RAN Fleet Air Arm,

which had only been formed in 1948, had done extremely well.

In late January 1952 *Sydney* transferred aircraft and stores to *Glory*, which had returned to Hong Kong after its refit. On 6 February 1952 she sailed for Singapore with a deck cargo of RAF Spitfire and Vampire fighters and then returned to Australia. In late August 1952 *Sydney* sailed in company with a number of RAN warships to join a Commonwealth task force off the Monte Bello Islands, North West Australia. Her aircraft flew extensive patrols to ensure that the area was clear of shipping while HMS *Plym*, a River Class frigate fitted with the first British atomic bomb, was moored and prepared for detonation. The atomic device inside *Plym* was detonated at 0930 on 3 October 1952 and could be seen from *Sydney*, which was 60 miles to seaward. She returned to Sydney later in the month after visits to Fremantle, Melbourne and Jervis Bay.

On 24 March 1953 *Sydney* sailed for the UK to represent the RAN at the Coronation Fleet review at Spithead. She had 817 (Firefly) NAS embarked and carried the whole Australian contingent for the

Coronation ceremonies. The cruiser HMNZS *Black Prince* joined her on passage. The opportunity was taken to carry out exercises with the MF, which included *Indomitable* and *Illustrious*, in April 1953 before arriving in the UK in May. On 15 June 1953 she was one of nine Commonwealth aircraft carriers present at the Coronation Review by HM Queen Elizabeth II, and 817 NAS took part in the fly past. After the Review she crossed the Atlantic in company with *Magnificent* and returned to Australia via Halifax, Baltimore, Jamaica, the Panama Canal, Pearl Harbor and Auckland. The outer sections of her gun sponsons had to be cut off to allow her to pass through the Panama Canal. She returned to Sydney in August and subsequently worked-up with the fleet in the Hervey Bay areas, her aircraft successfully bombing and sinking the target ship *Kuramia* in the process. In September she carried out the first of several patrols to enforce the armistice off Korea, interspersed with visits to Japanese ports and Hong Kong. In April 1954 she carried out exercises with USN and RN ships off Japan and then proceeded to Iwakuni, where the Sabres of 77

HMAS *Sydney* bound for Vietnam, loaded with trucks and equipment. HMAS *Melbourne* is just visible in the distance, above the starboard lower yardarm. (RAN)

Squadron RAAF were embarked for passage to Singapore. At one stage she had sixty-eight aircraft on board. At Singapore twelve new Sea Furies and stores were transferred to her from *Perseus* for passage to Australia and she handed over the armistice patrol duty to *Warrior*. From October 1954 she was used mainly as a training carrier, but in March 1956 she embarked 805 (Sea Fury) and 816 (Firefly) NAS to operate for the last time as a fixed-wing carrier. New pilots were deck qualified and aircraft handlers were worked-up to operational standard for service in *Melbourne*. Subsequently she acted as a training ship for new recruits to the RAN, but plans to modernise her to the same standard as *Melbourne* were cancelled. She paid off into reserve at Sydney on 30 May 1958 and was moored at Athol Bight, near Bradley Head, where the foremast of her First World War namesake stands on shore.

Following a requirement stated by the Australian Army for adequate sea-lift to move troops, weapons, stores and equipment, *Sydney* was brought out of reserve, refitted and recommissioned for the role. The flight deck could be used for helicopters, but unlike the RN commando carriers she did not embark squadrons of specialised assault helicopters. An extra crane was fitted to the port side of the flight deck, and pontoons were carried for landing Army vehicles. The ship's company was reduced to a minimum to make space available for the embarked forces. Her first activity comprised the movement of ANZAC troops to an exercise in Queensland during July 1962. In May 1963 she ferried Army and RAAF personnel to Malaysia for service in the Confrontation against Indonesia, after which she settled into a routine of visits and joint exercises until 27 May 1965, when she sailed to carry the First Battalion Royal Australian Regiment with its vehicles, stores and ammunition to Vung Tao Harbour in South Vietnam for combat duty. She sailed at 0100 to avoid anti-war protestors and was escorted by *Duchess*. In total *Sydney* ferried 827 troops, 1,879 tons of cargo, 400 vehicles and two aircraft to South Vietnam during 1965 and earned the nickname 'Vung Tao Ferry'.

For a number of years *Sydney* was committed to supporting Australian operations in Vietnam. In 1966 she carried 723 troops, 609 tons of cargo, 521 vehicles and twelve aircraft. She was usually covered by *Melbourne* and a naval task force, but when the carrier was in refit and not available she showed her versatility, in December 1967 for instance, by embarking the antisubmarine helicopters of 725 and 817 (Wessex) NAS for her own protection. Statistics for 1967 included the transport of 2,622 troops, 248 tons of cargo and 249 vehicles. In 1968 she ferried 3,147 troops, 207 tons of cargo and 173 vehicles. The figures for 1969 included 3,015 troops, 369 tons of cargo, 196 vehicles and two aircraft, and with *Melbourne* back in commission she no longer embarked the Wessex helicopters. In 1970 she ferried 1,475 troops, 687 tons of cargo and 178 vehicles.

The year 1971 brought some variety, and in July she visited the USA and Canada to pick up ten new Skyhawk fighters and take part in the British Columbia Naval Assembly hosted by the CAF. By September she was back on the Vietnam run, and during 1971 she ferried 3,828 troops, 1,605 tons of cargo and 586 vehicles. Many of these were being returned to Australia as forces were withdrawn from South Vietnam. *Sydney* sailed for her twenty-second and last Vung Tao run on 14 February 1972, but diverted on 5 March to answer a distress call and go to the aid of MV *Igara*, which had struck a reef and sunk 60 miles east of Singapore. She returned to Australia carrying 457 troops, 149 tons of cargo and 72 vehicles. Except for a few advisors left behind, these were the last Australians to leave Vietnam. In April *Sydney* visited New Zealand on a training cruise, but in May she began a major refit. Maintenance works had been scheduled to fit around the trooping schedule for seven years, but this work was intended to prepare her for prolonged service since, despite her age, she was in good condition.

The refit was completed in October 1972, and in November she sailed for South Vietnam with a cargo of non-military humanitarian aid. After its delivery she went to the aid of a disabled Panamanian freighter, the SS *Kaiwang*, and towed her into Hong Kong. After returning to Australia she embarked helicopters of 723 (Bell Iroquois) NAS and infantry from 7 Battalion Royal Australian Regiment, to evaluate the addition of embarked assault helicopters to her range of capabilities. Exercise assaults at Waionui in New Zealand confirmed the major advance this would give the Australian Defence Force, but in a surprise announcement on 20 July 1973 the ship's company were informed that *Sydney* was to be disposed of immediately as a savings measure, without replacement. During her service in the RAN she had steamed 711,549 miles, of which 395,591 were in the trooping role. There were attempts to preserve her as the centrepiece of a maritime museum in Sydney, but none of these came to anything, and on 7 October 1975 she was sold to the Dong Kuk Steel Mill Company of South Korea for $673,516, to be broken up for scrap. She was towed out of Sydney Harbour for the last time on 23 December 1975.

CHAPTER 22
MALTA CLASS

The *Malta* Class marked a major change in British aircraft carrier design. Work on them started after the Joint Technical Committee recommended that future naval aircraft should be allowed to grow in both size and weight up to a maximum of 30,000lb to provide improved performance. The Future Building Committee had already considered the impact such aircraft would have on the design of the ships that would operate them, and ordered new designs. Previous British carriers had been designed around the assumption that the aircraft complement would be the maximum number of aircraft that could be stowed in the hangar, and that aircraft would be launched in small numbers over a long period. Experience by 1942 had shown that many more aircraft needed to embarked, and that they would often need to be launched in large numbers for strike operations. The Admiralty accepted at this time that embarked fighters represented a better air defence for the fleet than either guns or armour. The armoured double hangar limited the size of the flight deck, and the medium-range-gun mountings on their sponsons aft narrowed it still further, limiting the size of any deck park and the maximum number of aircraft that could be ranged for take-off at any one time. Despite the acceptance of a low maximum speed for the 1942 light fleet carriers, it was believed that fleet carriers must be able to accelerate rapidly to 30 knots in order to launch large, heavy aircraft, and that powerful machinery would be needed for them.

Technical background

Design studies began in February 1943 with consideration of a lengthened *Ark Royal*, but were soon expanded to consider ships with single or double hangars, up to 900ft long and 54,000 tons deep load. Hangars with open sides like the USN *Essex* Class were considered, but DNC recommended against them as closed hangar designs, even if the sides were not armoured,

represented a more efficient and lighter hull. A ship's hull can be considered as a hollow beam which is stressed by the distribution of buoyancy caused by wave motion. In closed-hangar ships the flight deck is the upper part of the beam; in open-hangar ships the flight deck is built as superstructure and the hangar deck becomes the upper part of a smaller beam. The deeper beam of the closed hangar represents the stronger and lighter structure; it is capable of resisting greater loadings, and the difference between the two can be considerable. Against this, the Admiralty was aware that the USN was able to run aircraft engines in its open-hangared ships and bring them rapidly to the flight deck to increase the size of a launch. It was also believed to be easier to move aircraft in the large, open hangars of American ships than in the relatively cramped closed hangars of existing British ships, but many other factors would have to be taken into consideration if an open-hangar design was to be considered seriously. Both four- and five-shaft layouts were considered and various applications of armour were investigated.

The initial Design A was considered too small and replaced by Designs B and C, which were put before the Admiralty Board on 17 July 1943. Design B featured a single closed hangar and C a double closed hangar at 55,000 tons deep load. It was to operate 108 aircraft in a fifty/fifty mixture of fighters and TBD requiring a ship's company of at least 3,300. An open-hangar equivalent was sketched and submitted for comparison; it had an unarmoured flight deck but armour in the hull under the hangar deck. It was calculated at 61,060 tons at deep load. Design C, although not yet fully developed, was approved by the Board on 8 October 1943. Such was the importance placed on these ships by the Board that the order for a fourth unit of the *Audacious* Class was changed to a *Malta* on 12 July 1943, and three others were ordered on 15 July so that no time would be lost while the design was finalised. Design C was ready for Board approval by April 1944, but the Fifth Sea Lord, responsible for air matters, reopened the question of an open hangar design after urgent

representations from aircrew with extensive operational experience. The matter was discussed again, and the Board decided at its meeting on 19 May 1944 that the operational advantages of an open hangar were sufficiently compelling for it to be substituted for design C. DNC objected that the change of policy would delay the ships' construction by eight months and demonstrated how aircraft could be warmed up in the after part of the upper hangar to allow large launches from Design C, but the requirement for an open hangar stood.

A new Design X was prepared and submitted to the Board in August 1944. At 60,000 tons deep load it had a hangar that was open-sided aft but plated-in forward to prevent water ingress in rough weather. There was no flight deck armour, but it had 6in protection over the citadel under the hangar deck; there were two centreline and two side lifts. The latter were virtually impossible to fit in a closed-hangar design and had become appreciated by the Americans as one of the big advantages of the open design, as they allowed rapid aircraft movements while flying operations were in progress. As logistic resupply in the Pacific grew in importance it was also appreciated that the side lift allowed stores to be transferred rapidly into the hangar by jackstay transfer from a stores ship alongside and then distributed throughout the hull.

The design differed from all previous British carriers in that the flight deck would be built as superstructure and, therefore, needed to incorporate expansion joints. The island had grown to accommodate new radars under development and the air direction rooms and operations rooms to make use of them. By Design X it was split in two to allow an expansion joint approximately amidships. Advantage was taken of the gap to make both sections into aerofoil shapes to smooth the airflow away from the landing area aft. The 190,000shp machinery design of Design C was increased to

The armoured protection designed for the *Malta* Class in 1945. (AUTHOR'S COLLECTION)

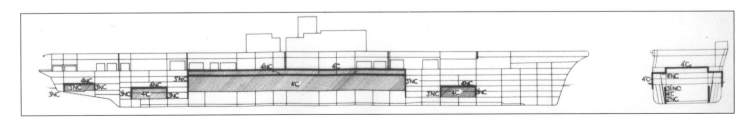

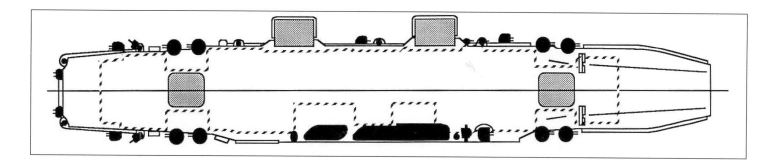

The final version of *Malta*'s flight deck design in 1945. The dotted lines show the dimensions of the single-deck hangar below it. (AUTHOR'S COLLECTION)

220,000shp for Design X but slightly reduced to 200,000 for Design X1, the final iteration; it would have been of an advanced, highly superheated design that was superior to the machinery fitted in *Ark Royal*. This would have given a speed in excess of 32 knots clean at deep load, and rapid acceleration.

The sixteen 4.5in guns were to be mounted in eight turrets, two on each quarter as in previous fleet carrier designs, but the requirement for them to fire across the deck was recognised as impractical and dropped. They would have been fitted in Mark 7 turrets, internally similar to the Mark 6 fitted to the majority of postwar British destroyers and frigates, but with a larger, 14ft-diameter roller path. Externally they would have been circular with a flat roof flush with the flight deck, like those in *Implacable* and *Indefatigable*. Like these earlier ships they would have been strong enough for aircraft to taxi over them or even to be parked with a wheel on the turret roof. Close-range armament included eight six-barrelled and seven single 40mm Bofors. Directors were mostly sited on or near the island so that they did not encroach on the rectangular shape of the flight deck or project above it, where aircraft wings might hit them. 'Less than perfect' fire control arrangements were accepted in the interests of optimal flying operations from the deck. The radar outfit would have been a considerable improvement on previous carriers, and was to include Type 960 air-warning, Type 982 intercept and Type 983 height-finding radars as well as Type 293M target indication radar and a number of target-tracking radars for the gunnery systems. Type 961 carrier-controlled approach radar for recoveries at night and in bad weather would also have been fitted.

Malta's open hangar design in 1945 compared with the USS *Essex* and the closed hangar in the *Ark Royal* that was under construction at the time. (AUTHOR'S COLLECTION)

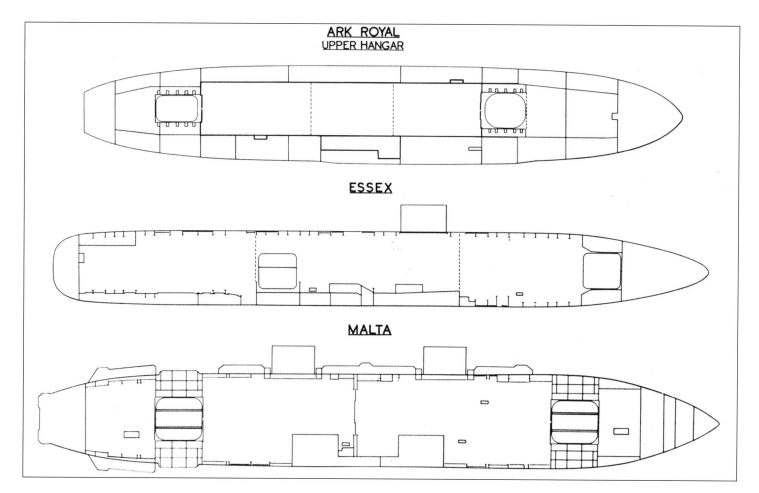

Design X offered the largest flight deck yet designed for a British warship, at 938ft long overall, 6ft longer than that of the contemporary USS *Midway*, CV-41. However, there were fears that such a large ship would be unable to enter either Portsmouth or Devonport Dockyards, and alternative hulls 850ft and 750ft long were considered. Both offered less aircraft operating capability than Design X, and thus less value for money. A compromise hull 888ft long and 56,800 tons deep load, designated Design X1, was adopted. It was the shortest hull that could realistically have two side lifts, both on the port side, but was at the upper limit of size for the dry docks available in the Royal Dockyards. On 27 February 1945 DNC was tasked with completing the new design, and it was worked out in detail for Board approval on 12 April 1945.

The final design, X1, was intended from the outset to operate 30,000lb aircraft in large numbers, especially on long-range strike operations, and the Future Building Committee accepted that the requirements of aircraft operation dictated the design. This was in marked contrast to the armoured carriers of the *Illustrious* group, in which the ship design had dictated the size and type of aircraft and the way that they could be operated. It was appreciated that heavy aircraft, and especially jets, would need to be launched by catapult, and two were specified capable of launching 30,000lb aircraft at ends speeds of up to 130 knots in quick succession. This was a big ask, and *Eagle*, completed in 1951 with two BH5s, the most powerful British hydraulic catapults, could only achieve end speeds of 75 knots at this weight. The Admiralty's early enthusiasm for the steam catapult is explained by the limitations on aircraft launch weights posed by legacy catapults.

The Admiralty decided in June 1944 that the flight deck should be constructed of mild steel plate on top of transverse beams that would provide the main strength, and that it should be covered with wood planking, following the USN practice. This gave a good non-slip surface that could easily be replaced after minor damage and aircraft accidents, but subsequent iterations of Design X1 may have reverted to a non-armoured steel deck, in line with the light fleet carriers. There would have been sixteen arrester wires reeved to eight operating units, each to be capable of stopping a 20,000lb aircraft at an entry speed of 75 knots. The three barriers would have had the same weight and entry speed parameters but a pull-out limited to 40ft. Movement of aircraft would have been easier than in any previous British design, with two centreline lifts, each 54ft long and 46ft wide, capable of lifting 30,000lb. The side lifts were 54ft long by 36ft wide and capable of lifting 30,000lb; aircraft positioned on them could overhang the ship's side.

Their length was reduced from 60ft in Design X in order to support the sides of the lift opening on main transverse bulkheads. They were positioned one forward of the barriers and one aft and, during aircraft recoveries, it was intended that 'side-tracking' gear on the flight deck would allow aircraft that had just landed on to be moved on to the after side lift and struck down into the hangar quickly while the recovery continued. Others would taxi into Fly 1 ahead of the barriers, allowing large numbers of aircraft to be landed-on in a single recovery. The aircraft struck down could taxi and shut down their engines in the hangar parking area. Conversely, during launch operations, about seventy aircraft could be ranged aft on the flight deck and taxi forward to be catapulted; others would be run-up in the hangar, brought up to deck level on the forward side lift and moved into line with the catapults on the 'side-tracking' gear to be launched quickly. The ideas were novel, founded on experience, but were never tried because the *Gibraltars* were cancelled and the angled deck and steam catapults were adopted before newer ships were completed.

The guides for the deck-edge lifts were outside the main hull, and in their lower position at hangar-deck level they would have been vulnerable to wave damage. However, this seems not to have been a problem with the single side-lift in the USN *Essex* Class, and the novelty of the design may have caused DNC to overstate the potential problem. The side lifts were designed to be hinged up for entry into harbour and docking.

There were concerns about the effect of fire in an open hangar, and it was designed to be divided, if necessary, into four sections, each of which could be isolated by steel doors. Each section had its own lift which could be used to evacuate aircraft, and the normal spray arrangements were provided. DNC believed that it would be possible to continue flying operations in action while fire in a single section was brought under control. While the deck area of *Malta*'s hangar was larger than the upper hangar in *Ark Royal*, the funnel uptakes made significant inroads on the starboard side because the funnel uptakes were brought as far to port as possible to avoid the uptake problems that had contributed to the loss of *Ark Royal* in 1941.

Without armoured sides to the hangar there was little point in armouring the flight deck, although the question was raised again in May 1945, following hits by kamikaze aircraft on British carriers in the Pacific. Adding armour to the flight deck would have required another major redesign, and idea was finally rejected by the First Sea Lord in a statement to DNC on 20 May 1945. Armour was concentrated on the hangar deck and ship's sides. Since the hangar deck was penetrated by access hatches to the deck below, the 4in armour was concentrated in the centre of the deck as an uncompromised 'slab' over the machinery. Armour of the same thickness was taken down the ship's sides to create an armoured 'box' over the machinery spaces. The magazines for 4.5in ammunition and the steering gear compartment lay outside this armoured citadel and were armoured with their own 4in inverted 'boxes' with 3in end bulkheads. In addition the design included a number of transverse bulkheads to limit the effect of underwater explosions and the subsequent flooding. The machinery was divided into forward and aft boiler room groups separated by auxiliary machinery, with an engine room further aft. The 'sandwich' underwater protection, effectively an interior 'bulge' 20ft thick, was based on a complete re-examination of the subject, and differed from the that fitted in earlier fleet carriers. Designed to protect against charges up to 1,200lb exploding 10ft below the deep waterline, it featured a water/water/air 'sandwich' backed by a holding bulkhead installed at an angle to the vertical. This had the advantages of grading the protection to meet the increased damaging effect as depth increased, and making it easier to provide the desired level of protection forward and aft of amidships.

Suspensions and cancellation

The change to an open-hangar design led to delays in laying down these ships. The Admiralty Plans Division effectively suspended *Africa* and *Gibraltar* in its 1944 construction programme, and expected *Malta* to be laid down at the end of 1944 and *New Zealand* in April 1945. The suspended ships were to be undertaken only if the work did not interfere with orders for other urgently needed warships. A report by the Controller in October 1944 clearly had the end of the war against in Germany in sight and anticipated Japanese defeat by December 1946. He recommended that *Malta* and *New Zealand* should still be laid down and proceeded with slowly, but that *Africa* and *Gibraltar* should remain suspended. The Board gave its approval for the revised plan in November 1944. A Paper on the composition of the postwar navy was prepared by Plans Division on 29 May 1945; it made no changes, but the reality of postwar austerity forced the Admiralty to make drastic cuts in the following weeks.

On 29 September 1945 the Controller recommended the outright cancellation of *Africa* and *Gibraltar*, together with the four ships of the *Hermes* Class that had not yet been laid down and large numbers of cruisers, destroyers, sloops and submarines that were accepted as surplus to postwar requirements and on which little work had been done. The Admiralty Board gave its approval for the cancellations on 15 October 1945. *Malta* and *New Zealand* were eventually cancelled on 13 December

1945, and some writers have taken the delay to indicate that work on them might have started. If this is so, there can have been very little metal on the slipway and the later date probably indicates little more than the growing pressure on the Admiralty to reduce the size of its residual building programme in a period of extreme austerity, and to make slipways available for mercantile construction.

A lost potential?

The potential offered by the *Gibraltar* class design is enigmatic. After two years' design effort they had reached the point where the design was mature enough to start in mid-1945, but three other large carriers and a number of smaller ones were actually being built and the Admiralty assumed, wrongly as it transpired, that the legacy *Illustrious* group, the largest of which were only two years old, could be modified at reasonable cost to operate the new generation of jet aircraft. A decade later it was realised that the armoured carriers, including *Ark Royal*, *Eagle* and *Victorious*, were extremely difficult and very expensive to adapt to take the new generation of carrier equipment including steam catapults, angled decks, larger radars and bigger operations rooms. With hindsight, the *Maltas* could have been modified in a shorter timescale at considerably less cost, and would have been more effective operational ships with the first- and second-generation jet strike fighters, just like the contemporary USN *Midway* Class. Their more modern machinery would also have given them a distinct advantage. It is difficult not to surmise that the RN would have been better off building two *Maltas* rather than the two *Audacious* Class ships that were retained and built to modified designs after 1945.

Malta Class technical details

Details are for the final X1 design, ready for construction to begin in August 1945. Had they been built, the finished ships would have differed in significant detail.

Displacement:	56,800 tons deep load
Dimensions:	length 897ft
	beam 136ft
	draught 34ft 6in
Machinery:	4 shaft Parsons geared turbines
	8 Admiralty three-drum boilers
	200,000shp developing 33 knots
Armament:	16 x 4.5in Mark 5; 48 x 40mm Bofors in 6-barrelled mountings; 7 single 40mm Bofors; 4 x 3pdr saluting guns
Protection:	4in hangar deck over citadel and belt on sides; 4in 'boxes' over 4.5in magazines and steering gear.
Fuel:	7,000 tons FFO and diesel
Endurance:	7,100 miles at 20 knots
Complement:	3,052 as a flagship

Aircraft operating data

Flight deck:	888ft x 121ft 9in
Hangar:	440ft x 90ft (maximum) x 17ft 6in
Catapults:	2 new-design hydraulic 30,000lb at 130 knots (would probably have been fitted with 2 BH5 30,000lb at 75 knots)
Arrester wires:	16 x 20,000lb at 75 knots; 3 barriers
Lifts:	centreline forward 45ft long x 46ft wide, 30,000lb
	side-lift forward 54ft long x 36ft wide, 30,000lb
	side-lift aft 54ft long x 36ft wide, 30,000lb
	centreline aft 45ft long x 46ft wide, 30,000lb
Aircraft:	108
Aircraft fuel:	190,000gal avgas
Air weapons:	Extensive bomb rooms designed to support operations by the latest aircraft in 1945. Exact loading not finalised, but staff requirement specified four loads for each strike aircraft and included torpedoes, 2,000lb, 1,000lb and 500lb bombs, bomb clusters, rocket projectiles, depth charges, mines, 20mm cannon ammunition, flares and pyrotechnics

Individual ship histories

Gibraltar

Although the design was not yet mature, the Admiralty allocated its Job Number J 4971 to the ship which was to be named *Gibraltar*, and placed on order for her with Vickers-Armstrongs' Walker Naval Yard on the Tyne on 15 July 1943. The firm allocated its Yard Number 82 to the design, but delayed laying her down until receipt of the final design drawings. Given the lack of a final design,

DNC advised Vickers to suspend orders for materials on 27 April 1944 and, although some preparatory work was probably carried out, she was never laid down. The Admiralty cancelled the contract on 15 October 1945 as part of the immediate postwar run-down of orders. Such material as had been assembled was either scrapped or used on other projects.

Malta

Allocated Admiralty Job Number J 1624, *Malta* was ordered from John Brown's Clydebank Yard on 15 July 1943 and allocated the Yard Number 624. John Brown's records show that manpower was originally allocated to begin work on the project at the beginning of 1944, when work on the escort carrier *Nairana* was completed. The keel laying had to be deferred because of the lack of final design drawings, but by April 1945 men were working on her. Doubt exists about whether metal was actually laid down on the slipway for her, but when the order was cancelled on 13 December 1945 such material as had been assembled was used for other projects or scrapped.

New Zealand

The third ship, to be named *New Zealand*, was allocated Admiralty Job Number J 3696 and ordered from Cammell Laird of Birkenhead on 15 July 1943. She was given Yard Number 1159 but there is no evidence that the firm did any work on her in the absence of final drawings. On 22 July 1944 the contract was transferred to Harland & Wolff in Belfast, which allocated the new yard Number 1304, although the Job Number remained the same. It is unlikely that she was laid down, although long-lead items might have been prepared, and the order was eventually cancelled on 13 December 1945. Such material as had been assembled was either scrapped or used in other shipbuilding projects.

Africa

Admiralty Job Number 11722 was originally ordered as a fourth, unnamed unit of the *Audacious* Class from the Fairfield Shipbuilding & Engineering Company of Govan, but on 12 July 1943 the order was changed to a *Gibraltar* Class ship. The name *Africa* was allocated by the Admiralty in keeping with the names chosen for the first three ships of the class, and the builder gave the project the Yard Number 722. Despite being on the order book for over two years, the lack of a final design meant that the project made little progress, and the order was cancelled on 15 October 1945. Such material as had been prepared was scrapped or used on other projects.

CHAPTER 23

A COMPARISON WITH AIRCRAFT CARRIERS IN OTHER NAVIES

By 1945 only the victorious RN and USN operated aircraft carriers. The Imperial Japanese Navy had been destroyed, and the other Axis powers owed their defeat in large measure to their failure to fight effectively in three dimensions at sea. Both Germany and Italy had attempted to build carriers, but political opposition from their land-based air forces hampered progress until it was too late. Their designs make an interesting comparison with British and American concepts, however.

Germany

Work on the design of an aircraft carrier began in 1934, a year after Hitler's Nazi party came to power, and the subsequent London Naval Treaty of 1935 allowed Germany to build aircraft carriers up to a total standard tonnage of 47,250, with individual ships limited to 23,000 tons. The design was the responsibility of Wilhelm Hadeler,

who had never flown or been on board an aircraft carrier but used images and drawings of foreign ships to calculate the size of hangars and lifts. His work was confirmed by a German naval mission that travelled to Japan in 1938 and witnessed flying operations from the recently rebuilt *Akagi*. The Japanese also gave deck-landing instruction to a handful of German pilots.

Two ships were funded, and the first, *Flugzeugtrager A*, was laid down in mid-1937 and launched in December 1938, when the second, *Flugzeugtrager B*, was laid down. The design was unusual and included a wide beam to improve stability and underwater defence, with the consequence that machinery of enormous power was required to achieve the designed high speed. Like her British, French and Japanese contemporaries she had two hangars, and the original design included a flying-off deck forward of the upper hangar. By the late 1930s the shortcomings of such an arrangement had become obvious and the deck was deleted. The flight deck

The USS *Essex*, CV-9, shortly after completion, showing how the side lift could be folded up to reduce the ship's width in pilotage waters. The flight deck is a simple rectangle uncomplicated by the cut-out segment built into British aircraft carriers to improve guns' arcs of fire. The heavy anti-aircraft armament is mounted on sponsons below flight-deck level. (A D BAKER III)

was extended forward and modified to incorporate two Deutsche Werke catapults. Aircraft were to be launched from these using trolleys which formed part of a system that reflected concerns about the safe operation of aircraft in rough weather. 'Railway lines' flush with the deck surface connected the stowage areas in the hangar with the forward lifts, and a similar system of rails ran along the centre of the flight deck, linking with those on the centre lift and running to a 'junction' aft of the forward left from which the two, parallel lifts were fed by separate tracks. Once the aircraft had been launched, the trolley would come to rest in a shuttle on transverse rails which moved to align the empty trolley with a 'siding' parallel with the

Graf Zeppelin at Gotenhaven in 1941, after work on her was suspended.
(AUTHOR'S COLLECTION)

catapult track from which, once the launch was over, the trolleys could be taken aft for reuse. It is difficult to imagine this cumbersome system working quickly enough to be practical and, except in the most adverse weather, it is difficult to imagine aircraft using anything but a free take-off technique.

Both electric and hydraulic arrester-wire mechanisms were evaluated at an experimental air station at Travemunde and the latter was selected, although probably never installed. The flight deck comprised wood planking laid fore and aft in the Japanese style over mild steel plating, and there were three octagonal lifts, aft, amidships and forward, all of them connecting to both hangars. The design included sixteen 5.9in guns mounted in twin casemates at the 'corners' of the upper hangar as a defence against surface ships, and twelve 4.1in guns in twin mountings sited three forward and three aft of the long island on the starboard side. By contemporary standards the armament was obsolescent and would not have been as practical as the dual-purpose weapons fitted in British and American carriers. There were also a number of smaller quick-firing anti-aircraft weapons.

The hangars were long, but incorporated workshops and accommodation as well as the casemates along the sides, reducing their practical width, but they had a greater deck area than in the British *Ark Royal*, designed in 1934 to operate a larger air group. The machinery was the most powerful installed in any warship before the USN *Iowa* Class battleships, and the sixteen Lamont boilers had their pressure increased to 1,250psi to achieve a design speed of over 33 knots, which was never tested in full power trials although she is believed to have moved under her own power at least once. The intended air group in 1940 comprised Messserschmitt Bf 109T (T for *Träger* or 'carrier') fighters and Junkers Ju 87T dive-bombers. Small batches of each were actually converted from land-based variants but used ashore

by the Luftwaffe when *Graf Zeppelin* was not completed.

Thankfully for the Allies, work on *Graf Zeppelin* was halted in 1940 when she was 90 per cent complete, and *Flugzeugtrager B* was broken up on the slipway. Construction was resumed in 1942 when it became obvious that battleships could not hope to operate against Allied carriers, but halted again in 1943. She was towed to Stettin to be used a floating anti-aircraft battery, with her gunners living in the completed accommodation areas. On 24 April 1945 she was scuttled with extensive damage to her machinery and bulkheads, but with only a few feet of water under the keel most of the hull remained above the surface. Russian engineers subsequently salvaged and refloated her, and in August 1947 she was towed into the Baltic for a series of weapons trials, during which she was attacked by aircraft, motor torpedo boats and destroyers. A torpedo from one of the latter caused the fatal damage which sank her in deep water on 18 August 1947.

The German aircraft carrier programme is one of the Second World War's great enigmas. Much of the opposition came from the political leadership of the Luftwaffe, which refused to cede control of any aspect of aviation to a naval task force. Had they not done so, and had *Graf Zeppelin* been completed in time to sail with *Bismarck* in May 1941, the Battle of the Atlantic might have taken a very different turn.

Graf Zeppelin technical details

Displacement:	33,550 tons deep load
Dimensions:	length 861ft 3in
	beam 118ft 9in
	draught 27ft 8in
Machinery:	4 shaft geared turbines
	16 boilers

	200,000shp delivering 33.8 knots designed speed
Armament:	8 twin 5.9in casemates; 6 twin4.1in mountings; 22 x 37mm; 28 x 20mm Oerlikon in quadruple, twin and single mountings
Protection:	60mm (2.36in) deck over magazines; 40mm (1.6in) deck over machinery; 20mm (0.79in) flight deck over hangar; 100mm (3.9in) waterline belt
Fuel:	6,156 tons FFO
Endurance:	8,000 miles at 18 knots
Complement:	1,760 ship's company; aviation complement never confirmed

Aircraft operating data

Flight deck:	787ft x 88ft
Hangars:	upper 600ft 5in x 52ft 6in x 16ft approx
	lower 557ft 9in x 52ft 6in x 16ft approx
Catapults:	2 x 11,000lb at 72 knots end speed, trolley method
Arrester wires:	2 (4?) 13,200lb at 78 knots entry speed. Never installed
Lifts:	3 octagonal, all with maximum dimensions 50ft long x 47ft wide
Aircraft:	40
Aircraft fuel:	large bulk stowage for avgas
Air weapons:	stowage designed for torpedoes; bombs; 20mm cannon and 7.9mm machine-gun ammunition; flares and pyrotechnics

Italy

The Italian Naval Staff ordered the design of an aircraft carrier to begin in 1932 but, as in Germany, the air force high command managed to persuade the political leadership to stop the project. However, in June 1940, when Italy entered the Second World War on the side of the Axis, a simpler plan to convert the transatlantic liner *Roma* into an auxiliary carrier was put forward. Authority for a rapid conversion with a flush deck and small hangar was given at the end of 1940, but in 1941 it was decided that a far more comprehensive conversion would be required to produce an effective aircraft carrier with a viable

The derelict *Aquila* at Genoa at the end of the war. (AUTHOR'S COLLECTION)

Aircraft operating data

Flight deck:	694ft 3in x 82ft 8in
Hangar:	524ft 11in x 59ft x 16ft approx
Catapults:	2 x 11,000lb at 72 knots end speed, trolley method
Arrester wires:	4 x 13,200lb at 78 knots entry speed
Lifts:	2 both 50ft x 50ft maximum dimensions
Aircraft:	51
Aircraft fuel:	avgas in cylindrical, non-structural tanks
Air weapons:	torpedoes; bombs; cannon and machine-gun ammunition; flares and pyrotechnics

air group. A design team subsequently visited the incomplete *Graf Zeppelin* in Germany and obtained what data they could from the Japanese, who also carried out conversions of liners.

The resulting design was certainly extensive but was incomplete when Italy surrendered in 1943. Renamed *Aquila* (Eagle), the original hull was gutted and new machinery and a hangar were fitted in amidships. Bulges with a layer of concrete inboard were fitted to give a measure of defence against torpedoes, and horizontal armour was fitted over magazines and the avgas stowage. The latter followed the British practice of placing the volatile liquid in cylindrical tanks inside water-filled compartments. The hull was given a considerably increased level of watertight subdivision and increased pumping capacity as its primary defence against damage, since fitting armour-layered anti-torpedo protection was not practical. The flight deck ended short of the bows and was to have been fitted with the same catapults and 'railway' system as *Graf Zeppelin*, together with four widely spaced arrester wires. The single hangar was high and it was intended to suspend up to fifteen reserve aircraft from the deck head, leaving room underneath them for aircraft to be ranged and struck down into the hangar in the normal way. The British *Argus* had had an overhead crane system to move aircraft over aircraft parked in the hangar, but no space for the overhead stowage of complete airframes. As in *Graf Zeppelin* the lifts were octagonal, but unusually they were placed close together by the island with the intention that, in the absence of a barrier, they could be used to strike aircraft down into the hangar quickly after a recovery.

The original liner machinery was replaced by four sets of geared turbines from two cancelled cruisers of the *Capitani Romani* Class, expected to drive the ship at up to 30 knots in service. Eight 5.4in low-angle guns came from the same source, to which were added a number of 65mm and 20mm close-range anti-aircraft weapons.

Aquila was essentially complete and being prepared for sea trials on 8 September 1943 when the Italian Government concluded an armistice with the Allies. She was sabotaged by members of her own ship's company a day later to prevent her falling into German hands, but remained afloat. In April 1945, however, she was scuttled by the Germans to block the port of Genoa. Raised in 1946, she was towed to La Spezia in 1949 and some consideration was given to completing her, but this came to nothing and she was finally broken up for scrap in 1952.

Aquila technical details

Displacement:	28,800 tons deep load
Dimensions:	length 759ft 2in
	beam 98ft 7in
	draught 24ft 3in
Machinery:	4 shaft geared turbines
	8 boilers
	151,000shp designed to deliver 30 knots
Armament:	8 x 5.3in; 12 x 2,56in; multiple 20mm
Protection:	30 to 80mm (1.2 to 3.2in) deck over magazines and avgas stowage
Fuel:	3,660 tons FFO
Endurance:	5,500 miles at 18 knots
Complement:	1,420

Japan

The IJN produced a large number of aircraft carriers that were built as such or converted from mercantile hulls, seaplane tenders and even the *Shinano*, originally laid down as the third battleship of the *Yamato* Class and the largest aircraft carrier built outside the USA. *Taiho*, ('Great Phoenix'), was one of Japan's last designs, and is included for comparison with contemporary British and American ships. The only unit to be completed of a projected class of eight, she represented an approach that differed from the ships described in Chapter 8 and was clearly influenced by the British armoured carriers of the *Illustrious* Class, which were under construction when she was ordered in 1939 and which had already demonstrated their worth when she was laid down in 1941. By then Japanese industry already lacked the resources to build any more of the class.

Taiho had two hangars but, unlike the British ships, their sides were not armoured. The flight deck between the two centreline lifts was constructed with 3in armour similar to that of the British ships. The upper hangar deck was unarmoured, but the lower had horizontal protection of about 1.25in thickness. The waterline belt varied between 2.2in abreast the machinery spaces and 6in abreast the magazines. An internal anti-splinter bulkhead about 2in thick ten feet inboard of the outer plating of the hull was the only protection against torpedoes. As usual in Japanese designs, the avgas stowage was the weakest link, and the problem was made worse in this ship by the inadequate training of her ship's company, late in the war, with regard to damage

The only known photograph of *Taiho*, taken off Singapore. Unfortunately it is of poor quality. (AUTHOR'S COLLECTION)

control techniques. Avgas was stowed in bulk tanks, integral with the hull, under the two lift wells fore and aft. The only concession to wartime experience was to fill the spaces around the tanks with poor-quality cement, which was liable to crack as the hull hogged and sagged and gave only minimal protection against splinters. Worse, it filled the only 'overflow' space if the tanks split.

The Japanese also adopted an enclosed bow to improve seaworthiness and improve the airflow over the flight deck, and built an island that was substantially increased in size on the starboard side amidships. Apart from the funnel, which was canted about 45 degrees to starboard with the aim of carrying smoke away from the flight deck, *Taiho* closely resembled a ship of the *Illustrious* Class. She was considerably heavier at deep load, however, and the effect of the weight of the double hangar structure and armour was that the lower hangar deck was only a few feet above the waterline. The lift wells, the deck of which formed part of the roof of the avgas stowage tanks, were actually below the waterline.

The armoured flight deck meant that *Taiho* could operate heavier aircraft than her predecessors, and the lifts were stressed to take 16,500lb. As in British and American carriers, arrester wires were fitted forward as well as aft so that aft-facing landings were possible. The Allies found that the forward units were seldom used and had removed them by 1945, but *Taiho* had eight units aft and six forward right up to her loss. All were of the same 13,200lb capacity at 78 knots as the earlier designs. Like all Japanese carriers, *Taiho* had no catapults. There were three barriers, two at the after end of the island and one at the forward, the latter intended for use with the forward arrester wires. The armoured deck meant that only two lifts could be installed, one at either extremity of the

hangars, and both served both hangar decks. The hangars were enclosed like those of British-built carriers and the original design air group was eighty-four, but in practice, due to the limited wing-fold of many IJN aircraft, the maximum practical number was sixty. By 1944 the IJN had insufficient aircraft and pilots to fill its carrier air wings, so the maximum number was seldom a problem.

Taiho was equipped with the new Japanese 3.9in dual-purpose gun, mounted in six twin turrets, three on each side of the flight deck. A number of 25mm light anti-aircraft weapons were mounted in sponsons below flight-deck level. She had the most powerful machinery ever fitted in a Japanese warship, 180,000shp, which exceeded the original design estimate and delivered 33.34 knots on initial trails in light condition over a measured mile. She had the potential to be a good design, but her loss typified everything that was wrong with Japanese carrier operations.

She was completed on 7 March 1944 and worked-up in the areas off Singapore, where fuel oil was available from refineries in Sumatra. On 19 June 1944 she was hit by a single torpedo from the US submarine *Albacore* while steaming with other warships northwest of Yap Island. The weapon detonated abreast the forward lift, split the forward avgas tank and cracked the cement that surrounded it. Flooding trimmed the carrier's bow down by five feet, sinking the lift well further below the waterline. It filled with a mixture of seawater and avgas from the cracked tank below. Portable pumps were used to try to clear the volatile mixture, but could not keep pace with the flooding. No attempt was made to cover the liquid in the lift well with foam to prevent the spread of petrol vapour. Worse was to follow. The forward lift had jammed halfway between the flight deck and the upper hangar deck, and the over-zealous flight-deck damage control party had planked over the hole in the deck to allow flying operations if required. This meant that, even if the after lift were lowered, a

natural flow of air through the hangars to remove the petrol vapour was not possible. The damage control officer therefore took the disastrous decision to open all the doors and hatches into the hangar in an attempt to create a draught, thereby permeating petrol vapour throughout the ship. To add to his error he then switched on all the ship's electric fans in a further attempt to clear the vapour. Only a spark was needed to cause a deadly explosion, and five hours after the torpedo impact a catastrophic explosion blew out the hangar bulkheads and even split the hull below the waterline. The armoured deck split but had the effect of reflecting the blast downwards into the hull. The blazing wreck sank an hour later, taking 1,650 of her men with her. The ship that represented the ultimate Japanese aircraft carrier technology was lost through a fatal weakness in her design and the ineptitude of her damage control personnel.

Taiho technical details

Displacement:	37,270 tons deep load
Dimensions:	length 854ft 8in
	beam 110ft 3in
	draught 31ft 5in
Machinery:	4 shaft Kanpon geared turbines
	8 boilers
	180,000shp delivering 33.3 knots on trials
Armament:	6 twin 3.9in mountings; 45 x 25mm on build, more added
Protection:	80mm (3.14in) armoured flight deck between lifts; 32mm (1.25in) lower hangar deck; waterline belt 55mm (2.2in) abreast machinery, 152mm (6in) abreast magazines
Fuel:	5,700 tons FFO
Endurance:	10,000 miles at 18 knots
Complement:	1,751

Aircraft operating data

Flight deck:	844ft 10in x 98ft 5in
Hangars:	both 500ft x 74ft x 14ft approx
Arrester wires:	8 aft, 6 forward all 13,200lb at 78 knots, 3 barriers with shorter pull-out
Lifts:	2 both 45ft 11in long x 45ft 11in wide
Aircraft:	up to 63
Aircraft fuel:	150,000gal avgas in bulk stowage
Air weapons:	torpedoes; bombs; 20mm cannon and 7.7mm machine-gun ammunition; flares and pyrotechnics

United States of America

US carrier designs make particularly interesting comparisons with their British contemporaries as both navies used similar criteria to develop their staff requirements and, as close allies, became increasingly aware of the strengths and weaknesses of each others' ships. By 1944 the USN was sufficiently impressed by British armoured decks to build them into its new *Midway* Class. The RN, on the other hand, was so impressed with the operating potential of USN open-hangar designs that it accepted a twelve-month delay in laying down the *Malta* Class to incorporate this feature into their design. Both features had their merits and demerits.

Essex Class

The most capable ships in the fast carrier task forces that dominated the Pacific in 1945 were the *Essex* Class, which resulted from one of the biggest industrial programmes of the war. Conceived in 1939 as an improvement on the previous *Yorktown* design, eleven were ordered in 1940 and a further twenty-one by 1944, although six that had not yet been laid down were cancelled in March 1945 and two that had been laid down were cancelled in August 1945 and scrapped on the slipway. The twenty-four that were completed achieved some remarkable build times, notably *Franklin*, CV-13, in fourteen months; *Hancock*, CV-19, in fourteen and a half months; and *Yorktown*, CV-10, in sixteen

and a half months. Only one of those finished in wartime took over twenty-four months, although the seven completed after the war obviously had less urgency and took longer. This remarkable achievement was made possible by the ruthless application of production-line techniques using standardised main and auxiliary machinery in hulls ordered from only five yards, Newport News, Bethlehem Steel, New York Navy Yard, Norfolk Navy Yard and Philadelphia Navy Yard. Newport News built seven of the first eleven ships on four slipways between April 1941 and October 1944, in an average building time of seventeen and a half months per hull.

Although referred to as a single class, there were in fact two distinct versions. The first ships were the 'short-hulled' type with an overall length of 872ft; most of the later ships were of the 'long-hulled' type with an overall length of 888ft. Both were longer than the *Illustrious* Class but with a narrower beam, the ratio of fineness helping to give a high speed of over 32 knots on trials. The flight deck was an optimal rectangular shape with no concessions to wind-flow or encroachments for the gun armament, making it much wider than that of *Illustrious*. The flight deck was constructed of wood planking laid athwartships, with the usual channels for lashing points over beams and steel plating. The main horizontal protection was

2.5in armour plate on the hangar deck over the machinery and magazines, with a further 1.5in on the main deck and extended to meet the top of the 5in waterline belt. Anti-torpedo protection comprised an effective vertical 'sandwich' of fuel, air and splinter bulkheads which filled the underwater beam outboard of the machinery spaces.

The machinery comprised a four-shaft layout with standardised Westinghouse geared turbines and Babcock & Wilcox boilers. The engine and boiler rooms were alternated boiler room/engine room/boiler room/engine room, so that a torpedo hit would not disable one complete type of machinery. The boilers used forced-draught arrangements to allow a reduction in the size of the funnel compared with previous classes, and chemicals were used with 'soot-blowing' techniques to clean the uptakes, reducing the amount of time spent boiler cleaning considerably below that considered necessary by the RN before 1945. The armament comprised four twin 5in dual-purpose mountings, two forward and two aft of the island on the starboard side, with four single 5in on port-side sponsons. A large number of 40mm in quadruple, twin and single mounts were mounted on sponsons, together with some 20mm. The comprehensive radar outfit included an SK air warning set with a range of 120 miles; a shorter-range SC set and an SP height-finding radar which

The USS *Bennington*, CV-20, in December 1944. The twin 5in mountings fore and aft of the island are conspicuous, as are the raised W/T masts. (A D Baker III)

was used from 1944 for fighter control; IFF and 'YE' aircraft homing beacons were all fitted as standard and, as the kamikaze threat developed in 1945, several ships were fitted with upwards-facing aircraft radar sets in a successful attempt to detect suicide aircraft in the immediate 'overhead' before they started their dives.

The aircraft operating arrangements were unrivalled for their time, and allowed air groups of up to 108 aircraft in the long-hulled ships. The flight deck was built as superstructure over the armoured hull and did not contribute to overall hull strength. The sides were partly plated in, but large openings allowed aircraft engines to be run in the hangar and, most importantly, the open hangar design allowed the installation of a deck-edge lift outside the floor area of the hangar on the port side amidships. This feature in particular impressed RN pilots as they became involved in Pacific operations alongside the USN. Openings in the hangar side also allowed the installation of an athwartship catapult in three ships, but it was seldom used and later removed. The other two

The *Essex* Class aircraft carrier USS *Wasp*, CV-18, on 9 June 1945. The structures supporting the side lift guides are clearly visible, as is the opening into the hangar. The white patches on the side of the island are charts showing the ship's company her former achievements in the Pacific Theatre of Operations. (A D BAKER III)

lifts were conventional centreline platforms at the fore and aft extremities of the single hangar that were locked at flight-deck level for flight operations, leaving lift wells in the deck below them. There were two parallel H-IVB hydraulic catapults forward of the forward lift, each capable of launching 18,000lb aircraft at an end speed of up to 78 knots from a 'stroke' of 86ft. There were eight arrester wires aft, each capable of stopping a 12,000lb aircraft at 75 knots entry speed relative to the deck, and three barriers with similar limits but a shorter pull-out. Six further arrester wires could be rigged forward if required to support aft-facing landings. The pull-out distances on USN arresting gear were significantly shorter than those accepted by the RN for its own gear, and consequently placed higher *g* loadings on aircraft as they were arrested. The original air group comprised thirty-six fighters, thirty-six scout/dive-bombers and eighteen torpedo-bombers. As fighters grew in size and capability they were able to take over more of the strike and search missions, with the result that by 1945 the standard air group ratio had changed to seventy-three fighters and fifteen of each of the other types. By August 1945 some ships were operating with ninety-three fighters and fifteen torpedo bombers.

No *Essex* Class carrier was sunk, but a number were damaged; two by torpedoes and eight by

kamikaze attack. On 19 March 1945 *Franklin*, CV-13, was operating off Kyushu, having returned to service only in January after repairs to damage suffered in the previous October. She was hit by two bombs, which exploded in the hangar among fuelled and armed aircraft, which exploded. The forward avgas system was secured, but the after system was in use and within a few seconds there was a tremendous fuel vapour explosion. Fire filled the hangar, killing all but two of the men in it, and the shock caused the thirty-one fuelled and armed aircraft running in the flight range to smash into each other. They too caught fire and their weapons exploded, some of them falling through holes into the hangar. However, the armoured hangar deck protected the hull beneath; power was maintained to pumps and the ship continued to move under her own power. She survived, and the Bureau of Ships subsequently described her damage as the most severe survived by any US warship during the course of the Second World War. She was able to steam home under her own power for repairs in New York Navy Yard, a testament to the soundness of the design and the resolution of her damage control teams, the damage having corresponded closely with the fatal damage that sank three Japanese carriers at Midway. Although reconstructed, she was placed in reserve in 1947 but never reactivated. She was sold for scrap in 1964.

Essex Class technical details

Displacement:	34,800 tons deep load
Dimensions:	length 876ft (first group); 888ft (second group)
	beam 147ft 6in
	draught 28ft 6in
Machinery:	4 shaft Westinghouse geared turbines
	8 Babcock & Wilcox boilers
	150,000shp delivering 33 knots
Armament:	4 twin and 4 single 5in; 17 quadruple 40mm Bofors; numerous twin and single 40mm and 20mm mounts
Protection:	Flight deck 1.5in; hangar deck 3in; main deck 1.5in; waterline belt 2 to 3in; bulkheads 2 to 3in; gun turrets 1.5in
Fuel:	6,300 tons FFO
Endurance:	14,100 miles at 20 knots
Complement:	3,448

Aircraft operating data

Flight deck:	866ft x 90ft
Hangar:	580ft x 71ft x 17ft 6in
Catapults:	2 H-IVC 16,000lb at 74 knots. Athwartship hangar installation in *Essex*, *Yorktown* and *Bunker Hill*
Arrester wires:	9 aft, 6 forward, all 12,000lb at 75 knots entry speed. 3 barriers with shorter pull-out
Lifts:	2 centreline lifts, each 47ft long x 47ft wide; deck edge lift 60ft long x 47ft wide
Aircraft:	up to 108
Aircraft fuel:	192,895gal avgas in bulk stowage
Air weapons:	torpedoes; rocket projectiles; depth charges; bombs; 0.5in machine-gun ammunition; flares and pyrotechnics

Independence Class

Like the RN, the USN could not produce fast fleet carriers quickly enough to meet its requirements and filled the gap by building 'emergency' light fleet carriers. The RN considered cruiser conversions but elected to build the *Colossus* and *Majestic* Classes from scratch to provide more-effective ships. The USN had ordered no fewer than thirty-six light cruisers of the *Cleveland* Class in 1940/41, and elected to convert some of these into light carriers. At 10,000 tons standard displacement they were considered to be the smallest hulls that could embark a viable number of aircraft and have the high speed required of fleet units.

The cruiser hull was completed up to the forecastle deck but modified to incorporate extra accommodation, bomb rooms, aviation stores and avgas stowage. The four-shaft 100,000shp cruiser machinery was retained, and gave the heavier ship a speed of about 31 knots, slightly less than those of the *Essex* Class but considerably more than the British light fleet carriers. The only armament comprised quadruple, twin and single 40mm Bofors in sponsons under the deck edge. Bulges were added to the hull sides to improve stability, and horizontal armour up to 3in thick over magazines was built in at hangar deck level, meeting the 2in waterline belt, which was thickened to 5in outboard of magazines. The waterline belt was omitted in *Independence* and *Princeton*, presumably because of weight considerations. Again, ruthless production-line techniques produced some remarkable build times, some ships being built in as little as thirteen months. All were built by the New York Shipbuilding Company, and all nine ships were completed by the end of 1943. Two larger conversions of heavy cruisers followed but were too late for war service.

The wooden flight deck was 525ft long, surprisingly stopping short of the open bow, and had a usable width of 73ft. It was built as a superstructure with the flight deck forming the roof, and was partly open at the sides with the area forward plated in. They had two hydraulic catapults forward and eight arrester wires aft, all to the same specifications as for the *Essex* so that the same aircraft types could be operated, but in smaller numbers. Both lifts were on the centreline at the extremities of the hangar, and they were too small to be fitted with a side lift. The hangar proved to be a disappointment; at only 215ft long and 58ft wide it was smaller than those of some of the larger escort carriers and too small to support the original air group of forty-five aircraft. When larger Hellcats replaced the Wildcat the air group comprised twenty-four fighters and twelve torpedo bombers, but by 1945 they operated standardised air groups of thirty-six fighters.

Only one ship of the class was lost, the USS *Princeton*, CVL-23. She was hit by a 551lb bomb dropped by a Japanese dive-bomber off Luzon on 24 October 1944. It penetrated the flight and hangar decks before detonating, but started a severe fire in the hangar, where six fully fuelled and armed aircraft intensified the blaze. Internal ventilation trunking spread heat and smoke throughout the hull and forced the ship to be abandoned except for firefighting parties backed up by ships lying alongside, which played hoses on to the fires. By mid-afternoon it appeared that she might be saved, but the torpedo warheads exploded, inflicting serious damage on the cruiser *Birmingham* alongside, which suffered 600 casualties. A further 108 men had been lost in *Princeton*. The wreck was finally sunk by a torpedo from the cruiser *Reno* half-an-hour later; the weapon detonated near the forward avgas tank which had, up to then, been undamaged. The subsequent petrol vapour explosion broke the hull in two and it sank within forty-five seconds.

Independence technical details

Displacement:	14,300 tons
Dimensions:	length 622ft 6in
	beam 109ft 3in
	draught 26ft
Machinery:	4 shaft GE geared turbines
	4 Babcock & Wilcox boilers
	100,000shp delivering 32 knots on light trials
Armament:	2 quadruple and 9 twin 40mm Bofors. Numerous smaller added
Protection:	main deck 3in; lower deck 2in; waterline belt 5in amidships tapering to 1.5in (not in *Independence* and *Princeton*); 5in bulkheads
Fuel:	2,460 tons FFO
Endurance:	7,600 miles at 20 knots
Complement:	1,569

Aircraft operating data

Flight deck:	525ft x 73ft
Hangar:	215ft x 58ft x 17ft 6in
Catapults:	2 H-IVC 16,000lb at 74 knots end speed
Arrester wires:	8 x 12,000lb at 75 knots, 2 barriers
Lifts:	2 centreline, both 43ft long x 42ft wide
Aircraft:	45 designed, 36 practical
Aircraft fuel:	101,800gal avgas
Air weapons:	torpedoes; rocket projectiles; depth charges; bombs; 0.5in machine-gun ammunition; flares and pyrotechnics

Midway Class

The *Midway* Class is included briefly for comparison with the British *Malta* Class and later designs. It was intended to launch the largest, practical deckload strike, and the three ships were originally designated 'battle carriers' or CVB, capable of operating air groups of up to 140 aircraft.

Evolved from 1942, the design included an armoured deck inspired by study of the British carriers rebuilt in Norfolk Navy Yard after action damage and, in turn, they clearly inspired British thinking that evolved into the *Malta* Class. Despite the armoured deck, the hangar was open and a side lift was fitted on the port side amidships. The 5in dual-purpose guns were fitted in single turrets sited at hangar deck level so that the largest unobstructed flight deck could be built on to the hull. There were also a considerable number of quadruple and twin 40mm Bofors mountings at the same level for close-range anti-aircraft defence.

The concept was far from universally popular with the USN at first, and the President initially refused to sanction their construction. Many officers felt that a larger number of smaller carriers would be more effective, but eventually three were approved and constructed. Like the *Lexington* and *Saratoga* before them, they demonstrated their worth when complete and became an essential part of the postwar strike fleet. The *Midway* Class proved able to accommodate the postwar requirement for heavy jet attack aircraft and their supporting workshops and ammunition, including atomic and nuclear weapons, and acted as the prototype for the concept of the very large carrier intended for global strike operations that led to the *Forrestal* and *Nimitz* classes. Size, especially volume, had become an important factor, but with the rise in the cost in other areas such as radar and command systems it was not, necessarily, a 'cost driver'. The cost of the extra steel to produce a bigger 'box' would not add as much to the cost of a new carrier design as equipment such as fire-control for anti-aircraft guns or missiles. When Lockheed P2V-3 Neptune twin-engine patrol bombers were modified to launch from a carrier deck in the atomic strike role, one of these aircraft took off from the USS *Coral Sea*, CVB-

43, in March 1949 at a record weight of 74,000lb; something that could not have been achieved with any other class of carrier. (They were not intended to land back on the deck after their mission.) Their open hangar also allowed the relatively straightforward modification to incorporate the postwar British inventions of the angled deck, steam catapult and mirror landing aid. They were also rebuilt with *Illustrious*-style enclosed bows, known as 'hurricane bows', and no fewer than three deck-edge lifts, two to starboard and one to port, the original centreline lifts having been removed.

Some of the *Essex* Class were modernised successfully with all these features but were unable to operate heavy aircraft such as the McDonnell Douglas F-4 Phantom, like the *Midway* or subsequent classes.

Midway Class technical details (as completed)

Displacement:	60,000 tons deep load
Dimensions:	length 968ft
	beam 136ft
	draught
Machinery:	4 shaft Westinghouse geared turbines (GE in F D Roosevelt) 12 Babcock & Wilcox boilers operating at 565psi, 850°F 212,000shp delivering 33 knots
Armament:	18 single 5in; 21 quadruple 40mm Bofors and numerous smaller
Protection:	flight deck 3.5in; gallery deck 3.5in; hangar deck 80lb plate; waterline belt 7.6in; bulkheads 6.3in; armoured 'box' over steering gear
Fuel:	9,276 tons FFO
Endurance:	20,000 miles at 15 knots
Complement:	4,104

Aircraft operating data

Flight deck:	924ft x 113ft
Hangar:	692ft x 95ft x 17ft 6in
Catapults:	2 H4-1, 16,000lb at 74 knots end speed
Arrester wires:	14 x 30,000lb at 78 knots entry speed; 6 barriers
Lifts:	2 centreline, both 54ft x 54ft deck-edge lift 46ft x 46ft
Aircraft:	136
Aircraft fuel:	332,000gal in bulk stowage
Air weapons:	torpedoes/ASW homing torpedoes; rocket projectiles; bombs; depth charges; 20mm cannon and 0.5in machine-gun ammunition; flares and pyrotechnics

In May 1946 C E Sherwin RCNC gave a talk to the DNC in which he gave his contemporary view on British and American designs. While talking about protection he said that, in his opinion, the 3.5in flight-deck armour in the *Midway* Class gave meagre protection for the hull below and that, overall, the ships could not be regarded as well protected. The *Malta* Class differed in not having an armoured flight deck:

It appeared to us necessary, even if an armoured flight deck were fitted in an open hangar carrier, that we must also provide efficient deck armour on the main hull below. Weight was not available to do both. In addition it seemed desirable that as far as possible the deck armour should be at hangar deck level; however, mainly to compromise on the problem of access, the armour did not extend right across the hangar deck. Both horizontal and vertical armour was to be of the same

The *Independence* Class light carrier USS *Cabot*, CVL-28. (AUTHOR'S COLLECTION)

thickness. In addition, *Malta* would have been fitted with transverse bulkheads very closely spaced constructed with 60lb plate up to the lower deck. It seemed essential to fit thick bulkheads of that nature, not only to limit the effects of underwater explosions but to confine, as far as possible, the effects of heavy weapons which might pierce the 4in armour and explode in the ship's vitals.

On the subject of hangars he said: 'The open hangar is not necessarily a great deal wider than a closed hangar. There are all sorts of obstructions along its sides, including the deep frames for supporting the flight deck; access ladders to the gallery deck above; hatches to give access to the decks below and even winches, bollards etc.' He pointed out that the hangars in *Ark Royal* were 67ft wide and in *Essex* only 3ft wider.

In the *Malta* class we did as much as we could possibly do to prevent the spread of fire through the hangar. The hangar is divided into four distinct sections; each section can be isolated by means of steel doors, but each section has its own lift. It was hoped that a fire, even a serious fire, in one section of the hangar could be kept to that section and that the operation of aircraft from the carrier whilst the fire was being fought would still be possible. It will be observed that the obstruction in the hangar caused by the funnel uptakes is rather more pronounced in *Malta* than in American ships. We did not think it wise to have our holes in the hangar deck for the uptakes too far from the middle line.

The USS *Coral Sea*, CVB-43, in June 1949. (A D Baker III)

One significant difference had emerged between the two navies' operating practices by this time. The RN continued to devote space in sponsons alongside the hangar for dedicated boat stowage. In the USN, boats, when required, were stowed in the hangar on trolleys, brought up to the flight deck when required and lowered by crane. As

The USS *Midway*, CVB-41, on 20 October 1945. (Author's collection)

many or as few boats as necessary could be embarked for the type of operation projected. This was an inherently better system.

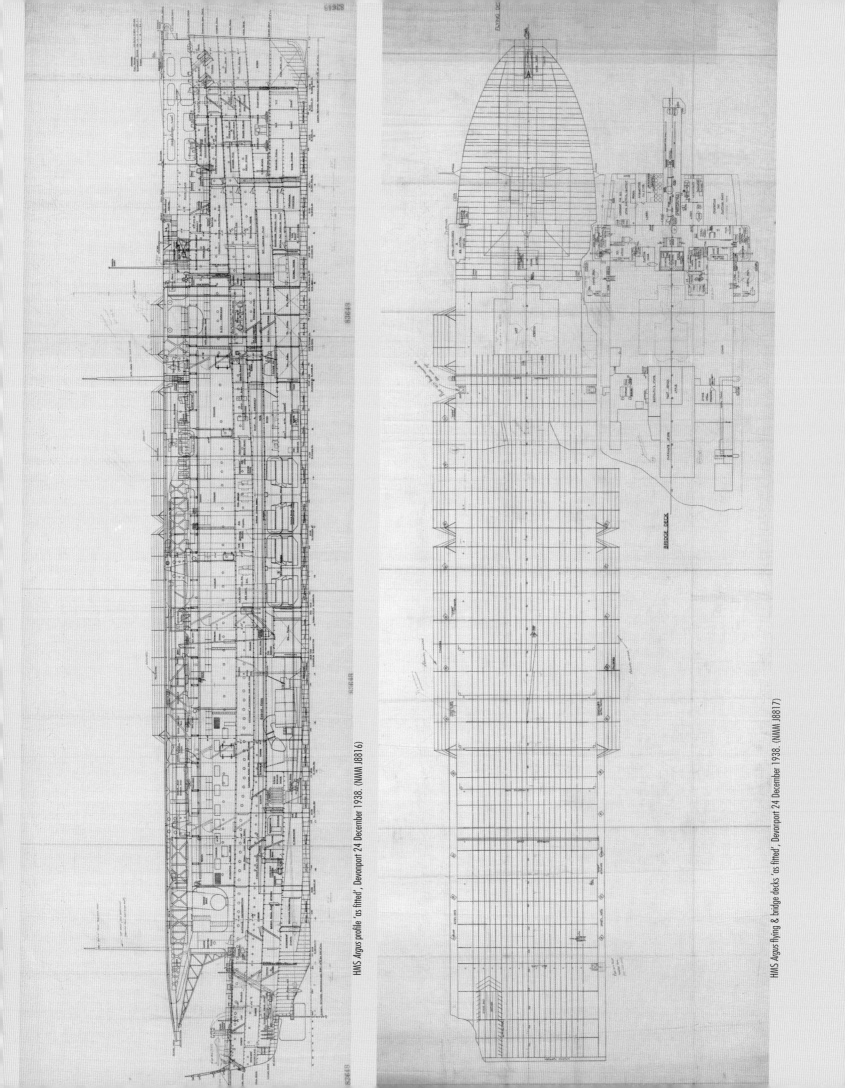

HMS *Argus* profile 'as fitted', Devonport 24 December 1938. (NMM J8816)

HMS *Argus* flying & bridge decks 'as fitted', Devonport 24 December 1938. (NMM J8817)

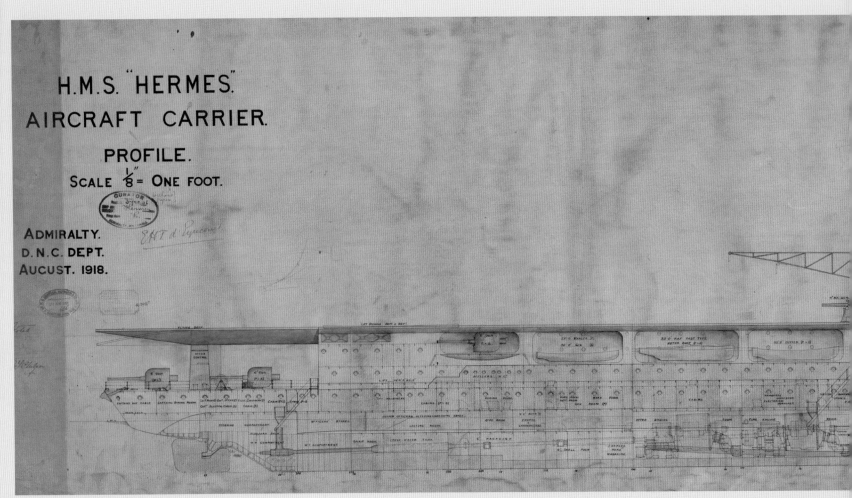

H.M.S. "HERMES."
AIRCRAFT CARRIER.

PROFILE.

SCALE $\frac{1''}{8}$ = ONE FOOT.

ADMIRALTY.
D.N.C. DEPT.
AUGUST. 1918.

HMS *Hermes* profile, Admiralty DNC Dept, August 1918. (NMM J8814)

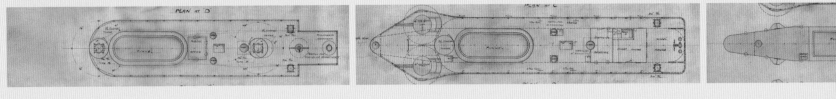

TOPSIDES.

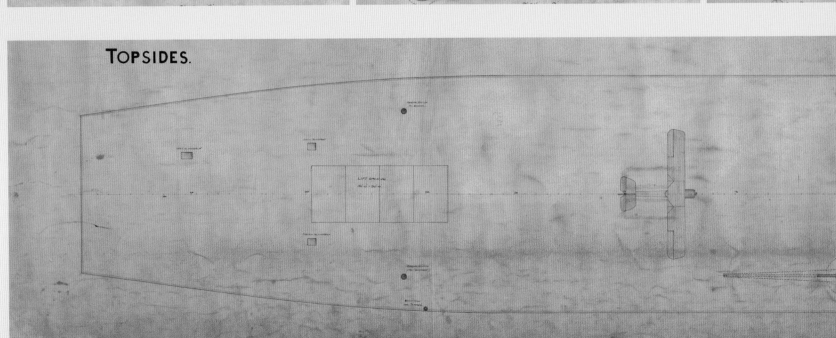

HMS *Hermes* plan of bridge structure & topside, Admiralty DNC Dept, August 1918. (NMM J8814)

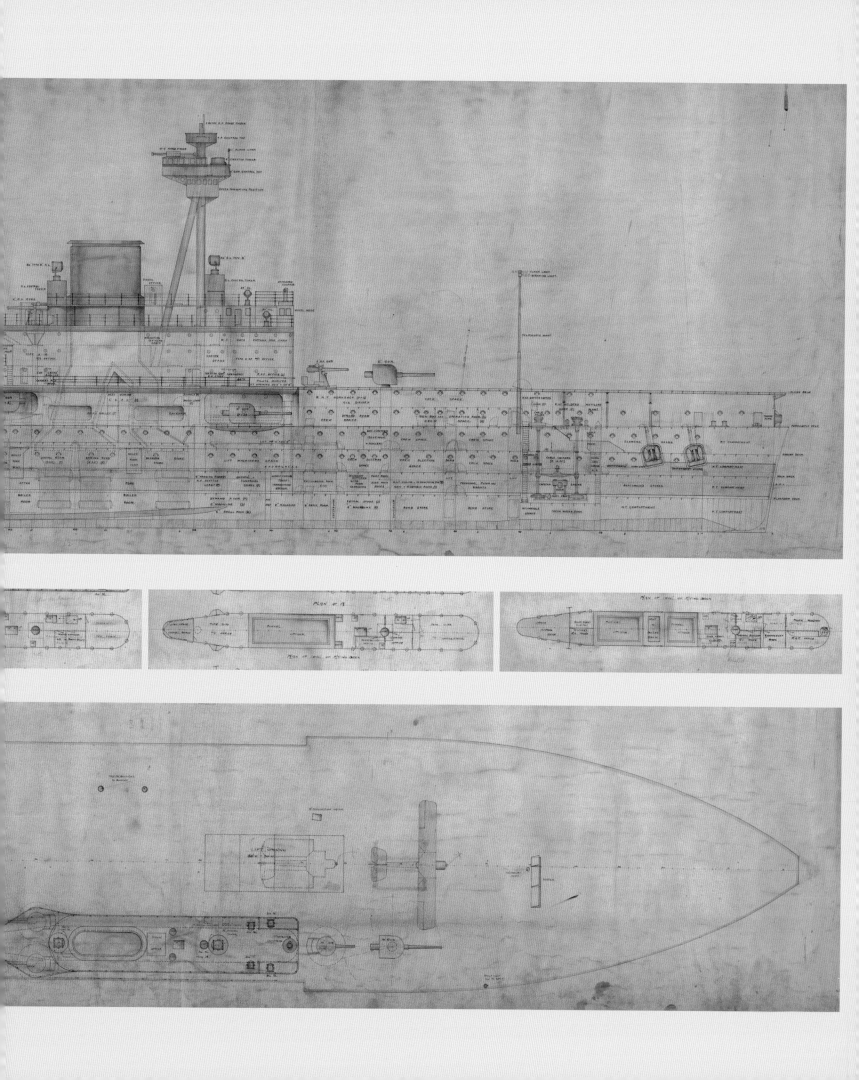

H.M.C.S. "MAGNIFICENT."

PROFILE.

(AS FITTED)

SCALE :- ⅛ = 1 FOOT.

DRG. Nº 6.

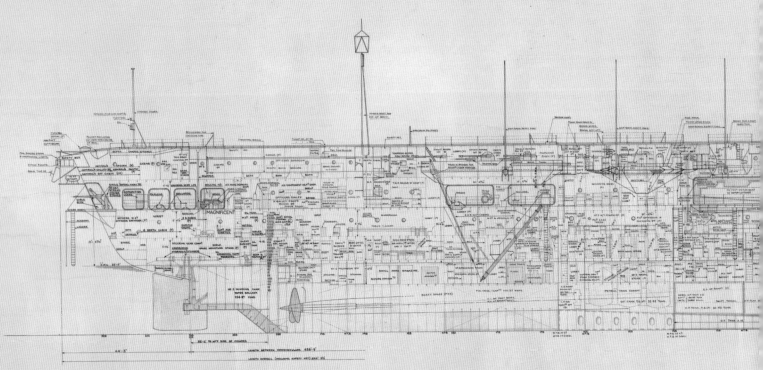

HMCS *Magnificent* profile 'as fitted', Harland & Wolff, Belfast, 20 July 1948. (NMM J8810)

FLIGHT DECK

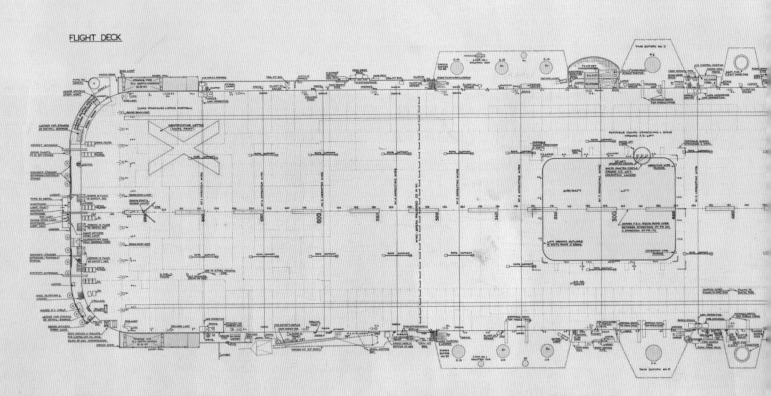

HMCS *Magnificent* flight deck & bridges 'as fitted', Harland & Wolff, Belfast, 20 July 1948. (NMM J8810)

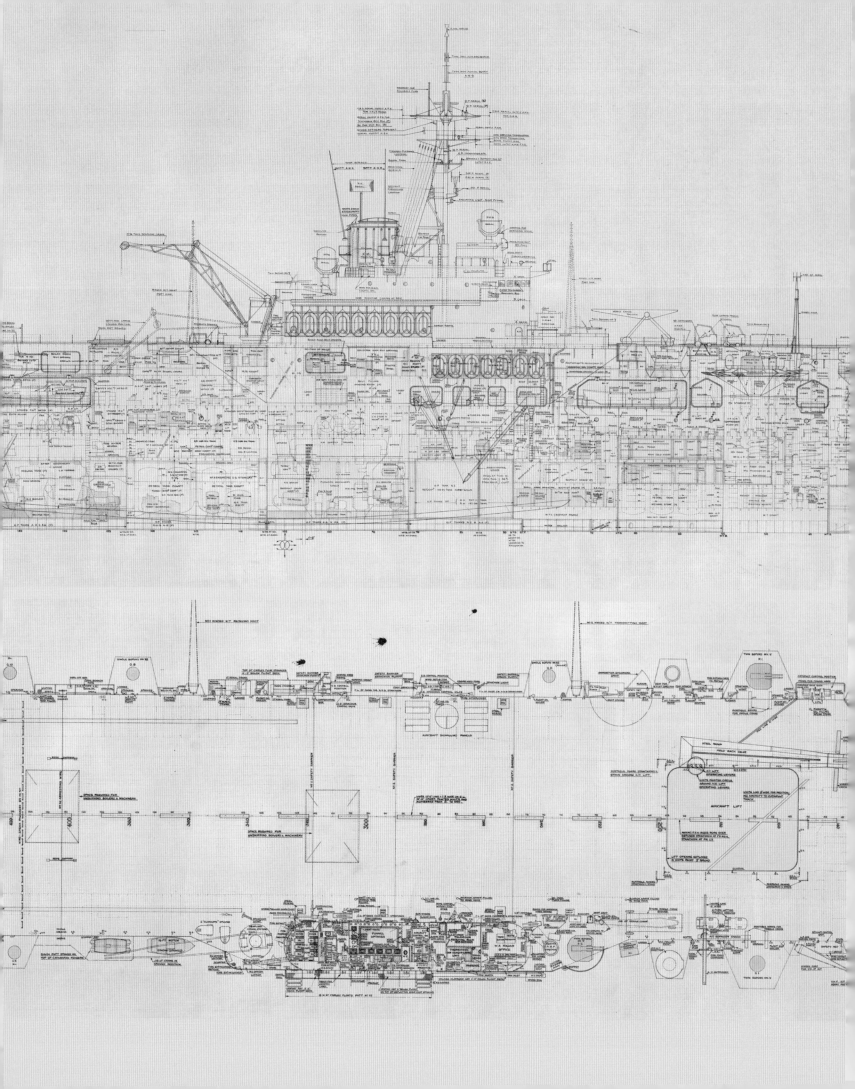

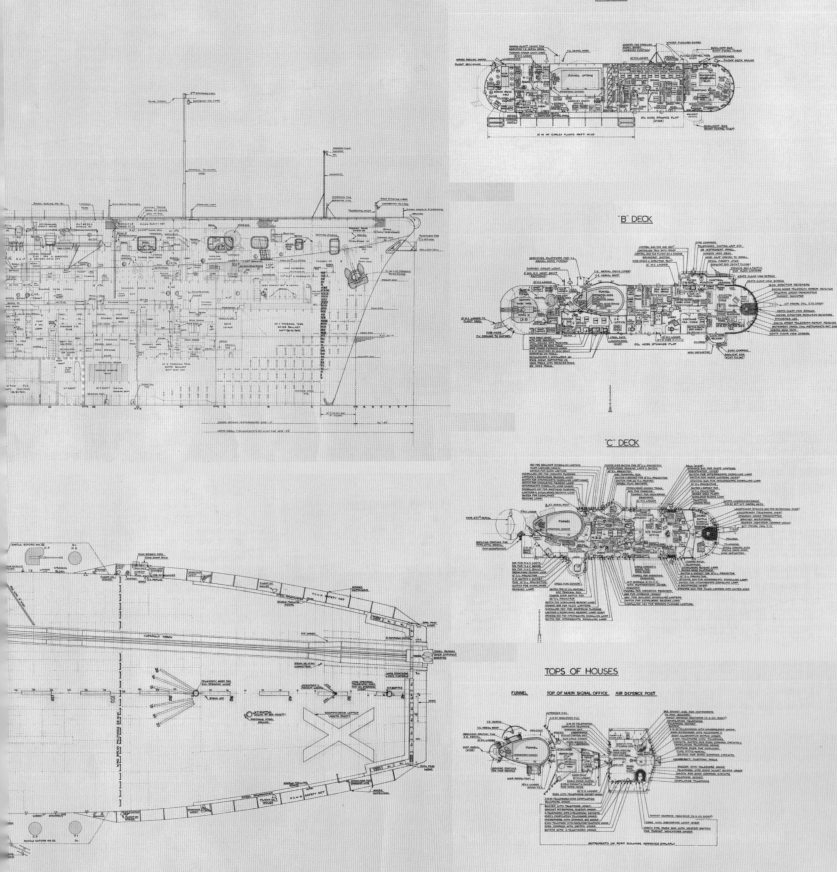

"A" DECK

"B" DECK

"C" DECK

TOPS OF HOUSES

FUNNEL   TOP OF MAIN SIGNAL OFFICE   AIR DEFENCE POST

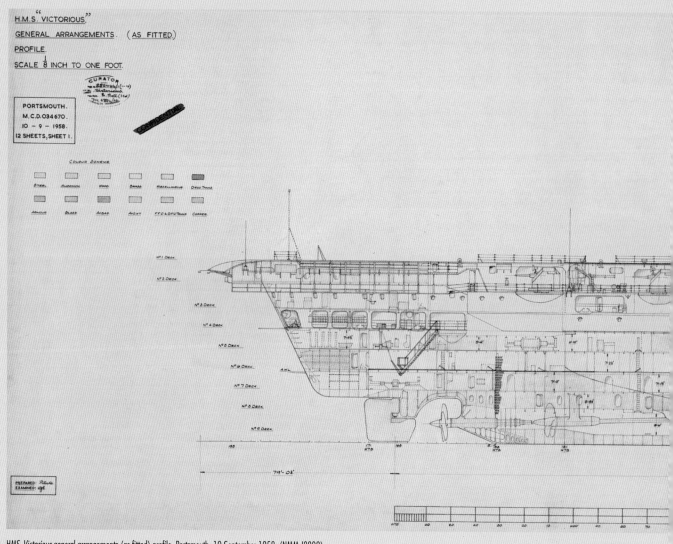

HMS *Victorious* general arrangements (as fitted) profile, Portsmouth, 10 September 1958. (NMM J8808)

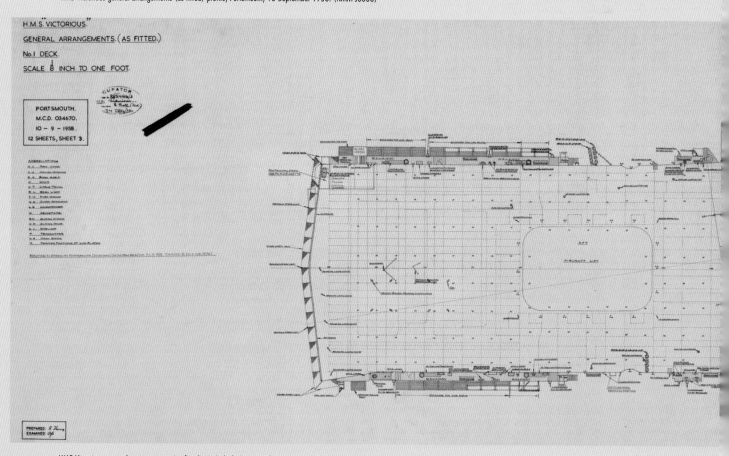

HMS Victorious general arrangements (as fitted) No 1 deck, Portsmouth, 10 September 1958. (NMM J8809)

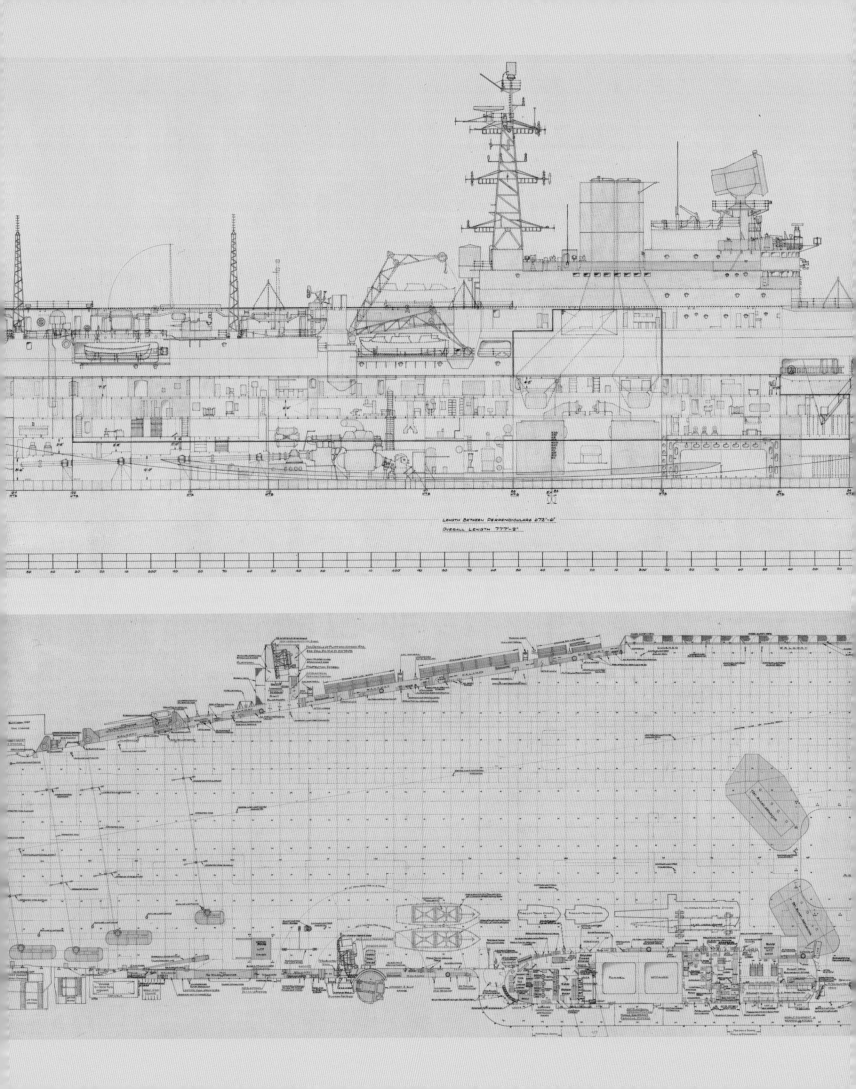

LENGTH BETWEEN PERPENDICULARS 672'-6"
OVERALL LENGTH 777'-2"

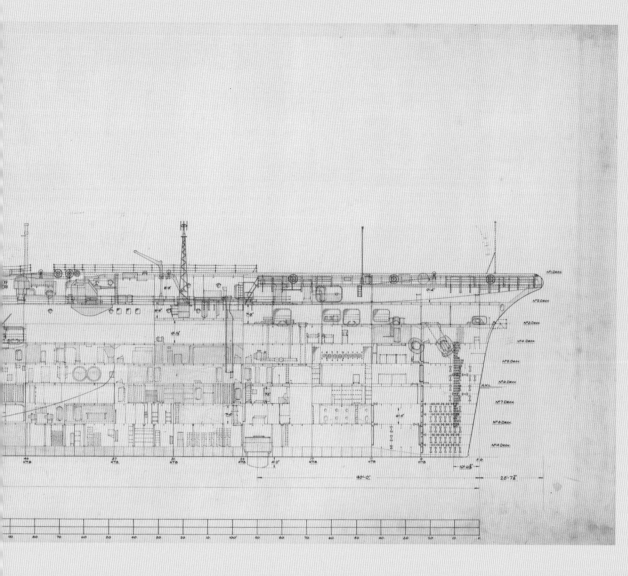

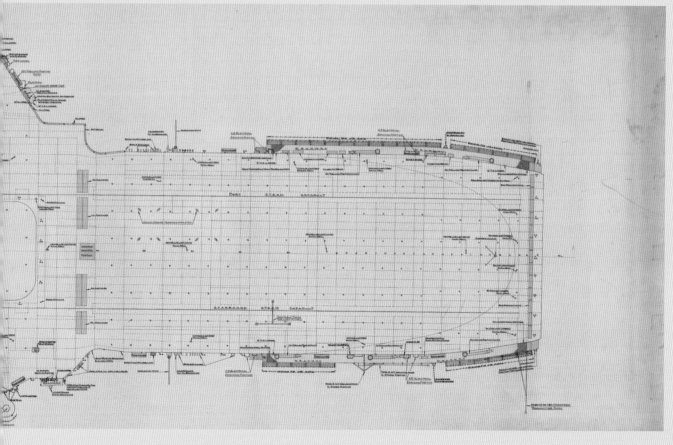

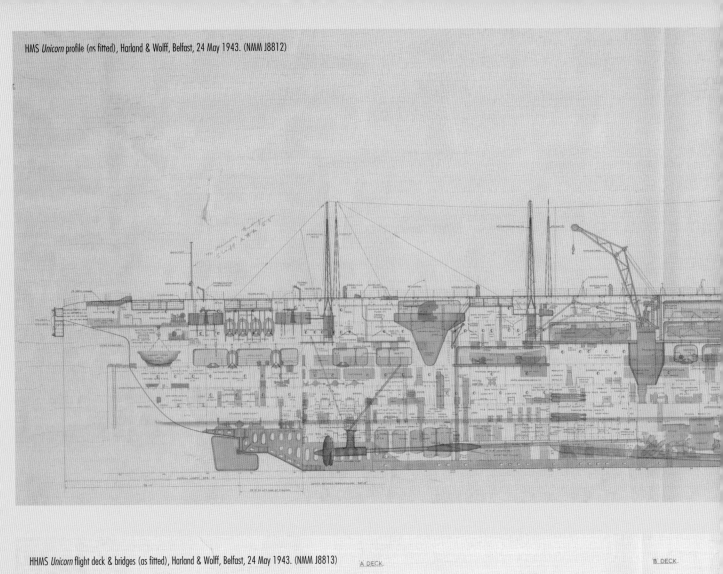

HMS *Unicorn* profile (as fitted), Harland & Wolff, Belfast, 24 May 1943. (NMM J8812)

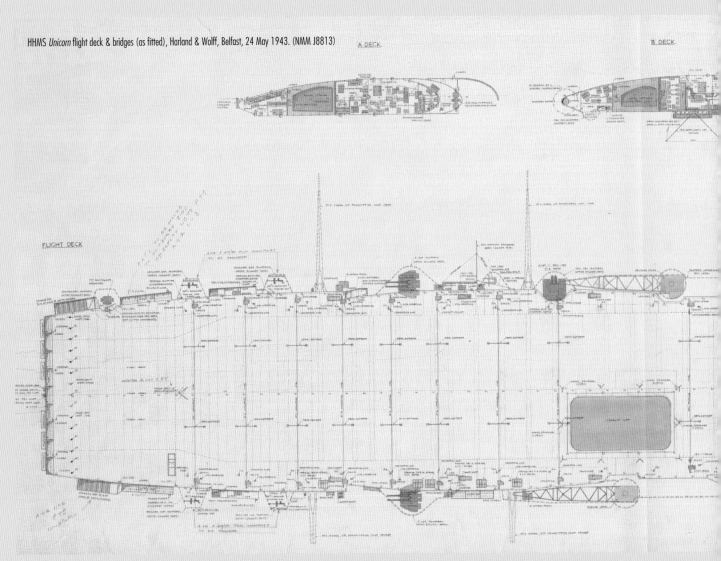

HHMS *Unicorn* flight deck & bridges (as fitted), Harland & Wolff, Belfast, 24 May 1943. (NMM J8813)

'A DECK.

'B' DECK.

FLIGHT DECK

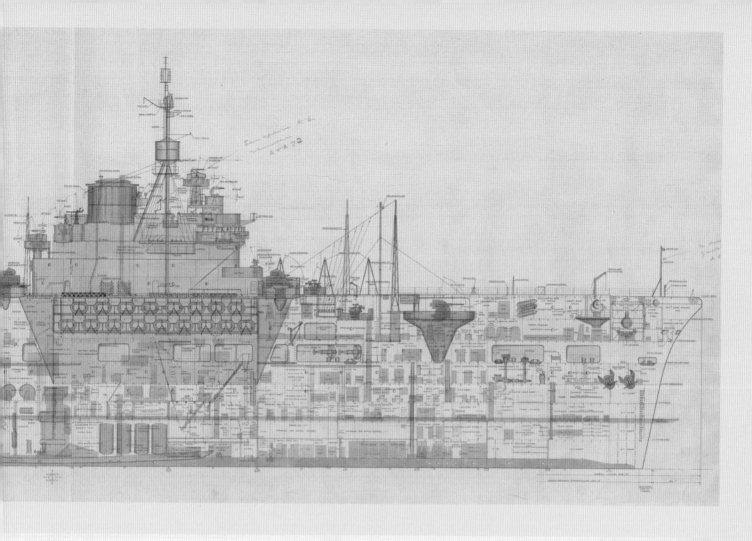

C' DECK.   D' DECK.   SIGNAL HOUSE TOP, ETC

FLIGHT DECK

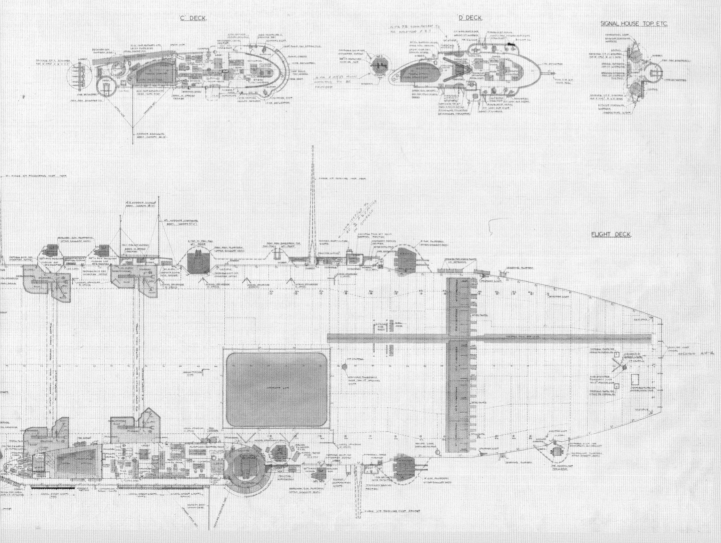

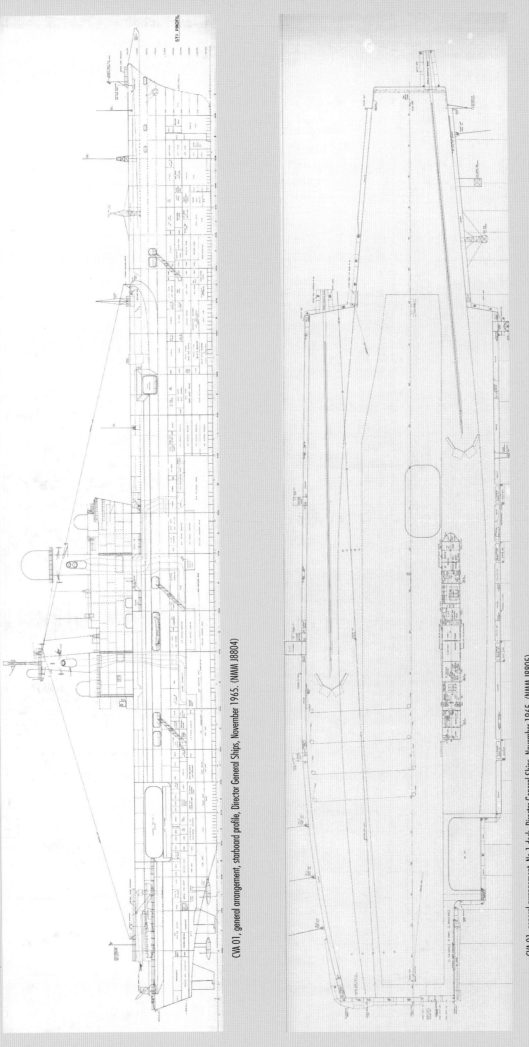

CVA 01, general arrangement, starboard profile, Director General Ships, November 1965. (NMM J8804)

CVA 01, general arrangement, No 1 deck, Director General Ships, November 1965. (NMM J8805)

THE MAINTENANCE CARRIERS
UNICORN, *PIONEER* AND *PERSEUS*

The concept of using a maintenance carrier to support the operations of a carrier strike fleet deployed at some distance from a main fleet base had its origins in the Abyssinian Crisis of 1935-36, when the reinforced MF was based in the Eastern Mediterranean. It was calculated that a single fleet carrier could lose up to 20 per cent of its air group lost or damaged beyond repair in a single operation, and that a further 10 per cent could be grounded by the need for major repairs that could not be carried out in the carrier. Although based on theory because the crisis did not end in conflict, these numbers proved to be reasonably accurate in the subsequent operations of the BPF. They were bad enough when applied to prewar carriers such as *Glorious* and *Ark Royal* with air groups of forty-eight and sixty aircraft respectively, but the new armoured carriers of the *Illustrious* Class were only projected to operate thirty-six. If one third of these were damaged beyond repair, support and replacement on a large scale were clearly necessary. The man who conceived the armoured carriers was also responsible for the solution to this problem.

Admiral Sir Reginald Henderson insisted that the armoured carriers and their embarked squadrons must be supported by a depot ship, in the same way that submarine and destroyer depot ships supported their flotillas. He was also far-sighted enough to insist that the ship should have all the essential features of an operational carrier, thus giving the fleet an extra deck when needed. Henderson was forced by ill health to resign in March 1939 and died only two months later, but by then the design work had been completed and approved.

Technical background

Unicorn, the first maintenance carrier, proved to be a very complicated ship to design. Preparatory work took over a year before an order was placed with Harland & Wolff for her to be built in the company's Belfast yard. She was intended to carry stocks of replacement aircraft and to carry out extensive and complicated repair and maintenance work to relieve pressure on the engineering staffs in the fleet carriers. The designed load was forty-eight aircraft, most of which were to be preserved and struck down into the lower hangar while the upper hangar was to be used for maintenance and repair; there was space for aircraft to fold and

Unicorn with Seafires on deck in 1943. (AUTHOR'S COLLECTION)

spread their wings. In addition to a large engine repair workshop there was a test compartment forward, just under the flight deck, in which engines could be fitted to a test stand and run at full power after reassembly. She was also fitted out with an extremely comprehensive range of airframe, radio, metalwork, woodwork, fabric, electrical and safety equipment workshops and test facilities, together with a stores complex capable of carrying spare parts for the entire contemporary range of front-line aircraft in service with the RN.

The support went beyond aircraft maintenance work, however, and she was equipped with a large sick bay, an operating theatre and a dental surgery. Space for two emergency medical stations was provided to cope with action casualties. Her armament of four twin 4in mountings and 2pdr 'pom-poms' was in line with contemporary depot ship practice but emphasised defence against air attack. *Unicorn* was fitted with an elaborate system of overhead hoists and transfer rails in both hangars to facilitate heavy component repair in aircraft undergoing maintenance, and the after end of the

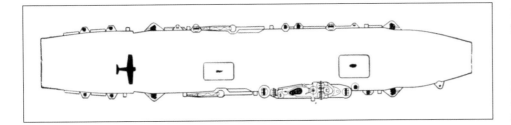

Unicorn's flight deck as designed; the aircraft is a Grumman Martlet/Wildcat to give scale. (AUTHOR'S COLLECTION)

upper hangar was open to allow engine runs to take place without the aircraft having to be taken to the flight deck. The flight deck itself extended a long way aft of the opening, so that a self-propelled lighter could be suspended beneath it. This could be lowered flush with the upper hangar deck so that aircraft could be moved on to it and, once it was lowered into the water, conveyed to another carrier or shore base. Alternatively, aircraft could be lowered on to it by crane once it was in the water; it made the ship self-supporting while moored in a forward base without shore support.

She was the first aircraft carrier in the world to be built for a specific, defined, purpose rather than for general aviation duties, and in appearance she resembled a foreshortened but taller *Illustrious* Class fleet carrier. Throughout her eventful career she had the highest bridge in the RN at 95ft, and the tallest masthead at 167ft. Although not intended for combat operations, she was nevertheless fitted with a 2in armoured flight deck and had 2in crowns and 3in sides fitted as 'boxes'

over her magazines. There was no waterline belt, but she had a 1.4in internal bulkhead to protect the machinery against an underwater explosion. The two-shaft machinery installation, similar to that installed in the 'War Emergency' destroyer classes, gave a trial speed of 24 knots and a sea speed of 22 knots, which was adequate for her intended role as a depot ship. She was the first ship to be fitted with Type 281B air warning and fighter control radar, and had a Type 72 homing beacon as well as fire-control radars for the 4in gun directors.

The single BHIII hydraulic catapult was capable of launching 14,000lb aircraft at an end-speed of 66 knots, using the tail-down method with a strop. Six arrester wires aft were each capable of stopping 20,000lb aircraft at an entry speed of 60 knots, and the single barrier had similar limits but a shorter pull-out. The forward lift was widened so that aircraft without folding wings could be struck down into the hangars. She could embark up to about eighty aircraft when operating in the ferry role.

In 1944 American-built aircraft were joining RN air squadrons in increasing numbers, and *Unicorn* had to be modified to maintain them effectively before joining the BPF. They differed from British-built aircraft in a number of ways, not least in having different threads on nuts and bolts and different electrical systems. Even washers differed, and a new range of general and specific stores items had to be stocked on board. Aircraft artificers and mechanics intended for work on American-built aircraft had to undergo special training, some of it in the USA for key senior ratings, and were issued with different US-specific toolkits. Technical ratings were all issued with their own toolboxes and task-specific tools in the days before tool control was introduced. These were formed into Special Repair Parties (SRPs), several of which were drafted to *Unicorn*. They found that the ship was not laid out well for concurrent work on the two different varieties of aircraft, and she was modified in Durban in November 1944 to create two 'production lines' and two different engine shops, one each for British and American aircraft

Unicorn in Trincomalee during February 1944, with Corsairs and Barracudas on deck. *Renown* and *Illustrious* are moored beyond the anti-torpedo nets (AUTHOR'S COLLECTION)

types. She left Durban on 1 January 1945 able to maintain the five types in service with the BPF — Corsairs, Hellcats, Avengers, Seafires and Fireflies. She already possessed facilities to repair Barracudas, the sixth type, which would arrive in the light fleet carriers in July.

Unicorn's usefulness in the Korean conflict led the Admiralty to make plans to include a replenishment carrier as a permanent part of the postwar fleet. In 1951 plans were prepared for her modernisation; they included the installation of a steam catapult with a stroke of 103ft and deck strengthening to allow aircraft up to 25,000lb be launched and up to 22,000lb to be recovered. A new crane capable of lifting third-generation jets was specified and, since both hangars were relatively low, consideration was given to creating a single, high hangar out of the two, with an accommodation deck over it, immediately under the flight deck. This was similar to the plans being prepared for the modernisation of *Implacable* and *Indefatigable*. Once the enormous cost of such a change was understood, however, it was dropped from the plan, but a fully angled flight deck was included. In October 1951 the Admiralty Board decided to proceed with the modernisation, and work was due to commence in July 1954. However, by July 1952 the cost and complexity of modernisation work on *Victorious* was causing serious concern, and the Admiralty came to the conclusion that money would be better spent on modernising operational carriers. The projected modernisation of *Unicorn* was cancelled.

Unicorn technical details

Displacement:	20,300 tons deep load
Dimensions:	length 640ft
	beam 90ft
	draught 24ft 10in
Machinery:	2 shaft Parsons geared turbines
	4 Admiralty 3-drum boilers
	40,000shp delivering 24 knots
Armament:	4 twin 4in; 4 quadruple 2-pdr
	'pom-pom'; twin and single
	20mm Oerlikons
Protection:	2in flight deck; 2in magazine
	crowns; 4in to 4.5in magazine
	sides; 1in lift platforms; 1.25in
	internal anti-torpedo bulkhead
Fuel:	3,000 tons FFO
Endurance:	7,500 miles at 20 knots
Complement:	1,200 including aircraft repair
	department

Aircraft operating data

Flight deck:	640ft x 90ft
Hangars:	upper 324ft x 65ft x 16ft 6in
	lower 360ft x 62ft x 16ft 6in
Catapult:	One BH3 12,500lb at 66 knots
	end speed
Arrester wires:	6 x 20,000lb at 60 knots entry
	speed; 1 barrier
Lifts:	fwd 46ft long x 36ft wide
	aft 46ft long x 26ft wide
Aircraft:	35 as an operational carrier
	24 undergoing repair

Unicorn serving with the BPF in 1945. She has Corsairs and Avengers on deck, and the two rectangular openings just below the flight deck right forward allow air to flow through the engine test bay so that engines can be run-up to full power inside. The BPF pennant number R108 is just visible below the after forecastle opening, on the panel of darker paint. (AUTHOR'S COLLECTION)

	up to 80 in the ferry role
Aircraft fuel:	98,600gal avgas
Air weapons:	depth charges, 20mm cannon
	and 0.303in machine-gun
	ammunition; flares and
	pyrotechnics

By 1943 it was becoming obvious that the fleet to be built up in the Pacific to fight alongside the USN against the Japanese would need more aircraft maintenance capability than *Unicorn* alone could provide. The Admiralty Board considered options including the conversion of *Furious*, which was coming to the end of her useful life, and the construction of specialised depot ships. The former was rejected as too difficult, and the latter course would have taken too long. The possibility of using escort carriers was considered but rejected, as it was calculated that three would be needed to equate to the facilities provided by *Unicorn* and, since it was not the purpose for which the US Government had provided them under the Lend/Lease agreement, difficulties would have to

Corsairs and Fireflies in *Unicorn*'s lower hangar in 1945. They are in a state of preservation and not yet prepared for issue to operational units. (AUTHOR'S COLLECTION)

be overcome before the conversions could be carried out. Ultimately it was decided that the requirement was sufficiently important to justify the conversion of two of the 1942 light fleet carriers already under construction in Vickers' yards into aircraft maintenance ships. *Edgar* and *Mars* were renamed *Perseus* and *Pioneer* and converted for the new role, retaining their original machinery. Since there was no longer any need for sponsons, the ships' sides were left 'clean' and the light anti-aircraft armament mounted on the upper deck. Apart from this distinguishing feature they retained the appearance of their sister ships, except for the generally 'lighter' island and mast, which lacked search radars and homing beacons since it had been decided not to retain an aircraft-operating capability. This allowed the revised design to provide the largest possible maintenance facilities in the minimum time, utilising all the available hull volume, but the upper deck was still referred to as the 'flight deck' despite its inability to operate fixed-wing aircraft, and the two lifts were retained to move aircraft between this deck and the hangar/workshop complex below. The island was enlarged across the deck by a large box-like structure which contained air offices, a ground equipment store and recreational facilities including a cinema. At the after end of the 'flight

deck' was a rectangular structure which contained the oxygen production plant and stowage for spare aircraft engines.

Surrounding the hangar and running the full length of the ship were two decks, the upper known as the gallery deck and the lower as the hangar deck. Each of these was divided into various compartments. For instance the gallery deck housed the radar and electrical offices and repair shop; the ready-use stores; the instrument repair shop; the spark-plug servicing shop; woodworkers'

shop; dope store; blacksmiths' and welders' shops. The hangar deck contained the ground equipment and tool stores; the fabric workers' shop; the hydraulic and oleo leg shop; dope shop; engine repair shop and fuel pump shop; armament offices; metalworkers' shop; machine shop; propeller shop and the parachute hanging and packing room. The decks below the hangar contained the machinery spaces and somewhat cramped accommodation. The lack of operational air weapons, aircraft handling parties, gunnery and action information sailors freed some space compared with the standard light fleet carriers, but it was not enough.

The maintenance carriers were not intended to carry out their tasks under way with the fleet but, rather, moored with other depot ships in a forward base to which aircraft were brought by ferry and replenishment carriers. They formed part of what was known as the FAMG within the Fleet Train of the BPF in 1945. It grew to be such a large element of it that they became a specialised sub-element known as the Air Train, commanded by a Commodore RN. Two aircraft lighters, stowed on the 'flight deck' at sea and lowered into the water by crane, were used to move aircraft to and from these ships; they had flat decks 48ft long by 12ft wide with lashing points to secure aircraft in transit, and were powered by two 40hp V8 petrol engines. The carriers also carried two 23-knot 'skimmers', each powered by a 45hp diesel engine, two fast motorboats for personnel and stores transfers, a motor cutter and a pinnace. There were also several 'Jumbo' mobile cranes to move crated stores, components and equipment to any part of

Unicorn alongside *Ocean* at Kure during the Korean war. (AUTHOR'S COLLECTION)

Unicorn laid up in reserve in the River Tamar by Devonport on 10 September 1956. (Author's collection)

the upper deck or hangar, in addition to the 'seaplane crane' aft of the island. *Pioneer* had a further, distinctive, crane fitted on the port side of the 'flight deck' forward.

As soon as an aircraft arrived on board it was taken on charge by the Receipt and Dispatch Section; guns were made safe and any bombs, rocket projectiles or pyrotechnics removed to the magazines. All items designated 'Appendix A', such as instruments, radio, safety equipment and armament, were then removed and the aircraft's log books thoroughly checked. At this stage the aircraft was still on the 'flight deck', and it would undergo a preliminary inspection to decide whether or not it was worth repairing or preparing for issue to a front-line squadron. As a rough rule of thumb, an aircraft that needed more than 1,000 man-hours of work would not be repaired. For those that were deemed worthy of repair a Board of Survey would follow to provide a complete assessment of damage, functionally test the electrical and hydraulic systems and ground-run the engine to assess its serviceability. Alternative choices of action were to carry on with repairs, transfer the aircraft if possible to a ferry carrier for work to be carried out at an RN air yard ashore, or strip it of useful components and push it over the side.

Aircraft that were to be repaired or refurbished on board were then taken down into the hangar, where the aircraft repair section would take it on charge. Components allocated to specialised component repair ships would be removed and shipped across by lighter; others requiring less work could be repaired on board. As the aircraft was worked on by different teams of men it moved progressively along the hangar from aft to forward until it reached the reassembly bay. As it did so its components made their own way through workshops. Electrical equipment was stripped and cleaned or, if necessary, replaced. Batteries were charged in a room in which two motor generators driven from the ship's ring main supplied current at up to 40V DC. Instruments such as the air speed indicator were removed and recalibrated. Radios and wireless sets were recalibrated in specialist test rooms equipped with artificial aerials. Hydraulic equipment such as oleos were tested on static rigs and replaced if they were found to be unserviceable. Damaged airframes were repaired using the resources of the metal repair shops, which were equipped with wheeling and raising machines, guillotines, bending machines and rolls, metal nibblers, bench drills and all the necessary work benches. Fabric repairs were carried out in extensive fabric repair shops equipped with sewing machines and large worktops. Once reassembled the aircraft

would be taken to the 'flight deck' and test run; guns would be fitted and radios checked. It would then be near an operational condition but would have to be taken ashore by lighter for a compass swing and test flight before entering the supply chain for issue to the operational fleet. It is arguable that, if the catapult had been retained, fixed-wing aircraft could at least have been launched from the deck, but it would have required manpower and maintenance that were both impractical.

This was a very sophisticated system, but it was biased heavily towards repairs, based on RN experience in the early war years. In practice the maintenance carriers spent most of their time preparing new aircraft, brought to them by ferry carriers, for onward shipment in replenishment carriers and issue to the fleet at sea.

The USN with its larger production base relied much more heavily on replacement than repair, although had the war continued into 1946 it might not have been able to do so to the same extent. It had no equivalent to the maintenance carriers, and relied on large numbers of ferry carriers that restocked supply pools in the forward area. Interestingly, the US Army Air Force (USAAF) commissioned aircraft maintenance ships to support the B-29 squadrons that operated from remote islands in the Pacific. These were comparable to the RN's Air Train but were manned by merchant navy sailors and USAAF maintenance personnel. In addition to lighters, much larger than those used by the British, they used Sikorsky R-4 helicopters to ferry passengers

and light stores between ship and shore; they were the first ships to operate helicopters regularly. Their task was eased, however, by the fact that their 'customers', the B-29 squadrons, operated permanently ashore from a fixed airfield.

Other aircraft maintenance ships built by the RN

Despite the complexity of the three maintenance carriers, the RN was still concerned at the scale of the repair task that might confront the BPF, and ordered several out of a number of mercantile hulls under construction as fleet auxiliaries in Canada to be completed as aircraft component repair ships. Others were converted from existing auxiliaries, and one of these, *Deer Sound*, a merchant ship requisitioned for use as a minelayer in 1939, was converted into an aero-engine repair ship, becoming the only one to see war service with the BPF. The function of these ships was to keep the aircraft maintenance carriers supplied with serviceable and tested components, carry out emergency repair work and produce the components needed to implement authorised modification programmes. Between them they were fitted with radar repair and test shops; metalworkers' and welding shops; coppersmiths' shops; woodworking shops; fabric shops; propeller and propeller-balancing shops; dope and paint shops; oxygen and carbon-dioxide bottle charging and test shops; machine shops; battery and accumulator repair and charging shops; electrical

Pioneer in Sydney Harbour in 1945, showing the many differences between her and her half-sisters, the light fleet carriers. She has no sponsons, and single 20mm Oerlikons are mounted in 'tubs' around the upper deck edge. The distinctive crane on the port side forward is clearly visible, as is the box-like structure to port of the island. (RAN)

Pioneer and *Perseus* technical details

Displacement:	16,500 tons deep load
Dimensions:	length 695ft
	beam 80ft 4in
	draught 23ft
Machinery:	2 shaft Parsons single-reduction geared turbines
	4 Admiralty 3-drum boilers
	40,000shp delivering 24.5 knots
Armament:	numerous 20mm Oerlikon in open mounts
Protection:	none
Fuel:	3,196 tons FFO
Endurance:	8,500 miles at 11 knots

Aircraft maintenance data

Flight deck:	space for parking and engine runs
Hangar:	275ft x 52ft x 17ft 6in
Lifts:	two, both 45ft long x 35ft wide. Both 15,000lb max load
Aircraft:	about 20 under repair; about 60 could be ferried
Aircraft fuel:	some tanks retained for maintenance use and transfer to other ships
Air weapons:	none, but magazine space for weapons removed from aircraft under repair

repair shops; instrument repair shops; oleo and hydraulic, mainplane, control-surface and empennage workshops. They were never used to their full capacity in the BPF, and the concept was not repeated after 1945, since when the RN has relied on air yards ashore for support.

Engine repair ships including *Deer Sound* were intended to carry out the complete overhaul, rectification and modification of all the British and American engine types used by front-line RN aircraft. As well as an extensive array of workshops similar to those in other component repair ships, they had comprehensive facilities to receive unserviceable engines, strip, clean and test them. There were benches for engine accessory, carburettor and petrol testing and component rectification, and there was floor space for reassembly, testing and the stowage of serviceable engines. Engines were received from maintenance carriers or fleet carriers and taken into the receipt store. From there they

were taken to the stripping shop, where they were reduced to their component parts, which were taken to the cleaning bay before moving to the viewing shop for a thorough visual and magnetic inspection. Next, the parts would move through specialised areas such as the cylinder bay, valve-servicing bay and crankshaft bay. Parts found to be unserviceable in the viewing process would be rectified or replaced by serviceable components. From there they would move to the component assembly bay and then be built up on one of two assembly lines that ran along either side of the ship, one for British engines and one for American. They met in the electrical shop, where engines were completed with the fitting of appropriate ignition systems. Once assembled, engines were taken to one of two test benches for trial runs before being put into a state of preservation internally and externally and then stored, ready for issue.

Unicorn was unique in that she was capable of carrying out all these function within a single hull that was also capable of operating aircraft. The other ships were capable of only part of the overall package.

Perseus in Sydney with the BPF in 1946. (RAN).

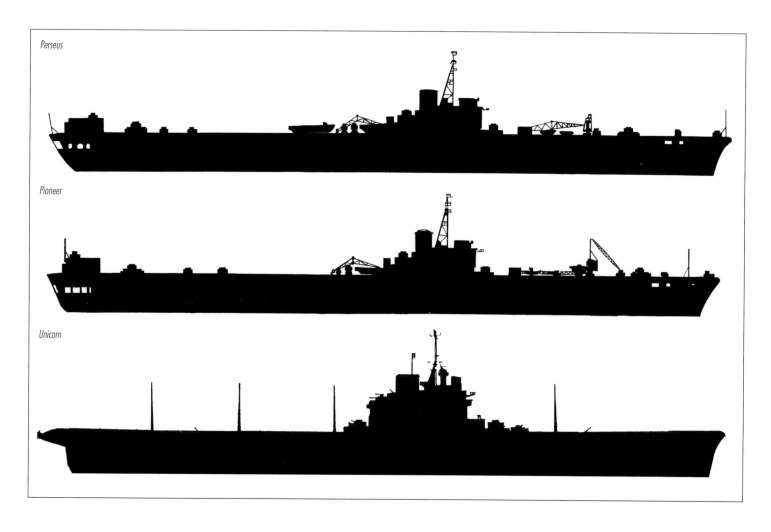

Perseus

Pioneer

Unicorn

These three silhouettes were used by the RN to show the differences in detail between these ships. They give a clear idea of the cranes and other upper deck detail. (AUTHOR'S COLLECTION)

Individual ship histories

Unicorn

Unicorn was ordered from Harland & Wolff's Belfast yard on 14 April 1939 as a 'Fleet Air Arm Supply and Repair Ship', allocated Admiralty Job Number J 3746 and Yard Number 1031. Her designation was subsequently changed to the less complicated 'Aircraft Maintenance Carrier'. Her order was clearly anticipated, and she was laid down on 29 June 1939 and launched on 20 November 1941. Construction was delayed slightly by an instruction in 1940 to give priority to the construction of escorts, but in 1942 the Admiralty ordered work on her to be hastened for completion as an operational carrier, without the

complete outfit of workshop equipment.

She was completed on 12 March 1943 and worked-up off Lamlash for service with the HF. Her first operational sortie was in May 1943, when she embarked 887 (Seafire) NAS together with 818 and 824 (Swordfish) NAS to form part of the escort for convoy MKF 15 to Gibraltar and ferry RAF Beaufighters to the Rock. She was attacked by a Focke-Wulf Fw 200 Condor, which dropped bombs that fell close to her starboard side but did no damage to *Unicorn* or any ship in the convoy. On return to the UK she joined *Illustrious* in Scapa Flow for Operation *Governor*, and sailed with the same air group in July for a feint against the Norwegian coast intended to divert German attention from the landings in Sicily. The material effects of this operation were minimal, but it did demonstrate that a carrier task force could now operate with impunity off the enemy-held coast of Norway.

On her return she embarked 809 and 897 (Seafire) NAS to add to 887 and retained a detachment of 818 NAS for antisubmarine protection, working-up with them in the Clyde before sailing in August to join *Attacker, Battler, Hunter* and *Stalker* in Gibraltar. Together they formed Force V under Rear Admiral Sir Philip

Vian to provide fighter cover for Operation *Avalanche*, the Allied landings at Salerno, with a total of 110 Seafires embarked in the five carriers. The Force moved to the operational area via Algiers and an intensive work-up off Malta. The assault began as planned on 9 September 1943, and *Unicorn* flew seventy-five sorties on the first day. Events ashore did not go as planned, however, and the carriers had to continue to give cover over the beach head for several days. Low winds and limited sea room complicated recoveries by the inexperienced pilots in the escort carriers, but *Unicorn* with her higher speed and bigger deck was better placed. She flew sixty sorties on the second day, forty-four on the third and only eighteen on 12 September. Force V retired to Bizerta, where it stood by in case of need, but it was not required and *Unicorn* returned to the UK on 20 September. In October she returned to Harland & Wolff's yard for a refit and completion in her intended role as a maintenance carrier.

While she had been at sea a selected team of her officers and men had been sent to air yards in the Home Air Command to train for their new tasks, which were usually carried out by Admiralty civilians ashore. They rejoined their ship in

The structure housing the prototype BXS-1 steam catapult on *Perseus* during a test with a 'light shot'. The pole mast has an anemometer on top of it to give accurate wind speeds over the deck near the catapult. (AUTHOR'S COLLECTION)

Her first task was to ferry every available reserve aircraft and engine from Cochin and Colombo to Sydney, the main base of the BPF, where she arrived on 12 February 1945. As she was the only efficient aircraft support facility in the new BPF at the time, her men were hard-pressed to prepare aircraft to replace those lost by front-line squadrons in the Palembang strikes, but they succeeded just in time. The ship also had to take on board all available stores to support the BPF carriers from the forward base in Leyte Gulf during the ensuing operations in support of the Okinawa landings. On 28 February she sailed for Manus in the Admiralty Islands, carrying the BPF reserve aircraft pool to support the fleet's work-up. Ferrying aircraft between carriers by lighter proved difficult in the prevailing swell, and a Seafire was lost and several other aircraft damaged. On 27 March *Unicorn* arrived at the forward base in San Pedro Bay, Leyte Gulf, to support *Illustrious*, *Victorious*, *Indomitable* and *Indefatigable*. After the first phase *Formidable* arrived to replace *Illustrious*, and for a brief spell five ships had to be supported. While this large force anchored together for replenishment from 23 April 1945 onwards, *Unicorn*'s two aircraft lighters had to work a non-stop day and night ferry service carrying aircraft between herself, the ferry and replenishment carriers and the fleet carriers for over seven days.

Perseus at anchor while carrying out steam catapult trials in 1951. The full size of the false deck installed to house the prototype catapult is evident. The funnel smoke shows that her bow is into wind, and aircraft are ranged aft ready to taxi forward on to the catapult. They include an Avenger, Sea Fury and two Sea Hornets. The fact that aircraft are to be catapulted into a low natural wind from a stationary carrier shows how powerful the new steam catapult was, and the confidence the trials team had in it by this stage. (R A BURT COLLECTION)

December, and on 29 December 1943 sailed with 818 (Swordfish) NAS embarked to join other ships including *Illustrious* for passage to join the EF. She passed through the Suez Canal on 12 January 1944 at the head of a line of battleships, and arrived at RNAS Cochin in southern India on 27 January to deliver a consignment of aircraft to the Receipt and Despatch Unit (RDU). While on passage her engineers had assembled new Barracudas and she had provided a spare deck for *Illustrious*' new fighter pilots to practise deck landing. On 2 February she moored in 'Repair Alley' in Trincomalee, close to other depot ships, to carry out her intended role in support of *Victorious* and *Indomitable* when they arrived, as well as *Illustrious*. In addition to repair work she often sailed to give deck-landing training for the growing number of pilots passing through the RN operational training units based in Ceylon. She proved her worth, and it is doubtful whether the EF carrier squadrons

could have remained in action without her. In March she visited Colombo to take a new outfit of spares on board, and she was refitted in Bombay in May. Barracudas and Corsairs were maintained in the hangars using rolling-production-line techniques that worked well. A test party was maintained ashore at RNAS China Bay, where aircraft that had completed repair were taken for test flights and compass swings. In August 1944 818 NAS disembarked for the last time, as there was no longer adequate room for an embarked squadron. She left Trincomalee for the last time in November 1944 with 817 (Barracuda) NAS embarked for antisubmarine defence, and arrived in Durban on 19 November, greeted by Miss Perla Siedle Gibson, the 'White Lady' who gave her the famous singing welcome. While there she was modified to be able to support US-built aircraft in large numbers, before sailing on 1 January 1945 to join the BPF.

Seafire VP460 about to be launched in 1951 without a pilot as a 'dead weight' during RN evaluation of *Perseus*' prototype steam catapult. The outer wings were removed to ensure that the aircraft did not fly very far but, surprisingly, some of these 'retired' aircraft did not give up without a struggle and flew a considerable distance! (AUTHOR'S COLLECTION)

Fortunately the sea was calmer than it had been off Manus, but the effort was worthy of note and Admiral Sir Bernard Rawlings, Second-in-Command of the BPF, who commanded the Task Force at sea, signalled his appreciation of the effort, without which further carriers strikes would not have been possible.

At the end of Operation *Iceberg*, the landings on Okinawa Island, the BPF returned to Sydney for replenishment and repairs. *Unicorn* left the anchorage at Leyte Gulf on 22 May and arrived in Sydney on 1 June. For six days she embarked aircraft and stores from RN air stations ashore, and then sailed for Brisbane on 6 June, where she was docked to have her bottom cleaned and repainted. On completion she sailed for Manus, arriving on 22 July to join *Pioneer* and *Deer Sound* to form an expanded and effective Air Train. *Pioneer* specialised in work on Corsairs and Avengers; *Unicorn* concentrated on the other types, with Seafires growing in importance now that *Implacable* had joined 1 ACS. *Unicorn* was still at Manus on VJ Day, and her tasks changed with the end of hostilities and the need to run-down forward bases. Her own repair department was landed to make more space available, and she evacuated the RN air station on Ponam Island and the aircraft pool on Pityilu Island in October, taking aircraft to RNAY Archerfield, where surplus aircraft and equipment were to be concentrated. She was back in Sydney in November, after which she sailed for the UK, having been away since December 1943. During this two-year wartime commission *Unicorn*'s aircraft repair department had worked on 626 aircraft and 283 aero engines. She arrived back at Devonport Dockyard in January 1946, her ship's company dispersed and she was reduced to reserve, moored in the River Tamar.

In 1949 she was recommissioned to ferry aircraft, stores and equipment to the FEF, which had replaced the BPF in 1948. Specifically she was intended to support *Triumph*, the aircraft carrier on station, and she sailed from Devonport on 22 September 1949 with a load of Seafire FR.47s and Firefly FR.1s and a considerable outfit of stores. On 25 June 1950 she was in Singapore Dockyard, preparing to return to the UK, when the communist North Korean Army attacked South Korea in an unanticipated act of aggression which was immediately condemned by the UN. *Triumph* was with the bulk of the FEF carrying out exercises with the US Seventh Fleet, and joined in striking North Korean targets from 3 July 1950. The creation of the BPF was a recent memory, and it was clear that the lessons learnt applied directly to this new conflict. *Unicorn* was ordered to remain with the FEF as the nucleus of an Air Train, and she re-embarked aircraft and spares to support operational carriers while consideration was given to how best to employ her. She could operate moored at a forward base as she had done at Leyte Gulf and Manus in 1945, or she could land her aircraft repair department, workshop equipment and stores to RNAS Sembawang in Singapore and operate as a replenishment carrier. The latter alternative was considered the more efficient and was adopted, although she retained a light repair and maintenance capability. She sailed from Singapore on 11 July, arriving in Sasebo, which was to be used by the Commonwealth navies as a forward base, on 20 July to transfer seven Seafires and five Fireflies to *Triumph*.

The range of capabilities *Unicorn* offered were quickly utilised and she began a series of voyages to ferry aircraft, ammunition, troops and stores into the war zone. In the UK the light fleet carrier *Warrior* was recommissioned to support her by ferrying aircraft, stores and personnel to the Far

East. In August 1950 *Unicorn* was in Hong Kong, being loaded with stores as diverse as aero engines, rum, flour and ammunition, when the UK Government took the decision to commit ground troops to the conflict. She embarked the Headquarters of 27 Infantry Brigade and the First Battalion of the Middlesex Regiment; most of the Brigade's vehicles were packed tightly into her lower hangar. She was joined by the cruiser *Ceylon*, carrying the First Battalion of the Argyle & Sutherland Highlanders, and the two ships entered Pusan, the last port in UN hands, on 29 August. She returned to Singapore in September to carry out a delayed refit, after which she returned to the war zone in December with a further 400 troops plus aircraft for *Theseus*, which had replaced *Triumph*. As in the BPF, she provided a spare deck for pilots, who had joined the fleet as replacements, to practise deck landing, leaving the operational carrier to concentrate on its primary role.

In 1951 she ferried Meteor jet fighters for 77 Squadron RAAF from Hong Kong to Iwakuni, across the bay from Hiroshima, where there was also a small RN detachment that maintained a pool of serviceable aircraft to support the operational carrier. Later in the year, between ferry runs in which she carried more RAAF Meteors as well as replacement RN fighters and thousands of troops into the war zone, she acted as an accommodation ship in Sasebo for Commonwealth naval personnel. She was 'adopted' by the Middlesex Regiment after a continuous close association. She crossed the 38th Parallel to bombard North Korean coast-watchers with her 4in guns and remains, at the time of writing, the only aircraft carrier of any nation to have carried out a shore bombardment under wartime conditions. She often used the Shimonoseki Strait on passage between Sasebo and Iwakuni and, despite careful checks on the state of the tide, she struck power lines that stretched between Honshu and Kyushu on 2 October 1951 because they were covered in snow and ice due to unseasonably cold weather and were sagging much lower than normal. Replacing them took weeks, and *Unicorn* invariably sailed to the south of Kyushu after that. Later in October she had to sail to ride out Hurricane Ruth, encountering 100-knot winds and waves 50ft high.

On 24 November 1951 a new ship's company recommissioned her in Singapore Naval Base; they had steamed *Warrior* out from the UK and *Unicorn*'s former ship's company steamed her home.

Perseus alongside in Portsmouth with a Whirlwind helicopter of 848 NAS landing on. She is already loaded with stores and replacement Sea Furies for the Far East Fleet. The aircraft are cocooned, but the single-decker buses and cars do not seem to have been protected against the elements. (AUTHOR'S COLLECTION)

Changing aircraft-carrier ship's companies on station became commonplace a decade later, but it was a novel concept in 1951. After a refit she resumed her varied duties, giving support to each new operational carrier as it arrived on station, including HMAS *Sydney*, which drew replacement aircraft from RN FEF stocks. In March 1952 she played the part of a light fleet carrier in Exercise *Vortex*, which tested the defences of Hong Kong, and in April she was presented with the Regimental March of the Middlesex Regiment and a special regimental Order of the Day, both of which were mounted on the quarterdeck next to *Unicorn*'s battle honours. The only other British warship to have been similarly honoured by a regiment was the battleship *Vanguard*. *Unicorn* sailed on several war patrols with *Ocean*, acting as a spare deck to recover unserviceable or damaged aircraft without interrupting the strike carrier's deck cycle, and using 'borrowed' Sea Furies to maintain a CAP over the task force. After a further refit she was present in Singapore Roads with a number of ships from the FEF to celebrate the Coronation of HM Queen Elizabeth II. On 17 July 1953 she sailed for Japan with a load of replacement Sea Furies and Fireflies, but while on passage on 26 July a 'Mayday' signal from the SS *Inchkilda* was intercepted, saying that she was under attack by pirate gunboats. *Unicorn* immediately went to her aid, closing the scene at high speed with all armament manned, and circled the pirate gunboat at 3,000 yards with all her medium- and close-range weapons trained on it. This was too much for the pirates, who reboarded their vessel and fled to the west. *Inchkilda* was returned to her master and went on her way little the worse. *Unicorn* remains, at the time of writing, the only aircraft carrier to have directly intercepted a pirate ship in defence of innocent shipping.

A day later, on 27 July 1953, the armistice that ended fighting in the Korean War was signed. After four years away from the UK and two separate commissions in the FEF, *Unicorn* left for home in October 1953. She had delivered a remarkable performance, having ferried more than 600 aircraft and 6,000 troops into the war zone. On 17 November 1953 she arrived back in Devonport and rejoined the reserve fleet. She was kept partly manned at short notice but redesignated a ferry carrier. After plans to modernise her were cancelled she was reduced to extended reserve in March 1957; her small ship's company was removed and she was no longer

maintained. Surprisingly, perhaps, in view of the internal space she had for the stowage of vehicles and equipment as well as aircraft, she was not considered for conversion to a commando carrier, and in 1958 she was placed on the Disposal List. She was sold to Arnott Young in 1959 and towed from Devonport in June for Dalmuir, where she was stripped out. The hull was scrapped at Troon in 1960.

Pioneer

Laid down and launched as *Mars*, her early details are included in Chapter 20. She was renamed in July 1944, after the decision had been taken to convert her into an aircraft maintenance ship, and completed on 8 February 1945. After commissioning as *Pioneer* in Barrow-in-Furness she worked-up in the Clyde and sailed for Australia on

Perseus in Malta on her way back to the UK from the BPF in 1946, loaded with aircraft and equipment for reuse. (AUTHOR'S COLLECTION)

31 March 1945, arriving in Sydney on 13 May. In June she sailed for her first task, to establish the RN forward aircraft pool at the US naval air station on Pityilu Island, near Manus. This was completed on 11 July, and she joined *Unicorn*, *Deer Sound* and the air stores issuing ships *Fort Langley* and *Fort Colville* at Manus to form the BPF Air Train. They provided 1 ACS with twenty-eight replacement aircraft before it sailed north to attack targets in Japan, and 155 further replacement aircraft to replenishment carriers in seven loads. Fifty-two unserviceable aircraft were brought back to the Air Train for repair. Before *Unicorn* arrived on 21 July, *Pioneer*'s two aircraft lighters were the only means of moving aircraft over the three-mile haul between the fleet anchorage and Pityilu, and they were run non-stop. A third, unserviceable, lighter had been embarked in Sydney and was brought into use after a great deal of work, but even with this and *Unicorn*'s lighters the number was still insufficient, and big USN lighters, each capable of carrying four aircraft, frequently had to be borrowed to move aircraft and load replenishment carriers.

While at Manus *Pioneer* repaired twenty-four aircraft in eight weeks. After they were test-run on deck they were taken by lighter to Pityilu for test flight, a small test party being kept ashore for the task. *Pioneer* was at Manus on 15 August 1945 when the Japanese surrendered, and she remained there until early September, when she sailed to join the BPF task force that was reoccupying Hong Kong. Maintenance ships and their technical sailors were particularly useful in getting the Colony's infrastructure working, and *Pioneer* spent two periods in Hong Kong during October and November, with a brief return to Manus in between. She returned to Sydney in December 1945 for a short defect rectification period, after

which she sailed for Singapore, en route to the UK, on 17 February 1946. On arriving home she was immediately reduced to unmaintained reserve and was never brought forward into service again, despite being redesignated a ferry carrier in June 1953. After being placed on the Disposal List she was sold to T W Ward in September 1954 and towed to Inverkeithing, where she was broken up for scrap.

Perseus

Laid down and launched as the light fleet carrier *Edgar*, details for which can be found in Chapter 20. After being launched on 26 March 1943 she was renamed *Perseus* in June 1944, after the decision to convert her into an aircraft maintenance ship. She differed only in detail from her sister ship *Pioneer*, the most obvious external variation being the different type of crane mounted on the port side, forward on the former flight deck. She was completed on 19 October 1945, too late for war service, and commissioned at Walker Naval Yard in Newcastle on the day of her completion. She arrived in Portsmouth on 24 October and, after a short work-up, sailed to join the BPF on 17 November, arriving in Sydney on 17 December. The Air Train was formally stood down on 28 February 1946, and *Perseus* visited Melbourne in March before returning to the UK, ferrying a load of BPF aircraft to the RN aircraft repair organisation. She arrived at Rosyth Dockyard on 17 May 1946 and was reduced to reserve.

The Admiralty had funded the development of the steam catapult, which it saw as the best method of launching the next generation of aircraft, which were expected to have maximum weights of up to 30,000lb. A test unit, designated BXS-1, was manufactured after 1946 and *Perseus*

was selected as the trial ship for it. The catapult was installed during a special refit in Rosyth during 1950, fitted into a superstructure running from the bow to a point level with the after end of the island structure on top of the upper deck, the original flight deck. It necessitated the removal of the structure to port of the island, but the structure aft, containing the spare engine store and oxygen manufacturing plant, was retained. A series of sea trials were carried out in conditions of great secrecy, during which 1,560 catapult launches were achieved. Of these, more than 1,000 used wheeled dead loads, the weight of which could be carefully controlled and steadily increased. Once confidence was established, unmanned aircraft were launched with their outer wings removed so that they would ditch shortly after launch. Most were Seafires and Sea Hornets that were surplus to operational requirements, and they were not recovered. Lastly, manned, operational aircraft were launched; these had to be craned on board like the dead weights and pilotless aircraft because *Perseus* was capable only of launching, not recovering, them.

The USN had followed the trials with keen interest, and sent observers to witness launches. On 31 December 1951 *Perseus* sailed from Rosyth for Philadelphia Navy Yard, where the BXS-1 was to be demonstrated to the USN. She arrived on 14 January 1952 and, once again, 'shots' with USN dead loads preceded live launches with operational types. Incidentally, USN dead loads were identified by six-digit numbers, whereas RN dead loads were given names such as 'Flossy' and 'Noah'. In total, 127 British and American piloted aircraft were launched before the trials ended successfully. *Perseus* sailed from Philadelphia on 10 March 1952 and arrived back in Portsmouth on 21 March. She was taken into dockyard hands and the prototype catapult, all her remaining workshop equipment and the superstructure at the after end of the flight deck were removed. She was recommissioned for use as a ferry carrier. With no fixed-wing aircraft and a large, unobstructed flight deck she became an ideal helicopter carrier, and on 10 December 1952 she sailed for the Far East with 848 (Whirlwind) NAS embarked, which was to be disembarked for service in Malaya. Subsequently she ferried Avengers from the USA which were allocated to the RN under the MDAP. In 1953 she was redesignated a ferry carrier, but her flight deck was covered with seating galleries from which VIPs and the press were invited to watch the Coronation Review of the Fleet at Spithead. After the seating was removed she ferried aircraft, personnel and stores to the FEF, arriving in

Singapore on 23 September and leaving for the UK on 9 November.

On 20 January 1954 she became a helicopter carrier again, and embarked the Westland Whirlwind antisubmarine helicopters of 706 NAS with their dipping sonar, known at the time as ASDIC. She sailed with them for sea trials to evaluate whether antisubmarine helicopters were a viable weapons system. Based in Northern Ireland, she operated out of Belfast and Bangor with ships and submarines of the JASS, based in Londonderry. The trial proved so successful that 706 NAS, a second-line unit normally based ashore, was redesignated a front-line unit, 845 NAS, on 15

March 1954. The new squadron embarked in *Perseus* on 21 April 1954 for passage to the MF, where it disembarked to RNAS Hal Far in Malta. It subsequently embarked in several MF carriers including *Eagle*, *Centaur* and *Albion*. *Perseus* herself continued to the Far East with relief supplies for Korea. Surprisingly in view of her suitability and availability, she saw no further use as a helicopter carrier after returning to the UK in July 1954, and was taken to Rosyth by a steaming party to be reduced to reserve. She was relieved by *Glory* in the ferry role from August 1954. The intention had been to convert her into a submarine depot ship along similar lines to *Triumph*, which was

Unicorn arrives at Pusan on 29 August 1950 with men and vehicles of the Middlesex Regiment embarked; the first British troops to arrive in Korea. (AUTHOR'S COLLECTION)

converted into a fleet maintenance ship. She was towed to Belfast in 1955 for work to start in Harland & Wolff's yard, but the 1957 Defence Review then reduced the number of projected submarine depot ships, and work on her was abandoned. She was towed to the Gareloch and placed in extended reserve to await disposal. In May 1958 she was sold to Smith & Houston for scrap and towed to Port Glasgow to be broken up.

CHAPTER 25

HERMES CLASS

The *Malta* Class dominated aircraft carrier plans for the 1943 construction programme, but the Admiralty also hoped to order eight light fleet carriers of an improved *Majestic* Class to supplement them. However, the Joint Technical Committee's recommendation at the end of 1942 that restrictions on the size and performance of naval aircraft she be eased ruled out repeat *Majestics*. The most significant changes were an increase in weight to 30,000lb and an increase in the entry speed into arrester wires to 75 knots. While the *Malta* design could absorb these changes and the *Majestic* Class could be modified to operate aircraft over 20,000lb, the new light fleet carriers of the 1943 Programme would have to be substantially redesigned to meet the new criteria.

Technical background

The hull had first to be enlarged to take aircraft of larger dimensions, with a larger hangar and larger lifts capable handling the new weights. Improved catapults and arrester gear would have to be provided, together with larger bomb rooms for the greater weight of ordnance that the new aircraft were expected to carry. Significantly, machinery of greater power would be needed to increase the wind over the deck, both to bridge the gap between the hydraulic catapult end speed and the stalling speed of the new aircraft, and to reduce the potential gap between the arrester-wire entry speed and the speed at which aircraft would fly their final approach. An increase in speed would also bring these ships closer to the tactical speed of a contemporary task force than their 1942 predecessors. There was insufficient capacity to design new machinery, so it was decided to use half the *Ark Royal* installation to deliver 78,000shp on two shafts, saving cost and ensuring standardisation in ships that were expected to have long postwar lives. The resulting design came close to the size and operating capability of *Illustrious*, and it was felt that it should include a greater amount of passive protection than the dispersed machinery spaces in earlier light fleet carriers. The flight deck was constructed with 1in hardened

A flight-deck tractor pulls out *Albion*'s fourth arrester wire for maintenance in January 1960. the helicopter parked aft is a Whirlwind. (AUTHOR'S COLLECTION)

Albion soon after completion. Unusually, the aircraft parked aft include a single Firefly T.7 trainer and two Sea Vampire T.22 trainers, types that usually operated from RN air stations ashore. (AUTHOR'S COLLECTION)

steel, which helped to provide the strength needed to operate the new generation of aircraft. Similar protection was provided on the middle deck over the machinery spaces, on the lower deck over the avgas stowage and in longitudinal protective bulkheads. The watertight subdivision of compartments was particularly effective, and after model tests it was claimed that 1943 light fleet carriers could stay afloat with six main compartments flooded amidships, or with five flooded at the bow or stern. The DNC thought that this aspect of the design was superior to that of *Ark Royal*.

With the ultimate cancellation of the *Malta* Class this became the first British aircraft carrier design in which the demands of aircraft operation dominated the design. The 1942 light fleet carriers had evolved successfully from an economical hull without complicated weapons systems. The need for space, speed and a more capable flight deck drove up the basic requirements for the 1943 ships dramatically, but they were still estimated to cost rather less than half a *Malta*. The flight deck was to be 730ft by 90ft, and the two centreline lifts were each to be 54ft long by 44ft wide and capable of moving 35,000lb aircraft. The original design specified twelve arrester wires, each capable of stopping a 30,000lb aircraft at an entry speed of 75 knots with four barriers. The two BH5 hydraulic catapults could each launch 30,000lb at

75 knots. Avgas stowage was to be 80,000gal in the standard tanks, and bomb rooms were to be capable of containing thirty-two torpedoes, over 120 bombs ranging in size from 2,000lb to 250lb, 2,000 rocket projectiles and thousands of rounds of cannon ammunition. Bomb lifts could move 4,000lb, and the original staff requirement called for sixteen aircraft to be rearmed on the flight deck in forty minutes. The significance of the increase in aircraft size projected by the JTC is shown by the fact that, even after all these increases, the 1943 ships were still expected to operate exactly the same number of aircraft, twenty-four, as the 1942 classes, but they were larger, more effective strike aircraft.

The improved design was essential if these ships were to be capable of operating the new generation of aircraft, and there was little point in ordering them if they were not, but the First Lord, A V Alexander, thought the design too elaborate and initially refused to sanction orders without Cabinet approval. When this was given, seven ships were ordered on 12 July 1943. An eighth was added on 11 August 1943 when it was decided that Devonport Dockyard had the capacity to lay down one of these ships after the launch of *Terrible* in 1944. The Programme anticipated, optimistically, that all eight would be completed in 1946. However, shipyard manpower capacity was insufficient to start work on all these ships because of the large orders that had been placed for landing craft intended for operations in the Pacific. By early 1944 the Admiralty gave instructions that work was to proceed on four ships; two more were to be started in the first quarter of 1945 and the

last two deferred. The four selected for progress were *Albion*, *Centaur*, *Elephant* and *Monmouth*, but Fairfield proved unable to start work on the latter in 1944 and no work was done on her. Harland & Wolff did have the capacity, so *Bulwark* was laid down in 1945 and *Monmouth* deferred. One of the deferred ships was *Polyphemus*, and Devonport Dockyard had carried out preliminary work and ordered machinery from Parsons with the intention of laying her down in October 1944, immediately after the launch of *Terrible*. After the deferral no further work was done. The name ship of the class, *Hermes*, was another of the deferrals, so *Elephant* was renamed. The four deferred ships were finally cancelled on 15 October 1945; none had been laid down and it is arguable that the Admiralty had maintained them in the 1943 Programme only as 'numbers' to be cancelled after hostilities in order to save ships that had been started for the postwar fleet. There was certainly little chance that the whole class could have been taken forward without cancelling other important projects in the overstretched shipbuilding industry of 1944 Britain.

After the end of hostilities, work on the four survivors slowed and was actually halted after they were launched. *Hermes*, ex-*Elephant*, was longest on the slipway, and she was reconstructed during build into an entirely new design which is described in Chapter 28. *Centaur* was the only ship to be completed to the original design with an axial, 'straight' flight deck; after trials she was immediately taken in hand for modification to have an interim angled deck fitted. This entailed extension of the flight deck to port amidships and

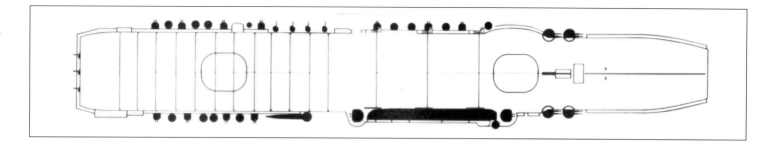

the removal of several 40mm Bofors mountings from sponsons on the port side. *Albion* and *Bulwark* were built to this standard, and thus completed slightly later. All three were fitted with the new mirror landing aid. By 1954 they had been under construction for ten years, but they proved to be useful fleet units with air groups made up with first-generation jet fighters and turboprop antisubmarine aircraft, together with the first AEW aircraft and antisubmarine helicopters. They ideally complemented the larger fleet carriers *Ark Royal* and *Eagle*, and were equipped with the same radar outfit, Types 960, 982 and 983 feeding displays in a similar two-level operations room/ADR. When the two *Implacables* were found to be too complicated and expensive to modernise they were paid off into reserve and their ship's companies used to man the new 1943 light fleet carriers.

Their original hydraulic catapults were incapable of operating the second generation of jet fighters, the Supermarine Scimitar and de Havilland Sea Vixen, due to enter service in the late 1950s, however, and a modification programme was prepared to refit the ships with steam catapults, improved arrester wires and improved radars. *Centaur* was the first to be modified, steam catapults being fitted in 1957, after which she was able to operate the new aircraft successfully but only in small numbers. It was therefore decided in 1962 that she would operate a single, large squadron of Sea Vixens which would specialise in the fighter role but be capable of strike missions, rather than a mix of two small squadrons. *Centaur* could not have operated Blackburn Buccaneers without considerable modifications that would have to bring her close the design of the much-modified *Hermes*.

Before the other two ships could be taken in hand, the 1957 Defence Review reduced the number of aircraft carriers that were to be retained in the operational fleet. It was therefore decided to modify them into the commando-carrier role pioneered by *Ocean* and *Theseus* at Suez in 1956.

Albion sailing for the Mediterranean in 1958 with 42 RM Commando and vehicles embarked. More than a thousand extra eyebolts had to be welded to the flight deck to allow the vehicles to be lashed securely in place. (AUTHOR'S COLLECTION)

Plans to convert two 1942 light fleet carriers into the role, possibly *Glory*, *Leviathan* or *Magnificent*, were therefore scrapped, and modifications prepared for *Bulwark* and *Albion*. The two ships were known as commando carriers or, more formally, as Landing Platforms (Helicopter) (LPH) in the NATO brevity code. They were intended to be able to carry a single Royal Marines Commando unit with its supporting artillery and engineer elements, totalling about a 1,000 men, and an RN assault helicopter squadron with sixteen aircraft. Four Landing Craft (Assault) were fitted to davits installed on the port and starboard sides aft to land vehicles and bulky stores that could not be carried by helicopter. The Type 960 radar was retained, but the 982 and 983 were removed and the air direction room was converted into an amphibious-operations room. The ship's company was reduced in size and much of the former air group

The *Hermes* Class flight deck design as intended in 1945. Note the three barriers, twelve arrester wires, central catapult and medium-range guns forward. The close-range armament along the port side and starboard side aft was impressively large but expensive in terms of manpower. The eventual design to which some of these ships were completed evolved and was very different. (AUTHOR'S COLLECTION)

accommodation was modified for use by the embarked force. A second RM Commando unit could be carried for a 'quick dash' under austere conditions. The former bomb rooms and aircraft equipment stores were modified to stow ammunition and assault stores ranging from sandbags and barbed wire to toilet paper and composite ration packs. Some aircraft support infrastructure had to be retained for the single RN helicopter squadron, but all fixed-wing facilities were removed, including the catapults and arrester

wires. The ships were expected to sustain assault operations for up to a week and low-intensity operations such as peacekeeping for a month within their own resources. They were, however, expected to operate within an amphibious task force with the new LPDs and RFAs, which could keep them supplied with fuel and stores when necessary. Theoretically, their helicopters could be fitted with dipping sonar to allow the ships to operate in the antisubmarine role, but, lacking observers, skilled sonar operators and a suitably equipped and manned operations room, their use in the short term would have been doubtful until a work-up with new personnel had been completed.

Bulwark was the first ship to be modified, and proved her worth in the Kuwait crisis of 1961 in more ways than one. Firstly, she was able to deploy her commandos into the operational area and keep them supplied by helicopter. Troops that arrived later by air had no logistical support and had to improvise before they became an effective fighting unit. Secondly, she was able to co-ordinate the movements of warships offshore, including those that were to provide naval gunfire support. Lastly, she had the only air warning radar available to British forces in Kuwait so, even when RAF fighters were flown in, they relied on *Bulwark* for intercept information and air traffic control. These tasks were taken over by the strike carrier *Victorious* when she arrived, but *Bulwark* had demonstrated the need for the commando carrier to function as a joint command centre. One consequence of this was that, when her sister ship *Albion* was modified, her Type 960 radar was removed and replaced by a Type 965 'bedstead' at the top of her lattice mast.

Centaur technical details

Displacement:	27,800 tons deep load
Dimensions:	length 737ft
	beam 123ft
	draught 28ft 3in
Machinery:	2 shaft Parsons geared turbines
	4 Admiralty 3-drum boilers
	76,000shp delivering 28 knots
Armament:	4 twin 40mm Bofors; 2 single
	40mm Bofors; 4 single 3pdr
	saluting
Protection:	1in to 2in flight deck; 1in
	magazine crowns; 1in funnel
	uptakes
Fuel:	3,500 tons FFO
Endurance:	5,000 miles at 20 knots
Complement:	1,390

Aircraft operating data

Flight deck:	733ft x 84ft abreast island; 5.5°
	angled deck
Hangar:	274ft plus 55ft extension fwd of
	fwd lift x 62ft x 17ft 6in
Catapults:	two BS4 steam with 139ft
	stroke capable of launching
	40,000lb aircraft at 94 knots
	end speed
Arrester wires:	six 35,000lb at 103 knots entry
	speed; nylon emergency barriers
	capable of being rigged in 5min
Lifts:	fwd 54ft long x 44ft wide,
	37,000lb
	aft 54ft long x 44ft wide,
	40,000lb
	both 22sec cycle
Aircraft:	Up to 42 depending on type
Aircraft fuel:	295,000gal avcat; 50,000gal
	avgas (for helicopters)
Air weapons:	Firestreak air-to-air missiles
	(AAM); Sidewinder AAM;
	Bullpup air-to-surface missiles
	(ASM); Mark 30/44/46 homing
	torpedoes; 2,000lb, 1,000lb and
	500lb bombs; 3in rocket
	projectiles with 28lb and 60lb
	warheads; 2in podded rocket
	projectiles; 30mm and 20mm
	cannon ammunition; 'Glow-
	worm' illuminant rocket
	projectiles; flares and
	pyrotechnics

Albion aircraft operating data as a fixed-wing carrier

Flight deck:	732ft x 84ft abreast island; 5.5°
	angled deck
Hangar:	274ft plus 55ft extension fwd of
	fwd lift x 62ft x 17ft 6in
Catapults:	Two BH5 hydraulic capable of
	launching 30,000lb aircraft at
	75 knots
	end speed
Arrester wires:	Six 30,000lb at 75 knots entry
	speed; emergency nylon barriers
	capable of being rigged in 5min
Lifts:	Two, both 54ft long x 44ft
	wide, both 35,000lb
Aircraft:	Up to 42 depending on type
Aircraft fuel:	309,750gal avcat
Air weapons:	Mark 30 homing torpedoes;
	2,000lb, 1,000lb and 500lb
	bombs; 3in rocket projectiles
	with 28lb and 60lb warheads;
	Mark 11 depth charges; 20mm
	cannon ammunition; flares and
	pyrotechnics

Bulwark aircraft operating data as a commando-carrier

Flight deck:	733ft x 84ft abreast island,
	axial
Hangar:	274ft plus 55ft extension fwd of
	fwd lift x 62ft x 17ft 6in
Lifts:	two, both 54ft long x 44ft
	wide, both 35,000lb
Aircraft:	30 helicopters in 1971
Aircraft fuel:	299,000gal avcat; 50,000gal
	avgas (or fuel for embarked unit
	vehicles)
Air weapons:	SS-11 ASM; SS-12 ASM; Mark
	44 homing torpedoes; 2in
	rocket projectiles; Mark 11
	depth charges; 7.62mm
	machine-gun ammunition;
	flares and pyrotechnics

Individual ship histories

Hermes

The original name-ship of the class, *Hermes*, was allocated Admiralty Job Number J 3656 and ordered from Cammell Laird of Birkenhead on 12 July 1943. She was allocated the Yard Number 1158, but no work had been done on her when the builder was instructed to defer construction in early 1944. The contract was formally cancelled on 15 October 1945.

Centaur

Allocated Admiralty Job Number J 3939, *Centaur* was ordered from Harland & Wolff on 12 July 1943. The firm allocated the Yard Number 1280 to the hull, which was laid down on 30 May 1944 and launched by HRH the Duchess of Kent on 22 April 1947. Work on the ship was suspended for two years while other, more immediate, work was carried forward, but she was eventually completed on 1 September 1953; the first of the class to complete and the only one to the original design. She was commissioned in Belfast on 17 September 1953.

In October 1953 she carried out post-build and first-of-class trials in the Portsmouth areas and was then taken in hand by Portsmouth Dockyard to have an interim 5.5-degree angled deck fitted. She emerged in May to take part in Operation *Loyalty*, acting as escort to HM Queen Elizabeth II as she approached the UK on her return from her Australian and Pacific tour. In September 1954 she embarked 806 (Sea Hawk), 810 (Sea Fury) and 820 (Avenger) NAS plus a ship's SAR Flight Dragonfly

RIGHT *Centaur* was taken in hand soon after completion and modified with an interim angled deck, which required a small port extension to the flight deck and the removal of some close-range weapons. In this photograph, taken on 12 May 1954, she has not yet been fitted with a mirror landing aid. (AUTHOR'S COLLECTION)

helicopter and deployed to join the MF. In October she withdrew the last British troops stationed in Trieste, and in early 1955 she carried out exercises with the US Sixth Fleet in the Mediterranean, returning to the UK for a docking and maintenance period in June 1955.

In January 1956 she embarked a new air group comprising 803 and 806 (Sea Hawk), 814 (Gannet) NAS and the ship's flight Dragonfly, and sailed to join the FEF. When she returned in May she was taken in hand by Devonport Dockyard for a limited modernisation which included fitting steam catapults and an improved ADR/operations room. She recommissioned in Devonport on 3 September 1958 and embarked 801 (Sea Hawk), 810 (Gannet) and 891 (Sea Venom) NAS and joined the HF after a work-up. In May 1959 she visited Copenhagen before deploying to join the FEF. In July she visited Karachi, and in August she flew the flag of FO2 FEF while taking part in a series of large-scale Commonwealth naval exercises, the biggest of their kind since 1945. When they ended, she visited Brisbane and took part in the city's centenary celebrations. In March 1960 she took part in Exercise *Jet 60*, another large Commonwealth naval exercise.

In April 1960 her aircraft went into action as part of Operation *Damon*, a series of air strikes against pirates and arms smugglers in the western part of the Aden Protectorate. By June she was back in UK waters, and at the end of August she arrived in Portsmouth Dockyard for a refit to prepare her to operate the next generation of naval fighters. She recommissioned on 3 March 1961 and embarked 807 (Scimitar), 893 (Sea Vixen), 849A (Gannet AEW) and 824 (Whirlwind) NAS before preparing for service with the MF. In July, however, she deployed into the Persian Gulf to replace *Victorious* as part of Operation *Vantage*, the British measures that prevented a threatened Iraqi invasion of Kuwait. By September the crisis was over and she returned to Devonport before returning to the Middle East on October. In November 1961 she took part in flood-relief operations in Kenya, during which her helicopters evacuated casualties and operated a 'flying doctor' service to remote areas.

In January 1962 she joined the FEF, and on 27 January went to the aid of the Greek tanker *Stanvac Sumatra*, which had broken in two 250 miles

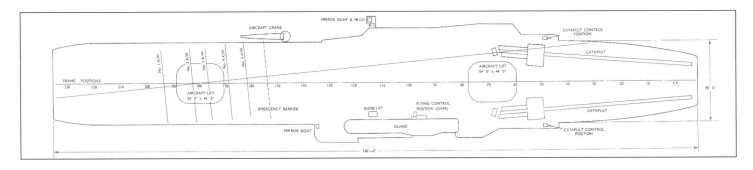

ABOVE *Centaur* as modified, with an interim angled flight deck. (AUTHOR'S COLLECTION)

LEFT *Centaur*'s mirror landing aid has been fitted in this photograph, and shows up clearly on the port side, despite the aircraft from which it was taken being lined up with the axial, rather than the angled deck. (AUTHOR'S COLLECTION)

southeast of Saigon in the South China Sea. In February she was in Singapore Dockyard for a maintenance period, and in February took part in Exercise *Jet 62*, the latest in the annual series of Commonwealth naval exercises. In April she sailed for the UK, carrying out exercises with the MEF en route before arriving home in May. After a short refit in Portsmouth she rejoined the MF at the end of July to take part in NATO Exercise *Riptide* in August, after which she carried out a series of port visits and returned to the UK. On 19 November 1962, while carrying out flying operations in the Irish Sea, she suffered a disastrous steam leak in 'A' boiler room which killed the four men on watch and the engineer officer of the watch, who was carrying out his rounds. The ship had to carry out a docking in Portsmouth to repair the damage, and in February 1963 she sailed to rejoin the FEF with 892 (Sea Vixen), 849B (Gannet AEW) and 815 (Wessex) NAS embarked. She returned for a refit in May, during which a Type 965 radar was fitted on a new lattice foremast stepped at the forward end of the island and improvements were made to her air defence operations room. She sailed with the same air group to rejoin the FEF in December, with the same air group. In January 1964 she was off Aden when units of the Tanganyika Rifles mutinied, and the Government asked the UK for immediate aid. *Centaur* embarked 45 RM Commando, the 16/5 Lancers, two RAF Belvedere

TOP RIGHT *Centaur* with Sea Hawks ranged on deck in 1959. (AUTHOR'S COLLECTION)

RIGHT *Centaur* off East Africa in January 1964, with the armoured vehicles of 16/5 Lancers on the starboard side of Fly 1 and two RAF Belvedere helicopters aft in addition to her normal air group, much of which is on deck to provide space in the hangar for the men of 45 RM Commando to sleep on camp beds. (AUTHOR'S COLLECTION)

helicopters plus vehicles and ammunition, in addition to her full air group. A plan known as Operation *Squeeze* was prepared so that Gannets and fighters could be launched if necessary, and the sonar sets were removed from the Wessex so that they could carry assault parties of marines ashore. A dawn assault on Colito Barracks proved completely successful and the mutineers surrendered. In March *Centaur* rescued survivors from the Greek liner *Lakonia*, and in April her Sea Vixens carried out strikes against rebellious tribesmen in the Radfan area, north of Aden. Later in the year she took part in Exercise *Fotex 64* and carried out anti-invasion patrols off Malaysia during the Confrontation against Indonesia. During October she exercised with the USN in the Subic Bay areas. After a very successful commission she returned to the UK on 21 December 1964.

In 1965 she sailed from the UK to work-up off Gibraltar, and then became flagship of the MF for visits to Naples and Istanbul before taking part in NATO Exercise *Aigrette* in June. After returning to the UK she visited the Clyde in August for a Fleet Review by HM the Queen, after which she visited Liverpool and returned to Portsmouth to pay off for the last time on 27 September 1965. Despite the fact that she was only twelve years old she was used, with a small administrative ship's company of her own, as an accommodation ship

during *Victorious*' 1965/66 refit and then towed to Devonport to act as an accommodation ship for *Eagle*'s refit in 1966. In 1967 she was a tender to the RN Barracks, HMS *Drake*, as an accommodation ship. Later in the year she was towed back to Portsmouth to act as an accommodation ship for *Hermes*' refit. In April 1970 she was back in Devonport, still in use as an accommodation ship, but her material state had deteriorated significantly and she was finally laid up in the River Tamar in December and placed on the Disposal List. On 11 August 1972 she was sold to the Queenborough Shipbreaking Company and towed to Cairnryan in Wigtownshire be broken up for scrap.

Albion

Allocated Admiralty Job Number J 4970, *Albion* was ordered from Swan Hunter on 12 July 1943. She was given the Yard Number 1721 and laid down in the company's Wallsend-on-Tyne yard on 23 March 1944. Work slowed after 1945, but she was launched by Mrs Violet Attlee, wife of Prime Minister Clement Attlee, on 6 May 1947 and immediately laid up at moorings in the Tyne. Her machinery was in place, but otherwise she was an empty shell with canvas covers over her empty lift wells. In August 1949 it was announced that work

Albion in Scapa Flow during March 1971, clearly showing the landing craft on the starboard side. One is already in the water and the second is being lowered. The Type 965 radar on top of her mast distinguished her from her sister ship *Bulwark*. (AUTHOR'S COLLECTION)

on her would be resumed for a planned completion date in 1953. Before it could begin, however, she needed a bottom clean, and it was decided to tow her to Rosyth Dockyard for the work to be carried out before returning her to Swan Hunter's yard for completion. She was towed into the North Sea by three tugs in deteriorating weather conditions on 17 October 1949, and in the subsequent storm with 85 knot winds her port navigation light was extinguished and she did not show 'not-under-command' lights. At 0415 on 18 October 1949 she collided with the 2,000-ton collier *Maystone*, which sank with the loss of all but four hands, leaving *Albion* with a hole 15ft long in the port side and a flooded engine room. A salvage tug and destroyer were sent from Rosyth to help, and the damaged carrier arrived there late on 19 October. Litigation subsequently found Swan Hunter and the tug owners to be at fault, and criticised the decision to sail at all, given the atrocious weather forecast.

She sailed for contractor's sea trials in June 1953, largely with an unpainted axial flight deck, but was modified afterwards with a 5.5-degree interim angled deck and mirror landing aids. She can thus claim to be the world's first carrier to be completed with these features built in, rather than fitted later. She was commissioned into the RN at Wallsend-on-Tyne on 26 May 1954 and accepted as complete after a full-power trial a day later. She subsequently embarked 813 (Wyvern), 815 (Avenger), 849C (Skyraider), 890 (Sea Venom) and 898 (Sea Hawk) NAS and joined the MF in September after working-up. In October 1954 she hoisted the flag of FOAC and carried out a series of exercises with the US Sixth Fleet before returning to the HF. In January 1956 she sailed for the FEF, still flying FOAC's flag, with the specific intention of operating with the Indian Navy, which was considering purchasing the incomplete

light fleet carrier *Hercules*. She took part in Exercise *Sea Dragon* in the South China Sea with Commonwealth warships and the French carrier *Lafayette*. In May she returned to Portsmouth for a planned refit which had to be shortened because of the Suez Crisis.

In September she began to work-up with 800 and 802 (Sea Hawk), 809 (Sea Venom) and 849C (Skyraider) NAS embarked. From 1 November 1956 she took part in Operation *Musketeer*, the Suez intervention, with *Eagle*, *Bulwark*, *Ocean*, *Theseus* and the French *Arromanches* and *Lafayette*. *Albion*'s aircraft struck first at Al Naza Airfield, six miles from Cairo and 130 miles from the fleet, and then continued operations for several days. The RN deployed only a third of the Allied ground-attack aircraft, but flew two-thirds of the missions

because of the carriers' proximity to the targets. On 5 November 1956 carrier fighters gave cover to the parachute assault on Gamil Airfield near Port Said; helicopters and Skyraiders flew in water, medical supplies and even barrels of beer to support the assault forces once they were ashore. Helicopters also evacuated the seriously wounded to the fleet and, for the first time, delivered operation orders around the fleet on a clear, dark night. After the Suez operation *Albion* returned to Malta on 29 November, and returned to the UK in March 1957, when she was visited by the Duke of Gloucester. She subsequently joined the HF, with 824 (Gannet) NAS added to the air group.

In May 1957 she took part in a Royal Review of the Home Fleet in the Cromarty Firth and later visited Oslo before entering Portsmouth Dockyard for a refit in November 1957. After its completion she was working-up in the Moray Firth in July 1958 when the Iraqi Revolution occurred. She hastened back to Portsmouth, having disembarked her air group, and prepared to embark 42 RM Commando and the Headquarters elements of the Army's 19 Infantry Brigade. Over 1,000 eye bolts had to be welded to the flight and hangar decks to provide lashing points for the 500 vehicles she was to carry. The greater part of the hangar was made into a dormitory with steel-frame bunks. She sailed with the force on 22 July 1958 and delivered them to Malta, where they increased the British capability to intervene in the Eastern Mediterranean if necessary. The whole evolution, from the time of receipt of the warning signal off Scotland to the unloading of the last vehicle in Malta, took nine days. After removal of the extra eye bolts and other repairs she embarked 804 (Sea Hawk), 809 (Sea venom), 849C (Skyraider) and 820 (Whirlwind) NAS and prepared for service in the FEF. She flew the flag of FO2 FEF for a spell, took part in several SEATO and Commonwealth naval exercises and visited ports in Australia and New Zealand. She also operated with the USN off Subic Bay and cross-decked aircraft with the USS *Yorktown* during Exercise *Sea Demon*. On her way back to the UK she visited Madagascar in May 1959, flying the flag of the C-in-C South Atlantic, and then went on to visit Rio de Janeiro in Brazil, circumnavigating the globe before returning to Portsmouth for a refit in August 1959.

She recommissioned for the last time as a fixed-wing carrier in December 1959, and worked-up in the Mediterranean with 806 (Sea Hawk), 894 (Sea Venom), 849D (Skyraider) and 815 (Whirlwind) NAS embarked. In March 1960 she embarked King Paul of Greece, an honorary admiral in the

Bulwark only days after completion in November 1954. She is not yet fitted with a mirror landing sight, and the multiple Bofors mounting aft of the island is cocooned. (AUTHOR'S COLLECTION)

RN, to witness flying operations, and passed through the Suez Canal to join the FEF, flying the flag of the C-in-C during visits to Hong Kong and Japan. Again exercises with Australian and New Zealand warships were carried out to strengthen alliances, and a series of port visits promoted British interests in the region. On the way back to the UK she took part in CENTO Exercise *Midlink 3* in the Middle East, and then disembarked her air group before arriving in Portsmouth on 17 December 1960. This commission had marked the last operational deployment of the Sea Hawk, Sea Venom and Skyraider by the RN.

In January 1961 she was taken in hand in Portsmouth for conversion into the second commando carrier. The work was completed in August 1962, when she was recommissioned by HRH the Duke of Edinburgh. Afterwards she worked-up in her new role with 845 (Wessex), 846 (Whirlwind) NAS and 40 RM Commando embarked, before sailing to join the FEF. In November 1963 she was visiting Mombasa when the Brunei Revolt occurred. She was ordered to Singapore with despatch to embark RM commandos and other Commonwealth forces, and

landed them with her helicopters in Borneo for operations ashore. Her time was then spent supporting operations in support of forces ashore in Borneo. In April 1964 she returned to the UK for a refit, but was back in the FEF with 848 (Wessex) NAS embarked for further operations in the Confrontation with Indonesia over Malaysian areas of Borneo. In August 1966 she left Singapore for a further refit in the UK, and when it was completed in 1967 she sailed for the FEF with 848 (Wessex) NAS embarked again. She sailed from the UK in some secrecy and by May was positioned off the coast of Nigeria, where a civil war had broken out, and spent some weeks poised ready to evacuate British nationals if it proved necessary. The RM battle-group was prepared to move ashore and hold a bridgehead to protect the evacuation, but it proved unnecessary and she returned to the UK to prepare for service with the FEF again. She sailed in September, but by then the Confrontation was over, but she was needed to form, with *Eagle* and *Hermes*, part of the task force which covered the withdrawal of British forces from Aden in October 1967. Helicopters of 848 NAS lifted off commandos of 45 RM Commando, the last unit to

Bulwark taking the damaged tanker Melika in tow in September 1958. Aircraft on deck include a Whirlwind helicopter, Sea Hawks and Sea Venoms. The frigate Puma is standing by to port. (AUTHOR'S COLLECTION)

leave. In December she left the Aden area and proceeded to Singapore, and in 1968 she took part in a number of exercises and visited ports in Australia, Japan, Korea and Cambodia.

A further UK refit was carried out from August 1969, and when it was completed she worked-up with 848 (Wessex) NAS embarked from March 1970. In September she took part in exercises in the Eastern Mediterranean and then rejoined the FEF for the last time in March 1971. She left Singapore with *Eagle* and a number of other ships in October 1971, when the FEF was stood down, and returned to the UK via the Persian Gulf and Cape Town. In January 1972 she started a refit in Portsmouth, after which she sailed for exercises with what was now the WF in the Mediterranean. In July 1972 845 (Wessex) NAS replaced 848, and in September she took part in NATO Exercise *Strong Express* off Norway. In October she sailed from the UK for exercises in Canada with 845

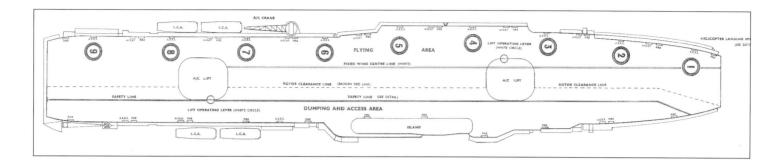

Bulwark after conversion into a commando carrier, with nine helicopter spots marked on the flight deck and space for RM vehicles and equipment to be stowed. (AUTHOR'S COLLECTION)

Bulwark in her early days as a commando carrier with the Far East Fleet. She has Whirlwind helicopters ranged forward, about to start up, and RM vehicles parked aft. She is refuelling the minesweeper *Woolaston*. (AUTHOR'S COLLECTION)

(Wessex) NAS and 42 RM Commando embarked, after which she visited Halifax, Quebec and Montreal, becoming the largest warship ever to pass through the St Lawrence Seaway at that time.

Albion arrived in Portsmouth on 24 November 1972 to pay off as the result of a Defence Review which led to a reduction in the size of the RN surface fleet. She was destored and finally

decommissioned on 2 March 1973 before being placed on the Disposal List and moored in Fareham Creek. In October she was sold to Wilson Walker Engineering, which intended to convert her into a heavy-lift vessel to support the growing North Sea oil industry. After she had been towed to the Clyde for conversion, however, the scheme fell through and she was moored in the Clyde. After a few weeks she was sold for scrap and towed to Faslane, where she was finally broken up.

Bulwark

The contract for *Bulwark* was placed with Harland & Wolff by the Admiralty on 12 July 1943. Her Admiralty Job Number was J 3906, and the builder allocated her Yard Number 1281. In 1944 she was one of four units of the *Hermes* Class that were deferred, but when Fairfield proved unable to take *Monmouth* forward, Harland & Wolff were instructed to start work on *Bulwark* in the spring of 1945. She was laid down on 10 May 1945, but work on her slowed after the war's end. She was launched on 22 June 1948 by the Countess of Granville, the sister of Queen Elizabeth, the Queen Mother, and completed to a modified design, with a 5.5-degree angled deck and fewer Bofors guns on port-side sponsons, on 4 November 1954. She had already been commissioned in Belfast on 29 October.

In November she moved to Portsmouth to carry out post-acceptance trials and was fitted with a mirror landing aid. In February 1955 an Avenger from 703 NAS at RNAS Ford was the first aircraft to land on board, and she replaced *Illustrious* as the trials and training carrier. In June she demonstrated her operational potential by embarking 800 and 811 (Sea Hawk) and 751 (Avenger) NAS for the HF Summer Cruise, after which she visited Oslo. In August 1956 she was brought up to operational standard again to embark 804, 810 and 897 (Sea Hawk) NAS and work-up with the MF for operations in the eastern Mediterranean. From 1 November 1956 she took part in Operation *Musketeer*, the brief Suez Intervention. Operating an all-Sea Hawk air group simplified her deck operations, and she flew 580 sorties against Egyptian airfields and military installations. In December 1956 she returned to

Portsmouth for a refit, emerging in May 1957 to join the HF as an operational carrier, the trials and training task being taken over by *Warrior*. Her air group comprised 801 and 898 (Sea Hawk), 849D (Skyraider) and 820 (Gannet) NAS initially, 845 (Whirlwind) NAS being added in August. In September she joined *Ark Royal* to take part in NATO exercise *Strikeback*, a major demonstration with the USN of NATO carrier striking power. Her recent refit had included the fitting of a flight deck magnetic loop communications system, and during *Strikeback* she was the first carrier to use it operationally. In December 820 disembarked and disbanded, leaving her with only rotary-wing antisubmarine aircraft.

In March 1958 she flew the flag of the C-in-C HF during Exercise *Maple Royal* with the RCN, and in May she left the UK to join the FEF. In July 1958 *Bulwark* was visiting Mombasa when the crisis in the Middle East caused by the Iraqi Revolution began. She was used first to ferry a British infantry battalion with its stores and vehicles from Kenya to Aden. Next, during August, she ferried another infantry battalion from Aden to Aqaba in Jordan in response to a request for help. On 13 September 1958 she was operating off the Strait of Hormuz when two tankers collided and the *Melika* caught fire. Helicopters of 845

NAS ferried firefighting parties under the command of *Bulwark*'s first lieutenant to assist the damaged ship, which was eventually towed safely to Muscat by the carrier. For its achievements on this day, 845 NAS was awarded the Boyd Trophy for 1958. *Bulwark* returned to Portsmouth in November 1958 and paid off into Dockyard hands for conversion into a commando carrier.

The conversion took a year, and she recommissioned on 23 January 1960 in her new role, subsequently embarking 848 (Whirlwind) NAS and 42 RM Commando for an operational work-up in the MF. In April 1960 HRH the Duke of Edinburgh, Captain-General of the Royal Marines, embarked to witness a major assault landing exercise on the coast of Libya that was the culmination of the training. In July 1961 she was visiting Karachi when Iraqi forces threatened to invade Kuwait and the British Chiefs of Staff ordered Operation *Vantage* into effect. *Bulwark* was ordered to Kuwait 'with all despatch', and used her helicopters to deploy 42 Commando on to the border within twenty-four hours. They then supported them with water, food and combat logistics. The squadron also had to support army units as they arrived by air. In October 1961 *Bulwark* was recommissioned in Singapore with a new ship's company flown out from the UK, and

Bulwark with an Alpha Range on the flight deck, including an RM Commando unit with its supporting arms and equipment in addition to the ship's own helicopter squadron. Note the 105mm pack-howitzers right forward and the neatly parked Land Rovers aft. (AUTHOR'S COLLECTION)

in January 1962 she took part in Exercise *Tombstone*, an amphibious assault exercise in northwest Australia. In March she exercised in the Persian Gulf with the Amphibious Warfare Squadron, and in April she embarked Wessex helicopters of 815 NAS from *Ark Royal* for type familiarisation. In May she played a major part in Exercise *Common Assault 3*, training troops of the Hong Kong garrison in new assault techniques in the New territories. In July she took part in the Commonwealth naval Exercise *Fotex 62*, and in October she visited Kuwait. In November she met *Albion* off Aden to transfer stores and equipment before leaving the FEF, and in December she began a refit in Devonport. She had played a considerable part in introducing the new doctrine and tactics of amphibious warfare to the RN and Commonwealth naval forces.

Bulwark recommissioned in Devonport in December 1963 and subsequently worked-up with 706 *Bulwark* (Wessex) Flight and 43 RM

Commando embarked before demonstrating operational readiness in Exercise *Sandfly* 2 on the coast of Libya. In April 1964 she relieved *Albion* as the FEF commando carrier off Aden; 706B amalgamated with 845 (Wessex) NAS, which transferred from *Albion*. From April onwards she provided support for Commonwealth operations ashore in Borneo. Half of 845 NAS operated ashore in bases constructed at Sibu, Nanga Gaat and Simanggang, earning it the Boyd Trophy for 1964. In March 1965 she took part in Exercise *Fotex* 65, one of the largest Commonwealth naval exercises, which included ships from the RN, RAN, RNZN and R Malaysian N with *Victorious*, *Eagle* and *Melbourne* providing the strike element. A visit to Western Australia followed before she returned to the UK for a refit in September 1965. She recommissioned in April 1966, and in June carried out successful trials with a prototype Hawker P.1127 short-take-off-and-vertical-landing (Stovl) fighter integrated with helicopter operations, but the type was not, then, selected for production. Later in the moth she took part in Exercise *Dry Fly* on the west coast of Scotland with 845 (Wessex) NAS and 42 RM Commando embarked, and in August she sailed for the FEF, relieving *Albion* south of the Suez Canal. Confrontation between Indonesia and Malaysia ended in October 1966 and she withdrew the 845 NAS detachments from Borneo and then took part in Exercise *Barrawinga* on the Queensland cost of Australia.

In June 1967 *Bulwark* and *Fearless* carried out a demonstration landing of 3 RM Commando brigade at Kuantan in eastern Malaysia, and in October she was recommissioned in Singapore with a new ship's company flown out from the UK. She finally returned to the UK in March 1968, via South Africa because the Suez Canal had been blocked during the 1967 Middle East War. In June she took part in Exercise *Polar Express* to demonstrate the UK's capability to reinforce NATO's northern flank, and then commenced a refit in August 1968, during which the ship's company was accommodated in *Centaur*. After recommissioning she sailed for the Mediterranean with 845 (Wessex) NAS and 41 RM Commando embarked to take part in Exercises *Grecian Vase* and *Olympic Express*. After a period back in UK waters she rejoined the FEF in January 1970 with 848 (Wessex) NAS embarked to take part, during June 1970, in Exercise *Bersatu Padu*, which involved over fifty warships, 200 aircraft and 20,000 men from Australia, New Zealand, Malaysia, Singapore and the UK; 40 RM Commando was landed from *Bulwark* at Penarek. When it was over she sailed for the UK via Djakarta, Fremantle, Durban and Gibraltar, and started a refit in August 1970.

In May 1971 she embarked 845 (Wessex) NAS and sailed for Stockholm and Helsinki, flying the flag of the C-in-C WF, before taking part in Exercise *Dry Fly III* in Loch Fyne during June. Later in the month she moved to the Mediterranean for NATO Exercise *Deep Furrow 71* in Turkish Thrace, together with amphibious units from the USA, Turkey and Italy. In November, during a visit to Trieste, a serious fire damaged 'B' boiler room and she had to return to Devonport for repairs.

In January 1972 she sailed for Malta to act the HQ ship for Operation *Exit*, the planned withdrawal of British forces. She subsequently spent two-and-a-half months moored in Grand Harbour, during which time a detachment of 845 NAS carried out over 1,000 deck landings. Negotiations between the British and Maltese Governments succeeded at the last moment, however, and British forces continued to use Malta as a base for a further seven years. In March *Bulwark* deployed to the Caribbean with 845 NAS and 41 RM Commando embarked for Exercise *Rum Punch* in the USMC training area on Vieques Island, east of Puerto Rico. After its completion, 41 RM Commando was landed to be based in Malta and 845 NAS transferred to *Albion*. In July 1972 she took part in Exercise *Westward Ho*, and in September deployed to the Mediterranean with 848 (Wessex) NAS and 42 RM Commando embarked for exercises. In early 1973 she sailed for the USA with 848 NAS and 40 RM Commando embarked. In February 1973 she visited Charleston, South Carolina, flying the flag of FOCAS, becoming the largest warship to sail under the Cooper Bridge. After the visit she took part in Exercise *Rum Punch 73* on Vieques Island. In April she deployed to the Mediterranean and embarked 41 RM Commando from Malta for exercises in Cyprus. On completion of these she returned to the UK, having landed the Commando in Malta, then disembarked 848 NAS and embarked 814 and 820 (Sea King) NAS before sailing for antisubmarine exercises with the USN inside the Arctic Circle. In July 1973 she took part in exercise *Sally Forth 73* in the Firth of Forth, a combined RN/RAF demonstration of versatility to UK Government Ministers and the Military Committee of NATO. This eventful year continued with Exercise *Deep Furrow 73* in the Mediterranean during September, with 848 NAS and 42 RM Commando embarked; it involved fifty-four warships and 50,000 marines and soldiers from the UK, USA, Greece, Turkey and Italy.

A deployment to the Caribbean followed in January 1974. *Bulwark* deployed to the Caribbean with 848 NAS and a force of Dutch Marines embarked, landing them in Curacao for exercises. She became the largest warship to visit Cartagena in Colombia. In February 1974 she took part in Exercise *Caribtrain*, a gathering of fourteen RN warships off Virgin Gorda Island. Both the First Sea Lord and C-in-C Fleet were embarked. She

returned to Devonport Dockyard in March for a refit which lasted until February 1975. After working-up she deployed to the Mediterranean with 848 NAS and 41 RM Commando embarked for exercises with the US Sixth Fleet. In June she took part in Exercise *Dawn Patrol* with 1 Amphibious Combat group of the Dutch Marine Corps embarked, and in September she took part in Exercise *Deep Express 75* in Turkish Thrace. On completion she visited Istanbul in company with *Hermes*. After returning to the UK she took part in Exercise *Triple Jubilee* during November 1975, in which a NATO amphibious force in the English Channel supported UK, US and Dutch marines operating in the Dartmoor, Lulworth and Salisbury Plain battle-training areas. In January 1976 *Bulwark* embarked 848 NAS, 40 RM Commando, the Dutch 1 ACG and the band of the Royal Green Jackets and sailed for the Caribbean again for exercises in Curacao, Puerto Rico and the Bahamas.

In April 1976 she made a ceremonial return to Portsmouth, after which she was reduced to reserve status in Portsmouth with a ship's company of about 200 to maintain equipment. However, when *Ark Royal* paid off in 1978 none of the new *Invincible* Class was complete and *Bulwark* was refitted for further service. She recommissioned on 23 February 1979 in the presence of HRH the Prince of Wales, and then worked-up with 846 (Sea King Commando) and 826 (Sea King ASW) NAS embarked for use in both the commando and antisubmarine support roles. In June 1979 she took part in Exercise *Whiskey Venture* in the Baltic, with 820 (Sea King ASW) NAS added temporarily to the other squadrons. She deployed to the Mediterranean in September for exercises with the Cyprus garrison, and in January 1980 she deployed to the USA with 814, 820 (Sea King ASW) and a detachment of 846 (Sea King Commando) NAS embarked. At the time she was the only aircraft carrier in operational service in the RN. In February 1980 she took part in Exercise *Safe Pass*, an antisubmarine training period with the USN off the US Atlantic coast. In March, however, an accidental fire destroyed A1 boiler room and she had to return to Portsmouth for restorative work, although the boiler room was not repaired and lower speed was accepted. In April 1980 she deployed to the Mediterranean with 846 NAS and 45 RM Commando embarked for NATO exercise *Dawn Patrol* off Sardinia, after which she returned to the UK for a maintenance period. In August she took part in NATO Exercise *Teamwork 80*, an antisubmarine training period in the North Atlantic, after landing 40 RM Commando non-tactically in Norway for exercises ashore.

After her return to Portsmouth a major fire damaged the forward part of the hangar and several messdecks while she was alongside. Concerns about her obviously poor material state, especially with regard to wiring, led to her withdrawal from service six months earlier than planned, and cancellation of a visit to the USA. She did, however, take part in Exercise *Cold Winter 81* off the Norwegian coast in early 1981, with 846 NAS and 42 RM Commando embarked. She entered Portsmouth for the last time on 27 March 1981 and was paid off and destored for disposal. While lying empty she was used by RM commandos to practice demolition techniques, which caused further deterioration in the state of the hull and machinery, but in May 1982 consideration was given to fitting her out as an aircraft maintenance carrier for service in the South Atlantic War, towing her if necessary to the area of operations. It was soon obvious, however, that her poor material state and the fact that RN Aircraft Repair Yards ashore would need to be stripped of equipment to outfit her, thus causing a wider problem, made the idea completely impractical, and the plan was not taken forward. She was sold for scrap in 1984 and towed out of Portsmouth in April for Cairnryan, where she was subsequently broken up.

Elephant (renamed, launched and operated as Hermes)

Ordered from Vickers-Armstrongs' Barrow-in-Furness shipyard on 12 July 1943 and named *Elephant* after Nelson's flagship at the Battle of Copenhagen in 1801, she was allocated Admiralty Job Number J 3295 and the builder's yard number 928. One of the four ships of the class authorised for construction in 1943, she was laid down on 21 June 1944. After the cancellation of the lead ship of the class, however, she was renamed *Hermes* on 5 November 1945 to perpetuate the famous name. She was subsequently reconstructed before launch and built to an entirely different design; her history will be found in Chapter 28.

Arrogant

The name *Arrogant* was given to Admiralty Job Number J 4973, ordered from Swan Hunter's Wallsend-on-Tyne shipyard on 12 July 1943. She

was given the builder's Yard Number 1723 but her construction was deferred in late 1943. No work seems to have been done towards her construction and she was never laid down, eventually being cancelled on 15 October 1945.

Monmouth

Admiralty Job Number J 11721 was ordered from the Fairfield Shipbuilding & Engineering Company of Govan, Glasgow, on 12 July 1943. She was allocated builder's Yard Number 721 and was one of four ships of the class that the Admiralty gave instructions to proceed with in late 1943, but the pressure of other orders, especially for landing craft, prevented Fairfield from laying the ship down. No work had been done by the end of 1944 and in the spring of 1945 the Admiralty decided to instruct Harland & Wolff to take *Bulwark* forward instead. *Monmouth* was formally cancelled on 15 October 1945 without any work having been done on her.

Polyphemus

An eighth ship of the class, to be named *Polyphemus*, was ordered from Devonport Dockyard on 11 August 1943. As a dockyard project she was allocated the Dockyard Number D 1226 and had no yard Number. The intention was to lay her down as soon as *Terrible* was launched, but the Admiralty decided to defer her construction in late 1943, although the machinery had already been ordered from Parsons Marine Engineering. (Interestingly, the slipway needed to be lengthened slightly for her, and the Admiralty compulsorily purchased Fore Street in Devonport to extend it. The street was walled in but never used before being handed back to the City of Plymouth in 2005. It was found to be a 'time capsule' of banks, shops and offices as they were in 1943, and generated considerable historic interest.) The contract was formally cancelled on 15 October 1945, by which time the machinery contract had also been cancelled.

Centaur leaves Portsmouth in her final configuration during 1963, with Type 965 radar mounted on a new foremast. The carrier in the background is HMCS *Bonaventure*. (AUTHOR'S COLLECTION)

CHAPTER 26

BRITISH CARRIERBORNE AIRCRAFT AND THEIR OPERATION

A Gannet AEW.3 launches from *Victorious'* starboard catapult. (AUTHOR'S COLLECTION)

The first operational aircraft to land on a British aircraft carrier was a Beardmore-built Sopwith Pup, which had a maximum launch weight of 1,225lb and carried 24gal of petrol for its single 80hp Le Rhône rotary piston engine. The last 'conventional' fighter to operate from a British carrier deck was the supersonic McDonnell Douglas Phantom, which had a maximum launch weight of 56,000lb, two Rolls-Royce Spey turbofans each delivering 20,515lb thrust with reheat, and an internal fuel capacity of 2,000gal of avcat which could be supplemented by external drop tanks. It was succeeded by the longest-serving RN carrierborne fighter, the 'unconventional' Stovl British Aerospace Sea Harrier, which had a maximum weight of 26,200lb and was powered by a single Bristol/Rolls-Royce Pegasus turbofan delivering 21,500lb thrust and had an internal fuel capacity of 660gal of avcat. The Pegasus's swivelling nozzles and the aircraft's 'puffer jet' controls allowed it to hover, once weight had been reduced below engine thrust, and then land vertically like a helicopter on to a carrier deck. Between these

extremes, there were a considerable number of variations in the first century of British carrier operations, but it would be a fair generalisation to say that before 1942 the design of the available carriers strongly influenced aircraft design. It would be fair to say that, after the Joint Technical Committee's relaxation of future aircraft parameters in 1942, larger and more capable aircraft designs became the strongest influence on the design of aircraft carriers, the differences between the 1942 and 1943 light fleet carriers being the most obvious examples of the change.

The first generation of shipborne aircraft required very little deck run to become airborne, and could even take off from short platforms fitted on to the gun turrets of battleships. Their very lightness was a deck-handling problem, however, and the fore-and-aft retaining wires fitted in the early carriers were intended to hold aircraft on deck after landing, rather than arrest their forward movement. Wing loadings were so low that they 'fluttered' like kites when the pilot stepped out, and had to be held firmly or lashed to ring bolts let into the deck until struck down into the

hangar. Fortunately aircraft weights increased rapidly, solving this particular problem, although even in the twenty-first century aircraft have to be lashed down because of ship movement, and delicate items such as helicopter rotor blades have to be firmly secured so that they are not damaged by gusts of wind. Before 1927 aircraft had no brakes, and had to be positioned for take-off by handling parties, since pilots could not taxi accurately out of a range into position. Take-off runs were longer because a certain amount of momentum was lost before the engine could be run up to full power when the handlers removed the chocks once the aircraft was on the centreline. Early rotary engines tended to overheat without airflow through them, and start-up was only practical once the ship was into wind. Sometimes engines simply refused to start. On the basis of flying trials carried out on the incomplete *Eagle* in 1920, the Admiralty decided that six was the

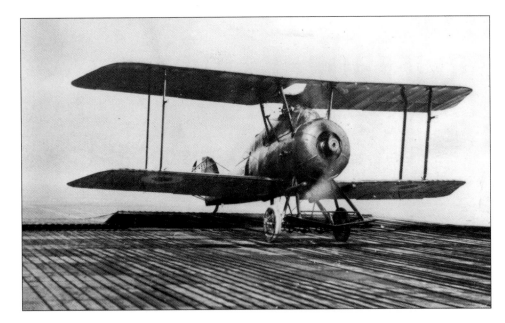

A Parnall Panther lands into the fore-and-aft retaining wires on *Argus* during 1919. (AUTHOR'S COLLECTION)

maximum number of aircraft that could be launched or recovered in a single evolution, and embarked air groups were made up with units which each consisted of six aircraft, until the present system of larger squadrons was introduced in 1933. Aircraft brakes made a big difference; they could be used to shorten the deck run on landing but, more importantly, they allowed pilots better control of their aircraft when taxying. Aircraft ranges could be more densely packed with three abreast in 'herring-bone' fashion; pilots could

be marshalled to taxi forward accurately on to the centreline and run-up to full power before releasing their brakes, shortening the deck run and checking the engine performance before being committed to launch. Ranges could be much larger than six in the same ships, the forward end of the range being dictated by the minimum deck run needed by the first aircraft to get safely airborne. Most important of all, they allowed the unpopular retaining gear to be removed.

In 1924 *Argus* carried out 108 deck landings,

of which thirty-three resulted in accidents, most of which were minor. A year later, after the Trenchard/Keyes agreement led to the majority of pilots being naval officers, carriers carried out a total of 1,457 deck landings, of which 802 were for training, but the accident rate fell to only 6 per cent. In 1929 the carrier force carried out a total of 5,372 deck landings, of which only 237 were for training, and the accident rate fell to 0.6 per cent.

Monoplanes needed a longer deck run for free take-off, but it could still be kept within manageable limits by turning the carrier into wind and increasing speed to create sufficient 'wind over deck' (WOD). The Fairey Fulmar, for instance, needed a roll of 420ft in nil-wind conditions, but this was reduced to 260ft with a WOD of 25 knots. By the 1940s the number of aircraft in the range could be increased if the first aircraft were catapulted. After 1945 turbojet-powered aircraft needed far greater deck runs to achieve a free take-off, and catapult launches became the normal method. Heavily loaded strike aircraft needed longer runs to take off. A Fairey Swordfish fitted with a torpedo needed a roll of 540ft to get airborne in still air, reducing to 345ft with 25

Fairey Flycatchers over *Furious*. This was one of the few aircraft types able to launch from the small flying-off deck. (AUTHOR'S COLLECTION)

A batsman in *Unicorn* gives the 'come on' signal. The square 'permission to land' signal below the range-finder 'bandstand' on the rear of the island is showing the 'affirmative' signal. (AUTHOR'S COLLECTION)

knots WOD. The last generation of piston-engined strike aircraft, such as the Fairey Barracuda, Grumman Avenger and de Havilland Sea Mosquito, all needed a WOD of at least 20 knots to get airborne, and could not take off fully loaded in still-air conditions.

The first night deck landing in any navy took place on *Furious* on 6 May 1926, using a system of Admiralty-designed lights that threw a 'wash' of soft white light over the deck to give pilots visual cues similar to those they had by day. Amber lights indicated the deck edge. Lighting methods improved through the 1930s, and by 1940 the majority of pilots were skilled in night deck landing techniques. Acquiring and maintaining those skills took constant practice, however, and the percentage of night-qualified pilots dropped in the war years.

A report on USN progress with the *Langley* from the British Naval Attaché in Washington was received by the Admiralty in 1927. It spoke positively about the system of cross-deck wires attached to friction devices which were engaged by aircraft tailhooks lowered by a control in the pilot's cockpit. When the hook was lowered, an elastic stay held it down and prevented 'hook bounce' when the bill impacted the deck, making it more likely that it would pick up a wire. Work started

on producing a British equivalent, despite opposition from the RAF, which advised that arrested landings would impose undue stress on airframes, and trials on a prototype model, the Mark I, were carried out in *Courageous* in 1931. The more effective Mark III arresting gear replaced it in 1933, and was subsequently fitted in all contemporary British carriers, making arrested landings a matter of routine. In 1932 the Admiralty proposed fitting a safety or 'crash' barrier in *Courageous* to allow faster aircraft

recoveries, since aircraft could taxi over it into a parking area forward, rather than having to be struck down into the hangar on the forward lift. In *Langley* the USN had found that the barrier, which could be raised after each landing to protect the aircraft parked forward, had reduced the interval between aircraft landings from five minutes to under one minute. Again the RAF objected, and it was not until 1938, as the Admiralty resumed full control of its own carrierborne flying after the Inskip Award, that first barrier was first fitted to a British carrier, *Ark Royal*. Its design differed from that used in the USN in that it relied on heavy stanchions which were raised from a flush position on the deck to hold the barrier in place when an aircraft engaged it. The 'give' in the wire was the only effective pull-out, stopping aircraft in about 40ft.

The change of organisation after the Inskip Award gave the RN a firmer grip on its own air arm and the means for making its own improvements in the deck operation of aircraft. The responsibility for doing so added greatly to the interest all naval officers took in matters that had been partly outside their control since the RNAS had been amalgamated into the RAF in 1918. The new administration brought with it new air stations, establishments and schools to address naval technical needs. These included units that taught operational flying techniques, torpedo attack, fleet fighter tactics, observers and telegraphist air gunners and deck-landing skills. These resulted in intense and specialised study by their staffs of many problems that had previously

The deck-landing mirror sight that replaced the batsman. (AUTHOR'S COLLECTION)

Left The deck-landing projector sight that replaced the mirror from 1960 onwards. (Author's collection)

Above De Havilland Vampire LZ551/G, the first jet aircraft to land on a carrier, lands on *Ocean* in December 1945. (Author's collection)

Below Supermarine Type 510 VV106 makes the first deck landing by a swept-wing jet aircraft. (Author's collection)

to obey. It was the DLCO's responsibility to get pilots safely on to the deck, having guided their approach from the turn on to finals and given the order to 'cut the throttle' at the right point over the arrester wires. His signals included the 'come on' with level arms, but raised arms meant 'go higher' when the approaching aircraft was low; lowered arms meant 'go lower' when the aircraft was high. A bat pulled swiftly across the chest meant 'cut the throttle', and bats waved over the head were an instruction to 'wave off', climb away and fly another circuit. The greatest crime was to arrive late for a briefed recovery time, but the second, of only marginally less significance, was to land against a 'wave-off' signal by the DLCO. Other signals could be used to indicate 'lined up left/right', 'hook not down', 'wheels not down', 'flaps not down' and other situations. A sailor, trained as 'talker', supported the DLCO; his job was to examine each aircraft turning finals through binoculars to check that aircraft were as they should be, calling 'Wheels down, flaps down, hook down' to the DLCO and pointing out any that failed to do so. He watched the aircraft right into the wires and called out which wire the hook caught, when the barrier went down, and when it was back up so that the next aircraft could land. 'Three wire, centre, barrier down' would be a typical call, followed by 'barrier up'. The DLCO would have his eyes fixed on the next aircraft thirty seconds away, and would rely on the 'talker' telling him the deck was ready or whether to order a 'wave-off'. Every landing was graded, and a second sailor was trained as a 'writer' to write down the DLCO's brief comments on a note-pad. Thus 'high in close' was written as HIC, 'lined up left' as LUL, and so on. The system of controlled landings was difficult to enforce at first among the small number of long-serving pilots who had extensive experience of landing-on without it, but its adoption as part of the pilot training syllabus for the large number of new pilots joining the RN and its reserves resulted in an immediate and noticeable improvement in deck-landing technique, and a marked drop in the number of accidents. The DLCO was able to contribute positively to improving the design of naval aircraft to make them safer to deck-land within the competency of the average pilot.

Some general aircraft developments were of particular importance to carrierborne aircraft, with their requirement for low landing speeds and short take-off runs. The first was the 'slat' patented by Frederick Handley Page in 1919. This comprised a small retractable aerofoil section fitted on the leading edge of a wing. When deployed, it moved out a small distance from the wing to create a small gap, through which smoothed airflow passed over the upper surface of the wing to prevent it from stalling at high angles of attack and at slow speeds.

gone almost untouched in the days of divided control. They were not modifications of RAF doctrine applied *ad hoc*, but a professional treatment of naval problems that required naval solutions. The opening of the deck-landing training school coincided with the introduction of monoplanes into naval service and Admiralty realisation of how far RN techniques had lagged behind those employed by the USN.

The system was introduced by the Admiralty from 1937, and differed from that in use in the USN, which used hand signals from which pilots 'took advice' and remained responsible for their own landings. Under the USN system the batsman's arms held level meant 'approach fine, come on'; arms raised indicated 'you are high', and arms lowered indicated 'you are low'. Under the new RN system, experienced pilots acting as deck-landing control officers (DLCOs or 'batsmen') gave mandatory orders which the approaching pilot had

By the 1930s a number of aircraft, including the Fairey Swordfish, were fitted with slats which activated automatically when airflow over the wing reduced pressure on the wing leading edge, allowing small springs to deploy the slats. A cockpit control allowed the pilot to lock them when combat manoeuvres might cause unwanted asymmetric extension.

Another important development was the trailing-edge flap, which came into general use in the late 1930s with the introduction of monoplanes, with their thinner wings. These are deployable surfaces on wing trailing edges that reduce the stalling speed of a wing when they are extended by increasing its camber and, therefore, the wing's maximum lift coefficient. They also increase the drag coefficient because they alter the planform of the wing when extended, causing greater induced drag and, in some cases, increasing the wetted area of the wing to increase parasitic drag. Flaps can be selected to give high lift with minimal extra drag for take-off, and high lift with more drag for landing. The introduction of flaps on monoplanes led to the adoption of a powered final approach in place of the earlier glide technique. This required the naval pilot to slow down to a few knots above the stall when downwind abeam the ship. Full flap was selected before starting the final turn on to the approach, after which the aircraft was flown in a 'three-point' attitude just above stalling speed. Height was controlled by varying the throttle, using more power to reduce the rate of descent when below the ideal glideslope and less power when high. Speed was controlled by using the elevator to make fine adjustments, nose down for more speed, nose up for less.

Unlike aircraft operations from an airfield ashore, landing and take-off from a carrier are only possible when the ship has turned into wind to give the required WOD for the weight of the aircraft recovering and arrester wire capability. All aircraft would be given a briefed recovery time, known as a 'C' or 'Charlie' time, and would orbit the ship until it was into wind ready to recover them; shown by flag 'F' being prominently displayed. Once the ship was steady into wind all aircraft would join the circuit to land-on in the shortest time, and the ship would already be turning out of wind as the last aircraft taxied out of the wires into the parking area.

The armoured carriers posed particularly severe restrictions on aircraft dimensions, as lift platforms could not be armoured and were designed to be small, since the lift wells constituted gaps in the horizontal protection. The Swordfish had a wingspan of 45ft 5in when spread, but this reduced to 17ft 3in when folded. After the relaxation in aircraft dimensions the Sea Mosquito of 1945 had a spread wingspan of 54ft 2in and a folded span of 27ft 3in. The weights more than doubled from 9,250lb for the Swordfish to 21,000lb for the Sea Mosquito, and these changes required lift platforms to be made larger and capable of moving the heavier weights. Flight-deck armour became more a method of providing the strength to operate bigger and heavier aircraft, and by 1952 it was accepted that the provision of horizontal armour that could defeat all forms of attack was no longer a practical proposition.

Apart from needing more deck space and improved catapults and arrester gear, turbojet aircraft affected carrier design in a number of other, less obvious ways. The Supermarine Seafire LIIC

had an internal fuel capacity of 85gal and the Hawker Sea Fury 200gal, but the similarly-sized Hawker Sea Hawk had an internal capacity of 395gal, with a further 200gal in drop tanks. Ultimately, the Phantom had a capacity more than three times greater than that. Fortunately jet aircraft used avcat (aviation catoline spirit), which had a higher flashpoint than avgas and could be stowed in bulk tanks integral with the hull, like the ship's fuel oil. After 1945 the weight of carrierborne aircraft grew rapidly. The Sea Fury weighed 12,350lb; its successor the Sea Hawk 16,200lb; the Supermarine Scimitar that replaced it 40,000lb and, ultimately, the Phantom 56,000lb. The Sea Harrier reversed the trend in 1980 at a mere 26,200lb. Increased aircraft weight affected carrier design in many ways, the most obvious being the need for hangar and flight decks strong enough to take the heavier static loads. The flight deck had also to be able to absorb the impact of a burst tyre or crash on deck, when an oleo or some other point loading of the aircraft mass would impact the deck in a small area. 'Jumbo', the salvage crane, and the ships other cranes would have to be capable of lifting aircraft, although in most cases the load could be lightened by disarming and/or defuelling the aircraft.

The increase in aircraft weight was not just caused by the larger quantity fuel required for adequate endurance with the new jet engines, but also by the increasing amount of equipment needed for aircraft to conduct strike warfare at long ranges with sophisticated weapons. Radar, guided

Sea Hawks starting up together in *Eagle*; the smoke is the exhaust from their cartridge starter units. (AUTHOR'S COLLECTION)

A Buccaneer with its air brakes open turns on to final approach astern of *Eagle*. It is to starboard of the wake but lined up with the angled deck. (AUTHOR'S COLLECTION)

specified role of reaching targets at long range, high speed and low level. They were not, however, powerful enough to give a short take-off, and the Buccaneer had to be catapulted from a carrier deck. Its specification was the first to be issued by the RN that did not call for the aircraft to be capable of a free take-off from the deck, and when disembarked ashore the Buccaneer S1 required a long runway to get airborne. The size of the wing was kept relatively small and the landing speed was kept within practical limits by the use of boundary layer control, which used bleed-air from the engines to blow a smooth airflow over the wings, flaps and tailplane to reduce the aircraft's stalling speed. It had to be accepted that recovery performance with one engine out, for whatever reason, and the other having to provide thrust as well as all the bleed air for the boundary-layer system, was marginal at best. Overshooting after a baulked approach, or 'bolting', as it was known, would not have been possible, and without a diversion airfield ashore, S1s landed into a nylon safety barrier rigged across the deck after a single engine failure. The Buccaneer S2 had two Rolls-Royce Spey turbofans which delivered a combined 22,000lb of thrust with even better specific fuel consumption, and a far better single-engine performance. Buccaneers had distinctive 'clamshell' airbrakes at the rear of the fuselage. These were opened for landing, allowing the throttles to remain at a high power setting so that sufficient bleed-air could reach the boundary-layer system without causing the aircraft speed to increase. In the event of a 'bolter' the aircraft climbed away initially by closing the air brakes rather than opening the throttles. The brakes were kept open on deck and in the hangar, as this significantly reduced the aircraft's length.

The Scimitar and Sea Vixen were capable of operations at high speed over great distances, and needed new tactics that were the focus of an air warfare weapons system. This, too, affected carrier design and required a command, control and communications (C3) system capable of interfacing with the aircraft to achieve the optimum strike effect. The Comprehensive Display System (CDS) fitted in *Victorious*, *Hermes* and *Eagle* was the most sophisticated example of an air warfare control environment in the pre-computer age. It included the three-dimensional Type 984 radar and advanced displays in a large two-tier acoustic data recorder (ADR) and operations room built into the island aft of the compass platform and Admiral's bridge. The Sea Vixen was the first British fighter to be designed as part of a weapons system, and the

missiles, electronic countermeasures and the need for a second crewmember in fighters all had an impact. Sustained operation at low level led to the Blackburn Buccaneer having a greater structure weight than previous naval aircraft, and longer aircraft lives also led to far heavier structures than the lightweight aircraft of the 1940s and early 1950s. In turn, the increasingly sophisticated avionics fitted in naval aircraft required specialised workshops and sailors to man them. With the introduction of the de Havilland Firestreak AAM, first carried by the de Havilland Sea Venom in *Victorious* in 1958, the ship's air department had to

be capable of supporting weapons that were as sophisticated as the aircraft that carried them. The modernised *Victorious* was also the first RN warship to deploy with nuclear weapons; the *Red Beard* tactical bomb that could be carried by the Scimitar and Sea Vixen. The Buccaneer was one of the most sophisticated aircraft designed for the RN and operated from its carrier decks. The S1 version achieved a low-level radius of action of over 500 miles with two de Havilland Gyron Junior turbojet engines which gave a combined total of 14,000lb thrust with very low specific fuel consumption, just enough to achieve the aircraft's

A drawing of the SR-177RN. The rocket motor was mounted over the single reheated turbojet engine. (AUTHOR'S COLLECTION)

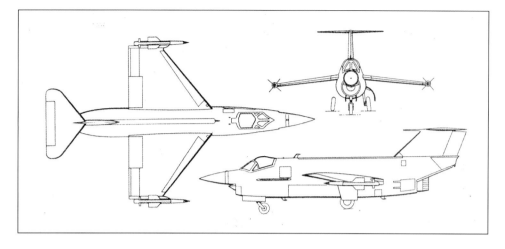

Fairey Gannet AEW 3 could data-link airborne radar information to the ADR, as well providing autonomous control for fighters and strike aircraft on missions. A number of ultra-high-frequency (UHF) radio circuits allowed communication with aircraft in the vicinity of the task force, and HF radio enabled long-range communication with strike aircraft. To allow operation in most weather conditions by day and at night, carriers were fitted with Type 963 carrier-controlled approach radar and carried a dedicated team of air traffic control officers to co-ordinate movements.

As strike warfare grew in sophistication, carriers were required to carry an increasingly complex array of weapons, including AAMs, nuclear weapons, homing torpedoes, and ASMs intended for attacks on both land and ship targets, with anti-radiation variants for use against hostile air defence environments. 'Dumb' bombs with a variety of fusing options had to be carried in large numbers and be available at short notice. These changes required bomb-rooms that had been designed to hold simple weapons in bulk to be modified to contain the new weapons and to allow the movement of their handling apparatus. Bomb lifts had also to be modified to cater for the new shapes and handling equipment. Nuclear weapons handling arrangements had to be fully understood and carefully rehearsed. The new weapons needed increased numbers of weapons supply and ordnance maintenance ratings, known colloquially as 'bomb-heads'. Preparations for a major strike could take some time, with the required weapons needing to be checked, brought up on deck, fused and prepared before being loaded on aircraft. The possibility of load changes had to be catered for by keeping a variety of prepared weapons on the flight deck near the aircraft parking areas. This could be dangerous if adequate safety measures were not followed.

Two roles that are now widely adopted were pioneered by the RN in the UK armed forces. The first airborne early warning (AEW) aircraft was the Douglas Skyraider AEW 1, the first of fifty being provided by the USN under MDAP arrangements in 1951. In USN service the aircraft flew with a pilot and two technicians who transmitted the picture from the aircraft's AN/APS-20 radar to the parent carrier and other warships by data-link. The RN retained the data-link but replaced the technicians with observers who were trained to direct fighters, strike aircraft and warships on to targets, evolving the AEW aircraft into a flying command and control station. The Skyraider was replaced in 1960 by the Fairey Gannet AEW 3, using a developed version of the same radar and a

similar crew. It was developed from the antisubmarine version and, like it, had an Armstrong-Siddeley Double Mamba turboprop engine, one section of which could be shut down in flight at any time to conserve fuel. Gannets were withdrawn from service in 1978 when *Ark Royal* was paid off, but the successful low-level attacks on the fleet by Argentine aircraft during the South Atlantic Conflict of 1982 showed the lack of AEW to be a tragic mistake. Sea King helicopters fitted with Searchwater radar were hastily converted and rushed into service; the derivative Sea King ASaC 7 is due to remain in RN service until 2016. In the early 1970s the RAF began to fit AN/APS-20 radars from stock held in reserve for the Gannets to Avro Shackletons, with the intention of replacing the naval aircraft once carriers were withdrawn from service after the 1966 Defence Review. The RAF found, instead, that AEW was of considerable value to its own operations, and subsequently procured the Boeing E-3 Sentry airborne warning and control system (AWACS).

The second new role was airborne refuelling or 'tanking'. Experiments had been undertaken with Sea Hawks using modified drop tanks and the 'probe and drogue' system, after the successful introduction of the capability by the USN. In this, the donor aircraft carries a pod with a small fuel tank of its own connected to the aircraft fuel system; a hose wound on to a drum is fitted at the rear of the pod, at the end of which is a 'drogue' or 'basket'. Power for the operation of the hose drum is provided by an alternator driven by a impeller at the front of the pod. The receiver aircraft has a probe, usually fitted to the forward part of the fuselage where the pilot can see it. In operation, the aircraft fly in close formation and the receiver pilot pushes his probe into the basket. When it is locked into position, fuel can flow from the tanker to the receiving aircraft. Care obviously had to be taken to leave sufficient fuel in the tanker to recover to its carrier with sufficient reserve for a bolter, but the system worked well. From 1958

Scimitars, Sea Vixens and Buccaneers were all fitted with what was known as the 'buddy' refuelling system manufactured by Flight Refuelling Ltd of Bournemouth in the UK. Tankers could be used to extend strike operations, to prolong fighters on their CAP stations, or as an emergency source of fuel for waiting aircraft if the flight deck became temporarily blocked by a crash on deck or similar emergency. Tankers could be held, manned, at short-notice standby on deck or launched to give an even quicker response during recoveries, especially at night or in bad weather. Several aircraft in every squadron had the plumbing fitted to act as tankers when necessary, but a specialised tanker unit, 800B NAS, was operated from *Eagle* between 1964 and 1966 to support the Buccaneer S1s of 800 NAS. The launch performance of the S1s was improved by catapulting them with a low fuel state and tanking them full once airborne. In the tanker role a Scimitar carried a total of 1,765gal of avcat in internal tanks, three 200gal drop tanks and the 'buddy' refuelling pod. Royal Air Force Vickers Valiant bombers, modified to act as tankers, entered service after 1960.

Two aircraft types that did not enter service would have had a great impact on carrier design had they done so, and the preparations carried out for them are unique to the RN. The first was the Supermarine Type 508, which first flew in 1951 but was never given a name. It was intended to land without an undercarriage on to an inflatable rubber 'mat' over the landing area of a carrier flight deck. After landing it would be lifted on to a trolley so that it could be handled and launched by a steam catapult. The concept was actually tested using specially-built de Havilland Sea Vampire F.21 fighters, which had airframes strengthened to allow them to land with their wheels retracted on a mat fitted to *Warrior* in trials from 1948. While the idea actually worked, it proved far too slow to be practical, since it took about five minutes for a crane to lift a single fighter off the mat on to a

trolley, compared with intervals of under a minute for conventional fighters to land into arrester wires and taxi clear. There were also unanswered questions of how to land undercarriageless fighters away from RN carriers or specially fitted air stations, and how to land propeller-driven aircraft, helicopters and even jets fitted with underwing weapons and drop tanks on to rubber-'mat'-fitted flight decks. The idea had originated because the first generation of jet engines had poor acceleration, making them difficult to operate in the carrier circuit. The problem was solved by the rapid development of jet engines, which behaved perfectly well in the second generation. The Type 508 was designed with an undercarriage for trials purposes and eventually metamorphosed into the Types 525, 529 and 544, to enter service in 1958 as the Scimitar.

The second design was the Saunders-Roe P-177, a fighter designed with a de Havilland Gyron Junior turbojet of 7,100lb thrust and a de Havilland Spectre 5A rocket engine of 8,000lb thrust. The idea was to use the jet for high-speed cruise and the fully-controllable rocket for take-off, climb and high-altitude acceleration. The rocket would have used high-test hydrogen peroxide (HTP) as an oxidant, with avcat injected into the expanding gases to increase the thrust. An earlier Saunders-Roe design, the SR.53, demonstrated the feasibility of the concept with less powerful engines in 1957/58, and achieved an electrifying performance above 35,000ft that has never been equalled by an aircraft designed in Britain. The developed P-177 was designed with an air intercept radar and a specified armament of *Red Top* AAMs on wingtip rails, plus underwing pylons for more *Red Tops*, air-to-ground missiles, bombs or drop tanks. It was designed to be a common aircraft for service with the RAF as well

as the RN, and twenty-seven prototypes were ordered in September 1956. These comprised nine basic development airframes, nine for RAF development and nine for RN development. The design produced greater commonality than the American General Dynamics F-111 and British Hawker P.1154 joint projects of the 1960s and the twenty-first-century Lockheed Martin F-35 Lightning II joint strike fighter. At a time when the Sea Hawk was still the RN's principal fighter, the P-177 was designed to be capable of climbing from a catapult launch to 50,000ft in a little over two minutes and accelerating from Mach 0.9 to Mach 1.4 while turning in a further half minute. An alternative version with a single, larger reheated turbojet and HTP tanks modified to contain avcat was considered, and Germany had entered negotiations to procure the type for the Luftwaffe. Unfortunately the P-177 was cancelled in 1958 after the notorious 1957 Defence Review's assumption that there was no further need for manned fighter aircraft. The Germans decided that there was, and bought the American-designed Lockheed F-104 Starfighter.

In 1957 work was being carried out to produce drawings for *Eagle*'s modernisation and, with the P-177 project progressing rapidly, work was done to design tanks for HTP stowage and to establish safe handling arrangements for the liquid, which is corrosive to human skin if touched. Specially lined tanks, pipes and pumps were worked on, together with safe methods of replenishment at sea. Rubber suits were designed for refuelling personnel. At least HTP had the merit that its decomposition produced steam and it was more likely to extinguish a fire than start it. One of the SR.53 development aircraft crashed on take-off at the Aeroplane and Armament Experimental Establishment (A&AEE) at Boscombe Down, and

An example of the tactical flexibility given by the 'buddy' air-to-air refuelling system. This Sea Vixen of 893 NAS from *Hermes* is refuelling two RAF Lightnings of 74 Squadron from Singapore, enabling them to take part in a Far East Fleet exercise in the South China Sea. (AUTHOR'S COLLECTION)

the resulting fire was extinguished by steam from the HTP.

Experiments with helicopters had begun during the Second World War, but regular detachments of the Westland Dragonfly HR.3 in aircraft carriers did not begin until the early 1950s, when they replaced the Supermarine Sea Otter amphibian for air/sea rescue duties. The RN used Sikorsky HRS-2 helicopters, designated Whirlwind HAR.21, ashore in Malaya from 1953 and evaluated the Sikorsky HO4S-3, designated the Whirlwind HAS.22, with its dipping sonar, in the antisubmarine role during 1954. Both types were provided by the USN under MDAP. The evaluation proved so successful that in October 1955 the Admiralty Board accepted that helicopters had become better antisubmarine aircraft than the fixed-wing Fairey Gannet, which was just entering front-line service. It was agreed that the Westland Whirlwind HAS.7, a licence-built version of the Sikorsky design, would be put into production as a gradual replacement of the Gannet although, surprisingly, the lightweight Short Seamew AS.1, intended for use from austere carriers for convoy protection, continued in development until 1957, when it was cancelled.

At first it was hoped to operate both fixed- and rotary-wing antisubmarine aircraft from support carriers, like the *Essex* Class CVS in the USN. However, the wartime carriers had by then been laid up in reserve and would have been too expensive to bring forward and operate; the 1942 light fleet carriers were thought to be coming to

The prototype Supermarine Type 508 carrying out flying trials in *Illustrious*. The developed version was originally intended to operate without an undercarriage. (AUTHOR'S COLLECTION)

the end of their practical lives, and it was decided to add antisubmarine helicopters to the air groups of strike carriers. This had the merit of providing the best antisubmarine defence for the carrier while it launched and recovered its strike aircraft, but failed to give the area capability provided by other nations' CVS air groups.

The disadvantage of this approach was that Whirlwind helicopters proved difficult to incorporate into deck operations alongside the fixed-wing launch and recovery cycle. Doubts that mixed air groups would be practical led the Admiralty to order a trial embarkation in *Bulwark* during 1958, in which she embarked an air group that included day and night fighters, AEW aircraft and antisubmarine helicopters. The trial proved

entirely successful, and for the next two decades antisubmarine helicopter units embarked in strike carriers. The commando carrier conversions allowed RN helicopter assault units to embark alongside Royal Marines Commandos. Since the 1960s the majority of warships and auxiliaries have been fitted with helicopter decks, some of the latter large enough to carry up to five helicopters on prolonged deployments. The Whirlwind was replaced by the larger and more capable, gas-turbine-powered Westland Wessex, which was, in turn, replaced by the AgustaWestland Sea King in the antisubmarine, assault, SAR and, ultimately, airborne surveillance and control roles. Powered by two Rolls-Royce Gnome engines, it weighed 21,400lb, had a rotor diameter of 62ft and gave

outstanding service in the RN from 1969 to a planned out-of-service date in 2016. It was replaced in the antisubmarine role, and eventually in the assault role, by the AgustaWestland Merlin HM.1 and its derivatives. These weigh 32,120lb, are powered by three Rolls-Royce Turbomeca RTM322 engines and have a rotor diameter of 61ft. Smaller helicopters such as the Westland Wasp and the AgustaWestland Lynx and Wildcat have been procured to operate from the decks of destroyers and frigates, but not from aircraft carriers.

CHAPTER 27

POST-1945 AIRCRAFT CARRIER DESIGNS THAT WERE NOT BUILT

The cancellation of *Malta* and *New Zealand* in December 1945 was seen by the Admiralty as a temporary setback caused by short-term financial constraints, but the long-term need for such ships was rightly considered essential and development work on fleet carriers continued. Experiments with undercarriageless fighters, the potential for vertical take-off and landing and the advent of turbojet and turboprop aircraft made it clear that radical changes to carrier design would be necessary to accommodate aircraft of increasing size and complexity. The wartime fleet carriers and some of the light fleet carriers could be modernised, but it was clear that they could never be as efficient as a new design. Surprisingly, in view of the delay caused to the *Malta* Class by insistence on an open-hangar design, the Admiralty now accepted DNC advice that future fleet carriers should be designed with enclosed hangars, although side lifts were considered to be a valuable new feature after studying American experience with the *Essex* Class in the Pacific.

Sketches of the radical 'flexible deck' and other novel features

In February 1952 a meeting was held in the Admiralty at which DNC and the Naval Air Department within the Royal Aircraft Establishment (RAE) were tasked to examine the possibilities for improving the aviation arrangements in a future carrier. Schemes including both the operation of conventional wheeled aircraft and 'undercarriageless' fighters were considered, with both straight and angled decks. In January 1953 the Director of Air Warfare (DAW) in the Admiralty proposed that the landing area should be angled by 7.5 degrees to starboard, with a small island on the port side aft. Funnels were to be situated below flight-deck level on the starboard side. This arrangement was believed to have the merit that, from a normal left-handed carrier circuit, an aircraft's final turn would be through only 170 degrees, rather than the 190 degrees when the deck is angled to port;

funnel smoke would be outboard and away from the aircraft's flight path on final approach. Assumptions made for the study were that flight-deck length was to be a maximum of 870ft; the wingspan of the largest aircraft embarked was to be 65ft; and that there were to be two side lifts and one on the centreline, and three steam catapults with 200ft stroke, at least one of which was always to be available for use, even when landing-on aircraft.

The studies went to considerable lengths to examine radical solutions that would make it possible to recover and launch aircraft concurrently. These produced some elegant solutions which have never, subsequently, been used by any navy. Among them was the idea of inclining the flight deck upwards slightly from the stern towards the bow, to help in bringing aircraft

The proposed small carrier design that was to be capable of conversion to operate Vtol aircraft. (AUTHOR'S COLLECTION)

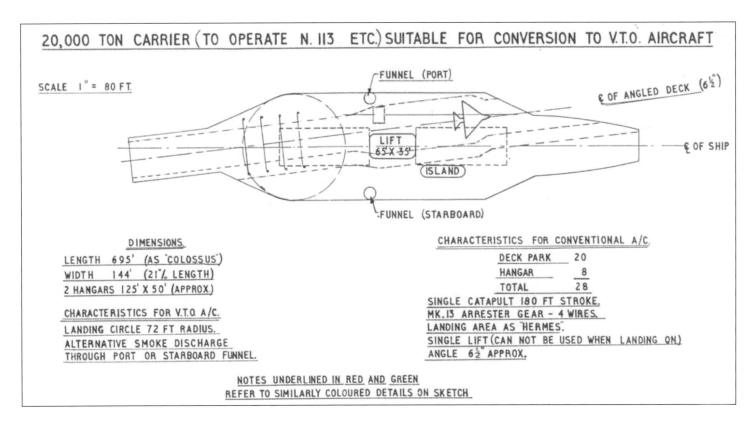

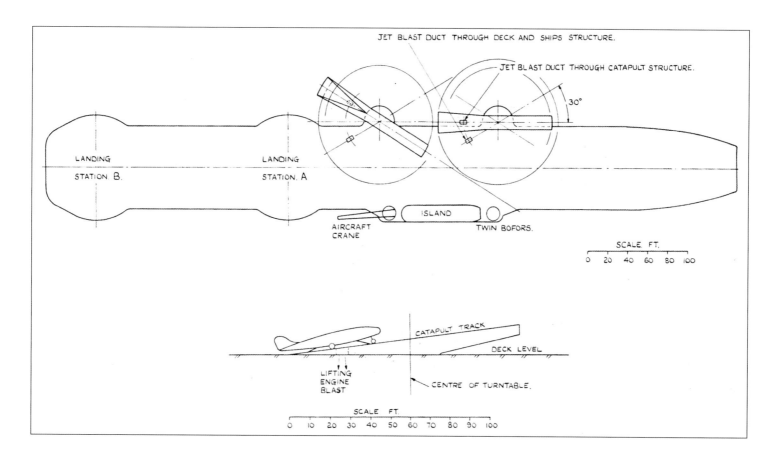

Proposed scheme for fitting rotatable steam catapults and vertical landing spots in *Warrior* for the operation of Vtol aircraft. (AUTHOR'S COLLECTION)

to a standstill while they were being arrested. More radically, they sought to separate launch and recovery operations by launching most aircraft from the hangar. This would have needed open hangar sides, but the noise would still have been horrific. The two hangar catapults were angled outwards slightly to keep aircraft separated during rapid launches and, most innovatively, they were mounted on a 5.5-degree upwards incline, giving many of the advantages of the later 'ski-jump'. On the other hand, maintenance in the after part of the hangar would have been impossible, and the blast effect on aircraft in the hangars would have been significant.

It should be borne in mind that these were not ship-design studies but concept drawings of operating possibilities for the flight deck and hangar. Most would have been completely impractical if they were ever translated into hardware, but they are no less fascinating for that.

The 1952 fleet carrier sketch design

During the late 1940s a number of sketch ship designs were prepared which incorporated the most practical of the new possibilities. The flexible

deck was eventually discarded, together with the schemes that had been considered in order to try to make it workable, but as new British ideas including the angled deck, originally referred to as the 'skew deck', matured they were incorporated. Originally a flight deck 1,000ft long was considered necessary to allow sufficient space for a deck park forward of the barrier, giving space aft of it for the extended arrester wire pull-out needed for the faster-landing jet fighters. The angled deck solved this problem and allowed shorter decks to be considered viable. None of the early sketches were taken forward, but during the period of British rearmament that followed the outbreak of the Korean War the Ship Design Policy Committee was tasked in June 1952 to define the characteristics that would be required in a new fleet carrier. By then it was realised the reconstruction of *Victorious* was proving difficult, and opinion was hardening that the funds that were available would be better spent on new ships than on the complicated reconstruction of the remaining ships of the *Illustrious* group. Steel was in short supply in 1952, and it was decided to scrap *Formidable* and a number of early *Hunt* Class destroyers immediately to provide a sufficient quantity to start one new carrier. Optimistically, a completion date of 1958 was aimed at because 1959 was widely believed to be the 'year of maximum danger', in which hostilities with the

Soviet Bloc would be most likely to break out. Although the physical features of the *Malta* design were not repeated, the same constraints rapidly emerged, as there was no money to build new dry docks and other support infrastructure. The Admiralty believed at the time that the best new carrier design was the smallest ship that would allow the effective operation of the largest or most heavily loaded naval aircraft. Effective operation, however, meant that aircraft needed to be carried in viable numbers to fulfil a number of tactical functions, so a design of at least *Malta* size was inevitable. The Admiralty considered strike warfare to be the critically important role, and the new ships were required from the outset to be capable of carrying large aircraft equipped with nuclear weapons for use against enemy warships and strategic targets ashore.

The USN was also concentrating on nuclear strike warfare, and the Admiralty followed the design of the huge *Forrestal* Class with keen interest. The American ships were intended to operate jet bomber designs of up to 70,000lb that evolved into the Douglas A-3 Skywarrior, at that time the largest aircraft ever designed for carrierborne operation, and the Admiralty had to consider the likelihood that in any major conflict the RN would have to absorb USN aircraft provided under the MDAP agreement, since the run-down British aircraft industry would be fully absorbed building

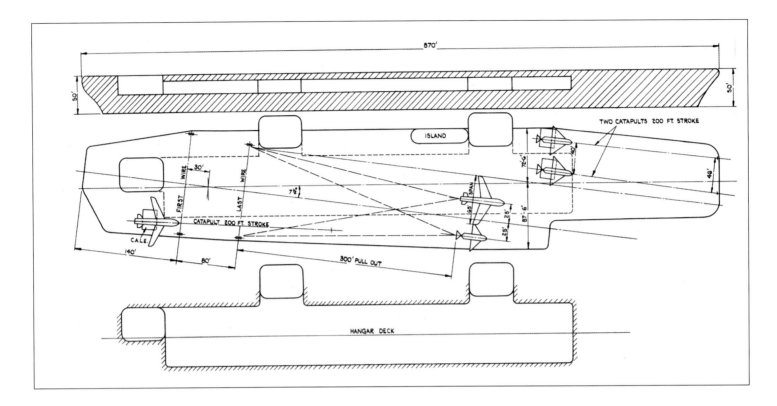

The following labels appear on the diagram: 870', 50', 50', ISLAND, TWO CATAPULTS 200 FT STROKE, 30', FIRST WIRE, LAST WIRE, 7½', 40', 75'6, 46', 65' SPAN, 25', 87'-6", 25', C.A.L.E., CATAPULT 200 FT STROKE, 140', 80', 300' PULL OUT, HANGAR DECK

aircraft for the RAF. This meant that the new British carrier under consideration had to be capable of carrying the same types of aircraft as the *Forrestal*, and of operating them efficiently in some numbers. The new RAF English Electric Canberra jet bomber was used a yardstick against which the ship design was compared. It had a maximum take-off weight of 50,000lb, a wingspan of 64ft, a length of 65ft and a height 15.5ft. It was not intended to develop a naval version of the Canberra but, rather, to note that this was the weight and shape that could be expected for any practical nuclear strike aircraft with a strategic capability. The actual staff requirement stated that the ship was to be capable of operating the A-3 Skywarrior at weights up to 70,000lb with steam catapult end-speeds up to 150 knots. The aircraft's height of just under 23ft was reduced by a folding fin, which would have allowed it to fit comfortably into the proposed hangar height of 22ft specified for the British design.

The single, enclosed hangar was initially required to have a total deck area of 55,000ft², similar to the *Ark Royal* or *Malta* designs and, with a deck park, the operation of an air group of about ninety aircraft would have been practical in 1958. Aviation fuel stowage was to be 250,000gal of avgas and 500,000gal of avcat, about one-third more than *Ark Royal* or the modernised *Eagle*, and comparable with the amount designed for *Forrestal*. A hull form based on that of the battleship *Vanguard* was evaluated in the Admiralty experimental tank at Haslar; it would

have given the required internal volume and a waterline length of 850ft was considered at first, but this would have meant that, in the UK, Number 10 Dock in Devonport and the Gladstone Dock in Liverpool would be the only dry docks that could handle the new ship. Docks in Gibraltar, Singapore and Sydney could take an even larger hull but were not ideal for primary technical support. Consequently the waterline length was reduced to 815ft to increase the number of usable docks, with considerable flight deck overhangs fore and aft, like the reconstructed *Victorious*. Width on the waterline was 116ft, with an overhang to port to support the angled deck which increased overall width to 160ft. The deep displacement was estimated at 53,150 tons. The Engineer-in-Chief's staff calculated that a four-shaft arrangement with 200,000shp could give the required 32 knots clean, and 30 knots six months out of dock in tropical waters. Advances in technology meant that the machinery would weigh roughly the same as the 152,000shp machinery in *Eagle*, about 3,600 tons, but the additional condensers, generators and air-conditioning plant required for the newer design would add another 200 tons. The boilers were to be capable of providing sufficient extra steam to provide a margin to operate three of the new steam catapults. The machinery arrangements were novel in that the inner shafts were driven by two units sited forward, with the engine rooms forward of the boiler rooms. A magazine separated the forward machinery units from two others sited

A 1953 concept design for an aircraft carrier capable of operating conventional wheeled aircraft and helicopters. The deck was angled to starboard rather than port to reduce the finals turn from a port, left-hand circuit from 190 to 170 degrees, making line-up with the deck potentially easier. The island is on the port side and there are two catapults forward and one on the starboard side aft. The hangar is open-sided with side-lifts to port. (AUTHOR'S COLLECTION)

further aft which drove the outer shafts. In their case the engine rooms were positioned aft of the boiler rooms. The vulnerable outer shafts were thus kept as short as possible, and the longer shafts inboard had the greatest amount of protection. In some sketches a second magazine was sited forward of the forward machinery; in others in was sited aft of the after machinery group with corresponding changes in the positions of the bomb lifts on the flight deck and in the hangar. The split machinery was intended to provide a redundancy of power in the event of underwater damage to either group, but led to exhaust smoke being trunked from each of the boiler room groups through funnels 150ft apart in separate islands on the starboard side, giving the design a distinctive and unusual appearance that was subsequently copied, for similar reasons, by the *Queen Elizabeth* Class sixty years later.

Each of the two islands was initially intended to be fitted with a type 984 radar, the two being arranged to rotate 'back-to-back' to provide a faster data rate, but, as in the ships that were built or converted with this radar, weight constraints would have limited the number of aerials to one, sited forward over the bridge to be clear of funnel smoke. They would also have had fire control, and navigation and carrier controlled approach radars that were technically superior to some of the radars fitted in contemporary USN carriers, but a USN-supplied tactical air navigation (Tacan) beacon was supplied to provide accurate aircraft homing in place of the earlier 'YE' beacon equipment. Early sketches included eight Mark 6 twin 3in 70-calibre gun mountings, still very much under development at the time, sited quadrantally like the 4.5in mountings in the *Illustrious* group, *Eagle* and *Ark Royal*. These complicated mountings were expected to fire 120 rounds per minute through their watercooled barrels, and were eventually fitted in the trials cruiser *Cumberland* and the *Tiger* Class cruisers, but they were to prove difficult and unreliable weapons in service.

Four design sketches were produced, identified as A, B, C and D, all of them with 2in armoured flight decks. Designs B and D, the preferred options, differed mainly in the positioning of lifts: B had a side lift at the forward end of the angled deck sponson on the port side and another slightly further aft just forward of the forward island on the starboard side; D had a side lift aft of the after island and a centreline lift aft of the two bow catapults, the arrangement that was used a decade later for CVA-01. A disadvantage of B was that, with both lifts forward, a number of aircraft would have to be ranged and then replaced to extract a serviceable aircraft that was parked in the after end

of the hangar with unserviceable aircraft forward of it. The arrangement in D would have been more flexible, allowing more straightforward access to larger areas of the hangar. It also enabled the third steam catapult on the angled deck sponson to be sited further forward, so that more aircraft could be ranged aft of it for a large launch. The full 8-degree angled deck would have allowed a large strike to be parked after landing-on in Fly 1, the forward deck park, Fly 2 abeam the island, and Fly 3 aft of the island while aircraft where still landing-on. In D both lifts could be used to strike aircraft down into the hangar while the recovery continued, another advantage over B, in which the port side lift could not be used if aircraft were recovering.

After the initial sketch designs were presented to the Admiralty Board in September 1952 a number of problems were found to complicate further progress. The DNC's design staff was pressured by a number of projects, and had insufficient people to take them all forward to the design drawing stage. Industrially only three yards, John Brown, Cammell Laird and Harland &Wolff, had slipways big enough for the proposed ships; none was immediately available and none had sufficient electricians or welders to meet the required build time. The proposed Y300 machinery was not yet fully developed and could not be ready before 1958; nor would the 3in gun mountings. The proposed carrier never reached the stage of having a name allocated, and it is generally referred to as the '1952 fleet aircraft carrier', two

of which were in the long-term programme. Despite the recognition of these shortcomings, work continued to refine the design, broadly reflecting realism. Maximum aircraft launch weight was reduced to 60,000lb, allowing a significant reduction in the strength and, therefore, weight of the structure needed to support the flight deck. Weight was also saved by reducing the hangar height to the standard 17ft 6in, and accepting that the larger American aircraft could not be operated at their maximum all-up weight. The armament of twin 3in/70-calibre mountings was reduced from eight to six, and the two turrets furthest forward were deleted, although four were retained in the two groups aft. In addition to the flight deck, the hangar deck and sides were to have 2in non-cemented armour, and 3.5in armoured 'boxes' around the magazines and steering gear were proposed. The machinery relied on its dispersion for protection, and the hull would have been extensively compartmentalised with 'sandwich' anti-torpedo protection at the sides. The other major change was the removal of one of the steam catapults, leaving one of 150ft stroke on the starboard side of Fly 1, intended to launch aircraft ranged to starboard aft, and one of 200ft

An alternative 1953 concept design for an aircraft carrier with a starboard angle as shown in the previous drawing but fitted with a 'rubber deck' capable of recovering fighters without undercarriages. Note the transverse platform intended to move aircraft away from where they came to rest on the mat on to the side lift. (AUTHOR'S COLLECTION)

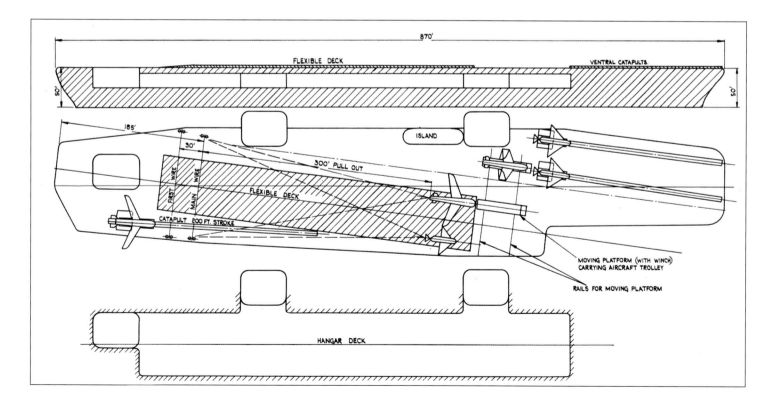

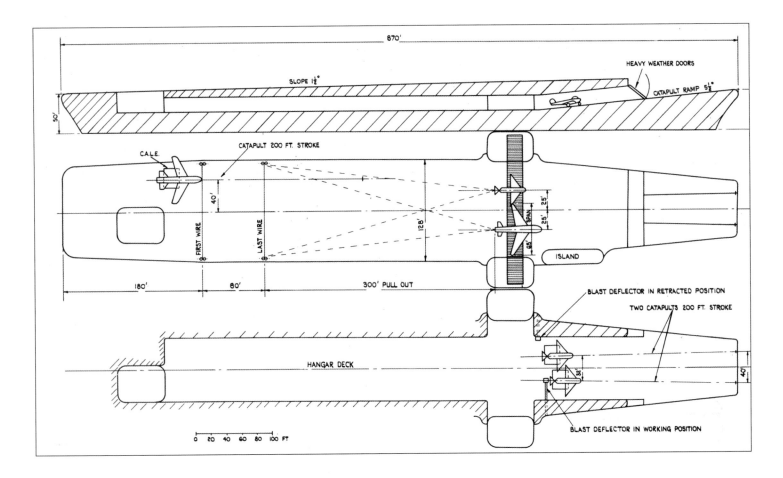

A more radical 1953 concept design for a 'straight-deck' aircraft carrier capable of launching aircraft from a 'second deck' in the open hangar. Note the transverse rolling mat intended to clear aircraft after landing on the upper deck on to the side lifts, and the inclined catapults intended to achieve the same effect as the later 'ski-jump'. These design studies were never taken forward but showed more imagination than most other designs before or since. Of course, not all the ideas would have been practical; the 'rubber deck' certainly was not, and the noise of jet aircraft running in the hangar would have been horrendous. (AUTHOR'S COLLECTION)

stroke on the forward part of the angled deck for launching the stream of aircraft ranged aft to port. A fleet carrier built to the revised design was calculated to cost £26 million, but was unlikely to be operational before the mid-1960s. The size of the air group was to be twelve nuclear strike aircraft, a mix of thirty-six day or night fighters, eight antisubmarine aircraft and two SAR helicopters.

The project was terminated in July 1953, however. With the end of the Korean War the government sought considerable economies and had begun a 'Radical Review' of British defence requirements which sought to replace conventional forces with a nuclear deterrent.

Much smaller carriers

Even before the termination of the 1952 project the DAW asked for studies to examine the cost and capability of carriers about the size of the 1942 light fleet carriers which had performed so well in Korean operations. The first of these depicted a ship capable of operating twenty-eight aircraft the size of the Supermarine N-113 Scimitar. A 6.5-degree angled deck would give the same landing area as that designed for the reconstructed *Hermes*, with four Mark 13 arrester wires on a 20,000-ton hull. A single steam catapult with 180ft stroke was

positioned on the angled deck sponson to port, and the small island was well inboard, allowing aircraft to taxi outboard of it. Although the hull was similar to that of the *Colossus* Class the design was proposed for new-build ships, not reconstructions, and machinery of greater power was to give them a maximum speed of 28 knots. The flight deck had large overhangs to port and starboard which allowed sufficient space for a deck park of twenty aircraft, which increased the overall width from the 112ft 6in of the earlier light fleet carriers to 144ft, 21 per cent of the ship's length. Overall length remained 695ft. There was only one lift, 65ft long by 35ft wide, situated almost exactly amidships. It served two small hangars, one forward and one aft, each 125ft long, 50ft wide, 17ft 6in high and capable of taking four aircraft. The lift obtruded into the landing area and could not be used during aircraft recoveries. A typical air group was to comprise twelve Scimitars, twelve Sea Vixens and four AEW aircraft, with two small SAR helicopters.

The most interesting feature of the design was that it was intended to be 'suitable for conversion to operate VTO [vertical take-off] aircraft'. These were an exciting prospect at the time, although no design was mature enough to offer the prospect of operational capability in under a decade. It was assumed that VTO aircraft would always land with

their nose into the relative wind, but that the ship need not turn into wind for it to do so. A circle 72ft in diameter was projected at the centre of deck movement on which VTO aircraft would land and then taxi clear into the deck park, leaving room for the next aircraft to land seconds later. So that funnel smoke would not interfere with cross-deck landing, the design included two funnels, the one furthest from the landing circle being selected for use as appropriate. Details of how to mount masts, radar arrays and aerials on the small island were not worked out in detail but, viewed in hindsight, the design has more merit than the later *Invincible* Class, in which cross-deck landing was severely impractical but not impossible. Not all aircraft types would have become VTO at once, of course, and these ships might have offered a 'cross-over' capability if they had retained their catapult and arrester wires, giving the latent ability to operate a mix of Kestrel/Sea Harrier/AV-8 and Gannet AEW aircraft with helicopters and legacy fighters such as the Sea Vixen, used for electronic attack.

Unfortunately, as things turned out, the design was not taken forward because VTO technology was considered to be too immature to justify the cost of investment and there was too little potential for strike warfare with large aircraft like the projected Blackburn NA-39, which was to become the Buccaneer. Like the 1952 carrier, this sketch was never given a formal name.

Undaunted by the rejection of the N-113/VTO convertible carrier, the DAW made another suggestion in late 1953, aimed at producing an inexpensive trade-protection carrier capable of operating the new generation of high-performance fighters. It would also be capable, when required, of embarking suitable aircraft to augment the strike fleet. Like the small carrier just described, the new sketch produced by DNC in February 1954 was based on the 1942 light fleet carrier hull, and there is evidence in their ships' covers that consideration was given to converting some ships to this standard. The key to the operation of heavier and more powerful aircraft was acceptance of the fact that they could not be launched and recovered at the same time. A landing area angled 2 degrees to port was to be offset slightly to port of the centreline, with its sponson's weight balanced by a long sponson on the starboard, giving room for a deck park around the new island

structure in Fly 2. Two new lifts stressed for heavier aircraft would have been installed closer together than those in the 1942 design; the after one was forward of the four Mark 13 arrester wires. A new steam catapult with 180ft stroke was projected for the starboard side of Fly 1, with the catapult aircraft line-up equipment (CALE) gear aft of it, level with and to starboard of the forward lift. Both lifts obtruded into the landing area and needed to be up during a recovery; the forward lift needed to be up during catapult launches. Some space on the starboard side of Fly 1 was available for use as a deck park during recoveries, but the angle was not great enough to make much of it available. The only defensive armament would have been twin Mark 5 Bofors mountings, one sited forward and aft of the port and starboard sponsons. The island, masts and radar arrays were not worked out in detail, but would probably have resembled smaller versions of those with which the 1943 light fleet carriers were completed at about the same time. The air group would have been about twenty, with a smaller deck park than the earlier concept but a larger hangar.

Medium aircraft carrier studies

Drawings were produced by the DNC to show that the new generation of aircraft could be operated from a ship 'grown' to about 24,000 tons from the 1942 light fleet carrier design. He argued, however, that a larger hull would give a steadier

flight deck, would be less cramped, would have better sighting opportunities for radar and other essential equipment, better aircraft handling and control arrangements and, not least, allow space to absorb new, as yet unknown, generations of aircraft. In November 1954 a design study for a 28,000-ton carrier was presented to the Admiralty Board for comment. It had an angled deck and was expected to have a similar aircraft complement to the redesigned *Hermes*, at about thirty-eight aircraft. Again costs were constrained by limiting the defensive armament to four twin Mark 5 Bofors mountings, as there was insufficient space for Mark 6 twin 3in mountings. Machinery developing 100,000shp on two shafts was to deliver 28 knots at deep load six months out of dock. The DNC did not regard this as a balanced design, and at their meeting in December 1954 the Board described the design as 'too big for a small carrier and too small for a big carrier'. It was not taken further.

Subsequent interest centred on the design of a larger carrier of about 35,000 tons, the same as the reconstructed *Victorious*. By 1955 this was considered to be the smallest ship that could operate modern aircraft in effective numbers, and

A 1953 concept design for an aircraft carrier with an angle to starboard capable of launching aircraft out of the hangar using the two inclined catapults. A third catapult is on the flight deck, starboard side aft. (AUTHOR'S COLLECTION)

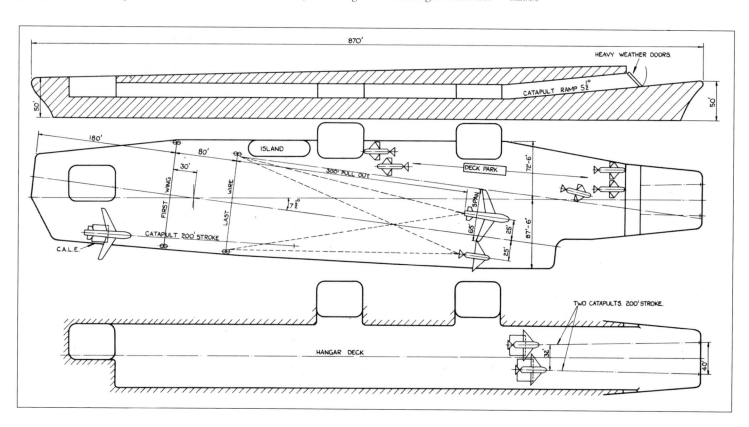

was described by the DNC as 'in effect a general-purpose carrier which, while not being so large as to be wasted in the trade protection role, could carry a considerable strike force as an alternative when required'. A typical air group could include up to forty-eight aircraft. The larger tonnage led to a three-shaft arrangement being proposed, developing 135,000shp to produce 30 knots six months out of dock. Defensive armament was to be a mix of Mark 6 twin 3in/70-calibre mountings and six-barrelled Bofors. The design underwent continuing development, and three ships appeared in the 1959-60 Long-term costing, for completion between 1970 and 1973. Initially they were intended to cost £18 million each, but as the detailed design evolved the weight increased and more equipment was added. From the time Lord Mountbatten became First Sea Lord in 1954 he took a close interest in the design and insisted that anti-aircraft missiles be added, as it appeared unlikely that the Admiralty would gain funding for a class of missile cruisers intended for task force defence. The design incorporated 2,700 tons of armoured plate and eventually grew to a deep-load displacement of 45,000 tons. These ships were never formally cancelled, but the requirement was eventually superseded by aircraft carrier Project 35, which became known as CVA-01. Despite searches of the relevant ships' covers at Woolwich, no sketch drawing of the design has been located.

The 'escort cruiser'

One other project deserves to be mentioned, although it was not considered by the Admiralty to be an aircraft carrier. This was the escort cruiser which grew out of fears in the mid-1950s that flight-deck operations in strike carriers would be degraded by the need to operate helicopters and fixed-wing jets alongside each other. Sketch designs started with destroyers able to operate six helicopters but otherwise armed only with Bofors guns, but grew rapidly to incorporate larger guns, anti-aircraft missiles, flag and task force command facilities with a conventional flight deck and a starboard-side island. Tonnage grew from 5,000 tons to over 13,000 tons. Although the fears about

mixed rotary- and fixed-wing operation were proved to be unfounded in a trial conducted in *Bulwark* during 1958, the project developed its own momentum, perhaps fuelled by the Sea Lords' inability to gain funding for new-construction aircraft carrier projects. Lord Carrington, the First Lord, found that descriptions of the ships as helicopter/guided missile/command ships lacked focus, and coined the term 'escort cruiser' to describe them in his briefings for the Ministry of Defence (MoD) in 1959. The concept was, however, ill-founded and the incorporation of fleet command capability and helicopters undermined the case for the new fleet carriers that the Admiralty had tried to fund for so long. Worse, the term 'escort' seemed to imply to politicians that the big carriers were so vulnerable that they required a big, sophisticated and expensive escort force with its own flagship to defend it against submarine and air attack. The later design studies were for a ship that had evolved from an escort into a high-value unit which needed to be escorted itself.

The escort cruiser evolved rapidly. By December 1961 the Chiefs of Staff Committee was briefed on design 21L2, which was to be capable of operating nine Sea King sized helicopters. It had a conventional flight deck and starboard island with a single centreline lift amidships giving access to the hangar, which was capable of stowing all nine aircraft. Armament comprised a GWS-1 Sea Slug launcher aft; two GWS-20 Seacat launchers on the island and a Mark 6 twin 4.5in mounting forward of the island on the starboard side. Comprehensive radar, command and communications systems were specified on a hull displacing 13,250 tons. Steam machinery of 60,000shp would have delivered 28 knots 'deep and dirty'. At an estimated £20 million each, these ships were almost as expensive as the recent medium carrier studies, but were to be paid for by deleting the last planned units of the *County* Class destroyer programme and reducing two of the new *Tiger* Class cruisers, only just completed but widely considered to be irrelevant in modern warfare, into extended reserve. Four were authorised to be placed into the long-term costings with the possibility of a fifth, timed to be completed when

the first entered long refit for the first time in order to maintain fleet strength. In July 1962 a major redesign was ordered to substitute the CF-299 Sea Dart missile system for Sea Slug and to enlarge and strengthen the flight deck to operate up to four Boeing-Vertol Chinook helicopters, since it was thought at the time that a version of this large twin-rotor helicopter might be procured as a Wessex replacement in the antisubmarine role. Austere accommodation arrangements were to be incorporated to allow up to 700 Royal Marines to be embarked in an emergency. Work was also ordered to reduce the size of the ships, in the mistaken belief that this would decrease their cost.

In the event, however, the escort cruisers were not built; the decision in February 1963 to procure four Polaris-missile submarines meant that the DNC's available resources had to be redirected on to them, and the escort cruisers were deferred. The subsequent decision to cancel the CVA-01 aircraft carrier project in February 1966 led to a period of chaos in which a Future Fleet Working Party was tasked to set in train a further series of studies which may well have been influenced by the escort cruisers but decided to build larger 'command cruisers'. Viewed with hindsight, the escort cruiser project was ill-judged and unfortunately named, but at least the final iteration showed the merit of the basic aircraft-carrier hull design pioneered by the RN for helicopter as well as fixed-wing flying operations. They appeared at a time when helicopters were rapidly growing in importance, and the majority of warships and RFAs would have the capability to operate them to lesser and greater extents within the next decade, thus expanding the number of helicopters available to the fleet without a dedicated helicopter ship. At about the same size as the later Italian *Giuseppe Garibaldi*, they could have been useful ships with the ability to operate Sea Harrier-type Stovl aircraft in small numbers in due course, but they were not what the RN needed for its strike, sea-control, amphibious warfare and trade-protection tasks. In fact they detracted from other, more relevant projects and confused the Admiralty's arguments for procuring more potent warships.

CHAPTER 28

THE RECONSTRUCTION –
VICTORIOUS, *HERMES* AND *EAGLE*

Admiralty attention had focused on new carrier designs to operate the generation of large, heavy jet and turboprop aircraft planned for the 1950s, but failure to fund them meant that the 'legacy' carriers of the *Illustrious* Class would need to be modernised to fill the gap if they were to be retained in service. In the short term the *Colossus* Class ships with their greater hangar height and more modern facilities were capable of operating piston-engined fighters more efficiently and economically than the fleet carriers, and they did so with considerable success throughout the Korean War. Another source of effective carriers would be the extensive modification of some ships that were still under construction, including *Hermes* and *Ark Royal*.

Technical background

After the cancellation of the *Malta* Class the Admiralty took stock of its existing carrier fleet in 1946. All six ships of the *Illustrious* group had survived the war, but some still bore the scars of considerable damage and extensive worldwide service. *Indomitable* and *Implacable* were the only fleet carriers to embark operational air groups in the immediate postwar years, both with piston-engined fighters after limited refits to improve their capabilities. The single-hangar ships had hangars only 16ft high; *Indomitable*'s upper hangar was 14ft high and the smaller lower hangar 16ft. In the last two ships both hangars were only 14ft high. The first four ships could operate aircraft

weighing up to 14,000lb, the last pair aircraft up to 20,000lb. Aircraft fuel stowage was totally inadequate to support jet operations, and the small lifts of the earlier ships were a significant limitation. Newer carriers all had hangar heights of 17ft 6in and could operate aircraft up to 30,000lb, and these were accepted as the minima to which the existing fleet carriers should be rebuilt. The question of 'closed' or 'open' hangars arose again, but by 1947 a committee set up by the Assistant Chief of the Naval Staff (ACNS) (Air)

Victorious in dry dock early in her reconstruction, showing the extent to which she was cut down before being rebuilt. (AUTHOR'S COLLECTION)

to make recommendations about fleet carrier modernisation had accepted the merits of the 'closed' design; this reflected the fact that the USN had shifted towards closed hangars after its experience of typhoons in the Pacific during 1945. Their decision also reflected the conclusions drawn from the Bikini Atoll atomic bomb tests, which showed clearly that aircraft needed to be protected from the blast effects of a distant atomic explosion.

The ACNS (Air)'s committee took the view that only a full modernisation could be justified, as this would give the ships a further twenty years' life, which would keep them effective 'into the mid 1960s' for a cost of 'about half that of a new carrier' for each ship. At first they took the view that all six ships should be rebuilt in the order *Formidable*, *Victorious*, *Indomitable*, *Illustrious*, *Implacable* and *Indefatigable*, but noted that some had a considerable number of unrectified defects that would complicate their reconstruction. In April 1947 the committee recommended the full reconstruction of *Formidable* and *Victorious* to the Admiralty Board, describing the end result as resembling a 'fast, armoured *Hermes* type' capable of operating forty-eight aircraft, compared with the forty-five expected in *Hermes* and eighty-four in *Ark Royal*. Money was still extremely tight, although easier to justify for the modification of existing ships than for the construction of new ones, and Admiralty approval for the work was not given until January 1948. Detailed work on the design, which would involve dismantling the hull down to hangar-deck level and the construction of a 'new' ship on top of the old lower hull, began in February 1948. It was not completed until June

1950, by which time a full survey of both ships had been carried out and revealed that *Formidable* had a distorted flight deck, propeller shaft defects and a considerable amount of internal structure that had been damaged by kamikaze hits in 1945 but only hastily repaired or patched over. Since March 1947 she had been laid up in unmaintained reserve, and her hull was found to have deteriorated significantly as a consequence. In 1950 it was decided, therefore, to modernise *Victorious* first. She had been running as a training ship until recently and her hull was in a far better shape.

As work on *Victorious* continued, the complexity and cost of modernisation became apparent and the Admiralty was forced to accept that modernisation of the entire class was not financially viable. By 1951 work on *Victorious* was expected to be complete by 1955 and work on *Implacable* to start

in November 1953, for completion to a similar design in April 1957. More limited modernisation of the light fleet carriers *Warrior* and *Theseus* was to be carried out between April 1952 and September 1953 for the former, and April 1953 and September 1954 for the latter. The maintenance carrier *Unicorn* was to be modernised between July 1954 and December 1955. By 1952 the cost of work on *Victorious* was 'giving the Admiralty cause for concern', and work on *Implacable*, *Theseus* and *Unicorn* was postponed for two years. In June 1952 it was cancelled completely, and *Victorious* was to be the only ship of her group to be modernised. With the remaining legacy carriers unable to operate the new jet fighters, and no new carriers authorised, her modernisation had become too important to lose, and work on her continued.

Victorious reconstruction

The detailed design was completed in June 1950, and work on *Victorious* began in Portsmouth Dockyard on 23 October 1950. Initially the modernisation work was to be completed in 1954. However, the work spanned a period of dramatic change in carrier design and capability, with the result that several successive design modifications were made which extended both the time required and the cost to complete what became almost a new ship. Some changes required work already completed to be dismantled and started again; work on her modernisation was not finally

Victorious' new island being built up. The trough in the flight deck in the foreground is for the port steam catapult. (AUTHOR'S COLLECTION)

Victorious' port sponson being installed. (AUTHOR'S COLLECTION)

completed until 1958. The initial design required the hull to be cut down to the hangar deck and then rebuilt to give a new hangar height of 17ft 6in. She was to operate aircraft of up to 40,000lb, so the new flight deck was supported by deep beams 8ft high and the space between them formed a new gallery deck containing accommodation, Admiral's staff quarters, radar offices, an air operations office and briefing rooms. The staff requirement also called for a side lift on the port side forward and an enlarged centreline lift aft, two steam catapults and the substitution of 3in Mark 6 mountings for the twin 4.5in mountings. The extra height of the hangar and gallery deck was compensated for by reducing the thickness of the hangar side armour to 1.5in from 4.5in but the flight deck was to retain 3in armour plating. The changes were expected to increase the deep-load displacement from 31,000 to 33,000 tons.

In June 1953 the Board formally approved the fitting of a full 8.5-degree angled deck to port, following the successful trials in *Triumph* and the USS *Antietam*. This required the fitting of a large sponson and the refitting of the arrester wires to lie across the new landing area. The continued addition of weight, however, brought the deep-load displacement up to 35,500 tons, raising the waterline significantly above the original level. This put the hangar deck only 14ft above the deep waterline and made it impossible to fit a side lift since, with any significant wave motion, the structure under the lift platform would impact the water and judder. At the same time, installation of the new Type 984 radar was authorised, to be supported by the Comprehensive Display System (CDS) and digital plot transmission in the aircraft direction room (ADR), and the substitution of USN 3in/50-calibre mounting for the British 3in Mark 6, which was suffering considerable development delays. The new radar and its control systems required considerable rewiring and added to the need for greater electrical generation capacity. The USN Tacan was also specified and fitted. The most embarrassing change to the design followed in December 1953, after the realisation that the boilers were largely worn out and incapable of providing sufficient steam for concurrent high speed and steam catapult operation; their life was due to expire in 1964. Unfortunately the hangar and gallery deck structure, together with the new armoured flight deck, had just been completed when it was decided that reboilering was essential, and a hole large

enough to get the old boilers out and new ones in, with their associated auxiliary machinery, had to be cut and then filled. Had the requirement been highlighted earlier, the work could have been done when the ship was originally stripped down, with a considerable saving in time and expense.

The error highlighted poor liaison within the dockyard, which was reorganised as a consequence, but pressure of work also contributed to the delays in modernising *Victorious*. The need to provide large quantities of avcat led to the creation of hull tanks capable of holding 285,000gal. Later, the decision that she was to operate piston-engined Skyraiders and Whirlwinds led to the need to stow considerable quantities of avgas in protected tanks, but when this requirement lapsed it proved possible to increase the aviation fuel stowage

arrangements to 327,800gal of avcat. Two new centreline lifts were installed; the forward was 58ft long by 40ft wide and the after 54ft long by 34ft wide, and both were capable of lifting 42,000lb and more than double the size of the original lift platforms. A new bow, similar to that of the light fleet carriers, and a considerable flight deck overhang aft, extended the length of the flight deck by 22ft to 765ft. The twin 3in mounts were fitted in similar fashion to those of the proposed new fleet carrier, with two on the port side aft, two on the starboard side aft and one each on the port and starboard sides forward. A single six-barrelled Bofors mounting was sited forward of the two 3in mounting on the starboard side aft. Electrical generation capacity was more than doubled to 5,000kW, with eight steam and four diesel

Victorious listed 12 degrees to starboard during her post-reconstruction inclining experiment. (AUTHOR'S COLLECTION)

The scale of the new port-side sponson and the Type 984 radar aerial mounted on the island are evident in this photograph, taken as *Victorious* entered Malta in 1959. On deck are Scimitars, Sea Venoms and Skyraiders. (AUTHOR'S COLLECTION)

played an effective role in a number of operational tasks, especially in the Far East.

Victorious technical details

Displacement:	35,500 tons deep load
Dimensions:	length 778ft 3in
	beam 145ft 9in
	draught 31ft
Machinery:	3 shaft Parsons geared steam turbines
	6 Admiralty 3-drum boilers
	110,000shp delivering 31 knots
Armament:	6 twin 3in USN Mark 33; 1 sextuple 40mm Bofors
Protection:	3.5in flight deck; 4.5in waterline belt and hangar sides; 2.5in hangar deck.
Fuel:	4,180 tons FFO
Endurance:	11,000 miles at 12 knots
Complement:	2,400

Aircraft operating data

Flight deck:	775ft x 145ft; 8.5° angle
Hangar:	360ft plus 52ft extension forward of forward lift x 62ft 6in x 17ft 6in
Catapults:	2 x BS4 steam catapults, both 145ft stroke capable of launching 50,000lb at 97 knots end speed.
Arrester wires:	5 x 35,000lb at 103 knots entry speed. Emergency nylon barriers
Lifts:	forward 58ft long x 40ft wide aft 54ft long x 34ft wide; both 42,000lb
Aircraft:	36
Aircraft fuel:	327,800gal avcat
Air weapons:	Red Beard nuclear bomb; Firestreak AAM; Sidewinder AAM; Red Top AAM; Bullpup ASM; Mark 30, 44 and 46 homing ASW torpedoes; 1,000lb MC bombs; 500lb bombs; 28lb practice bombs; 3in RP; 2in RP; Mark 11 depth charges; aircraft mines; 30mm gun ammunition; 20mm gun ammunition; flares and pyrotechnics

generators. Bulges 4ft wide were added below the waterline to maintain stability, improving the original three-layer 'sandwich' system of underwater defence, but the side belt armour was reduced in thickness from 4.5 to 2in and extended to cover the enlarged bulk fuel installation.

The last major changes followed in 1954, and reflected the growing complexity of naval aircraft and their weapons. *Victorious* was fitted with two of the new mirror landing aids; one to port and one to starboard of the landing area, the latter acting as a standby. To get the port unit into an optimal position it had to be fitted on to a pronounced sponson built out from the after part of the angled-deck sponson. She became the first British warship to be fitted with magazine handling arrangements and workshops to support guided weapons, the de Havilland Firestreak intended for use by Sea Venom and subsequently Sea Vixen fighters. Later modifications had to be made for Sidewinder and Bullpup missiles provided by the USN under the MDAP. Major changes to the aircraft engineering workshops were made after 1956 to support radars in the Sea Venom, Sea Vixen, Gannet and Skyraider. She was also the first British warship fitted to deploy a nuclear weapon; the *Red Beard* tactical bomb that was carried by Scimitar and Sea Vixen fighters in the strike role.

The modernisation of *Victorious* was the largest task ever undertaken in a Royal Dockyard up to that time, and the sheer complexity of the project contributed to the inadequate planning that preceded it. There was a shortage of shipwrights in Portsmouth, so the new gallery deck and island were constructed in 30-ton blocks at Devonport Dockyard and carried in barges up the Channel before being moved into position by crane and then welded into place. The cost of the modernisation rose dramatically as more layers of work were continually added to the original package. Before work started the estimate was £5.4 million; it rose to £7.7 million once work had started and the Dockyard had more reliable data on which to base calculations. By March 1952 the figure was £11 million, and after reboiling and new radar were factored in this had risen to £14.16 million. The final figure in 1958, when work was complete, was a little over £30 million. A new ship built at the same time would have been subject to some of the design changes but would not have incurred work to strip down the hull, reboiler and replace old machinery. Nor would new equipment have to be 'shoe-horned' into an older hull not designed for it. *Victorious* had many of the advantages of a new ship but lacked the expectation of hull life that would have come with it. However, she proved to be a very successful ship, capable of operating the full range of contemporary RN aircraft in significant numbers, together with those still in development, including the Buccaneer. Smaller than the new American carriers, she nevertheless had better radar and aircraft direction systems. Together with the angled deck, mirror landing aid and steam catapults this gave her a fair claim to be one of the world's best-equipped aircraft carriers in 1958. She

The ceremony during which *Hermes* was formally handed over to the RN by Vickers off the south coast of the UK in 1959. (AUTHOR'S COLLECTION)

Hermes' modernisation during her extended build

Originally, *Hermes* was expected to be completed in 1952 to the same design as *Centaur*. However, the Admiralty instructed Vickers that greater priority was to be given to *Melbourne* and work on *Hermes* was generally slow, stopping altogether for significant periods. This gave an opportunity for the ship to be reconstructed on the slipway to bring it up to the latest standards, with changes that were sufficiently major to require Admiralty Board approval before they were implemented. In 1951 approval was given to install two steam catapults instead of the original BH5 hydraulic catapults, improved arrester gear and a side lift instead of the original forward centreline lift.

The side lift was not easy to incorporate because, in a closed-hangar design, the sides of both hull and hangar resist shear forces and prevent the whole structure from buckling, and cutting a large hole in the ship's side would potentially weaken the structure considerably. A solution was devised at the Naval Construction Research Establishment, using what was then the 'cutting-edge' technology of photoelasticity, in which a large model of the structure was made out of Perspex, illuminated with polarised light and placed under load. Bands of light and dark showed the stress patterns and their magnitude. The model was easy to modify, and amendments could be made until the ideal solution was obtained. The hole in the ship's side was constructed before launch, with a sliding steel door to close the hangar when necessary to keep it weather tight and as a fire precaution. Unlike *Victorious*, *Hermes'* hangar deck was sufficiently high above the waterline to make the side lift viable but, even so, it could be a problem when the platform was in the down position in rough weather or when rolling slightly to port during a turn to starboard. Because of this only 5 degrees of rudder (of a potential 35 degrees) were used when the lift was in the down position. The structure needed to support the steam catapults also needed design effort, especially with regard to the need to absorb the impact of the shuttle and stop it within a few feet at the forward end of the catapult stroke. A test structure for the BS4 steam catapults to be installed in *Ark Royal* was built ashore, and loads of up to 2,000 tons were applied to it. The lessons learned were applied to the installations in *Hermes*.

After launch in 1953 design work began on a further series of modifications which were to bring the ship close to the standard of the modernised *Victorious*, albeit with a slightly smaller air group. These included the installation of a sponson on the port side to support an 8-degree fully-angled flight deck; installation of Type 984 radar, CDS and digital plot transmission, mirror landing aids and Tacan. The mirror landing aids were subsequently replaced by the improved projector landing sights during a refit. The additions raised the estimated deep-load displacement from 23,800 tons to 27,800 tons, the acceptable limit of what could be achieved. Some of the proposed new equipment was not yet fully developed and gave rise to concerns that the tonnage might rise still further. To counter this, some fairly extreme weight-saving measures were incorporated. These included the use of plastic-coated, rather than lead-coated, cabling, which saved 50 tons, and the use of aluminium alloy rather than steel for the reconstructed forward part of the island structure. Careful attention to detail over a further seventeen items of installed equipment saved another 120 tons. The increased deep-load displacement caused a slight reduction in *Hermes'* economical endurance figures when compared with her lighter sister ships. Also, it was found in service that continual use of the steam catapult while the ship was steaming at high speed, conditions which were common in the Far East, caused a reduction of about a knot in top speed. Admiralty Board approval to complete the ship to this greatly modified design was given in September 1955, and the ship had to be partly dismantled to incorporate all the changes.

Hermes technical details as a fixed-wing carrier

Displacement:	27,800 tons deep load
Dimensions:	length 774ft 3in
	beam 147ft 11in
	draught 27ft 10in
Machinery:	2 shaft Parsons geared steam turbines
	4 Admiralty 3-drum boilers

	76,000shp delivering 28 knots
Armament:	2 quadruple GWS-22 Seacat
	SAM in 1968
Protection:	1 to 2in flight deck; 1in
	magazine crowns
Fuel:	3,500 tons FFO
Endurance:	5,000 miles at 20 knots
Complement:	2,100

Aircraft operating data

Flight deck:	744ft x 144ft; 8° angle.
Hangar:	356ft x 62ft x 17ft 6in
Catapults:	2 x BS4 steam catapults
	port 175ft stroke; starboard
	151ft stroke; both 50,000lb at
	94 knots end speed
Arrester wires:	5 x 35,000lb at 103 knots entry
	speed; emergency nylon barriers
Lifts:	side-lift forward 54ft long x
	34ft wide
	centreline aft 54ft long x 44ft
	wide; both 40,000lb
Aircraft:	30 in 1968
Aircraft fuel:	332,000gal avcat
Air weapons:	Red Beard/WE-177 nuclear
	bombs: nuclear depth charges;
	Firestreak AAM; Red Top
	AAM; Sidewinder AAM;
	Bullpup ASM; Mark 30, 44, 46
	ASW homing torpedoes;
	1,000lb MC bombs; 500lb

bombs; 28lb practice bombs;
3in RP; 2in RP; 30mm cannon
ammunition; 7.62mm
machine-gun ammunition;
flares and pyrotechnics

Hermes subsequent modifications

In 1971 *Hermes* was withdrawn from service as a conventional carrier for political reasons and modified for use as a commando carrier. Changes included the removal of the steam catapults, arrester gear and projector landing sights, the Type 984 radar and the CDS. A single Type 965 'bedstead' radar on a pole mast replaced the 984 on the island, and the ADR was refitted to act as an amphibious operations room. Bomb rooms were modified to take ammunition for the embarked RM Commando unit and its supporting artillery battery, and accommodation was modified. Had it not been for the political antagonism towards any form of aircraft carrier prevalent in the UK at the time, she could have been a far more effective ship if at least one steam catapult, arrester wires and the Type 984/CDS system had been retained, enabling her to operate aircraft such as the Gannet AEW 3, Sea Vixen and allied aircraft as well as, or instead of, commando helicopters when necessary. The air group now comprised a single, large squadron of Wessex helicopters and a small squadron of Sea

King antisubmarine helicopters.

In 1977 she was further modified to become an antisubmarine carrier with the capability to revert to the commando role at short notice when required. The operations room was fitted with the computer-aided antisubmarine information system, a command system originally intended for ASW frigates, and stowage was provided for antisubmarine weapons including nuclear depth bombs, conventional depth charges and homing torpedoes. Sonobuoys were carried in substantial numbers. Air groups now comprised one or more squadrons of Sea King and a smaller squadron of Wessex.

Hermes' last modification in the RN, completed in 1981, saw her fitted as a support carrier (CVS) able to operate Sea Harrier fighters and antisubmarine and commando Sea King and Wessex helicopters. She was fitted with a 12-degree ski-jump and a deck approach projector sight; a derivative of the deck-landing projector sight intended to bring Stovl fighters to a hover alongside their landing spot, rather than to a point on the deck where a hook could engage the target arrester wire. Workshops were modified to support the Sea Harrier and bomb rooms had the ability to carry air weapons restored. These included 1,000lb 'iron bombs', Sidewinder AAMs, Sea Eagle ASMs and the WE-177 free-fall nuclear bomb.

The flight decks of *Hermes* and *Victorious*, showing the differences between the two modernised ships. (AUTHOR'S COLLECTION)

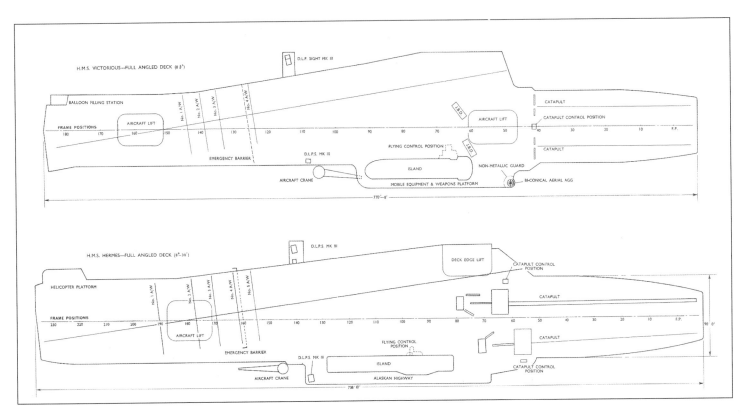

A Phantom from 700P NAS at RNAS Yeovilton over *Hermes* in the Channel in 1968. It was the requirement to operate Phantoms from *Hermes'* relatively small deck that led to the UK variant being re-engined with Rolls-Royce Spey turbofan engines. (AUTHOR'S COLLECTION)

As a conventional aircraft carrier *Hermes* was well-equipped and efficient, but her air group was criticised by some as being too small. Against this, she could be positioned over most of the Earth's surface to make the best use of it, and must be considered an affordable, effective aircraft carrier. She played a fundamental part in the task force that liberated the Falkland Islands in 1982, proving to be a far more versatile ship than the later *Invincible* Class. It is worth noting that she carried more than twice as many aircraft as *Invincible* despite having a hull of similar internal volume. She remains an effective unit of the Indian Navy in 2013, over fifty years after her completion.

Eagle modernisation

Aircraft carrier technology advanced rapidly after *Eagle*'s completion, and by 1953 she could be considered obsolescent without steam catapults and improved arrester gear, although she was fitted with an interim 4-degree angled deck. A modernised design to bring the ship fully up to the latest standard was prepared in 1955, but it was estimated to cost £16.5 million, only slightly less than a new ship, and this was considered unacceptable. The failure to obtain approval for a new carrier, however, meant that *Eagle* was too valuable a ship to lose, and a less-extensive scheme was prepared which would take four rather than six years in dockyard hands to complete. This was accepted by the Admiralty Board in July 1958, and work started on her in Devonport Dockyard in mid-1959. The complexity of the modernisation was eased by the fact that she already had hangars an acceptable 17ft 6in high.

Work was still extensive, however, and involved the complete removal of the island and its replacement by a new structure, the fitting of a large sponson to port to allow a full 8.5-degree angled deck, removal of the four forward 4.5in gun turrets and replacement of the close-range Bofors anti-aircraft guns with GWS-20 Sea Cat missile systems. The new air group was expected to comprise twelve Blackburn NA.39 Buccaneers, ten de Havilland Sea Vixens, twelve Saunders-Roe SR-177 rocket-powered fighters, fourteen Gannet antisubmarine aircraft and two SAR helicopters. At the time the SR-177 was an important project, with both turbojet and rocket motors to give it an electrifying performance, especially in the climb and at high altitude. The oxidant for the rocket motor was HTP, which had to be stowed in

exceptionally clean facilities. Four pure aluminium tanks capable of storing 283 tons of it were designed into the space formerly occupied by the forward 4.5in magazines, and special aluminium pipes were designed. When the SR-177 was cancelled for political reasons in the 1957 Defence Review, more-conventional avcat tanks were installed instead. Other modifications included reducing the thickness of the flight-deck armour from 4in to 1.5in and strengthening the flight deck to take a static load of 45,000lb and a dynamic load of 150,000lb. The replacement of avgas by avcat meant that over 487,000gal of the latter could be carried in bulk tanks. As in *Victorious* and *Hermes*, Tacan and Type 984 radar were to be installed but, unlike them, *Eagle* was to have the first computer-assisted action information system in the RN, known as Action Data Automation (ADA), rather than CDS. Unlike the other conversions, *Eagle* had sufficient capacity to allow a double Type 965 'bedstead' radar to be mounted on a lattice mast aft of the Type 984 on the island. This was rotated to give 'back-to-back' coverage of the area 'behind' the Type 984 as it rotated, doubling the rate at which data was acquired. Although it lacked the range and height-finding capability of the Type 984 it proved to be a useful addition. The operations room and ADR were the most advanced to be fitted into any carrier at the time, and a step beyond the other reconstructed ships. Electrical generating capacity

was increased by 3,000kW to 8,250kW, but this was to prove barely adequate to meet the requirements encountered in service. *Eagle*'s redesigners had to accept a complicated DC/AC mix of electrical arrangements because of the age of the basic design, much of which had to be retained in an attempt to hold down costs. For the same reason she was not reboilered, and steam quantities and conditions were below the ideal to provide high speed and continuous operation of the two steam catapults, but arrangements were made to make it possible to control the whole propulsion system from a central machinery control room to allow passage through an area of nuclear fallout. A novel change was the replacement of the traditional ship's steering wheel with a small 'joystick', the first to be fitted in an RN warship. By October 1959 the estimated cost of reconstruction had risen to £23.5 million, and by the time the work was complete it had cost £31 million, or roughly the estimated cost of a new ship which would not have had the electrical and boiler limitations.

A side lift was considered, but the lower hangar deck was too near the waterline; an installation like the one fitted to *Ark Royal* on build could only have served the upper hangar and would have interfered with the angled deck. *Ark*'s was not a success and had been removed, so it was decided not to fit *Eagle* with one. Both centreline lifts were upgraded to accept 40,000lb aircraft, and the

aircraft cranes were upgraded to 35,000lb with an overload capacity of 45,000lb. Originally the two steam catapults were to be fitted in the bow/Fly 1 area, but neither would have had a stroke long enough to launch the heaviest aircraft. Instead, a BS5 with 151ft stroke, capable of launching 50,000lb at an end speed of 91 knots, was fitted on the port bow, and another BS5 of 199ft stroke and capable of launching 50,000lb at 105 knots end speed was fitted on the port side of the angled deck sponson. The new arrangement proved more adaptable to bringing aircraft forward out of the range than the earlier double-bow arrangement. New arrester wires capable of stopping aircraft of 35,000lb with an entry speed of 103 knots were installed, and workshops were brought up to the best standard possible in the space available to support the technically complex aircraft specified for the new air group. New jet-blast deflectors were installed aft of the catapults, but these would have needed to be replaced by new watercooled units to operate the Phantom safely. During her 1966/67 refit she was fitted with a single direct-acting DAX II arrester wire capable of stopping the Phantom fighter so that she could carry out

trials with the new aircraft. *Ark Royal* was fitted with a complete set of DAX II units in her refit, and the need for *Eagle* to be fully so fitted was a major factor in the political decision to withdraw her from service early.

Accommodation standards were improved with extensive air conditioning, but the need to introduce considerable quantities of new wiring and plumbing into an old hull led to a lowering of headroom and cramped conditions in some areas. That said, her overall habitability was probably the best of her generation in the RN, and she was undoubtedly the most capable carrier to have been deployed by the Service. Her early withdrawal from service was for purely political reasons, since the Government of the day would only allow one carrier to be retained. *Ark Royal*, by then a much less capable ship overall, was being modified to operate Phantoms. *Eagle* would have needed refits to her workshops, jet-blast deflectors, arrester gear and bomb rooms to do so, so the politicians insisted that the less-capable ship was retained and the better ship with a longer life expectancy discarded. The British management of one of the nation's most potent

Eagle's rebuilt and much-improved flight deck can be seen clearly in this 1965 overhead view. (AUTHOR'S COLLECTION)

weapons systems has never been logical or easy to comprehend.

Postscript

Eagle was laid up in the River Tamar near Devonport Dockyard in 1972 and used as a source of spares for *Ark Royal*. In 1978 consideration given to fitting her with a ski-jump and towing her to sea to launch Sea Harriers from various ski-jump angles between 5 and 15 degrees to select the optimal one for *Hermes* and the *Invincible* Class. On inspection, however, the unmaintained flight deck was found to be badly corroded, with grass growing on it, and the interior of the hull was in poor condition. Welding a new structure on to it and then making it safe for the take-off and

Eagle's flight deck after modernisation. (AUTHOR'S COLLECTION)

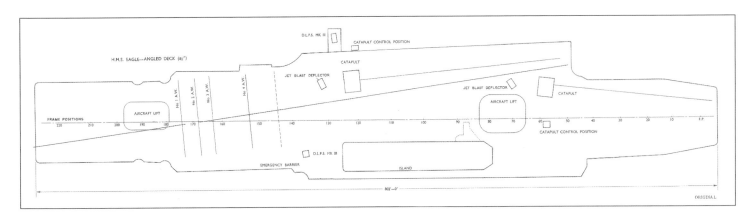

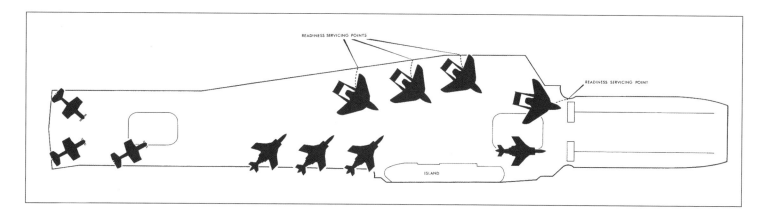

A typical launch range on *Victorious*. (AUTHOR'S COLLECTION)

landing of aircraft was deemed to be an unwise and expensive measure, and it was not taken forward.

Eagle technical details as modernised

Displacement:	50,536 tons deep load
Dimensions:	length 813ft 5in
	beam 171ft
	draught 34ft 6in
Machinery:	4 shaft Parsons geared steam turbines
	8 Admiralty 3 drum boilers
	152,000shp delivering 30.5 knots
Armament:	4 twin 4.5in Mark 6DP turrets;
	6 quadruple GWS-22 Seacat SAM;
Protection:	1.5in flight deck; 4.5in waterline belt; 1.5in hangar sides.
Fuel:	3,200 tons FFO
Endurance:	7,000 miles at 14 knots
Complement:	2,750

Aircraft operating data

Flight deck:	800ft x 160ft; 8° angled deck
Hangar:	upper 364ft plus 45ft extension forward of forward lift x 67ft x 17ft 6in
	lower 172ft x 54ft x 17ft 6in
Catapults:	Forward BS5 steam, 151ft stroke capable of launching 50,000lb at 91 knots end speed
	waist BS5 steam, 199ft stroke capable of launching 50,000lb

Victorious refuels at sea from RFA *Orangeleaf.* (AUTHOR'S COLLECTION)

	at 105 knots end speed
Arrester wires:	4 x 35,000lb at 103 knots entry speed; emergency nylon barriers
Lifts:	forward 54ft long x 44ft wide centreline aft 54ft long x 33ft wide, both 40,000lb
Aircraft:	44 in 1964
Aircraft fuel:	487,480gal avcat
Air weapons:	WE-177 tactical nuclear bomb; nuclear depth charges; Red Top AAM; Firestreak AAM; Sidewinder AAM; Bullpup ASM; Mark 44 and 46 ASW homing torpedoes; 1,000lb MC bombs. 500lb bombs; 28lb practice bombs; 3in RP; 2in RP, Mark 11 depth charges; 30mm cannon ammunition; 7.62mm machine-gun ammunition; flares and pyrotechnics

Individual ship histories

Victorious after modernisation

Victorious arrived in Portsmouth and landed stores and ammunition from March 1950, passing into Dockyard administration from 30 June. Work on her started in October 1950 and was not completed until 1 January 1958, when she moved out of dry dock. Throughout her modernisation the incomplete light fleet carrier *Leviathan* was moored close by to provide a spare gear store, offices and other facilities for dockyard staff.

She was commissioned in Portsmouth on 14 January and sailed for sea trials on 3 February with two Whirlwind helicopters and a Gannet of 701C NAS embarked, the latter being moved about the deck and hangar to test facilities and compatibility.

Victorious in the Johore Strait in 1967, flying a paying-off pennant before entering Singapore Naval Base for what proved to be the last time. Aircraft on deck are Buccaneers, Sea Vixens, Gannets and Wessex helicopters. (AUTHOR'S COLLECTION)

Later in the month she moved to the Clyde, where she carried out 'measured mile' steaming runs in company with the destroyer *Contest*. On 28 February a Scimitar of 700 NAS, the carrier trials unit, piloted by Lieutenant Commander Lambe, carried out 'touch-and-go' landings, and the ship returned to Portsmouth a day later for catapult dead-load and other trials to be carried out. Towards the end of May 1958 she sailed for a Families' Day in the Channel, followed by further sea trials. On 23 June Commander S J A Richardson carried out the first arrested landing in a Gannet of 700 NAS and then taxied forward to make the first 'live' catapult launch. Several days of air trials followed which included the recoveries and launches of a variety of aircraft including an early-production Sea Vixen. She visited Le Havre on 27 June before resuming flying trials, returning to Portsmouth on 11 July. The full trials programme was eventually completed on 5 September 1958, their length underlining the complexity of the 'new' carrier and her systems.

On 23 September *Victorious* began to embark the ground parties for the squadrons that would comprise her new air group, which was to comprise 803 (Scimitar), 893 (Sea Venom), 849B (Skyraider)

and 824 (Whirlwind) NAS. A day later the helicopters of 824 NAS were embarked while the ship was still alongside in Portsmouth, and she sailed on 25 September to embark the remainder of the air group, which had gathered at RNAS Yeovilton. The CO of 803 NAS, Commander J D Russell, was the first to land-on but, tragically, the arrester wire parted before bringing the aircraft to a standstill and it went over the side. The SAR Whirlwind managed to drop its diver on to the Scimitar's cockpit, but neither he nor the pilot could open it, and commander Russell sank with the aircraft. The other aircraft were sent back to Yeovilton, but the cause of the failure was quickly ascertained and the air group embarked without incident later in the day. Two days later a Whirlwind ditched after an engine failure while the ship worked-up in Lyme Bay, but its crew got out safely. After her short work-up, *Victorious* deployed to join the MF and secured next to *Eagle* in Malta on 13 October. Visits to Toulon and Messina fell either side of a period in Malta after two further Whirlwinds ditched because of engine failure. Problems with the Alvis Leonides engines of the Whirlwind HAS.7 were a fleet-wide problem, and the type was grounded until a solution was found in the UK. Two Cyclone-engined Whirlwind HAR.3s were 'borrowed' from 848 NAS at RNAS Hal Far to act as SAR 'plane-guards' while the HAS.7 problems were sorted out.

During November *Victorious* carried out 'search and strike' exercises with *Eagle*, and in December

893 NAS Sea Venoms carried out the first high-seas firings of the Firestreak missile, against pilotless target aircraft launched from Hal Far. They proved to be extremely successful and gave the ship and her air group an unprecedented air-defence capability. By this stage the Whirlwinds were back in operation, and they contributed to a period during December when the air group flew without a break for fifty-eight hours and carried out night strikes against *Sheffield* and *Ulysses*. In January she took part in a MF air defence exercise in which RAF Canberra bombers from Malta acted as the 'enemy'. In January she returned to Portsmouth and flew-off her squadrons to their parent air stations to give leave and carry out a short maintenance period before returning to the MF in February 1959 to participate in Exercise *Dawn Breeze IV* with ships of the MF, HF, French and Dutch navies. The carrier task force comprised *Victorious*, *Eagle* and *Centaur*, and between them they successfully defended the fleet against 'attacks' by RAF V-bombers and Canberras from Malta.

In March engine problems grounded the Whirlwinds of 824 NAS again and they were transferred to *Eagle* by lighter for passage to the UK, and replaced by six aircraft from *Eagle's* 894 (Sea Venom) NAS. Later in March *Victorious* returned to Portsmouth for a docking and assisted maintenance period which lasted two months. In May she worked-up in the English Channel with three Sea Vixens from 700Y NAS, the intensive flying trials unit embarked in addition to the

Victorious in refit in Singapore Dockyard's King George VI dry dock.
(AUTHOR'S COLLECTION)

normal air group. At the end of the month she took part in a HF air defence exercise in the North Sea in company with *Centaur*, during which RAF Bomber Command provided the 'enemy'. A series of 'Shop Window' demonstrations of her new aircraft and equipment followed, after which she took part in air-defence exercises with the HF, Dutch and Danish navies in June. After that she visited ports in Norway and Denmark and welcomed Prince Bernhardt of the Netherlands and King Olav V of Norway on board. At the end of June she sailed for the USA, flying the flag of Rear Admiral Sir Charles Evans, FOAC, to demonstrate her Type 984 radar, CDS and the Scimitar strike fighter to the USN, arriving off Norfolk Navy Yard on 10 July in company with *Scarborough*, *Tenby* and *Salisbury*. On 14 July 1959 she joined ships of the US Second Fleet for exercise *Riptide* under the command of Vice-Admiral Smedberge USN, who flew his flag in the USS *Northampton*. United States Navy carriers in the exercise included *Saratoga*, *Essex* and *Wasp*, and both aircraft and admirals were exchanged between the RN and USN carriers as the exercise progressed. After visits to Boston and New York, *Victorious* returned to Portsmouth in August.

In September 1959 she took part in Exercises *Blue Frost* and *Barefoot* in the Norwegian Sea in company with *Armada*, *Dunkirk*, *Trafalgar*, *Talent* and *Tideflow*; both exercises were intended to test NATO's ability to react to Soviet aggression in Northern Norway. On 22 September a Skyraider ditched after engine failure and its crew of three was rescued by a Soviet trawler. In October *Victorious* returned to Portsmouth for a brief period during which the Radio Luxemburg programme *Take Your Pick* was broadcast from the hangar. After exercises in Lyme Bay she returned to the Mediterranean to take part in exercises during November with the US Sixth Fleet, which by then included *Saratoga*. She returned to Portsmouth in December to prepare for deck-landing trials with the new Blackburn NA.39 Buccaneer. These took place in January 1960, thirty-one successful recoveries and launches being carried out by two aircraft. On 29 January she anchored off Greenock, and in early February she took part in rough-weather antisubmarine exercises off Iceland in company with *Salisbury*, *Torquay*, *Paladin* and *Tenby*. The First Sea Lord, Admiral Sir Charles Lambe, joined her on 11 February to witness flying operations in severe weather. After a visit to Hamburg she returned to Portsmouth to refit and recommission.

The next commission began in Portsmouth on 14 September 1960, after which she carried out a brief work-up in UK waters. The new air group, comprising 803 (Scimitar), 892 (Sea Vixen), 849B (Gannet AEW) and 825 (Whirlwind) NAS, embarked on 18 September, after which she deployed to the MF to work-up to full operational efficiency. On 5 November Rear Admiral Smeeton, FOAC, transferred his flag from *Ark Royal* to *Victorious*, and at the end of the month she took part in Exercise *Royal Flush IV*, a NATO war-at-sea exercise involving the British and American strike carriers *Victorious*, *Ark Royal*, *Hermes*, *Saratoga*, *Independence* and *Intrepid* operating in the western Mediterranean. On its completion the three British carriers were filmed and photographed manoeuvring together off Malta,

and in December *Victorious* took part in Exercise *Pink Gin III*, a training exercise in support of British Army units based near Tobruk. In December she took part in Exercise *Decex*, a fleet training period off Cape Bon in company with *Ark Royal* and *Albion*, the latter having been relieved in the FEF by *Hermes*. On 11 December she rode out a storm off Gibraltar during which an underwater object struck her rudder and jammed it; divers removed the obstruction a day later. On 15 December she embarked the new First Sea Lord, Admiral Sir Caspar John, to witness an air-defence exercise against aircraft from *Ark Royal*. On 19 December she returned to Portsmouth to give Christmas leave, but on 20 January she sailed for

live Firestreak firings off Aberporth. She then sailed for the South Atlantic, flying the flag of FOAC, giving a 'Shop Window' demonstration to South African VIPs on 17 February, after which she visited Cape Town. A new Queen's Colour for the South Atlantic and South America Station was presented on *Victorious'* flight deck on 19 February 1961, and after the visit she sailed for Aden to take part in Exercise *Sea Sheikh* in March. This was an air-defence and army co-operation training period carried out in company with *Hermes*; FOAC transferred his flag to *Hermes* when it was over.

At the end of March the air group was disembarked to RAF Tengah on Singapore Island and *Victorious* entered Singapore Dockyard for a maintenance period. On 19 April she re-embarked the air group except for 825 NAS, which embarked in *Bulwark*; *Victorious* hoisted the flag of

FO2 Far East, Rear Admiral Le Fanu, and sailed for Exercise *Pony Express*, a major SEATO amphibious training period that included *Bulwark*, *Melbourne*, *Coral Sea* and *Thetis Bay* as well as *Victorious*. After the exercise she returned to Singapore and moved into the King George VI dry dock in the dockyard for a refit which lasted until June. On 26 June 1961 she sailed for Hong Kong in company with *Cassandra* and *Carysfort*, but on 29 June she was ordered to proceed to the Persian Gulf 'with all despatch' following the Iraqi threat to invade Kuwait. She refuelled from RFA *Wave Ruler* off Sumatra on 8 July, by which time *Bulwark* with 848 NAS and 42 RM Commando had already arrived off Kuwait. By 8 July *Victorious* and her battle group arrived to join Operation *Vantage*, which successfully deterred an Iraqi invasion. She provided the ability to strike at

Victorious turning at speed and accelerating; hence the black smoke as more fuel is sprayed into the boilers. The aircraft on deck are Buccaneers, Sea Vixens and Gannets. (AUTHOR'S COLLECTION)

enemy forces on the ground and defend the region's air space, including control for RAF Hawker Hunters in Bahrain which would otherwise have operated 'blind'. Temperatures were so hot that chefs demonstrated the ability to fry eggs on the flight deck, but *Victorious* and her aircraft coped well. By 31 July the immediate threat had passed, and *Victorious* was relieved by *Centaur*, which had moved to the area from the MF. In August she moved to Mombasa for a rest period, after which she deployed to Zanzibar, where she landed two 825 NAS Whirlwinds to help police deal with civil unrest. Scimitars also provided support by flying low over 'dissident' villages.

In September *Victorious* returned to Singapore Dockyard for an assisted maintenance period, after which she took part in Exercise *Fotex 61*, a period of intensive Commonwealth naval sea training. Later in the month she carried out the delayed visit to Hong Kong and then joined Exercise *Crosstie*, a period of strike warfare and cross-deck training with the USN in the Subic Bay areas off the Philippine Islands in company with *Ticonderoga*. In November she returned to Singapore Naval Base and then sailed for Aden, but was diverted to Mombasa so that two 825 NAS Whirlwinds could assist in flood relief work on Lamu Island. On 1 December she met *Centaur* in the Gulf of Suez and embarked two Whirlwinds from her 824 NAS. *Centaur* subsequently recovered the two that were left ashore in Kenya on flood relief work. After passing through the Suez Canal *Victorious* took part in Exercise *Royal Flush V* off Malta in company with units of the US Sixth Fleet. On its conclusion she visited Malta briefly to embark 815 (Whirlwind) NAS from *Ark Royal* for passage back to the UK, and arrived in Portsmouth on 19 December to give leave. She had been away for just under a year and had steamed 82,000 miles. In February she sailed for Gibraltar to take part in Exercise *Dawn Breeze VII* in March 1962. This was a NATO training period off northwest Spain, during which her aircraft practised cross-deck operations with the French carrier *Clemenceau*. The First Sea Lord and C-in-C of the French Fleet were embarked to witness operations. On 2 April 1962 she disembarked her air group and entered

Portsmouth to pay off and carry out a refit, during which the flight deck was to be strengthened to allow her to operate the new Buccaneer strike aircraft. The mirror landing aids were to be replaced by the improved projector sight systems, and more extensive air conditioning was to be installed in the accommodation areas. Her second commission after modernisation had seen her undertake unprecedented levels of activity for a major British warship in peacetime, 323 days out of a total of 594 being spent at sea.

The third commission began on 29 June 1963, when she recommissioned in Portsmouth. In July she carried out post-refit trials followed by flying trials with the Buccaneer S1s of 801 NAS. A month later she embarked a new air group comprising 801 (Buccaneer), 893 (Sea Vixen), 849A (Gannet AEW) and 814 (Wessex) NAS, and was to operate with the same squadrons for the rest of her time in service. In August she deployed to rejoin the FEF, passing through the Suez Canal on the 21st. In early September she worked-up off Aden, using aircraft from RAF Khormaksar as adversaries, and later in the month relieved *Ark Royal* off Singapore. By then Commonwealth forces were defending the new state of Malaysia against Indonesian 'Confrontation', and *Victorious* operated in a deterrent role off the east coast of Malaysia during October. In November she exercised with the USN in the Subic Bay areas off the Philippines, and in December she participated in Exercise *Kit Kat*, an air-defence training period off Malaysia. Over the Christmas period she was in Singapore Naval base, before taking part in Exercise *Cocktail*,

an army support training period which, again, took place off the east coast of Malaysia. In January 1964 *Centaur* was ordered to embark 45 RM Commando from Aden to put down mutinies by East African army units, and *Victorious* was ordered to Mombasa from Singapore to act in support, anchoring off Kilindini Harbour on 26 January. Two days later she was ordered to Dar-es-Salaam to relieve *Centaur*, arriving on 29 January, when she embarked 45 RM Commando and the two RAF Belvedere helicopters, remaining offshore while the situation ashore eased. Later that month she returned to Kilindini and disembarked the air group to Nairobi Airport to retain flying currency. On 9 February 45 Commando and the RAF helicopters were transferred to *Albion*.

In March 1964 *Victorious* joined a large Commonwealth fleet to take part in Exercise *Jet 64*, a major training period with ships from the UK, Australia, Canada, India and New Zealand; FO2 FES embarked off Langkawi Island. In April she took part in an air-defence training period with *Centaur* before visiting Hong Kong and launching a fly-past on ANZAC Day, 25 April. In May she visited the USN naval base at Yokosuka in Japan and carried out exercises with *Kitty Hawk* off Okinawa before skirting Typhoon Viola and carrying out further exercises in the Subic Bay areas. At the end of the moth she participated in Exercise *Ligtas*, a SEATO war-at-sea training period with warships from the USA, UK, Australia and New Zealand. She moved into the King George VI dock in Singapore Dockyard in June 1964 for a refit, and her ship's company moved into barrack accommodation in HMS *Terror*. For the first time, a major British warship was recommissioned on the Far East Station and a new ship's company was flown out from the UK in batches, the men they replaced being flown home as they were relieved. The evolution took three weeks with effective help from the FEF Staff and went very smoothly.

Victorious' next commission began in August 1964, and after post-refit trials she visited Australia, joining several other British warships to pass through the Lombok Strait between Indonesian islands to demonstrate their international right of innocent passage, and during a visit to Fremantle over 14,000 people visited the ship in single day. Subsequently, exercises were held in the Indian Ocean with the US ships *Enterprise*, *Long Beach* and *Bainbridge*, the USN's first 'all-nuclear' battle group. *Victorious* had to withdraw from a subsequent exercise with *Centaur* in the Indian Ocean during September when

Victorious being broken up for scrap at Faslane in 1969. Although she was considered to be old, the material being removed in this photograph had been constructed less than two decades earlier. (T FERRERS-WALKER COLLECTION)

rudder problems forced her to return to Singapore Dockyard for defect rectification work. While she was in dock her air group operated ashore, considerably strengthening the defence of Malaysia. Gannets flew searches over large areas of sea, Sea Vixens intercepted intruders at night or in bad weather and the helicopters operated in support of security forces in the jungle. The Buccaneers practised ship attacks and posed a lethal threat to any Indonesian warships that attempted to threaten Commonwealth units patrolling against infiltrators. With the defect fixed, *Victorious* took part in exercises with the USN off Subic Bay in January 1965. On 6 January an F-4 Phantom from the USS *Ranger* did a touch-and-go roller on *Victorious* with its hook up, becoming the first Phantom to land on a British aircraft carrier. The type had just been ordered for the RN as a Sea Vixen replacement, and the event caused considerable interest. In March she took part in Exercise *Fotex 65*, a Commonwealth sea training period that started off Pulau Langkawi and continued for two weeks. The opportunity was taken to make a massive statement of Commonwealth support for Malaysia against Indonesian 'Confrontation', with *Eagle*, *Victorious*, *Melbourne*, *Bulwark*, the former carrier *Triumph* and thirty-five other warships taking part.

On 27 March *Victorious* put on Exercise *Showpiece*, a demonstration of British naval air power off Singapore for the Malaysian Prime Minister, Tungku Abdul Rahman. In April 1965 she visited Kobe in Japan; 15,000 people toured the ship in a single day and many others had to be turned away. May saw *Victorious* taking part in exercise *Sea Horse*, a SEATO training period that simulated the escort of an ocean convoy from Manila to Bangkok. Other ships included the carriers *Melbourne* and *Bennington*. On 26 May she returned to Singapore, and on 30 June she sailed for the UK after nearly two years in the FEF, meeting *Ark Royal*, which was to relieve her, off Aden in July. *Victorious* returned to Portsmouth on 27 July 1965 and moved into D Lock for a major refit. While she was away she had steamed 125,000 miles and her aircraft had carried out 10,000 deck landings.

Victorious recommissioned, for what was to be the last time, in Portsmouth on 7 April 1966. Several days later she sailed for post-refit trials in Lyme Bay, followed by an air group work-up in the Moray Firth, using RNAS Lossiemouth as a diversion. By then 801 NAS had re-equipped with the Buccaneer S2, the first unit to take the type to sea, and 893 NAS operated the Sea Vixen FAW.2. On 8 July she sailed from Portsmouth to join the FEF, visiting Malta briefly, passing through the Suez Canal on 28 July and arriving in Singapore on 16 August after exercises off Penang with *Eagle* before relieving her on station. By then

'Confrontation' was over, and in September she hoisted the flag of FO2 FES and sailed for exercises with the USN in the Subic Bay areas. After a visit to Hong Kong in October she took part in Exercise *Sword Hilt* in October. This included *Melbourne* and twenty-three other ships from the RN, RAN and USN in a series of tactical exercises off the east coast of Australia. On 27 October 1966, aircraft from *Victorious* and *Melbourne* flew over Sydney Harbour, with Vice-Admiral Mills, FO2 FES, and Vice-Admiral McNicol, Chief of Staff of the RAN, among the aircrew. After the recovery both carriers entered harbour. During this visit *Victorious*' ship's company raised the money to purchase a Fairey Firefly from RANAS Nowra to bring back to the UK for presentation to the Fleet Air Arm Museum at RNAS Yeovilton.

From Sydney *Victorious* sailed though the Southern Bight for a visit to Fremantle, after which she returned to Singapore Dockyard, where she began an assisted maintenance period in December. Over the Christmas period in HMS *Terror*, the barracks ashore, members of the ship's company staged a pantomime, *Vic Whittington*, which proved very popular. In January 1967 she sailed for flying exercises in the South China Sea, visited Hong Kong and then carried out exercises with the USN off the Philippines. On 15 February she went to the aid of the Thai-registered ship *Maha Thevi*, which was aground on rocks at Permanggil, 85 miles northeast of Singapore. A Wessex of 814 NAS lowered two officers from HMAS *Vampire* on to the wreck and they were able to get the survivors ashore. Helicopters then took them to *Victorious*, which took them to Singapore. In March she took part in Exercise *Fotex 67*, and in April *Victorious* visited Hong Kong, where she was hit by the Star Ferry *Mao Tin* in fog but neither vessel was damaged. Further exercises with the USN in the Subic Bay areas took place later in April, after which she returned to Singapore Naval Base. *Victorious* sailed for the UK on 4 May 1967. She refuelled in Malta on 24 May, but her passage home was delayed and she was held in the Malta areas as tensions in the Middle East grew. She remained off Malta throughout the Arab/Israeli Six-Day War, but was not called upon by the UK Government to take action. Passage to the UK was resumed on 12 June. On 19 June her air group flew off to their parent air stations and their maintainers were put ashore by lighter in Plymouth Sound. A day later *Victorious* entered Portsmouth Dockyard and commenced a planned refit.

On 11 November 1967 a fire broke out in No.13 Mess on the gallery deck, caused by a tea urn that had been left switched on and boiled dry. It caused the death of CPO J C Nicol and minor damage to wiring and structure. The damage was not serious and the refit could have been completed on time, but the Government, which had decided

not to build new carriers, seized on the opportunity to dispose of *Victorious* and claim that the remaining force was too small to be sustainable. The resultant loss of a valuable ship that had some years of potential service before it reflects little credit on those who initiated the move or did not speak out against it. The recommissioning ceremony planned for 24 November 1967 was cancelled and replaced by a ship's company families' day. On 5 December the immaculate ship was cold-moved from D Lock to Middle Slip Jetty, where she was destored. On 13 March 1968 the white ensign was lowered for the last time at sunset, after which aircraft of 801 and 893 NAS flew over the ship in salute. Having taken the decision to dispose of her, the MoD moved swiftly, and she was sold to ship breakers on 11 July 1968 and towed from Portsmouth to Faslane. FONAC, Vice-Admiral H R B Janvrin, a former captain, flew over her in a Swordfish in a last salute as she was towed out of Portsmouth. It was a sad end for a famous ship with an outstanding record of achievement.

Hermes

Laid down by Vickers at its Barrow-in-Furness shipyard as *Elephant* on 21 June 1944, she was renamed *Hermes* on 5 November 1945, retaining the Admiralty Job Number J 3295 and the Yard Number 928. Work proceeded slowly, but she was substantially modified on the slipway before being launched by Mrs Clementine Churchill, wife of the Prime Minister Winston Churchill, on 16 February 1953. Once she was in the water, work started on a more elaborate redesign and to dismantle part of the hull and reconstruct her to a considerably altered and more modern design in 1955. After fifteen years in the builder's hands she was finally ready for contractor's sea trials in May 1959. These were completed on 18 November 1959, and she sailed on the same day for Portsmouth, where she commissioned on 25 November 1959.

A period of trials and a 'shake-down' cruise to Gibraltar followed, after which the first landings were carried out by Sea Furies from the Fleet Requirements Unit at RNAS Yeovilton on 10 February 1960. Flying trials followed in May; the first operational aircraft to land-on was a Gannet AEW 3 of 849C NAS, and the first jet was a Sea Hawk. The full air group embarked for the first time on 5 July 1960; it comprised 804 (Scimitar), 890 (Sea Vixen), 849C (Gannet AEW) and 814 (Whirlwind) NAS, and *Hermes* sailed for an operational work-up in the Mediterranean. After a spell in the Malta areas she took part in Exercise *Royal Flush III* with *Ark Royal* and ships of the USN Sixth Fleet including *Forrestal*. This was to be her Operational Readiness Inspection (ORI), and having passed it satisfactorily she visited Algiers and

Hermes carrying out flying trials in 1981 after being fitted with a 12-degree 'ski-jump' forward and a new Stovl runway angled one degree to starboard. The projector sight forward of the side lift on the port sponson was part of a trail organised by the author to evaluate its suitability as a Sea Harrier landing aid. It was subsequently adopted and named the 'deck approach projector sight', intended to guide aircraft to a hover position rather than to a point on deck to catch a wire. (AUTHOR'S COLLECTION)

the UK, arriving in Portsmouth on 19 April. On 29 May 1961 she sailed and embarked her air group in the Channel. A day later her aircraft took part in the Paris Air Show and then she gave a 'Shop Window' demonstration in the Channel for VIPs. In June she took part in Exercise *Fairwind VI*, a NATO exercise which simulated a task force passage through a nuclear fallout area. At the end of June a planned visit to Norfolk, Virginia, was cancelled because of the commitment of *Victorious* and *Centaur* to Operation *Vantage* in support of Kuwait, and *Hermes* was ordered to Gibraltar, where she stood by in case she was needed in the Middle East. On 24 July she was released from standby, and in August she visited Oslo, where King Olav V toured the ship. Later in August she operated in Lyme Bay to carry out trials with two Buccaneers from A&AEE Boscombe Down. One of them ditched seconds after a catapult launch and was unfortunately lost with its crew. In September *Hermes* operated in the Channel again for her aircraft to participate in the Farnborough Air Show on the 10th. A day later she returned to Portsmouth, where her first commission ended and she began a major refit.

The refit was completed on 20 April 1962, and she recommissioned on 24 April, after which she worked-up and sailed for the MF flying the flag of FOAC. Her new air group comprised 803 (Scimitar), 892 (Sea Vixen), 849B (Gannet AEW) and 814 (Wessex) NAS, and they worked-up off Malta in June. In July the ship visited Beirut and then carried out an ORI as part of Exercise *Barbican II*, an army support exercise in Cyprus with *Centaur* acting as the 'enemy'. After its successful conclusion she took part in Exercise *Riptide II* off Portugal in August. This was a NATO strike Fleet training period in company with *Centaur* and the US carriers *Enterprise* and *Forrestal*. In September she took part in Exercise *Falltrap* in the Aegean, in company with British, Italian and US warships. *Hermes* returned to Portsmouth for a self-maintenance period in October, and on 11 November 1962 FOAC, Rear Admiral F H E Hopkins, hosted a Taranto Night Dinner on board at which the guest of honour was Admiral Sir Caspar John, the first pilot to be appointed as First Sea Lord. The last serviceable Swordfish was craned on board for the occasion, and it was retained on board until the ship sailed on 13 November, when it took off from the deck,

returned to the UK at the end of August, disembarking 814 NAS before taking part in Exercise *Swordthrust* in September, an air-defence exercise in company with *Ark Royal*, *Gambia* and several destroyers against opposition provided by the USN. In October 1960 she added 824 (Whirlwind) NAS to the air group for Exercise *Rum Tub III*, an antisubmarine training period in the Western Approaches. On its completion she returned to Portsmouth to give leave from 17 October.

On 7 November 1960 she sailed for the FEF with her original air group, transiting through the Suez Canal on 6 December. Six days later she gave a 'Shop Window' demonstration off Aden for VIPs, her air group being the first to deploy Scimitars,

Sea Vixens and Gannet AEW 3s east of Suez. She arrived in Singapore Naval Base on 31 December 1960 and then sailed on 12 January 1961 for exercises with the USN in the Subic Bay areas and a visit to Hong Kong in company with *Voyager*, *Yarmouth* and *Rocket*, flying the flag of FO2 FES. In February she arrived in Trincomalee to begin Exercise *Jet 61*, one of the largest Commonwealth naval exercises ever held. It included *Melbourne*, *Belfast* and a number of other warships from Australia, New Zealand, India, Pakistan, Ceylon and the UK. On 15 March she took part in Exercise *Sea Sheikh* with *Victorious*, which was to relieve her in the FEF, and sailed through the Mediterranean, visiting Naples before returning to

A clear view of *Hermes'* flight deck as she enters Singapore Naval Base in 1968. The 'Alpha Range' includes Gannets, Sea Vixens, Buccaneers and Wessex helicopters. (AUTHOR'S COLLECTION)

the last occasion on which a Swordfish was launched from a carrier at sea. After embarking the air group she was to embark VIPs to witness flying operations in the Irish Sea but, unfortunately, the SAR Whirlwind helicopter ditched while ferrying guests back to RNAS Brawdy and two of its passengers, Lord Windlesham and an RAF officer, were drowned. At the end of the month *Hermes* left UK waters for the FEF, taking part in Exercise *Poker Hand* with the US Sixth Fleet as she passed through the Mediterranean.

After arriving in Singapore, *Hermes* embarked FO2 FES and sailed in January 1963 for exercises with the USN off Subic Bay which included cross-deck operations with the USS *Ranger*. At the end of the month she took part in Exercise *Tussock*, demonstrating the ability of carrierborne aircraft to support troops in the New Territories of Hong Kong. A brief stop in Singapore was followed by Exercise *Jet 63*, the latest in a series of big Commonwealth naval training periods, during February. In March she returned to Singapore for a docking, and in April she joined fifty-seven other warships for the SEATO Exercise *Sea Serpent*. *Melbourne* and *Yorktown* also took part. In May she operated with a number of USN warships off Okinawa, but in June a planned visit to Tokyo had to be cancelled so that she could return to Singapore Dockyard for urgent defect rectification. On 7 July 1963 she took part in Exercise *Birdcage*, after which she was relieved by *Ark Royal* in the FEF and sailed for the UK, but she was ordered to remain off Aden until relieved by *Victorious* because of the deteriorating 'confrontation' situation with Indonesia over the creation of Malaysia. On 21 July she was released from standby and entered the Mediterranean, where 819 (Wessex) NAS was embarked from RNAS Hal Far in Malta to replace 814 NAS in the air group. In September she took part in Exercise *Unison*, a HF convoy protection exercise, and then moved to the MF for exercises with the USS *Independence*, followed by a visit to Barcelona in October. At the end of November she took part in exercise *Limejug* with the HF in the Atlantic, and in January 1964 she took part in Exercise *Phoenix*, a HF air-defence training period. *Hermes'* second commission ended with Buccaneers and Sea Vixens embarked from the A&AEE for trials in Lyme Bay before she entered Devonport Dockyard for a long refit and modification period on 24 February 1964.

After 108 days at sea *Hermes* looked rather weatherbeaten, and is seen here being joined by *Illustrious* on her arrival back in UK waters. The aircraft on deck are Sea Harriers and Sea King helicopters. (AUTHOR'S COLLECTION)

Hermes recommissioned in Devonport on 14 May 1966 and began post-refit trials. In September she embarked a new air group comprising 809 (Buccaneer), 892 (Sea Vixen), 849B (Gannet AEW), 814 (Wessex) NAS plus two Whirlwind SAR helicopters and a carrier on-board delivery (COD) Gannet. She worked-up in the Moray Firth after a visit to Hamburg, and in November took part in Exercise *Roedean*, a period of antisubmarine training with British and Canadian escorts, but had to be docked in Portsmouth to investigate a cracked propeller. In January 1967 she sailed for the FEF, taking the

opportunity to participate in Exercise *Dawn Clear* with the USS *Shangri-La* as she passed through the Mediterranean. After visits to Greece and Cyprus she passed through the Suez Canal and relieved *Victorious* off Aden, giving support to British forces ashore during a period of heightened terrorist tension in the protectorate. On 20 May she left for Gan, the British island base in the Indian Ocean, but on 3 June she was ordered back to Aden when the Six Day War between Israel and its Arab neighbours broke out. When it became clear that intervention by the Western Powers was not an option, she was ordered back to Gan with her

Hermes sails for the South Atlantic with the RN Task Force on 5 April 1982. On deck are Sea Harriers and Sea King helicopters. (AUTHOR'S COLLECTION)

battle group and finally arrived in Singapore on 22 June after sixty-six days at sea and on standby for action. In July she exercised with USN ships off Subic Bay, and after visits to Hong Kong and the Cocos Islands she visited Fremantle in Western Australia, where 11,000 people toured the ship in a single day while she was open to visitors. After that she was due to return to the UK and, since the Suez Canal had been blocked in the recent fighting, she sailed for an 11,500-mile voyage around southern Africa on 4 September, arriving back at Portsmouth on 2 November 1967 to give leave. However, on 31 November she sailed, embarked her air group, and carried out a fast passage around the Cape of Good Hope to the Middle East. On 9 November she was off Muscat and Oman, where British forces were still based after the withdrawal from Aden; once there she joined *Bulwark*, *Barrosa* and *Devonshire* in support of British interests. On Christmas Day 1967 she moved into the Persian Gulf with *Bulwark* to operate off Sharjah, and then returned to the area off Aden. On 3 January 1968 the British task force covering Aden was dispersed and *Hermes* sailed for the UK via the Cape of Good Hope. She returned to Portsmouth on 19 February 1968. Since recommissioning in May 1966 she had steamed 122,448 miles, and her passage time from

Fremantle to Portsmouth had been a postwar record for a British warship.

In March 1968, following her premature withdrawal from service, many of *Victorious*' ship's company were transferred to *Hermes* and she was recommissioned in Portsmouth on 17 May 1968 after a short refit. On 31 May she embarked a new air group which had been intended for *Victorious*; it comprised 801 (Buccaneer), 893 (Sea Vixen), 849A (Gannet AEW), 814 (Wessex) NAS and a COD Gannet. The work-up to ORI standard was carried out in the Moray Firth. On 17 July an RN Phantom fighter from the A&AEE made several 'touch-and-go' landings while *Hermes* was in the Channel, after which she deployed to the FEF via Cape Town. She arrived off Penang on 18 August 1968 and worked-up with RN and RAN ships of the FEF; air opposition was provided by aircraft from RAAF Butterworth in Malaysia. On 23 August four Buccaneers of 803 NAS landed-on. They had flown non-stop from RNAS Lossiemouth in Scotland to Gan using air-to-air refuelling, and thence to *Hermes* in order to prove the capability to reinforce an operational carrier at sea if necessary. The 'observer' in one of these aircraft was Admiral Sir Michael Le Fanu, the First Sea Lord, who had undergone training at the RN Strike School to fit him for the task. Vice-Admiral O'Brien, the Commander FEF, Rear Admiral Griffin FO2 FEF and Rear Admiral Fell FOAC were on board to witness this important and historic event. On the last day of the month *Hermes* arrived in Singapore

Naval Base for a maintenance period.

In mid-September she sailed for exercises in the South China Sea with a number of RN and RAN warships, and then joined an amphibious task force in the Celebes Sea. This comprised *Albion*, *Intrepid*, *Triumph* and the RFA *Tidespring* in addition to *Hermes* and, once worked-up, the task force took part in Exercise *Coral Sands* from 30 September onwards. This began off the Admiralty Islands and continued to the south, down the eastern coast of Australia. It was the largest war-at-sea exercise ever held in the region up to that date, with opposition provided by *Sydney*, USN warships and both Australian and US aircraft. The ceremonial entry into Sydney Harbour on 14 October 1968 was the largest fleet arrival since 1945; *Hermes* berthed alongside Garden Island Dockyard with part of her air group disembarked to RANAS Nowra. She sailed on 31 October and re-embarked the air group off Jervis Bay; combined RN/RAN exercises followed, during which RAN A-4 Skyhawks and S-2 Trackers carried out practice deck landings and catapult launches to prepare them for embarkation in *Melbourne*, which was nearing the end of its modernisation. In November *Hermes* sailed north with *Diana* as plane-guard for exercises with the USN, visiting Okinawa and then Hong Kong at the end of the month. Christmas was spent in Singapore, and in January *Hermes* took part in Exercise *Fotex 69*, a training period off Penang with a large number of RN and RAN escorts and opposition provided by aircraft from RAAF

Butterworth and RAF Tengah. She returned to Singapore on 8 February 1969. She left Singapore for the last time on 12 February and sailed for a visit to Fremantle in Western Australia, where over 12,000 people visited the ship in a single day. After further exercises with the RAN she sailed for the UK, stopping briefly at Cape Town on the way. *Hermes* returned to Portsmouth on 1 April 1969 for a docking and maintenance period, during which the ship's company was accommodated in *Centaur*. She was rededicated on 29 August 1969 and sailed for Portland to work-up, after which the air group re-embarked and she underwent an ORI in Scottish waters. In November she took part in Exercise *Decamp* with *Eagle*, and entered Gibraltar with her at the end of the month. After a brief return to the UK, *Hermes* returned to the Mediterranean in January 1970 for exercises off the North African coast. After visits to Malta, Villefranche, Istanbul and Cyprus she took part in exercise *Dawn Patrol* in June with ships of the US and Italian navies in the Ionian Sea. This was her last period of operations as a conventional carrier, and she returned to Portsmouth on 22 June 1970 to pay off into 'care and maintenance' to await conversion into a commando carrier.

Hermes taking part in a four-ship replenishment at sea with the Far East Fleet while the author was serving in her in 1968. From left to right the ships are the destroyer Diana, a Tide Class RFA tanker, Hermes and the air-stores ship RFA Reliant. Stores from the last-named are being taken on to the side lift, from where they are easily taken into the hangar and struck down. Aircraft on deck are Sea Vixens, Buccaneers, Gannets and a Wessex helicopter. (AUTHOR'S COLLECTION)

In October 1970 she was towed to Devonport Dockyard, and in March 1971 she was taken in hand for conversion. *Hermes* recommissioned as a commando carrier in Devonport on 18 August 1973, and after a period of trials she embarked a new air group, which comprised 845 (Wessex) and 814 (Sea King ASW) NAS. Exercise *Swift Move*, an amphibious training period off Norway in October, was followed by a period of arctic warfare training off Northern Norway in January 1974. In February she took part in Exercise *Dawn Patrol* in the Mediterranean, and in June she was training with commando forces in Canada when she was ordered to the eastern Mediterranean at short notice. During July 1974 she evacuated 900 British nationals from Cyprus during fighting between Greek and Turkish factions on the island. In September she took part in the NATO Exercise *Northern Merger* in the Atlantic. In February 1975 *Hermes* sailed from Devonport with the same air group and 45 RN Commando for training in Canada and visits to Montreal and Quebec, returning to the UK in June. In September she took part in Exercise *Deep Express* in the Aegean Sea, and in November she took part in Exercise *Ocean Safari*, a large-scale NATO war-at-sea training period in the Atlantic. After a maintenance period in Devonport she took part in Exercise *Atlas Express* off Norway in January 1976, with 45 RN Commando embarked. In May 1976 she was taken in hand in Devonport Dockyard for conversion into an antisubmarine carrier, retaining a commando-carrying capability. After conversion she embarked the same squadrons but 814 NAS was increased in size.

Hermes recommissioned in Devonport on 10 December 1976, and in January 1977 she carried out trials with Harriers in the English Channel, intended to identify the ideal visual and blind approach aids to support Stovl aircraft operations at sea. In March she sailed for an antisubmarine work-up in the Mediterranean, after which she returned to the UK to take part in HM Queen Elizabeth II's Silver Jubilee Fleet Review at Spithead, flying the flag of FOCAS. Other carriers present were *Ark Royal* and *Melbourne*. After the Review she took part in Exercise *Highwood*, an international maritime air defence training period. In October she took part in Exercise *Ocean Safari 77* in the Atlantic, and in February 1978 she took part in Exercise *Spring Train* in the Gibraltar areas. In March she took part in Exercise *Safe Pass*, and in May in Exercise *Open Gate*. The major NATO Exercise *Northern Wedding* followed in September, after which she carried out further Harrier trials. After a refit she carried out further series of trials with development Sea Harriers and aircraft of 700A NAS, the Sea Harrier Intensive Flying Trials Unit. In 1980 *Hermes* was taken in hand in Portsmouth Dockyard for conversion into a general-purpose carrier, able to operate Sea Harrier fighters, Sea Kings in the antisubmarine and commando roles and Wessex in the latter. She sailed for post-conversion trials in June 1981, after which she embarked her new air group, which comprised 800 (Sea Harrier) and 826 (Sea King ASW) NAS. After working-up she was undergoing a maintenance period in Portsmouth during March 1982 when Argentine forces invaded the Falkland Islands and other British

Royal Navy Sea Harriers and RAF Harriers ranged on *Hermes* during the South Atlantic Conflict in 1982. (AUTHOR'S COLLECTION)

dependencies in the South Atlantic. Hastily prepared and stored, she embarked an enhanced air group alongside and sailed on 5 April 1982 as flagship of the task force despatched to the South Atlantic in company with *Invincible* and other warships. Her air group included aircraft from 800 and 899 (Sea Harrier), 826 (Sea King ASW) and 846 (Sea King commando) NAS. While in the South Atlantic she was further reinforced by Sea Harriers of 809 NAS, Harriers of 1 Squadron RAF and Lynx helicopters of 815 NAS. Her operations were central to the success of the task force and she spent 108 days continuously at sea, a record for a British carrier, beaten subsequently only by *Invincible*. Between them the two carriers flew 2,000 operational Sea Harrier sorties in which thirty-two enemy aircraft were confirmed destroyed in air-to-air combat for no losses, although some Sea Harriers were lost to anti-aircraft fire and operational accidents. *Hermes* returned to a memorable welcome in Portsmouth on 21 July 1982.

Hermes' interrupted refit was resumed in August 1982 and lasted until November. In January 1983 she re-embarked 800 (Sea Harrier) and 814 (Sea King ASW) NAS to work-up in Scottish waters for exercise *Roebuck*, a NATO training period in which ships of the British, US, Dutch, Canadian, Norwegian and German navies took part in appalling weather. A visit to Hamburg followed in February, after which she took part in Exercise *Cold Winter*, during which RM and Dutch commandos were landed in Norway. In April she sailed for the USA and visited New York, after which a number of 'Shop Window' displays were staged at sea for American VIPs. In May the ship visited Mayport in Florida, where it was granted the freedom of the city of Jacksonville Beach. Exercise *United Effort* with the USN was followed by a visit to Norfolk, Virginia, in May 1983 to prepare for the large NATO Exercise *Ocean Safari*, during which she returned across the Atlantic as part of the antisubmarine support group for the strike fleet. On return to the UK 814 NAS was disembarked and the ship took part in exercises in Swedish waters, during which 800 NAS Sea Harriers operated with and against Swedish fighters. After a visit to Gothenburg, Harriers of 1 Squadron RAF were embarked to operate with 800 NAS in Exercise *Mallet Blow* in the North Sea. Further exercises in the North Sea with 845 NAS Wessex were followed by a period of deck-landing practice for IN Sea Harriers in Start Bay during July. In September she embarked 845 (Wessex) and 846 (Sea King commando) NAS, together 40 RM Commando Group, for a planned exercise with Spanish marines in Malaga.

This was cancelled, but the ship and its task group continued to the Mediterranean for Exercise *Display Determination* in Turkish waters. On completion she steamed through the Dardanelles to visit Istanbul and then returned to Cyprus, where exercises were carried out with the British garrison. Exercises with Egyptian armed forces and a visit to Alexandria followed in October, and then *Hermes* sailed to visit Gibraltar for the last time in November 1983. She finally arrived back in the UK, flying her paying-off pennant, on 22 November 1983. A week later, after ammunition and stores had been landed, she sailed for Devonport, where she underwent a refit. This was completed on 6 April 1984 and she sailed with a reduced ship's company for trials in the Channel, after which she was taken into Number 3 Basin in Portsmouth Dockyard with a ship's company of about 100 to 'preserve her by operation' alongside. She was to be kept at thirty days' notice for sea until the new *Ark Royal*, third ship of the *Invincible* Class, was completed in July 1985, after which she was to be at reduced readiness and offered for sale.

In May 1986 it was announced that she had been sold to the IN for £60 million, the cost to include a year-long refit in Devonport. When that was completed, on 12 may 1987, she was commissioned into the IN as INS *Viraat*. She arrived at Mumbai on 21 August 1987 after a work-up in the UK, and operated an air group which comprised 300 NAS with Sea Harriers and 330 NAS with Sea Kings. She has proved to be as effective in operation with the IN as she was in the RN, and is still in service during 2013, fifty-four years after her original completion. Delays with the carriers being procured to replace her may yet keep her in service for several more years after 2013.

Eagle after modernisation

Eagle was taken in hand by Devonport Dockyard on 30 October 1959, having paid off in May. She recommissioned temporarily on 16 January 1964 for sea trials, but the dockyard work was not finally completed until May. She was recommissioned fully on 14 May 1964 and sailed five days later for post-modernisation trials. The first aircraft to land-on were de Havilland Tiger Moths from Britannia Royal Naval College Dartmouth, which took the opportunity to land on her big deck on 20 June, but the proper flying trials programme began in Lyme Bay on 14 July, with aircraft of her new air group carrying out a number of arrested landings and catapult take-offs. The air group comprised 800 (Buccaneer), 800B (Scimitar), 849D (Gannet AEW), 820 (Wessex) and 899 (Sea Vixen) NAS and a single COD Gannet. Fittingly, her first foreign visit was to Brest during a break in her trials programme, which was eventually completed at the end of October. On 1 December she sailed to join the FEF with FOAC embarked, passing through the Suez Canal on 12 December. After exercises off Aden she spent Christmas in Mombasa, and eventually arrived in Singapore on 13 January 1965.

In February *Eagle* sailed for antisubmarine exercises in the Singapore areas, followed by exercises with the USN off Subic Bay. In March she hoisted the flag of FOAC again and took part in Exercise *Fotex 65* in company with *Victorious*, *Melbourne* and *Bulwark* and a number of other RN, RAN and RNZN warships. At the height of the 'Confrontation' with Indonesia over the newly independent Malaysia this was a powerful statement of Commonwealth intent. At the end of

Scimitars, Gannets, Sea Vixens, Buccaneers and a Wessex helicopter on *Eagle's* flight deck after a recovery. (AUTHOR'S COLLECTION)

the month Exercise *Showpiece* was staged for Malaysian VIPs. During the rehearsal two of 820 NAS' Wessex ditched, leading to a temporary grounding of the type, but the demonstration subsequently went well, with the Prime Minister of Malaysia, Tungku Abdul Rahman, embarked. On 20 April she left the FEF for the UK, visiting Beirut and Malta before returning to Devonport on 24 May 1965. She underwent a docking and maintenance period before sailing to rejoin the FEF on 24 August. After a work-up in the western Mediterranean she took part in Exercise *Quick Draw* with ships of the MF and the US Sixth Fleet. Unfortunately a Sea Vixen and its crew were lost on 8 September. After a visit to Malta she passed through the Suez Canal and carried out exercises off Aden; 820 NAS landed helicopters to assist the security forces ashore, but a Buccaneer flown by two USN exchange officers was lost due to fuel problems. Both aircrew ejected safely. On 13 October *Eagle* arrived in Mombasa for a visit, after which she returned to the Aden area to fly missions in support of the army ashore. Next she arrived in Singapore on 12 November, a day after the unilateral declaration of independence (UDI) by the Government of the British Colony of Rhodesia. As part of the British response *Eagle* was ordered to sea on 18 November and proceeded to Gan, where she embarked FOAC and his staff. She proceeded to the East African coast, ready to land Sea Vixens, Scimitars and Gannets for the air defence of Zambia if the situation ashore degenerated into conflict. In the event they were not needed, and in mid-December *Eagle* sailed to Mombasa, where she carried out a maintenance period and spent a second Christmas.

On 10 January 1966 *Eagle* sailed to return to Aden again, where her aircraft operated in support of the army ashore. She returned to Singapore in February, and in March she joined the FEF in exercises off Penang, but on 5 March she was ordered to relieve *Ark Royal* on the 'Beira Patrol', enforcing UN sanctions against Rhodesia by preventing tankers from entering the port of Beira in Portuguese East Africa to unload oil for the illegal regime. She remained on station until 4 May, when she handed over to *Ark Royal* and returned to Singapore for a maintenance period. *Eagle* had spent seventy-one days at sea, a new record for a British warship, during which she had steamed 30,000 miles and flown 1,880 sorties which had identified 767 ships, including 116 tankers. After Singapore she visited Hong Kong, then sailed to Subic Bay in June for exercises with the USN. After a further period in Singapore she sailed for exercises off Penang, then returned for a

visit to Mombasa before passing through the Suez Canal again on her way home. She returned to Devonport on 22 August 1966. During her year with the FEF she had steamed 108,000 miles and spent 248 days at sea. Her ship's company moved into *Centaur* and she was taken over by the Dockyard for a refit.

Eagle's ship's company moved back on board in March and she recommissioned on 6 April 1967. She began sea trials on 8 April, but on 11 April, while steaming on the measured mile off Cornwall, she suffered a serious electrical fire in 'B' boiler room and had to go back into Devonport Dockyard for repairs. These were completed on 27 May, and she resumed her trials programme. In late June she embarked her air group for an operational work-up in the Moray Firth. It remained the same except for the removal of 800B NAS, which had been disbanded. The work-up culminated with a successful ORI in August, after which she sailed for the Middle East, via the Cape of Good Hope, to cover the withdrawal of British forces from Aden. Over 10,000 people visited the ship during her refuelling stop in Cape Town. She arrived in

Singapore on 6 October 1967 and then sailed for Aden on 23 October, spending nine weeks at sea as part of the task force that covered the British withdrawal as Aden gained its independence. Air defence was taken over from the RAF on 7 November. From 26 November four Sea Vixens were kept airborne continuously until the Royal Marines' rearguard were embarked on 28 November, ending 128 years of British rule. *Eagle* returned to Singapore on 2 December. After a rest period she sailed for exercises off Penang in January 1968 before taking part in Exercise *Partner* with ships of the RN, RAN and RNZN in the Indian Ocean and then visiting Fremantle in February. An intensive period of flying exercises off eastern Malaysia followed, after which she visited Hong Kong in March. She was meant to have exercised with the USN off Subic Bay in April, but was ordered to Aden at short notice to protect British interests, including a BP oil refinery, from the threat of violence. After some weeks at sea she handed over to *Albion* and sailed for the UK via Cape town, as the Suez Canal remained closed after the 'Six-day' Arab/Israeli War. She arrived back in

Hermes, followed by *Eagle*, leaves Gibraltar in 1970. (Author's collection)

Devonport on 18 June 1968. She had been away from the UK for 308 days, 220 of which had been spent at sea. On 23 August *Eagle* sailed for Exercise *Silver Tower*, a major NATO exercise in which she was the only strike carrier, effectively attacking a number of simulated targets on land and at sea. She returned to Devonport in October to pay off for a further refit.

Eagle recommissioned for what was to be the last time on 5 March 1969 in Devonport. A few days later she sailed to work-up with 800 (Buccaneer), 826 (Wessex), 849D (Gannet AEW) and 899 (Sea Vixen) NAS embarked. After her ORI she carried out Phantom deck-landing trials in the English Channel during June 1969 with two aircraft from A&AEE Boscombe Down. Sixty-one successful arrested landings were carried out in the two-week trial. Later in the month she crossed the Atlantic to visit Norfolk, Virginia, and then Boston, Massachusetts, before returning to take part in the Royal Review of the newly-formed WF, an amalgamation of the former HF and MF, on 28 July 1968, flying the flag of the C-in-C WF. New colours were presented to the Fleet by HM The Queen in *Eagle*'s hangar on 29 July. In September *Eagle* deployed to the Mediterranean to take part in Exercises *Peace Keeper* and *Deep Furrow 69*, interspersed with visits to Gibraltar, Malta, Naples and Toulon. In October she took part in NATO training periods in the Aegean Sea, and in November she took part in Exercise *Decamp* in the Atlantic in company with *Hermes*. In early 1970 she took part in a training period in the Moray Firth, followed by a visit to Liverpool, after which she returned to Devonport for a period of docking and essential defect repair, with the ship's company accommodated in *Centaur* again.

The maintenance period ended on 26 September 1970 when her air group re-embarked; it differed slightly in that 826 NAS had re-formed with Sea Kings. Returning to Devonport after her initial work-up, *Eagle* grounded near Drake's island and had to be docked for the replacement of a propeller and repairs to hull plating. She was at sea again in November and visited Southampton before returning to Devonport in December. On 19 January 1971 she sailed for the Mediterranean for a work-up that culminated in a successful ORI, and then visited Villefranche in February before taking part in exercise *Perfect Princess* before returning to Devonport to prepare for her final deployment to the FEF. She sailed on 26 May for Cape Town, and finally arrived in

Sailors enjoying a recreation break lend scale to *Eagle*'s flight deck and the aircraft parked on it off Tanzania in 1965. (Author's collection)

A Buccaneer of 800 NAS makes a low pass over *Eagle*. Wingtip vortices like these are common at high speed in the moist air close to the sea surface. (AUTHOR'S COLLECTION)

Singapore on 8 July. The FEF was about to be disbanded, and Singapore Dockyard had already been sold to commercial interests; *Eagle* sailed for a series of goodwill visits to Australia and New Zealand at the end of the month. Unfortunately she suffered a fire in one of her liquid oxygen plants which led to the death of a sailor, but the visit to Sydney went ahead on 4 August. A visit to Wellington in New Zealand followed, after which she visited Fremantle and then returned to Singapore in September. In a short ceremony the Queen's Colour of the FEF was paraded for the last time and transferred to *Eagle* for the passage back

to the UK. In October *Eagle* sailed for exercises with the USN off Subic Bay, but on passage she responded to a distress call from the SS *Steel Vendor*, which had run aground and was breaking up off Loatia Island, west of the Philippines, in appalling conditions. Four Sea Kings from 826 NAS managed to winch all forty of her crew members to safety. Afterwards the exercises went ahead as planned.

Next, *Eagle* visited Hong Kong and then returned to Singapore, where her air group carried out a fly-past to mark the final British withdrawal from the base at the end of October 1971 before taking part in Exercise *Curtain Call* with *Albion* and RN, RAN and RNZN warships off the Malacca Strait, after which the entire fleet enjoyed a barbeque on Langkawi Island. From there *Eagle* steamed across the Indian Ocean to the area off

Masirah where she was to provide cover for the withdrawal of British forces from the Persian Gulf. She eventually visited Durban in December after spending fifty-six days at sea carrying out routine flying operations in case of a need which, in the event, did not arise. Over the Christmas period 20,000 people visited the ship, and she sailed for the UK on 4 January 1972. Her air group disembarked on 23 January, and she entered Portsmouth Dockyard three days later, flying the flag of FOCAS and a 450ft-long paying-off pennant. After destoring she was towed to Devonport and laid up off Cremyll in the River Tamar to be a source of spares for *Ark Royal*. She was eventually sold for scrap and towed from the Tamar on 4 September 1978 to Cairnryan in Scotland to be broken up for scrap. Demolition was complete by 1980.

CHAPTER 29

CVA-01: THE UNBUILT *QUEEN ELIZABETH*

The succession of new aircraft carrier designs in the 1950s were never formally cancelled, and the requirement for four new fleet carriers remained in the long-term costings under the generic title of 'guided-missile equipped aircraft carriers'. In 1958 the DNC pointed out to the Admiralty Board that, notwithstanding the modernisations then being carried out, the existing carrier fleet had a finite life, and that at some stage new construction would be necessary to supplement and eventually replace it. Despite the arguments over carrier size since 1944, the Naval Staff was still unable to decide between a larger number of relatively small carriers or a smaller number of large carriers, and in January 1960 the FRC was tasked to study the question and make recommendations. A wide range of numbered studies were distilled down to just six for presentation to the Board, of which the smallest was Study 27, for a 42,000-ton ship that could carry twenty-seven Buccaneer or Sea Vixen sized aircraft and have a defensive armament of Seacat missiles. The others were Studies 23D and E for ships of 48,000 tons, Study 29 for a ship of 50,000 tons, Study 24 for a ship of 55,000 tons, and Study 30 for a ship of 68,000 tons. All of the larger ships were to be armed with US Tartar missile systems and would be able to carry significantly more aircraft, which could be operated in worse weather and sea conditions. It was estimated that four Study 27 carriers would cost £180 million to build, compared with four Study 24 ships, which were estimated to

cost £240 to build. There were clear advantages in size, however, and it was calculated that Study 24 would be capable of operating forty-nine aircraft compared with the twenty-seven in Study 27. This gave better value for money with a 'ship-build cost' of £1.2 million per aircraft in a single Study 24 ship, but a higher figure of £1.6 million per aircraft in a single Study 27 ship. The MoD and the Government would, of course, have to be persuaded that the higher total cost of construction was affordable, but the small percentage rise in cost for such a considerable increase in operation performance was felt to be a powerful argument.

In January 1961 the Board decided that a ship of at least 48,000 tons would be needed, and the Ship Characteristics Committee was instructed to work out a detailed Staff Requirement, amalgamating several of the earlier studies into a new one identified at first as Study 35. They were to assume that the first ship would have its sketch design approved in late 1962, and that provisional orders for the hull and machinery would be placed in 1963. Building drawings were to be completed in 1965, when metal would be cut for the first ship. Launch was to be in 1967, with a trials programme starting in 1970 for operational service from late 1971. The carrier designs in the 1950s had been based on general-purpose aircraft carriers capable of providing aircraft for a wide range of fleet duties. Study 35 had one important difference, however, in that the Board decided that the new ship's primary purpose was to

be a strike carrier capable of attacking both ships and land targets with nuclear and conventional weapons. It was allocated the NATO brevity code CVA for a strike carrier, rather than CV for a general-purpose carrier. From this time onwards the project was referred to as CVA-01, later ships of the class being designated CVA-02 and -03. Other roles included the operation of fighters both to escort the strike aircraft and provide air defence over large areas of sea, and the operation of radar-equipped AEW aircraft capable of searching for air and sea targets. Significantly, the Board accepted that antisubmarine helicopters added value to the air group and were vital for the close-range defence of the carrier task force against submarine attack, making the continued interest in escort cruisers at the time even more difficult to understand.

To help finalise the Staff Requirement and evolve the design process, work proceeded on the basis that the new carrier would have a displacement similar to that of the modernised *Eagle* at about 50,000 tons but, having a more modern and efficient hull design, would represent a significant measure of improvement. A number of further design studies were produced and compared with the 75,900-ton USN *Forrestal* design and the 31,000-ton French *Foch* design, which represented the opposite extremes of new carrier construction. The former was deemed too large for existing British infrastructure to support it and too expensive to build; the latter was rejected because of doubts about its stability if all of the thirty aircraft projected were embarked. Five studies were laid before the Board. The first four of these were identified as Study 50 for a 50,000-ton carrier, Study 52 for a 52,000-ton ship, Study 53 for a 53,000-ton ship, and Study 55 for a 55,000-ton ship. As can be imagined, the final Study 58 was for a 58,000-ton ship. The sketch design with the optimum features derived from these studies emerged in April 1962 and was studied in detail by the Board. It was for a carrier that would be 890ft long at the waterline, with a maximum width outside the angled deck of 177ft and a nominal displacement of 50,000 tons. In response the Board asked for quick studies to be made of designs up to 60,000 tons; the implication of using commercial docks for the new carrier's maintenance and a comparison with the modernised *Eagle*. The studies found that a larger carrier would

An artist's impression of CVA-01. (AUTHOR'S COLLECTION)

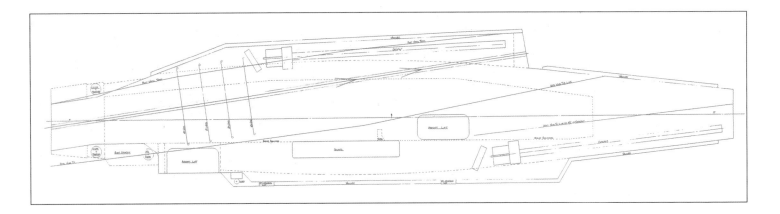

The 1962 Design Study 53 for CVA-01's flight deck with a conventional angled deck. (AUTHOR'S COLLECTION)

have a construction cost beyond what the Government was prepared to contemplate, refits in commercial yards would be expensive because only the Royal Dockyards had the infrastructure to support high-technology equipment such as radar and electronics, but that docking might be a practical possibility. The comparison with *Eagle*, as might be expected, showed that a later design based on the growing wealth of jet operating experience would be more efficient but cheaper to operate than the older ship, even after its modernisation. It also recognised that *Eagle* had reached, or even exceeded, its design margins and that the new design had room for growth over the succeeding decades.

Given the results of its quick studies, the Board decided that Study 53 represented the best compromise and should be developed into a mature design to replace *Victorious* in service. Cost was estimated at between £55 and £60 million for the first ship, and the Board accepted that this must represent a 'ceiling' figure, with no alterations or additions made during the design and build process that would add to it. Study 53 was expected to operate an air group of thirty-six strike aircraft, fighters and AEW aircraft, plus six antisubmarine helicopters and two SAR helicopters. The fact that separate studies throughout the 1950s and 60s had come to the same conclusion that a carrier of about 53,000 tons represented the best operational value for money indicates that this figure was a minimum, not a maximum, if the ship was to be effective over its planned life. The early *Illustrious* Class ships showed what could happen if ships were built to too small a margin. Ominously, there was one dissenting voice within the Board, Lord Carrington the First Lord, political head of the RN and the man who would have to make the case for the new carriers to the Government through the MoD. He suggested that the Board should look again at carrier designs of about 40,000 tons capable of operating twenty-four aircraft, showing that he was unimpressed by

the arguments about the cost-effectiveness of larger designs, but throughout 1962 he bowed to the professional opinions of his naval Board colleagues. It is interesting that he thought in terms of size and related this to cost. He did not think in terms of the requirement and the sophisticated electronic equipment now needed to achieve it, and this somewhat naive view came to be shared by a number of politicians who eventually terminated the project without ever understanding the vital need for it, its value, or even where the true costs lay.

In early 1963 there were still four ships in the long-term costings, but the decision in April to procure four nuclear submarines equipped to carry the American Polaris intercontinental ballistic missile (ICBM) as a national deterrent caused a reappraisal, and the number was reduced to three. The sketch design was approved by the Admiralty Board in July 1963, and the Government approved development work on the first of class but, with the reduction to three from four as the eventual size of the carrier force, the Admiralty was told to replace both *Victorious* and *Ark Royal* with the first ship. A sum of £1.6 million was allocated to cover development and design costs, but as each item fell due for payment the Treasury tried to block it, resulting in delays and further nugatory expenditure. Progress was also slowed by the fact that the Admiralty's Ship Department at Bath lacked the design staff to carry forward all the work that was now required, since the Polaris SSBNs (ship, submersible, ballistic [missile], nuclear [powered]) had to be in service by 1968. It is worth noting that politicians accepted without question that these SSBNs were the optimum design to carry sixteen Polaris missiles, patrol with them for long periods and launch them when required; their tonnage was, thus, much greater than that of any previous RN submarine. A similar comprehension of the new carrier design was never achieved.

By 1963 no single shipyard had facilities large enough for the new carrier, and work would be required to dredge fitting-out berths and to both lengthen and widen slipways. No single shipyard had enough draughtsmen to prepare construction

drawings, and even the combined staff of two, such as John Brown and Fairfield, would still have left a shortfall in electrical specialists. Despite this the work was achievable and the project could have proceeded, albeit at a slower pace than originally intended. Technically the ship reflected the years of careful thought that had gone into the development process. She was considered to be just too large for a two-shaft arrangement, so a three-shaft system was selected. This had the added value of redundancy in the event of action damage, and allowed high speed to be maintained on two units while a third was shut down for maintenance during long periods at sea. The steam plant was the most advanced ever designed for the RN, and would have run at 1,000psi and 1,000°F. Electrical power output was to be 20,200kW; when compared with the 8,250kW in the modernised *Eagle* this shows both the limitation on upgrading an older design and the rapid contemporary increase in the need for electrical power. An innovative exhaust system for the boilers was designed for CVA-01, with smoke carried above the island in two combined 'mast and smoke-stack' structures known as 'macks'. Vortex generators in the starboard side of these caused the smoke to be led away to starboard, well clear of the flight deck. The arrangement worked well in windtunnel model tests. The island structure consisted of two separate blocks, each with a 'mack' exhausting the separated boiler rooms. The space between the blocks was used as a 'garage' for flight-deck tractors and other equipment, and had roller shutters to close it if required. Above the 'garage' the blocks were joined to give space for offices and ready rooms, giving the appearance of a single continuous island slightly larger than those on USN carriers. Radars and the Tacan aerial were carried on top of the 'macks'. The planned long-range surveillance radar was the Anglo-Dutch Type 988 'three-dimensional' array, in a large and distinctive dome on top of the forward 'mack'. This was cancelled when the Dutch elected not to purchase the British Sea Dart missile system and, had she been built, CVA-01 would probably have had an improved version of the Type 984 with transistors replacing valves.

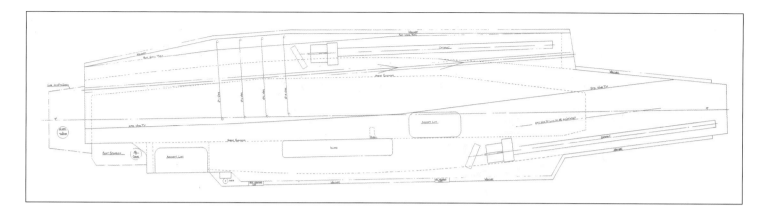

The alternative parallel deck design for CVA-01 that was accepted by the Admiralty Board in 1963. (AUTHOR'S COLLECTION)

The decision that, as the high-value unit to be defended, CVA-01 should be fitted with the best defensive weapons, proved to be one of the design's cost drivers, but it seems never to have been questioned by politicians. The design included both the CF-299 area-defence missile system, later named Sea Dart, and the Ikara antisubmarine missile system developed in Australia. Both needed 'special to class' launchers, missile handling systems and extensive magazine arrangements. Again the likelihood is that, had she been built, CVA-01 would have been fitted 'for, but not with', or not at all with either system. While the Sea Dart launcher was similar to the version fitted in Type 82 and Type 42 destroyers it was to be loaded horizontally from a 'travelling box' that was loaded from the handling system aft of the magazine and raised level with the launcher arms. Its development would not have been cheap. At first the design had no armour, but it did have new and effective anti-torpedo protection based on work by the Naval Construction Research Establishment (NCRE). During the design process armour was worked into the design; it included a 3in flight deck, 3in hangar sides, 1.5in bulkheads around magazines and 'splinter-proof' steel bulkheads. This took the design about 1,000 tons over the politically charged 53,000 tons, but that figure was still used to describe the new carrier 'under standard operating conditions', that is with some fuel and ammunition expended. The 3.3kV electrical distribution system would have been new to the RN and used step-down transformers.

The design work was completed on 27 January 1966 and approved by the Admiralty Board, which 'warmly congratulated' the staff of DG Ships who had achieved it. Orders for long-lead items costing a total of £3.5 million, mainly machinery, had been placed despite Treasury tardiness in allocating the money. The detailed plans were ready for dispatch to shipyards for the competitive tender process, and CVA-01 had been named *Queen Elizabeth* although the Board had, unfortunately, elected not to announce it until the order was placed. The name *Duke of Edinburgh* was allocated to CVA-02, reportedly at the insistence of HM The Queen, and CVA-03 was allocated the name *Prince of Wales*. Unfortunately the new Labour Government of the day failed to comprehend the RN's vital requirement for CVA-01, and cancelled the entire project in February under the cover of an ill-considered and inadequately explained Defence Review. The same Government subsequently allocated a considerable amount of public money to try to maintain jobs in the shipyards that could have built the *Queen Elizabeths* but had attracted few commercial orders. Yet more public money was spent in futile attempts to replace the lost capability with ships such as the cruiser *Tiger*, which was expensively modified to carry just four Sea Kings

Considerable thought went into the design of CVA-01's aviation arrangements, and the hull and flight deck were, in many ways, more advanced than in the USN *Nimitz* Class. The large single hangar had an opening right aft through which aircraft could be moved on to the small quarterdeck to carry out ground runs, rather than having to be moved on to the flight deck, where they would have interfered with flying operations. It was served by two lifts; the forward one was inboard but to starboard of the centreline so that it did not obtrude into the landing area. It used a new 'scissors' arrangement under the platform to raise and lower it, rather than the previous, heavier designs in which the platform was suspended from chains. It was one of the few features of the CVA-01 project to be carried forward to another design, two similar lifts being fitted in each of the *Invincibles*. They proved to be problematical in service and needed time, expense and development before they could be considered reliable. A side-lift suspended more conventionally from chains was fitted on the starboard side aft. Both lifts were specified to take a 75,000lb load. The island was designed well inboard, leaving space outboard of it, known as the 'Alaskan Highway', along which aircraft could be taxied, allowing a circular movement from the parking areas, either aft to the side-lift to be struck down or forward to the bow catapult. Early iterations of the design had a large sponson to port to take an 8-degree angled deck, but in 1962 the Fleet Work Study Team proposed extending the sponson forward and aft to shift the whole landing area to port, creating a 'parallel deck' angled at only 3 degrees. This small angle was retained to ensure that aircraft that missed the arrester wires and bolted would pass well clear of aircraft in the parking area to starboard. In effect, the flight deck was divided into two lanes with the parking area to starboard increased by 15 per cent and an unobstructed landing area to port. It would also have made recovery in poor visibility easier, since aircraft would have been lined up close to the wake for their carrier-controlled approach. Another advantage of the 'parallel deck' was that it moved the recovery area forward so that the arrester wires were positioned closer to the centre of pitch than in the angled-deck design, thus helping recoveries in bad weather when the ship was pitching. Here again the 53,000-ton design had merit, as the ship was nearly 1,000ft long and less susceptible to pitch motion than a smaller, shorter ship. The simultaneous launch and recovery of aircraft in what the USN calls the 'battle flexi-deck' was entirely practical, although parking would have become tight with larger numbers. The flight deck was to be stressed to take aircraft up to 70,000lb.

The philosophy behind the design and the planned air group of thirty-six strike fighters, four AEW aircraft, six antisubmarine helicopters and two SAR helicopters was that about two-thirds of the air group could be stowed in the hangar and about two-thirds could be parked on deck. This left a 'spare third' that could be filled by a squadron deployed to reinforce the carrier, as 803 (Buccaneer) NAS demonstrated on *Hermes* in the Indian Ocean in 1968. The RN also hoped that it might prove possible to embark RAF squadrons to provide a surge reinforcement capability, especially in the Far East, and successively proposed joint forces of Hawker P.1154, Buccaneer and Phantom aircraft. All were rejected by the RAF, which refused to see any requirement for its aircraft to operate at sea.

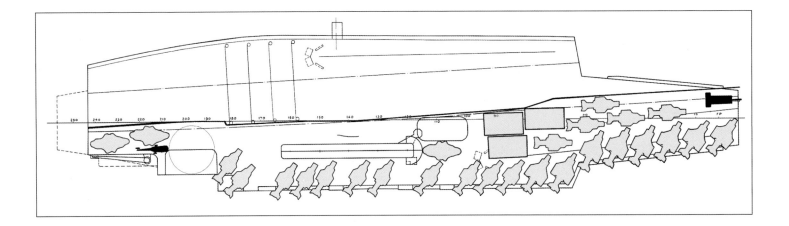

Interestingly, politicians never found it necessary at the time to question this viewpoint or wonder if the ideas might save taxpayers' money with common aircraft and joint capability. Every aspect of the design was carefully studied and modelled if necessary, including the diamond-shaped flying control position (Flyco) which gave an unprecedentedly good view of the deck and aircraft in the visual circuit and on approach. Lighting and flight-deck floodlighting for night operations were to a new design which was eventually fitted to the modernised *Ark Royal*.

The two steam catapults each had a stroke of 250ft and were capable of launching a 55,000lb aircraft at an end speed of 115 knots, the longer stroke giving a smoother acceleration than the shorter stroke of earlier British steam catapult installations. Experience with *Victorious* and *Hermes* had shown that the catapult aircraft line-up equipment (CALE) installation aft of the catapults was unnecessary, and it was omitted from CVA-01, but new watercooled jet-blast deflectors were designed to be positioned aft of the catapults to protect aircraft moving out of the range from the reheated jet thrust of aircraft taking off. These were another element of the design that actually saw service; two were fitted in *Ark Royal* during her modernisation. The catapults were positioned on the starboard bow to launch aircraft ranged on the starboard side and on the port waist to launch aircraft raged to port. During flexible launch and recovery operations aircraft ranged in Fly 3 could taxi forward along the Alaskan Highway outboard of the island to launch from the bow catapult while aircraft landed on the angled deck, turning to taxi into Fly 2 to clear the runway. Both lifts could be used while these operations were in progress to strike down unserviceable aircraft or bring up serviceable replacements. There were four arrester wires, each capable of stopping a 40,000lb aircraft at an entry speed of 112 knots; all were of the new direct-acting design. A single projector landing aid was fitted on a sponson

which projected out to port from the angled deck; a spare sight was positioned aft of the island on the starboard side.

The operations room and ADR were sited on 5 deck, and a lift connected them to the bridge so that the captain and his senior aviation and warfare officers could move quickly between them if necessary. CVA-01 had fewer boats than previous British carriers, they were stowed to starboard of the Sea Dart launcher on the quarterdeck, aft of the flight deck, and could be lowered into the water by the aircraft crane, which was sited just aft of the side-lift, forward of the boat deck. The crane was capable of recovering a ditched but floating helicopter and lifting it on to the side-lift, it was cleared to lift 40,000lb. The side lift was also to be used for the movement of stores during solids replenishment operations at sea (RAS). For these the lift would be in the down position with the jackstay wire attached a strong point on the side of the deck above it. Stores would have been taken straight into the hangar, moved by mechanical handling equipment and struck down into dedicated stores areas using specialised lifts instead of manpower. There were four bomb lifts, each able to service both the hangar and flight deck.

Unbuilt *Queen Elizabeth* technical details

Displacement:	54,650 tons deep load
Dimensions:	length 963ft
	beam 231ft 4in
	draught 33ft 4in
Machinery:	3 shaft geared steam turbines
	6 boilers
	135,000shp delivering 28 knots
Armament:	1 x GWS-30 Sea Dart SAM system with 2 Type 909 target-tracking radars
	1 x GWS-40 Ikara ASW missile system

A 1965 drawing of *Queen Elizabeth*, CVA-01, showing thirty representative aircraft parked to starboard of the parallel deck which could still be used for launch and recovery operations. The three boxes represent the maximum dimensions allowed for the Gannet AEW.3 replacement, which would probably have been an improved version, the AEW.7. The black object at the port bow is 'Jumbo', the mobile crane, placed where it can still move to a crashed aircraft in the landing area. Note that space is still available in Fly 2 to park more aircraft if necessary. (AUTHOR'S COLLECTION)

Protection:	3in flight deck and hangar sides; 1.5in magazine sides and bulkheads; 1.5in splinter-proof bulkheads
Fuel:	6,200 tons diesel
Endurance:	6,000 miles at 20 knots
Complement:	3,230

Aircraft operating data

Flight deck:	930ft x 230ft
Hangar:	660ft x 80ft (maximum) x 18ft with two bays at 19ft to allow aircraft to fold or spread for maintenance
Catapults:	2 x BS5 with 250ft stroke capable of launching 55,000lb at an end speed of 115 knots
Arrester wires:	4 x 40,000lb at 112 knots entry speed. Emergency nylon barriers
Lifts:	forward 70ft long x 35ft wide aft 70ft long x 32ft wide, both 75,000lb load
Aircraft:	47 designed, with capability to embark 15 more for surge operations
Aircraft fuel:	600,000gal avcat
Air weapons:	WE-177 nuclear bombs; 1,000lb MC bombs; 500lb bombs; Red Top AAM; Bullpup ASM; Mark 44/46 ASW homing torpedoes; napalm tanks; Mark 11 depth charges; flares and pyrotechnics.

CHAPTER 30

ARK ROYAL — CONTROVERSY,
A SINGLE CARRIER AND HER AIRCRAFT

Technical background

Ark Royal was originally laid down as a unit of the *Audacious* Class, and her early development was described in Chapter 19. Work on her stopped in 1946 while the design was reviewed; it was hoped that she could be brought, as far as possible, up the standard of the cancelled *Malta*, but this proved to be difficult in a hull that was over 10,000 tons lighter and already close to its original design limit. She could operate the same aircraft and would be fitted with the same radars, operations room and ADR, but the design showed its limitations in the stowage available for aircraft fuel and air weapons. Less than two days' supply of fuel for the air group was available in the protected avgas tanks, but the rapid adoption of turbojet and turboprop aircraft relieved the situation because jet fuel had a higher flash point and could be carried in bulk stowage like FFO or diesel. The low air-weapon numbers would have to be taken care of by frequent replenishment at sea from armament stores ships. Here too progress helped, as later, larger generations of aircraft were embarked in smaller numbers which reduced the need for bulk weapons stowage. On the other hand the increasing use of technically complex weapons including nuclear bombs and guided missiles increased the need for workshops and more complex magazines and weapon handling arrangements.

Side lifts, like those designed for *Malta*, were considered essential, and considerable design and construction effort went into achieving one abeam the island on the port side. In a closed hangar design two side lifts would have been impossible, and achieving one required considerable structural alterations. The same photoelastic modelling technique was used as in *Hermes* to design the side-lift structure, which had to cut into the armoured hangar side amidships without weakening the hull. Only the upper hangar could be served, as the lower hangar would place the lift platform too close to the waterline, and the steelwork to maintain the integrity of the hull reduced the height of the opening to 16ft 6in, a foot lower than the hangar the lift was to serve. Despite these drawbacks the side-lift was considered essential for what was then a straight-deck carrier design, as the landing area for jet aircraft was using up more of the deck, shrinking the parking area in Fly 1 forward. The ability to strike down aircraft as they landed using a lift that was clear of the centreline, without interrupting the recovery, was so important that the Admiralty Board agreed the change in August 1950. The side-lift machinery space took up a substantial part of the of the lower hangar, and the structure around the opening caused the down-takes to A and B boiler rooms to be rerouted less efficiently. Two sextuple Bofors

Ark Royal in May 1957. She still has the side lift, but the port 4.5in gun turrets have been removed and the flight deck has been extended over their sponson. Aircraft on deck include Sea Hawks, Wyverns, Gannets and Skyraiders. Note the sailors forming 'ARK' just aft of the forward lift. (AUTHOR'S COLLECTION)

mountings had to be landed. The whole situation changed with the introduction of the angled deck; *Ark Royal* was fitted with an interim 5.5-degree angled deck, which moved the parking area to starboard of the landing area, away from the side lift. Worse, the lift obtruded into the landing area and had to remain locked at flight-deck level during every recovery, making it useless for its original purpose. It was removed during the ship's 1958 refit. On completion, the port forward 4.5in-gun mountings were plated over because they were on the angled-deck centreline. In 1958 they were removed and extra accommodation was built into the space vacated. The starboard forward mountings were removed soon afterwards.

The most important change to be approved was the incorporation of two BS5 steam catapults in place of the original hydraulic units. The date of her completion was dictated by the delivery and installation of the first two catapults, and she was the first carrier in the world to be completed with them. The development of a water ram to

293

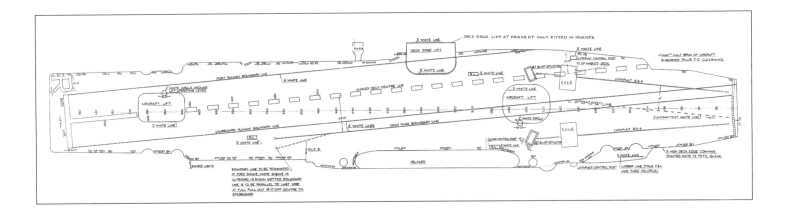

decelerate the catapult pistons and absorb the impact of stopping them was carried out ashore, and the resulting structure was fitted in all British carriers equipped with steam catapults. *Ark Royal* was also the first carrier in the world to be completed with the angled deck and mirror landing aids built in, as opposed to being fitted after completion. In order, the first three ships to be completed fitted with these major British inventions were *Ark Royal* on 25 February 1955, the USS *Forrestal* on 1 October 1955, and HMAS *Melbourne* on 8 November 1955. A number of other improvements were built into the design,

including a lattice foremast and radar to contemporary British standards. One aspect that could not be improved was internal volume, and she was always a cramped ship with a poor standard of accommodation. The original design assumption had been that aircraft would be stowed in a relatively large hangar area and brought up to the flight deck in relatively small groups for flying operations over a prolonged period. By 1945 this concept had been overtaken by the need to launch large ranges of aircraft for strike operations, and *Ark Royal* was always going to compare unfavourably with big-deck,

Ark Royal's flight deck before the removal of the side lift and her special refit. The markings applied to RN carrier decks are shown in considerable detail. (AUTHOR'S COLLECTION)

single-hangar USN carriers, but the key fact was that she existed and was able to play an important role in postwar RN operations around the globe.

Ark Royal refuels at sea in 1957 from RFA *Wave Master*, with the destroyer *Dainty* on the other side of the tanker. (AUTHOR'S COLLECTION)

In this 1956 photograph *Ark Royal's* port forward gun turrets are still in place but have been plated over to extend the angled runway. (AUTHOR'S COLLECTION)

angled deck and two new steam catapults identical to those fitted in *Eagle*. All gun armament was removed to save weight, reduce the number of sailors needed to man and maintain them and make space available, although three hardpoints capable of taking GWS-20 Seacat launchers were fitted. Two new lattice masts were stepped, each carrying a Type 965Q 'double-bedstead' air surveillance radar. A new Type 993 radar was fitted and the old Types 982 and 983 were retained, but the command and control systems were not updated and she retained the obsolescent 'picture compilation' system with which she had been completed because modernisation to the Type 984 radar and action data automation system fitted in *Eagle* would have required conversion to AC electrical supply and complete rewiring. One major advance was the fitting of the USN AN-SPN 35 carrier-controlled approach radar, giving a big improvement in night and bad weather recoveries, as it could track incoming aircraft in elevation as well as azimuth. Despite the lack of a new command system and the retention of the original island, the refit included the addition of 3,000 tons of new structure, 1,200 miles of new cabling and the creation of twenty-six new mess-decks equipped with bunks and limited air conditioning. After the refit she was one of the first ships in the RN to be fitted with a satellite communications system, and she remained an anomalous mixture of old and new technology to the end.

Her 'special refit' was calculated to cost £32.5 million, about half the estimated cost of CVA-01. Taken with the £20 million spent to give the cruisers *Tiger* and *Blake* a mediocre helicopter capability to replace the cancelled carriers, it is difficult to understand how the Government at the time managed to convince itself that it was saving money.

Despite the predictions that she could not be kept in service beyond 1974, *Ark Royal* fulfilled a vital role in the RN as the last conventional strike carrier and was kept in service until 1978, albeit with frequent machinery failures and technical problems, all of which were overcome by her hardworking ship's company, with dockyard assistance. Despite politicians' promises that alternative weapons would be procured to replace the big carriers, none were, and *Ark Royal* kept naval aviation alive during a period of traumatic decline in RN capability. Even with her faults she was a valuable ship that played an important role, and her withdrawal from service at the end of 1978 marked the end of an era.

Another weakness that was not immediately apparent on her completion was caused by *Ark Royal's* twelve-year period of construction, during which she was inadequately preserved. She was found to be prone to material defects and major machinery breakdowns, and repairs were made difficult by the fact that much of her machinery was already old at the time of her completion, and had been made to wartime standards without adequate quality control by firms that no longer existed. Hard usage and minimal maintenance in her early years had added to the problems, which had been solved in her modernised contemporaries by extensive replacement of old machinery by new material, but, given the unexpectedly high cost of modernising *Victorious* and *Eagle*, the Admiralty Board decided that modernising *Ark Royal* to the same standard was not a viable option. By 1963 the Naval Staff was talking about the need to replace her with a new ship, despite the fact that she was only eight years old, although cynics might say that this was an attempt to strengthen the case for getting new construction started, rather than a hard necessity. It is noticeable throughout this period that the Admiralty tended to under- rather than over-estimate the potential lives of ships in service. She had been completed as a DC electrical ship, so if she was to be retained in service beyond 1966 she would have to be fitted with additional AC generators to support improved communications and sensor fits. Accommodation would always be poor, but more extensive air conditioning was a staff priority to allow continued service in the Middle and Far East in rotation with other carriers.

A two-year refit was planned for 1966, which was intended to do the minimum amount of work necessary for her to operate the latest generation of aircraft safely until 1972, when CVA-01 was expected to be complete. Further work to keep her in service until 1974 was predicted to extend the refit to three years. The cancellation of CVA-01 in February 1966 changed the whole picture, and after considerable argument the Government allocated funding for a 'special refit' that would allow *Ark Royal* to operate the new Phantom fighter and Sea King ASW helicopter in addition to Buccaneers, Gannet AEW aircraft and Wessex SAR helicopters. Lasting from 1967 to 1970, the refit included the installation of an 8-degree

Ark Royal leads ships of the Far East Fleet through the Johore Strait to Singapore Naval Base. The 'Alpha Range' has been improved by tensioning two Scimitars on the catapults; other aircraft in it include Gannets and Wessex helicopters. 'Jumbo' the crane is parked aft of the island. (AUTHOR'S COLLECTION

Technical details (after 1970)

Displacement:	50,786 tons deep load
Dimensions:	length 845ft
	beam 166ft
	draught 36ft
Machinery:	4-shaft Parsons geared steam turbines
	8 Admiralty 3-drum boilers
	152,000shp developing 30.5 knots
Armament:	Fitted for, but not with, 4 GWS-20 Seacat; 4 single 3pdr saluting guns
Protection:	4in flight deck over hangar; 1.5in remainder of deck; 4.5in waterline belt; 1.5in hangar sides; 2.5in hangar deck; 1.5in longitudinal bulkheads
Fuel:	5,500 tons FFO
Endurance:	7,000 miles at 14 knots
Complement:	2,640

Aircraft operating data

Flight deck:	790ft x 120ft; 8.5 degree angle
Hangars:	upper 364ft plus 45ft extension forward of forward lift x 67ft x 17ft 6in
	lower 172ft x 54ft x 17ft 6in
Catapults:	forward BS5 steam, 151ft stroke; 50,000lb at 91 knots end speed
	waist BS5 steam, 199ft stroke; 50,000lb at 105 knots end speed
Arrester wires:	4 x DA2 40,000lb at 115 knots entry speed
Lifts:	forward 54ft long x 44ft wide aft 54ft long x 33ft wide, both 40,000lb
Aircraft:	38 in 1975
Aircraft fuel:	522,000gal avcat
Air weapons:	WE-177 tactical nuclear bombs; Sparrow AAM; Sidewinder AAM; Martel ASM; 1,000lb MC bombs; 540lb bombs; 500lb bombs; 2in rocket projectiles; Mark 44/46 torpedoes; Mark 11 depth charges; flares and pyrotechnics

Individual ship history

Ark Royal

Ark Royal was launched by HM Queen Elizabeth, later Queen Elizabeth the Queen Mother, on 3 May 1950 and completed on 25 February 1955 after contractor's sea trials. She was handed over to the RN and commissioned by the Queen Mother in Devonport a day later, on 26 February, and allocated to the C-in-C Plymouth for initial Service trials. When these were completed she carried out flying trials in the Mediterranean in June and then embarked her first air group on 21 July 1955. It comprised 800 and 898 (Sea Hawk) together with 824 (Gannet ASW) NAS, and she joined the MF. There were delays in getting some of the new types for her air group into service, but 849B (Skyraider) NAS joined on 8 December 1955 and 891 (Sea Venom) NAS joined on11 February 1956. In March she took part in Exercise *Dawn Breeze* with

other NATO ships in the Western Mediterranean and then returned to the UK to join the HF. Having launched and commissioned the ship, the Queen Mother maintained a relationship with *Ark Royal* and visited her in Portsmouth in April before the ship moved to Devonport for a refit which was to prevent her taking part in the Suez intervention later in the year.

After the refit was completed in November 1956 she rejoined the HF with an air group comprising 802, 804, 898 (Sea Hawk), 815 (Gannet ASW), 831 (Wyvern) and 849B (Skyraider) NAS. Sea Venoms had some development problems, and her nightfighter squadron did not join until some months later. In February 1957 problems with her steam turbines, the first of many machinery problems that were to affect her throughout her life, forced her to return to Devonport Dockyard for repairs, which were completed in May. On 27 May 1957 she was one of a number of ships that concentrated with the HF in Cromarty Firth, and on that day she was visited by HM Queen

Elizabeth II and the Duke of Edinburgh. Two days later she sailed with HM The Queen embarked to witness flying operations in the Moray Firth. On 30 May she sailed for the USA to take part in the International Naval Review at Hampton Roads, Virginia; visits to Norfolk Navy Base and New York were made, and cross-deck operations were carried out with aircraft from the USS *Saratoga*. On her return to UK waters at the end of June she transferred 898 NAS to *Bulwark* at sea, using Whirlwind helicopters to transfer personnel, stores and luggage after the aircraft had recovered to their new ship; this was a 'first' for a RN jet fighter squadron.

On her return to the UK 893 (Sea Venom) NAS joined the air group on 28 August 1957, and the ship took part in Exercise *Strikeback*, a NATO training period for the Strike Fleet. In October she secured in Southampton to act as host for a visit to the port by the USS *Forrestal* and her six escorting destroyers. On 27 January 1958 she embarked 800 (Sea Hawk) NAS, making her air group one of the largest ever operated by a British carrier. A day later *Ark Royal* rejoined the MF to take part in a series of NATO exercises, the first of which was Exercise *Marex* in March, followed by a visit to Genoa and then a maintenance period in Malta. Exercise *Apex*, intended to practice the art of screening a carrier task force against submarine attack, followed in April, and then Exercise *Shotgun* saw the air group providing air support for

Ark Royal after her special refit, showing the white rectangles painted alongside the angled deck, intended to help pilots orientate their line-up during night deck landings. They showed up well under the low-intensity floodlights mounted on the island and, when clean like this, were very effective. On deck are Buccaneers, Gannets and a Sea King helicopter. (AUTHOR'S COLLECTION)

amphibious landings on the coast of Sardinia. A visit to Naples followed, and then a BBC crew came on board to film footage for the TV series *Skylarks*. *Ark Royal* returned to Portsmouth in June 1958 and then moved to Devonport on 5 July to prepare for a major refit, during which the side-lift was to be removed and modifications were to be made to facilitate the operation of the Scimitar strike fighter. HM Queen Elizabeth The Queen Mother visited the ship on 7 July, and the refit began on 21 July 1958.

In April 1959 a fire broke out on board, delaying completion of the refit, but it was finished by the end of the year and she recommissioned at Devonport on 28 December 1959. After sea trials she embarked a new air group on 4 March 1960 comprising 800 and 807 (Scimitar), 820 and 824 (Whirlwind), 892 (Sea Vixen) and 849A (Gannet AEW) NAS and sailed for Malta to join the MF. Feed water problems caused a machinery breakdown, and a planned visit to Naples had to be cancelled so that she could be docked in Malta to cure the problem. In April she carried out strike exercises with the US 6th Fleet, and in early June she gave a 'Shop Window' demonstration of her capability for Spanish VIPs off Barcelona. Later in the month she embarked a squadron of French Navy Aquilons, a licence-built version of the Sea Venom, for joint exercises off Toulon. In return, the two Whirlwind squadrons were disembarked for antisubmarine exercises with the French Navy ashore. After a visit to Palma *Ark Royal* returned to the UK to participate in the NATO Exercise *Swordthrust* in company with *Hermes* and a number of Allied warships and aircraft. She returned to Devonport in October to give leave and carry out an assisted maintenance, after which she embarked a changed air group which comprised 800 and 807 (Scimitar), 824

(Whirlwind), 849A (Gannet AEW) and 831 (Gannet ECM) NAS, the latter embarking for the first time. In November she returned to the Mediterranean for Buccaneer trials which were meant to follow a short visit to Malta, during which some of her aircraft were disembarked to RNAS Hal Far. The trial was delayed, however, because of difficulties with the Buccaneer that had to be resolved before it could take place. A visit to Toulon was cancelled and the stay in Malta extended into a ten-day maintenance period. More aircraft were needed ashore for continuation flying, so Scimitars and Gannets were launched by catapult while the ship was moored in Grand Harbour, the first time swept-wing jets had been launched from a stationary ship by the RN.

The Buccaneer trials eventually took place from 15 November 1960; thirty-six deck landings were achieved by the two aircraft, but their engines suffered reliability problems and the trial was terminated early. Later in November 893 (Sea Vixen) NAS joined the air group and *Ark Royal* took part in Exercise *Royal Flush II* in company with *Victorious* and *Hermes*. This was an air-defence exercise with the USN 6th Fleet, and was unusual in that the RN had more participating carriers than the USN. It was followed by Exercises *Pink Gin III* and *Decex*, after which *Ark Royal* went alongside in Gibraltar for a FOAC inspection. Later in the month she embarked the First Sea Lord to give a demonstration of carrier capability with *Victorious*, after which she spent Christmas in Malta. In January 1961 she moved into the Atlantic to carry out Arctic Trials off Greenland. These were intended to evaluate how conditions of extreme cold affected flying operations, with special emphasis on men and equipment. They ended on 9 February and, after a short visit to New York, *Ark Royal* returned to Devonport to end

Ark Royal was not fitted with Type 984 radar and CDS, but had the two Type 965Q double arrays shown here. The 'dustbin' shape at the highest point of the mast is a Tacan homing beacon. (AUTHOR'S COLLECTION)

what had been a short but interesting commission, during which 8,632 aircraft sorties had been flown in a variety of weather conditions ranging from the benign to the extreme.

After a docking and maintenance period, *Ark Royal* recommissioned in September 1961 and embarked a new air group in November after sea trials and a work-up. It comprised 800 (Scimitar), 815 (Wessex), 849C (Gannet AEW) and 890 (Sea Vixen) NAS. After embarkation the ship sailed for the Mediterranean to work-up to the standard required for her ORI until January, when she returned to Devonport to prepare for service with the FEF. Unfortunately she grounded entering harbour because two marker buoys were out of position, and repairs took until March, when she sailed for the Far East. When she passed through the Suez Canal at the end of the month she was the largest RN warship to have done so. At the time the canal had not been widened or deepened, and there were concerns that she was a tight fit. When she completed the passage her captain sent a signal to the Admiralty that simply said 'pop'. *Ark Royal* arrived in Singapore on 12 April 1962 after thirty-four days at sea. Later in the month she participated in exercise *Fantail* to practise giving support to 3 Commando Brigade in the Malayan Jungle, before sailing to join *Melbourne* and the USS *Bennington* for the SEATO Exercise *Sea Devil*. On conclusion of the exercise on 2 May 1962 a fourteen-mile-long column of thirty-four warships, led by the carriers, steamed in Manila Bay, the largest fleet ever to visit the city. A longer visit to the US base at Subic Bay was followed by a short stay in Hong Kong and then exercises with the USN off Okinawa. In July she took part in Exercise *Fotex 62* with a number of RN, RAN and RNZN warships. The C-in-C FES visited *Ark Royal* and was flown ashore to Singapore in a Gannet.

In August *Ark Royal* took part in Exercise *Showboat* off Singapore, a demonstration of RN capability for regional heads of state and VIPs, after which she visited Fremantle in Western Australia, where 15,000 visitors toured the ship in a single day and a ship's company dance ashore was attended by over 3,000 people, many of whom had travelled great distances. In October flying exercises were continued in the Singapore and Hong Kong areas. She finally left Singapore on 25 October, carrying the guns, transport and equipment of 34 Regiment RA on the flight deck in addition to the air group for passage to Aden. The Regiment was disembarked on 4 November, and after flying exercises *Ark Royal* visited Mombasa, where the captain hosted a visit by

tribal chieftains who had travelled a considerable distance to see the ship. She returned to Devonport on 16 December 1962 to carry out a self-maintenance period, after which she sailed on 4 February 1963 for flying trials in Lyme Bay. These included the first deck landings by the prototype Buccaneer S2, and a series of night 'touch-and-go' landings by a Sea Vixen to evaluate new flight-deck floodlighting that had been installed during the maintenance period. On 8 February a prototype Hawker P.1127 Kestrel V/Stol fighter made the world's first vertical landing by a jet aircraft on an aircraft carrier off Berry Head. It was flown by company test pilot Bill Bedford, who had no previous deck landing experience. Trials continued for several days, during which the aircraft carried out a number of vertical and rolling take-offs and landings.

Early in 1963 the creation of Malaysia led to 'Confrontation' with Indonesia, and *Ark Royal* was allocated to the FEF to join *Hermes* and *Centaur* after taking part in exercise *Dawn Breeze VIII* and docking in Gibraltar. She carried out flying exercises off Aden in May and visited Mombasa

before arriving off Malaysia to take part in Exercise *Birdcage* in the Andaman Sea with ships of the RN, RAN and RNZN. After a short maintenance period in Singapore she took part in Exercise *Fotex 63*, but her participation was cut short by turbine problems in 'Y' engine room and she had to return to Singapore Dockyard for repairs. Once repaired, *Ark Royal* visited Hong Kong and then sailed for the Persian Gulf, where she took part in Exercise *Biltong* before visiting Mombasa and Karachi. In November she joined the USS *Essex* for Exercise *Midlink* with ships from the UK, USA and Pakistan. She subsequently visited Zanzibar for its independence celebrations in December, called at Mombasa again and then sailed for the UK, arriving at Devonport on 3 January 1964 for a refit.

Post-refit trials began in November 1964, and she embarked a new air group comprising 803 (Scimitar), 819 (Wessex), 849C (Gannet AEW) and 890 (Sea Vixen) NAS, ready to start her full work-up in the Moray Firth during January 1965. After her ORI she took part in the NATO Exercise *Pilot Light* in company with *Karel Doorman* and ships of the US, Norwegian, Canadian and Dutch Navies.

Even a big ship like *Ark Royal* could pitch noticeably in a big swell; her bows are seen here 'digging in'. Landing with this amount of deck movement could be exciting. (AUTHOR'S COLLECTION)

A ceremonial entry into Bergen by the combined fleet followed on 10 March. Later in the month she carried out the carrier qualification trials for the Buccaneer S2, one of them being launched at its maximum all-up weight of 50,000lb, the first time the RN had launched an aircraft at this weight. She had a Families' Day off Devonport in May, and sailed for the FEF in June to relieve *Victorious*. She arrived in Singapore on 19 July 1965 and subsequently took part in Exercise *Fotex 65* before visiting Subic Bay and joining the USN in Exercise *Guardrail*. In September she carried out flying exercises close to the coast of Vietnam, and had to ride out tropical storm Agnes off Hong Kong in September before visiting the Colony.

Ark Royal was in Singapore on 31 October 1965 when fire broke out in 'B' boiler room and spread to the funnel uptakes. Repairs required

Ark Royal's two hangars photographed from the forward lift at its mid position. Buccaneers used the lower hangar; Phantoms, Gannets and Sea King helicopters the upper. (AUTHOR'S COLLECTION)

Dockyard assistance, and the ship's participation in Exercise *Warrior* off Australia was cancelled. Further feed-water problems were subsequently encountered, and she was not operational again until mid-December, by which time Rhodesia had declared UDI and *Eagle* had established the Beira Patrol. In late December *Ark Royal* visited Fremantle, and in early March she relieved *Eagle* off the Mozambique Channel. *Eagle* returned later in the month so that *Ark Royal* could return to Singapore for maintenance, the intention being that she would return to the Beira Patrol in mid-April. Mechanical defects proved a problem again, however, and prevented her sailing until the end of April. She finally relieved *Eagle* on 4 May 1966. During this second period her aircraft searched 12 million square miles of ocean, located 500 ships, and *Ark Royal* had steamed 12,000 miles. On 30 May she left the area to return to the UK, arriving at Devonport on 13 June to join the HF. In August she took part in the NATO Exercise *Straight Lace*, and on 20 September 1966 she embarked HM The Queen Mother off Aberdeenshire for day at sea,

during which she witnessed a firepower demonstration. A fortnight later *Ark Royal* returned to Devonport, arriving on 4 October, to be destored and pay-off into Dockyard hands for a major modernisation to equip her to operate the next generation of naval aircraft.

Work on installing a fully angled deck, new steam catapults, direct-acting arrester gear and new maintenance facilities within what was already an elderly hull began in early 1967 and was completed in February 1970. She was recommissioned on 24 February 1970 by HM The Queen Mother, and sailed for post-refit trials on 4 March. During these, problems were found with the jet-blast deflectors, the bow catapult and the arrester gear, which had to be set right in Devonport. A visit to Liverpool took place in June, after which her new air group, comprising 809 (Buccaneer), 824 (Sea King), 849B (Gannet AEW) and 892 (Phantom) NAS, joined the ship. Her ORI was successfully achieved on 29 July. During a further work-up in the Irish Sea during September, *Ark Royal* stood by the burning coaster

Ark Royal taking part in Exercise *Ocean Safari* in 1977. (AUTHOR'S COLLECTION)

St Brenden until the destroyer *Cavalier* arrived to tow it to safety. Next came the NATO Strike Fleet Exercise *Northern Wedding* and a visit to Oslo, after which a Sea King of 824 NAS rescued the crew from a disabled German merchant ship, the *Leda*. She then deployed to the Mediterranean and was in Malta when the new Government announced that she would be retained in service until the late 1970s to maintain RN capability. From 29 October 1970 *Ark Royal* took part in exercise *Lime Jug 70*. The Soviet *Kotlin* Class destroyer *Bravyy* was shadowing her, a common practice during the Cold War era, but inexplicably turned across the carrier's bow during a night launch. Only prompt action by *Ark Royal*'s captain prevented a tragedy, but her bow still impacted the destroyer's port quarter, and seven Soviet seamen were seen to fall or jump off their ship into the sea. Five were recovered, but a search initiated for the other two found no trace of them. *Ark Royal* had some damage to her stem about four feet above the waterline, and returned to Malta for this to be repaired. Before her arrival, however, she stood by the destroyer *Fife*, which suffered a major fire in her gas turbine room; Sea Kings ferried foam and other fire-fighting equipment from *Ark Royal* to help. When the repairs in Malta were complete she sailed for flying exercises near the island. On 29 November 1970 Lieutenant T Adams, normally a Gannet pilot in 849B NAS, was launched from the flight deck in his hot-air balloon to land mail in Malta; the only known occasion when such an 'aircraft' was used for this purpose. After a visit to Naples she returned to Devonport for a maintenance period in December.

The work was completed in April 1971, and she sailed to embark her air group and work-up in the Moray Firth. In May she embarked RAF Harriers for a ten-day trial to see if their operation from an aircraft carrier was viable; this was the first time RAF fighters had taken-off from an RN carrier since the Second World War, and while their embarkation was not without its difficulties it was shown to be perfectly practical. For periods during the trial, Government ministers, senior officers and representatives of nine other navies, including the USN, embarked to see how it progressed. After a brief return to Devonport, *Ark Royal* sailed for the Caribbean on 2 June 1971. Later in the month she and her aircraft took part in live missile firing exercises in the USN Atlantic

Fleet Weapons Range (AFWR), and provided the opposition for the USS *America*'s ORI. At the end of the month she carried out the first of a series of visits to Fort Lauderdale that were to culminate in *Ark Royal* being given the Freedom of the City. A maintenance period in the US Naval Station Mayport was followed by exercises with the USN in the AFWR and a brief visit to St Thomas in the US Virgin Islands before *Ark Royal* returned to UK waters, where she embarked a BBC television crew in Lyme Bay to film a live broadcast, 'At sea with the Royal Navy', from the ship. She returned to Devonport in September for a Families' day and maintenance period before sailing later in September for NATO Exercise *Royal Knight*, in which she operated as part of the Strike Fleet supported by US, German, Dutch and Norwegian warships. After the 'wash-up' in Rosyth she joined the USS *Independence* in the North Sea for Exercise *Magic Sword IV*, flying the flag of the C-in-C WF. In October she visited Portsmouth, and on 4 November 1971 she deployed to the Mediterranean for Exercise *Med Passex*, during which she cross-operated aircraft with the USS *Independence* in the Ionian Sea. After further intensive flying exercises and visits to Malta and Gibraltar she returned to Devonport on 7 December.

She sailed again in late January for exercises with the USN in the Caribbean, but in mid-Atlantic she was ordered to close the self-governing colony of British Honduras in

reaction to the threat posed by large Guatemalan Army units that had massed on the border. Some British troops were flown in, but there was nothing the RAF could do to support them. *Ark Royal* was ordered to proceed 'with all despatch' to close the area as soon as possible and demonstrate British resolve and capability. On 28 January 1972 she launched two Buccaneers of 809 NAS from a position southwest of Bermuda, tasked with overflying the capital, Belize City, to reassure the residents that Britain intended to defend them. Buccaneer tankers refuelled them in flight on the outward and inbound legs, and the mission involved six hours of continuous flying on a round trip of 2,600 miles with no politically acceptable diversion. Repeat launches were prepared as the ship closed the colony, but were not needed. The first flights caused the threat of invasion to evaporate; Guatemala did not wish to fight a nation with a strike carrier it could not match. It was a classic demonstration of sea power, for which 809 NAS was awarded the Boyd Trophy in recognition of its achievement. By early February the crisis was over, and the ship proceeded north for a planned visit to New York before exercising with the USN in the AFWR. In late February *Ark Royal* participated in Exercise *Lantredex*, in which

An interesting comparison. *Ark Royal* alongside in Norfolk Navy Base, Virginia, in 1978, next to the USS *Nimitz*. (USN)

Ark Royal about to enter Norfolk Navy Base, Virginia, while taking part in the US bicentennial celebrations in 1976. The author was serving in her at the time. (AUTHOR'S COLLECTION)

she provided the opposition for the USS *Franklin D Roosevelt*'s ORI. This realistic exercise included attacks with live weapons on a decommissioned USN destroyer, which was sunk by British Buccaneers and Phantoms. In March *Ark Royal* returned to Devonport for a maintenance period, sailing again in June 1972.

She took part in Exercise *West Hoe* in July as part of the preparation for her ORI, after which she took part in Exercise *Strong Express* in August; this was the largest NATO exercise ever held at the time, involving 300 ships and over 64,000 men. *Albion* and the US carriers *John F Kennedy* and *Intrepid* also took part. *Ark Royal* attended the 'wash-up' in Rosyth before carrying out flying exercises in the North Sea and visiting Oslo. In November two Buccaneers from A&AEE Boscombe Down were embarked to carry out trials with the new Martel ASM, and *Ark Royal* then deployed to the Mediterranean for Exercise *Corsica 72*, a UK amphibious training period with *Bulwark*, *Fearless* and *Intrepid* which included simulated opposed landings on the west coast of Corsica. In January 1973 she sailed for the NATO Exercise *Sunny Seas* off Portugal with ships from Canada, Norway, Holland, the USA and UK. This was followed by the national Exercise *Medtrain 73* in the Western Mediterranean with a large concentration of RN warships. After an extended visit to Malta she returned to the UK for a maintenance period before

deploying to the AFWR in April. A passage exercise was carried out with the French carrier *Foch* in mid-Atlantic. Exercise *Lantredex* was followed by a visit to Fort Lauderdale and further intensive flying operations off Florida, during which a number of mechanical problems with evaporators became apparent, but the ship was able to continue operations. In July she crossed the Atlantic to take part in Exercises *JMC 168* and *Sallyforth 73* off Scotland before returning to Devonport for a major refit which started at the end of the month.

The discovery of unexpected machinery defects delayed completion of the refit, but *Ark Royal* was able to sail in April 1974 for trials, and began her work-up in July. After that she deployed to the Mediterranean for intensive flying exercises. She was back in Devonport in December to prepare for a deployment to the western Atlantic, and sailed in January 1975 to exercise with the USN in the AFWR, during which cross-deck operations were carried out with the USS *Independence*. In May *Ark Royal* steamed south for exercises with the Brazilian Navy during which she embarked a Brazilian Navy Sea King squadron before visiting Rio de Janeiro, joining an RN task force from the Far East led by the cruiser *Blake*, which had steamed around the Cape of Good Hope. *Ark Royal* arrived back in Devonport in June. She sailed again in September for a work-up in the Moray Firth, during which HM The Queen Mother visited the

ship to witness flying operations. In November she took part in another large NATO training period, Exercise *Ocean Safari* in the Norwegian Sea, with over seventy-five Allied warships and auxiliaries, including *Hermes*. In February 1976 she sailed for Exercise *Springtrain* off Gibraltar with a BBC film crew on board who made the successful television series *Sailor*, after which she sailed for exercises with the USN in the AFWR again. She then underwent a maintenance period in Mayport. Catapult defects led to a further period of repair in Norfolk Navy Yard before the ship returned to the AFWR. After a second, scheduled visit to Norfolk, *Ark Royal* returned to the UK in July. She sailed again in September for Exercise *Teamwork* off Scotland, then visited Lisbon before entering the Mediterranean for NATO Exercise *Display Determination* with warships from Portugal, France, Italy, Turkey, the USA and UK. The other carriers taking part were *Nimitz*, *America* and *Clemenceau*. After visiting Toulon and Gibraltar she returned to the UK at the end of October to prepare for her final refit, which was planned to last from November 1976 to June 1977.

The refit was completed on 1 June 1977 as

Phantom XT865 on *Ark Royal's* forward lift, demonstrating how tight a fit this fighter was in a carrier originally designed in the mid-1940s. Note the catapult bridles stowed on the bulkhead to port of the lift platform. (AUTHOR'S COLLECTION)

planned, and after trials she took part in the Silver Jubilee Fleet Review for HM Queen Elizabeth II in the Solent on 28 June 1977, flying the flag of the C-in-C Fleet. Other carriers in the Review were *Hermes* and *Melbourne*. In September she worked-up in the Moray Firth, with a visit by HRH The Prince of Wales on 21 September during which he was launched in the observer's seat of a Buccaneer of 809 NAS. In October she visited Hamburg and then returned to the Moray Firth for the final phase of the work-up and ORI. Exercise *Ocean Safari*, another large NATO training period, was followed by Exercise *Isle d'Or*, a French-sponsored international training period, and a visit to Malta in November. After a visit to Naples she returned to Devonport in December. She sailed again on 18 February 1978 for a work-up and inspection by FOCAS, and in April she sailed for her final deployment to the western Atlantic, to the Caribbean and the USA. Exercises with the USN in the AFWR were interspersed with visits to the Virgin Islands before Exercise *Solid Shield* in May, during which *Ark Royal* provided opposition for the USS *John F Kennedy*. A visit to Port Everglades was followed by further exercises, during which problems with the evaporators made the supply of fresh water difficult. In June she visited Mayport but, despite considerable maintenance effort, condenser problems in 'Y' unit were added to the evaporator problems. In August she visited Norfolk Navy Yard for pre-exercise briefings, and subsequently took part in Exercises *Common Effort* with the USN and *Northern Wedding*, a NATO training period which involved over 200 warships and auxiliaries in a passage by the Strike Fleet from the USA to the Norwegian Sea.

On 20 September 1978, while *Ark Royal* was in the Moray Firth, The Queen Mother paid a final visit to 'her' ship at her own request. She was presented with a miniature replica of the ship's silver bell by the captain, after which she addressed the ship's company and said: 'It might seem strange to some people that a man-made floating construction of steel and weaponry should evoke the intensity of feeling, and indeed emotion, which I am sure we are all feeling'. Her words exactly captured the feelings of many people who had encountered this great ship during her important years of service. *Ark Royal* then deployed to the Mediterranean for her last period of training, the NATO Exercise *Display Determination*, during which she operated efficiently alongside the US carriers *Forrestal* and *John F Kennedy* before visiting Naples. A visit to Piraeus in Greece was followed by flying exercises with the USS *Saratoga*. She then made a final visit to Malta, sailing on 16 November 1978 flying her paying-off pennant. A brief visit to Palma was carried out, after which she sailed for the UK, disembarking the air group for a flight home across France on 27 November 1978, that day marking the RN's last steam-catapult launch. Ammunition was back-loaded to RFA *Regent* as she crossed the Bay of Biscay, and *Ark Royal* returned to Devonport on 4 December 1978 to end an era and meet an emotional welcome. She was subsequently destored and paid off for the last time on 13 February 1979. On 4 June she was moored to the buoys off Cremyll in the River Tamar, where her sister ship *Eagle* had lain for several years. Suggestions that she might be preserved came to nothing because of the cost involved, and in March 1980 it was announced that she had been sold for scrap. She set off under tow to Cairnryan on 22 September 1980, arriving six days later.

CHAPTER 31

SMALL CARRIER DESIGNS FOR A FUTURE FLEET

During the 'Radical' Defence Review of 1953 the First Sea Lord, Admiral of the Fleet Sir Rhoderick McGrigor, stated when giving evidence that he: '. . . must finally point out the disastrous results which would follow if, in spite of the strategic need, fleet aircraft carriers were abolished from the Royal Navy. In the eyes of the rest of the world we would cease to be a major naval power, and I must ask you to bear in mind the effect of this on the morale of the navy and on its confidence in any Board of Admiralty which agreed to such a measure.' Subsequent Boards kept faith with this view, and in August 1963 a later First Sea Lord, Admiral Sir David Luce, outlined his Board's philosophy in a letter to Commanders-in-Chief and Flag Officers. In this, he explained that the Admiralty Board were convinced that aircraft carriers and a viable Fleet Air Arm operating from them must continue to be integral parts of the fleet if it was to remain effective. True to this belief, he resigned when *Queen Elizabeth*, CVA-01, was cancelled in 1966. Unfortunately his successor, Admiral Sir Varyl Begg, failed to understand the relevance of aircraft to all forms of warfare and the vital need for aircraft carriers to operate them from the sea, and his opposition added to the RN's post-CVA-01 trauma. The new First Sea Lord set up a Future Fleet Working Party (FFWP), which was instructed to adopt an 'anti-carrier' focus intended

to change the fundamental and long-standing structure of the fleet.

The possibility of creating a viable fleet without carriers had been examined in 1962 for comparison with the arguments in favour of CVA-01. The study group had reported that such a fleet would be very expensive to create and very limited in capability. Without AEW aircraft, the fleet's anti-aircraft missiles would be limited to engagements within the ships' radar 'line of sight', making them particularly vulnerable to pop-up low-level attacks under the radar horizon. The fleet would have no defence against shadowing aircraft that remained outside missile range, and would be unable to destroy missile-firing aircraft before they launched their weapons. Sea search and probe missions like those that initiated the Beira Patrol would no longer be possible beyond the helicopters' radius of action. A surface-to-surface missile (SSM) would have to be developed or procured to replace strike aircraft in the anti-surface-vessel role, but even this would be of limited value without AEW aircraft to provide targeting information. The DNAW stressed to the FFWP the value of embarked AEW aircraft in all forms of warfare, and began to consider the potential of Stovl strike fighters such as the Hawker Siddeley Kestrel and its successor, the Harrier.

By 1966 the SSBN project was sufficiently far

advanced to allow DG Ships some flexibility to work on new sketch designs. Four escort cruisers and two replacement commando carriers remained in abeyance within the long-term costings, and as early as March 1966 the Naval Staff put forward a paper that recommended amalgamating the two designs. It was thought that six commando cruisers could result, which could either carry an embarked military force with its associated helicopters or an air group comprising a mix of antisubmarine, AEW and missile-carrying helicopters, probably Sea Kings. For the first time, serious consideration was recommended into the use of Stovl fighters to be exchanged for helicopters on a one-for-one basis. In May 1966 the FFWP followed the paper with a request for studies into the alternative assumption of building six command/commando/escort cruisers, each to be capable of embarking six P.1127 Kestrels or six helicopters. Studies were also set up to evaluate the possibility of fitting AEW radar into helicopters such as the Sea King or, surprisingly, the much larger twin-rotor Chinook, which had just entered service with the US Army. Design work was backed by a Naval Staff Target for the commando cruiser prepared in April, but as soon as DG Ships began to work on potential ship design it immediately became apparent that the requirement to operate and support any sort of fighter, even a Stovl one and even in modest numbers, drove the tonnage considerably above that proposed for the escort cruiser only three years earlier. The first sketch design was for a ship of 15,000 tons with an external hangar that formed part of a large starboard-side island, capable of housing six Sea Kings or four Kestrels and two SAR helicopters. The choice of an external hangar limited the number of aircraft that could be carried but allowed a large amount of mess-deck space under the flight deck for a commando group of up to 600 men in addition to the ship's company. With the hangar doors open, jet blast or the downwash from helicopter rotors would have made working in the hangar particularly difficult, and it would have been more difficult to keep the ship darkened with the large vertical hangar doors than

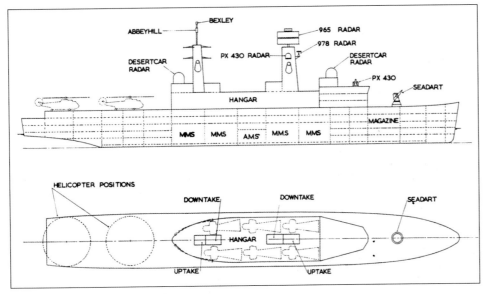

1966 Design 5 for a small helicopter-carrying cruiser. Note the combined mast and funnels like those in the CVA-01 design. (AUTHOR'S COLLECTION)

Top 1966 Design 6 for a larger helicopter-carrying cruiser with a 'through deck' and hangar in the relatively large island. (AUTHOR'S COLLECTION)

MIDDLE 1966 Design 7 for a 15,000-ton helicopter-carrying cruiser with a small hangar under the after flight deck in addition to the one in the island. The greater tonnage allowed more CVA-01 technology, including the Type 988 *Broomstick* radar on the foremast, to be incorporated. (AUTHOR'S COLLECTION)

BOTTOM A 1966 design for a cruiser-carrier. This design was sufficiently large to have potential for Stovl aircraft operations in addition to helicopters. (AUTHOR'S COLLECTION)

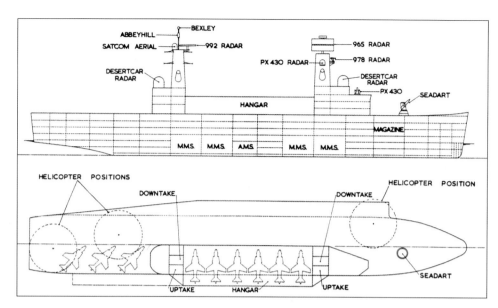

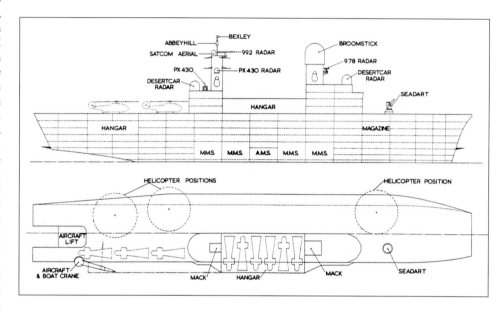

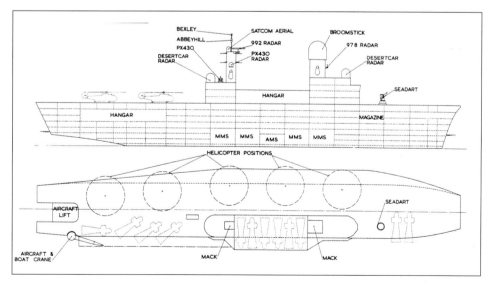

with the conventional hangar arrangement under the flight deck, in which lighting could be turned off in the lift wells during aircraft moves.

The sketch design resembled a scaled-down CVA-01 but with a larger island which also incorporated the soon-to-be-cancelled Type 988 radar. There was also to be a Sea Dart launcher aft, a 4.5 in Mark 8 gun forward of the island and a Sea Wolf SAM launcher aft of the island. Both SAM systems had their full outfit of target indication and tracking radars, and the ship was to have sonars Type 182, 184 and 185. She was to have an operations room to the latest standard, fitted with the Action Data Automated Weapons System (ADAWS), and was to be capable of operating as a flagship in command of naval task forces. Communications to the latest standard were required, including sets capable of working with the commando force ashore during an assault. Two-shaft steam machinery of 60,000shp was intended to deliver 28 knots six months out of dock, and the hull was to be 645ft long on the waterline, slightly shorter than a 1942 light fleet carrier, with a flight deck 100ft wide at its widest point, and an overall beam of 125ft. Unsurprisingly the cost was put at over £30 million. It was not intended that this ship was to be capable of operating in both the commando and antisubmarine roles concurrently. If used in the helicopter or Stovl fighter roles they would have been very expensive ships for the modest aircraft capability they deployed. If used in the commando role their lack of landing craft, assault helicopter numbers and support facilities would have put them at a considerable disadvantage when compared with the light fleet carrier conversions they would have replaced, which had good qualities in all these areas. Again, they would have been very expensive ships for the modest capability they delivered. Their missile and gun armament put them in the destroyer category, but without an antisubmarine weapon, except those carried by helicopters if embarked, these ships would have needed to be escorted rather than having their own capability as escorts. Lacking a ship-killing weapon, they were never cruisers in the historical sense of the name.

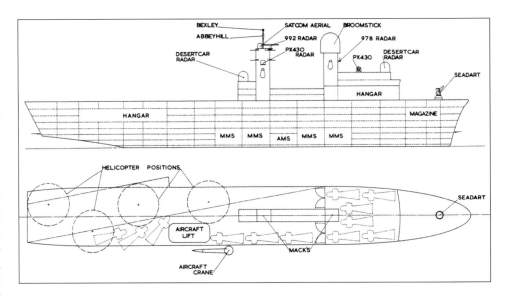

The FFWP noted the design and called for further work to address its weaknesses. The resulting changes included an increase in the number of embarked aircraft from six to eighteen, and an increase in the size of the embarked commando force to 650. Of these, 325 were to be accommodated to the latest RN standards and a further 325 to be given basic, bunk-only accommodation. To accommodate the extra aircraft a half-hangar was added on 4 deck under the after part of the flight deck to accommodate six Sea Kings or Kestrels. The original design had featured an external hangar in the island to remove the need for complicated lift platforms to penetrate the flight deck, but the revised design required a lift at the rear end of the deck that was suspended aft of the main hull so that it did not take up valuable hangar space. It was to be stressed to take 30,000lb to allow some aircraft growth, but its location aft meant that the Sea Dart launcher and its systems had to be moved forward. Other changes included the addition of ballistic protection around the machinery spaces and increased fuel stowage to meet the staff requirement for a 'fast deployment' endurance of 5,000 miles at 25 knots. These changes forced the standard displacement up to 17,000 tons and the estimated cost to over £38 million. An initial air group was envisaged as comprising six antisubmarine Sea Kings, four AEW or electronic warfare Sea Kings and eight surface search/strike Sea Kings equipped with the Martel ASM. Later the air group was expected to comprise six antisubmarine Sea Kings, four AEW Sea Kings and eight Kestrel Stovl strike fighters. Six aircraft were to be stowed in each hangar, with six more in a deck park.

The First Sea Lord, through the FFWP, criticised the design as 'looking too much like an aircraft carrier'. The DG Ships advised that, since the function dictates the form, this design had many advantages over other possible alternatives, but the FFWP ordered alternative studies into designs that could not be mistaken for aircraft carriers. This puerile instruction must represent the lowest point of British warship specification in the post-sailing era, but DG Ships did produce several designs, including one with a superstructure on the centreline aft, which looked rather like a super tanker, and another with the superstructure on the centreline forward, which looked like an oil rig support ship (or the later RFA *Argus*). A third design had the superstructure on the centreline amidships like the 1917 *Furious*.

As they ignored the hard-won lessons of the past, these designs deserved to be rejected, and they were. The design caused DG Ships to lose confidence in the naval staff, however, and the Directorate produced its own sketch design for a 20,000-ton commando carrier. To be built to mercantile standards, it was intended to establish the optimum size and cost for a 'cheap' ship capable of deploying a commando unit and its vehicles without the sophisticated and expensive command and weapons systems specified for the commando cruiser. The basis for the hull design was a study for a submarine depot ship intended to be built to Lloyd's rules; a small starboard-side island with a 'mack' combined mast and smokestack was included for minimal command and control, again reminiscent of CVA-01. Propulsion would also have made use of the steam technology developed for CVA-01, with 25,000shp delivering 20 knots six months out of dock and an endurance of 5,000 miles at economical speed. Two hangars under the

flight deck could have taken nineteen Wessex helicopters, exchangeable with a similar number of Kestrels. A garage in-between the hangars could have accommodated thirty-two Land Rovers and sixteen trailers, and other vehicles could have been stowed on the flight deck. The hull was slightly larger than that of a 1942 light fleet carrier but did not include sponsons in its basic form, in order to maintain commonality with the depot ship. Had they been included, an even more effective flight deck could have been created for relatively little extra expense. There were designed spots on the flight deck for eight Sea Kings to run concurrently and, as in *Bulwark* and *Albion*, four LCVP landing craft were to be carried on the port and starboard quarters to provide flexibility in assault landings.

The most bizarre of the 1966 'not an aircraft carrier' designs for a cruiser-carrier. (AUTHOR'S COLLECTION)

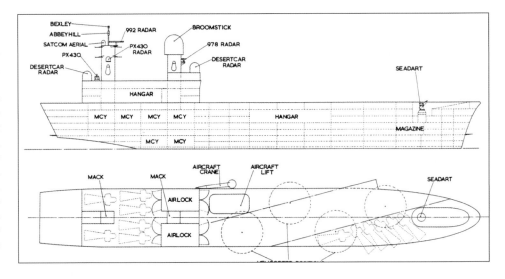

The practical 1966 design for a commando carrier. (AUTHOR'S COLLECTION)

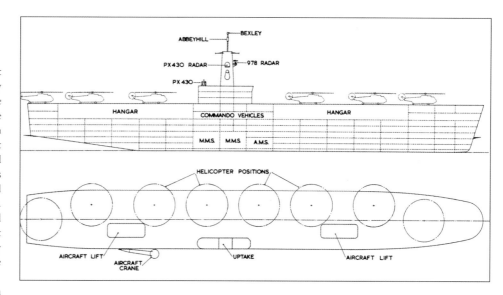

The design provided a capability similar to that of the USN *Iwo Jima* Class LHAs, with the ability to carry 650 commandos plus 250 more in austere accommodation. The ship's company had to be relatively high at 750 because of the steam machinery. Build cost was estimated to be about £20 million, less than half that of the proposed command/commando/cruiser, but modifications would have been needed before this design could have operated Stovl strike fighters successfully. They were possible, however, and the design would have had export potential. It was by far the most practical of the designs to emerge in this dreary period, but it was not taken forward. Nor were the command/commando/cruisers.

If nothing else, the FFWP designs had shown the naval staff that attempts to combine so many roles into a single ship design were never going to be economical or even practical. In June 1967 the idea of a command cruiser, able to act as a flagship for the largely frigate-equipped navy that was expected to remain after the carriers were phased out in the mid-1970s, emerged and gained support from the Secretary of State for Defence, Dennis Healey. Despite his earlier open opposition to CVA-01, he now found himself able to describe command cruisers to the First Secretary of the Treasury as having: '… a number of capabilities which are essential if the shape of the fleet, based mainly on relatively lightly armed frigates, is to be credible in the 1970s; in particular the command of aircraft, aircraft control facilities and the larger antisubmarine helicopters which will be increasingly important weapons, especially against nuclear submarines. … I am entirely satisfied that we must find room in our future naval plans for some ships of the cruiser type.' To fund these new ships he was content to limit the construction of the new Type 82 destroyers to the single prototype ship on order, even though a new class would have to be designed to carry the Sea Dart missile system in its stead. Following this enthusiasm the FFWP ordered a series of exploratory studies that looked at the qualities required from a helicopter-carrying command cruiser, which was tentatively given the NATO designation CCH. More than fifty-two different sketch designs were produced, ranging from an 8,300-ton ship with a two-spot flight deck aft of a box-like hangar capable of containing four Sea Kings but with no gun or missile armament and estimated to cost £20 million, to an 18,750-ton design with internal hangarage for nine Sea Kings or Stovl fighters under the flight deck, Sea Dart, torpedo tubes, chaff dispensers and close-range guns. The latter was to be powered by steam turbines capable of high speed and long endurance, and was estimated to cost £36 million, over half

the cost of CVA-01 for a fraction of the capability.

The costing of new designs intended to meet the FFWP vision became a major issue, and on 12 July 1968 DG Ships gave a presentation on the subject to Admiral Begg and his Board colleagues. In it he said:

> It has become abundantly clear to us in recent years that our predictions of unit cost for projected new ship designs cause both pain and surprise to Board members. The pain obviously arises from high costs versus limited budgets. The surprise shows a lack of common ground between Board Members and ourselves in terms of judging the potential costliness of a given warship concept as a whole and of individual features of that concept both in an absolute sense and in comparison with other designs and with merchant ship types. Some of this may even be due to diverging mental pictures of the ship package to which the cost is attached.

The specific factor that had triggered this issue was the apparent imbalance of cost between CVA-01, estimated at £60 million, and the 18,750-ton CCH estimated at £36 million but with considerably less capability. The Board had associated cost with tonnage, but now they were forced to realise that the bulk of the cost lay with systems, including computer assisted command and communication systems, missiles, high-technology radars and machinery. The cost of the steelwork had become a secondary issue, and it was arguably cheaper to build a larger hull to make the installation of systems easier. There is evidence to show that attempts to reduce the tonnage and volume of CVA-01 proved to be more expensive than allowing a modest increase in size would have been. The point DG Ships was making was that

CVA-01 had been a 'cost-effective' design; the package was expensive but you got a considerable amount of fighting capability across the whole range of modern warfare for it. The command cruiser designs emerging from the FFWP deliberations contained the same command systems, missiles, radars and aircraft support arrangements, the last being required whether it was intended to operate nine aircraft or forty-nine. Given the grudging aspirations to operate a variety of aircraft for essential tasks, the biggest differences between the carrier and the larger command cruiser designs were internal volume and the steel needed to encapsulate it. The first was free and the second not expensive. The planners and, indeed, their political masters, had failed to understand that the systems were more expensive than the structure.

A secondary but nonetheless important factor was that CVA-01 was a completed design ready to go out to the shipyards for competitive tender. About £3 million had been spent, and lost after cancellation, on long-lead items and, apart from the work needed to produce detailed production drawings, production could have started in months. The new command cruiser designs laid before the FFWP represented 'clean sheet of paper' concepts that would require design and development work that could take years. Design work on the carrier had been funded and lost; design work and construction of the command cruiser had still to be funded. The DG Ships could see no simple solution to the problem, but it was agreed that his department would, in future, inform the Board through the planning staff of the likely cost implications of specified warship systems in more detail than previously. This process started with the command cruiser design that evolved into the *Invincible* Class aircraft carriers, and detailed breakdowns of weight, space and cost were prepared.

A 1968 design for a helicopter-carrying command ship, showing how the cruiser designs were evolving towards the design that became the *Invincible* Class. (AUTHOR'S COLLECTION)

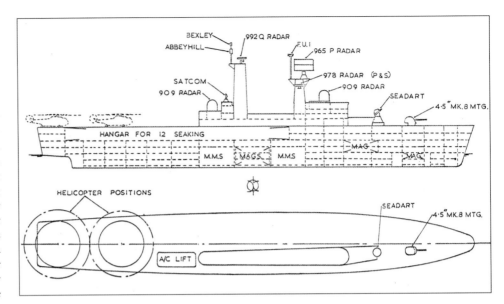

In 1968 Admiral Sir Michael Le Fanu replaced Admiral Begg as First Sea Lord. A former Controller who had championed the replacement carrier programme, he steered the cruiser design studies away from the smaller, less-capable ships towards larger designs with an unobstructed flight deck and starboard-side island capable of operating Stovl fighters. He was ably assisted by Admiral Sir Frank Hopkins, a naval pilot who had been a tower of strength in supporting carrier aviation, first as DNAW and then as 5th Sea Lord/DCNS under a succession of First Sea Lords. His support for 'carrier-shaped ships' must have been particularly difficult to maintain in the Begg years, and the RN owes him a great deal for his perseverance.

In 1970 a new Conservative Government was elected, and called for an evaluation of the possibility of running on the existing carrier force to fulfil a promise it had made in the election campaign. The evaluation had to be carried out in some haste, as the Government required the answer to be given in time for it to be included in the spring Parliamentary debate on the Navy Estimates. The previous Labour Government had failed to honour its promise to provide replacement weapons systems for the carriers, so on the face of it the decision to run on the carriers should have been obvious, but the limitations imposed by the new Government were to have a critical impact on the Admiralty Board's decision. There was still to be no new carrier, making the whole evaluation process seem little more than the management of a wasting asset. *Eagle* and *Ark Royal* would be allowed to run on until 1979, but *Hermes* was still to be converted into an LPH, although the reason why was not made clear. *Victorious* had already gone prematurely to the scrapyard, so was already beyond being saved but, surprisingly, *Centaur* was not considered for retention either as a CV or as a commando carrier, despite being only seventeen years old. Perhaps the cost was considered too high, although she had far greater potential than

any of the command cruiser designs put forward to the FFWP. The Government also stipulated that all Phantoms and Buccaneers were to be handed over to the RAF as planned by their Labour predecessors, so new aircraft would need to be procured to operate alongside the remaining Gannets, Sea Vixens and Sea Kings. There was to be no new money to replace the afloat support ships and dockyard facilities that supported the carriers, as their removal had already been identified as savings measures. The two commando carriers *Albion* and *Bulwark* were not included in the study and were expected to run on.

These crippling reservations meant that the provision of core capabilities on which the RN had relied since the Second World War would be difficult and expensive to maintain, but arguably the Board should have opted to retain the largest possible number of carriers because they represented the only option guaranteed to maintain the RN's capability for another decade. The case for retaining *Hermes* as a CVA could have been argued strongly, replacing her LPH conversion with *Centaur*. Still traumatised by the arguments over CVA-01, however, the Board was concerned that the design effort needed to plan refits for *Eagle* and

Ark Royal, the conversion of *Hermes* and the reprovision of afloat support would be large and might delay work on the command cruiser. They decided to compromise by retaining *Ark Royal* with sufficient Phantoms and Buccaneers for her air group until the late 1970s, as described in Chapter 30. The remaining Phantoms and Buccaneers would go to the RAF as previously planned, and *Eagle* would be discarded because, despite being the better ship, she was due a large refit before *Ark Royal*. Irrationally, it was thought that *Eagle's* planned refit would have led to an early gap in capability, but this view failed to take into account the fact that a single carrier could not provide complete continuity and there would inevitably be gaps after the reduction of the carrier force.

With the fate of the existing carrier force decided, Board attention turned to the command cruiser, since the Board felt that, after the bruising battles of the 1960s, it was unable to seek political approval to design and build a true aircraft carrier. The large cruiser design seemed the only viable option, and work on the design was ordered with some urgency. The development of the *Invincible* Class that evolved from it is described in detail in chapter 33.

CHAPTER 32

SHORT TAKE-OFF AND VERTICAL LANDING

This iconic image shows a prototype Hawker P.1127 in the hover before making the world's first vertical landing by a fast-jet on an aircraft carrier. It took place on *Ark Royal* on 8 February 1963. (AUTHOR'S COLLECTION)

In 1945 the Admiralty drafted a staff requirement for a quick-reaction, vertical-take-off fighter capable of carrying out last-minute interceptions against Japanese kamikaze aircraft that had broken through the fleet's CAP. They would have been aware, through captured examples, of the German Bachem Ba 349 Natter point-defence interceptor, which was launched vertically up a railed structure, had an initial rate of climb of 35,000ft/min but an endurance of only 2min with its Walter HWK 109 rocket motor. It was intended for use against daylight bombers at altitude; once the pilot had fired his rocket armament at a target he ejected himself and the motor to parachute to the ground, leaving the wooden airframe to crash.

The Admiralty required a somewhat more rational fighter, and the Fairey Aviation Company put forward a sketch design for a small turbojet powered delta-wing fighter that was to achieve vertical take-off by being boosted up rails at the edge of the flight deck by rockets before reaching sustained flight with the jet engine. It would have landed 'more or less' conventionally on the flight deck, using a tail hook catching arrester wires. The

end of the war against Japan took the urgency out of the requirement, but it continued as a postwar research project as the Fairey Delta 1, with some interest from the RN and RAF. A number of half-scale models were launched from a vertical rail structure at the Weapons Research Establishment at Woomera in Australia. There was some USN interest in tail-sitters at the same time, but these also came to nothing.

By the late 1940s the RAE at Farnborough was concentrating considerable research into the problems associated with high-speed flight, and its scientists came to the conclusion that future supersonic aircraft would need very small, thin wings optimised for high-speed flight that would lead to very high landing speeds. This would make conventional take-off and landing on a carrier deck extremely difficult, if not impossible. The Admiralty had already seen landing speeds rise dramatically with the introduction of the first generation of jet fighters, and had no reason to doubt the RAE's advice that vertical landing would be the only practical way to operate future jet generations. The potential Stovl carriers described in chapter 27 were one response, and the Admiralty was always

conscious that the concept might have to be allowed for. It was thought that the time would come, probably in the late 1970s, when there would be no other way of operating fast jets. The concept had nothing to do with simplified deck operations or improving rough-sea landing capability. In fact the RAE scientists were proved wrong, and advances in wing design have continued to make it possible for fast jets to land conventionally on aircraft carriers.

NATO also became interested in VTOL strike fighters, but for a different reason. A growing belief that its airfields were vulnerable if the Red Army launched an attack on Western Europe led to a theory that aircraft should be dispersed into the field, close to the troops on the front line, despite the evidence from two world wars and the recent Korean conflict that it was extremely difficult to render airfields inoperable. The theory failed to take into account the logistical support problems posed by the need to get fuel and

A P.1127 demonstrates its ability to land across the deck with a relative wind on the port beam. While this proved practical on *Bulwark* in 1966, it was to prove much less practical in the narrower *Invincible* Class. (AUTHOR'S COLLECTION)

sophisticated weapons to widely dispersed sites close to the enemy in the front line. Nor did it take into account a number of considerations such as bad-weather recovery; homing through enemy or even friendly air space; and command of, communication with, and defence of the dispersed aircraft. A revised theory that VTOL aircraft would operate from an airfield main base where they would refuel, rearm and be briefed before moving forward into a dispersed site was even less realistic because reliance was placed on the continued use of the 'vulnerable' airfield. In the mid-1950s NATO naively sought to standardise Allied equipment from rifles to radar and, among others, two Basic Military Requirements were written for aircraft capable of operating from dispersed sites away from airfields. Requirement NBMR 3 called for a lightweight, single-role VTOL strike fighter capable of carrying a tactical nuclear weapon on short-range missions. It had to take-off and land on unprepared fields near the forward edge of the battle area. The less well-known NBMR 4 sought a tactical transport aircraft in the Lockheed C-130 Hercules class, able to support the NBMR 3 aircraft dispersed into the field. The UK, France, Germany and the USA put effort into NBMR 3, but only the UK put any significant effort into NBMR 4, the USA taking the view that the C-130 already provided sufficient rough-field capability to meet its requirements.

The British Hawker P.1127, French Dassault Mirage IIIV and German VAK-191 were all flown for evaluation, and paper studies of operational derivatives based on them were submitted for the glittering prize of standardised NATO production. The British Treasury hoped that production by an international consortium would radically reduce the cost of procurement and ownership for a new generation of battlefield support aircraft, but the NATO Standardisation Committee had no power to order aircraft, it could only recommend a solution. Sensitive to the international issues at stake, it declared the British and French aircraft 'Joint Technical Winners', and left the various governments to make of that what they would. By 1961 the British design had evolved into the Hawker Siddeley P.1154, which was supersonic at altitude and could carry a useful load from a short take-off. A vertical take-off was possible, but offered only limited payload and endurance. It would have been an expensive and very specialised aircraft to develop and, with an engine optimised to give a thrust-to-weight ratio better than 1:1 on landing, its specific fuel consumption in cruising

flight would have been inferior to that of contemporary foreign fighters. Its export potential would have been negligible. To complicate matters still further, in 1961 the UK Defence Secretary insisted that the P.1154 form the basis of a joint project to replace the de Havilland Sea Vixen in RN service and the Hawker Hunter in the RAF. This despite the fact that the former specified a two-seat, twin-engine, high-flying fighter with a very powerful radar and AAM armament, and the latter a single-seat, single-engine, low-flying ground-attack aircraft without radar, intended to carry a nuclear store or conventional bombs. Worse, the naval version had to be stressed for catapulting, although its vertical landing capability meant that it did not require an arrested landing. It needed a large fuel load to give endurance on CAP, and sufficient weapons to carry out two interceptions. The RAF version needed less fuel and a lighter structure to give 'quick dash' strike capability. Two years were wasted trying to

produce a common airframe that met these two very different requirements before the RN managed to convince the Government that the USN F-4 Phantom II was the only aircraft capable of delivering the sort of operational capability it required to face the threat posed by the Soviet Bloc; a batch was ordered and the P.1154RN was cancelled. Eighteen months later the simpler P.1154RAF version was also cancelled, and the RAF gained approval to buy F-4 Phantoms, showing that a common aircraft of the type envisaged by the RN had been possible all along if only the air staff had had the vision to accept it. A projected transport aircraft design to meet NBMR 4, the Armstrong Whitworth Type 681, was cancelled at the same time, as no other nation was interested in its 'niche' vertical landing capability and it would have been far more expensive than the C-130 to develop, procure and operate.

Some operational analysis of Stovl operations was carried out in 1965 using nine aircraft derived

A P.1127 makes a hover-landing on *Bulwark* in 1966. The jet efflux and the spray it is causing are evident below the aircraft. (AUTHOR'S COLLECTION)

from the P.1127 prototype and named Kestrel. Three each were purchased by the Governments of the UK, USA and Germany to form a Tripartite Evaluation Squadron which operated at RAF West Raynham. Pilots and maintenance personnel were drawn from the RAF, USAF, Luftwaffe and the USN; the RN chose not to be represented. One of the aircraft crashed, but when the squadron was disbanded six of the remaining eight aircraft, designated AV-8As, went to the USA for further evaluation, and two continued development work in the UK. The USAF and Luftwaffe both concluded that operations from hardened shelters on conventional airfields by conventional aircraft were both cheaper and more efficient than dispersed operations by VTOL aircraft. Had there

A P.1127 carries out a running take-off from *Bulwark* in 1966. The jet blast has no effect on the Wessex helicopter parked on 9 spot with its blades spread. (AUTHOR'S COLLECTION)

Sea Harriers ranged aft in *Invincible*. (AUTHOR'S COLLECTION).

been any operational merit in dispersed Stovl operations, the USAF would undoubtedly have hastened them into service during the Vietnam War, which was growing in intensity and had already led to urgent requirements for new combat aircraft. After all the funding, some interest in Stovl operations remained in the UK, and a developed version of the Kestrel went into service with the RAF in 1969. This had little to do with the cost-effective delivery of an interdiction/strike capability and more with the contemporary Labour Government's wish to provide some work for the British aviation industry, which had suffered a series of cancelled projects in the preceding months. The new version was given the name Harrier, originally intended for the P.1154; eighty-four were ordered in the first batch, but significantly the RAF ordered 200 more-capable but conventional SEPECAT Jaguars to form the main component of its tactical strike force.

In retrospect, the British fascination with the platform rather than the required operational effect it was intended to achieve is difficult to understand. It contrasts unfavourably with the US and German decision to focus on the more efficient and affordable capability offered by conventional aircraft operating from hardened conventional airfields, albeit further from the front line. The NATO planners' assumption that concrete runways were the vulnerable part of the equation is even more difficult to understand. Dispersed aircraft near the front line and the hundreds of men and vehicles needed to make them work would have been vulnerable to small-arms, mortar and artillery fire in addition to missile and air attack; the weather in Europe would have been a significant limiting factor. The initial outfit of a Harrier squadron in Germany included over 200 support vehicles which proved impossible to hide. The idea of dispersed operation was quietly dropped after 1970.

At sea, however, Stovl operations proved far more efficient and practical. The USMC invested in a small number of AV-8A Harriers because they were impressed by the aircraft's undoubted ability to deliver bombs over short ranges in the ground-attack role to support infantry in an amphibious assault. Far from being dispersed, AV-8s embarked in an LPH were at the centre of the action, surrounded by a layered defence system and able to move ashore with the marines like helicopters. Workshops and magazines in the LPH were concentrated close at hand. Cynics have also

A Sea Harrier of 801 NAS leaves *Ark Royal*'s 12-degree 'ski-jump'. (AUTHOR'S COLLECTION)

A Sea Harrier landing from the hover on *Illustrious*. (AUTHOR'S COLLECTION)

commented that the AV-8A was so highly specialised in the ground-attack role that it could not be 'mis-employed' on naval missions, as other USMC fighters such as the Chance-Vought F-8 Crusader and F-4 Phantom often were. Despite a licence agreement between Hawker Siddeley and McDonnell Douglas, the AV-8A was procured in such small numbers that all were built in the UK. The RN began to take a close interest in the Harrier after the cancellation of CVA-01, and the operation of Stovl aircraft began to be a driver for some of the larger command cruiser designs.

The proponents of Stovl fighters claimed they could be operated from small, simple and therefore cheap ships which came to be known as 'Harrier carriers', to provide fighter capability at sea without incurring the cost of a true carrier. A study carried out by DNAW in the late 1960s revealed a more balanced picture. It compared the Harrier with the version of the Jaguar under development at the time for the French Navy. It noted that Harriers were more expensive than Jaguars in the ratio of 8:5. Eight Jaguars could be purchased for the same price as five Harriers, an imbalance which explained why the RAF bought more of the former. Furthermore, because it was designed to optimise cruise efficiency rather than landing performance, the Jaguar could carry a larger weapon load further. In this era before the introduction of 'smart' weapons, fewer Jaguars than Harriers would be needed to ensure hits on a given target, and Jaguars had the radius of action to reach targets that the Harrier could not. The study compared two weapon effort planning scenarios; one a strike intended to sink a destroyer-sized warship, the other a strike intended to destroy a bridge. Different parameters were used, some favouring the Harrier and some the Jaguar, and on average it was found that twelve Harriers would be needed to perform the same task as eight Jaguars, and that there were a significant number of options the latter could employ that the former could not. Cost-effectiveness factors of 96 against 40 were derived, making the Harrier more than twice as expensive as the Jaguar for a given task, but the Jaguar could not be operated from a 'simple' Stovl ship. The study took the contemporary cost of steam-catapult and arrester-wire systems and modified the cost-effectiveness factors accordingly. For a *Hermes*-sized carrier fitted with two steam catapults and four arrester wires, the revised numbers were 96 against 50, and such

a ship had the advantage of being able to operate viable AEW aircraft and cross-deck a range of Allied fighters as well, something the 'Harrier-carrier' could not do. It was still very much more expensive to procure the less-capable Stovl aircraft and the 'cheap' ship has been bought by the higher expenditure on an expensive aircraft. Numbers vary, but the same argument holds good in the twenty-first century. The USN is not interested in the Stovl variant of the F-35 Joint Strike Fighter because its own 'tail-hook' carrier version is cheaper and carries a larger weapon load further. The USMC wants the Stovl variant because it is the only aircraft available capable of moving ashore with the Marines alongside helicopters in an amphibious assault. Despite questions about the variant's cost and over-engineered design, the USMC really has no alternative.

The British decision to procure the Stovl variant of the F-35 for the *Queen Elizabeth* Class described in chapter 35 owes more to political factors than any selection process intended to identify the ideal, cost-effective carrier-borne

Boeing, and small numbers were exported to Spain, Italy and Thailand, who continue to operate them in the twenty-first century. In addition, AV-8Bs were built by BAE Systems to replace the earlier generation of Harriers in the RAF.

The Sea Harrier was not the best fighter that the RN could buy at the time, but it was the only aircraft that the British Government of the time would allow it to buy, regardless of cost-effectiveness or capability issues. In practical terms it was the only fighter that could be operated at sea once the RN was forced to order ships of such limited size as the *Invincible* Class but, fortunately, the RN retained a skill base from its earlier Phantom and Buccaneer pilots to make it work effectively and 'fight above its weight' in the South Atlantic Conflict to liberate the Falkland Islands. The Sea Harriers embarked in *Hermes* and *Invincible* were fundamental to British plans, and twenty-eight out of the total of thirty-two that had been procured at the time were deployed in four NAS, one of them formed at short notice. They flew 2,000 operational sorties and achieved thirty-two confirmed 'kills' over enemy aircraft in air-to-air combat. They also carried out effective strikes against enemy shipping and shore targets. None were lost in air combat, but two were lost to anti-aircraft fire and others in accidents. An overall serviceability in excess of 90 per cent was maintained. The ability of Sea Harriers to recover on to their small carriers in rough weather was fortuitous, since it had not been called for in the Staff Requirement for the aircraft. Comparisons with *Ark Royal* and her air group, which had been decommissioned three years earlier, were not entirely appropriate because she was at the end of a long life in which very much more capability had been achieved than her original designers would have thought possible. The real comparison should be made with *Queen Elizabeth*, CVA-01, the ship the RN had tried for so many years to procure in order to deter, or if necessary fight this war or any other in which the nation had to take decisive action at short notice. She was designed to operate in rough weather, with strike operations in the Barents Sea in mind, and would have been better able to operate aircraft in the South Atlantic than *Ark Royal*, *Hermes* or *Invincible*. In historical terms the RN made the Sea Harrier work, and the RN can be justly proud of its achievement. In terms of the capability the nation needed and should have been able to afford, there were better solutions.

The *Invincible* Class was originally designed to operate Sea Harriers from a runway 450ft long and angled 1 degree to port so that the aircraft cleared the Sea Dart missile launcher and its protective

aircraft. For similar reasons the procurement of a navalised version of the Harrier in the late 1970s was political in that it was the only aircraft that the Government would allow the RN to operate from its projected command cruisers. With an effective limit of 20,000 tons on these ships they could not, realistically, have operated any conventional carrier aircraft that was available.

The navalised Harrier was given the name Sea Harrier, which was originally to have been given to the RN version of the P.1154. It entered front-line service with radar and other modifications for use in the fighter, reconnaissance and strike roles, the last including the ability to carry the WE-177 nuclear weapon. The Sea Harrier was deployed at first in squadrons of only five aircraft, but it was

immediately apparent that the new type was far more effective in its mobile base than its shore-based cousin had been in dispersed operations. The command, control, communications, workshop support and magazines needed to support sustained strike fighter operations had the effect of changing the command cruiser into an aircraft carrier, however, and it proved not to be a 'cheap' ship. Sea Harriers operated effectively from all three *Invincible* Class ships and *Hermes*, but the only export success was India, which bought Sea Harriers together with *Hermes* in the mid-1980s. The USMC developed and procured an advanced version of the AV-8A, designated AV-8B, for use in the ground-attack role. It was manufactured in the USA by McDonnell Douglas, now part of

ABOVE An overhead view of the P.1127 after landing on *Ark Royal*'s deck on 8 February 1963. (AUTHOR'S COLLECTION)

RIGHT A Sea Harrier of 801 NAS lands on the USS *Ranger*.

'zareba' just aft of the open forecastle. After lining up at the after end of the deck the aircraft would accelerate along the runway, reaching the forward end at about 90 knots. With a typical wind of 20 knots over the deck this gave an end speed of 110 knots as the aircraft left the deck, well below the stalling speed of the small wing. To compensate, the pilot selected the nozzles down to about 50 degrees from the horizontal and raised the nose slightly to give optimal wing incidence. Much of the aircraft's weight was thus borne by engine thrust, but a proportion of thrust was still directed aft and accelerated the aircraft away in slightly climbing flight. Seconds later, when speed had increased to the point where the wing provided sufficient lift for normal flight, the nozzles were rotated fully aft and the aircraft was flown conventionally. This short-take-off technique allowed the aircraft to launch about 30 per cent heavier than a vertical take-off would have allowed. This technique is used today by USMC AV-8B Harriers launching from LPH, but the RN improved on it with a 'ski-jump'. Like the angled deck, mirror landing aid and steam catapult, this was the idea of a serving naval officer, in this case Lieutenant Commander D R Taylor RN. In addition to the RN, the technique has been used by the Indian, Russian, Spanish, Italian, Thai and most recently Chinese navies on the their carriers, although the Russians and Chinese use it to launch conventional rather than Stovl fighters.

The Harrier family has been particularly well suited to this form of launch since, being designed to hover, they have a system of duplicate flying controls that operate when the wing is not giving lift and the normal control surfaces have no airflow on which to act. In wingborne flight the Harrier is controlled by conventional elevators, ailerons and rudder. When the engine nozzles are rotated below 10 degrees these surfaces continue to move but, in addition, a series of 'puffer' jets fed with bleed-air from the engine through a series of pipes provide forces which control the aircraft in pitch, roll and yaw. The pilot makes inputs to the 'puffer' jets by moving his controls in the normal manner to activate both types of control. When the nozzles are returned to the horizontal the 'puffer' jets are selected off, and only the conventional control surfaces remain active. The USMC elected to retain its 'flat launch' technique, as it allows more level space for the operation of helicopters from its ships, which have the advantage of a deck run nearly twice as long as that in *Invincible*. The 'ski-jump' comprises a curved structure at the forward end of the flight deck over the bow which causes the aircraft to leave the deck after nozzle rotation at a speed very much less than that required for a flat deck take-off. This effect translates into a shorter deck run or higher launch weight, or both. At the high aircraft weights associated with strike missions a 'ski-jump' represents about a 30 per cent reduction in the end speed required, which, because distance depends on speed squared, reduces the deck run required by about 50 per cent. At the lower weights typical of fighter missions the decreased end speed requirement leads to a 40 per cent reduction in velocity, requiring a deck run of only about a third of that needed for a flat deck launch. Alternatively, from a longer deck run the end speed remains

comparable with a flat deck launch; only about 4 knots is lost 'climbing the hill'. The aircraft is, thus, effectively launched with 30 knots 'excess' end speed and can carry 30 knots multiplied by 66lb per knot, roughly 2,000lb, extra payload compared with a flat-deck launch.

The concept was first tested using a 'ski-jump' erected from Fairey medium girder bridge components at RAE Bedford. A 15-degree 'ski-jump' was found to impose a 2.5g vertical loading on a Sea Harrier, but no structural changes to the airframe were deemed necessary, though the compression ratio of the undercarriage was altered to give a better performance. Theoretically, launch performance continues to improve with increased 'ski-jump' angles, but in practical terms there was found to be an optimum end speed corresponding to maximum launch weight, and this was achieved by a minimum angle, the size of which was derived from the radius which avoided the undercarriage being a limiting factor at that weight. This effectively sized the 'ski-jump', since excess load factor was proportional to end speed squared divided by the radius of the curve. In practice, the ideal radius for the Sea Harrier lay in the range 600 to 800ft. The application of Euclid's theory then determined how long and how high the actual 'ski-jump' structure needed to be for a given exit angle. The size of the structure grew markedly after 12 degrees, and this was a disincentive to considering larger angles. *Hermes* and *Ark Royal* were fitted with 12-degree 'ski-jumps' from the outset. Worries that the 'ski-jump' might blank the firing arcs of the Sea Dart launcher to port led to an initial, timid 7-degree structure being fitted on build in *Invincible* and *Illustrious*, but both were subsequently refitted with 12-degree 'ski-jumps'. The interface problem was finally resolved when Sea Dart was removed.

CHAPTER 33

INVINCIBLE CLASS

Invincible being relieved by *Illustrious*, the nearer ship, in the South Atlantic during 1982. The narrowness of the deck is clearly evident; *Invincible* has four Sea Harriers and a Sea King in the narrow Fly 2 alongside the island. *Illustrious* has three Sea Kings and a Sea Harrier. The deck markings were designed for their purpose by the author, who ran the flying trials in both ships. They differed from previous designs in having no circles to mark designated landing spots. (AUTHOR'S COLLECTION)

*I*nvincible was originally conceived as a command cruiser with aviation facilities, but the requirement to operate both large helicopters and Stovl fighters by day and night in any weather inevitably transformed the design into a small aircraft carrier. During the design process it was referred to as a 'through-deck cruiser', but the term drew some ridicule and the illusion that the ship could be described as any sort of cruiser was finally dispelled when the first ship was completed in 1980 and given an 'R' rather than a 'C' pennant number.

Technical background

The design that finally emerged from over fifty considered was a 19,500-ton ship with an excessively long island on the starboard side, set so far inboard that it severely limited the parking space in Fly 3. The wasted space outboard of it was used for boats on their davits. The narrow flight deck was just big enough to allow a runway for Harrier-sized fighters but, surprisingly, there was an open forecastle forward, rather than a Fly 1 parking area. Aft of this a Sea Dart launcher and its surrounding protective 'zareba' were mounted in the most inconvenient place when attempts

were made to park aircraft forward of the island or, as it transpired, fire a missile from it. There was a generation gap between this design and the last carrier project; a fact that added some complexity and the need to relearn hard-won knowledge that had been discarded. The political requirement to keep the tonnage at or below 20,000 added cost and complexity, with the result that these ships had to have a structure of unusual lightness to remain inside the weight limit.

A comparison with earlier designs shows that the cruiser *Tiger* had an internal volume of 1,412,586ft³; the aircraft carrier *Centaur* 3,248,949ft³ and *Invincible* 3,178,320ft³. Weight-saving measures were achieved by the use of finite element analysis and a ruthless policy of using lightweight equipment, such as the scissors lifts, which saved the weight of the counterbalances used in previous designs. Even then the steel weight was 10,000 tons, but its erection amounted to only 15 per cent of the total manhours consumed in *Invincible*'s construction. From these figures it can be seen that an increase in hull size, but with the same outfit of equipment, would have led to a modest increase in the amount of steel used and an increase in production cost of about 2 to 3 per cent, but would have dramatically improved

the design's ability to operate aircraft. A decision on the choice of machinery was taken only after prolonged arguments between advocates of advanced steam units derived from CVA-01 technology, diesel-electric plant and gas turbines. The eventual choice of four Rolls-Royce Olympus gas turbines had many benefits, not least commonality with contemporary destroyer designs including the Type 42, and the ability to change engine units at sea. On the other hand, they needed intake and exhaust trunking of five times the cross-sectional area that would have been required for steam machinery. Each Olympus had its own lift to bring it up to hangar-deck level so that it could be replaced, giving the ship a total of six lifts. The engine lifts severely constricted the central part of the hangar into a 'dumb-bell' shape.

The possibility of operating a navalised version

Illustrious on 31 August 1983, with a Sea Harrier and Sea King helicopter on deck. Note the Vulcan Phalanx CIWS mounted temporarily on the flight deck to provide defence against sea-skimming missiles. (RAN)

of the Harrier was included in the design from its inception, and in 1968 the Controller, Admiral Sir Horace Law, envisaged a ship with a carrier-style flight deck and an air group of five navalised Harriers, nine antisubmarine Sea Kings and three AEW Sea Kings, not all of which could be stowed in the hangar. The exact number of aircraft and types embarked could be altered to suit tactical requirements, but it was obvious from the outset that fighters required much more comprehensive facilities than even large helicopters in terms of workshops, control, carrier-controlled approach and the sheer variety and number of weapons they could carry. The ships were expected to have a life of twenty to twenty-five years, and the planners anticipated that they would have to embark the aircraft that would replace the Sea King and Sea Harrier from the late 1980s. The hangar was therefore designed to be 20ft high to give a margin for growth, and the flight and hangar decks were made stronger than strictly necessary for the first aircraft to be embarked. Taken with the machinery access and inlet/exhaust trunking, these 'drivers' gave the *Invincible* Class the highest freeboard of any ship in the RN, and a very high beam-to-draught ratio. The 'cruiser' anchors and cable originally specified proved immediately to be inadequate and had to be replaced with heavier, more appropriate gear.

The four Olympus TM 3B gas turbines were to be capable of delivering a continuous 94,000shp though two shafts. At 47,000 this was to be more shp per shaft than any previous British warship. The comparative figure for the *Ark Royal*, paid off in 1979, was 38,000; *Victorious* was 36,000; the battle cruiser *Hood* was 36,000; the battleship *Vanguard* was 32,000; the cruiser *Belfast* was 20,000 and the 1952 destroyer *Daring* was 27,000. When combined with a volumetrically large hull

of unusually light construction, it is easy to see why the first two ships suffered from vibration and why the third ship had to have 500 tons of additional steel added to the shaft area in an attempt to cure the problem. Similar 'fixes' were applied to the other ships in refit.

Despite its innovative features and the fact that many people saw the 'cruiser' as a means of disguising what was really an aircraft carrier and 'smuggling' its construction through the estimates, *Invincible* and her sister ships had a mediocre aircraft operating capability for their size. Their internal hull volume was nearly identical to those of *Centaur* and *Hermes*, but they could operate only half the number of aircraft. Part of the problem, apart from the political bias against aircraft carriers, was the lack of a single aim for the aircraft carrying cruiser options out of which the design evolved. Requirement NSR 7097, which was eventually written around the final design, was

An 'Alpha Range' on *Ark Royal*, with Sea Harriers and both AEW and antisubmarine Sea King helicopters on deck. (AUTHOR'S COLLECTION)

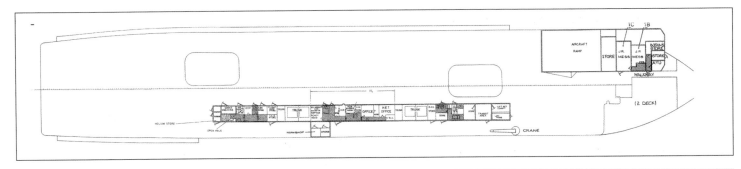

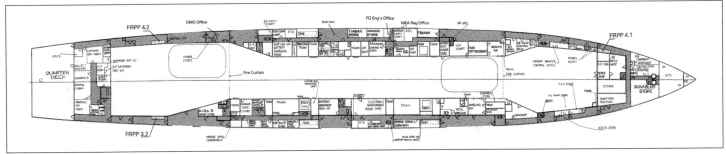

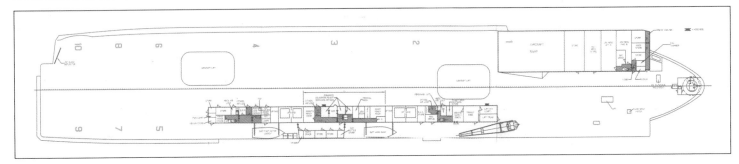

very much a product of its time. It stated that the ships were to command a task force and control the operation of land-based aircraft; to act as the force ASW commander of a NATO task group and to operate large ASW helicopters for area defence; to deploy Sea Dart SAGW for area defence; to deploy a surface reconnaissance capability and to deploy a quick-reaction contribution to limited air defence, probe and strike capability with Stovl aircraft. Fixed-wing aircraft were thus initially given the least priority by the staff, but their operation had the biggest influence on the design. The project lacked a chief executive like Vice-Admiral Mackenzie who dominated the Polaris submarine project. It therefore became vulnerable to continual changes of concept and, in effect, became a 'dumping ground' for every aspect of surface warfare. *Invincible* had the sea-boats of a cruiser, the missile system of a destroyer, and the sonar system, but not the ASW weapons, of a frigate, but she had the only relatively big flight deck in the fleet. No other ship could operate the aircraft she could, but it took a decade of experience for this to be accepted by the Staff. The systems and the men to man them led to a cramped hull and clashes of priority until they were gradually removed in

refits; first the sonar, then Sea Dart, allowing more magazine space for air weapons and accommodation for aircraft maintainers.

The opening paragraphs of NSR 7097 read like a defence review, but they explain many of the shortcoming that subsequently limited *Invincible* as an aircraft carrier. The embarked task force commander was to respond with force only when specifically directed, presupposing tight political control and carefully regulated rules of engagement. It was envisaged that non-firing operations may last for up to three months, during most of which maritime contingency forces might be constituted. If escalation continued, firing operations might be expected to last a further month, the last week of which would see widespread operations at an intensive level. This very specific concentration on the period of transition leading to war was very much a product of the way the Cold War was perceived in the early 1970s, and reflected the way in which a number of NATO exercises were constructed. Politicians had forgotten the possibility of 'brush-fire' wars, and thought only in terms of the risk of a nuclear exchange following an 'incident' within the NATO area and the tightly-controlled steps that

TOP *Ark Royal's* flight deck in 1985. (AUTHOR'S COLLECTION)

MIDDLE *Ark Royal's* hangar deck in 1985. (AUTHOR'S COLLECTION)

BOTTOM *Illustrious'* flight deck in 2012, showing the final, extended design with more parking space forward. (AUTHOR'S COLLECTION)

would follow. Designing a ship around the period of transition to war, rather than the ability to fight a prolonged war, led to a minimal designed outfit of air weapons for fixed-wing aircraft, the NSR's lowest priority. The initial outfit was for only forty AIM-9 Sidewinder AAMs; eighteen ASMs; eighteen conventional 1,000lb bombs; and some 30mm cannon ammunition, flares and pyrotechnics. The higher-priority Sea Kings were allocated only twelve nuclear depth-bombs, fifty-four homing torpedoes and twenty-four Mark 11 depth charges, the last not even enough to give each Sea King one full load. Fortunately it proved difficult to 'design down' to such a limited specification, and the bomb rooms were drawn to give a floor area capable of taking these weapons. It was therefore possible to increase the numbers significantly by stacking and the use of shelving. The removal of the Sea Dart system later made more magazine space available.

The end of the Cold War and British involvement in a number of conflicts led to a reappraisal of aircraft carriers and their value. A series of modifications to the *Invincible* Class gave the improved aircraft operating capability that the ships should have had from the outset. The removal of Sea Dart allowed the parking space forward of the island to be extended forward and the space under it to be used for the construction of enlarged briefing rooms, intelligence offices and sortie planning facilities. Some design shortcomings could not be repaired, however. The light hull meant that sponsons could not be added to increase the size of the deck, and ruled out the installation of a side lift. The two centreline lifts both obtruded into the runway and, if the forward one was down, it was near enough to the 'ski-jump' to prevent rolling take-offs by Sea Harriers. Unfortunately, for the first decade of operation the lifts' scissors operating mechanism was unreliable and they often stuck halfway down, sometimes with the platform at an awkward angle which made recovery of the aircraft on it difficult. The early focus on the period of transition before conflict led to the naval staff insisting that no aircraft homing aid be fitted 'since it would not be switched on'. This led to the loss of at least one or two aircraft that were unable to locate their ships, and was remedied by the introduction of Tacan in later refits.

By the end of their lives these ships were capable of operating about twenty aircraft and could be used as strike, commando or antisubmarine platforms. Extensive joint command and communications facilities were fitted, although accommodation for the staff, an air group and the ship's company was tight. One of three junior rates' dining halls was converted into a command planning room, men having to eat in shifts in the remaining two. They were among the first RN warships to include women in their ships' companies after 1990, which led to some changes in the mess-deck and bathroom arrangements, and from 2005 they no longer operated their own air groups but embarked tailored air groups (TAGs), made up of RN, Army and RAF Sea Harriers, Harriers and helicopters to undertake specific missions. The RN and RAF Sea Harrier and Harrier squadrons had been formed into a joint force in 2000, but in 2006 the Sea Harriers were withdrawn from service as part of a Government reduction in defence expenditure. At the time it was thought that the F-35 Joint Strike Fighters intended to replace them would be in service by 2012, but delays in development have meant that the type is unlikely to be in service before 2020. From 2006 to 2010 the RN operated a Wing, nominally of two naval air squadrons, equipped with ground-attack Harriers, but from 2004 to 2009 these spent time operating ashore in Afghanistan as part of the British contribution to the NATO-led campaign. The loss of the Sea Harriers left the RN with no embarked fighters for the first time in a century, and the Harriers spent very little time embarked. *Illustrious* 'kept the art alive' by embarking USMC, Spanish and Italian naval Harriers from time to time in exercises. From 1981 the British Government had planned to run two ships with the third in reserve; a more permanent reduction had originally been intended and *Invincible* was sold to Australia, but after her part in the Falklands Conflict the Australian Government released the British from the contract and she was retained.

Invincible was reduced to reserve in 2005 and not recommissioned. A Defence Review by the new Coalition Government in 2010 led to the surprise immediate withdrawal of *Ark Royal* and the entire RN/RAF Harrier force. *Ark Royal* had been intended to run on until 2014. The last of the class, *Illustrious*, which was to have run on until 2016, was retained to act in the LPH role, while *Ocean* refitted in 2013 but will be discarded in 2014. The *Invincible* design was not the best the RN could have had, nor the one that offered the taxpayer the best value for money, but they were there when they were needed, with just enough capability to succeed. As their individual ship histories show, they played a key role in the RN during the last decades of the twentieth century and the first of the twenty-first.

Invincible technical details on completion

Displacement:	19,500 tons deep load
Dimensions:	length 677ft 9in
	beam 104ft 6in
	draught 29ft
Machinery:	2 shaft, each with reversible gearbox
	4 Rolls-Royce TBM3 Olympus gas turbines
	112,000shp delivering 28 knots designed
Armament:	GWS-30 Sea Dart
Protection:	none
Fuel:	3,000 tons diesel
Endurance:	5,000 miles at 18 knots
Complement:	1,100

Aircraft operating data

Flight deck:	550ft x 65ft
Hangar:	500ft (including lift wells) x 74ft max/40ft min x 20ft
Lifts:	Two 54ft long x 31ft 8in wide 'scissors-type', both 35,000lb
Aircraft:	Up to 20, depending on type
Aircraft fuel:	250,000gal avcat
Air weapons:	WE-177 tactical nuclear bombs and nuclear depth charges; Sidewinder AAM; Mark 46 homing torpedoes; 1,000lb MC bombs; BL-755 cluster bombs; 2in RP; Mark 11 depth charges; 30mm cannon ammunition; 7.62mm GPMG ammunition; flares and pyrotechnics; modified after build to take Sea Eagle ASM

Individual ship histories

Invincible

Laid down on 20 July 1973 at Vickers' yard in Barrow-in-Furness, *Invincible* was launched by HM Queen Elizabeth II on 3 May 1977. She was officially completed on 11 June 1980 after moving to Portsmouth to prepare for extensive first-of-class trials, interspersed by visits to Lisbon, Brest and Gibraltar and basic sea training at Portland. The First of Class Flying Trial took place in October, and the first-ever 'ski-jump' launch at sea was carried out on 29 October 1980 by an instrumented aircraft from A&AEE Boscombe Down. After a docking and the issue of aircraft operating clearances she embarked 800 (Sea Harrier) and 820 (Sea King ASW) NAS in February 1981 for a shake-down period and further trials in the Mediterranean. She returned to Portsmouth in June and was declared operational on 19 June 1981. Later in the month she embarked her permanent air group, 801 (Sea Harrier) and 820 (Sea King ASW) NAS, and carried out operational sea training at Portland. In July she sailed for the Western Atlantic, and in August visited Norfolk Navy Base, from where she sailed to take part in NATO Exercise *Ocean Venture*, flying the flag of FOF 3 as part of antisubmarine group 2. The exercise 'wash-up' took place in Bergen, after which she took part in Exercise *Ocean Safari* in September, followed by a visit to Ferrol before returning to Portsmouth on 24 September for an assisted maintenance period.

The air group was re-embarked in November for a passage exercise with French warships, followed by live Sea Dart firings off Aberporth and passage to Plymouth, where 40 RM Commando was embarked for amphibious trials intended to prove the ship's capability to act as an LPH for short periods when required. After the Nott Defence Review in late 1981 it was announced

Invincible sails from Portsmouth with the South Atlantic Task Force on 5 April 1982, cheered by crowds ashore. (AUTHOR'S COLLECTION)

that the RN carrier force was to be reduced, and in early 1982 *Invincible* was sold to the RAN for £175 million, a sum believed to be less than her estimated build cost. After the Argentine invasion of the Falkland Islands, however, she sailed for the South Atlantic on 5 April 1982 with a task force including *Hermes*. Her air group was augmented by aircraft and personnel from 899 NAS, the Sea Harrier training unit at RNAS Yeovilton. On the way south she had to change an engine, something an earlier carrier could not have done, and the British-declared Total Exclusion Zone around the Falkland Islands was entered on 1 May, the day strikes were flown against Argentine positions in Port Stanley. On 4 May 820 NAS Sea Kings helped to rescue the ship's company of *Sheffield* after she was hit by an Exocet missile and, as the conflict progressed, Sea Harriers of 809 NAS were added to the air group. By the end of the fighting her Sea Kings had flown 3,099 operational sorties, nearly all of them antisubmarine, and her Sea Harriers had flown 599 combat missions, claiming seven enemy aircraft confirmed shot down and three probables. *Invincible* spent 160 days at sea, a new record for a British carrier, before returning to Portsmouth on 17 September 1982 to be greeted by HM Queen Elizabeth II, one of whose sons, HRH Prince Andrew, had served as a pilot in 820 NAS. A day later the ship began a short refit, during which Vulcan Phalanx close-in weapon systems (CIWS) were added on the forecastle and the starboard after quarter of the flight deck, the latter somewhat limiting the number of available helicopter operating spots and aircraft parking. The Australian Government agreed not to hold the UK to the contracted sale, and she was retained by the RN, although only two carriers were to be in commission at any one time, with the third in refit or reserve. The work was completed in February 1983, and after working-up she sailed for exercises in the Caribbean and with the USN off the coast of the USA.

On 1 September *Invincible* sailed from the UK as flagship of the 'Orient Express' deployment to the Far East, which was intended to demonstrate and practise the capability to project force at long distances from the UK. Three frigates, two tankers and a store ship accompanied her. Exercise *Jolly Roger* took place off Gibraltar before passing through the Suez Canal on 22 September for visits

Invincible's narrow deck and large, inboard island can be seen in this photograph of the South Atlantic Task Force in April 1982. (AUTHOR'S COLLECTION)

A Sea Harrier is towed into the small parking area forward of *Invincible's* island. It had an important function as somewhere to put aircraft that went unserviceable during a multiple Sea Harrier launch using the runway, and was often referred to as the 'graveyard' in consequence. Note how the forward lift obtruded into the runway close to the 'ski-jump', preventing its use when the lift was down. (AUTHOR'S COLLECTION)

Indies and USA in the spring of 1986 as a training ship, with 240 Dartmouth cadets and 80 artificer apprentices on board. The only aircraft embarked were three Wessex of 845 NAS. She carried out a live Sea Dart firing in the AFWR and returned to Portsmouth in March. Between 7 and 18 April 1986 she was moored in the Solent for first-of-class underwater shock trials, during which charges were detonated near the ship to evaluate the effect of explosions on her machinery and equipment. Later in the moth she moved to Devonport, where she was taken in hand for a major 'modernisation' refit that brought her up to the standard of *Ark Royal*, the third unit of the class, with a 12-degree 'ski-jump'; Goalkeeper CIWS and enhanced command and control arrangements. Since commissioning she had steamed 260,000 miles.

Post-refit trials in November 1988 were followed by a shake-down with aircraft embarked in February 1989. *Invincible* was recommissioned in Portsmouth on 18 May 1989 by her patron, HM Queen Elizabeth II, and subsequently worked-up to operational efficiency with a new air group that had formerly served in *Illustrious*; it comprised 800 (Sea Harrier), 814 (Sea King ASW) and 849A (Sea King AEW) NAS. Her ORI took place in August, after which she sailed for a deployment in the Western Atlantic on 16 October 1989. A visit to Wilmington, North Carolina, was followed by Trial *Punish* in the Atlantic Undersea Test and Evaluation Center (AUTEC) range, during which 814 NAS tested new equipment and tactics against British and USN nuclear submarines; 800 and 849A disembarked to NAS Cecil Field for air combat exercises with the USN. A visit to Fort Lauderdale later in the month was followed by operational training with the USN in the AFWR and visits to Mayport and Norfolk in December and January 1990. Later in January she took part in Exercise *Fleetex 1/90* with the USN. After a brief visit to Barbados in February she returned to Portsmouth on 23 February and disembarked the air group to prepare for operation as an LPH. She subsequently showed her growing versatility by embarking 845 and 846 (Sea King Commando) NAS, elements of 42 and 45 RM Commandos and the staff of Commodore Amphibious warfare; sailing for exercise *Cold Winter* in the Norwegian littoral on 5 March. After that she reverted to her primary role, re-embarked the standard air group and sailed in the summer for exercise *Dragon Hammer* in the

to Bombay, Penang and Singapore. In November the task force took part in Exercise *Valiant Usher*, after which it visited Fremantle before joining RAN ships for a series of war-at-sea exercises. Later in the month there was a visit to Jervis Bay, and then the task force moved to Wellington in company with an RNZN frigate for more exercises, followed by a visit to Auckland. In December 1984 a visit to Sydney was complicated by popular disquiet over whether she might or might not be carrying nuclear weapons, but by then vibration aft was causing problems, and in January 1985 she moved to Singapore where repairs were made to the shaft area by Sembawang Shipyard, the former Royal Dockyard. In February she visited Penang but then returned to the UK early, arriving in early March for urgent work to

cure the vibration. In April she visited Hamburg and then took part in a series of exercises for the rest of the year.

The first of these was Exercise *Cold Winter*, an amphibious exercise in Norway with 42 RM Commando embarked. Exercise *Hardy Crab* in May provided deck-landing and 'ski-jump' training for the Harriers of 1 Squadron RAF. Another amphibious exercise, *Rolling Deep*, again with 42 RM Commando, took place in September, followed by Exercise *Autumn Turn*, a NATO antisubmarine training period in October. In November Exercise *Iles d'Or* was carried out with French and USN warships in the Mediterranean. The busy year ended when the air group was disembarked on 4 December 1985; after ceasing to be fully operational she deployed to the West

Sea Harriers were stowed in *Invincible*'s forward hangar. Four can be seen under the overhead gantry in this photograph. Evolved from the prototype P.1127, the Sea Harrier was not 'maintainer friendly', in that the wings had to be removed as a single structure before the engine could be lifted out, leaving the fuselage in a specially built cradle; hence the need for the heavy-duty overhead gantry. The inverted-'V' structures visible at top left are the 'scissors' units that support, raise and lower the forward lift. (AUTHOR'S COLLECTION)

Mediterranean, during which Sea Harriers carried out cross-deck operations with the AV-8s embarked in the Spanish carrier *Principe de Asturias* and the Italian carrier *Garibaldi*, and all three worked with the USS *Dwight D Eisenhower*. In May she visited London for the first time, having to pass through the barrier to moor near the old RN College at Greenwich. In the late summer of 1990 she took part in Exercise *Teamwork* in the North Sea in company with *Ark Royal* and eighty-five other ships from eight NATO nations, after which she visited Scapa Flow in the Orkney Islands. On 29 November 1990 women joined her company and she became the first British carrier to have a mixed ship's company. Early in 1991 she carried out a deployment to the Western Atlantic to carry out a period of training with USN and Dutch warships, and visit Barbados before returning to the UK.

In August 1991 she sailed from Portsmouth to carry out Exercises *Vendetta* and *North Star* and live Sea Dart firings during September, before visiting Lisbon. In October she entered the Mediterranean to take part in the big NATO Exercise *Display Determination* with FOF 3 embarked. Later in the month she visited Alexandria and carried out Exercise *Nile 91* with ships of the Egyptian Navy before joining them for the Egyptian Navy Days celebrations in Alexandria. At the end of October she visited Istanbul with the C-in-C Fleet embarked, and then visited Palermo and Gibraltar before returning to Portsmouth in mid-November. After a period of maintenance she prepared for another Far East deployment, took part in operational sea training off Portland and then in Exercise *Teamwork* in the North Atlantic.

Invincible sailed from Portsmouth on 5 May 1992 for the *Orient 92* deployment flying the flag of the Commander UK Task Group (COMUKTG), in company with other warships and auxiliaries. At the end of May she took part in Exercise *Dragon Hammer* in the Eastern Mediterranean and then visited Piraeus before passing through the Suez Canal. In June she visited Mombasa, and in July she took part in Exercise *Sea Copra*, providing cover for a training amphibious assault landing on Diego Garcia by 40 RM Commando. In mid-July she arrived in Singapore for a visit, and after a few days sailed for a visit to Yokosuka in Japan, followed by exercises with the Japanese Maritime Self Defence Force during which she embarked a Japanese admiral and his

staff. In August she arrived in Pusan, South Korea, where she hosted a British Defence Sales exhibition. From there she visited Hong Kong and then returned to Singapore, where she prepared for Exercise *Starfish* with other members of the Five-Power Defence Agreement in September. Integrated Air Defence Exercise 92/4 followed, involving fighters from the RAF, RAAF, RNZAF and R Malaysian AF. During the exercise Sea Harriers flew ninety-six sorties. A banyan on Pulau Tioman Island was followed by a visit to Penang in October 1992 and then a visit to Abu Dhabi, where she took senior officers from the United Arab Emirates to sea and hosted a British Defence Day in which twenty-six companies set up displays in the hangar. *Invincible* passed north through the Suez Canal on 4 November 1992, after which she visited Haifa. From there she moved to Cyprus to take part in an air defence exercise with two Italian Navy TAV-8Bs and a Sea King embarked in addition to her own air group. She arrived back in Portsmouth on 27 November for a dockyard assisted maintenance period.

The air group re-embarked on 27 March 1993 for a shake-down period which ended with a continuation sea training period with Flag Officer, Sea Training (FOST) at Portland. In May she took part in Exercise *JMC 932* off the coast of Northern Scotland, returning to Portsmouth briefly before sailing on 22 July for the Adriatic, where she was to relieve *Ark Royal* in Operation *Deny Flight*, enforcing a no-fly zone over Bosnia and supporting British forces ashore operating with the UN in the former republic of Yugoslavia. Carrier tasking was shared with the French *Clemenceau*, one of the two always being on task with the other close at hand but able to participate in training periods and carry

out port visits. The carriers were able to move into clear areas when UN aircraft ashore were grounded by bad weather. *Invincible* visited Corfu and spent Christmas 1993 in Malta. She was relieved in turn by *Ark Royal* in February 1994, and returned to Portsmouth for a maintenance period and to give leave. She was back in the Adriatic again to relieve *Ark Royal* in August 1994 with, in addition to her earlier air group, a detachment of 801 NAS embarked, equipped with the first Sea Harrier F/A.2 fighters to enter operational service. During breaks from the front line she visited Naples and Trieste. Several Sea Harriers came under fire, including two in November whose pilots evaded missiles by using chaff and flares. Christmas 1994 was spent in Malta, and *Invincible* was relieved in February 1995 by *Illustrious*, returning to Portsmouth for a refit in which a new sewage treatment plant and improved galleys were installed. Workshops were improved to support the Sea Harrier F/A.2, which would now equip a full squadron.

In May 1995 *Invincible* worked-up to deploy for a third period of duty in the Adriatic. By then NATO had taken over operations ashore on behalf of the UN. In September Bosnian Serb forces laid siege to the city of Sarajevo, and *Invincible* joined the US carriers *America* and *Theodore Roosevelt* to strike at Serb-held positions around the city. During this ten-day period, Sea Harriers of 800 NAS flew twenty-four bombing sorties, forty-two CAP sorties and twenty-eight reconnaissance missions, helping to achieve a successful outcome when Serb forces complied with UN Resolutions to withdraw their heavy weapons from around the city. The Sea Harrier F/A.2 was widely praised for its effective multirole capability. During a period away from operations *Invincible* took part in exercise *Infinite Courage* with the USS *America* and other Allied ships before returning to the UK after her relief by *Illustrious*. She arrived in Portsmouth on 9 December 1995 for a maintenance period. When it ended, in March 1996, she was ordered to stand by for operations in the Adriatic, but was not immediately required there because a peace treaty had been signed between the warring factions in the former Yugoslavia. In June she visited Amsterdam and then embarked RAF Harrier GR.7s for Operation *Hornpipe*, an evaluation of the type's capability to carry out prolonged embarkation in a carrier, with especial regard to night operations and the alignment of its navigational systems at sea. Exercise *JMC 962* followed off the north of Scotland, with over forty Allied warships and 150 aircraft, followed by a visit to North Shields and a series of demonstrations as part of Staff College Sea Days. In the autumn she took part in the NATO Exercise *Northern Lights* off Norway, followed by a passage to the Mediterranean for exercise *Dynamic Mix*, which involved *Invincible*, *Principe de Asturias* and *Garibaldi* working together, the 'enemy' being provided by US and French units. When it ended she passed through the Suez Canal and moved into the Persian Gulf to join the USS *Enterprise* battle group and the RN Armilla Patrol Group for Exercise *Gulfex 98*, a major joint exercise that concentrated on air warfare. She then demonstrated the British commitment to the region by visiting Dubai, Kuwait and Al Jubayl in Saudi Arabia. After a successful deployment she returned to Portsmouth on 19 December 1996.

In January 1997 *Invincible* was presented with the 'Wilkinson Sword of Peace' by HRH The Prince of Wales, awarded to her jointly with *Illustrious* for their operations in the Adriatic. She spent the first half of the year in UK waters before taking part in Exercise *JMC 972* off northwest Scotland in June, after which she took part in Staff College Sea Days and sea power demonstrations to MPs and prominent businessmen off the Isle of Wight. The Prince of Wales spent a day at sea in August. On 2 September *Invincible* sailed for Exercise *Tapon* and embarked 800 (Sea Harrier), 849A (Sea King AEW) and two aircraft of 814 (Sea King ASW) NAS plus, for the first time on an operational deployment, five Harriers of 1 Squadron RAF. The remaining Sea Kings of 814 NAS embarked in RFA *Fort Victoria*. Effectively, this marked the first deployment of what would become known as a TAG in the next decade. The exercise took place off southern Spain and also involved *Principe de Asturias* and her AV-8Bs. When the exercise ended, in September, 1 Squadron disembarked to its UK base and *Invincible* set a heading for the USA, launching three Sea Harriers with air-to-air refuelling to fly

ahead. She visited Norfolk and was due to carry out exercises with the USN and visit Mayport and Caribbean ports, but a crisis over the issue of UN weapons inspectors and their work in Iraq arose, and *Invincible* was ordered to join a build-up of US and British forces in the Persian Gulf. Initially, Britain's air contribution was to comprise RAF Panavia Tornadoes, but they were denied the use of bases in Turkey and Saudi Arabia for any attack on Iraq, and *Invincible* was ordered to Gibraltar with all despatch in order to be prepared to provide a viable British strike capability as part of Operation *Bolton*. She rendezvoused with *Illustrious* to take on stores, personnel and the Commander UK Task Group, entered Gibraltar for a few hours to embark more stores, and sailed to embark 1 Squadron RAF on 20 November 1997. Her air group now comprised 800 (Sea Harrier), 849A (Sea King AEW) and part of 814 (Sea King ASW) NAS, and 1 Squadron RAF (Harrier). The remainder of 814 stayed in RFA *Fort Victoria*, which continued to be part of the battle group. After a work-up off Sardinia she carried out a brief patrol in the Adriatic but remained on standby for the Gulf. Christmas was spent anchored off Akrotiri in Cyprus, and she subsequently visited Palermo before beginning another Adriatic patrol. On 4 January 1998 the order came for her to proceed to the Persian Gulf for Operation *Bolton*, the threat of Allied force to back-up UN Resolutions against Iraq. *Invincible* entered the Gulf on 25 January 1998 and used her aircraft to implement the southern no-fly zone in concert with aircraft from USN carriers. In the event the UN managed to end the crisis, albeit temporarily, and air strikes were not required. Visits were made to Dubai and Bahrain, and on 1 March 1998 *Illustrious* arrived to take over as the spearhead of the British military presence in the area. *Invincible* sailed for the UK and arrived in Portsmouth on 26 March for a period of maintenance. She was one of the first ships to be worked on by Fleet Support Limited, the new company running the dockyard maintenance and repair organisation.

After sailing for a shake-down, *Invincible* entered the Baltic to visit Gdynia in Poland. At the time Poland was seeking to join NATO after the fall of the Eastern Bloc, and 11,000 visitors toured the ship on a single day. She returned to Portsmouth to take part in the International Festival of the Sea, and subsequently remained in UK waters for the remainder of the year. Another critical situation then developed in the Persian Gulf, however, and *Invincible* was ordered to sail for the Middle East on 9 January 1999. She embarked her 'standard' air group on this occasion, with no RAF Harriers, and passed through the Suez Canal on 21 January. On arrival in the Northern Gulf she began to fly air patrols in Operation *Southern Watch*, the enforcement of the southern no-fly zone

over Iraq, together with USN carrierborne aircraft. She left the Gulf for the UK on 1 April 1999, but on 9 April she was diverted to the Ionian Sea to take part in Operation *Allied Force*, the NATO air attacks on Serb military targets in Kosovo, including bridges, roads, ammunition and fuel dumps, and command and communication sites. The first missions were flown on 14 April, and *Invincible*'s aircraft remained in action until 21 May, when sufficient NATO aircraft were available ashore to allow her to return to the UK. She arrived in Portsmouth on 27 May to begin a major series of alterations, including the removal of the Sea Dart launcher and the conversion of the SAM magazine to take air weapons, and the extension of the flight deck forward to give more parking space to facilitate the embarkation of RAF Harriers in a deck park with enhanced aviation facilities including a 100-seat briefing room in the space under the new flight deck. Command, control and communications were improved to allow her to operate as a joint task force command ship, and workshops were modified to support the new Merlin antisubmarine helicopter. She could now operate up to sixteen Sea Harriers and Harriers regularly to function as a strike carrier or CVA.

Invincible sailed for post-refit trials on 7 March 2000 and carried out sea training in May. In June she joined other warships in touring UK ports on a 'Meet the Navy' tour, culminating in a visit to London in July. Later in the month she took part in Exercise *JMC002*, but a planned deployment to the Western Atlantic was cancelled and she was deployed to the Mediterranean to be prepared for action because of another deteriorating political situation in the Balkans. Her standard air group was again reinforced by 1 Squadron RAF. In September she joined NATO forces near the Adriatic, and when, on 26 September 2000, the Greek ferry *Express Samina* hit rocks and sank, helicopters from *Invincible* helped with the rescue operations in difficult conditions at night, saving a number of survivors. The political situation subsequently eased, and *Invincible* was able to return to Portsmouth on 18 November, having travelled 9,000 miles and visited Cyprus, Haifa, Majorca, Malaga and Malta. In early 2001 she carried out trials with a modified Harrier operated by QinetiQ to evaluate proposed automatic carrier-recovery and navigation avionics for the Future Carrier Borne Aircraft intended to replace the Sea Harrier. In February she embarked aircraft of 845, 846 (Sea King Commando), 847 (Lynx/Gazelle) NAS and RAF Chinooks, together with elements of 42 RM Commando, for an amphibious training period off Norway that included a visit to Harstad.

Despite the carriers' important role in events in the Mediterranean and Middle East, the Government had decided to maintain only one ship as a front-line carrier ready for any eventuality, with the second ship at less-immediate notice and the third in refit or reserve. *Invincible* returned to Portsmouth in April and landed all stores and ammunition to reduce to a state of 'preservation by operation' with a reduced ship's company. On 23 July she sailed to Rosyth to begin a major refit which was to include strengthening the flight deck to operate Merlin helicopters, the installation of networked IT systems and updating of the command systems, and the overhaul of the main machinery. Post-refit trials in the Moray Firth began in February 2003, by which time it had been announced that she would be withdrawn from service and placed in reserve in 2005, rather than 2010 as originally planned. At the time it was expected that *Queen Elizabeth* would be in service by 2012 and the remaining two carriers would be sufficient to fill the gap. Defects were made good in Rosyth before the ship returned to Portsmouth on 14 March. In April she took part in the 60th Anniversary celebrations of the Battle of the Atlantic off Liverpool, then moved to the Clyde to take on stores and ammunition before beginning an extensive work-up, starting off Plymouth where FOST now had his headquarters. The air group, comprising 801 (Sea Harrier), 814 (Merlin) and 849B (Sea King AEW) NAS, embarked for operational training in the North Sea leading up to the ORI.

In September 2003 *Invincible* took part as high-readiness fleet flagship in the NATO Exercise *Northern Light*, which demonstrated the capability of the new NATO Response Force. In October she visited Tenerife and then sailed for a training period off Scotland from 16 October with aircraft of 800 NAS and 3 Squadron RAF added to the air group. During this training period *Invincible* launched nine Sea Harriers and seven Harriers in five minutes, which was believed to be a record for the class. A final rededication ceremony was planned for 12 December 2003, with HM The Queen in attendance, but three days before the event Her Majesty had to undergo a knee operation and HRH Prince Andrew stood in for her. On 23 February 2004 she sailed for amphibious exercises off the south coast with 845 (Sea King Commando) and part of 3 Commando Brigade embarked, before taking part in Exercise *Joint Winter 04* off Narvik in Norway. Visits to Tromso and Copenhagen followed, and on 26 April HM The Queen was able to fly out to the ship in the Channel to have lunch with the captain and meet some of the ship's company. On 6 May 2004 the ship left Portsmouth for Exercise *Aurora*, a major deployment of Allied ships to the Western Atlantic involving *Invincible*, *Ocean* and ships from the USA, Australia, Canada, Denmark, France, Germany, Holland, Italy, Norway and Peru. In addition to her normal squadrons, *Invincible* embarked the Harriers of 3 Squadron RAF. The

force concentrated at Norfolk, Virginia, before the main training period, codenamed Exercise *Rapid Alliance*, an amphibious training period with *Invincible*'s aircraft providing close air support for the landings. After the exercise she visited New York on 1 July before returning to Portsmouth on 16 July.

In September she deployed to the Mediterranean to take part in Exercise *Destined Glory* with other NATO high-response forces to practise crisis response and peace support missions, returning to the UK on their completion. On 17 January 2005 *Invincible* sailed from Portsmouth to take part in a series of strike exercises in the Mediterranean and Middle East given the overall title of *Marstrike 05* and designed to demonstrate the UK's ability to deploy, operate and sustain a maritime strike force away from the UK. She embarked a TAG comprising 801 (Sea Harrier), 849B (Sea King AEW) and a single Sea King COD from 771NAS, with Harriers from 4 Squadron RAF flying out to reinforce it from the UK for short periods. In addition, ASW helicopters were embarked in Royal Fleet Auxiliaries (RFAs) that formed part of the task force. A month-long training period known as Exercise *Magic Carpet*, with the full TAG embarked, took place off Oman in February. It was the largest strike exercise carried out to that date by a ship of the *Invincible* Class, and by 2 March 196 fixed-wing sorties had been flown. *Marstrike 05* was *Invincible*'s last major deployment, and after her return to the UK her last task was to act as flagship of the Trafalgar 200 Fleet Review in the Solent on 28 June 2005. After that she carried out a series of series of visits to Southampton, Crombie, London and North Shields before returning to Portsmouth for the last time on 1 August. She was decommissioned on 3 August 2005, six months earlier than previously planned, and was replaced as high-readiness fleet flagship by *Illustrious* a day later. She was subsequently destored and reduced to a state of extended readiness in Portsmouth before a planned final withdrawal from service in 2010. Nominally she was at eighteen months' notice for sea, but in practical terms she was gradually stripped of equipment to provide spares and replacements for her two sister ships. She was not returned to service, and in February 2011 it was announced that she had been sold for scrap to Leyal Ship breakers at Aliaga in Turkey. She was towed out of Portsmouth on 24 March 2011 and demolition was complete within a year.

Illustrious

Illustrious was laid down by Swan Hunter at its Wallsend-on-Tyne shipyard on 7 October 1976, and launched by HRH Princess Margaret, the Queen's sister, on 1 December 1978. She was

originally due to be completed in November 1982, but the urgent need for another aircraft carrier in the South Atlantic Conflict led to her completion being achieved on 18 June 1982. Having already carried out contractor's sea trials in January, she sailed for Portsmouth on the day of her official completion. On 20 June 1982 she was commissioned at sea, the first RN warship to do so, and began a period of urgent preparation for war service. She was fitted with two Vulcan Phalanx mountings, one on the forecastle and one on the starboard after quarter of the flight deck, and an improved command and control system. By then the Argentine garrison in the Falkland Islands had surrendered, but there was considered to be an urgent need to patrol the islands to prevent another attack. She embarked a new air group during her operational sea training which comprised 809 (Sea Harrier), 814 (Sea King ASW) and 824D (Sea King AEW) NAS. The last was the world's first helicopter AEW unit, and formed with two aircraft that had been fitted with a modified Searchwater radar in only eleven weeks and tested. Fortunately a number of former Gannet observers were able to bring the capability to life in the short time available. The unit subsequently recommissioned as 849 NAS which, like its fixed-wing predecessor, detached flights to operational carriers.

In August 1982 *Illustrious* relieved *Invincible* off the Falkland Islands and remained in a position where she could provide air defence or strike at an enemy force. On 21 October 1982 she handed over responsibility for the air defence of the islands to RAF fighters which had arrived to operate from a base ashore, and began the voyage home. In November she visited Puerto Rico, Fort Lauderdale and Philadelphia before returning to the UK. On 6 December 809 NAS disembarked to RNAS Yeovilton to disband, and the helicopters disembarked to RNAS Culdrose. *Illustrious* returned to Portsmouth a day later, having been at sea for 143 days and carried out 7,127 deck landings since sailing. She then began a maintenance period during which work was carried out on parts of the ship the builders had not had time to finish. The work was finished in early March 1983 and she carried out a period of sea training off Portland. On 30 March 1983 a rededication service in Portsmouth attended by HRH Princess Margaret provided the ceremonial beginning to her Service career that the original commissioning service at sea in June 1982 had lacked. After this she carried out the extensive post-build trials programme for her Sea Dart, electronic warfare and command systems that had not been possible earlier, with a single Wessex of 845 NAS embarked. In May 1983 she embarked aircraft of 899 (Sea Harrier) and 846 (Sea King Commando) NAS and visited Newcastle so that the men who had built her could see the finished product. She then took part in air-defence exercises in the North Sea, working with RAF fighters and radar units ashore. Sea Dart firings took place off Aberporth on 16 May, and on 20 May 1983 she embarked 801 (Sea Harrier) and 820 (Sea King ASW) NAS for a work-up in the South West Approaches, ending with a visit to Lisbon which started on the last day of the month.

On 7 June 1983 *Illustrious* joined *Hermes*, *John F Kennedy* and *Foch* in the major NATO Exercise *Ocean Safari* in the Atlantic. During the exercise a Sea Harrier pilot failed to locate her and, short of fuel, landed on the 2,500-ton Spanish freighter *Alraigo*, incurring some damage and considerable publicity. The aircraft was subsequently recovered and repaired for further service. The exercise 'wash-up' was held in Brest, after which *Illustrious* returned to Portsmouth for a maintenance period. In August she was present for Navy Days and then embarked 800 (Sea Harrier) and 814 (Sea King ASW) NAS for a work-up. The squadrons had served previously in *Hermes*, but were now allocated to *Illustrious* as her standard air group. In September she deployed to the Mediterranean for Exercise *Display Determination*, which began on 24 September. On 4 October, however, the after lift broke down and she had to go into the Italian dockyard at Taranto for repairs. After visits to Athens, Genoa and Gibraltar she arrived in Devonport for several days before taking part in Exercise *Ready Rob* in the South West Approaches. She returned to Portsmouth after a visit to Hamburg in December for more comprehensive repairs to the after lift. In January 1984 she sailed

Illustrious alongside the carrier berth in Portsmouth Naval Base during 2012. (Crown Copyright/MOD 2012)

for a deployment to the Western Atlantic, visiting New York and Norfolk before taking part in Exercise *United Effort* with the USN from 16 February. From 6 March 1984 *Illustrious* took part in the NATO Exercise *Teamwork*, during which she crossed to the Eastern Atlantic and embarked aircraft from 899 (Sea Harrier) and 810 (Sea King ASW) NAS in addition to her air group, bringing the total number of aircraft embarked to twenty-two. Sea Harriers flew four-hour CAP sorties with air-to-air refuelling by aircraft from the USS *Independence*. The 'wash-up' was held in Bergen, after which she had a brief maintenance period in Portsmouth before sailing for Exercise *Open Gate* off Gibraltar on 25 April 1984. Exercise *Distant Hammer* followed on 7 May, after which 800 and 814 NAS were jointly awarded the Australia Shield for their intensive professional embarked operations in 1983/84. After a visit to Palma and live Sidewinder AAM firings on 27 May, *Illustrious* returned to Portsmouth on 30 May.

On 27 June she sailed for Exercise *JMC 842* off Northern Scotland, afterwards visiting Copenhagen and Amsterdam. On 12 July she embarked an instrumented Sea Harrier from the A&AEE off Plymouth for trials of the Sea Eagle ASM, and the decommissioned destroyer *Devonshire* was sunk by a Sea Eagle on 16 July to prove the weapon's operational effectiveness. A change of role followed, with 819 (Sea King ASW), 845 and 846 (Sea King Commando) NAS embarking at the end of July for Exercise *Remount*, a period of amphibious training. On 20 August she returned to Portsmouth for maintenance before sailing on 17 September to embark the air group for exercise *Autumn Train* in the Mediterranean. After visiting Gibraltar and Lisbon she sailed to Rosyth to prepare for Exercise *JMC 843* in November, after which she disembarked 814 NAS

on 21 November and embarked 846 (Sea King Commando) NAS, together with Commodore Amphibious Warfare and 1 ACG of the Dutch Marine Corps for Exercise *High Tide*. After the exercise she visited Hamburg and then disembarked the air group and amphibious forces on 11 December before a maintenance period in Portsmouth.

With work completed she sailed on 23 April 1985 with the air group embarked for a work-up period culminating in an ORI on 4 June. At the end of July she sailed for the Western Atlantic, carrying out Exercise *Pilgrims' Progress* on passage. Philadelphia was visited in August, followed by a briefing in Norfolk before Exercise *Ocean Safari*, during which she recrossed the Atlantic with the NATO Strike Fleet; the 'wash-up' was in Bergen, after which she returned to Portsmouth. The usual deployment to the Mediterranean for Exercise *Autumn Train* followed in October, after which she visited Gibraltar and sailed to Rosyth to prepare for Exercise *JMC 853* in the waters off Scotland. She returned to Portsmouth in December to give leave. Exercises *JMC 861* and *Western Change*, before the end of February 1986, were followed by a period of maintenance. On 2 April she embarked her air group while still alongside in Portsmouth before sailing, but a day later a serious fire broke out in the starboard gear room and, after disembarking the air group, she had to return to Portsmouth for repairs. These took until 14 July, when she carried out machinery trials, and on 21 July she re-embarked the air group and sailed for the *Global 86* deployment, taking part in exercises with the Greek Navy before passing through the Suez Canal on 4 August. On 6 August she suffered a fire in the port outer Olympus gas turbine, which had to be replaced. She visited Singapore on 18 August and Fremantle in October after taking part

Illustrious operating in the LPH role with marines moving out to five Sea Kings running on spots. A further four Sea Kings in Fly 2 have tractors attached, ready to pull them out on to spots from which they will be launched as a second assault wave. The small parking space in Fly 1 has RM Land Rovers stowed in it. (AUTHOR'S COLLECTION)

in several multinational training exercises. In November she visited Bombay after exercises with the IN, and at the end of the month took part in exercise *Saif Sarees* off Masirah. From there she passed back into the Mediterranean and returned to Portsmouth for a maintenance period.

Illustrious sailed on 27 April 1987 and embarked 800 (Sea Harrier), 814 (Sea King ASW) and 849A (Sea King AEW) NAS to work-up ready for an ORI in June. After a visit to Amsterdam she returned to Portsmouth to prepare for participation in Exercise *Ocean Safari* and then visited Devonport and Hamburg before Exercise *Offshore Remount*. In October she prepared for the LPH role and embarked 845 and 846 (Sea King Commando) NAS for Exercise *Purple Warrior*, a large-scale UK national amphibious training period. After leave in December she re-embarked the normal air group in mid-January 1988 for Exercise *Aswex 1/88* in the Iceland/Faroes Gap before visiting Rosyth and Newcastle and returning to Portsmouth. In April she sailed to the Mediterranean for exercises with the Spanish Navy, followed by cross-deck operation with the Italian carrier *Garibaldi*. Exercise *Dragon Hammer* in May followed a visit to Naples, and by the end of the month she was back in Portsmouth. Rosyth Navy Days in June were followed by Exercise *JMC 882* and a period of preparation in Portsmouth for a deployment to the Western Atlantic which began on 3 October. She visited Mayport on 18 October and then participated in Trial 'Baste 88' in the AUTEC Range. In November she visited Charleston, South Carolina, and then took part in exercise *Fleetex 1/88* with the USN. After a visit to Fort Lauderdale she returned to the UK, arriving in mid-December. Exercise *Water Baby* in January 1989 was followed by Exercise *JMC 891* in early February, a visit to Amsterdam, and exercise *North Star* in late February.

After visiting Hamburg she transferred her air group on 22 March 1989 to *Invincible*, which had just emerged from modernisation, and moved into Portsmouth for a defect rectification period. On 30 June she moved into 3 Basin and paid off into reserve for two years' 'preservation by operation' with a small ship's company. In 1991 she was moved to Devonport to be taken in hand for a major modernisation which lasted until May 1994. After initial trials she participated in the Review of Ships in the Solent on 6 June 1994 to mark the 50th anniversary of the D-Day Landings. She then worked-up to operational standards and deployed

to the Adriatic in February 1995 with 801 (Sea Harrier), 820 (Sea King ASW) and 849B (Sea King AEW) NAS embarked to relieve *Invincible*. *Invincible* relieved *Illustrious* again at the end of May 1995. The two carriers were jointly awarded the Wilkinson Sword of Peace for their activities. *Illustrious* returned to relieve *Invincible* again on 9 December 1995, but the situation ashore began to ease, and on 15 February 1996 the UK Task Force reverted to national control and was withdrawn from the Adriatic, although NATO could call for a carrier to return within twenty-one days. After a period of maintenance *Illustrious* became the flagship of a UK Task Group in April 1996 for a Western Atlantic deployment that was to include Exercise *Purple Star*, a US/UK bilateral amphibious exercise. She returned to Portsmouth in June.

In January 1997 *Illustrious* sailed as flagship of the *Ocean Wave 97* Deployment to the Middle and Far East with the Commander UK Task Group and a joint force headquarters team embarked. In March 1997 Harriers of 1 Squadron RAF flew out to join the air group and *Illustrious* took part in Operation *Jural*, enforcing the no-fly zone over Southern Iraq. Twenty-eight sorties were flown, eighteen of them over Iraq. The RAF aircraft disembarked at the end of March and flew back to the UK as the task group headed east. Exercise *Setia Kawan II* (Loyal Friends) followed in April; this was a Five-Power Defence Agreement training period which included an amphibious landing by Royal Marines with cover given by Sea Harriers. In May came Exercise *Flying Fish*, which incorporated the regular Exercise *Starfish* and an

Preparing 1,000lb bombs in *Illustrious'* Fly 1 for Harriers of the Naval Strike Wing. (Crown Copyright/MoD 2012)

air-defence training period with over forty warships and 140 aircraft of the Five-Power Defence Agreement (FPDA). In June she visited Singapore while other ships of the task group visited a number of other ports, and on 30 June 1997 *Illustrious* provided distant cover 'over the horizon' during the ceremonies that marked the handing of the Colony back to China. On 1 July the Royal Yacht *Britannia*, which had been in Hong Kong harbour with HRH The Prince of Wales embarked, joined the *Illustrious* group at sea for a short period. *Illustrious* returned to Portsmouth at the end of August 1997.

After a maintenance period in Portsmouth, *Illustrious* sailed for the Mediterranean on 18 January 1998 with Harriers of 3 Squadron RAF added to her normal air group, to prepare to relieve *Invincible* in the Gulf, should it prove necessary. In March she did so, and her aircraft flew missions over the no-fly zone, but the crisis over weapons inspectors was resolved by the UN and *Illustrious* left the Gulf on 17 April. On her return she was taken in hand by Fleet Support Limited in Portsmouth for a major upgrade, which included removal of the GWS-30 Sea Dart missile system and the lengthening of the flight deck forward of the island in Fly 1. New facilities, including a 100-seat briefing room and a strike planning office, were built into the space underneath the new area of deck, and the former Sea Dart magazine was modified to provide stowage space for air weapons. A new bomb-lift was installed within the envelope of the former Sea Dart hoist assembly. Improvements were also made to the action-data automated weapon system (ADAWS). She was brought out of dry dock on 4 February 1999 and began post-refit trials on 16 March. Operational sea training and a work-up followed with 801 (Sea Harrier), 820 (Sea King ASW) and 849B (Sea King AEW) NAS embarked, and in June she took part in exercise *JMC 992*.

In January 2000 *Illustrious* sailed as part of the Aurora 2000 deployment to carry out training in the Far East with a group of RN and French warships. On her return she visited Haifa and Malta before returning to the Atlantic to take part in the NATO Exercise *Linked Seas* with RAF Harriers embarked in addition to the normal air group, but on 8 May 2000 she was diverted with her battle group to proceed to Sierra Leone with all despatch as part of Operation *Palliser* to intervene in the crisis there. It was followed by the UK amphibious ready group, which had been exercising off Gibraltar. Rebels had threatened to overthrow the elected government, and the British intervention allowed the evacuation of UK

nationals and the insertion of troops to restore calm and allow UN peacekeeping forces to resume their duties. In March 2001 *Illustrious* took part in Exercise *JMC 011* and then visited Newcastle. In April, with the other two ships in refit, she became the only 'ready RN carrier' in commission.

Illustrious acted as flagship of another large deployment in September 2001 in which twenty-six ships took part; named the Argonaut 2001 Deployment. Royal Air Force Harriers were added to the air group to form a TAG, and a visit to Malta was made while passing through the Mediterranean, after which an air group work-up with live weapons firing took place in the eastern Mediterranean. Exercise *Saif Sareea II* (Swift Sword) off Oman followed in October, working with the

ARG, which included *Ocean* and had elements of 3 Commando Brigade embarked together with Omani forces. At the end of the month the task force was held in the Arabian Sea for possible operations in the NATO campaign developing in Afghanistan. She was re-roled as an LPH in just twenty-four hours and her fixed-wing aircraft flew back to the UK, leaving her as the flagship for the UK contribution to Operation *Enduring Freedom*, with helicopters embarked. *Illustrious* and her destroyer escort were stood down to spend Christmas in Kenya before returning to the Arabian Sea. Relieved on station by *Ocean*, she returned to Portsmouth in March 2002 after seven months away. She was taken in hand for a refit in what had by then become the Babcock Yard at Rosyth in September 2002, during which her command and communication systems were improved with the addition of a third, or mizzen, mast at the after end of the island to take the added aerial arrays. Flyco was replaced by a new structure with considerably more glazing to give a better view of the flight deck. She also had a new 'ski-jump' and the upgraded facilities needed to operate Merlin antisubmarine helicopters and the GR.9 version of the Harrier, which was to be operated by both the RN and RAF after 2006, when the Sea Harrier was scheduled to be withdrawn prematurely from service.

The work was completed in late 2004, and *Illustrious* began a series of trials and shake-down periods to bring the new equipment into use. She usually embarked a Sea King to act as a COD aircraft, but from thenceforth her operational aircraft embarkations were to be structured as TAGs for specific missions. Her first exercise was the newly titled Exercise *Neptune Warrior*, formerly known as *JMC*, off the coast of Scotland in early June 2005. She acted as the flagship of the RN contingent, with ships and aircraft of fourteen other nations taking part, and the training period brought her up to the standard required to assume the duty of R2 ready strike carrier at two days' notice for operations. She was rededicated at a service attended by Lady Sarah Chatto, Princess Margaret's daughter, and replaced *Invincible* as fleet flagship on 4 August 2005. In November 2005 she was in Malta for a visit timed to coincide with the state visit of HM The Queen for the Commonwealth Heads of Government Meeting, during which she provided the venue for a party hosted by The Queen. She subsequently returned to the UK via Gibraltar to prepare for a deployment to the Indian Ocean, designated *Aquila 06*.

Illustrious sailed for the deployment on 29 March 2006 with a TAG that included the Harriers of the recently re-formed 800 NAS, 814 (Merlin) and 849A (Sea King AEW) NAS. In the Mediterranean the group was joined by a French destroyer, and after passing through the Suez Canal took part in Exercise *Magic Carpet* off Oman and

Illustrious marks the 80th birthday of HM Queen Elizabeth II in 2006. The aircraft on deck are Harriers. (Crown Copyright/MOD 2012)

visited Dubai in early April. Later that month *Illustrious* visited Mumbai and then took part in Exercise *Konkan 06*, the first bilateral UK/Indian naval exercise for nearly forty years. After the exercise the task group participated in Operation *Calash*, a multinational commitment to providing security for shipping passing through the Indian Ocean. At the end of June the group sailed to return to the UK, passing through the Suez Canal on 28 June. Visits were made to Athens, Algiers and Gibraltar, where it was planned to embark families in *Illustrious* for the voyage back to Portsmouth. The plan was cancelled at short notice, however, because the Israeli invasion of Southern Lebanon had caused a rapidly deteriorating situation in the country. *Illustrious* was ordered east across the Mediterranean to lead a UK task group close to the Lebanese coast, and on 16 July 2006 she was ordered to implement Operation *Highbrow*, the evacuation of UK citizens, as the situation ashore worsened. Her average speed on passage was nearly 30 knots and she was joined by two destroyers, a frigate and RFA and even a nuclear submarine. Off Gibraltar, 800 NAS was disembarked and a new TAG of aircraft from 845 and 846 (Sea King Commando) NAS and RAF Chinooks was embarked, having flown from RNAS Yeovilton to Cyprus to intercept the carrier. A British team was landed in Beirut under fire and established communications with the Principal Joint Headquarters (PJHQ) in the UK and the task group. Over 4,000 refugees, half of them UK citizens, were embarked from the waterfront and taken to Cyprus, from where they were flown back to the UK by the RAF. The last embarkations took place on 22 July, after which the group moved out to sea, maintaining a presence 'over the horizon' in case of need. Subsequently a NATO task group including the Italian carrier *Garibaldi* took over the task, and *Illustrious* returned to the UK via Gibraltar.

From 2007, RN Harriers were deployed to Afghanistan in rotation with RAF Harrier detachments from Joint Force Harrier (JFH), with the result that embarked Harrier operations became rare. The situation was made worse by a disagreement between the RN and RAF over manning the second RN Harrier unit, designated 801 NAS. In the end the personnel appointed to 801 were added to 800 NAS to form what became

known as the Naval Strike Wing. Harriers of 4 Squadron RAF carried out deck-landing practice in March, and one of the increasingly rare fast-jet embarkations as part of a TAG was Exercise *Neptune Warrior 071* in April 2007, in which *Illustrious* took part as a CVA and *Ark Royal* as an LPH, with warships of nineteen other nations reflecting the training period's growing importance to NATO as a test of operational readiness. Conducted off Cape Wrath in Scotland, it included the use of live weapons. On completion the UK task group, including *Illustrious*, took part in the major NATO Exercise *Noble Mariner* off Denmark in May and June 2007. At the end of May she was the first British carrier to visit Tallin in Estonia. On 24 June 2007 *Illustrious* sailed with a TAG comprising 857 (Sea King AEW) and Sea Kings of 771 NAS in the COD role to cross the Atlantic to visit New York and take part in the USN Exercise *Bold Step*, followed by Exercise *Carrier Strike Group 10* in July with the US carriers *Harry S Truman* and *Dwight D Eisenhower*. Her escort, the destroyer *Manchester*, became the first

RN ship to be fully integrated into a USN battle group. *Illustrious* had no strike fighters of her own, but embarked sixteen USMC AV-8B Harriers of VMA-542 to form a third battle group. During the exercise a USMC Bell Boeing V-22 Osprey landed-on, making *Illustrious* the first RN carrier to recover a tilt-rotor aircraft; the landing was also the first to take place on a non-US warship. It had to land aft of the island, the central area of flight deck being the only space big enough for it. Another fact for the record books was that VMA-542's aircraft were the largest embarkation of foreign aircraft ever to embark in a British carrier. The deployment was extremely successful, and in one twelve-hour period *Illustrious* flew 152 sorties, exceeding the record of 123 in twenty-four hours

Illustrious operating in the LPH role during 2012. Helicopters on deck include both commando assault and ASaC Sea Kings and an AAC Apache in Fly 1. The latter shows how the extension of the flight deck to starboard of the 'ski-jump' has transformed it into a viable helicopter operating spot. (Crown Copyright/MoD 2012)

set by the light fleet carrier *Glory* in April 1953, an outstanding achievement. On completion, *Illustrious* recrossed the Atlantic, returning to Portsmouth in August to prepare for a further deployment.

In mid-September 2007 she sailed for the Mediterranean to take part in Exercise *Noble Midas* in the Adriatic from 1 October, intended to provide training for the NATO Rapid Reaction Force. *Illustrious* acted as the UK flagship, but JFH was unable to provide aircraft for her TAG, so AV-8s of the Spanish Navy's 9 Squadron were embarked to provide her ship's company with fast-jet operating experience. Italian AV-8s were also embarked for a spell. She returned to Portsmouth in December to prepare for a major deployment to the Indian Ocean in 2008, codenamed *Orion 08*, which was to bring together UK, US, French and Spanish ships under RN control. The deployment was meant to begin in January 2008, but *Illustrious'* departure was delayed by defects in her refrigerator and oily water separation systems. She finally sailed to join the remaining ships in February, visiting Malta on her way east. Her TAG comprised 814 (Merlin) and 854 (Sea King AEW) NAS. A 'force integration training period' was held in the Eastern Mediterranean before passing through the Suez Canal to visit Muscat in March. She sailed on 19 March and embarked four Harriers of the Naval Strike Wing to join the TAG for Exercise *Hajjar Osprey* off Oman. The Harriers departed to fly back to the UK on 11 April, where they were to prepare for a deployment to Afghanistan, and *Illustrious* crossed the Indian Ocean to participate in Exercise *Konkan* with the IN. In April she conducted security patrols in the Gulf of Aden as part of Operation *Calash*, and then exercised with the Royal Saudi Navy in the Red Sea. From there she sailed for Cyprus and then Izmir in Turkey, where her visit was timed to coincide with a state visit by HM The Queen and *Illustrious* hosted an official reception. She arrived back in the UK, after a brief stop in Gibraltar, on 30 May 2008. During the deployment TV Channel 5 had made the documentary series *Warship* on board, which was shown after her return. She took part in Navy Days at Portsmouth in July with a Merlin and a full-sized wooden model of an F-35 Joint Strike Fighter on deck.

On 17 October she visited Liverpool, and on 4 November 2008 she moored at Greenwich to play a central role in ceremonies to mark the 90th Anniversary of the end of the First World War. The wooden F-35 remained on deck. In May 2009 she returned to Greenwich to take part in celebrations that marked the centenary of aviation in the RN. After that she moved into the Baltic with a TAG that included Harriers, Merlins and Sea Kings to take part in Exercise *Loyal Arrow* with Allied forces in Northern Sweden. Later in the month she

visited Tallin again, and then Oslo, before returning to Portsmouth. In October she visited Liverpool and then moved to the Clyde to take part in Exercise *Joint Warrior 092* (the former *Neptune Warrior/JMC*) with warships from Canada, the USA, Denmark, Brazil and Turkey. Aircraft of the Naval Strike Wing formed part of the TAG together with Merlins and AEW, now retitled Airborne Surveillance and Control (AS&C), Sea Kings.

In February 2010 *Illustrious* arrived in the Babcock Yard at Rosyth for an upgrade and maintenance period. The work was expected to take over a year, and was intended to keep her viable as a strike carrier until a projected 'out-of-service' date in 2016. It included the installation of a defensive anti-torpedo system; new command and communications software; a structural survey; the replacement of pipework and wiring, and complete repainting. She was relieved as fleet flagship by *Ark Royal*. The focus of the work changed in late 2010, however, as part of the Coalition Government's Strategic Defence and Security Review, which withdrew *Ark Royal* and the entire RN/RAF Harrier force from service with immediate effect, leaving the RN with no operational carrier or embarked fighters for the first time since 1915. The Government accepted a ten-year gap before *Queen Elizabeth* and the F-35 Lightning II were due to enter service, during which the threat to the UK was expected to be 'low'. A short study was announced to consider whether *Illustrious* or *Ocean* should be retained as the fleet's only helicopter platform. It was decided that *Ocean* should be retained for the longer term, but that *Illustrious* should be retained as an LPH until 2014 to cover a period in which *Ocean* was planned to be in refit. *Illustrious* emerged for sea trials in May 2011, and began sea training and an operational work-up as a helicopter carrier in July, after which she stayed alongside in Portsmouth. In March 2012 *Illustrious* took part in the NATO Exercise *Cold Response* off Northern Norway, but had to return to the UK early after a tug gashed the ship's side. Next she participated in another Exercise *Joint Warrior*, and on 1 October 2012 she sailed for the Mediterranean as flagship of a Response Force deployment codenamed *Cougar 12*. The force contained a number of amphibious ships and embarked RM units from 3 Commando Brigade. *Illustrious'* TAG included 814 (Merlin), 854 (Sea King ASaC), 845 and 846 (Sea King Commando) NAS, plus 656 (Boeing Apache) Squadron of the Army Air Corps. During Exercise *Corsican Lion* in October she was joined by the French carrier *Charles de Gaulle* to help in forming the construction of an Anglo-French Rapid Response Task Force by 2016. The deployment included a visit to Malta, with which *Illustrious* inherited close ties from her predecessor. The Task

Force Commander stated that throughout the deployment his ships remained at five days' notice to deploy anywhere in the world, able to get within twelve miles of 147 nations, three out of every four countries in the world.

Extant in 2013, she is due to be taken out of service in 2014, by which time she will be thirty-two years old, making her the longest-serving British aircraft carrier. She has been operational for a third of the century in which the RN has operated aircraft from ships at sea.

Ark Royal

Originally, the third ship of the *Invincible* Class was to have been named *Indomitable*, but it was changed, with royal approval, to *Ark Royal* when the last conventional British aircraft carrier returned from her last deployment. She was laid down by Swan Hunter in its Wallsend-on-Tyne shipyard on 14 December 1978 and launched by HM Queen Elizabeth the Queen Mother on 2 June 1981. In September 1982 she was docked for installation of propellers, rudders and stabilisers and then moved to the Walker Naval Yard for completion, the last ship ever fitted-out there. Contractors' sea trials were carried out from October 1984, and final machinery trials were carried out off the Tyne in April 1985 with a Wessex of 707 NAS embarked for helicopter delivery service (HDS) duties. Nominal completion was achieved on 24 June 1985, and the ship's company moved on board a day later. After embarking a single Swordfish by crane from RNAS Lee-on-Solent to mark the continuity of her famous name, she sailed for Portsmouth on 28 June, arriving on 1 July with a Sea Harrier of 899 NAS on deck with the Swordfish. Trials and a period of sea training at Portland were then carried out before the ship was commissioned in Portsmouth by HM Queen Elizabeth the Queen Mother on 1 November 1985.

Flying trials subsequently took place in the Mediterranean, during which a wreath was laid on 14 November over the spot where the wartime *Ark Royal* sank. Visits to Marseilles and Suda Bay followed trials on the Fleet Operational Readiness and Calibration System (FORACS) Range in Crete. After passage exercises with French and Italian naval units and a brief stop in Gibraltar, she returned to Portsmouth on 16 December 1985. Further sea trials and a visit to Amsterdam took place in January 1986, followed by sea training in February and an air group work-up off Western Scotland with 801 (Sea Harrier) and 820 (Sea King ASW) NAS embarked during April, culminating in her ORI. On 17 June 849B (Sea King AEW) NAS was added to the air group, and *Ark Royal* sailed for a deployment to the western Atlantic. She took part in Exercise *Liberty Train* on passage

across the Atlantic, and arrived in New York on 28 June, flying the flag of FOF3. On 3 July 1986 she took part in the International Naval Review to mark the rededication of the Statue of Liberty by President Reagan, then sailed for exercise *Aswex 1/86* with the USN. A visit to Fort Lauderdale was followed by Trial *Baste 86* in the AUTEC Range in the Bahamas in August, and then a visit to Norfolk Navy Base. NATO Exercises *Northern Engagement* and *Northern Wedding* took up most of August and September, with a 'wash-up' in Amsterdam in September. After a brief spell in Portsmouth the ship sailed for the Mediterranean and Exercise *Autumn Train* in October before visiting Gibraltar, where a rock concert was held on the flight deck, and Lisbon. On 5 November 820 NAS disembarked and was replaced by 845 (Sea King Commando) NAS, and two days later Dutch marines embarked for amphibious training at Garelochhead. The marines were disembarked to Valkenburg on 13 November and *Ark Royal* visited Hamburg. *Ark Royal* was back in Portsmouth for a maintenance period on 20 November 1986.

She sailed for another Western Atlantic deployment on 12 January 1987, with Exercise *Caribtrain* later in the month, followed by a visit to Barbados in February and Exercise *Aswex 1/87* Part 1 with the USN. Another USN training period, Exercise *Fleetex*, a visit to Puerto Rico and *Aswex 1/87* Part 2 followed in quick succession, then *Ark Royal* visited Mayport in March. Later in

the month Trial *Punish* took place in the AUTEC Range and the ship visited Charleston, South Carolina, before returning to Portsmouth, arriving on 9 April for a docking and maintenance period. She was at sea again for Exercise *Aswex 2/87* in May, and in June she visited London, becoming the largest warship to date to pass through the Thames Barrier. Later in the month she took part in Exercise *JMC 872* off Scotland and then Exercise *Hadrian's Wall* before returning to Portsmouth again. Another air group work-up followed by an ORI took place in October, and on 3 November *Ark Royal* sailed and embarked an enhanced air group for the large UK national Exercise *Purple Warrior*. It comprised 800 and 801 (Sea Harrier), 849B (Sea King AEW) and part of 826 (Sea King ASW) NAS, plus Harriers of 1 Squadron RAF. *Ark Royal's* port inner gas turbine failed on 8 November, but she was able to remain part of the exercise. The RAF Harriers were disembarked on 12 November and the remaining aircraft on 18 November. After a brief visit to Cherbourg, *Ark Royal* returned to Portsmouth for leave and a maintenance period.

She was at sea again for a shake-down period with her normal air group embarked on 26 January 1988. After brief visits to Newcastle and Rosyth she took part in Exercise *JMC 881* during February, and visited Hamburg after training with *Illustrious* in the North Sea during March. Later in March she took part in Exercise *Mallet Blow*, during which Sea Harriers achieved 104

A Sea Harrier of 801 NAS leaves *Ark Royal's* 12-degree 'ski-jump'. (AUTHOR'S COLLECTION)

interceptions in twenty-five sorties. After visiting Rotterdam she returned to Portsmouth to prepare for a period in the Far East, and on 13 June 1988 sailed to the Far East for Deployment *Outback 88* as flagship of an RN task force. Exercise *Jolly Roger* took place in the Mediterranean, followed by a visit to Malta. She arrived in Singapore on 23 July 1988 and sailed on 8 August to give a British Defence Export Day at sea for 100 VIPs. From 13 August she took part in exercises with the USN off Subic Bay, then visited Hong Kong at the end of the month. In early September she took part in Exercises *Setia Kewan* off Brunei and *Lima Bersatu* before landing a guard on Possession Island on 17 September to form part of an Australian rededication ceremony at the Captain Cook Memorial. She then carried out exercises with the RAN and RAAF before visiting Brisbane. On 27 September *Ark Royal* entered Sydney Harbour with Sir James Rowland, Governor of New South Wales, on board. On 1 October she took part in the Australian Bicentennial Fleet Review in Sydney Harbour, inspected by HRH The Duke of York; the air group took part in the fly-past. A week later she sailed for exercises with the RAN in Jervis Bay, but a subsequent planned visit to Melbourne had to be cancelled because high winds and a tug strike prevented her from berthing. After a visit to

Fremantle on 23 October *Ark Royal* sailed for Bombay, where she gave another Defence Export Sea Day before sailing for a passage exercise with *Nimitz*. After passing through the Suez Canal she took part in a war-at-sea exercise with the French carrier *Clemenceau*, then visited Gibraltar before returning to Portsmouth on 15 December 1988.

A period of leave and maintenance followed as she prepared for the LPH role, sailing on 26 February 1989 to embark 845 and 846 (Sea King Commando) NAS and 45 RM Commando for Exercise *Cold Winter* off Northern Norway. She returned to Portsmouth in March and sailed on 1 April with her normal air group re-embarked for Exercise *Spring Train* in the Mediterranean. By May she was back in Portsmouth before taking part in Exercise *Square Nut*, a training period with a Dutch task force. A visit to Hamburg was followed by deck-landing training by 4 Squadron RAF's Harriers and Exercise *Vendetta*. She was back in Portsmouth for Navy Days in June, then sailed for exercise *JMC 892* and joint RN/Spanish Navy Sea Harrier/AV-8B operations in the North Sea. A maintenance period in July was followed by a work-up and Exercise *Sharp Spear*, after which *Ark Royal* acted as host for the Spanish carrier *Principe de Asturias* in Portsmouth. Visits to Brest and Lisbon were followed by a docking in Portsmouth and then a work-up and ORI in February/March 1990. On 18 April *Ark Royal* sailed for a deployment to the Western Atlantic as flagship of an RN task force, starting with exercise *Jolly Roger*. A visit to New York in May was followed by exercise *Marcot* and visits to Halifax in Nova Scotia

and Boston before returning to the UK in July. Exercise *Teamwork 90* took place in September, followed by a 'wash-up' in Oslo. A brief visit to Gibraltar ended the year, and *Ark Royal* was back in Portsmouth in December 1990.

On 10 January 1991 *Ark Royal* sailed to the eastern Mediterranean to join Allied forces securing the area against the threat of attack by Iraq, which had over-run and occupied Kuwait. Her battle group worked closely with the US Ships *Virginia*, *Philippine Sea* and *Spruance*, and spent fifty-one days at sea standing by, but subsequent hostilities during what became known as the First Gulf War were confined to the Gulf and *Ark Royal* was not required to take action. On her way home she visited Athens, Naples and Palma before returning to Portsmouth in April. She was at sea again in May for exercise *JMC 912* and then NATO Exercise *Ocean Safari 91*. On 10 September she sailed with an RN task force for a Western Atlantic deployment that began with visits to Bermuda and Fort Lauderdale. At the end of the month she participated in Trial *Woking* in the AUTEC Range, intended to prove the avionics in the new HAS.6 version of the Sea Kings that equipped 820 NAS. A visit to Mayport in October ended the deployment, after which *Ark Royal* sailed for Gibraltar and then returned to UK waters for deck-landing trials with RAF Chinook helicopters. She returned to Portsmouth on 18 November and was visited by HM The Queen Mother two days later, after which she began a maintenance period.

In February 1992 she carried out post-

Ark Royal as she finally appeared, with a mizzen mast containing a precision approach radar and Tacan for aircraft recovery. Both were mounted inside the cladding to protect them from the elements with no loss of capability. The deck approach projector sight can be seen mounted just aft of Flyco, and the tube-like objects on the after island bulkhead are the rear flight-deck floodlights. These were a poor feature of the *Invincible* Class design because they were mounted too low and shone in pilots' eyes when they landed-on after spots, and cast long shadows beyond parked aircraft. (CONRAD WATERS COLLECTION)

maintenance trials and was visited by HRH The Princess Royal during a shake-down in the Channel. After sea training and a visit to Greenock she visited Copenhagen and then took part in Exercise *Purple Monarch* in June. Another brief visit to Gibraltar was followed in September by a deployment to the Western Atlantic, during which exercise *Fleetex 1/92* with the USN was followed by a visit to Norfolk Navy Yard. Weapons training in the Jacksonville areas followed, and then a visit to Mayport and trials in the AUTEC Range off the Bahamas. She visited Nassau at the end of the month before sailing for the UK, arriving in Portsmouth on 6 November 1992. On 16 November 1992 the Admiralty Board held a Royal Dinner on board for HM Queen Elizabeth II in honour of the 40th anniversary of her accession to the throne, and the ship then settled into a maintenance period.

After a work-up at Portland in January 1993 *Ark Royal* deployed to the Mediterranean in April for a brief visit to Naples, after which she moved into the Adriatic as flagship of Task Group 612.02 to provide support for UN peacekeeping

A Merlin helicopter ferries stores to *Ark Royal*. She was the only ship of the class to retain Vulcan Phalanx CIWS guns; her two sister-ships were refitted with 'Goalkeeper' systems. (AUTHOR'S COLLECTION)

operations in the Former Republic of Yugoslavia. On 24 April 1993 her Sea Harriers were declared to the UN and NATO as being capable of dropping laser-guided bombs, and she took part in Operation *Deny Flight*, enforcing a no-fly zone over the former Yugoslavia, in support of British troops in the peacekeeping force and in support of Allied ships in the area against the threat of attack by surface vessels. She had to remain close to the operating area, but was released for short visits to Bari and Corfu in May. A short self-maintenance period was carried out in Malta in June and, once she was back in the Adriatic later in the month, cross-deck operations were carried out with *Garibaldi*. A brief visit to Suda Bay in July was followed by more time at high alert in the operational area. In August 1993 she was relieved on station by *Invincible* and returned to Portsmouth for an assisted maintenance period. In November she was back at sea again for a work-up and deck-landing trials with two development Sea Harrier F/A.2s. On 28 January 1994 she sailed for the Mediterranean again to relieve *Invincible* as the 'on-call' carrier available for operations as part of the British Operation *Hamden* in the Adriatic at short notice. From 13 February her Sea Harriers flew up to fourteen sorties a day to prevent either warring faction from using aircraft in what had become a siege around Sarajevo. They also provided an important reconnaissance capability, providing the UN and NATO commands with photographs of the movement of tanks and guns. The pressure of operational flying led to planned visits to Naples and Toulon being cancelled, but she did visit Piraeus for a short maintenance period in April. While she was there, Serb forces in Bosnia attacked the town of Gorazde, and she returned immediately to the operating area. On 16 April 1994 two Sea Harriers were tasked to attack a tank which was firing at British troops from a wooded area near the town, but were forced to make several passes to identify it positively. One of them was shot down by a missile, but fortunately the pilot was able to eject.

In May *Ark Royal* moved away from the operational area to take part in Exercise *Dynamic Impact*, the largest NATO exercise in the Mediterranean since the end of the Cold War,

Ark Royal's hangar, looking from aft to forward, with the 'scissor' arms of the after lift in the 'up' position in the foreground. A Sea King and Sea Harrier are secured in the narrow part of the hangar, which was made so by the need for Olympus engine removal lifts, air intakes and exhausts. (AUTHOR'S COLLECTION)

involving ninety-three warships from ten nations. At the end of the training period she visited Palma, and after a ceasefire in the Bosnian conflict, agreed at Geneva in June, she visited Istanbul, Crete and Malta. She returned to Portsmouth on 2 September. Later in the month she visited Newcastle and then returned to Portsmouth, where she paid off into reserve and was laid up in 3 Basin with much of her equipment removed for use in other ships. A major refit had been planned to start in 1997, but was delayed for financial reasons.

Ark Royal was eventually towed to Rosyth in May 1999 to begin an extended refit that would bring her up to the standard of her two sister ships. After being taken into 1 Dock her hull was extensively surveyed and a considerable amount of work was found to be necessary to rectify deterioration caused by the period in reserve, nearly doubling the size of the work package. The gearboxes were replaced, the old Flyco was removed from the island and a new one with more glazing fitted. The ADAWS was upgraded and a

Ark Royal operating RAF Chinook helicopters in the Northern Gulf during the Second Gulf War in 2003. The extended Fly 1 parking area allows a Chinook and Sea King ASaC.7 to be parked in it comfortably. Note the amount of space taken up by the Chinooks, which do not have folding rotor blades. (AUTHOR'S COLLECTION)

Flag Officer, Sea Training (FOST) staff, who were now located at Plymouth. Some weeks later the death of HM Queen Elizabeth The Queen Mother was keenly felt, and at her funeral on 9 April 2002 the captain acted as a pall-bearer and a number of the ship's company attended to represent 'her' ship. In May the ORI was successfully achieved and she was declared the operational fleet carrier at R2 readiness, capable of operating any TAG ordered but with a nominal air group comprising 801 (Sea Harrier), 849B (Sea King AEW) and 814 (Merlin) NAS. By then the Sea Harrier squadrons had been absorbed into JFH, and it had been announced that they would be phased out by 2006 and replaced by two squadrons of Harrier GR.9s, with another two operated by the RAF also capable of embarking.

On 16 May 2002 she deployed to the Mediterranean for Exercise *Dynamic Mix 02*, a major NATO maritime, amphibious and air training period that included forces from thirteen nations. A visit to Alicante followed the exercise, and by mid-June she was back in Portsmouth. On 27 June 2002 she was visited by HM Queen Elizabeth II in one of the ceremonies timed to mark the 50th Anniversary of her accession. After an assisted maintenance period in July and August she sailed on 2 September for Exercise *Argonaut 02*, a NATO training period that began in the Bristol Channel and ended in the Mediterranean, after which she visited Malta to mark the 60th Anniversary of the wartime *Pedestal* convoy to the Island. In October she visited Barcelona and then returned to the UK to prepare for NTG-03, a planned naval task group deployment to the Far East for training with Commonwealth and Allied forces in 2003, to be led by *Ark Royal*. However, the deteriorating situation between the UN and Iraq over the freedom of weapons inspectors to search for weapons of mass destruction caused the UK to make preparations for the alternative Operation *Telic*, the UK contribution to Allied conflict with Iraq in which *Ark Royal* was to play a significant part.

An enhanced NTG-03 sailed for the Mediterranean in January 2003 to ensure the readiness of a broad range of military capabilities. *Ark Royal* deployed in her secondary LPH role, with RAF Chinooks of 18 Squadron and 849A (Sea King ASaC) embarked, in company with *Ocean* and other amphibious ships which, between them, carried 3 Commando Brigade comprising 40 and 42 Royal Marines Commandos and their supporting elements. As the situation continued

new operations room constructed, together with a Joint Force Headquarters. The GWS-30 Sea Dart missile system was removed and the flight deck extended forward into the space made available, the space under it being used for new, larger briefing and flight planning rooms, extra magazines and a new bomb-lift. The lifts were modified to eradicate the earlier problems, and new workshops were constructed to support the Sea Harrier F/A.2, Harrier and Merlin. Other work included the replacement of galleys, installation of a new sewage treatment plant, and modification of fuel tanks to allow more avcat to be stowed at the expense of diesel. The ship that emerged in 2001 was a capable, if small, strike carrier; a much more

useful national asset than the limited antisubmarine carrier launched twenty years earlier.

The ship's company began to move on board at the end of March 2001, and on 13 July *Ark Royal* sailed from Rosyth for post-refit trials. She moved to Portsmouth in September and then began to work-up, with a visit to Cherbourg in between periods of flying. She returned, officially, to fleet duty on 2 November and was rededicated on 22 November 2001 with HM The Queen Mother as Guest of Honour. The aviation work-up continued with 814 (Merlin) NAS carrying out a period of deck-landing training. On 23 February 2002 she started a period of operational sea training with to deteriorate, the force, comprising over thirty RN and RFA ships with forty-five embarked helicopters, moved into the Northern Persian Gulf. Hostilities began on 19 March 2003 with missile strikes, some of them from RN submarines, against the Iraqi command, control and air-defence systems. Helicopters from *Ark Royal* took part in an amphibious assault against the Al Faw Peninsula on 21 March in which 40 and 42 Commandos were landed by air and sea in a very successful operation. When the combat phase of the conflict ended, a number of RN ships left the Gulf, and *Ark Royal* arrived back in Portsmouth on 17 May 2003. She was relieved as high-readiness fleet flagship by *Invincible* in September, and spent the autumn in low-key refresher flying in the North Sea, visiting Amsterdam and North Shields on the Tyne before returning to Portsmouth for Christmas.

In February 2004 *Ark Royal* sailed with 800 (Sea Harrier), 849B (Sea King ASaC) and two helicopters of 771 (Sea King) NAS embarked for a work-up off Scotland before visiting London and Hamburg. The Sea Harriers of 800 NAS left the ship for the last time at the end of March, and *Ark Royal* returned to Portsmouth to be reduced once more into reserve, or 'extended readiness' as it was now known, from April 2004. In July 2005 she was towed to Rosyth for a restorative docking period and a package of enhancements intended to improve her capability as an LPH, so that she could cover for *Ocean* while she underwent her first major refit. The most obvious change was a new mizzen mast sited at the after end of the island, made of 'tuned composites' which allowed the radar and communications equipment fitted inside to 'see out' while being protected from the weather, unlike earlier equipment fitted outside masts. Among other equipments it was fitted with SPN-720 precision approach radar for aircraft, Tacan and the new UK Bowman HF and VHF communications system. After years in a 'mothballed' state, her hull-mounted Type 2016 sonar was finally removed and ADAWS was further upgraded. The programme slipped behind schedule, and efforts to regain time led to a hasty conclusion of work, but harbour acceptance trials began in July 2006 and she sailed on 29 September for post-refit trials. Restoration of the ship's systems after the compressed maintenance period led to problems, and the port inner gas turbine failed within a few days and had to be changed. The first aircraft sorties were completed in October, and on 26 October *Ark Royal* moved to Portsmouth, having taken on ammunition to complete her trials programme and to work-up.

A three-week period of flying trials included landings by Harriers from Boscombe Down, and RAF Chinook helicopters followed, after which she undertook operational sea training as an LPH in

early 2007. She was deemed to be operationally ready after Exercise *South West Marines* in March, with two companies of 40 Royal Marines Commando and a variety of helicopters embarked to form a TAG, and replaced *Ocean* as the R2 LPH. On 20 April she sailed for Exercise *Cockfight*, acting as a target for the Submarine Commanding Officers Qualifying Course or 'Perisher' off Scotland. After that she took part in Exercise *Neptune Warrior 071* with elements of 824 (Merlin) and 848 (Sea King Commando) NAS embarked; both were operational training units which used the experience to train students. 847 (Lynx) NAS also embarked to take part in amphibious operations. Visits to Copenhagen and Gothenburg followed, after which she took part in Exercise *Noble Mariner*, a training period for NATO's high-readiness response force in an area of Poland. The scenario involved the evacuation of civilians, amphibious operations and humanitarian relief, after which *Ark Royal* took over duty as Fleet Flagship, visited Gdynia and Hamburg and then returned to Portsmouth in June. In mid June she visited London before returning to Portsmouth for a maintenance period.

She was back at sea on 17 September 2007 to take part in Exercise *Grey Heron* in the Solent with 45 RM Commando embarked. The next two exercises, *Komodo Dragon* in the Irish Sea and *Chameleon* in the Channel, practised her ability to embark a JFHQ and the RAF Chinooks of 7 Squadron and to work with special forces. Part of the TAG was formed by 848 (Sea King Commando), with 702 (Lynx) NAS embarked to give deck-landing training for its student pilots. Operation *Hound* subsequently covered maritime security operations in the Bay of Biscay, making use of the passage time outbound to Lisbon in November. Once there, a conference of the Maritime Analysis and Operations Centre – Narcotics was held on board, and an International Agency set up to combat drug trafficking at sea. After returning to the UK she gave amphibious training to 1st Battalion The Rifles with 848 (Sea King Commando) NAS embarked, and deck-landing training for 845 (Sea King Commando) NAS. A maintenance period in Portsmouth followed, ending on 5 February 2008 when she sailed for a visit to Newcastle and a training period in the North Sea, after which she embarked 824 (Merlin) NAS and sailed for the NATO Exercise *Armatura Borealis*, an amphibious training period off Norway. Her main task with 824 NAS was the antisubmarine protection of the operating area. She subsequently visited Faslane, where 824 NAS was landed, and on 15 March 2008 she sailed for a deployment to the Western Atlantic, arriving at Norfolk Navy Base on 24 March, where she prepared to embark a USMC TAG for participation in the UK/US Exercise *Constant*

Alliance. She sailed on 1 April 2008 with HMM-774 (Boeing Vertol CH-46 Sea Knight), two Sikorsky MH-60S Knighthawk helicopters of HSC-26 and 'Group India' of 3rd Company, 8th Marines, embarked. She was escorted by two USN destroyers. The exercise ended with an assault in the Camp Lejeune area and was judged a great success. After a visit to Norfolk she returned to the UK in late June to begin a low-key period of support for operational training squadrons and maintenance alongside in Portsmouth. In June she visited Liverpool and provided a DLT deck for 702 (Lynx) and 771 (Sea King utility) NAS. Next she visited the Isle of Man before preparing for another deployment to the USA in which she was to take part in Exercise *Brimstone*, a joint task force exercise with the USN. The need for constant embarkation of foreign marines and aircraft reflected the fact that the UK's own Royal Marines and RN helicopters were heavily committed to the conflict in Afghanistan and had little time to practise their primary role.

Ark Royal was due to sail on 2 July 2008, but her departure was delayed by twenty-four hours so that the she could be used as the venue for Baroness Taylor, the Minister for Defence Equipment & Support, and industry chiefs to sign the contract for the new *Queen Elizabeth* carriers. She finally sailed with only 854 (Sea King ASaC) NAS embarked, arriving in Norfolk later in the month. The USMC put a command and communications team on board and she was to operate the same TAG and embarked force she had embarked earlier in the year. She sailed from Norfolk on 21 July at action stations for a successful training period that lasted a week, after which she briefly visited Mayport and then sailed for the UK on 1 August. No tanker was available and she had to make a slow, economical passage, using 854 NAS to carry out maritime surveillance and arriving in Portsmouth on 24 August for a routine maintenance period. The programme for the remainder of the year was limited by budget cuts, but she did take part in Exercise *Joint Warrior* off Scotland in October with 854 (Sea King ASaC) NAS embarked again and a USN battle-management staff. At the end of October she embarked three Merlins of 820 NAS and deployed to Gibraltar for exercise *Aswex 082*, but the operating area had to be moved to the South West Approaches, which caused cancellation of a post-exercise visit to Lisbon. Back in Portsmouth in December she was allocated to Operation *Adana*, the national quick-reaction-alert force designed to counter intruders into UK airspace.

Ark Royal sailed again on 12 January 2009 for a visit to Liverpool, after which she went alongside at Glen Mallen in the Clyde to land her stocks of ammunition. On 26 January she visited Scapa Flow, and on 29 January she visited Newcastle and then took part in an air-defence exercise in the North Sea with the new destroyer *Daring* and RAF fighters during her passage back to Portsmouth. From February to September she was docked in Portsmouth for a contractor supported refit to refurbish systems and prepare the ship for regeneration in the strike role. The work started without an agreed schedule and was, therefore, at some risk of slippage, but she came out of dock on time on 4 August 2009 and sailed in October for a shake-down before operational sea training in November. On full-power trials she achieved 31.7 knots, partly due to her new 'Intersleek' hull paint. In late November she embarked helicopters of the Maritime Counter-terrorism Group, including a Chinook, Sea Kings and Lynx, for deck-landing qualification by day and night. Early in 2010 she began an operational work-up to prepare for duty as the UK high-readiness strike carrier and fleet flagship. The duties were assumed from 25 January, allowing *Illustrious* to pay off for a refit in Rosyth, although she had not actually completed her ORI and until 8 February her precision approach radar and Tacan were not cleared for operation. She arrived at Glen Mallen to embark carrier strike ammunition on 15 February, and assumed R2 readiness from then. On 1 March 2010 she embarked six Harriers of the Naval Strike Wing and two Merlins for her final operational work-up which culminated in a successful ORI on 15 March.

On 6 April 2010 *Ark Royal* sailed for Exercise *Joint Warrior* off Scotland with a TAG comprising aircraft from 800 (Harrier) NAS, 849 (Sea King ASaC), 814 (Merlin) and 815 (Lynx) NAS. Flying operations were hampered by the ash cloud from the eruption of the Icelandic volcano Eyjafjallajokull, but *Ark Royal* managed to move to a clear area. Without consultation the RAF's 1 Group, which administered all Harriers, ordered 800 NAS to disembark to a Scottish airfield, demonstrating the weakness of the way JFH was structured. *Ark Royal* remained in the exercise in a command role, but, with the ash cloud disrupting air travel across Europe, the Prime Minister ordered the RN to provide immediate sea lift and she was detached for Operation *Cunningham*. While she was on passage to the Western Channel a leak was discovered in a sea-water inlet to the engine room. Preparations had been made to lift 1,450 passengers, but in the end

she was stood down and not used. After returning to Portsmouth the leak was investigated and found to be serious. Although she had been meant to deploy immediately after *Joint Warrior* for a Western Atlantic deployment codenamed *Auriga*, she was docked on 27 April for work to begin. Work was completed on 5 May, and 857 (Sea King ASaC) and two helicopters from 815 (Lynx) NAS embarked alongside while she was refuelled the next day. She sailed for *Auriga* on 7 May, flying the flag of the Commander UK Carrier Strike Group, and picked up her original programme on 14 May, although a visit to New York was cancelled. After preparations at Norfolk Navy Yard she sailed on 18 May for exercise *Capella Strike*, embarking twelve AV-8B Harriers from Marine Air Group 14. The Marines' embarkation was extremely successful, and sorties were flown at a high rate across a range of capabilities from air-defence and strike to close air support. The Harriers disembarked on 27 May and the ship visited Mayport for a stand-down period. When she sailed for a UK/US antisubmarine training period in June she embarked six Harriers of the RAF's 1 Squadron, but their performance proved pedestrian, achieving in five days what the twelve USMC aircraft had achieved in two. Far more could have been achieved if a 'current' carrier squadron had embarked. The next phase of *Auriga* was the Canadian Exercise *Halcyon Rendezvous*, which took place between Norfolk and Nova Scotia.

Ark Royal arrived in Halifax on 23 June 2010 to host a series of meetings timed to coincide with the G-8 Summit, and to take part in the International Fleet Review that marked the RCN's first century. HM Queen Elizabeth II reviewed the Fleet from HMCS *St Johns*. On 30 June *Ark Royal* sailed for the final phase of the *Auriga* deployment, Exercise *Comptuex* with the USN, her battle group being joined by the UK high-readiness amphibious force led by *Ocean*. A short work-up was required, as the RAF pilots in 1 Squadron had been changed while the ship was in Halifax, but 849 (Sea King ASaC) and 814 (Merlin) NAS were able to fly effective sorties from the outset. A number of UK senior officers visited the ship during July to see the carrier strike force in action, and after the training period the ship visited Port Canaveral, having transferred her Lynx to *Ocean* and taken four Sea Kings in return. She left for the UK on 1 August and arrived in Portsmouth twelve

days later. After a leave period the ship spent September preparing for Exercise *Joint Warrior 10-2*, during which Army Air Corps Apache 'gunship' helicopters of 656 Squadron were to be embarked to gain day and night deck-landing qualification and explore how the use of attack helicopters from a sea platform could be improved. The exercise took place in October with a UK two-star battle staff embarked and the USN Commander Strike Training – Atlantic on board to witness the unusual operations. By 14 October the Apaches achieved initial maritime operating capability, and *Ark Royal* returned to Portsmouth for a maintenance period to prepare for a planned deployment in 2011 and ceremonies to mark the 25th anniversary of her first commissioning.

It was not to be. The Government's Strategic Defence and Security Review (SDSR) decided, apparently at the very last moment, that JFH and *Ark Royal* would be withdrawn from service with immediate effect to save money, leaving a ten-year capability gap before *Queen Elizabeth* and the F-35, which were not to be cancelled, could come into service. The captain and his ship's company heard the news on the radio on the morning of 19 October 2010; after speaking to his heads of department the captain cleared lower deck to tell his people what he knew. The MoD, which had enforced a press blackout, confirmed the news that she was to go within days. Despite this, HM Queen Elizabeth II visited the ship on 5 November 2010, wearing an *Ark Royal* brooch that had been worn by her mother at the ship's first commissioning in 1985. The ship sailed on 9 November to land her outfit of ammunition at Glen Mallen, and visited Newcastle and Hamburg. Four Harriers embarked for a short spell, the last of which was launched in flurries of snow on 24 November 2010, piloted by Lieutenant Commander J Blackmore RN. *Ark Royal* returned to Portsmouth on 3 December and her ship's company marched through the city on 22 January 2011. The captain and many of her ship's company were reappointed to *Illustrious*, and *Ark Royal* finally decommissioned on 11 March 2011. It was announced on 10 September 2012 that she had been sold for scrap to the ship-breaking firm in Turkey that had already broken up *Invincible*. *Ark Royal* was towed out of Portsmouth on 20 May 2013 and arrived in the Leyal Shipbreaking Yard in Turkey on 11 June.

CHAPTER 34

OCEAN – LANDING PLATFORM (HELICOPTER)

Ocean carrying out initial sea trials in the Irish Sea during 1998, still flying the red ensign before handover to the RN. The island shows far fewer aerials than it was to have a decade later, after extensive upgrades. (BAE SYSTEMS)

Although not technically an aircraft carrier, *Ocean* is included because she is a large 'flat top' capable of operating a range of helicopters and, potentially, Stovl fighters. Her inclusion allows comparison with the earlier generations of aircraft carriers used in the LPH role, including the previous *Ocean* and *Theseus*, *Bulwark*, *Albion* and *Hermes*, besides illustrating the increasingly important 'cross-over' capability of an LPH which has alternated with *Invincible* Class carriers to provide the UK with a deployable amphibious capability. As this book is being edited, *Illustrious* is acting as an LPH while *Ocean* is in refit.

Technical background

The previous generation of RN commando carriers had all been disposed of by the 1980s, but the South Atlantic Conflict showed the fundamental importance of such ships for power projection in limited war situations, and the provision of important options in higher-intensity conflict. The RN hoped to procure two new ships, known at first as aviation support ships, and the names *Ocean* and *Theseus* were allocated to them. Financial restrictions eventually limited the project to a single ship, and invitations to tender were issued in 1987 but allowed to lapse. Lack of funding severely limited the project and, arguably, the RN was fortunate to get the ship that it eventually did. The staff requirement was minimal and envisaged the ship taking part in three exercises a year with a modest amount of passage time at low speed. The contract for *Ocean* was finally signed with Vickers Shipbuilding and Engineering on 11 May 1993. The hull was built by Kvaerner at Govan, moving to Barrow-in-Furness under its own power in November 1996 for fitting-out and completion.

The design was based loosely on the *Invincible* Class but with an area aft of the hangar on 4 deck fitted as a garage for the stowage of up to forty Land Rovers, thirty-four trailers and six 105mm light guns. Access to it was provided through a ramp at the stern, the after aircraft lift or an inclined ramp to the flight deck with a crane aft of the island capable of lowering vehicles into landing craft. The hangar is capable of storing twelve Sea Kings and is on 5 deck, divided into three sections by fire curtains. It is larger than those in the *Invincible* Class ships and of a more regular and therefore useful shape. The island has a single funnel carrying the exhausts from the two Crossley-Pielstick 12-PC2.6V 400 diesels which deliver 18,360hp to two shafts, and there is also a bow thruster. The diesels give a much greater range than the *Invincible*'s gas turbines, 8,000 miles at 15 knots, but a much lower top speed of only 18 knots. She was finished with the ADAWS command system and a limited communications fit, but these have been steadily improved in a succession of refits. Magazines and storage spaces were designed to take the ammunition and material required by a commando group in an amphibious assault and to sustain it in operations ashore, and are not entirely suitable for strike operations by Sea Harriers or their equivalent. Four landing craft for vehicles and personnel, LCVP Mark 5, are carried on davits in cut out-out areas of the hull, and the ship also carries two Griffon hovercraft. The original design included a

Ocean being launched at Govan on 11 October 1995. (Author's collection)

significant amount of empty space which could be used up through life for improvements to accommodation and the installation of new equipment, and this has proved extremely useful. The ship's company is considerably less than that of the LPH *Bulwark* at 285 including 9 Assault Squadron Royal Marines, who man the LCVPs. Besides the vehicle garage, other improvements include the design of wider passages in the assault routes, to make it easier for fully equipped marines to make their way from the assembly areas to the flight deck, hangar or boat decks.

The aviation arrangements were designed to support an embarked TAG of up to twelve Sea King (Commando) helicopters in the assault role and six smaller Lynx or Apache helicopters

operating in the reconnaissance and antitank roles. The flight deck is strong enough to operate RAF Chinook helicopters, although their size limits their numbers and they cannot be struck down into the hangar. The relatively large flight deck has six helicopter operating spots with more parking space than an *Invincible*, so that it is possible to launch a heliborne assault in a single wave of twelve helicopters, tractoring the second six on to spots as the first six lift off. The deck is completely flat, without an open forecastle forward of it, although for some unknown reason the forward part of Fly 1 has been made pointed like the 1920s *Eagle* and *Hermes*, significantly reducing the amount of parking space available for aircraft, vehicles and pre-prepared underslung loads. The

deck is marked with a runway centreline and Sea Harriers could land-on easily and theoretically carry out a flat deck running take-off, but the Vulcan Phalanx gun at the bow would represent a hazard for an aircraft that drifted to the right on take-off. *Ocean* has no fixed aircraft workshops like those in aircraft carriers, but uses instead a containerised amphibious support package which can be modified to suit the TAG embarked. The lack of relevant workshops and weapons handling arrangements would limit practical operations by Stovl aircraft without a change of role supported by a major refit.

In the absence of an RN strike carrier, *Ocean* showed flexibility during operations off Libya in 2011 by embarking a TAG comprising Army Air Corps (AAC) Apaches to carry out ground-attack missions, RN ASaC helicopters to give situational awareness in the area of operations, and USAF SAR helicopters to recover aircrew brought down behind enemy lines. Despite successive governments' stated intention to improve the UK's ability to deploy a strike force with global capability, it seems remarkable that no serious attempt has been made to create and deploy a dedicated combat SAR capability like that fielded by the US and French armed forces.

Libyan operations in 2011 showed that *Ocean*, like any big 'flat top', has the flexibility to operate in more ways than the original staff requirement stipulated or that politicians had thought they would need. She was cheap to build at slightly more than the cost of a contemporary frigate, and can carry a commando group with its artillery and light vehicles to the area of operations and land it using helicopters and small landing craft. UK policy still calls for tanks and other armoured vehicles to be landed as part of an all-arms task force, however, and these have to be carried in the LPDs *Bulwark* and *Albion*, which carry large landing craft Mark 10 in their floodable docks capable of landing heavy vehicles. Each ship can carry six main battle tanks and about thirty all-terrain armoured vehicles on its vehicle deck. Aviation facilities were severely limited in these ships to save cost, so they have only a small deck with two Sea King-sized spots, no hangar, limited fuel and no support capability. Thus even a modest amphibious operation would require the RN to deploy two ships, one to provide the helicopters and the other to provide the heavy armoured vehicles. By comparison, the French *Mistral* Class

Ocean at anchor in a Norwegian fjord during Exercise *Cold Response* in 2010. Unlike a carrier she has an 'L' pennant number. Note the unnecessarily pointed bow with a Vulcan Phalanx mounted on it. (Crown Copyright/MoD 2010)

An AAC Apache attack helicopter is manhandled on to *Ocean's* after lift. The rows of small circles on deck mark the positions of ring bolts to which aircraft are lashed to keep them secure against damage caused by ship movement. (AUTHOR'S COLLECTION)

LHD can carry as many helicopters, up to twelve main battle tanks landed by four landing craft from a dock aft, and a much smaller ship's company. *Ocean* compares even less favourably with the larger Spanish *Juan Carlos* Class LHDs, two of which have been bought by Australia for the RAN, which can carry even more aircraft and vehicles than a *Mistral* with a ship's company that is slightly smaller than that of *Ocean*. Although the ship has given far better service than the pedestrian specification gave the RN a right to expect, one has to be disappointed at the lack of vision within the UK MoD that prevented the RN from having a ship as good as or better than those operated by the nation's contemporary allies. However one looks at it, the political pressures that forced the RN to buy cheap ships of limited individual capability have led to what amounts to an expensive but second- or even third-rate amphibious capability in the twenty-first century. The export successes of French and Spanish LHDs to Russia and Australia have served to emphasise how out of touch with practical reality British naval procurement has become.

Ocean technical details in 2010

Displacement:	21,758 tons deep load
Dimensions:	length 667ft 4in
	beam 112ft 10in
	draught 21ft 4in
Machinery:	2 shaft Crossley Pielstick 12
	PC2.6V 400 diesels
	18,360hp delivering 18 knots
	single-propeller Kamewa bow
	thruster; 612hp
Armament:	4 twin BMARC 20mm; 3
	Vulcan Phalanx 20mm; 4
	Miniguns 7.62mm; 4 GPMG
	7.62mm
Protection:	none

Fuel:	2,000 tons diesel
Endurance:	8,000 miles at 15 knots
Complement:	285 ship
	972 embarked force plus 300 in
	austere conditions

Aircraft operating data

Flight deck:	550ft x 104ft
Hangar:	365ft x 69ft x 20ft
Lifts:	Two centreline, both 54ft 8in
	long x 31ft 8in wide
	Both 35,000lb
Aircraft:	Up to 18 helicopters in a
	variable TAG, depending on
	size
Aircraft Fuel:	200,000gal avcat (quantities of
	mogas also carried for vehicles)
Air weapons:	Hellfire ASM; 30mm cannon
	ammunition; 0.5in machine-
	gun ammunition; 7.62mm
	machine-gun ammunition;
	palletised loads of military
	ammunition to support the
	embarked force ashore.

Individual ship history

Ocean

Ocean is expected to have a number of years left in service. The following notes on her history are, therefore, necessarily incomplete. Their brevity also reflects her operational use as an amphibious ship rather than an aircraft carrier in the full sense of the description, but should give a sense of her operational activity.

The contract for a single amphibious helicopter carrier was placed with Vickers Shipbuilding and

Engineering on 11 May 1993. The hull was built by Kvaerner at Govan, the first steel being cut on 30 May; fabrication began on the slipway just over a year later, in June 1994. She was launched on 11 October 1995 and hit the bottom while sliding off the slipway, with the result that she had to be docked for repairs to the underwater damage. Machinery was installed alongside Clydebank and she moved to Barrow-in-Furness in November 1996 for completion. She left Barrow for sea trials in early 1998, but in April a submerged log hit one of her propellers and damaged the associated shaft, so she had to be taken into Portsmouth, where she was docked for repairs. She moved to her home port in Devonport in May and resumed the trials programme in June 1998. On 30 September 1998 she was formally commissioned in Devonport, and subsequently continued her trials programme, which included deck landings by Sea Kings and Sea Harriers. In October she sailed with a TAG of Sea King helicopters for a shake-down deployment to the Caribbean which was to include hot-weather trials, but she was diverted to give humanitarian aid to Honduras and the Mosquito Coast area of Central America after Hurricane Mitch caused devastation. Her helicopters helped to provide food and medical assistance to communities up to 100 miles inland, and she provided up to 300 tons of fresh water per day.

By December she was back in Devonport, and in January 1999 she sailed for cold-weather trials off Norway. These were followed by the last of the flying trials, in which an RAF Chinook from A&AEE Boscombe Down carried out 227 deck landings to clear the ship to operate the type. She could now embark a TAG comprising a mix of Sea King, Lynx, Gazelle and Chinook helicopters. After her final period of operational sea training in April she was declared to be operational in July 1999. For her first deployment she embarked 845 (Sea King Commando) and 847 (Lynx/Gazelle) NAS and 40 RM Commando, and sailed in August with a number of other RN warships and auxiliaries for Deployment *Argonaut* 99 to the Eastern Mediterranean to participate in NATO Exercise *Bright Star*. On 17 November she was diverted to the Turkish coast to conduct emergency relief operations following a major earthquake centred on Duzce, returning to the UK at the end of the year. In early 2000 she led a further deployment of the amphibious ready group to the Mediterranean codenamed Deployment *Aurora 2000* with 846 (Sea King Commando), 847 (Lynx) NAS and 42 RM Commando embarked for a series

Ocean alongside her normal berth in Devonport Naval Base. The large openings in the ship's side are where the assault landing craft are secured to davits; there are a further two on the port side. They are usually lowered while in harbour to allow their crews to train with other RM assault units. (CROWN COPYRIGHT/MoD 2012)

of exercises. The first was Exercise *Rock Wader* in Gibraltar, intended as a shake-down exercise. Next came Exercise *Pine Wader* in Portugal from 10 April, and Exercise *Ambrose Hill* at Camp de Canjeurs, a large artillery range in Southern France, from 26 April. On 5 May *Ocean* and her amphibious group were warned to stand by for Operation *Palliser* in support of British nationals in Sierra Leone and to protect UN peacekeepers under attack by rebel forces. The exercise was terminated and the group left France on 7 May, arriving off Sierra Leone on 14 May, where it joined *Illustrious*. The UK Spearhead Battalion, 1 Parachute Regiment, had been flown into the country, and *Ocean*'s landing craft and helicopters were used to support operations ashore. A few days later 42 RM Commando was landed to help bring stability to the war-torn country, and the operation was regarded in Whitehall as a model use of force to stabilise the situation and bring peace to what could have been a serious 'brush-fire' situation. Other British troops were subsequently flown in and the amphibious group returned to the UK, arriving in June. *Ocean* was back in the Eastern Mediterranean in the autumn for the NATO Exercise *Destined Glory*, and in November she was diverted to Sierra Leone again for Operation *Silkman* as an overt show of strength in support of the Government. Landing operations by 42 RM Commando were carried out near Freetown in a high-visibility show of force, and underpinned a

ceasefire which was agreed between the Government and the rebels. *Ocean* remained in the area for another week and then returned to Devonport on 1 December.

In August 2001 *Ocean* sailed as part of the *Argonaut 2001* Deployment, working-up off North Devon and then visiting Lisbon, Cartagena and Malaga before moving into the Indian Ocean to take part in the UK/Omani Exercise *Saif Sareea II* (Swift Sword II). Intended to demonstrate the capability of the UK Rapid Reaction Force to intervene in the Middle East, the exercise took place in October

2001, not long after the September 2001 terrorist attack on New York. The USA began Operation *Anaconda*, attacks on terrorist bases in Afghanistan, at the same time, and requested support from the UK. Consequently Royal Marines were landed from *Ocean* to form Task Force *Jacana*, which took part in Operations *Ptarmigan*, *Snipe* and *Buzzard*. Subsequent UK operations were coded Operation *Oracle* and formed part of the wider US-led Operation *Enduring Freedom*. *Ocean* returned to the UK, leaving *Illustrious* in the Indian Ocean in the LPH role. She sailed from the UK to relieve *Illustrious* on 11 February 2002, with 45 RM Commando embarked. After exercises in the Gulf, 45 Commando was disembarked into Afghanistan in May to continue operations against terrorist bases. Since the campaign was becoming extended and shore-based support was growing, the decision was taken to reduce the size of the RN task force, and *Ocean* returned to Devonport in June. The latter part of 2002 was spent in Devonport undergoing maintenance and repairs delayed by the ship's unexpectedly high tempo of operations. The opportunity was taken to incorporate improved command and communications systems and to fit blisters, 164ft long, on either side of the hull, to improve her stability when lowering loaded landing craft from davits. The ship's company prepared for the planned 'NTG 03' Deployment, but UN

Ocean moored in the Thames during the 2012 London Olympic Games. The cranes visible to the right of the island are not part of the ship, but a construction project in the background. (CROWN COPYRIGHT/MoD 2012)

problems with Iraq over arms inspections led to changes and an enlarged 'NTG 03' prepared for possible conflict in the Middle East.

Ocean sailed from Devonport with 40 RM Commando and 847 (Lynx/Gazelle) NAS embarked on 16 January 2003. She arrived off Cyprus on 26 January and carried out four days of assault training including night operations, after which she sailed into the Gulf, arriving on 15 February, when she went into defence watches. Operation *Telic*, the second Gulf War, began on 21 March, and on that day Sea Kings of 845 NAS and RAF Chinooks landed the second assault wave, comprising 42 RM Commando, on to the Al Faw Peninsula, the first wave having been flown from *Ark Royal*. As the marines advanced they were supported by 847 NAS Lynx helicopters from *Ocean* which successfully attacked a number of Iraqi tanks with ASMs. By early April the war had moved deep inland and the RN task force was reduced. Command was transferred from *Ark Royal* to *Ocean*, but three weeks later *Ocean* was also withdrawn, taking 845 and 847 NAS back to the UK together with elements of 3 Commando Brigade. She arrived back in Devonport on 28 May 2003.

On 23 July 2003 HM Queen Elizabeth II presented a new Queen's Colour to the Fleet on board *Ocean* while the ship was anchored in Plymouth Sound with about twenty other ships in review order. The Trinity House vessel *Patricia* acted as a 'Royal Barge', and two tugs were positioned on *Ocean*'s quarters to keep her positioned so that the island structure could provide some shelter on a very wet and blustery day. Large crowds watched the proceedings from Plymouth Hoe. On 13 May 2004 *Ocean* sailed from Devonport with the ARG as part of the *Aurora 04* deployment to the Western Atlantic. After concentrating at Norfolk Navy Base the RN task force, which included *Invincible*, *Ocean* and the new LPD *Albion*, took part in Exercise *Rapid Alliance* to demonstrate that UK and US amphibious forces could work closely together. She returned to Devonport in July.

Ocean sailed from Devonport on 6 February 2006 for Arctic training off Norway with 45 RM Commando and a TAG made up with helicopters from the Joint CHF embarked, returning in April. She deployed again on 11 September for Operation *Vela 06* with 40 RM Commando, a TAG from the CHF and 849B (Sea King ASaC) embarked. The deployment included participation in Exercise *Grey Cormorant* off the South West coast of the UK in late September, and Exercise *Green Eagle 06* off

Ocean off Libya in 2011 with AAC Apaches on deck and airborne together with USAF Blackhawk combat SAR helicopters aft. The port after landing craft is turned out ready for lowering. (CROWN COPYRIGHT/MOD2012)

Sierra Leone. On passage, aircraft flew intelligence gathering missions to support international operations against terrorist groups. In March 2007 *Ocean* was deployed to the Caribbean with a TAG comprising 854 (Sea King ASaC) and 700M (Merlin) NAS on a tour of duty intended to counter the operations of drug-runners and provide security for Commonwealth nations in the region. She also carried a detachment of Royal Marines and high-speed raiding craft to carry out interceptions. In one interception, guided by a Sea King of 854 NAS, twelve bales of cocaine were winched into a Merlin from the sea where they had been dumped. Their street value was estimated at £28 million. She carried out several important diplomatic visits to places including Norfolk, Virginia, for the Azalea Festival. Her deployment was also timed to coincide with the hurricane season so that she could give aid, if necessary, to British Overseas Territories. When she returned to Devonport in July the high-readiness LPH role was taken on by *Ark Royal* and *Ocean* was taken in hand for her first major refit from September. Work included the fitting of new sections of propulsion shaft, improved accommodation for embarked forces and stowage areas for their kit, and provision of workshop and support facilities to operate AAC Apache gunship attack helicopters. Overall the refit was intended to allow her to remain in service as a viable amphibious unit for a further fifteen years.

The refit was completed in 2008, and she began post-refit trials on 24 September. After working-up and carrying out operational sea training, Ocean resumed the task of high-readiness LPH in 2009 before sailing on 18 February as part of the Taurus 09 deployment with 40 RM Commando and a TAG from 857 (Sea King ASaC), 820 (Merlin) NAS and the CHF. The first phase of the deployment included Exercise Egemen, an Allied amphibious training period in Turkey, after which Ocean continued to the Far East with her amphibious battle group for further exercises. These included jungle training for the embarked force in Brunei, and participation in the FPDA and Commonwealth Exercise Persama Shield off Malaysia in June. She was also present at the International Maritime Defence Exhibition in Singapore. The deployed force returned to the UK in August.

On 8 February 2010 Ocean took part in the annual cold-weather training period in Northern Norway with 45 RM Commando, after which she was one of a number of RN warships ordered to stand by to evacuate British travellers from Europe when the ash cloud from Icelandic volcano Eyjafjallajokull halted commercial aircraft movements. She was not used in the end, and joined the Auriga 10 Deployment in July to take part in major US/UK amphibious exercises off the eastern USA. During Exercise Kearsage USMC V-22 Osprey tilt-rotor and CH-53E Sea Stallion heavy-lift helicopters operated from Ocean during an assault training period off Norfolk. After the exercise she visited Mayport for a period of maintenance and to be reconfigured for further tasks, including a maritime and security patrol in the Caribbean. On 9 September she visited Rio de Janeiro for exercises with the Brazilian Navy and Marines, after which she hosted a UK Trade and Industry Exhibition and a formal UK/Brazilian Defence Agreement was signed on board. After leaving Brazil she crossed the Atlantic to visit Lagos in Nigeria, where she took part in a President's Fleet review to mark fifty years since the nation was granted independence by Great Britain. She returned to Devonport in the late autumn after maritime security operations in the Gulf of Guinea.

After the Strategic Defence and Security Review (SDSR) at the end of 2010 the UK's Coalition Government ordered a brief study into whether Illustrious or Ocean should be retained.

The decision, taken early in 2011, was that Illustrious should complete her refit and be retained as an LPH until Ocean completes her own major refit and upgrade in 2014. Illustrious would then be discarded and Ocean would run on until a suitable replacement, likely to be considered as one of the Queen Elizabeth Class in its secondary role, is in service. In May 2011 Ocean sailed from Devonport as part of the follow-up element of the Cougar 11 Deployment to the Mediterranean, which to was to include the amphibious Exercise Cypriot Lion, with a TAG comprising 857 (Sea King ASaC) NAS and 656 Squadron AAC. The 56th Rescue Squadron of the USAF with its Sikorsky HH-60G Pave-Hawk helicopters was added later, as Libya had become a focus of world attention when opposition forces tried to overthrow the Gaddafi regime and British forces were redeployed to the area as part of Operation Ellamy to implement a no-fly zone over Libya in accordance with UN Security Council Resolution 1973. After the immediate implementation of the SDSR the UK no longer had a strike carrier capability, but an eventual total of five AAC Apaches had been embarked in Ocean together with ASaC Sea Kings to provide a very limited attack capability, working alongside similar French helicopters operating from the LHD Tonerre. The first attacks were carried out in the Brega area on 4 June 2011, and eventually nine radar-guided Hellfire missiles were fired against maritime targets, all of which hit, and 550 rounds of 30mm gun ammunition were fired. She remained off Libya with her Apaches until September and then proceeded to Cyprus, where she was to change her embarked force for a deployment into the Red Sea for a period of maritime security

operations. She returned to Devonport in December 2011, by which time she had spent 229 days deployed, of which 176 had been spent at sea, a total that far exceeded the carrier operations described earlier in this book, even those in wartime. She was awarded the Fleet Trophy as the RN's most effective big ship (although, to be realistic given the few big ships left in service, that title hardly does her achievement justice).

On 4 May 2012 Ocean was moored in the Thames at Greenwich to practise her part in providing security arrangements for the London Olympics, including accommodation and helicopter support. At the end of May she sailed for visits to Hamburg for the Port Festival, and then Sunderland. She returned to Greenwich on 13 July to support the Olympic and Paralympic Games, and did not finally return to Devonport until 21 September. During that time she operated five RN and five AAC Lynx helicopters and also operated London Air Ambulance and Metropolitan Police helicopters. Four hundred RN and Army security personnel lived on board, and more than 100,000 meals were provided throughout the games. Once back in Devonport she prepared for a major refit which is scheduled to last until the end of 2013. When she rejoins the fleet in 2014, after trials and a period of working-up, she will take the LPH task back from Illustrious, which will be paid off. Ocean will be the only 'big-deck' warship left in the RN from 2014 until Queen Elizabeth begins her trials programme, still far from being operational, in 2016.

Ocean in the River Tamar, sailing from her base port in Devonport with tugs in attendance. (CROWN COPYRIGHT/MOD2012).

CHAPTER 35

QUEEN ELIZABETH CLASS

Technical background

The *Queen Elizabeth* Class, comprising two ships under construction at the time of writing, has evolved from one of the most complicated and protracted warship procurement programmes in British history. As with so many British aircraft carriers, their design has been dogged by politics, and while the ships are not perfect the nation will be fortunate to have them. Preliminary studies of potential new carriers had been carried out since the late 1980s, and the success of the *Invincible* Class in supporting operations in the Former Republic of Yugoslavia from the Adriatic, coming so soon after the vital role played by aircraft carriers in the South Atlantic Conflict of 1982, accelerated those studies as the new Labour Government carried out its Strategic Defence Review in 1997. When the Review was announced the Secretary of Defence stated: 'The current three *Invincible* Class carriers are to be replaced by two larger and more

flexible aircraft carriers. These ships . . . are to enter service in 2012 and 2015.' At last, it seemed, politicians had accepted that the structure of a modern warship, and therefore its tonnage, represented only about 20 per cent of its cost, the remainder being spent of command, control, communications and technical systems. Thus increased steelwork to provide a greater hull volume was likely to add only a small percentage to the build cost, but would lead to a far more flexible ship. The wise old shipbuilder's adage about hull volume, 'steel is cheap and air is free', is worth quoting.

Unfortunately the good ideas seem to have withered in the subsequent design phase. It should be noted that warship design by 1998 was the responsibility of the MoD Procurement Agency, not the RN, which had been transformed by then into an operational arm within an increasingly joint-force structure. The wealth of RN knowledge about conventional carrier operations with

An artist's impression of *Queen Elizabeth* with Lightning IIs and a Merlin Helicopter on deck (AIRCRAFT CARRIER ALLIANCE)

catapults and arrester wires before 1978 had been considerably diluted by more recent Stovl operations, and the UK was partly funding an Advanced Stovl-designed strike fighter with the USMC to replace the Sea Harrier within the life of the *Invincible* Class and the AV-8B in USMC expeditionary air wings embarked in amphibious carriers. The Government decision to move the Sea Harriers into a Joint Force structure under RAF administration led to further complications, as the higher command within the RAF remained institutionally averse to the operation of embarked fighters. However, by 2000 the Advanced Stovl project had been absorbed into the US Joint Strike Fighter Project, eventually designated the F-35 and given the name Lightning II, which was to be produced in three versions: the conventional 'A'

Queen Elizabeth's forward island is moved on to a barge for passage to Rosyth after its completion in Portsmouth. It arrived at its destination on 11 February 2013. (AIRCRAFT CARRIER ALLIANCE)

variant for the USAF, the Stovl 'B' variant for the USMC, and the carrier-capable 'C' version with tailhook and nose-tow catapult arm for the USN. The UK added yet more initials by naming its own requirement the Future Carrier-Borne Aircraft (FCBA) at first, and then the Joint Combat Aircraft (JCA) when the RAF joined the project. The UK partly funded the 'B' version as the only Level 1 international partner, but the advantages of the 'C' version, which had a greater radius of action, a larger internal weapons bay and the ability to bring a greater weight of unused weapons back to the ship than the vertical-landing 'B' in hot conditions, soon became obvious. Arguments were put forward that, since the UK wanted a carrierborne strike fighter, the 'C' was the better long-term version but, rather than take a decision, the MoD's procurement arm gave design contracts to two firms, BAE Systems and Thales UK. Each was instructed to produce two designs, one for a smaller Stovl carrier and one for a larger 'conventional' carrier. It was expected that the ensuing sketch designs would be evaluated and followed by a decision on which aircraft type to procure and which carrier design to operate it. It was immediately apparent that the conventional designs were more flexible ships with no limitation on the type of AEW aircraft that could be embarked and considerably more 'cross-over' capability to embark assault helicopters and an amphibious marine force in a secondary commando role. Since the UK had invested in the F-35 project

from the outset and it was expected to be developed by the time the first ship was in service, no thought appears to have been given to procuring alternative fighters such as the USN McDonnell Douglas (later Boeing) F/A-18E/F or the French Dassault Rafale for operation from the conventional designs. The idea behind building two ships had been to run one as a high-readiness strike carrier with the second ship available as an LPH, at a lower state of readiness as a strike carrier or in refit, thus ensuring a gapless capability. This was the arrangement under which the *Invincible* Class carriers had been run in their last years of

operation, but was never fully understood by the press and public.

The Ministry's subsequent decision was both complex and surprising. The small Stovl designs clearly lacked flexibility and were rejected; the Thales conventional design was selected as the basis for further development, but was to be built by a consortium of both companies and redesigned to operate the Stovl variant of the F-35 and a helicopter AEW aircraft. To answer critics who pointed out that these ships were projected to have a life of up to fifty years but were 'locked into a configuration that only Stovl aircraft can use', the MoD instructed that the ships were to be built to 'an innovative, adaptable design'. They were to be built with a ski-jump and associated equipment to operate the Stovl F-35B aircraft, but to an essentially conventional carrier design so that, after the F-35, they could be modified in refit to operate aircraft requiring a catapult launch and arrested recovery. In the 'small print' of the agreement, however, it was apparently specified that launch would be by the C-13 steam catapult and recovery by Mark 7 mod 3 arrester gear that was already in service in the USN *Nimitz* Class. Subsequent design work concentrated on such a ship, identified as Design D. The design demonstration phase was completed in 2007. 'Main Gate' Government approval to proceed with the project was given on 25 July 2007, but the final Government approval to start manufacture was not

The final bow section, the last part of *Queen Elizabeth's* flight deck, being lowered into place in Number 1 Dock in Rosyth on 8 February 2013. (AIRCRAFT CARRIER ALLIANCE)

Queen Elizabeth's forward island in place on 29 March 2013. (Aircraft Carrier Alliance)

given until May 2008. The 'team' responsible for the manufacture of the two aircraft carriers had evolved into the Aircraft Carrier Alliance. It comprised BAE Systems Surface Ships, Thales UK, BAE Systems (Marine and Insyte) and Babcock Marine, plus the UK MoD both as a partner and as the customer. A contract was signed between the Ministry and the Alliance on board *Ark Royal* on 3 July 2008. Within the Alliance, BAE Systems had responsibility for design integration, construction, commissioning and acceptance of the two ships; BAE Insyte was to be responsible for the design and installation of the command system; and Thales UK for the Stage 1 design, power and propulsion systems and the aviation interface.

Initially the lead ship was to be completed for trials in 2014 but, having ordered the ships, the Government announced on 11 December 2008 that completion of the first ship was to be delayed by two years to reduce expenditure in the short term although cost in the longer term would be considerably increased. A similar delay would, necessarily, be imposed on the second ship, which could not be assembled in Number 1 Dock in Rosyth until the first ship was floated out of it. The first metal for *Queen Elizabeth* was cut on 7 July 2009, and for *Prince of Wales* on 16 February 2011. In 2010 the new UK Coalition Government announced the result of a new SDSR, which withdrew *Ark Royal* and the remaining force of Harriers from service with immediate effect. The two *Queen Elizabeth* Class carriers were not cancelled, and it was explained that the SDSR had found the gap of ten years in naval strike capability before the first ship became operational to be acceptable given the present world situation. Bizarrely, however, the review placed great emphasis on a naval strike capability after 2020, and stated that the best aircraft for operation from the new ships would be the F-35C carrier variant, not the Stovl F-35B on which considerable sums had been spent and upon which the UK staff embedded in the project management team in the USA had had some influence on the design. This was, of course, the decision which should have been taken at the outset, but with over a year of fabrication completed it was too late to alter the design of *Queen Elizabeth*, and the changes to *Prince of Wales* would delay her entry into operational service until after 2020. The UK had by then ordered three F-35B pre-production aircraft, and negotiations were begun to swap the last of these for an F-35C. Having worked with the 'B' variant for over a decade, the UK had made no input into the 'C' variant, which was tailored around the USN *Nimitz* and CVN-21 designs. *Queen Elizabeth* was

to be completed with a flat deck and no ski-jump in 2016 for a two-year first-of-class trial programme, after which she was to run for a short period as what would have been the world's largest helicopter carrier until replaced by *Prince of Wales*, which would operate as a strike carrier with a TAG including F-35Cs. The decision whether to convert *Queen Elizabeth* with catapults and arrester wires at her first refit or not was to be taken at the next SDSR, planned for 2015.

For over a year the Alliance worked closely with the USN on the design and potential installation of catapults and arrester gear. It was decided not to install the USN model C13 steam catapults and standard USN Mark 7 arrester gear originally agreed but, rather, to install the new electromagnetic aircraft launch system (EMALS) and advanced arrester gear (AAG) designed for the new USS *Gerald R Ford*, CVN-78, due for completion in 2015. The first set of equipment was earmarked for her but, generously, the USN made the second set available for *Prince of Wales*. By early 2012, however, MoD sources were saying that the cost of installing EMALS and AAG in *Prince of Wales* had been estimated at about £2 billion, or half the original build cost of the ship. If it was decided to fit the equipment into *Queen Elizabeth* after her completion, a cost roughly the equivalent of the original build was quoted. Sources in the USN said that the actual cost of the equipment on a government-to-government sales basis would be about £450 million, although this was never confirmed in a contractual arrangement. The extra £1.5 billion was the cost of installation estimated by the Alliance, revealing that the design was never really adaptable once construction had started. On 10 May 2012 the UK Defence Secretary stated that the Government had elected to return to the Stovl F-35B for operations from these ships. Interestingly, the MoD never explained why it had not considered or costed the installation of steam catapults and Mark 7 arrester gear as specified in the carriers' build

contract; another facet of the procurement saga that is difficult to comprehend or explain. The decision to operate conventional carrier aircraft was undoubtedly the right one, but it should have been taken at the outset, allowing the design team to get on with producing a practical ship that could have operated a variety of affordable strike fighter and airborne-surveillance-aircraft designs. Instead of producing a ship that will be interoperable with Britain's US and French allies, the UK has produced an expensive alternative which is less capable and interoperable with neither. The 2012 decision has effectively locked these ships into a configuration that can be used only by Stovl aircraft. The installation of catapults and arrester gear to operate some future fighter or unmanned combat aircraft is likely to be no less expensive in some future refit than the figures quoted in 2012, and the concept of the 'adaptable' carrier design must be deemed an expensive and unnecessary failure.

Construction

The ships are being built in sections constructed by BAE Systems at Govan, Scotstoun and Portsmouth; Babcock in Rosyth and Appledore; Cammell laird in Birkenhead; and A & P on the Tyne. The sections are taken by lighter to Rosyth, where they are assembled in Number 1 Dock. Originally built in 1916, the dock is just large enough but needed to have the entrance widened from 124ft to 138ft and the sides reprofiled with the removal of angled steps to make the dock floor 30ft wider. A new overhead crane with a span of 394ft has been installed to straddle the dock and lift the smaller blocks into place. It is 223ft high and has two hooks capable of lifting 1,100 tons and a third capable of lifting 550 tons. The ship's two island structures are the result of machinery installations and their individual exhausts that are widely separated to provide redundancy in the event of action damage. The individual blocks fabricated under cover and fitted-out with machinery and subassemblies such as diesel generators, offices, cabins and galleys before they are moved to Rosyth. They have to fit each other precisely, and a tolerance of only 10mm is allowed. Each block forms a watertight section of the finished hull, enabling them to be floated into the dock before assembly and proving the integrity of their build quality from the outset. Work was provided to the different yards to provide, as far as was possible, an even and predictable flow of work, and the use of the latest cutting and welding technology has transformed the way in which the yards operate. The need to hire agency workers at peak periods, together with trailers and barges to move the blocks, imposes a strict discipline on completion dates, often years in advance, for every component. Each block is physically weighed before it is moved on to a barge. For instance, lower block 03 weighed about 8,000 tons, and lower block 04, which contains much of the machinery, about 11,000 tons. In early 2013 the project has been remarkable for completing every aspect on time at the predicted cost. The only variations to the original programme have followed the changes imposed on the project by politicians.

Design

Both ships have all-electric propulsion with power provided by two Roll-Royce MT-30 gas turbine alternators, each developing 36MW and four Wartsila auxiliary diesel generators, each developing 7MW. A number of 2MW emergency diesel generators are fitted throughout the ship. Two shafts are each driven by a 30MW electric motor, making the ship capable of a design speed of 26 knots. This is about a knot slower than the French carrier *Charles de Gaulle* but significantly slower than the 30-plus knots of a USN *Nimitz*. Speed might have been an issue when operating the F-35C at its maximum weight in light wind conditions, but is unlikely to be a problem in Stovl operations. The motors are situated in the after part of lower block 04 to minimise the length of the propeller shafts. Surprisingly, as a cost-saving measure, the *Queen Elizabeth*s are not fitted with azimuth thruster pods like other modern warships. Economical cruising speed is estimated at 15 knots, giving an endurance of 10,000 miles. The design calls for the ships to operate at maximum sustained effort for seven days without replenishment, have a maintenance interval of six months and a docking interval of six years. The two-island layout is unusual but not new to the RN; earlier British carrier designs in 1943 and 1951 had two separate islands, the latter incorporating exhausts from widely separated machinery, but both were cancelled before construction began. The CVA-01 would have been slightly longer but 10,000 tons lighter,

and would have had two separate exhaust 'macks' built into what started as separate islands that were joined in the centre during the design phase.

The air search radar is the three-dimensional Thales Type 1046, and other types are fitted for surface surveillance, target indication and navigation. For aircraft precision approach guidance SPN 720(V)15 radar is fitted. Tacan will be fitted to both ships. To save cost and minimise the requirement for weapon stowage and technical manpower, ship-fitted weapons were kept to a minimum and comprise only three Phalanx CIWS mountings to give a 'last-ditch' defence against sea-skimming missiles. Four miniguns are mounted on the quarters to give a defence against 'terrorist-manned boats' in confined waters, and hand-held weapons can be deployed for security if required. There are nineteen watertight compartments, and all machinery is controlled by an integrated platform management system which, together with the operations room and navigation and flight planning area, uses open architecture computers to allow continual upgrades to be applied to the systems.

The completed ships are to be 932ft long, with a waterline beam of 128ft and a width across the flight deck of 239ft. Height from the bottom of the keel to the masthead is to be 187ft and the deep-load draught is to be 33ft. Once the sections arrive in Rosyth each ship is expected to be in the dock for two years before being floated out into the adjacent non-tidal basin for completion. The projected ship's company of 679 compares very favourably with 726 in the smaller *Illustrious* and even more favourably with 4,660 in the larger USS *Gerald R Ford*. An embarked air group will increase this number by up to 1,000, with room for more in austere conditions. Four galleys with 67 catering staff serve four dining areas, the largest of which can serve 960 sailors with hot meals in an hour. Sailors from previous generations of aircraft carriers would be pleasantly surprised to find that these ships are equipped with a cinema, fitness suites and a shopping complex. All cabins will have access to the internet and e-mail. Junior sailors will live in six-berth cabins allowing a flexible male/female ratio. The majority of senior sailors and officers have single cabins with adjacent toilet and shower facilities. The sick bay includes an operating theatre, a dental surgery and an eight-bed ward with eleven full-time medical staff, with scope for considerable expansion when the ship operates in the humanitarian relief role. The size of the ship's company has been kept small by the use of automation to bring ammunition, stores and catering supplies out of bulk stowage using systems similar to those used by the logistics industry ashore.

The flight deck and hangar are the largest ever built in a British aircraft carrier, so it is

particularly disappointing that these ships are so limited in the types of aircraft they can operate, when a more dynamic and visionary project from 2008 could have produced ships that would have been so much more versatile. On the positive side, however, these ships restore a viable British carrier strike capability after a prolonged gap, and are capable of large-scale deployed operations as part of a national or international task force. The deck is large enough to allow the simultaneous launch and recovery of Stovl fighters and helicopters. A 12-degree ski jump is sited on the port side of Fly 1, with parking space to starboard of it, as in *Hermes*. The large, single-deck hangar allows a considerable amount of space for aircraft to be manoeuvred inside it. The two starboard-side deck lifts are each large enough to take a fully-spread Chinook or two F-35s. During replenishment operations at sea, stores and ammunition can be taken on to the side lifts and then struck down into storage areas from the hangar using the automated systems, again minimising the manpower needed. Having both lifts on the starboard side of the hangar is a slight limitation, but the hangar is sufficiently large that this will not pose a problem like the cramped hangars on earlier designs. The class was designed, like CVA-01, to take up to thirty-six strike fighters in the defining air group, together with four airborne surveillance and control helicopters and four antisubmarine helicopters, although in 2013 a TAG of thirty F-35Bs, six Merlin and four ASaC helicopters is predicted. In everyday peacetime operations it is likely that a naval air squadron of up to twelve F-35Bs will be embarked, with the potential for an RAF unit to embark for surge combat operations. In 2013 the MoD plans to operate the JCA as a joint force, like assault helicopters and the former Harrier force. There is no provision for combat SAR in strike operations. This task, if performed at all, will have to be undertaken by antisubmarine Merlins, whereas French and USN carriers can embark joint combat SAR units.

The ships can operate any helicopter in UK service, including Chinooks and Apaches, which can keep their rotors spread in the hangar, and are large enough to operate F-35s from the deck at the same time. The design includes large briefing rooms and mission planning rooms which can incorporate flight simulators in which pilots can 'fly' virtual missions before undertaking them in reality. The ship is controlled from the forward island and the flying control position or 'flyco' is in the after island, with emergency command positions in both to cater for action damage. The original contract between the Ministry and the Alliance called for two ships to be available on 584 days of every year, the balance of 146 reflecting one ship in refit or maintenance. This may change to

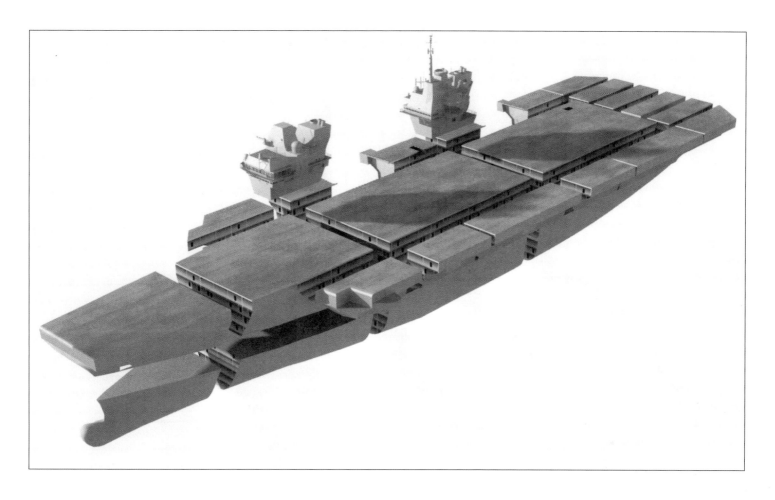

put one ship at lower readiness, but shows what is possible. The exact number of JCAs to be procured has not been announced, but in early 2013 orders had been placed for three pre-production examples and two production aircraft. The UK Defence Secretary has stated that aircraft will be available for *Queen Elizabeth*'s sea trials in 2018, and a squadron will be able to embark operationally in 2020 to restore the UK's carrier strike capability. The first British squadrons will have to form and train in the USA to take advantage of the established US F-35 autonomous logistic support system, but by 2018 this will need to be available in *Queen Elizabeth* and air stations ashore where the type will disembark when not at sea.

These ships are big and have enormous potential, not all of which has been used by the UK, as we have seen. This gives the design export potential, and a formal agreement was signed between the UK and French Governments in 2006 that will allow a conventional carrier based on the *Queen Elizabeth* design to be built in France after 2013. Significantly, it would be fitted with C-13 steam catapults and Mark 7 arrester gear within a build price quoted by a French source in 2012 as less than the cost of *Queen Elizabeth* to take EMALS and AAG! If built, it will demonstrate the ship that the RN could and should have had.

Queen Elizabeth technical details

Displacement:	66,600 tons deep load
Dimensions:	length 931ft 8in
	beam 128ft waterline; 239ft 6in
	across flight deck
	draught 36ft
Machinery:	2 shaft each driven by a 30MW
	electric motor
	2 Rolls-Royce MT-30 gas
	turbines each developing
	36MW
	2 Wartsila diesels each
	developing 7MW
	Emergency 2MW diesel
	generators
	electric propulsion delivering
	up to 26 knots
Armament:	3 x 20mm Phalanx; 4 x 30mm
	miniguns
Protection:	not released
Fuel:	9,450 tons diesel/avcat for ship
	and aircraft
Endurance:	10,000 miles at 15 knots
Complement:	675 ship + 1,000 air
	group/embarked force + 100
	battle staff

Queen Elizabeth was constructed in a number of blocks, built all over the UK, which were transported by sea to Number 1 Dry Dock at Rosyth for assembly. (AIRCRAFT CARRIER ALLIANCE)

Aircraft operating data

Flight deck:	925ft x 220ft amidships; 120ft
	at bow
Hangar:	508ft 6in x 109ft 11in x 22ft
Lifts:	90ft (average) long x 50ft wide;
	both 120,000lb max load
Aircraft:	40 designed TAG; more can be
	carried with a deck park
Aircraft fuel:	not released
Air weapons:	The weapon fits (US or UK
	weapons) for the F-35 have not
	yet been announced. The F-35
	is designed to carry US nuclear
	weapons but it has not been
	stated whether UK aircraft will
	do so. Stingray homing
	torpedoes; Mark 11 depth
	charges for Merlin helicopters;
	0.5in machine-gun ammunition
	for helicopters

CHAPTER 36

AIRCRAFT CARRIERS IN THE COMMONWEALTH NAVIES

The navies of Australia and Canada had evolved in the early part of the twentieth century from detached squadrons of the RN. During the Second World War both operated under the operational control of the Admiralty and, as the striking power of carrierborne aircraft grew, both began to consider ways to introduce aircraft carriers into their postwar fleets. The RCN, as explained earlier, provided the ship's companies for *Puncher* and *Nabob*, but under the terms of the US Lend/Lease Act the ships remained part of the RN. The air departments and embarked squadrons were provided by the RN. By 1945 agreement had been reached that the RCN would man a light fleet carrier which would be lent by the RN for operations in the Pacific. The unexpectedly early end of the conflict took the urgency out of the project, but the RCN eventually commissioned *Warrior* on loan from the RN in 1946, becoming the first navy outside the UK, USA, Japan and France to operate an aircraft carrier.

By 1945 nearly half the RN's aircrew came from the RCN, RAN, RNZN and their reserves, with the result that there were a number of trained pilots and observers who could be recruited into peacetime commissions with the Commonwealth navies when they acquired their own aircraft carriers. In the RCN the ship's air department and air engineering technical personnel were either recruited from the RN, or Canadians who wanted a peacetime naval career trained in the UK. *Warrior* operated an air group of Seafire fighters and Firefly fighter reconnaissance/antisubmarine aircraft at first, and could therefore rely on the RN for technical management of its fledgling naval aviation branch. The light fleet carrier was a good choice because its machinery was closely similar to that in the cruisers and destroyers already operated by the RCN and the amount of new technology to be absorbed was limited, largely, to the flight-deck machinery and the aircraft themselves. *Warrior* was returned to the RN and replaced by the improved *Magnificent*, which was capable of operating larger and heavier aircraft. Like *Warrior*, she was on loan to the RCN, but the terms of the agreement allowed her to be retained as long as Canada paid for her upkeep and refits. She operated British Sea Fury FB.11 fighters and Firefly AS.4 antisubmarine aircraft at first, maintaining close links with the RN, but the latter were replaced by TBM-3E Avengers.

By 1952 the advent of the angled deck and steam catapult meant that light fleet carriers would need to be extensively modified at Canadian expense, and the RCN obtained Government approval to purchase an incomplete ship and rebuild it to a new design, rather than modify *Magnificent*. Fortunately the RN had retained several incomplete light fleet carrier hulls after 1945, and one of the these, *Powerful*, was purchased outright for completion to a new, advanced design. Originally a sister-ship of *Magnificent*, she was very different when she was commissioned into the RCN as HMCS *Bonaventure* in 1957. She marked a transition, as technical support management links were retained with the RN for the ship but she operated aircraft of American design and, because of this, aircrew were trained in the USA rather than the UK. The McDonnell F2H-3 Banshee fighter gave a limited all-weather air-defence capability, and Trackers built under licence in Canada as the CS2F-2 were used for longer-ranging antisubmarine missions, with the Sikorsky HO4S-3 Whirlwind helicopter giving close-in antisubmarine defence. Unlike the RN, which concentrated on a strike capability for its carriers, the RCN concentrated on antisubmarine warfare

The hull of HMAS *Canberra* arrives in Australia from Spain, where it was built, on the heavy-lift ship *Blue Marlin*. (RAN)

HMAS *Canberra* being fitted-out in Melbourne. (RAN)

in the North Atlantic and was able to deploy a significant capability from a relatively small carrier. Despite its success, *Bonaventure* did not survive the transition to the unified CAF, and fell victim to similar arguments about the cost-effectiveness of carriers against shore-based aircraft that afflicted the UK and Australia at this time. *Bonaventure* made her last fixed-wing launch in December 1969 and was withdrawn from service in 1970. By then, Canada had developed sophisticated operating systems that allowed Sea King antisubmarine helicopters, originally purchased for the carrier, to operate from frigates, and embarked aviation developed along this route. In 2012 the Sea Kings are still in service despite a protracted and very delayed development programme with a successor type. Single services have been restored, albeit under joint operational command, with the result that the RCN operates a substantial force of destroyers and frigates, each capable of embarking helicopters flown by detachments from the RCAF.

The acquisition of an aircraft carrier for the RAN was somewhat more controversial at the outset, although the Australian Commonwealth Naval Board (ACNB) had pushed hard for a light fleet carrier capable of operating in the Pacific and as the logical focus of a postwar fleet from 1944. Unfortunately the British First Naval Member, Admiral Sir Guy Royle, who was a former 5th Sea Lord responsible for RN air matters, obtained Admiralty approval for the transfer on loan at no cost to Australia of one of the ubiquitous light fleet carriers 'in a quiet and unofficial way', without seeking Government approval. The Prime Minister, John Curtin, reminded Royle that communications on such matters should be made through Government channels. The idea was discussed when Curtin visited the UK for talks with Winston Churchill, but forceful British arguments led Curtin to suspect that, while the idea had merit, the RN was merely trying to solve its own manpower crisis by obtaining Australian sailors to man new ships that could not otherwise be commissioned in 1945. There was an element of truth in this, but the resulting lack of a decision delayed the creation of an Australian Fleet Air Arm. After the end of hostilities a study was set up by Admiral Sir Louis Hamilton, the last British admiral to be seconded to the RAN as First Naval Member. Chaired by Commander V A T Smith DSC RAN, who had served with the RN as an observer throughout the war, the study recommended the purchase of two light fleet carriers and the creation of an RAN Fleet Air Arm on RN lines.

'Cash-strapped' Britain could no longer afford to lend or donate carriers but, after negotiation, the Admiralty agreed to sell two suspended *Majestic* Class light fleet carriers for the estimated price of one. The purchase price was thus £2,750,000 for the two ships, plus £450,000 each for their initial outfits of stores. Against this could be set the £427,000 for a replacement HMAS *Sydney* raised by public subscription after the loss of *Sydney* II in 1941. *Sydney* was commissioned into the RAN at Devonport, where she had been built, in December 1948, but it was decided to delay her sister ship, *Melbourne*, to incorporate the latest technology, and she eventually emerged in 1955 to a very different design, operating an air group of Sea Venom FAW.53 fighters and Gannet AS.4 antisubmarine aircraft. She was the third ship in the world to be equipped with a steam catapult, angled flight deck and mirror landing aid during build, rather than retrofitted after completion. As in the RCN her squadrons were numbered in the RN sequence, and RN technical management of the ships and aircraft reduced the overhead cost of naval aviation. Also like *Bonaventure*, operating data and techniques were listed in CB 04484, the RN Aircraft Carrier Handbook.

As the RN moved towards larger carriers and aircraft, withdrawing its smaller light fleet carriers from service, Australia followed Canada in procuring USN aircraft for carrierborne operation; S-2G Trackers replaced the Gannets and A-4G Skyhawk strike fighters replaced the Sea Venoms. Sea Kings built under licence by Westland in the UK replaced Wessex antisubmarine helicopters. *Sydney* was not modernised, but provided a significant capability as an LPH during the Vietnam War, while the replacement of *Melbourne* became a major political issue in the 1970s. Several international designs were evaluated, but the British *Invincible* design was not taken forward

HMAS *Canberra* in BAE Systems' yard at Williamstown, near Melbourne, in May 2013. (AUTHOR'S COLLECTION)

because of its high cost and the complexity of the Sea Dart missile system, which was not used by the RAN. The preferred option was the USN *Iwo Jima* Class design, which was affordable, needed less than half the ship's company of *Melbourne*, was capable of operating large helicopters and could be modified with an antisubmarine command system without losing a significant amphibious capability as an LPH. Other contenders were the USN Sea Control Ship design, subsequently built by Spain and Thailand as small carriers, and the Italian *Garibaldi* design. However, after the 1981 Nott Defence Review the British Government decided to retain only two of its three *Invincible* Class ships, and *Invincible* herself was offered for sale at £175 million, considerably less than her estimated build cost. A study was instigated to decide whether to retain the GWS-30 Sea Dart system, and the balance of probability is that it would have been removed, since other RAN warships were fitted with the USN Standard SAM and Australia could not afford to support two separate systems. Royal Navy technical assistance would have been available and GWS-30 would have been removed to create more deck space, as it eventually was in the RN. The Australian Government never took the decision to procure Sea Harriers for operation from the ship, although, since she had a 'ski-jump' and support facilities for the type, its eventual operation would have remained an attractive option and RAN pilots on exchange duty had flown the type with the RN. The ship would have been recommissioned as HMAS *Australia* after being taken over by the RAN. It was not to be, however. After the Falklands Conflict the Australian Government offered to release the UK from the sales contract if it wished. The offer was accepted, *Invincible* was retained by the RN and *Melbourne* was withdrawn from service in 1982 without replacement.

Unlike Canada, however, Australia has decided to return to the operation of big-deck ships in the twenty-first century in order to expand its capability to project expeditionary forces over significant distances. By then the RN had lost its full-time design element, and realistically had nothing to offer, while the RAN had achieved Government support to procure two amphibious assault ships and was in a position to procure the best and most practical design. The USN LHA and LHD designs were too big and expensive, so the French *Mistral* and the Spanish *Juan Carlos* class designs were compared and evaluated. The latter was chosen in 2007 and two ships were ordered, to be named *Canberra* and *Adelaide*. Bizarrely, the traditional flagship name *Australia* was rejected by the Government because it feared adverse publicity if it should be damaged or even sunk in action. Their hulls were built by the design-lead shipyard, Navantia, at

Ferrol in Spain, and the first, *Canberra*, arrived at BAE Systems' shipyard at Williamstown in Australia on the heavy-lift ship *Blue Marlin* in 2012. BAE Systems will fit the locally-made island and outfit the ships ready for initial sea trials soon after this book is published. Their procurement reflects the RAN's ability to select and procure good warship designs and, more significantly from a British perspective, the rapid decline of the UK's ability to compete in that market, despite having once exported more aircraft carriers than any other nation, with 1942 light fleet carriers capable of operating in a variety of roles. The new Australian LHDs are capable of operating up to twelve NH Industries MRH-90 helicopters, with six operating spots. The hangar is linked to the flight deck by two lifts, one right aft and one on the starboard side forward of the island; both are clear of the 'runway' or aircraft operating area. In the Spanish Navy, *Juan Carlos* is capable of operating AV-8B Harriers and has a 'ski-jump' at the forward end of the runway. This has been retained in the design adopted by the RAN, allowing the ships to operate USMC, Spanish, Italian or Thai AV-8s if necessary, and the deck is stressed to operate F-35Bs. The Australian Government has plans to procure the F-35, but has emphasised that this is to be the landlocked USAF F-35A version. As can be imagined, this has been the subject of some debate and will, no doubt, continue to be so for some years to come. The MRH-90 multirole tactical transport helicopter is being procured in sufficient numbers to equip one naval air squadron and several squadrons of the Army Air Corps. While the Navy will be responsible for 'best practice' in embarked operations, large-scale amphibious operations will involve joint TAGs with Army helicopters including Chinooks. When required, the LHDs will also be able to embark, sustain and integrate the new SH-60R Seahawk sea control helicopters being procured for the RAN.

The LHDs have a vehicle deck or 'garage' underneath the hangar which is capable of accommodating 150 vehicles, including both main battle tanks and soft-skinned types together with containers and palletised stores. The dock aft is 227ft long by 52ft wide and accommodates either four landing craft Mark 8 or three landing craft and a single landing craft air cushion. Medical facilities include two operating theatres, an intensive care unit and a sick bay; they can be enhanced to give a significant humanitarian relief capability in addition to the ships' primary role of strategic power projection. The design features diesel-electric propulsion giving 35,000hp and a sea speed of a modest 19 knots; there are two podded propulsors giving greater man-oeuvrability than the shafts in the RN's new

Queen Elizabeth Class and greater survivability against underwater action damage. The ship's company is 245, about fifty fewer than the RN's *Ocean*, and it is difficult not to form the opinion that this is a better design than the UK's mediocre *Ocean* and the LPDs *Bulwark* and *Albion*, which have to operate together to provide a capability close to a single LHD.

India's was the last Commonwealth navy to adopt aircraft carriers, and its gradual rise in maritime power reflects its increasing wealth and influence as a nation over the past sixty years. A small shore-based Fleet Air Arm had been operated since independence, but in 1957 the Indian Government purchased the incomplete light fleet carrier *Hercules*. She had been built by Vickers-Armstrongs on the Tyne but laid up since 1946, and was towed to Harland & Wolff in Belfast for completion. The redesigned ship drew on the experience gained with *Bonaventure*, and she was completed as INS *Vikrant* in 1961 with a steam catapult, angled deck and mirror landing aid; the last of the 1942 light fleet carriers to enter service. Her initial air group comprised Sea Hawk FGA.6 fighters and French Alizé antisubmarine aircraft; they were later joined by Sea King helicopters. The IN had hoped to buy French Etendard fighters at first, but accepted Sea Hawks when they were offered at a bargain price as they were being withdrawn from front-line service in the RN. A subsequent batch of surplus Sea Hawks was bought from the Federal German Navy.

Unlike Canada and Australia, India moved away from British technical management to provide its own more nationally-centred support infrastructure, with which it obtained remarkable value for money from its Sea Hawks, which were not finally withdrawn from service until the 1980s. Indian naval air squadrons were never numbered in the RN sequence, and were given numbers in the 300 sequence. In the 1980s, however, India became the only export customer for the Sea Harrier, which replaced the Sea Hawk at a relatively modest cost. They were able to operate from *Vikrant*, which was fitted with a 12-degree 'ski-jump', and subsequently from *Hermes*, renamed *Viraat*, which was purchased from the UK for a bargain price in 1986. Australia had considered buying *Hermes* in the late 1960s and in the early 1980s, but had always rejected the idea because she was relatively old, expensive to operate and needed a large ship's company. That said, she is still in service with the IN in 2013, fifty-four years after her original completion, and must represent an excellent return on the Indian investment in purchasing her. She still operates an air group of Sea Harriers and Sea King helicopters, although they have been joined by Russian-built Kamov Ka-31 airborne surveillance and control helicopters.

The Russian influence has gradually grown, and in 1994 the Russian Navy offered one of its modified *Kiev* Class aircraft carriers for sale. The offer was not immediately taken up, but in 1999 the Russians offered the former *Admiral Gorshkov*, which had originally been completed in 1987, free of charge provided the Indian Government paid for her to be modernised and refitted in Russia. This proved a more attractive idea, and an agreement was signed in 2004 for the ship to undergo a five-year refit, during which missile systems in the area forward of the island would be removed and replaced by a 'ski-jump' and Fly 1 extension of the flight deck for parking. The original cost of the work was estimated at $US 625 million, but unforeseen problems were encountered which delayed the work and increased the cost to over $US 2 billion. In late 2012 the ship, by then renamed *Vikramaditya*, underwent sea trials that exposed a number of machinery problems which will need to be resolved before she enters service in 2013. Like similar ships in the Russian and Chinese navies, *Vikramaditya* is designed to operate aircraft using the short take-off but arrested recovery system (Stobar). This uses a 'ski-jump' to launch fighters off a short deck run, but arrester wires to recover tailhook fitted fighters in the conventional way. A conventional projector landing aid like that used by the USN is used to guide pilots, and Indian Navy pilots have undergone deck-landing training with the USN during 2012. She will operate a mixed air group of Mikoyan and Gurevich MiG-29K fighters and Kamov antisubmarine and ASaC helicopters. There can be no doubt that *Vikramaditya* will be a powerful addition to the Indian fleet, but the cost will have been high and she will be twenty-six years old when she

becomes operational, about the same age as *Viraat* when she was purchased.

Indian expansion plans include an indigenous carrier to be named *Vikrant* II. Laid down in 2009, this 37,500-ton ship has been designed with the help of Fincantieri in Italy and is to use the same two-shaft gas turbine propulsion system as the Italian *Cavour*. In 2013 the ship is afloat but work to fit her out is proceeding slowly, with completion tentatively scheduled for 2016. She is to be capable of operating the MiG-29K and the indigenous Indian naval variant of the indigenous Hindoustan Aeronautics Limited Tejas light strike fighter as well as helicopters.

Despite the large numbers of New Zealanders who flew with the FAA during the Second World War, the RNZN was never large enough to operate an aircraft carrier or form its own Fleet Air Arm, and a number of New Zealand citizens have served in the postwar RN and RAN as pilots and observers. Ships of the RNZN have operated helicopters since 1966, when the first *Leander* Class frigate entered service. At first Westland Wasps were procured and operated by RNZN pilots trained in the UK, with RNZAF maintenance technicians. With the introduction of the ANZAC Class from 1997, Wasps were replaced by the Kaman SH-2G Seasprite. These are flown by RNZN pilots and observers trained in new Zealand and supported by RNZAF technicians for embarked operations.

The early Canadian and Australian aircraft carriers are covered in the appropriate chapters with their RN sister ships because they were built in the UK and operated in close harmony with the RN. The twenty-first-century RAN LHDs, together with the latest IN carriers, are described briefly in this chapter for comparison. It is to be hoped that they, too, will have the chance to work closely with the RN.

INS *Viraat*, formerly *Hermes*, continues to serve with the Indian Navy in 2013, and is seen here with Sea Harriers and Sea Kings on deck. (USN)

Canberra Class LHD technical details

Displacement:	25,790 tons deep load
Dimensions:	length 752ft 3in
	beam 105ft
	draught 19ft 7in (lower when
	docked down)
Machinery:	2 podded propulsors
	Diesel-electric; 4V diesel driven
	alternators
	35,000hp delivering 19 knots
Armament:	4 x 25mm Typhoon
Protection:	none
Fuel:	diesel
Endurance:	9,000 miles at 15 knots
Complement:	243 plus up to 1,000 squadrons
	and embarked force

Aircraft operating data

Flight deck:	660ft x 105ft
Hangar:	10,000ft2
Lifts:	2 centreline each capable of
	lifting 29.7 tons
Aircraft:	Up to 30 depending on size; a
	typical assault air group could
	include 18 MRH-90 and 8
	Chinooks
Aircraft fuel:	jet aviation fuel
Air weapons:	7.62mm and 0.5in machine-
	gun ammunition, flares and
	pyrotechnics for helicopters.
	Substantial quantities of
	ammunition for the embarked
	forces

The refurbished Indian carrier *Vikramadtya* on trials in June 2012. (SEVMASH)

Vikramadtya technical details

Displacement:	45,500 tons
Dimensions:	length 928ft 6in
	beam 167ft 4in
	draught 32ft 8in
Machinery:	4 shaft GTZA 674 turbines
	8 KWG4 boilers
	200,000shp delivering 30 knots
Armament:	SAM and close-range guns, not yet finalised
Protection:	not announced
Fuel:	not announced
Endurance:	18,000 miles at 18 knots
Complement:	2,500

Aircraft operating data

Flight deck:	928ft x 160ft maximum with 14-degree 'ski-jump' forward; Stobar
Hangar:	600ft x 96ft x 24ft
Arrester wires:	3 x 48,000lb at 140 knots
Lifts:	alongside island 63ft long x 34ft wide; 60,000lb aft of island 60ft long x 15ft wide; 40,000lb
Aircraft:	20 in initial air group comprising 12 MiG-29K and helicopters
Aircraft fuel:	jet aviation fuel, amount not announced
Air weapons:	AAM; ASM; conventional bombs and rocket projectiles; 30mm cannon ammunition; flares and pyrotechnics

Vikrant II: Indigenous Indian aircraft carrier technical details

Displacement:	37,500 tons
Dimensions:	length 853ft
	beam 196ft 8in
	draught 27ft 6in
Machinery:	2 shaft General Electric LM 2500 gas turbines
	120,000shp delivering 28 knots
Armament:	SAM and close-range guns not yet announced
Protection:	not announced
Fuel:	not announced
Endurance:	7,500 miles at 18 knots

Aircraft operating data

Flight deck:	850ft x 180ft maximum; 14-degree 'ski-jump' forward; Stobar
Hangar:	dimensions not yet announced
Arrester wires:	3 x 48,000lb at 140 knots
Lifts:	2 side-lifts, one forward one aft of the island both approximately 50ft x 50ft; 60,000lb
Aircraft:	20 MiG-29K, Tejas and helicopters
Aircraft fuel:	jet aviation fuel, amount not announced
Air weapons:	as in *Vikramaditya*

Note: These three ships were not complete at the time this book was written, and the figures above were taken from advance information. On completion, therefore, there may be some differences in detail.

Chapter 37

BRITISH CARRIER CONCEPTS AND FOREIGN AIRCRAFT CARRIERS COMPARED

In the decade after 2003 that followed the beginning of extensive Allied land operations in Iraq and Afghanistan, most Western governments have come to regard the 'maritime contribution to joint operations' as the transport and supply of large military forces across a 'benign' maritime environment to protracted operations ashore. As these draw to a close in 2013 it is becoming evident that, in the future, the open sea is likely to be an element that is far from benign. As arguments about the possession of islands and their surrounding economic zones in the Far East, Indian Ocean and South Atlantic make the headlines, the recent dominance of the USN and its carrier strike groups is being balanced by the emergence, or re-emergence, of powerful regional navies, among which those of China, India and Russia now operate aircraft carriers and plan to build more. France, Spain, Italy, Brazil and Thailand also operate ships capable of operating fixed-wing fighters to a greater or lesser extent. It is likely that the ocean 'commons' will become far less 'conveniently benign' in the years ahead.

In 2013 the RN has no aircraft carriers in commission as such, although *Illustrious* is operating as an LPH until relieved by *Ocean* in 2014. *Queen Elizabeth* is unlikely to have a viable operational capability until 2020. Her role has changed since the original concept in 1998, and

the balance of capabilities has shifted towards power projection in all its forms, including helicopter-borne amphibious assault rather than operation primarily as a strike platform, like earlier British and contemporary USN strike carriers. She is likely to operate a much smaller number of F-35B Lightning II strike fighters than originally intended, perhaps only as few as twelve or less regularly, but despite that she will be of critical importance when confrontation and combat take place at sea, when British forces will have to fight for access to an area of sea or its adjacent land, either alone or as part of a coalition of allied nations. Whatever *Queen Elizabeth*'s designers expected her to do and whatever naval experts believe she should have been able to do, the ship that emerges in 2020 will have as its primary purpose the requirement to create the conditions under which other major components such as amphibious, antisubmarine and logistic support forces can operate. In conjunction with *Daring* Class destroyers she must achieve battle-space dominance, and no other British asset can do that. She may operate alone or as part of a coalition force, and this chapter compares other contemporary carriers with the British ships that are under construction.

Britain's two closest allies are the USA and France, both of which operate strike carriers. In

addition to the existing carrier navies, a number of other countries either have, or are building, big-deck helicopter carriers which have the latent 'cross-over' capability to operate Stovl fighters such as the AV-8B and the much larger and heavier F-35B. The following ships are included for comparison with *Queen Elizabeth*.

France

Charles de Gaulle

The only nuclear-powered aircraft carrier to be built outside the USA, *Charles de Gaulle* was ordered in 1986 as the first of two ships, but the second was cancelled as an economy measure. She was floated out of dry dock in 1994 and first commissioned in 2001. Her two K15 PWR nuclear reactors are the same as those fitted in *Le Triomphant* Class submarines and are capable of

The French nuclear aircraft carrier *Charles de Gaulle* with the British frigate *Montrose* in company. The aircraft on deck are Rafales and Super Etendards, and her island is noticeably further forward than in USN carriers. (Crown Copyright/MoD 2012)

The USS *George H W Bush*, CVN-77, last unit of the *Nimitz* Class, turning at speed. (USN

steaming the ship at 25 knots for seven years continuously before they need refuelling. Early teething troubles included the loss of a large section of the port propeller while steaming at high speed in 2001, but she has subsequently proved to be a very successful ship, taking part in strike operations in Afghanistan and Libya alongside USN and allied aircraft. French naval aircrew are trained by the USN, and her air group works closely with US carriers, cross-decking frequently during exercises. Much smaller and lighter than *Queen Elizabeth*, she is capable of embarking a flexible air group of about thirty-six aircraft including Rafale omni-role fighters; Super Etendard strike aircraft until the last examples are replaced by Rafales; E-2C Hawkeye ASaC aircraft and four helicopters, of which two usually come from a joint combat SAR force and two act as the ship's 'planeguard'.

Charles de Gaulle technical details

Displacement:	42,500 tons deep load
Dimensions:	length 857ft 6in
	beam 211ft 4in
	draught 30ft 10in
Machinery:	2 shaft K15 PWR nuclear
	driving GEC/Alsthorn turbines
	300 MW delivering 27 knots
Armament:	vertical launch SAM; PDMS; 4
	Giat 20mm guns
Protection:	not specified
Endurance:	7 years at 25 knots
Complement:	1,260 (plus 800 marines in
	temporary accommodation of
	necessary)

Aircraft operating data

Flight deck:	857ft 6in x 211ft at widest
	point
Hangar:	454ft x 96ft 6in by 20ft
Catapults:	2 C-13 steam each capable of
	launching 78,000lb at 150
	knots end speed
Arrester wires:	4 Mark 7 arrester wires, each
	50,000lb at 130 knots entry
	speed
Lifts:	2 side-lifts aft of the island on
	the starboard side both 62ft 4in
	long x 41ft wide, both
	72,000lb
Aircraft:	Up to 40 depending on air
	group composition

Aircraft fuel:	990,000gal avcat
Air weapons:	Magic and Mica AAM; SCALP-
	EG ASM; Sagem ASM; Exocet
	ASM; ASMP-A nuclear strike
	missiles; AS-30L laser-guided
	missiles; Paveway 2 PGM;
	conventional bombs; 30mm
	cannon ammunition; flares and
	pyrotechnics

PA-02

In 2003 the French Navy obtained approval to include a second aircraft carrier in the Defence Programming Law, but financial restrictions prevented it being laid down. An agreement was signed with the British Government in 2006 to build the ship at Chantiers de l'Atlantique to a design based on the *Queen Elizabeth* Class but modified to suit French requirements. The main difference is that she will be built with catapults and arrester wires from the outset and will have two C-13 steam catapults and a four-wire USN Mark 7 arrester wire system. She will also have French command, control and communications systems and the ability to stow French nuclear weapons. Interestingly, the French shipyard has quoted a lower price for the whole construction of this ship than the UK Aircraft Carrier Alliance quoted for modifying *Queen Elizabeth* to take EMALS and AAG. A cost for fitting C-13 catapults and Mark 7 arrester gear was never released by the British Government. As yet unnamed, PA-02 is designed to operate a flexible air group of about forty Rafales, E-2Cs and helicopters. If proceeded with, she might be laid down in mid-decade.

United States of America

Nimitz Class

In 2013 the USN operates ten *Nimitz* Class nuclear aircraft carriers, and each of them is capable of operating as many aircraft as a small national air force. Nuclear-powered, they can steam for one million miles before they need refuelling; and they need only one refuelling in the entire fifty-year projected life of each ship. The enormous hull has the aviation fuel stowage capacity to operate for sixteen days continuously without replenishment at sea, and magazine capacity to match. They are all configured to conduct both strike and antisubmarine operations for protracted periods, and a typical air group comprises up to forty-eight F/A-18A/C Hornet and F/A-18E/F Super Hornet strike fighters, four Boeing EA-18G Growler electronic warfare aircraft or, in the short term, the EA-6B Prowlers they replace, four E-2C Hawkeye ASaC and sixteen MH-60R/S Seahawk helicopters.

The first ship, *Nimitz*, was completed in 1975 and the last, *George H W Bush*, in 2009. The origins of the hull design go back to the aborted carrier *United States* in 1949, and many of their systems are manpower intensive. One of the drivers for changing production to the new CVN-21 *Gerald R Ford* Class was to produce redesigned systems within the same outer hull shape that require considerably less manpower. Ships like these would be beyond the capacity of any other navy except, perhaps, that of China to build, man and maintain.

An artist's impression of the USS *Gerald Ford*, CVN-78, showing the smaller island sited further aft than in the previous *Nimitz* Class.

Nimitz Class technical details

Displacement:	102,000 tons deep load
Dimensions:	length 1,092ft
	beam 252ft
	draught 37ft
Machinery:	4 shaft turbines
	2 Westinghouse/GE PWR
	A4W/A1G nuclear reactors
	280,000shp delivering over 30
	knots
Armament:	GMLS SAM; Sea Sparrow SAM;
	20mm Vulcan phalanx CIWS
Protection:	anti-torpedo 'sandwich'
	protection along hull sides;
	2.5in Kevlar armour on parts of
	ship's side and on 'box'
	protection over magazines and
	machinery spaces
Fuel:	some diesel carried for
	emergency generators.
Endurance:	1 million miles at high speed
	before nuclear refuelling is
	required
Complement:	5,750

Aircraft operating data

Flight deck:	1,090ft x 250ft maximum; 8-degree angled deck
Hangar:	684ft x 108ft x 25ft
Catapults:	4 C-13 steam catapults, each 310ft long capable of launching 78,000lb at 150 knots end speed
Arrester wires:	4 (later ships 3) Mark 7; each capable of arresting 50,000lb at 130 knots entry speed
Lifts:	4 side-lifts each 85ft long x 52ft wide; 200,000lb
Aircraft:	Up to 80, typical air group 70
Aircraft fuel:	Sufficient for 16 days continuous flying without replenishment
Air weapons:	Weapons are stowed in huge quantities; they include tactical nuclear weapons; Harpoon ASM; SLAM-ER ASM; Maverick ASM; HARM anti-radiation missiles; laser-guided bombs; JSOW; JDAM GPS-guided bombs; AIM-120 AAM; AIM-9 AAM; Mark 54 homing torpedoes; Hellfire ASM; depth charges; 20mm gun ammunition; 0.5in machine-gun ammunition; 7.62mm machine-gun ammunition; flares and pyrotechnics.

USS *Enterprise* during her final deployment in 2012, with the British destroyer *Diamond* in company. (Crown Copyright/MoD 2012)

Gerald R Ford

Known during the design phase as the CVN-21 Class, these ships are of the same hull dimensions and tonnage as the previous *Nimitz* Class, but the flight deck and interior layout have been redesigned to increase sortie generation rates and to be operable with considerably less manpower. A new operations room is designed to act as the nodal point of a flexible networked system sustaining multiple, simultaneous missions including integrated strike planning, joint/coalition missions and special warfare missions. Like their predecessors they are to have a hull life of fifty years.

The air group is expected to include about seventy-five aircraft, made up in the next decade of twenty-four F-35C Lightning and twenty-four F/A-18E/F Super Hornet strike fighters; six unmanned carrierborne combat air surveillance and strike system aircraft; four EA-18G Growler electronic warfare aircraft; four E-2D Hawkeye ASaC and sixteen MH-60R/S Seahawk helicopters. Compared with the *Nimitz* Class the island is moved further aft, there is one less lift and the four C-13 steam catapults are replaced by four EMALS. The Mark 7 arrester gear is replaced by AAG; CVN-21 was designed to take these systems from the outset and they will not be a retrofit as they would have been in *Queen Elizabeth*. The first ship is due to be launched in 2013, completed in 2015 and available for operational deployment from 2017 after trials. Two further units are planned, with the first expected to be laid down in 2014.

Gerald R Ford technical details

Displacement:	100,000 tons deep load
Dimensions	length 1,092ft
	beam 256ft
	draught 40ft 9in
Machinery:	4 shaft turbine
	nuclear powered, details as
	Nimitz
Armament:	as *Nimitz*
Protection:	as *Nimitz*
Fuel:	as *Nimitz*
Endurance:	as *Nimitz*
Complement:	4,660

Aircraft operating data

Flight deck:	1,090ft x 256ft maximum
Hangar:	as *Nimitz*
Catapults:	4 EMALS, each capable of
	launching 100,000lb at 130
	knots end speed
Arrester wires:	3 advanced arrester gear, each
	60,000lb at 130 knots entry
	speed
Lifts:	3, similar details to *Nimitz*
Aircraft:	up to 90
Aircraft fuel:	In excess of 16 days' supply for
	continuous operation
Air weapons:	as *Nimitz* but with revised
	bomb lifts and weapon
	handling arrangements.

An artist's impression of the USS *America*, LHA-6, showing just how thin the dividing line between an LHA with enhanced air facilities and an aircraft carrier with amphibious capability has become.

One other USN carrier worthy of mention, since it shows what a carrier can achieve, is *Enterprise*, which was deactivated in 2012 after a service life of fifty-one years. The largest mobile object ever built by man when she was completed in 1961, she was the first nuclear-powered aircraft carrier; longer but with a slightly smaller deep load displacement than *Nimitz*. She carried out twenty-five major deployments to the Mediterranean, Pacific and Middle East and served in nearly every major conflict that happened during her lifetime, starting with the Cuban Missile Crisis in 1962, followed by six deployments to the Vietnam conflict, through the Cold War to the Gulf wars. She launched the first American attacks in direct support of Operation *Enduring Freedom* in Afghanistan. Her long and illustrious career shows that the investment in a big deck carrier can be amply repaid by service in the national interest, and that a well-designed ship really can remain in service for a long time. Her life span makes an interesting contrast with the short average lives of British aircraft carriers. By the same standard set by the USN, *Queen Elizabeth* ought to remain in service until 2070.

The new *America* Class LHA also make an interesting comparison with *Queen Elizabeth* and illustrate the growing 'cross-over' capabilities shared by aircraft carriers and big-deck amphibious ships made possible by their embarkation of 'modular' air groups. They follow on from the *Wasp* Class with a hull of similar dimensions but with the dock aft omitted and replaced by an enhanced capability to operate Stovl fighters and storage space for military equipment and light vehicles. A second ship is expected to be completed to this design but, after her, later ships may be modified to incorporate a dock but with other compromises introduced. Due to be completed in 2014, *America* is designed primarily to operate an assault air group of ten F-35B Stovl fighters, twelve MV-22 Ospreys, eight Bell AH-1Z Viper attack helicopters, four CH-53E Sea Stallion heavy-lift helicopters and four MH-60S Blackhawk combat SAR helicopters. The ship, aircraft and embarked marine force are designed to attack targets from much further out at sea than more conventional amphibious ships, and bring a new dimension to amphibious assault. This longer range was part of the rationale for omitting the dock and its landing craft, since they could not function at the sort of ranges envisaged. Alternatively, she can operate as a sea-control carrier with up to twenty-two F-35B Lightning Stovl fighters and six MH-60R helicopters embarked. This multifunctional capability is further enhanced by a command system which is designed to be reconfigured between roles easily to help achieve this aim. The USN also states that she will also be capable of operating unmanned combat air vehicles of an unspecified type in due course. She will be powered by two LM2500 gas turbines developing 70,000shp and two electrical auxiliary propulsion motors each developing 10,000shp, which can be combined to give a top speed of 22 knots or operate independently to give a low-speed loiter. Endurance is 9,000 miles at 12 knots. The self-defence outfit of missiles and CIWS guns will be similar to the outfit in the *Nimitz* Class. There are two side-lifts, one on the port side amidships and one on the starboard side right aft. Planned complement is 1,059, with the capacity to embark 1,687 marines. She will, thus, have a flexible mix of capabilities and will be used in a variety of roles. Inevitably she will be compared with *Queen Elizabeth*, since *America* was designed from the outset as an LPH with potential strike capability and *Queen Elizabeth* was designed to be a strike carrier with the potential to deploy an amphibious capability. Adaptable carrier designs represent a modular approach, with embarked aircraft or marine forces offering capabilities across the spectrum of warfare and humanitarian relief from a common hull

with its small ship's company, automated storage facilities and medical facilities. They must represent the long-term future for every navy that aspires to be more than a coastal patrol force.

America technical details

Displacement:	44,850 tons deep load
Dimensions:	length 844ft
	beam 194ft across side-lifts;
	108ft waterline
	draught 28ft 6in
Machinery:	2 shafts; 2 GE LM2500 gas turbines delivering 70,000hp
	2 auxiliary propulsion motors delivering 10,000hp
	22 knots maximum speed
Armament:	2 Sea Sparrow SAM; 2 RAM SAM; 2 Vulcan Phalanx 20mm CIWS
Protection:	not specified
Fuel:	diesel
Endurance:	9,000 miles at 12 knots
Complement:	ship 1,059 plus 1,870 embarked military force

Aircraft operating data

Flight deck:	920ft x 118ft maximum
Hangar:	30,542ft2
Lifts:	2, one port amidships, one starboard side aft
	both open on three sides, 72,000lb
Aircraft:	typically 38 fighters and helicopters in the assault role

Aircraft fuel:	26 in the sea-control role
	1,300,000gal aviation turbine fuel
Air weapons:	large magazines capable of carrying Paveway LGM; JDAM; Maverick ASM; dual-mode bombs; conventional bombs; cluster bomb units; unguided rocket projectiles; AIM-120 AAM; AIM-9 AAM; 25mm gun ammunition; homing torpedoes; depth charges; 0.5in machine-gun ammunition; 7.62mm machine-gun ammunition; flares and pyrotechnics plus numerous other weapons as F-35B is introduced. Palletised military ammunition carried for disembarkation to operations ashore

Russian Federation

Admiral Kuznetsov

The only aircraft carrier serving with the Russian Navy at present, *Kuznetsov* was laid down in 1982 and completed in 1990. An incomplete sister ship, the *Varyag*, was sold to China and completed for the People's Liberation Army – Navy in 2012. Both use the Stobar launch and recovery system with a 14-degree 'ski-jump' forward, and an 8-degree angled deck with four arrester wires. Powerful steam machinery gives a top speed of over 30 knots, with a radius of action of 8,500 miles at

The Russian Navy's aircraft carrier *Admiral Kuznetsov* passes through the North Sea on her way to exercises in the Mediterranean, with the British destroyer *Liverpool* in the foreground. (CROWN COPYRIGHT/MOD 2012)

18 knots. For close defence she has four SA-N-9 'Gauntlet' SAM installations and eight Kashtan 30mm gun systems, each of the latter combined with SA-N-11 'Grisson' SAMs. Unusually for an aircraft carrier she has surface-to-surface missiles, the SS-N-19 'Shipwreck', which has a range of 280 miles and terminal radar guidance. The latter are mounted in twelve vertical launch tubes set into the flight deck aft of the 'ski-jump', which could not be used with aircraft parked in Fly 1. The SAMs are in vertical launch tubes in sponsons, port and starboard side forward and aft.

The normal air group comprises eighteen Sukhoi Su-33 'Flanker' strike fighters, four Sukhoi Su-25 'Frogfoot' ground-attack aircraft, fifteen Ka-27 'Helix' antisubmarine helicopters and two Kamov Ka-31 RLD airborne surveillance and control helicopters, although it is claimed that up to sixty aircraft can be operated. In 2008 the Russian Navy announced that it intends to build a new generation of aircraft carriers. It is believed that design work has started on the project, and construction of a new dry dock 1,350ft long has begun at the Severodvinsk shipyard where *Vikramaditya* was converted for the IN.

Admiral Kuznetsov technical details

Displacement:	58,500 tons deep load
Dimensions:	length 999ft
	beam 229ft 6in
	draught 34ft 3in
Machinery:	4 shaft geared turbines
	8 boilers
	200,000shp delivering 30 knots
Armament:	SS-N-19 'Shipwreck' SSM; SA-N-9 'Gauntlet' SAM;
	CADS-N-1
	30mm CIWS guns combined with SA-N-11 'Grissom' SAM
Protection:	not specified
Fuel:	diesel, amount not specified
Endurance:	8,500 miles at 18 knots

Aircraft operating data

Flight deck:	999ft x 220ft maximum
Hangar:	600ft x 96ft x 25ft
Catapult:	none but 14-degree 'ski-jump' at bow for Stobar launches
Arrester wires:	4 with similar capability to USN Mark 7

Lifts:	2 side lifts on starboard side, one forward and one aft of island, both 60ft x 60ft
Aircraft:	40 regularly embarked; up to 60 could be operated
Aircraft fuel:	not specified
Air weapons:	AAM; ASM; LGM; 30mm cannon ammunition; homing torpedoes; depth charges; unguided rockets; flares and pyrotechnics

Italy

Cavour

The Italian Government placed a contract with Fincantieri in 2007 for the construction of an aircraft carrier capable of operating Stovl fighters and, in addition, of acting as an amphibious assault ship and task force flagship. Less than half the tonnage of *Queen Elizabeth*, she can operate a flexible air group which typically comprises eight AV-8 Harriers and twelve Merlin or NH-90 helicopters configured in the antisubmarine and/or amphibious assault roles as well as for airborne surveillance and control. The design is said to take into account the eventual need to operate unmanned air vehicles, although no specific type has been named.

The two lifts are sited forward and aft of the island, the latter being a side-lift; both are clear of the fixed-wing runway and capable of lifting 60,000lb. The 12-degree 'ski-jump' is situated well forward to port, leaving a broad parking space in Fly 1 to starboard of it. The two-shaft gas turbine machinery produces 118,000shp, giving a maximum speed of 28 knots and an endurance of 7,000 miles at 16 knots. She has a defensive armament of Aster SAMs and OTO Melara 3in guns, and a command system based on that developed for the *Andrea Doria* (Horizon) Class destroyers.

The after part of the hangar is designed to be used as a vehicle 'garage' in amphibious operations, and is capable of carrying up to twenty-four main battle tanks and fifty amphibious assault vehicles. However, since she lacks a dock and landing craft (utility), she has to go alongside in harbour to land the heavy vehicles, rather than land them over a beach, but could use marine infantry in the assault

Admiral Kuznetsov with the British destroyer *York* in the background. This image shows the width of the flight deck across the angle and the prominent 'ski-jump' forward. (CROWN COPYRIGHT/MoD 2012)

The Italian *Cavour* with AV-8B Harriers and AW-101 helicopters on deck. (ITALIAN NAVY)

vehicles as part of an assault. Alternatively they could use the ro-ro ramps to transfer vehicles to lighters or LCUs from an LPD to take part in an assault. Access to it is gained through a ro-ro ramp aft, another one on the starboard side under the island, and the after lift. *Cavour*, the only ship in the class, was laid down in 2001, launched in 2004 and completed in 2006 for sea trials. The basic ship's company is 528, but there is accommodation for up to 1,205 to include embarked squadrons, battle-management staff and an embarked marine force. Overall, this is a well-thought-out and effective design which has shown itself to be capable of operations ranging from conflict to humanitarian relief. For different operations she can operate a larger number of AV-8s or helicopters. As in the US and Spanish navies, the ability to use embarked fighters to support helicopter-borne amphibious assaults from the same deck is a big advantage.

Cavour technical details

Displacement:	27,100 tons deep load
Dimensions:	length 772ft 10in
	beam 128ft
	draught 24ft 8in
Machinery:	2 shafts driven by 4 GE/Fiat
	LM2500 gas turbines
	118,000shp delivering 28 knots
	bow and stern thrusters
Armament:	Aster 15 SAM; 2 x OTO Malara
	3in guns
Protection:	none specified
Fuel:	diesel
Endurance:	7,000 miles at 16 knots
Complement:	528 ship's company; total 1,205
	including squadrons/military
	force

Aircraft operating data

Flight deck:	720ft x 110ft maximum
Hangar:	440ft x 69ft x 23ft 6in
Catapult:	none, but 12-degree 'ski-jump'
	forward for Stovl operations
Lifts:	fwd 70ft long x 46ft wide
	side-lift aft 49ft long x 46ft
	wide
Aircraft:	Up to 20 AV-8B Harrier (to be
	replaced by F-35B) fighters or a
	mix of
	Merlin/NH-90 helicopters and
	fighters
Aircraft fuel:	unspecified quantity of avcat
Air weapons:	Maverick ASM; AIM-120
	AAM; AIM-9 AAM; JDAM;
	LGM; 25mm cannon
	ammunition; homing
	torpedoes; depth charges; flares
	and pyrotechnics.

China

Liaoning

Originally laid down for the Soviet Navy in the Nikolayev shipyard, Ukraine, in 1985 as the second unit of the *Kuznetsov* Class, and to have been named *Varyag*, this ship was launched in 1988 but laid up incomplete after the break-up of the Soviet Union. In 1998 the Government of Ukraine sold her to China after an unsuccessful attempt by the Russian Navy to fund her completion. She subsequently entered the Dalian shipyard in China after being towed through the Bosporus in 2001. A massive programme of modernisation and upgrading followed, and was completed in 2012, when the ship carried out her first flying trials with arrested recoveries demonstrated by Shenyang J-15 fighters, a design based on the Russian Su-33 fighters embarked in *Kuznetsov*. She uses the same Stobar launch and recovery system as the Russian *Kuznetsov* and the slightly smaller Indian *Vikramaditya*.

During her long rebuild her main propulsion systems, shafting, propellers and rudders were replaced and she was fitted with new auxiliary systems. New radars, including the 'Dragon Eye' 3D phased-array system and electronic warfare systems, were fitted together with aircraft control and carrier-controlled approach radars. She has also been fitted with the FL-3000N short-range air defence system and Type 1030 30mm CIWS. After her long modernisation she was allocated the pennant number 16 and commissioned into the People's Liberation Army – Navy as *Liaoning*. It is believed that one reason for the prolonged period in shipyard hands was that Chinese engineers methodically 'reverse-engineered' the ship and its systems to facilitate the construction of a number of aircraft carriers in China. The ship and her potential air group give China a powerful new 'blue water' naval capability, and her development to full operational capability will be interesting to watch. *Liaoning*'s technical details and aircraft operating data are similar to those given above for *Kuznetsov*.

CHAPTER 38

CARRIERBORNE AIRCRAFT IN THE TWENTY-FIRST CENTURY

In 2013 only the USA, France, Russia and China are manufacturing the carrierborne strike fighters that have the potential to dominate conflict at sea and in littoral areas. The type which gains most of the headlines for both good and bad reasons is the US Lockheed Martin F-35 Lightning II, originally known as the Joint Strike Fighter (JSF). It evolved from the amalgamation of a number of earlier projects into a single-seat, single-engine strike aircraft with advanced sensors and reconnaissance systems, and is being produced in three distinct variants with as much commonality as possible. The UK has been involved with the F-35B Stovl variant since it subsumed the RN/USMC Sea Harrier/AV-8 replacement project in the late 1980s, and although other nations have joined the programme as more modest partners, the UK remains the only Level 1 partner with staff imbedded in the Integrated Project Team and a major contribution to development funding.

The F-35 has proved far more difficult to design and bring into service than was originally planned, however, and full operational capability from a British aircraft carrier will be nearly a decade later than originally intended, when it was envisaged that *Queen Elizabeth* would be at sea with the first squadron in 2012. The most capable and successful carrier strike fighter in the first two decades of the twenty-first century is undoubtedly the USN F/A-18E/F Super Hornet, which is the result of an exemplary development project that has delivered hundreds of aircraft at the planned cost and, in most cases, earlier than contracted. Had the *Queen Elizabeth* project overcome the timid approach evident in its early conception and been designed from the outset with catapults and arrester wires, this would have been the ideal fighter of choice, giving the RN advanced capability at a known and affordable cost with low development risk. The 'E' is a single-seat variant;

the 'F' is a two-seater with a naval flight officer/observer (NFO) in the rear seat. Super Hornet development began as 'low-risk' insurance to cover the failure or cancellation of more advanced projects including the A-12 replacement strike aircraft, the USN advanced tactical fighter and A/F-X. When these expensive stealthy projects were cancelled in the 1990s as part of the 'peace dividend' after the end of the Cold War, the F/A-18 became central to the USN's future plans. Development was assisted by the experience gained during development and production of the earlier or 'legacy' Hornet in four versions.

The Super Hornet is made of strong but lightweight materials including carbon epoxy (19 per cent), titanium (21 per cent) and steel (15 per cent). The airframe is covered in a signature-reducing coating, but has a higher possibility of detection than an aircraft designed with stealth characteristics from the outset. The aircraft is powered by two General Electric F414-GE-400 engines, each developing 22,000lb of thrust in full reheat; they are modular and 2,000 flying hours are allowed between replacement of the hot section for maintenance, and 4,000 hours between maintenance for the cold section. Both have full-authority digital engine control (Fadec). The airframe shows no great advance over those of earlier generations of jet fighters. For instance, the top speed is significantly less than that of an F-4J Phantom, but avionics represent a huge advance. Block II Super Hornets were the first fighters in the world to deploy operationally with an airborne electronically-scanned array (AESA) in 2006. This solid-state AN/APG-79 radar has no moving aerial dish, and shapes radar beams electronically using a number of static transmitter/receiver units. By comparison with earlier airborne radar arrays it is virtually maintenance free and may not need to be removed through the life of its parent airframe. Sensor information is fused into head-down screens, a head-up display and helmet-mounted cuing systems for both pilot and NFO. In the strike role an electro-optical targeting pod known as the shared reconnaissance pod (Sharp) can be mounted externally, as can an advanced tactical

An F-35C Lightning II joint strike fighter in flight, showing its two weapons bays open. (USN)

forward-looking infrared system (Atflir). An integrated defensive electronic countermeasures system includes an ALR-67(V)3 radar warning receiver, an ALQ-214 jammer, an ALE-47 countermeasures dispenser and an ALE-50 towed decoy. Communications systems include a secure V/UHF radio and the Link 16 joint tactical information distribution system (Jtids). The open-architecture computer system that forms the core of the avionics is designed to allow the straightforward installation of new lines of code for the incorporation of upgrades and new weapons.

Both the 'E' and 'F' versions are capable of operating in the fighter, strike and reconnaissance roles in a single sortie, although the single-seat 'E' tends to specialise in strike and the two-seater 'F' in fighter operations. The 'F' has the same capabilities as the 'E' but 942lb less fuel, to allow for the second cockpit. The NFO allows better use to be made of the information generated by the aircraft's systems and from off-board sensors through Link 16. From Block II aircraft in 2006, sensor information can be 'decoupled' to allow the two aircrew to fight different engagements. For instance, the pilot could use the radar and Atflir to engage a small 'pop-up' moving target on land, while the NFO uses off-board sensor information from another platform, such as a warship or E-2C Hawkeye control aircraft, to engage an airborne target. Both have helmet-mounted cuing systems that allow them to aim weapons off the aircraft's centreline without have to point it at a particular target. The F/A-18E/F has eleven external weapons

stations, which increase the aircraft's radar cross-section when in use. Weapons that can be deployed include tactical nuclear bombs; JDAM; JSOW, Maverick ASM; Harpoon ASM; any laser-designated or conventional bomb in US service; HARM anti-radiation missiles; AIM-120 AAM and AIM-9 AAM. External fuel can be carried in up to five 480gal tanks, giving up to 30,000lb of fuel on start-up if required. External dimensions of the two versions are identical; both have folding wings and a maximum take-off weight of 66,000lb. Both versions can carry buddy refuelling pods and act as tankers to extend the radius of strike aircraft, as Buccaneers, Scimitars and Sea Vixens formerly did in the RN, and also to act as recovery tankers, orbiting the carrier when necessary to provide fuel for returning aircraft that are low on fuel in bad weather and at night. With four AIM-120s, two AIM-9 AAMs and a centreline fuel tank an F/A-18F can maintain CAP 200 miles from the carrier for two-and-a-half hours with fuel for three combats during the time on

task. With four JDAM or laser-guided munitions, two AIM-120s, two AIM-9 sand a centreline tank an F/A-18E can act as its own escort, striking at targets out to 400 miles from the carrier. With three tanks it could strike at targets 800 miles from the carrier, and this could be extended to over 1,000 miles with air-to-air refuelling from a 'buddy'. Super Hornets have flown a high percentage of US fighter/ground-attack missions over Afghanistan.

The EA-18G Growler uses the same airframe and AN/APG-79 radar as the Super Hornet but has avionics derived from the EA-6B Prowler to operate in the electronic attack role. The type is in production in 2013 and has replaced about half of the EA-6B fleet, with two new squadrons forming every year. Following its usual policy of low-risk,

An F-35B makes a gentle approach to land on the USS *Wasp*, visible in the middle distance. (USN)

incremental improvement, the USN is developing a new Block II electronic attack system that will be fitted to upgraded versions of the Growler in due course. The USN remains the only navy that operates dedicated electronic attack aircraft, but the RAAF has announced the Australian Government's approval of its intention to modify twelve of its F/A-18Fs to Growler standard for maritime operations.

France has developed a very capable aircraft it describes as an 'omni-role' fighter, known as the Rafale. This project was contemporary with the Eurofighter Typhoon, and the French were astute enough to develop the Rafale for both air force and naval use, with obvious advantages in terms of common training, logistic support and tactics. The British decision to limit the Typhoon to landlocked RAF use failed to address the nation's important need to operate fighters at sea and at great distance from the UK. The Rafale has a neat, well-designed airframe with advanced avionics which give it its 'omni-role' capability. At their core is the Thales RBE2 radar, which gives multi track-while-scan air-to-air, ship tracking, terrain-following and synthetic aperture navigation modes. From 2013 the present scanner array will be replaced in service by an AESA derivative, keeping the Rafale at the technological forefront of capability. The Spectra electronic countermeasures suite includes a radar warning receiver, an active jammer; infrared missile approach warning, laser detection and chaff/flare dispensers. Passive target detection and identification is provided by a front-sector optronics sensor in a ball-shaped housing on the nose which contains a high-magnification TV camera and an infrared search and track sensor. A Damocles target designation pod and an NG/Areos reconnaissance pod can be carried externally, and information from both can be data-linked via Link 16 to other platforms. The fused data from all

sensors can be seen by the pilot in head-down or head-up displays and in a helmet-mounted sight.

Like the Super Hornet, the Rafale carries all its weapons externally, with a consequent increase in radar cross-section. Its thirteen hardpoints can carry up to a combined maximum total of 20,000lb of stores. The centre five can each be fitted with 330gal fuel tanks and the centre three can be fitted with 539gal tanks. If the latter are carried, however, the aircraft is limited to subsonic speeds and the g limit is reduced until they are empty. Rafale can be used as a buddy tanker like the F/A-18, and its extensive array of weapons includes Mica and eventually Meteor AAMs, ASMP-A and SCALP-EH ASMs, Exocet anti-ship missiles, the French AASM precision bomb and a 30mm cannon. It is powered by two Snecma M88-2E4 engines, each delivering 17,000lb thrust in full reheat. Maximum launch weight is 54,000lb and it has an impressive turning performance; it is capable of Mach 2.0 at altitude, making it faster than the F/A-18. Like the American aircraft, Rafale would have been a good investment for the RN, but the lack of UK industrial input would have deterred the British Government from procuring it. In 2013 the Aeronavale retains one Flotille of Dassault Super Etendard strike fighters, but these are to be replaced by Rafales in the near future, giving the French Navy an impressive force of three Rafale Flotilles.

The fighter selected by the UK for operation from the new generation of aircraft carriers after the *Invincible* Class is the Stovl variant of the F-35 Lightning II Joint Strike Fighter. This has had a long and complicated evolution which began with discussions in the late 1980s between the UK and US Governments about a potential joint advanced Stovl or Jastovl fighter to replace both the RN Sea Harrier and USMC AV-8B Harrier. In the early 1990s a number of other strike fighter projects were in the early stages of development in the USA, including the USN/USAF joint advanced-

technology strike fighter (Jast); the common affordable lightweight fighter (Calf); and the joint stealth strike aircraft (JSSA). In 1994, after the end of the Cold War, the US Government ordered that Jastovl, Jast, JSSA and Calf be merged into a single project with, it was hoped, 80 per cent commonality between the three different variants. In 1995 the new title joint strike fighter (JSF) was applied to the development, continued British interest in the Stovl variant being reflected in Level 1 partnership which included UK funding and personnel in the Integrated Project Team. Three industrial groups were funded to carry out concept demonstrations from December 1995, after which (surprisingly in view of their recent collaborative Stovl experience), the McDonnell Douglas/BAE Systems/Northrop Grumman Team was eliminated first when the US Government deemed that their design was not sufficiently technologically advanced; a decision that many would consider questionable in the light of subsequent experience. Boeing and Lockheed Martin were each funded to produce two demonstration airframes, designated X-32 and X-35 respectively. Subsequently Boeing bought McDonnell Douglas, and BAE Systems and Northrop Grumman joined the Lockheed Martin team. The X-35, redesignated F-35, was selected as the winning design and a development and demonstration phase of development was ordered on 26 October 2002. The three variants to be developed concurrently were the F-35A, a land-based aircraft for the USAF; the F-35B, a Stovl variant for the USMC, RN and RAF as an AV-8B/Sea Harrier/Harrier replacement, and the F-35C, a carrierborne version for the USN. The selection of a single-seat, single-engine design and basic dimensions were driven by the Stovl variant's need to hover on engine thrust to carry out a vertical landing. Had the Stovl variant not been absorbed into the project, the aircraft designed to meet the USAF and USN requirements would have been very different and, arguably, the Stovl variant could have been less sophisticated and expensive, since it was intended, primarily, to be a close-air-support aircraft capable of flying in close co-operation with marines on the ground, rather than flying deep-penetration strike missions.

Despite the obvious advantages of the F-35C for carrier operation, the UK stayed with the Stovl variant because of its recent Sea Harrier/Harrier experience and the early assumption that the type would have to operate initially from the *Invincible* Class. By the time the 2010 SDSR changed the requirement to the carrier variant it was too late to modify the first ship in build with catapults and arrester wires. There are, inevitably, compromises to achieve the performance required by each variant,

An F-35B in the hover before landing the USS *Wasp*. Note the rotating jet nozzle aft and the various doors that have to be open for the horizontal lift fan inlet and exhaust, together with the puffer jets. The horizontal fan's exhaust can be seen aft of the nose oleo. (USN)

but all of them incorporate stealth technology and have a low probability of detection by a range of sensors when operating without external stores on pylons. All are powered by a single Pratt & Whitney F135 engine with 43,000lb of thrust in full reheat, but the 'B' version's engine is modified with a swivelling nozzle aft and a power drive, through a clutch, to a horizontal lift fan aft of the cockpit. It also has a three-stage rather than a two-stage compressor. Doors above and below the fuselage open to allow air through the fan when it is engaged, and piping from the engine runs to roll-control 'puffer jets' in the wings to control the aircraft when it is not in wing-borne flight. The 'B' version sacrifices internal fuel capacity for the lift fan, and its drive shaft and has only 14,000lb of internal fuel compared with the 'A's 18,000lb, giving a radius of action of about 400 miles. The 'B' also has smaller internal weapons bays because of the need to reduce weight. Each can carry a single 1,000lb-class strike weapon and an AIM-120 AAM. The 'A' and 'C' variants have larger internal weapons bays, each capable of carrying a single 2,000lb-class strike weapon and an AIM-120. The 'C' version has a larger wing and tailplane to give lower carrier-compatible landing speeds, and has the largest internal fuel capacity at 20,000gal, giving the greatest radius of action of over 600 miles on internal fuel.

The F-35's defining role is long-range strike, using stealth to penetrate sophisticated air defences in the opening stages of a conflict against a 'near-peer' opponent, prior to theatre-entry amphibious assault. It achieves this by operating clean, with only internal fuel and weapons to minimise its radar reflective area. The design is enhanced by a non-radar-reflective coating said to be superior to the fragile coating applied on earlier USAF types such as the Northrop B-2 bomber and F-22 fighter, which has had an adverse impact on aircraft availability. Once an enemy's air defences have been suppressed, all three variants can be fitted with external pylons giving a total of eleven weapons stations including the internal bays. The type's radius of action can be dramatically improved by the 426gal fuel tanks that can be fitted on the inner wing stations. However, once fitted with external stores the F-35 becomes an orthodox but very expensive strike fighter with no more stealthy characteristics than the F/A-18 or Rafale. Since the USN can use F/A-18s as buddy tankers and the USAF has a large number of large land-based tankers, the F-35 has not been developed to carry a buddy air-to-air refuelling system. This does not affect the USN, but will

limit the type's attractiveness to export customers such as the UK, since it will not be the 'complete package' like the Super Hornet or Rafale. Unmanned combat air systems are examined in the next chapter, but it is worth noting here that the Northrop Grumman X-47B demonstration prototype is already flying and due to carry out carrier compatibility trials in 2013. It and its successors will have ranges and loiter times considerably in excess of manned strike fighters and need less compromises to achieve stealth characteristics. The 'window of opportunity' in which the F-35 represents the optimum strike and reconnaissance package may be a short one.

From a British perspective the F-35 Lightning will have to work through a number of compromises before it will be effective. First will be the need for focus. Initial plans are that the type will be operated by a joint force, with both RN and RAF squadrons operating in a similar way to the Harrier force from 2000 to 2010. This may produce a clash of interests if the joint command seeks to operate the type mainly ashore with occasional 'deployments' to sea in a carrier. After a decade without fixed-wing aircraft at sea the RN will need to concentrate on operations at sea and focus on making them effective. The erroneous concept that the *Queen Elizabeth* Class are 'ferries' to carry assets to scenes of action must be resisted if they are to realise their potential. Other compromises are more technical and will need to be resolved before the type enters operational service. Strike operations in the past decade have seen precision-guided air weapons used sparingly against 'pinpoint' targets to avoid the risk of collateral damage and civilian casualties. In

consequence strike aircraft have often brought back expensive, unused weapons to their operating base, and while this is straightforward for aircraft that land conventionally ashore and afloat it can be a major problem for aircraft that rely on engine thrust to hover before landing, especially in hot conditions. Airframes always increase in weight during their time in service, and Stovl aircraft are no exception. Increasing engine thrust to maintain the ability to bring back unused weapons will be expensive through the life of the aircraft, and it was the alleged inability of the Sea Harrier to land at high weights in hot conditions that caused it to be withdrawn prematurely from service in 2006. There is no guarantee that the F-35B will not suffer the same problem in due course and, significantly, to maintain commonality all three versions had to be redesigned to reduce airframe weight when it was found that the first prototype was too heavy to allow a vertical landing with unused weapons under certain conditions. The UK has considered developing a 'rolling vertical' type of landing that would retain some wing lift and allow the 'B' to recover on to its parent carrier with a greater weight of unused weapons. In 2013 this has yet to be funded or developed.

The F-35 is an 'all-electric' aircraft with the most extensive use of electric systems ever incorporated in a fighter. It has literally tens of millions of lines of software code which the US Congress has refused to release outside the USA, making the UK reliant on US input for software upgrades and modifications, and there is therefore an issue over the full 'sovereignty' of the aircraft's deployment and operation. To save money, the British Government has not developed software

An F-35B touches down on the USS *Wasp*. (USN)

that would allow RN aircraft to use British weapons. Until such software is developed, installed and tested, UK F-35s will have to use US weapons. All F-35 maintenance, logistic support and flight planning is controlled by a computerised autonomous logistic support system without which the type cannot be operated. At some stage before 2020 the British Government will have to buy into the US system, raising further questions about the aircraft's 'sovereignty', or replicate it at considerable expense with a British equivalent. The former is the only realistic option.

Two other carrierborne fighters are in service in 2013. The first is the Russian Navy's Sukhoi Su-33 'Flanker D', which operates from the *Kuznetsov*. The type first entered service in 1998 and only twenty-four were delivered. It has a maximum launch weight almost identical to that of the F/A-18 at 66,010lb, and has two AL-31F turbofans, each capable of 28,214lb thrust in reheat and giving a top speed in excess of Mach 2 at altitude, making it faster than its contemporaries. It can carry up to 14,300lb of external stores on twelve external hardpoints, including eight R-27, R-77 or R-73 AAMs, precision-guided munitions and ECM pods. It also has an internal 30mm cannon. The Chinese Shenyang J-15 has obvious similarities but is powered by two Shenyang Liming WS-10 Taihang engines and has a powerful Chinese multimode radar. The type operates from the Chinese carrier *Liaoning* and completed sea trials in 2012.

The slightly smaller MiG-29K has been procured by India for operation from its new generation of aircraft carriers, and it has been reported that the Russian Navy is interested in procuring the type. It has a maximum launch weight of 54,000lb and is powered by two Klimov/Sarkisov RD-33MK engines, each delivering 20,000lb of thrust in full reheat. The MiG-29KUB has two seats and slightly less fuel; the second cockpit has both flying controls and operational equipment, allowing the variant to be used for conversion training or operational missions from a carrier deck. Like the Su-33 and J-15, the MiG-29K uses the Stobar operating technique and has a deck-landing hook aft. It is coated with a radar-absorbent material which the manufacturer claims will reduce its signature by a considerable margin compared with earlier versions of the type. Its sensors include an 'electronic intelligence system', ECM, infrared countermeasures, a sophisticated navigation system and a Phazotron Zhuk-ME radar which has a detection range of about 80 miles against a five-square-meter target and the ability to engage up to four targets simultaneously. The type has an

extremely good turning performance and can carry eight different types of AAM and even more ASMs on eight underwing hardpoints and another on the centreline. The two inboard pylons can be fitted with tandem weapon racks. Radius of action is 450 miles with internal fuel and 700 miles with external tanks.

Most significant navies operate airborne surveillance and control aircraft, although only the USN and France operate a fixed-wing type for the purpose. Both use the Northrop Grumman E-2C Hawkeye, although the USN is developing a more advanced 'D' version and the French aircraft will be rebuilt to this standard. The E-2D first flew in 2010 and initial operational capability is due in 2015. The core element of the new aircraft and its systems is the AN/APY-9 radar, which operates in C band (US L band) and combines a rotodome rotating mechanically once every ten seconds to give 360-degree coverage with electronic scanning with the rotodome stopped to investigate a particular target or sector. The 'D' will also incorporate improved ESM, ECM, defensive aids and countermeasures, and will be able to share information with other platforms using Links 4, 11, 16 and the USN co-operative engagement capability (CEC). Hawkeyes have a crew of two pilots and three naval flight officers/observers. The 'D' will have a 'glass cockpit' with multifunction displays allowing the non-flying pilot to display tactical information and act as a fourth flight officer when necessary. Unlike the 'C', the 'D' will have an in-flight refuelling capability that will allow it to remain airborne for over seven hours when required, and the system will be retrofitted to 'legacy' 'C's until the planned fleet of seventy-five 'D's is fully in service. An initial clearance to use naval F/A-18 and C-130 tankers is to be followed by a clearance to use all allied tanker aircraft. The E-2D has a maximum launch weight of 56,500lb and the conventional airframe is

powered by two Rolls-Royce T56-A-427A turboprops, each driving an eight-bladed NP-2000 propeller and developing 5,100shp. The engines have full-authority digital engine control (Fadec) and a propulsion control monitoring unit which reduces vibration considerably below the levels found in earlier models. The basic airframe first flew in 1960 and is another good example of the USN flair for minimising cost by using incrementally advanced, open-architecture avionics in a well-proven but effective airframe.

Other navies, including those of the UK, Spain, Italy, India and Russia, use helicopters to provide an ASaC capability, and the Sea King ASaC.7 in service with the RN is typical. A number of Sea King airframes were converted from their former antisubmarine role in the mid-1980s because no other aircraft capable of carrying a suitable radar could operate from the small flight decks of *Invincible* Class carriers. The original AEW.2 variant was upgraded to ASaC.7 standard with the installation of the Cerberus mission system centred on the Thales Searchwater radar. This gives 360-degree coverage from an aerial which rotates inside an inflatable radome on the starboard side of the fuselage that is lowered after take-off; control is exercised through the Cerberus system using touch-screen displays with which the two observers can control the radar beam and call up any display they want with a maximum of three key presses. Unusually, Searchwater operates in I-band (US X-band), which gives a lower maximum range but a very narrow, precise beam which enables extremely accurate target identification. It is frequency-agile and has both pulse and pulse-doppler modes, the latter displaying small objects that have motion with no 'clutter' or 'sea return' obscuring the picture. The sweep speed and antenna angle can be adjusted to optimise the radar for the search in progress, and each observer can make changes but these will affect the picture both see. Without a

A night deck landing on the USS *Wasp* by an F-35B. The reheated jet efflux from the rotated nozzle aft is striking. The illuminated strips on the fuselage are formation lights to assist pilots in keeping station on other aircraft at night or in cloud. (USNM)

strike carrier in RN service after 2010, RN Sea King ASaC.7s have operated from the operational LPH, from *Daring* Class destroyers and ashore in Afghanistan in support of NATO forces. The radar is as effective over land as over the sea, and can even detect moving people and animals. Operational ASaC.7s have a maximum launch weight of 21,500lb and are powered by two Rolls-Royce Gnome 1400-1T engines. They have AN/AAR-57 missile warning systems, an ALQ-157 infrared jammer and M-147 chaff and flare dispensers. The British Government has studied replacement options since 1996 under the titles of the maritime airborne surveillance and control (MASC) project and project 'Crows' Nest', but in 2013 no decision has been taken other than to announce that the ASaC.7 is to be withdrawn from service in 2016. It therefore seems likely that this vital capability, and with it the skill level of its operators, will at best be 'gapped' when *Queen Elizabeth* comes into service. The Spanish Navy uses Sea Kings in this role; the Italian Navy a modified version of the Merlin, and both the Russian and Indian Navies have a version of the Kamov Ka-31 helicopter.

In the twenty-first century antisubmarine types have evolved into what are now known as sea control helicopters, with considerably wider mission capabilities, and a number of types are used by the majority of the world's navies. In the RN virtually every warship and auxiliary is capable of embarking a helicopter. Unlike most navies, however, the RN uses two different sea control helicopters, the large Merlin in big-deck ships and some frigates, and the smaller Lynx, to be replaced by the Wildcat, in others. With the introduction into service of the Wildcat from 2015 this split is expensive in terms of manpower training and logistic support but seems set to continue. In comparison, the much larger and better-funded USN uses the MH-60R/S duo for both tasks. The AgustaWestland Merlin HM.2 is bigger than other sea control helicopters such as the MH-60R Seahawk and NH-90, and has a maximum launch weight of 32,000lb. Much of the airframe is made of corrosion-resistant carbonfibre, and it is powered by three Rolls-Royce/Turbomeca RTM-322 engines, each delivering over 2,000shp; the other types mentioned have only two. The Merlin is fitted with the same folding light antisubmarine helicopter (Flash) sonar as the other two types, designated Type 2089 in RN service. This is claimed to be able to detect submarines down to their maximum diving depth and has range-scales from 1 to 26 miles; it uses high-resolution doppler processing techniques and shaped pulses to detect

targets moving as slowly as 1 knot. Extended duration frequency-modulated (FM) pulses are used to detect near-zero doppler targets. Other operational modes include active continuous-wave (CW) in pulses of up to 10sec, FM in pulses of up to 5sec, and passive listening and an underwater telephone capability for communicating with 'friendly' submarines. Like other sea-control helicopters, the Merlin uses active and passive sonobuoys and has a AQS-903A acoustic processor to analyse their input. Blue Kestrel radar gives 360-degree coverage and its software includes the ability to read the automatic identification system carried by the majority of the world's shipping. In the HM.2 variant it is modified to give synthetic-aperture and inverse synthetic-aperture images to improve surface-search capability, and a Wescam MX-15 electro-optical camera system. Sensors will be controlled by a new open-architecture computer system which will be easier to upgrade and adapt than earlier equipments. The aircraft has defensive aids plus chaff and flare dispensers. In the earlier version armament was limited to Stingray homing torpedoes, depth charges and a door-mounted 0.5in machine-gun, with the result that, although Merlins could detect a surface target, they had to call up a 'shooter' to engage it. The two other major sea control helicopters both carry ASMs, and this shortcoming will, hopefully, be set right in the HM.2 when it comes into operational service from 2013, and it will be able to carry the same future ASM as the Wildcat. The Merlin has a maximum endurance of six hours.

The USN SH-60R has a maximum launch weight of 23,000lb and is powered by two General Electric T700-GE-701C engines. It has the same Flash sonar, designated AN/AQS-22 by the USN, and an AN/UYS-2A modular signal processor that interprets information from both the dipping sonar and sonobuoys. The AN/APS-147 multimode radar gives 360-degree coverage and the aircraft has an electro-optical camera and a contemporary

outfit of ESM, ECM and defensive aids. Its armament comprises up to eight AGM-114A Hellfire ASM or two Mark 54 torpedoes, or a missile/torpedo mixture. The Hellfire missiles can be fitted with a variety of warheads and are intended for use against small, fast vessels in littoral waters. Larger targets would be engaged by strike fighters in the USN battle plan, but the open-architecture computer system allows the introduction of alternative ASMs and AAMs for export customers such as Australia. The MH-60S is a utility version of the Seahawk which is also embarked in carriers but is frequently detached to other ships in the battle group.

The NH-90 NATO Frigate helicopter is named the Caiman in the French Navy and is entering operational service in 2013. It will operate from the *Charles de Gaulle* in the sea-control role as well as in destroyers and frigates. It also has a variant of the Flash sonar, can deploy sonobuoys and is fitted with a TMS2000 acoustic processor, 360-degree radar an electro-optical camera system and defensive aids. It is smaller than the Merlin, with only two RTM 322 engines, and has a maximum launch weight of 24,000lb. Like the Merlin, the airframe makes extensive use of carbonfibre, but its potential weapon loads are more impressive, with the ability to carry two MU-90 torpedoes or two Marte Mark 2S ASMs. With a 150lb warhead these have a genuine 'ship-killing' capability against frigate-sized targets and, with a range of twenty miles, they can be fired outside most frigate defences. The NH-90 has larger doors and a bigger floor area than the MH-60R, making it a better platform for boarding of raiding parties of marines, even with the sonar equipment in place. The type has had development difficulties and is only just entering operational use in 2013 but, as well as France, it has been procured for the navies of Belgium, Finland, Germany, Holland, Italy, Norway, Portugal and Sweden.

CHAPTER 39

UNMANNED AIRCRAFT – A FAST-MOVING TECHNICAL AND TACTICAL REVOLUTION

The decade-long conflict fought by NATO forces against insurgents in Afghanistan saw a dramatic increase in the number of unmanned air vehicles (UAVs) used for reconnaissance, intelligence gathering and the selection of targets for strike aircraft. Some unmanned types, such as the General Atomics MQ-9 Reaper, have been armed with Hellfire missiles or small bombs to carry out small-scale attacks on time-sensitive moving targets that 'pop-up' during their extended patrols. These are 'flown' in real time by a remote pilot in the USA during the mission, but 'handed-off' to a local controller for landing. Smaller UAVs have been used in Afghanistan by the British Army, including the Elbit Hermes 450, but their operation has been far from trouble-free and the MoD has admitted that eleven have been lost in operational accidents, more than the total originally purchased. The RAF's 39 Squadron has operated up to thirteen MQ-9 Reapers, purchased from the USA under a £300 million US Foreign Military Sales contract, in Afghanistan, but three of these have been lost in accidents. The US armed forces have suffered similar attrition on a very much larger scale but, despite this, UAVs have performed a vital reconnaissance mission when there is a negligible ground threat and no air opposition. When an air threat exists, current UAVs are extremely vulnerable. In 2008, for instance, a Russian Air Force MiG-29 shot down a Georgian Hermes 450 similar to those used by the British Army. In October 2012 an Israeli Air Force General Dynamics F-16 shot down a UAV launched from the Lebanon, and in November 2012 two Iranian Sukhoi Su-25 fighters engaged an unarmed US General Atomics MQ-1 Predator UAV which was carrying out surveillance east of Kuwait, sixteen miles off the coast of Iran, but failed to shoot it down with guns.

Until recently this vulnerability has caused the USN to be cautious in its approach to the use of unmanned combat air systems (Ucas), but recently it has carried forward three major developments. The first is an unmanned helicopter designed to operate from destroyers and frigates, the Northrop Grumman MQ-8B/C Fire Scout, and is outside the scope of this book except to note that it was deployed operationally in 2012 both at sea and in Afghanistan. Failures of its autonomous recovery system caused problems that grounded the aircraft for a period but will be overcome. The 'C' variant uses a larger airframe based on the Bell 407, with the same avionics as the earlier version, but has a greater load-carrying capability.

The second project began in 2003 with the joint Ucas trial of three distinct aircraft types, the largest of which was the Northrop Grumman X-47A. The trial was terminated in 2006 but the USN invested $636 million dollars in the derivative X-47B for a project known as the unmanned combat air system demonstration (Ucas-D) from 2007. This tasked the manufacturer with producing two prototype tailless unmanned aircraft that will demonstrate the ability to be launched from a carrier and carry out arrested recoveries alongside conventional manned aircraft in 2013. The first aircraft flew in 2011, and launches by steam catapult and arrested recoveries were carried out at NAS Patuxent River, Maryland, in 2012 to prepare for carrier trials in 2013. The software that will control the X-47B in its recovery pattern to the deck was tested in a series of carrier landings by a modified F/A-18 test aircraft with a safety pilot, which proved both safe and effective. Although intended as a technology demonstrator, the X-47B can be fitted with a range of sensors including multimode synthetic-aperture and inverse synthetic-aperture radar, both electro-optical and infrared cameras and ESM. Two internal weapons bays can carry a total of 4,500lb of weapons, which could include six precision-guided small-diameter bombs. The aircraft has a maximum launch weight of 46,000lb, putting it in the same weight category as the RN Sea Vixen, and has a single Pratt & Whitney F100-PW-220U engine delivering 18,000lb thrust. Top speed is about 460 knots at low level, and the aircraft is designed to be stealthy across the detection spectrum. As well as carrier compatibility, the two aircraft will be used to demonstrate the ability to refuel in flight, both as a donor and as a receiver, using both the USN probe-and-drogue and USAF flying-boom techniques, paving the way for future long-endurance Ucas operations. With full internal fuel, sensors and strike weapons the X-47B has a planned radius of action in excess of 1,600 miles. Alternatively, fuel tanks could replace the weapons in the internal bays to give a 'clean' radius of action of 2,000 miles on reconnaissance missions. It could loiter over a target of interest 1,000 miles from the carrier for two hours.

Potentially, Ucas-Ds could make significant changes in the way carriers operate. Their long range and endurance allow the carrier to launch them from the open ocean and maintain

An X-47B in flight. (USN)

reconnaissance and precision strike capability from beyond the range of most anti-access systems. Initially, derivative Ucas's will rely on stealth to protect them from enemy defences, but defensive systems in more advanced applications than those being fitted to fighters such as the F-35 can be fitted to counter the threat in due course. Beyond the X-47B, the USN is defining an unmanned carrier-launched strike and surveillance system (Uclass), which is to be ready for the deployment of a six-aircraft squadron to a carrier air wing by 2020. The adoption of an operational derivative of the X-47 is not a 'given', and the USN is asking industry to propose affordable types capable of up to fourteen hours' endurance with an adequate fuel reserve to loiter waiting for recovery on return to the carrier. The aircraft selected must be able to use 'lethal precision weapons to suppress, defeat, destroy, deceive or influence a range of enemy targets', and is to have both folding wings and tie-down points for carrier stowage. Taxying with power on is to be achieved by aircraft handlers using remote-control units on deck.

As the cost of manpower becomes less affordable, the concept of a mixed air group comprising both manned and unmanned aircraft is extremely attractive. They can provide

intelligence and surveillance of potentially hostile targets thousands of miles from the carrier, operating if necessary as a continuous 'swarm', with artificial intelligence deciding when to refuel or replace individual aircraft. Unmanned systems would stay alert throughout long sorties, and without the need for a cockpit, life-support systems and pilot/machine interfaces the aircraft could have uncompromised stealth characteristics which would be more effective than those designed into the F-35. Manned aircraft will provide continuation training for flight-deck crews and operations teams, so savings can be made from the lack of any requirement to fly unmanned aircraft on non-operational sorties. The Uclass will not be lightweight, and nor will its unit procurement cost be insignificant, but it will offer huge advantages for carrier strike groups as more nations develop 'anti-access' missile systems a generation beyond those deployed by the Soviet Navy in the 1970s and 1980s. The Uclass may be engaged by enemy defensive systems until they are suppressed, and may have to operate in concert with submarine-launched cruise missiles and escorting fighters and electronic attack aircraft. It is likely to mark the start of a new era for strike operations from aircraft carriers that is as important as the first manned

An X-47B on the flight deck of the USS *Harry S Truman*, CVN-75, during the embarked compatibility tests that preceded launch and recovery trials. The other aircraft aft near the X-47 are F/A-18 Super Hornets and an MH-60 Seahawk helicopter. Three C-2 Greyhounds are parked forward of the island. (USN)

take-offs and deck landings a century ago.

The third major USN unmanned system is not designed to operate from a ship platform, but has relevance to strike carrier operations as part of the broad area maritime surveillance (Bams) concept. The unmanned Northrop Grumman MQ-4C Triton is designed to complement the Boeing P-8A Poseidon in providing continuous surveillance over large designated areas of ocean, transmitting a detailed analysis of the surface picture to other platforms and intelligence centres. Triton is another example of the USN's cost-conscious and careful approach. The airframe was derived from the USAF Northrop Grumman RQ-4B Global Hawk and modified with a new outfit of sensors. It has the same Rolls-Royce AE3007 engine delivering 7,000lb of thrust but, whereas the RQ-4 is intended to remain at high altitude throughout its long sorties, the MQ-4 may have to descend through cloud to use its electro-optical/infrared

An X-47B taxies around the flight deck of the USS *Harry S Truman*. It is directed by a 'yellow-jacket' marshaller in the normal way, but controlled by men with hand-held remote-control units. There are two of the latter in this photograph; one at the top left and one at the bottom centre. Both are facing the X-47. (USN)

An X-47B secured on the USS *Harry S Truman's* flight deck forward of the island. (USN)

camera to identify individual ships if necessary. It could therefore suffer from ice accretion on the wings and control surfaces, and has been fitted with engine and airframe anti-icing systems similar to those fitted to the P-8. Tritons are intended to maintain continuous surveillance over an ocean orbit, giving fleet and task force commanders battle space awareness with imagery,

multifunction radar and ESM transmitted in real time without a break, using a variety of data links including Link 16. The USN plans to buy sixty-eight MQ-4Cs, which will ultimately allow it to maintain five permanent orbits world-wide. Coverage could be maintained in the area of interest of a carrier battle group or amphibious ready group for its entire forward deployment.

An X-47B on one of the USS *Harry S Truman*'s side lifts. (USN)

Since 2009 five modified RQ-4 Global Hawks have been used by the USN in what started as a six-month Bams demonstration orbit. That orbit has been maintained for over three years, and is regarded as an essential element of current fleet operations. Each MQ-4 Bams orbit is expected to require 55,000 flying hours in a single year.

Individual MQ-4Cs can remain airborne for up to twenty-eight hours and have a maximum take-off weight of 32,000lb. They will be flown from designated airfields close to their orbit to carry out pre-programmed, autonomous flight paths which require a remote pilot only as a 'safety-number' for take-off and landing. The sorties will be overseen by controllers in the USA who can make inputs to designate targets or give new waypoints for the orbit but do not 'fly' the aircraft remotely, as with earlier UAVs. The most important element of the sophisticated avionics suite is the multifunction active sensor (MFAS), an electronically-scanned radar array that gives 360-degree track-while-scan coverage and is capable of following hundreds of discrete targets even in high-density shipping areas such the English Channel or the Straits of Malacca. Individual ship identification can be achieved using the electro-optical/infrared camera mounted in a turret under the aircraft's nose or by the Sierra Nevada ESM system, which contains an archive of 'signatures' which allow the identification of specific emitters. Real-time information will be distributed throughout the network-enabled fleet.

At the time of writing no other nation has ordered Bams or anything like it, and the RN has nothing to compare with the USN systems described except for a specification which has been drawn up for an unmanned helicopter capable of demonstrating operation from the flight deck of a frigate. The UK Government has made no statement about the potential operation of Ucavs from the *Queen Elizabeth* Class, but has funded the development of the BAE Systems Taranis, a Ucas demonstration aircraft about one quarter of the size of the X-47B, named after the Celtic God of Thunder. BAE Systems claims that it has long range and is potentially capable of carrier operation, but would require catapults and arrester wires. The UK Government decision to complete the two new carriers as Stovl ships will preclude them from operating Uclass or an equivalent unless or until an unmanned Stovl aircraft is designed or the ships are modified. An agreement has been signed with France to cover the joint design of future Ucavs, but since *Charles de Gaulle* will be able to launch and recover conventional tail-hooked aircraft it is unlikely that the French Navy will be interested in a Stovl variant which is likely to be less capable and more expensive. The British decision to concentrate exclusively on Stovl may well limit the RN's ability to buy into a Uclass capability as it evolves. At whatever pace unmanned carrier aircraft progress, their eventual use is one of the most interesting prospects for the present century.

CHAPTER 40

THE ROYAL NAVY'S FUTURE PROSPECTS: THE AUTHOR'S AFTERWORDS

In the preceding chapters we have seen British aircraft carriers grow from an innovative but experimental force that inspired other nations to imitate and improve on it, into an important tactical force acting support of battleships and then as a strategically important and effective strike force between 1945 and the late 1960s. We have also had illustrative examples of the aircraft that operated from them described, together with comparisons of British carriers with other nations' ships and methods of operation. Over the last half-century we have seen a gradual decline forced on the RN carrier force by politicians who have failed to understand, or implement, the value of a maritime strategy for the UK, while the ships themselves spent more and more time at sea acting in the national interest. Opposition has led, since 1961, to aircraft carriers becoming the most

studied weapons systems in the history of British procurement, and it is a testament to generations of senior officers who believe that the UK should have an effective navy that the *Queen Elizabeth* Class has survived at all. However, there can be little argument against pessimists who observe that British aircraft carriers have reached their nadir in the second decade of the twenty-first century.

Nevertheless, there are grounds for optimism in the longer term, and the British aircraft carrier story is far from over. Optimists draw strength from the fact that, despite their chaotic and long-delayed procurement programme, the *Queen Elizabeth* Class offer new possibilities for the operation of British tactical aircraft if politicians have the wit to understand their value and the RN and its sister Services can focus their collective imagination and drive to achieve the best from

them. In a world in which an increasing number of state and non-state powers threaten the use of force to achieve their objectives it is vital that the UK has such a capability if it is to continue to play a role commensurate with its status in world events as they unfold. Increasingly, the UK is likely to have to react, like the other permanent members of the UN Security Council and major states with global influence, to unforeseen crises with highly trained and capable forces at very short notice. The defence of our own shipping, citizens and interests,

An artist's impression of *Queen Elizabeth* alongside the carrier berth in Portsmouth Naval Base with HMS *Victory* and the iron frigate *Warrior* visible in the background. Both side-lifts are down to allow direct access from the jetty into the hangar for loading stores. She has Lightning IIs and a single Merlin on deck (AIRCRAFT CARRIER ALLIANCE)

as well as those of Commonwealth and allies, demands nothing less. The sort of effective reaction, in fact, that was achieved by aircraft carriers in the last century, combining, as they do, the sustainable reach of warships, the striking power and versatility of aircraft flown from a well-equipped mobile base, and the multirole capabilities of large structures that constitute deployable sovereign territory.

These ships will not emerge from the builder's yard as the strike carriers that were originally envisaged. Their tortuous specification and development process, the absence of a fully comprehended national concept of strike fleet operation for them, and the lack of any one person in charge of the project have condemned these ships to be late in service, over-budget and operationally suboptimal. The contrast with the appointment of a submarine-expert admiral as Chief Polaris Executive who overcame every obstacle to deliver the submarine-launched deterrent on time and budget in 1968 could not be more marked. The decision in 2012 to revert to the F-35B Stovl variant of the Lightning as the embarked fighter was driven by short-term cost-cutting criteria rather than a recognised need for strategic capability, but the decision to operate a variety of fixed-wing aircraft with catapults and arrester wires, rather than be limited by Stovl, should have been taken at the start of the project, not after construction of the ships had begun. It is likely that *Queen Elizabeth* will at first operate only a handful of RN Lightnings regularly to maintain core capability, relying on RAF reinforcements for surge operations that require a larger air group. The latter would require training and could not be deployed as quickly or as effectively as an all-RN Lightning force, but a joint approach may be the political price that has to be paid to maintain inter-Service harmony and Government acceptance. As we saw with JFH, a further limitation on embarked operations would follow the deployment of a large part of the force to protracted operations ashore; a single squadron cannot be in two places at once.

The way the *Queen Elizabeth* Class has been developed has not been good, and the limitations the ships will suffer compared with what they could have achieved are hardly things we should be proud of as a nation. They are the result of the UK's dysfunctional procurement system, which has ignored the wealth of experience accumulated by the RN over the previous century. These negative views must be set aside, however, and the new carriers must be considered with regard to the strength and versatility they will bring to UK defence, not to what they should have been or could have been if their procurement had been better managed. In earlier chapters the emergence of a 'cross-over' capability between big-deck amphibious carriers and strike carriers was

described, with ships such as the USS *America* able to provide both an amphibious force and air power from the sea in measures that are flexible and adjustable, a capability that analysts are referring to as 'triphibious' operations, combining land, sea and air operations in a single ship that operates as an operational 'hub'. *Queen Elizabeth* will be just such a ship, but will approach 'triphibious cross-over' from an original design as a strike carrier, whereas *America* began as an amphibious assault ship with an enhanced air capability. The two may well operate in a similar fashion and form the basis of a new approach to naval aviation in the twenty-first century, the big-deck air-capable ship with a number of roles, many of which can be carried out concurrently. The end of the aircraft carrier has been prophesied a number of times since the first practical example, HMS *Argus*, first went to sea in 1918, but the fact that other nations have never doubted their value and we are building new ones to fill an embarrassing gap in capability inflicted by our own Government shows how important such ships are now and are likely to remain. As an island nation totally reliant on seaborne global trade it must always be important that we keep the seas safe and open for the shipping upon which we rely. Even the USA can no longer defend the world's shipping routes alone, and other wealthy nations must be capable of contributing realistically to the task. We rely on warships to 'go into harm's way' to defend our interests; it would be callous to expect them to do so against any but the least sophisticated opposition without the element of integral air capability that they need to succeed.

Following the prolonged campaigns on land in the Balkans, Iraq and Afghanistan in which the UK has fought over the past three decades, both public and politicians have come to think of contemporary warfare in terms of land conflict. Even BR 1806, the RN *Statement of Maritime Doctrine*, refers to the 'maritime contribution to joint operations', implying a primary joint operation ashore and a secondary maritime element at sea which is not the focal point of conflict, rather than sea control and maritime conflict in their own right. As the twenty-first century progresses and several nations square up to each other to dispute the ownership of small islands and the resource-rich sea areas around them, from the South Atlantic to the South China Sea, the possibility of conflict at sea over resources is becoming more likely. China, India and Russia are building, or plan to build, new aircraft carriers for this reason, and Russia, Australia, South Korea and Japan are building big-deck LPHs with 'cross-over' potential. These are in addition to established navies that already have carrier capability. In their projected fifty-year lifespan it is likely that the UK's new carriers will have to project power in the UK national interest into sea areas dominated by

a potentially hostile battle group that may well contain one or more aircraft carriers, as well as other surface units and submarines, and the USA and France may not be able or willing to protect us. Little thought has been given to fleet-versus-fleet conflict since the end of the Cold War, and we are now entering an era when serious thought should be given to it before the RN's core capability becomes too atrophied to recover. Thankfully the decision to build large ships has made them adaptable, and it is worth recalling the considerable modifications that were worked into the *Invincible* Class that changed them from antisubmarine specialists into general-purpose carriers with a viable strike capability. The *Queen Elizabeths* have scope for even more and greater changes if required, and can evolve into many roles in due course if the Government recognises the need for them to do so.

More than any other British weapons system, the new carriers with the strike fighters and helicopters they embark will be able to create the conditions under which other forces can operate successfully to achieve the national aim. This may involve fighting hostile forces at sea and from the land at short notice, with forces trained for their tasks at peak proficiency. They will include both naval air squadrons and Royal Marines acting in combat formations that are, in effect, one of the ship's weapons. Of course units from the other Services will be needed to expand numbers in prolonged combat, but they must be trained to the standard of RN and RM units in fighting at and from the sea if they are to be effective in the same way that the Army gunners and engineers that form part of 3 Commando Brigade are. Nothing less will be good enough. This would give the UK an effective 'triphibious' capability that could bring rapid force to bear in a 'trouble spot' or 'brushfire war', and would be a national capability that would be envied by many as a 'force for good', deterring low-intensity conflict that might otherwise escalate. In essence, *Hermes* acted as an early example of such a capability in the South Atlantic Conflict of 1982, when she embarked and supported Sea Harriers, antisubmarine and commando assault helicopters, formations of Royal Marines and, during the latter part of the conflict, RAF Harriers brought out from the UK to join her. Had it not been for her the RAF Harriers would not have been able to get to the fight, a point that protagonists of exclusively land-based fixed-wing operations would do well to remember. As unmanned combat aircraft develop, British carriers are likely to be the most important option for deploying RAF elements to contribute to a sea-based conflict.

The ship's companies of *Queen Elizabeth* and *Prince of Wales* have much to be positive about when they first enter service. Like all big-deck ships they have more flexibility than their political masters have comprehended, and can deliver effects at short notice from humanitarian relief after a disaster, through the spectrum of peacetime alliance-building visits and exercises, to both low- and high-intensity conflict. They inherit a long and unrivalled tradition of operating aircraft at sea, often in the most difficult circumstances with little recognition for a job well done. In addition to the operation of RN aircraft and RM combat formations, they have enormous potential to act as joint bases for RAF and Army aircraft and numerous combat formations including special forces when needed. In the sort of high-tempo expeditionary operations proposed in SDSR this may be the only way such units can get into action at short notice, and the carriers should be welcomed in that light. Strategic airlift has a complementary role to play, but transport aircraft need airfields to land on and cannot do so against opposition. In the opening stages of a joint operation warships provide the necessary command, control and communications in the area of operations, allowing operations to unfold in the optimum manner once airfields and port facilities have been secured. Operation *Vantage*, the defence of Kuwait in 1961, may have happened fifty years ago, but accounts of it still make interesting reading for planning staffs, and it would be a foolish Service man or woman who dismissed such experience as 'mere history'.

These ships will have a flexible and adaptive capability that has the potential to serve the nation well in a range of likely scenarios, but it will take firm leadership, ingenuity and determination to achieve it. This has been visibly lacking in their procurement process, which has, of course, been outside the RN's control in the current era of centralised MoD procurement. There is an urgent and important need to demonstrate the new capability to our allies and to those who would oppose us. The latter need to be made to believe that we are expert in the maritime approach to warfare, good at what we do and have lost nothing in the last decade thanks to the support of our friends and allies. By taking control of the battle-space in an area of interest on, above and below the surface of the sea and both on and over any adjacent land, the new carriers can act as a national hub which will allow the deployment of larger joint national and coalition assets if and when they are needed. While conceding that cynics who say that the British Government has never really understood naval aviation and actually constitutes its worst enemy may have a point, I remain optimistic that aircraft carriers are too important a national asset to lose, and that capabilities vital to the UK's defence will be recreated with *Queen Elizabeth* and *Prince of Wales*.

APPENDIX A

Illustrative Royal Navy Carrierborne Aircraft 1912-2012

Aircraft	Length	Span (spread)	Span (folded)	Height	Internal fuel	Max Weight	Powerplant	Crew
Camel 2F.1	18ft 8in	26ft 11in	—	9ft 1in	37gal	1,530lb	150hp piston	1
Short 184	40ft 7.5in	63ft 6.75in	16ft 4.25in	13ft 6in	80gal	5,363lb	260hp piston	2
Flycatcher	23ft 1in	29ft 0in	—	12ft 0in	53gal	2,979lb	400hp piston	1
Dart	35ft 4.5in	45ft 6in	17ft 6in	12ft 11in	78gal	6,400lb	470hp piston	1
Swordfish	35ft 8in	45ft 6in	17ft 3in	12ft 4in	110gal	9,250lb	750hp piston	3
Skua	35ft 7in	46ft 2in	15ft 6in	14ft 2in	166gal	8,228lb	830hp piston	2
Barracuda	37ft 0in	50ft 0in	18ft 0in	14ft 9in	226gal	14,250lb	1,260hp piston	3
Avenger	40ft 0in	54ft 2in	20ft 8in	13ft 9in	278gal	16,400lb	1,750hp piston	3
Sea Fury	34ft 8in	38ft 4.75in	16ft 1in	15ft 0in	200gal	12,500lb	2,480hp piston	1
Sea Hawk	39ft 8in	39ft 0in	13ft 3in	16ft 8in (folded)	397gal	16,200lb	5,200lb-thrust jet	1
Gannet ASW	44ft 6in	54ft 4in	19ft 11in	13ft 9in	968gal	23,700lb	3,035shp double turboprop	3
Sea Vixen	55ft 7in	51ft 0in	22ft 3in	10ft 9in	1,300gal	46,750lb	2 x 10,000lb-thrust jet	2
Wessex	65ft 10in	56ft 0in	12ft 0in	15ft 10in	308gal	13,600lb	1,450shp shaft turbine	4
Sea King	55ft 9.75in	62ft 0in	15ft 6in	15ft 11in	800gal	21,400lb	2 x 1,500shp shaft turbine	4
Sea Harrier	47ft 7.5in	25ft 3.5in	—	11ft 10.5in	600gal	26,200lb	21,500lb-thrust jet	1

APPENDIX B

Examples of aircraft from other Services that have operated from RN aircraft carriers

In 1963 the Admiralty announced Government approval to proceed with CVA-01 and stated that the ship would not just be a fleet unit but a joint national asset capable of operating aircraft from all three Services. Unfairly, this statement was greeted with some ill-informed criticism by commentators who thought that the statement was an attempt to justify the construction of large 'Admirals' flagships'. The ability of aircraft carriers to embark, assemble, fuel, arm and launch a wide variety of tactical aircraft had actually allowed other Services to deploy operational aircraft into conflicts that would otherwise have been beyond their range for many years, and would continue to do so. Numerous examples will be found in the individual ship histories, but the following examples are mentioned here to give an easy reference that shows how commonplace such operations have been over the past century.

In December 1918 *Ark Royal* ferried an RAF Squadron to Somaliland, where it helped troops on the ground to put down a revolt by native insurgents.

Royal Air Force Fairey IIICs, Sopwith Camels, Short 184s, 1½ Strutters and Grain Griffins were deployed to Russia in several ships, including *Vindictive* and *Nairana*, in 1919 to take part in British operations against the Bolsheviks.

In the early 1920s *Ark Royal* ferried a number of RAF aircraft to the Dardanelles during the Chanak Crisis.

Early in the Second World War *Glorious* ferried RAF fighters to Norway and even recovered several of them during the subsequent withdrawal of British forces. A large number of aircraft were ferried to Takoradi in West Africa by *Furious*; from there they flew on to the Middle East. In 1942 others were deployed to the East Indies by *Indomitable* during attempts to build up forces that could halt the Japanese advance. Large numbers of Hurricanes and Spitfires were ferried to a position within flying range of Malta by *Ark Royal*, *Furious*, *Argus* and the USS *Wasp* and launched to strengthen the defences. In 1944 the escort carriers ferried the Mosquitoes of 618 Squadron RAF to Australia, from where they were to have embarked in a fleet carrier with their *Highball* bouncing bombs to attack Japanese warships. In the event the attack was cancelled because of US opposition to any but American aircraft attacking Japanese capital ships, but all the preparatory work was done and 618's pilots were deck-landing qualified and ready.

In 1950 *Unicorn* ferried Meteor fighters from Singapore to Japan, where they were used in the Korean War by 77 Squadron RAAF. The aircraft had been ferried to Singapore from the UK by RN ferry carriers.

The Suez landings in 1956 saw Whirlwind and Sycamore helicopters of the Joint Army/RAF Helicopter Development Unit embarked in *Ocean*, and they joined 845 NAS in *Theseus* to carry out the first operational helicopter-borne assault in history.

In 1964 *Centaur* embarked two RAF Westland Belvedere helicopters which were used to help put down mutinies by units of the Tanganyika Rifles. In 1966 RAF helicopters and AAC Auster light observation aircraft and Westland Scout helicopters were ferried to Borneo from Singapore in *Albion* and *Bulwark* during the 'Confrontation' with Indonesia. During the 1960s and 1970s a number of USN aircraft 'cross-decked' on to British carriers and RN aircraft reciprocated, to demonstrate compatibility in both the Pacific and Atlantic areas. *Ark Royal* had not quite finished her 'special refit' when 892 NAS, with its new Phantoms, was ready for sea, so the unit embarked for a successful period in the USS *Saratoga* in the Mediterranean.

In 1982 RAF Harriers were embarked in *Hermes* during the South Atlantic Conflict to liberate the Falkland Islands. A number of RAF Chinooks were embarked in *Atlantic Conveyor* and were lost with her, except for one, which was flown ashore and used operationally. In 2003 RAF Chinooks embarked in *Ark Royal* during the Second Gulf War and carried Royal Marines ashore during the assault on the Al Faw Peninsula. After 2000, Harriers and helicopters from the two new Joint Forces were regularly embarked in carriers and the LPH.

In 2007 USMC AV-8B Harriers and V-22 Ospreys embarked in *Illustrious*, followed a few months later by Spanish and Italian AV-8B Harriers. In 2010 AAC Apache helicopters embarked in *Ark Royal* and demonstrated their ability to operate from a carrier. Later in the same year she also operated USMC Harriers, and in 2011 AAC Apaches embarked in *Ocean* for operations in the Libyan littoral.

This list is by no means comprehensive, but it does highlight an important and often underrated national and collaborative capability that provides a preventive or reactive force when nothing else can and the need is urgent.

APPENDIX C

The proposed aircraft carrying mail steamer of 1923

In March 1923 Sir Eustace Tennyson d'Eyncourt, Director of Naval Construction, and John Narbeth, the constructor responsible for the early aircraft carrier designs, gave a presentation to the Royal Institution of Naval Architects in which they proposed the construction of an aircraft-carrying mail steamer. The DNC had clearly put considerable thought into the idea, and the resultant design drawings are included to allow comparison with designs that were taken forward.

The speakers started by explaining that they believed that there was already a synergy between fast merchant ships and aircraft. They said:

In case of need, passengers now occasionally leave London or Paris by aeroplane some time after the hour when the mail trains leave. The aeroplanes get to an aerodrome at the port in time to enable the passenger to alight and then embark on the liner with which the mail train connects, thus giving a very notable advantage in time saved to the traveller. The advantage will obviously be increased if the aeroplane, instead of alighting at an aerodrome and requiring the passenger then to proceed by some other conveyance to the ship, possibly by motor car and also by ferry steamer, could fly right on to the ship herself while she is proceeding on her voyage at sea. Should this be practical, flying on and off ships at sea opens up a great vista of future developments for combined aircraft and steamship services.

Although it was not discussed at the meeting, such a ship obviously had the latent potential to be requisitioned for use by the RN in time of war, since the carrier conversions in the First World War had all been made from fast merchant ships of varying sizes.

A detailed design was shown which had been the work of C J W Hopkins MBE RCNC. It was for a ship that was 600ft long between perpendiculars, with a waterline beam of 80ft and a draught of 28ft. It would have had oil-fired water-tube boilers capable of developing 50,000shp and stowage for 2,500 tons of FFO. This would have given the ship the capability to cross the Atlantic at 22 knots, roughly the same as other contemporary mail steamers. Holds were designed for about 1,500 tons of cargo, and the boilers were to be sited aft of the engines with uptakes led vertically to the underside of the flight deck and then horizontally aft to a large, common duct under the flight deck aft, from which flaps would have directed the funnel smoke to port or starboard or upwards through shutters in the flight deck, as required by the captain to give optimal conditions for steaming or flying. Given the failure of the ducted systems in *Argus* and *Furious*, this must be recognised as the weakest feature of the design and was unlikely to have been successful.

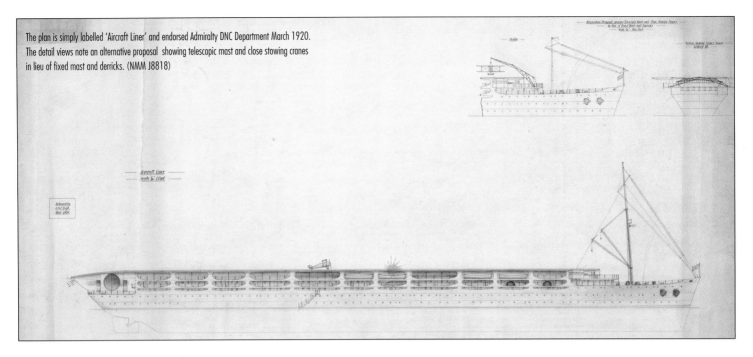

The plan is simply labelled 'Aircraft Liner' and endorsed Admiralty DNC Department March 1920. The detail views note an alternative proposal showing telescopic mast and close stowing cranes in lieu of fixed mast and derricks. (NMM J8818)

The flight deck was rectangular and about 565ft long and 100ft wide. It ended about 100ft aft of the bow, enabling 'very satisfactory navigating and cable arrangements to be made', and a foremast was proposed to carry navigation lights and to carry long derricks for hoisting cargo, aircraft, stores and baggage to the flight deck and holds. The designers were concerned that the mast 'may appear at first sight to be open to objection as being in the way of aircraft', but felt that this view was unsound because 'machines rise in a very few yards and after a very short time are well in the air and can be manoeuvred to either side of the mast and shrouds without any trouble'. For landing, it was considered that 'there is a flight deck 565 feet long and in the case of a failure to alight the machine would get away clear of the vessel long before reaching the mast position over the bow'. Readers will form their own conclusions about these arguments and, to be fair, alternatives were put forward in case the mast proved unacceptable.

The navigating bridge was under the forward edge of the flight deck, where it was well protected from weather but allowed a good view. A look-out tower for sighting aft was placed at each bridge wing, each being equipped with engine telegraphs for use when docking. Aft of the bridge were officers' quarters and a block of twelve lifeboats which could be launched from either side of the ship. Aft of them was a lift serving the forward hangar, the space around it designated an aircraft assembly area. Since the area under the flight deck was largely open, windbreaks were provided to protect aircraft that were being assembled or maintained. A

second block of twelve lifeboats was aft of this area, with the after lift and assembly area further aft again. Abaft the after lift was an emergency dynamo and the smoke duct.

On the next deck down the captain's quarters were aft of the forecastle, with first class accommodation for up to 138 people astern of them. There were suites of rooms amidships connecting to a library, ladies' drawing rooms, a lounge, smoke-rooms and a veranda cafe. The bulkheads surrounding the smoke ducts aft were water-jacketed 'where desirable' to prevent excessive heat in the adjacent passenger accommodation. Given the experience in *Furious*, it is likely that this design feature, too, would not have been entirely successful. Beneath this deck was further first and second class accommodation, forward and after hangars, holds, machinery, cold storage and mail rooms. The design included bulges to protect the hull against 'the results of damage by icebergs, collision or other misadventure in peacetime'. They would also give protection against mines and torpedoes in wartime, of course.

As in any aircraft carrier design, the number of aircraft that could be embarked depended on the types to be embarked and whether they could be folded like naval aircraft or dismantled to fit into the hangars. Since no commercial aircraft were designed for embarked service, the presentation used current naval types to illustrate capacity; it was assumed that all aircraft would be struck down into the hangars and that none would remain in a deck park. It was estimated that the forward hangar would have contained ten Sopwith T.1s or eleven Parnall Panthers; the after hangar

would have contained eight T.1s or ten Panthers. Comparisons were made with the commercial Bristol Ten-seater, de Havilland D.H.34 six-seater and de Havilland D.H.9C three-seater. Overall the ship was to have accommodation for a ship's company of 400 and up to 1,273 passengers.

Several advantages were put forward for such ships. Running from Great Britain to New York, such a ship could send off aeroplanes to reach Montreal in Canada before the ship reached New York. A corresponding gain would be made by Canadian steamers using the port of Halifax, which could launch aircraft to get passengers ashore well before the ship arrived. Ships running from Great Britain to Australia could land passengers without having to stop in Lisbon, Gibraltar, Algiers, Malta, Naples, Port Said, Aden, Port Sudan, Khartoum, Somaliland and, possibly, Bombay before arriving in Colombo. On the last part of the journey to Australia 'various other aerial services could be maintained'. A comparison between the cost-per-mile of various methods of transport for a ton of cargo was made which drew attention to the fact that a passenger steam train would cost 6 pence per mile, a first class liner would cost 51 pence per mile, and a privately chartered aircraft 492 pence per mile. A fusion of all three as described above would, therefore, not only be quicker but cheaper!

As we now know, the design was never considered as commercially attractive as the designers believed, and no such ship was ever built. It seems a pity, because it would have been interesting in its own right and would have assumed importance as a trade protection carrier in 1939.

APPENDIX D

Fighter Catapult Ships and CAM-ships

Although these ships were not aircraft carriers in the true sense of the definition, as they could not recover their aircraft once they were launched, fighter catapult ships were RN-manned and existed for the purpose of deploying fighters in defence of convoys. The CAM-Ships were merchant ships fitted to launch a Hurricane manned by an RAF or RN pilot in defence of a convoy; to intercept enemy aircraft they were fitted with radar and had RN personnel to man it. A brief description of both types follows, to give an idea of the desperate measures taken to compensate for the lack of trade protection carriers in the early years of the Second World War.

Fighter Catapult Ships

The heavy losses of shipping in convoy caused by German Fw 200 Condor bombers in the latter half of 1940 caused the Prime Minister, Winston Churchill, to order urgent priority to be given to both fighter catapult ships and CAM-ships. It was decided to modify four vessels fitting out as auxiliary war vessels with catapults and arrangements for embarking a single Fulmar or up to three Hurricane fighters for use against long-range enemy bombers or shadowing aircraft tracking convoys. As with the CAM-Ships, the Hurricanes were aircraft that had seen previous RAF service, modified with catapult spools. They were joined by the catapult trials ship *Pegasus* (formerly *Ark Royal*), which operated in the same role. The four ships were *Springbank*, which was originally to have been an auxiliary anti-aircraft ship, *Maplin*, *Patia* and *Ariguani*, which had been intended for use as ocean boarding vessels. They were considered the only immediate and practical solution for providing aircraft to protect convoys at short notice, but it is worth

noting that all their operational results combined were not as significant as those of the first escort carrier, *Audacity*, which was modified and taken into service at the same time. The embarked fighters all had naval aircrew and retained their normal, wheeled undercarriage. If they could not fly ashore after an interception, the aircrew had either to bale out or ditch and hope to be recovered by a surface escort. The aircraft was launched by a single catapult powered by cordite in *Springbank* and by rockets in *Ariguani* and *Maplin*; replacement aircraft were hoisted on to it by derrick. They were originally to have been fitted with two 6in guns, but these were replaced by more suitable anti-aircraft weapons, typically up to eight 4in guns in twin mountings, 2pdr pom-poms and 20mm Oerlikons with relevant control arrangements.

Brief individual ship histories

Patia

A ship of 5,355 tons originally completed in 1922, she was requisitioned in 1940 and completed as a fighter catapult ship on 21 March 1941. She was allocated to WAC, but on 27 April 1941 she was sunk off the Tyne by enemy bombing before she had even embarked any aircraft.

Springbank

A ship of 5,150 tons originally completed in 1926, she was requisitioned in 1940. Completed as a fighter catapult ship on 10 May 1941, she subsequently operated with convoys on the North Atlantic and Gibraltar routes, with a single Fulmar embarked. On 10 June 1941, while with HX 129, she launched a Fulmar against an Fw 200 which was intercepted but evaded into cloud. The Fulmar was able to fly to RNAS

Belfast and land. On 18 September 1941 she launched a Fulmar against another Fw 200 while in the vicinity of HG 73. The Fw 200 was intercepted and attacked but evaded into cloud, the Fulmar managing to fly to Gibraltar to land. After it had landed, seven of the fighter's eight machine-guns were found to have jammed because of faulty ammunition. On 27 September, while still with HG 73, *Springbank* was hit by a torpedo fired by U-201 west of Ireland in heavy weather, and sank.

Ariguani

A ship of 6,746 tons originally completed in 1926, she was requisitioned in 1940 and completed as a fighter catapult ship on 10 May 1941, equipped with a rocket-powered catapult and with a single Fulmar embarked. A Hurricane was added in August 1941. She operated on the North Atlantic, Gibraltar and Sierra Leone convoy routes, and on 27 August 1941 launched her Fulmar against an Fw 200 but, despite the fighter chasing the enemy aircraft for 45 miles under radar control through low cloud, it was not shot down. The fighter pilot subsequently landed in Ireland in bad weather, waited 20min for the weather to clear and then flew on to Eglinton in Northern Ireland. On 4 October 1941, while with OG 75, she launched her Fulmar against a Fw 200 which was intercepted and damaged but escaped into cloud. The Fulmar pilot baled out over the convoy and was picked up despite gale-force winds. On 26 October 1941 she was hit by a torpedo from a U-boat, damaged and subsequently towed to Gibraltar. She was subsequently reverted to her original design and reverted to commercial use in December 1941.

Maplin

The most successful of the fighter catapult ships, she was a ship of 5,824 tons originally completed in 1932. She was requisitioned for use as an ocean boarding vessel in 1940 but converted to a fighter catapult ship and completed as such on 18 June 1941 for service on the North Atlantic, Gibraltar and Sierra Leone convoy routes. She had a rocket-powered catapult and at first one, then three Hurricanes embarked. On 18 July 1941, while with OB 346, she launched a Hurricane against an Fw 200 which was shot down by the convoy's anti-aircraft fire just before the fighter intercepted it. The pilot was baled out and successfully picked up. A second Hurricane was then mounted on the catapult, a feat described by the C-in-C WAC as reflecting great credit on the ship's company in the difficult conditions at the time.

Another launch was carried out on 3 August 1941, while in the vicinity of SL 81. The Hurricane successfully intercepted an Fw 200 bomber and shot it down. Lieutenant (A) R W H Everett RNVR, the pilot, baled out and was successfully picked up by a surface escort; he was subsequently awarded the DSO for his action. On 14 September 1941 a Hurricane was launched against an Fw 200 about 100 miles southwest of Ireland. The pilot carried out a series of attacks for an hour, forcing the enemy aircraft to jettison its bombs and escape into cloud, but the Hurricane's machine-gun armament proved too light to inflict fatal damage on the enemy. The pilot baled out and was successfully picked up. *Maplin* ceased to be a fighter catapult ship in 1942 as escort carriers began to come into service, and reverted to mercantile use in June.

In total four fighter catapult ships, including *Pegasus*, operated from December 1940 to early 1942; they carried out ten operational launches, made seven interceptions, shooting down one enemy aircraft and damaging another. Their morale effect on the ships in convoy was much greater than their physical achievements, however.

CAM-Ships

The CAM-ships evolved from a 1940 idea that a number of merchant ships could be fitted with rudimentary rocket-powered catapults capable of launching Hurricane fighters to defend convoys against Fw 200 Condor bombers. The Admiralty agreed that the majority of the pilots would be provided by the RAF, and No.9 Group Fighter Command was given responsibility for the project, setting up a Merchant Ship Fighter Unit (MSFU) at RAF Speke near Blackpool for the purpose. The ships chosen were fitted with radar and VHF radios; the former either naval Type 286P or RAF CHL with fighter controllers provided by the appropriate Service to make best use of the relevant equipment. As VHF radios were in short supply, many came from Fighter Command stations that denuded their own stocks to provide them for merchant ships. The first CAM-Ship, *Michael E*, came into service in May 1941 and eventually thirty-five ships were fitted and at least two were given dummy catapults to confuse the enemy. They were used on the North Atlantic, Gibraltar and Russian convoy routes and achieved some success, but eleven CAM-ships were sunk by enemy action. All were fitted with Type P catapults and most had some form of light anti-aircraft armament.

Figures for 1942 indicate that in that year forty-three CAM-Ships carried out round voyages in the North Atlantic, twenty-five on the Gibraltar run and four on Russian convoys. On the Gibraltar route they shot down one Fw 200 and damaged another; on the Russian route they destroyed one Ju 88, one He 111 and two He 115s, damaging another He 111. No enemy aircraft were destroyed or damaged on the North Atlantic convoy routes. Sometimes both fighter catapult ships and CAM-Ships sailed in the same convoy, and when they did the former was responsible for command and control; the two had, therefore, to remain in visual signalling distance.

Vessels fitted and operated as CAM-Ships

Michael E*	*Empire Eve*
Primrose Hill*	*Empire Sun**
Empire Spring*	*Empire Health*
Empire Tide	*Empire Flame*
Empire Dell*	*Empire Clive*
Helencrest	*Empire Rowan*
Empire Rainbow*	*Eastern City*
Empire Ray	*Empire Spray*
Empire Faith	*Dalton Hall*
Empire Burton*	*Empire Day*
Kafiristan	*Daghestan*
Novelist	*Empire Foam*
Empire Stanley Empire Ocean	
Empire Shackleton*	*Empire Darwin*
Empire Moon	*Empire Franklin*
Empire Wave*	*Empire Gale*
Empire Hudson*	*Empire Morn*
Empire Lawrence*	

* Vessels sunk by enemy action.

CAM-Ship operational launches between 1941 and 1943

On 1 November 1941 *Empire Foam* launched against an Fw 200 while with HX 156. The enemy aircraft was driven off.

On 25 May 1942 *Empire Morn* launched against two enemy aircraft while with QP 12. A Ju 88 was shot down and a Bv 138 was driven off. The Hurricane pilot baled out too low and died before he could be rescued.

Also on 25 May 1942 *Empire Lawrence* launched against enemy aircraft while with PQ 16. One He 111 was shot down and a second severely damaged.

On 14 June 1942 *Empire Moon* launched while with HG 84. A single Fw 200 was driven off and probably damaged.

On 18 September 1942 *Empire Morn* launched against enemy aircraft while with PQ 18. One He 115 was shot down and a second forced to crash into the sea. The Hurricane pilot managed to fly to Archangel and land safely.

On 1 November 1942 *Empire Heath* launched while with HG 91. A single Fw 200 was shot down forty-three miles away from the convoy.

The last CAM-Ship launches took place on 28 July 1943, when both *Empire Tide* and *Empire Darwin* with SL 133 launched against enemy aircraft. One Fw 200 was shot down and a second severely damaged.

By 1943 escort carriers were coming into service in some numbers, and the CAM-Ships reverted to normal mercantile duties.

Between May 1941 and August 1943 CAM-Ships made 170 round voyages, during which there were only eight operational launches.

APPENDIX E

British aircraft carrier losses

Ben-my-Chree

While anchored off Castelorizo Island on 9 January 1917 *Ben-My-Chree* was engaged by Turkish shore batteries which scored hits and set her on fire. She was abandoned when the fires spread out of control, largely caused by the explosion of petrol vapour in two-gallon cans that had been thought to be empty. Another cause of fire was the wooden decking in the hangar and on the aircraft assembly deck aft, which was soaked with oil and petrol. The fires were still burning on 13 January after she had come to rest on the bottom, although her upper works, including the burnt-out shell of the hangar, remained above the surface. Bombs and ammunition had continued to explode while the fires burnt. She was raised in 1920 and subsequently sold for scrap. The lesson that petrol vapour was extremely dangerous was taken to heart by DNC and led to subsequent British ships having a number of safety precautions built in, including hangars that were enclosed and that could be entered only through air locks.

Courageous

The first British warship to be lost in the Second World War was the aircraft carrier *Courageous*, victim of the mistaken belief in the Admiralty that aggressive patrolling was the best way to counter the threat of U-boats. Experience was soon to show that specialised training and equipment were needed for antisubmarine warfare, and that using an important fleet unit to 'trail its coat' through dangerous waters was not a good idea. On 17 September 1939 she was torpedoed by U-29 at 2000 in position 50 degrees 10 minutes north, 14 degrees 45 minutes west, southwest of Ireland. She sank in less than fifteen minutes with the loss of 518 men. Swordfish had been airborne throughout the time that the U-boat was working into an attacking position, but had failed to see its periscope, and the two screening destroyers failed either to detect or sink U-29, which returned safely to Germany.

Glorious

On 8 June 1940 *Glorious* was returning to Scapa Flow from operations off Norway when she was intercepted and sunk by the German battle-cruisers *Scharnhorst* and *Gneisenau*, together with her two screening destroyers *Ardent* and *Acasta*. The decision to use her as a ferry carrier to evacuate seventeen RAF fighters, ten of which were obsolescent biplanes, rather than act as a strike carrier with her own full air group, was extremely questionable. Her captain's lapse in tactical awareness by not flying search aircraft while he was on passage with such a light escort was another contributory factor in the loss of this valuable ship. She was hit repeatedly by 11in gunfire from the two enemy warships after 1600 in position 68 degrees 45 minutes north, 04 degrees 30 minutes east, southwest of Narvik, before sinking at 1730 with very few survivors.

Ark Royal

Ark Royal was hit by a single torpedo from U-81 at 1540 on 13 November 1941, while returning from one of her numerous missions ferrying RAF fighters to Malta. Damage control was not well handled initially and, despite attempts to tow her to Gibraltar, she rolled over to starboard and sank at 0600 on 14 November, east of Gibraltar in position 36 degrees 06 minutes north, 05 degrees 07 minutes east. In 1967 the author attended a damage control course in Portsmouth during which the instructors were still using a model of *Ark Royal* to demonstrate how she could, and should, have been saved.

Audacity

At 2035 on 21 December 1941 the escort carrier *Audacity* was escorting convoy HG 76, roughly in position 44 degrees north 20 minutes west, some 500 miles west of Cape Finisterre, when she was torpedoed by the U-741 and sunk. At the time she was outside the convoy and had no escort of her own, possibly because the limited visibility from her bridge made it difficult to take station inside the convoy perimeter at night.

Hermes

The Japanese fast carrier task force attacked Trincomalee in Ceylon, now Sri Lanka, on 9 April 1942. *Hermes* had been ordered to disperse from the harbour, and she sailed south with the destroyer HMAS *Vampire* without aircraft embarked, relying on shore-based RAF fighters for protection. The two ships were discovered by chance some 65 miles south of the main target at 1100 and both were attacked by dive-bombers from *Akagi*, *Hiryu*, *Shokaku* and *Zuikaku*, which scored over forty hits with 500lb bombs, sinking both ships by 1130. The nearby hospital ship *Vita* was respected by the Japanese naval pilots and was able to rescue over 600 survivors.

Eagle

Eagle formed part of the fighting escort for the *Pedestal* convoy to Malta and was torpedoed by U-73 at 1310 on 11 August 1942, about 60 miles off the Algerian coast and 584 miles west of Malta, in position 38 degrees 05 minutes north, 03 degrees 02 minutes east. The U-boat had penetrated the destroyer screen and passed undetected under two lanes of merchant ships to carry out its attack. *Eagle* was hit by four torpedoes spaced 40ft apart, the first of which hit under P3 6in gun mounting and all of them abreast the port engine room. She immediately began to roll to port and sank bodily at 1315 with the loss of two officers and 158 ratings, nearly all of them in the machinery spaces. The destroyers *Laforey* and *Lookout*, together with the tug *Jaunty*, rescued 789 men.

Avenger

Returning to the UK from Operation *Torch*, *Avenger* was torpedoed by the U-155 in position 36 degrees 15 minutes north, 07 degrees 45 minutes west, to the west of Gibraltar, at 0415 on 15 November 1942. The Board of Inquiry found that splinters from the torpedo penetrated the bomb room and detonated bombs and depth charges which had been stowed against the ship's side plating. Other ships of the class were fitted as quickly as possible with longitudinal bulkheads to keep bombs ten to fifteen feet from the ship's side, and the USN made similar modifications. *Avenger* sank in under five minutes, and there were only twelve survivors.

Dasher

The last British aircraft carrier to be lost was not the result of enemy action, but of an internal explosion while she was anchored off Little Cumbraes Island in the Clyde on 27 March 1943 at 1645, shortly after returning from sea. The Board of Inquiry found the cause to be an accidental petrol explosion, possibly caused by someone smoking near a leaking valve in an avgas control compartment. She sank in three minutes, and there were only 149 survivors. All other US-built CVEs in RN service had significant improvements made to their avgas storage arrangements after this tragic accident.

APPENDIX F

Pennant Numbers and Deck Recognition Letters

Ship	Pennant Number	Deck Recognition Letter	Ship	Pennant Number	Deck Recognition Letter	Ship	Pennant Number	Deck Recognition Letter
Activity	D94		*Glory*	R62	L (1945) R (1946)	*Queen*	D19	Q
Albion	R07	Z (1954) A (1958)	*Hermes* (1924)	I95	HR	*Rajah*	D10	
Ameer	D01		*Hermes* (1959)	R12	H	*Ranee*	D03	F
Arbiter	D31		*Hunter*	D80		*Ravager*	D70	V
Archer	D78		*Illustrious* (1940)	R87	L (1940) Q (1945)	*Reaper*	D82	R
Argus	I49				D (1946) Y (1953)	*Ruler*	D72	
Ark Royal (1938)	91		*Illustrious* (1982)	R06	L			
Ark Royal (1955)	R09	O (1955) R (1958)	*Implacable*	R86	N (1945) A (1946)	*Searcher*	D40	S
Ark Royal (1985)	R07	R			C (1948)	*Shah*	D21	
Atheling	D51		*Indefatigable*	R10	S	*Slinger*	D26	
Attacker	D02		*Indomitable*	R92	W (1945) C (1946)	*Smiter*	D55	G
Audacity	D10				A (1947)	*Speaker*	D90	
Avenger	D14		*Invincible*	R05	N	*Stalker*	D91	
						Striker	D12	
Battler	D18	B	*Khedive*	D62		*Sydney*	R17	K (1949) S (1956)
Begum	D38							
Biter	D97		*Leviathan*	R97		*Thane*	D48	
Bonaventure	CVL-22	CVL-22				*Theseus*	R64	T
Bulwark	R08	B	*Magnificent*	CVL – 21	21	*Tracker*	D24	TR
			Melbourne	R21	Y (1956) M (1957)	*Triumph*	R16	P
Campania	R48	Z			21 (1969)	*Trouncer*	D85	I
Centaur	R06	L (1953) C (1954)				*Trumpeter*	D09	J
Chaser	D32		*Nabob*	D77				
Colossus	15	D	*Nairana*	D05	Y	*Unicorn*	R72 (1945) A195 (1953)	U (1945) Y (1946)
Courageous	50							
			Ocean (1945)	R68	O	*Venerable*	R04	V
Dasher	D37		*Ocean* (1997)	L12	O	*Vengeance*	R71	M (1945) Q (1946)
						Victorious	R38	P (1945) S (1945)
Eagle (1924)	94	EG	*Patroller*	D07	F			G(1946) V (1958)
Eagle (1951)	R05	J (1951) E (1958)	*Perseus*	R 51 (1945) A197 (1952)		*Vikrant*	R11	
Emperor	D98	E	*Pioneer*	R76 (1945) A198 (1953)		*Vindex*	R15	V
Empress	D42		*Premier*	D23	P	*Vindictive*		
			Pretoria Castle	F61				
Fencer	D64		*Puncher*	D79	N	*Warrior*	R31	W (1946) J (1953)
Formidable	R67	X (1945) R (1945)	*Pursuer*	D73	U			
Furious	47							
Glorious	77							

BIBLIOGRAPHY

ADM files held by The National Archives at Kew

ADM 1/22148 — Proposal to build angled landing decks in future carriers.
ADM 1/24145 — Aircraft Carriers, specifications for new designs, 1952.
ADM 1/24210 — Aircraft carriers, outline designs, 1931-32.
ADM 1/24212 — Preliminary investigations into carrier design.
ADM 1/24223 — HMS *Unicorn*, Board approval.
ADM 1/24508 — New design for a fleet carrier.
ADM 1/24623 — Deck landing, proposals for investigation of problems.
ADM 1/25057 — HMS *Glory*, return from Korea to the UK.
ADM 1/25058 — The future of HMS *Indomitable*.
ADM 1/25061 — HMS *Glory*, proposal to recommission.
ADM 1/25062 — HMS *Glory*, programme.
ADM 1/25067 — HMS *Glory*, proposal for use in Training Squadron.
ADM 1/25102 — Merchant aircraft carriers, a scheme by E H Watts.
ADM 1/25111 — HMS *Ark Royal*, approval for installation of angled deck, 1953.
ADM 1/25149 — Cheapest possible aircraft carrier to operate modern fighters, 1953-54.
ADM 1/25532 — HMS *Perseus*, January - February 1954.
ADM 1/25891 — 1954 Long-Term plans for the future RN.
ADM 1/25901 — Anti-Submarine Warfare, comparison of fixed and rotary-wing aircraft.
ADM 1/25933 — Trade protection carriers in 1955.
ADM 1/25934 — Surface strike potential in escort carriers, 1955-56.
ADM 1/25935 — Naval fighter development.
ADM 1/25987 — Cost of HMS *Centaur*.
ADM 1/26139 — Reserve ships, worth for retention, 1955.
ADM 1/26332 — HMS *Majestic* stores.
ADM 1/26373 — Revised island in HMS *Hermes*.
ADM 1/26450 — HMS *Ocean* - mass helicopter trials.
ADM 1/26496 — Sale of a carrier to Argentina, 1956.
ADM 1/26497 — Sale of HMS *Vengeance* to Brazil, 1957.
ADM 1/26842 — HMS *Hermes* Staff requirement.
ADM 1/26966 — HMS *Eagle*, catapult launch by voice, 1958.
ADM 1/27051 — Operation *Musketeer*, carrier operations.
ADM 1/27153 — HMS *Bulwark*, Staff Requirement for conversion into a commando carrier.
ADM 1/27359 — Steam catapult development 1953-56.
ADM 1/27685 — The case for the helicopter carrier/escort cruiser.
ADM 1/27871 — Aircraft complement of carriers.
ADM 1/28617 — RN amphibious capability 1966-72.
ADM 1.28639 — Aircraft carrier programme. Date for replacing HMS *Ark Royal*.
ADM 1/28644 — Aircraft carrier programme 1963-73.
ADM 1/28853 — Work-study report of flight deck layout for CVA-01.
ADM 1/28876 — Staff requirement for CVA-01.
ADM 1/29044 — Name for CVA-01.
ADM 1/29052 — CVA-01 development and design contracts.
ADM 1/29053 — Escort cruiser programme.
ADM 1/29065 — Long-term carrier plan 64A.
ADM 1/29132 — P-177 aircraft, bid to treasury.
ADM 1/29135 — Continued development of P-177.

Ships' covers held by the National Maritime Museum in the Brass Foundry at Woolwich

Furious, Glorious, Courageous
Argus
Eagle
Hermes (1924)
Ark Royal (1938)
Illustrious group
British-built escort carriers
American-built escort carriers
Audacious Class
1942 light fleet carriers
Malta Class
Unicorn
Hermes Class
Victorious
Hermes (1959)
Eagle (1951)
CVA-01
Ark Royal (1955)

Admiralty Handbooks and Publications

Aircraft Carrier Guide	1941 edition
Aircraft Carrier Handbook	1943 edition
Aircraft Carrier & Commando Ship Handbook	1966 edition
Aircraft Carrier Memoranda	1967 edition
Naval Aircraft Handbook	1958 edition

Naval Staff Histories

Battle Summary 5 — The Chase and Sinking of the *Bismarck*
Battle Summary 14 — Loss of HM Ships *Prince of Wales* and *Repulse*
Battle Summary 17 — Naval operations of the campaign in Norway
Battle Summary 27 — Operation *Tungsten* – naval air attack on the *Tirpitz*
Battle Summary 30 — Operation *Avalanche* – landing at Salerno
Battle Summary 38 — Operation *Torch* – invasion of North Africa
Battle Summary 43 — Operation *Dragoon* - invasion of the South of France
Battle Summary 47 — Operation *Iceberg* – naval operations Okinawa
War with Japan in six volumes.
Middle East Operations - Jordan/Lebanon 1958; Kuwait 1961
The Development of British Naval Aviation 1919-1945 Volume I
The Development of British Naval Aviation 1919-1945 Volume II
The Development of British naval Aviation 1919-1945, notes for unfinished Volume III
Naval Aircraft Progress and Operations - Periodical Summaries 1 to 11.
Progress in Naval Aviation/ Progress of the Fleet Air Arm – Summaries 1 to 8.
Director of Naval Air Organisation and Training's Quarterly News Letter on Naval Aviation, July 1949 to May 1958.
Flight Deck, The RN Journal of Aviation, 1944 to 1946 and 1952 to 2000.
DNC *Brief History of the Development of Aircraft Carriers and Arresting Gear*, September 1953.
'HMS *Invincible*, The First of a New Genus of Aircraft Carrying Ships', Royal Institution of Naval Architects Spring Meeting Paper, 1981.

Published sources

Allward, Maurice, *Buccaneer*, Ian Allen, Shepperton, 1981.
Anon, *Ark Royal, a Flagship for the 21st Century*, Catchline PR and Communications, Fife, undated.
Apps, Michael, *Send Her Victorious*, William Kimber, London, 1971.
Apps, Michael, *The Four Ark Royals*, William Kimber, London, 1976.
Askins, Simon, *From the Cockpit 7 – Gannet*, Ad Hoc Publications, Ringshall, 2008.
Baird, Bob, *Shipwrecks of the Forth and Tay*, Whittles Publishing, Dunbeath, 2009.
Barker, Ralph, *The Hurricats*, Pelham Books, London, 1978.
Benbow, Tim, *British naval Aviation – The First 100 Years*, Ashgate, Farnham, for the Corbett Centre for Maritime Studies, 2011.
Bennett, G H, *Hunting Tirpitz – Royal Naval Operations against Bismarck's sister ship*, University of Plymouth Press, Plymouth, 2012.
Blundell, W G D, *British Aircraft Carriers*, Model & Allied Publications, Hemel Hempstead, 1969.
Brown, David K, *The Grand Fleet, Warship Design and Development 1906-1922*, Chatham Publishing, London, 1999.
Brown, David K, *Nelson to Vanguard, Warship Design and Development 1923-1945*, Chatham Publishing, London, 2000.
Brown, David K, and Moore, George, *Rebuilding the Royal Navy, Warship Design since 1945*, Chatham Publishing, London, 2003.

Brown, Eric, *Wings on my Sleeve*, Weidenfield & Nicolson, London, 2006 edition.
Brown, Eric, *From the Cockpit 8 – Firebrand*, Ad Hoc Publications, Ringshall, 2008.
Brown, Eric, *From the Cockpit 13 – Seafire*, Ad Hoc Publications, Ringshall, 2010.
Brown, J David, *HMS Illustrious*, Warship Profile 11, Profile Publications, Windsor, 1971.
Brown J David, *Carrier Air Groups – HMS Eagle*, Hylton Lacy Publishers, Windsor, 1972.
Brown, J David, *HMS Eagle*, Warship Profile 35, Profile Publications, Windsor, 1973.
Brown, J David, *The Seafire*, Ian Allen, London, 1973.
Brown, J David, *Aircraft Carriers*, Macdonald and Jane's Publishers, London, 1977.
Brown, J David, *The Royal Navy and the Falklands War*, Leo Cooper, London, 1987.
Brown, J David, *Warship Losses of World War Two*, Arms and Armour Press, London, 1995 edition.
Brown, J David (edited by Hobbs, David), *Carrier Operations in World War II*, Seaforth Publishing, Barnsley, 2009.
Bruce, J M, Page, G and Sturtivant, Ray, *The Sopwith Pup*, Air-Britain (Historians), Tunbridge Wells, 2002.
Burke, Stephen and Olejnik, Adam, *Freedom of the Sea – The Story of Hitler's Aircraft Carrier Graf Zeppelin*, published by the authors, 2010.
Burns, Ian M, *Ben-my-Chree*, Colin Huston, Leicester, 2008.
Burns K and Critchley M, *HMS Bulwark 1948-1984*, Maritime Books, Liskeard, 1986.
Burt, R A, *British Battleships 1919-1945*, Seaforth Publishing, Barnsley, 2012.
Buttler, Tony, *The de Havilland Sea Vixen*, Air-Britain (Historians), Tunbridge Wells, 2007.
Carter, Geoffrey, *Crises do Happen – The Royal Navy and Operation Musketeer, Suez 1956*, Maritime Books, Liskeard, 2006.
Chartres, John, *Westland Sea King*, Ian Allen, Shepperton, 1984.
Chesneau, Roger, *Aircraft carriers of the World, 1914 to the Present, an Illustrated Encyclopaedia*, Arms & Armour Press, Lionel Leventhal Ltd, London, 1984.
Childs, Nick, *The Age of Invincible – The Ship that Defined the Modern Royal Navy*, Pen & Sword Maritime, Barnsley, 2009.
Clapp, Michael with Southby-Tailyour, Ewen, *Amphibious Assault Falklands – The Battle of San Carlos Water*, Orion Books, London, 1997.
Corbett, Sir Julian, and Newbolt, Henry, *Naval Operations – History of the Great War based on Official Documents* (5 volumes), Naval & Military Press undated reprint in association with the Imperial War Museum.
Cosentino, Michele, *Le Portaeri Italiane*, Storia Militaire, Albertelli Edizioni Speciali, Parma, 2011.
Cronin, Dick, *Royal Navy Shipboard Aircraft Developments 1912-1931*, Air-Britain (Historians), Tonbridge, 1990.
Cull, Brian, with Nicolle D and Aloni S, *Wings Over Suez*, Grub Street, London, 1996.
Dickens, Peter, *Narvik*, Ian Allen, Shepperton, 1974.
Doust, Michael J, *From the Cockpit 2 – Scimitar*, Ad Hoc Publications, Ringshall, 2006.
Doust, Michael J, *From the Cockpit 3 – Sea Hawk*, Ad Hoc Publications, Ringshall, 2007.
Doust, Michael J, *From the Cockpit 6 – Buccaneer*, Ad Hoc Publications, Ringshall, 2007.
Dyson, Tony, *HMS Hermes 1959-1984*, Maritime Books, Liskeard, 1984.
Ellis, Herbert, *Hippocrates RN, Memoirs of a Naval Flying Doctor*, Robert Hale, London, 1988.
Fazio, Vince, *Australian Aircraft Carriers 1929-1982*, undated monograph published by the Naval historical Society of Australia.
Fletcher, R G, *Front Line Avenger squadrons of the FAA*, published by the author, Bury St Edmonds, 1995.
Frame, T R, Goldrick, J V P and Jones, P D, *Reflections on the Royal Australian Navy*, Kangaroo Press, Kenthurst NSW, 1991.
Francillon, Rene J, *Tonkin Gulf Yacht Club – US Carrier Operations off Vietnam*, Conway Maritime Press, London, 1988.
Frere-Cook, Gervis, *The Attacks on the Tirpitz*, Ian Allen, Shepperton, 1973.
Friedman, Norman, *Carrier Air Power*, Conway Maritime Press, London, 1981.
Friedman, Norman, *US Aircraft Carriers, an Illustrated Design History*, United States Naval Institute, Annapolis, 1983.
Friedman, Norman, *The Post-war Naval Revolution*, Conway Maritime Press, London, 1986.
Friedman, Norman, *British Carrier Aviation – The Evolution of the Ships and their Aircraft*, Conway Maritime Press, London, 1988.
Friedman, Norman, *The Naval Institute Guide to World Naval Weapons Systems 1991/92*, Naval Institute Press, Annapolis, 1991.
Gillett, Ross, *HMAS Melbourne – 25 Years*, Nautical press, Sydney, 1980.
Gillett, Ross, *Wings Across the Sea*, Aerospace Publications, Sydney NSW, 2000.
Graham, Alastair with Grove, Eric, *HMS Ark Royal – Zeal Does Not Rest 1981-2011*, Maritime Books, Liskeard, 2011.
Grenfell, Russell, *Main Fleet to Singapore*, Faber & Faber, London, 1951.
Grove, Eric J, *Vanguard to Trident*, The Bodley Head, London, 1987.
Gunston, Bill, *Early Supersonic Fighters of the West*, Ian Allen, Shepperton, 1974.
Gunston, Bill, *F-4 Phantom*, Ian Allen, Shepperton, 1977.
Gunston, Bill, *Harrier*, Ian Allen, Shepperton, 1981.
Haarr, Geirr H, *The German Invasion of Norway, April 1940*, Seaforth Publishing, Barnsley 2009.
Haarr, Geirr H, *The Battle for Norway, April - June 1940*, Seaforth Publishing, Barnsley 2010.
Hall, Timothy, *HMAS Melbourne*, Allen & Unwin, Sydney, 1982.
Harding, Richard (ed), *The Royal Navy 1930-2000, Innovation and Defence*, Frank Cass, Abingdon, 2005.
Harrison, W, *Fairey Firefly*, Airlife Publishing, Shrewsbury, 1992.
Harrold, J E, *Dark Seas – The Battle of Cape Matapan*, University of Plymouth Press, Plymouth, 2012.
Hermon, Gill G, *Royal Australian Navy 1939-1945* (2 volumes), Australian War Memorial, Canberra, 1957 and 1968.
Hezlet, Sir Arthur, *Aircraft & Sea Power*, Peter Davies, London, 1970.
Hibbert, Edgar, *HMS Unicorn – The Versatile Air Repair Ship*, Arthur H Stockwell Ltd, Ilfracombe, 2006.
Hobbs, David, *Aircraft Carriers of the Royal and Commonwealth Navies*, Greenhill Books, London, 1996.
Hobbs, David, *Royal Navy Escort Carriers*, Maritime Books, Liskeard, 2003.
Hobbs, David, *Moving Bases – Royal Navy Maintenance Carriers and MONABS*, Maritime Books, Liskeard, 2007.
Hobbs, David, *A Century of Carrier Aviation*, Seaforth Publishing, Barnsley, 2009.
Hobbs, David, *The British Pacific Fleet*, Seaforth Publishing, Barnsley, 2011.
Hone, T C, Friedman, Norman and Mandeles, M D, *American and British Aircraft Carrier Development 1919-1941*, Naval Institute Press, Annapolis, 1999.
Horsley, Terence, *Find, Fix and Strike, the Story of the Fleet Air Arm*, Eyre and Spottiswoode, London, 1943.
Howard, Lee, with Burrow, Mick, and Myall, Eric, *Fleet Air Arm Helicopters since 1943*, Air-Britain (Historians), Tonbridge, 2011.
Howarth, Stephen, and Law, Derek, *The Battle of the Atlantic 1939-1945*, Greenhill Books, London, 1994.
Howse, Derek, *Radar at Sea – The Royal Navy in World War 2*, MacMillan Press, Basingstoke, for The Naval Radar Trust, 1993.
Jackson, Robert, *Strike From the Sea – A History of British Naval Air Power*, Arthur Barker, London, 1970.
Jackson, Robert, *Suez 1956: Operation 'Musketeer'*, Ian Allen, Shepperton, 1980.
Jackson, Robert, *The Malayan Emergency and Indonesian Confrontation – The Commonwealth's Wars 1948-1966*, Pen & Sword Aviation, 2011.
Jarrett, Philip, *Fairey IIIF – Interwar Military Workhorse*, Ad Hoc Publications, Ringshall, 2009.
Jellicoe, Admiral Viscount J of Scapa, *The Grand Fleet 1914-16 – Its Creation, Development and Work*, Cassell & Company, London, 1919.
Jenkins, C A, *HMS Furious*, Warship Profiles 23 and 24, Profile Publications, Windsor, 1972.
Johnstone-Bryden, Richard, *HMS Ark Royal IV – Britain's Greatest Warship*, Sutton Publishing, Stroud, 1999.
Jones, Ben, *The Fleet Air Arm in the Second World War, Volume 1, 1939-1941*, Ashgate, Farnham, for the Navy Records Society, 2012.
Jones, Colin, *Wings and the Navy 1947-1953*, Kangaroo Press, Kenthurst, NSW, 1997.
Jordan, John, *Warships after Washington – The Development of the Five Major Fleets 1922-1930*, Seaforth Publishing, Barnsley, 2011.
Kealy, J D F, and Russell, E C, *A History of Canadian Naval Aviation*, The Department of National Defence and The Queen's Printer, Ottawa, 1965.
Kemp, P K, *Fleet Air Arm*, Herbert Jenkins, London, 1954.
Knowlson, Joyce, *HMS Ocean 1945-1957 – Peacetime Warrior*, published by the author, 1998.
Lansdown, John R P, *With the Carriers in Korea 1950-1953*, Square One Publications, Worcester, 1992.
Layman, R D, *Before the Aircraft Carrier – The Development of Aviation Vessels 1849-1922*, Conway Maritime Press, 1989.
Leahy, Alan J, *From the Cockpit 5 – Sea Hornet*, Ad Hoc Publications, Ringshall, 2007.
Leahy, Alan J, *From the Cockpit 12 – Sea Fury*, Ad Hoc Publications, Ringshall, 2010.
Lehan, Mike, *Flying Stations – A Story of Australian Naval Aviation*, Allen & Unwin, St Leonards, NSW, 1998.
Lenton, H T, *British Battleships and Aircraft Carriers*, Macdonald, London, 1972.
Lind, Lew, *Historic Naval Events of Australia Day-by-Day*, AH & AW Reed Pty Ltd, French's Forest, NSW, 1982.
Lowry, T P, and Wellham, John W G, *The Attack on Taranto – Blueprint for Pearl Harbor*, Stackpole Books, Mechanicsburg, PA, USA, 1995.
Lyon, David, *HMS Illustrious*, Warship Profile 10, Profile Publications, Windsor, 1971.
Macintyre, Donald, *The Battle of the Atlantic*, Batsford, London, 1961.
Macintyre, Donald, *Wings of Neptune*, Peter Davies, London, 1963.
Macintyre, Donald, *The Battle for the Mediterranean*, Pan Books, London, 1970.
Macintyre, Donald, *Narvik*, Pan Books, London, 1971.
Macintyre, Donald, *Aircraft Carrier – The Majestic Weapon*, Macdonald, London, 1968.
Marriott, Leo, *Royal Navy Aircraft Carriers 1945-1990*, Ian Allen, Shepperton, 1985.
McCandless, Robert, *From the Cockpit 16 – Barracuda*, Ad Hoc Publications, Ringshall, 2012.
McCart, Neil, *HMS Albion 1944-1973 – The Old Grey Ghost*, Fan Publications, Cheltenham, 1995.
McCart, Neil, *HMS Eagle 1942- 1978*, Fan Publications, Cheltenham, 1996.
McCart, Neil, *HMS Centaur 1943-1972*, Fan Publications, Cheltenham, 1997.
McCart, Neil, *HMS Victorious 1937-1969*, Fan Publications, Cheltenham, 1998.
McCart, Neil, *Three Ark Royals 1938-1999*, Fan Publications, Cheltenham, 1999.
McCart, Neil, *The Illustrious & Implacable Classes of Aircraft Carrier 1940-1969*, Fan Publications, Cheltenham, 2000.
McCart, Neil, *HMS Hermes 1923 & 1959*, Fan Publications, Cheltenham, 2001.
McCart, Neil, *The Colossus Class Aircraft Carriers 1944-1972*, Fan Publications, Cheltenham, 2002.
McCart, Neil, *HMS Glory 1945-1961*, Maritime Books, Liskeard, 2002.
McCart, Neil, *Harrier Carriers Volume 1 – HMS Invincible*, Fan Publications, Cheltenham, 2004.
Mills, Carl, *Banshees in the Royal Canadian Navy*, Banshee Publications, Willowdale, Ontario, 1991.
Moore, George, *Building for Victory – The Warship Building Programmes of the Royal Navy 1939-1945*, World Ship Society, Gravesend, undated.
Moore, John, *The Fleet Air Arm*, Chapman & Hall, London, 1943.
Moore, Richard, *The Royal Navy and Nuclear Weapons*, Frank Cass, London, 2001.
Morgan, E, and Stevens, J, *The Scimitar File*, Air-Britain (Historians), Tunbridge Wells, 2000.
Norman, J G S 'Joe', *From the Cockpit 4 – Firefly*, Ad Hoc Publications, Ringshall, 2007.
Nott, Rodney, and Payne, Noel, *The Vung Tau Ferry and Escort Ships, Vietnam 1965-1972*, General Aviation Maintenance Pty Ltd, Essendon, Victoria, 1998.
Pack, S W C, *The Battle of Matapan*, Pan Books, London, 1968.
Pack, S W C, *Night Action off Cape Matapan*, Ian Allen, Shepperton, 1972.
Pack, S W C, *The Battle for Crete*, Ian Allen, Shepperton, 1973.
Partridge, R T, *Operation Skua*, Fleet Air Arm Museum, Yeovilton, 1983.
Payne, Donald, *From the Cockpit 10 – Swordfish*, Ad Hoc Publications, Ringshall, 2008.
Peattie, Mark R, *Sunburst – The Rise of Japanese Naval Air Power, 1909-1941*, Chatham Publishing, Rochester, 2001.
Phillips, Lawrie, *The Royal Navy Day By Day*, Spellmount, Stroud, 2011.
Polmar, Norman, *Aircraft Carriers* (2 volumes), first Macdonald, London, 1969, and second Potomac Books, Washington, 2008.
Poolman, Kenneth, *Illustrious*, William Kimber, London, 1955.
Poolman, Kenneth, *Ark Royal*, William Kimber, London 1956.
Poolman, Kenneth, *Escort Carrier 1941-1945*, Ian Allen, Shepperton, 1972.
Poolman, Kenneth, *The Sea Hunters – Escort Carriers v U-Boats, 1941-1945*, Arms and Armour Press, London, 1982.
Poolman, Kenneth, *Escort Carrier – HMS Vindex at War*, Secker & Warburg, London, 1983.
Popham, Hugh, *Into Wind – a History of British Naval Flying*, Hamish Hamilton, London, 1969.
Reece, Michael, *Flying Royal Marines*, Royal Marines' Historical Society, Eastney, 2012.
Reynolds, Clark G, *The Fast Carriers – The Forging of an Air Navy*, Naval Institute Press, Annapolis, 1992.
Roberts, John, *Safeguarding the Nation – The Story of the Modern Royal Navy*, Seaforth Publishing, Barnsley, 2009.
Roskill, Stephen W, *The War at Sea* (3 volumes), HMSO, London, 1954-1961.
Roskill, Stephen W, *Documents Relating to the Naval Air Service, Volume 1, 1908-1918*, Navy Records Society, Greenwich, 1969.
Rowan-Thomson, Graeme, *From the Cockpit 9 – Attacker*, Ad Hoc Publications, Ringshall, 2008.
Royal Institution of Naval Architects, *Selected Papers on British Warship Design in World War II*, Conway Maritime Press, London, 1983.
Schofield, B B, *The Russian Convoys*, Pan Books, London, 1964.
Schofield, B B, *Loss of the Bismarck*, Ian Allen, Shepperton, 1972.
Schofield, B B, *The Attack on Taranto*, Ian Allen, Shepperton, 1973.
Service Historique de la Marine, *Les Marines de Guerre du Dreadnought au Nucleaire*, Paris, 1988.
Smith, Peter C, *Task Force 57*, William Kimber, London, 1969.
Smith, Peter C, *Eagle's War*, Crecy Books, 1995.
Snowie, J Allen, *The Bonnie – HMCS Bonaventure*, Boston Mills Press, Ontario, 1987.
Stevens, David, *The Royal Australian Navy*, Oxford University Press, Melbourne, 2001.
Stevens, David, and Reeve, John, (eds), *The Face of Naval Battle*, Allen & Unwin, Crows Nest NSW, 2003.
Stevens, David, and Reeve, John, (eds), *The Navy and the Nation*, Allen & Unwin, Crows Nest NSW, 2005.
Stevens, David, and Reeve, John, *Sea Power Ashore and in the Air*, Halstead Press, Ultimo NSW, 2007.
Stevens, David, (ed), *Naval Networks: The Dominance of Communications in Maritime Operations*, Sea Power Centre – Australia, Canberra, 2012.
Stevens, David, (ed), *The Commonwealth Navies – 100 Years of Co-operation*, Sea Power Centre – Australia, Canberra, 2012.
Sturtivant, Ray, *British Naval Aviation – The Fleet Air Arm 1917-1990*, Arms & Armour Press, London, 1990.
Sturtivant, Ray, and Balance, Theo, *The Squadrons of the Fleet Air Arm*, Air-Britain (Historians), Tunbridge Wells, 1994.
Sturtivant, Ray, and Page G, *Royal Navy Aircraft Serials and Units 1911-1919*, Air-Britain (Historians), Tonbridge, 1992.
Sturtivant, Ray, and Cronin, Dick, *Fleet Air arm Aircraft, Units and Ships 1920 to 1939*, Air-Britain (Historians), Tunbridge Wells, 1998.
Sturtivant, Ray, with Burrow, Mick, *Fleet Air Arm Aircraft 1939 to 1945*, Air-Britain (Historians), Tunbridge Wells, 1995.
Sturtivant, Ray, with Burrow, Mick, and Howard, Lee, *Fleet Air Arm Fixed-Wing Aircraft since 1946*, Air-Britain (Historians), Tonbridge, 2004.
Thetford, Owen, *British Naval Aircraft since 1912*, Putnam, London, 1962 edition.
Till, Geoffrey, *Air Power and the Royal Navy 1914-45*, Jane's Publishing, London, 1979.
Watton, Ross, *Anatomy of the Ship – The Aircraft Carrier Victorious*, Conway Maritime Press, London, 1991.
Weaver, D G, *The History of HMS Queen – A World War II Lend-Lease Aircraft Carrier*, privately published by the author, 2004.
Woodman, Richard, *Malta Convoys 1940-1943*, John Murray, London, 2000.

Annual Publications
Jane's Fighting Ships
The World's Warships
Warships of the Royal Navy
Seaforth World Naval Review

GLOSSARY

A/A	Anti-Aircraft
A&AEE	Aeroplane and Armament Experimental Establishment
AAC	Army Air Corps
AAG	Advanced Arrester Gear
AAM	Air-to-Air Missile
AC	Auxiliary Collier (USN designation)
—	Alternating Current
ACA	Aircraft Carrier Alliance
ACG	Amphibious Combat Group (Dutch Marine Corps)
ACNB	Australian Commonwealth Navy Board
ACNS	Assistant Chief of the Naval Staff
ACS	Aircraft Carrier Squadron
ACV	Auxiliary Aircraft Carrier (alternative USN designation)
ADA	Action Data Automation
Adaws	Action Data Automated Weapons System
ADR	Aircraft Direction Room
AESA	Airborne Electronically-Scanned Array
AEW	Airborne Early Warning
AF	Atlantic Fleet
AFC	Air Force Cross
AFO	Admiralty Fleet order
AFWR	Atlantic Fleet Weapons Range (USN)
AIM	Air Intercept Missile
Alis	Autonomous Logistic Information System
AN/APS	Army-Navy/Airborne Pulse Search (radar) (USN designation)
ANZAC	Australia & New Zealand Army Corps
A/S	Antisubmarine
ASaC	Airborne Surveillance and Control
ASM	Air-to-Surface Missile
ASR	Air-Sea Rescue
Astovl	Advanced Short Take-Off/Vertical Landing (aircraft)
ASW	Antisubmarine Warfare
ASWEX	Antisubmarine Warfare Exercise
Atflir	Advanced Tactical Forward-Looking Infrared
AVG	Auxiliary Aircraft Carrier (USN designation)
avcat	Aviation catoline spirit
avgas	Aviation gasoline
avtur	Aviation turbine spirit
Babs	Blind Approach Beacon System
Bams	Broad Area Maritime Surveillance System (USN)
BAVG	Auxiliary Aircraft Carrier allocated to Britain (by the USN)
BBC	British Broadcasting Corporation
BCF	Battle Cruiser Fleet
BEF	British Expeditionary Force
BOAC	British Overseas Airways Corporation
BPF	British Pacific Fleet
BR	Book of Reference
BS	Battle Squadron
CAF	Canadian Armed Force
CAFO	Confidential Admiralty Fleet Order
CAG	Carrier Air Group
Cale	Catapult/Aircraft Line-Up Equipment
Calf	Common Affordable Lightweight Fighter
CAM-Ship	Catapult-Armed Merchant Ship
CAP	Combat Air Patrol
CB	Confidential Book
CCA	Carrier Controlled Approach
CCH	Helicopter-operating Cruiser (USN/NATO designation)
CDS	Comprehensive Display System
—	Chief of the Defence Staff
CEC	Co-operative Engagement Capability
CENTO	Central Treaty Organisation
CF	Channel Fleet
C-in-C	Commander-in-Chief
CIWS	Close-in Weapons System
COD	Carrier On-board Delivery (aircraft)
COMUKTG	Commander UK Task Group
CRBFD	Close-Range Blind Fire Director
CS	Cruiser Squadron
CV	Aircraft Carrier (USN/NATO designation)
CVA	Attack Aircraft Carrier (USN/NATO designation)
CVB	'Battle' Aircraft Carrier (USN designation)
CVE	Escort Aircraft Carrier (USN/NATO designation)
CVG	Carrier Air Group (USN designation)
CVL	Light Aircraft Carrier (USN designation)
CVN	Nuclear-Powered Aircraft Carrier (USN/NATO designation)
CVS	Support Aircraft Carrier (USN/NATO designation)
CW	Continuous-Wave
DAD	Director Air Department
DAW	Director of Air Warfare
DC	Direct Current
DCNS	Deputy Chief of Naval Staff
DG Ships	Director General Ships
DLCO	Deck Landing Control Officer
DLT	Deck Landing Training
DNAW	Director of Naval Air Warfare
DNC	Director of Naval Construction
DNO	Director of Naval Ordnance
DSC	Distinguished Service Cross
DSO	Distinguished Service Order
ECCM	Electronic Counter-Countermeasures
ECM	Electronic Countermeasures
EF	Eastern Fleet
EG	Escort Group
EIF	East Indies Fleet
Emals	Electromagnetic Aircraft Launch System
ESM	Electronic Support Measures
F/A	Fighter/Attack (aircraft)
Fadec	Full-authority Digital Engine Control
FAMG	Fleet Aircraft Maintenance Group
FAW	Fighter, All-Weather (aircraft)
FB	Fighter-bomber (aircraft)
FCBA	Future Carrierborne Aircraft
FEF	Far East Fleet
FES	Far East Station
FFO	Furnace Fuel Oil
FFWP	Future-Fleet Working Party
FGA	Fighter Ground Attack (aircraft)
Flash	Folding Lightweight Acoustic System for Helicopters
Flyco	Flying Control Position
FM	Frequency Modulated
FO	Flag Officer
FOAC	Flag Officer Aircraft Carriers
FOCAS	Flag Officer Carriers and Amphibious Ships
FOF	Flag Officer Flotillas
FO2	Flag Officer Second-in-Command
Fotex	Fleet Operational Training Exercise
FPDA	Five-power Defence Agreement (UK, Australia, New Zealand, Singapore, Malaysia)
FRS	Fighter, Reconnaissance and Strike (aircraft)
GF	Grand Fleet
GPMG	General-purpose machine-gun
GWS	Guided Weapons System
HAR	Helicopter Air Rescue
HAS	Helicopter Antisubmarine
HDS	Helicopter Delivery Service
HF	Home Fleet
—	High-frequency
HF/DF	High-frequency Direction Finding
HM	Her/His Majesty
HMS	Her/His Majesty's Ship
HMAS	Her/His Majesty's Australian Ship
HMCS	Her/His Majesty's Canadian Ship
HMNZS	Her/His Majesty's New Zealand Ship
hp	horsepower
HRH	Her/His Royal Highness
HS	Helicopter Antisubmarine Squadron (USN designation)
HTP	High-Test Hydrogen Peroxide
IFF	Identification Friend or Foe
IFTU	Intensive Flying Trials Unit
INS	Indian Naval Ship
IR	Infrared
JASS	Joint Anti-Submarine School
JAST	Joint Advanced Technology Strike Fighter
Jastovl	Joint Advanced Short Take-Off Vertical Landing (aircraft)
JCA	Joint Combat Aircraft
JDAM	Joint Direct Attack Munition
JFH	Joint Force Harrier
JHDU	Joint Helicopter Development Unit
JHF	Joint Helicopter Force
JMC	Joint Maritime Course
JSF	Joint Strike Fighter
JSSA	Joint Stealth Strike Fighter
KCB	Knight Commander of the Order of the Bath
knot	measurement of speed; 1 knot equals 1 nautical mile per hour
lb	pound (weight)
LCA	Landing Craft Assault
LCT	Landing Craft Tank
LCVP	Landing Craft Vehicles and Personnel
LHA	Landing Ship Helicopter Assault
LHD	Landing Ship Helicopter/Dock
LPD	Landing Platform Dock
LPH	Landing Platform Helicopter
LSO	Landing Signal Officer
MAC-Ship	Merchant Aircraft Carrier
MASC	Maritime Airborne Surveillance and Control (Project)
MC	Military Cross
MDAP	Mutual Defence Assistance Programme
MF	Mediterranean Fleet
MFAS	Multi-Function Active Sensor
MG	machine-gun
mm	millimetre
MoD	Ministry of Defence
MONAB	Mobile Operational Naval Air Base
MQ	Unmanned Maritime aircraft designation (USN)
MRH	Multi-role Helicopter
MV	Motor Vessel
MW	Megawatt
NAS	Naval Air Squadron
NATO	North Atlantic Treaty Organisation
NBMR	NATO Basic Military Requirement
NCRE	Naval Construction Research Establishment
NFO	Naval Flight officer (USN)
NTG	Naval Task Group
NPL	National Physical Laboratory
ORI	Operational Readiness Inspection
pdr	pounder (as in 12-pounder gun)
PGM	Precision-Guided Munition
PJHQ	Principal Joint Headquarters
psi	pounds per square inch
PWR	Pressurised Water-Cooled Reactor
QARNNS	Queen Alexandra's Royal Naval Nursing Service
RAA	Rear Admiral Aircraft (Grand Fleet)
RAAC	Rear Admiral Aircraft Carriers
RAAF	Royal Australian Air Force
RAE	Royal Aircraft Establishment
RAF	Royal Air Force
RAN	Royal Australian Navy
RANAS	Royal Australian Naval Air Station
RANR	Royal Australian Naval Reserve
RANVR	Royal Australian Naval Volunteer Reserve
RAS	Replenishment At Sea
Ratog	Rocket-Assisted Take-Off Gear
RCAF	Royal Canadian Air Force
RCN	Royal Canadian Navy
RCNAS	Royal Canadian Naval Air Station
RCNR	Royal Canadian Naval Reserve
RCNC	Royal Corps of Naval Constructors
RCNVR	Royal Canadian Naval Volunteer Reserve
RFA	Royal Fleet Auxiliary
Rimpac	'Rim of the Pacific' allied naval exercise
RM	Royal Marines
RMS	Royal Mail Ship
RN	Royal Navy
RNAS	Royal Naval Air Service
—	Royal Naval Air Station
RNAY	Royal Naval Air Yard
RNR	Royal Naval Reserve
RNVR	Royal Naval Volunteer Reserve
RNZN	Royal New Zealand Navy
RNZAF	Royal New Zealand Air Force
RNZNVR	Royal New Zealand Naval Volunteer Reserve
RP	Rocket Projectile
SAGW	Surface-to-Air Guided Weapon
SAM	Surface-to-Air Missile
SAR	Search and Rescue
SDR	Strategic Defence Review
SDSR	Strategic Defence and Security Review
SEATO	South East Asia Treaty Organisation
SG	Support Group
Sharp	Shared Aircraft Reconnaissance Pod
shp	shaft horsepower
SRP	Special Repair Party
SS	Steam Ship
SSBN	Nuclear-powered Ballistic missile Submarine
SSM	Surface-to-Surface Missile
SSN	Nuclear-powered Submarine
Stobar	Short Take-Off But Arrested Recovery
Stovl	Short Take-Off/Vertical Landing
Tacan	Tactical Air Navigation System
TAG	Telegraphist Air Gunner / Tailored Air Group
TAMY	Transportable Aircraft Maintenance Yard
TBR	Torpedo Bomber Reconnaissance (aircraft)
TE	Task Element
TEZ	Total Exclusion Zone
TF	Task Force
TG	Task Group
TS	Training Ship
UAV	Unmanned (uninhabited) Air vehicle
Ucas-D	Unmanned (uninhabited) Combat Air System – Demonstrator
Ucav	Unmanned (uninhabited) Combat Air Vehicle
Uclass	Unmanned (uninhabited) Carrier-Launched Airborne Strike, Surveillance System (USN)
UDI	Unilateral Declaration of Independence (Rhodesia/Zimbabwe)
UHF	Ultra High Frequency
UK	United Kingdom
US(A)	United States (of America)
USAF	United States Air Force
USMC	United States Marine Corps
USN	United States Navy
USS	United States Ship
UN	United Nations
VAD	Voluntary Aid Detachment (nurses)
VC	Victoria Cross
VHF	Very High Frequency
VE-day	Victory in Europe day
VF	Fighter Squadron (USN designation)
VJ-day	Victory over Japan day
VMA	Tilt-Rotor squadron (USMC)
VS	Anti-Submarine Squadron (USN designation)
V/Stol	Vertical/Short Take-off and Vertical Landing
VTO	Vertical Take-off
Vtol	Vertical Take-off and Landing
VU	Utility Squadron (USN designation)
WAC	Western Approaches Command
WF	Western Fleet
WOD	Wind Over Deck
W/T	Wireless telegraphy